PERSONALITY IN JAPANESE HISTORY

Published under the auspices of
The Center for Japanese and Korean Studies
University of California, Berkeley

The Center for Japanese and Korean Studies of the University of California is a unit of the Institute of International Studies. It is the unifying organization for faculty members and students interested in Japan and Korea, bringing together scholars from many disciplines.

The Center's major aims are the development and support of research and language study. As part of this program the Center sponsors a publication series of books concerned with Japan and Korea. Manuscripts are considered from all campuses of the University of California as well as from any other individuals and institutions doing research in these areas.

RECENT PUBLICATIONS OF
THE CENTER FOR JAPANESE AND KOREAN STUDIES

R. P. DORE
Education in Tokugawa Japan. 1964

JAMES T. ARAKI
The Ballad-Drama of Medieval Japan. 1964

MASAKAZU IWATA
Okubo Toshimichi: The Bismark of Japan. 1964

FRANK O. MILLER
Minobe Tatsukichi: Interpreter of Constitutionalism in Japan. 1965

MICHAEL COOPER, S.J.
They Came to Japan: An Anthology of European Reports on Japan, 1543–1640. 1965

GEORGE DE VOS AND HIROSHI WAGATSUMA
Japan's Invisible Race. 1966

RYUTARO KOMIYA, ED.
TRANSLATED FROM THE JAPANESE BY ROBERT S. OZAKI
Postwar Economic Growth in Japan. 1966

ROBERT A. SCALAPINO
The Japanese Communist Movement, 1920–1966. 1967

SOON SUNG CHO
Korea in World Politics, 1940–1950: An Evaluation of American Responsibility. 1967

KOZO YAMAMURA
Economic Policy in Postwar Japan: Growth versus Economic Democracy. 1967

C. I. EUGENE KIM AND HAN-KYO KIM
Korea and the Politics of Imperialism, 1876–1910. 1967

EARL MINER, TRANS.
Japanese Poetic Diaries. 1969

DONALD C. HELLMANN
Japanese Foreign Policy and Domestic Politics. 1969

IRWIN SCHEINER
Christian Converts and Social Protest in Meiji Japan. 1970

H. D. HAROOTUNIAN
Toward Restoration: The Growth of Political Consciousness in Tokugawa Japan. 1970

CHIE NAKANE
Japanese Society. 1970

PERSONALITY IN JAPANESE HISTORY

INTRODUCED AND EDITED BY

ALBERT M. CRAIG

AND

DONALD H. SHIVELY

UNIVERSITY OF CALIFORNIA PRESS

BERKELEY • LOS ANGELES • LONDON

1970

University of California Press
Berkeley and Los Angeles, California

University of California Press, Ltd.
London, England

Copyright © 1970 by
The Regents of the University of California

Library of Congress Catalog Card Number: 73–111420
International Standard Book Number: 0–520–01699–8
Printed in the United States of America

To Edwin Oldfather Reischauer

on his sixtieth birthday
with respect and affection
from a few of those who have been
his students

CONTRIBUTORS

John C. Pelzel
Professor of Anthropology, Harvard University

John W. Hall
A. Whitney Griswold Professor of History, Yale University

Donald H. Shively
Professor of Japanese History and Literature, Harvard University

Thomas C. Smith
Professor of History, Stanford University

Tetsuo Najita
Associate Professor of History, University of Chicago

Conrad Totman
Associate Professor of History, Northwestern University

Robert K. Sakai
Professor of History, University of Hawaii

George M. Wilson
Associate Professor of History, Indiana University

Albert M. Craig
Professor of History, Harvard University

Marius B. Jansen
Professor of History, Princeton University

George Akita
Professor of History, University of Hawaii

Akira Iriye
Associate Professor of History, University of Chicago

Peter Duus
Associate Professor of History, Claremont Graduate School

Howard S. Hibbett
Professor of Japanese Literature, Harvard University

CONTENTS

ix

Contents

INTRODUCTION: PERSPECTIVES ON PERSONALITY IN JAPANESE HISTORY

Albert M. Craig

Personality is a major dimension of history. Like institutions or culture, personality has its own structure, its own forces, and its own impact within the confluence of historical determinants. What a man is shapes his role in an institution just as the demands of the institution mold the personality. The relationship is two-way and dynamic. Also dynamic, as anthropologists long have noted, is the interaction between personality and culture.

Without considering the factor of personality there are many historical phenomena in Japan that we cannot understand. This becomes especially clear when we compare phenomena occurring at different times and places. Consider the following two examples:

1. There appear to be striking similarities among the *shishi*, the proemperor fanatics of the late Tokugawa era, certain groups of ultranationalist young officers in the 1930's, and the anarchic leftist student groups during the late 1960's—in spite of their different ideologies and differing historical contexts. In each case radical ideas and feelings of moral righteousness "cooked" within the group, ego reinforced alter, pressure built up, until action erupted in the form of assassinations or group violence.

2. Japanese energy or drive cannot be explained solely in terms of social or cultural factors. Occasionally it is self-destructive; at some periods of history it has been manifested in openly aggressive actions. But most of the time it is harnessed and bent to achievements that are socially approved: in the unrelenting pursuit of goals by political leaders, in the efforts by businessmen and bureaucrats to rise within their organiza-

1

tions, in the hard work performed by the Japanese laborer, and even in the productivity of artists. For the student of Japan to describe this drive—when it operates and when it does not—is not as satisfactory as to understand why it exists (for it does not exist in many other countries) and how it relates to the total personality.

The importance of personality to an adequate historical explanation in such particular cases, however, must not lead to a view of history in which personality impinges only in certain instances. We would view it, rather, as a constant. Most of history unfolds as gradually changing equilibrium among mature personalities, stable institutions, and slowly evolving culture. The Tokugawa era (1600–1868) is an example of this.

At the center of power was the Tokugawa superstate, called the Bakufu or Shogunate. Its head, the shogun, was the overlord of all Japan, ruling directly his own vast domain and indirectly as the lord to whom all other feudal lords were vassals. Apart from his domain there were about 260 other "feudal" states. At the top of each was a daimyo or feudal lord, who governed with the aid of the samurai class, a military aristocratic class, the upper reaches of which staffed the officialdom of the domain. (The daimyo domains are often referred to as han.) Beneath the samurai class—which constituted about 5 percent of the total population, far larger than the aristocracies of late feudal Europe—were the peasants who tilled the soil and made up the bulk of the population and the artisans and merchants who lived mainly in the cities and castle towns.

An earlier generation of scholars, seeking in Tokugawa society those characteristics that led Japan to become militarist in the 1930's, viewed it as a police state, rigid, military, and static, its only movement the growth of a merchant economy which, producing dislocations, led to the Meiji Restoration in 1868. This view is no longer held. Today scholars plumb the Tokugawa for the wellsprings of Japan's amazing growth in the modern era. They find slow, evolutionary changes occurring in every sector: in the land system, in law and government, in the intellectual life, in the arts, in education, and so on. In terms of personality we can say that the over-all stability of the system depended on men who could respond creatively to change and make adjustments. It depended on men who had an everyday, constant commitment to making the system work. Had the leaders been overly rigid, cumulative small changes would have led to an early breakdown.

To put this in a slightly different perspective, if we see the Tokugawa era as a 250-year dynasty, we are struck by the vitality it possessed even during its last years. The parallel to the Chinese "dynastic cycle," in fact, cannot be drawn in Japan for, far from experiencing a cycle of administrative decline and decentralization, the Tokugawa polity was marked from the start by considerable decentralization within the overarching framework of Tokugawa controls and subsequently by growing bureaucratization within the Bakufu and the local daimyo states. Communications improved immensely as the period wore on and government became competent in many new ways. There were signs of trouble, too—the rise of state debts, the poverty of lower samurai, sporadic droughts and famines, and increasing peasant uprisings. Yet there was no *crise de système*. Even after the arrival of Perry in 1853 destroyed the seclusion policy which had been basic to the Tokugawa scheme, the old regime did not collapse immediately. Rather, the period was marked by the emergence of vigorous personalities who attempted to cope with the new situation in realistic terms. A number of the studies in this volume illustrate some of these Tokugawa characteristics.

Two papers treat seventeenth-century political figures. John Hall treats Ikeda Mitsumasa, a daimyo who was regarded as one of the "Four Superior Lords" of the 1630's, the very model of an early modern daimyo. Working from the diary kept by the daimyo at a time of crisis, Hall finds that he was a serious and sober administrator who used his officials well and paid close attention to details; he was a doer, not a pawn "in the hands of the impersonal forces of history." Donald Shively writes on the much disparaged Tsunayoshi, who for his particular eccentricity was known as the "Dog Shogun" and has come down through history as a half-despotic and half-comic figure. Yet even Tsunayoshi is shown to have had a serious side, rationalizing his defects and aspiring to be a Confucian sage-king. Shively treats not only the character of the man but how the man contributed to the spirit of his time.

Two papers deal with lower ranking figures of the late eighteenth and early nineteenth centuries, the Bakufu retainer Ōshio Heihachirō and the farmer-scholar Ōkura Nagatsune. Both men were importantly shaped by Confucianism. Ōkura, as described by Thomas Smith, was a frustrated Confucianist who turned from the politics that was not the concern of his station to agricultural and sericultural studies. Ōshio, in the account by Tetsuo Najita, was a sage who, aspiring to an ethical ideal outside of history, became a rebel. Both men were concerned to serve the people: one by contributing to a new technology, one by sacrificing himself in the name of justice. The significance of both men for history is also ambiguous. Ōshio had in greater measure the intellectuality and dedication, along with anger and frustration, that in a lesser measure made other members of his class work for their polity. Yet his own sacrifice seems an omen, at least in retrospect, of the approaching doom of the system. Without the positive contributions of men like Ōkura from every walk of life, the Tokugawa equilibrium would not have lasted as long as it did. Yet in a longer perspective, the enlightened self-interest and concern with productivity that meant so much to the stability of the Tokugawa state take on a much more dynamic significance, and Ōkura's openness to change seems to presage tendencies of the early Meiji era. Or, to put it in the form of a question, we may ask whether the spread of Confucianism among commoners contributed to the stability of the Tokugawa society or whether it was a rationalizing force undercutting the system.

Another group of three papers treats historically interrelated figures who were active in politics in the pre-Restoration period between 1834 and 1858. Conrad Totman writes of the relationship between Abe Masahiro, the chief senior councillor of the Bakufu, and Tokugawa Nariaki, the daimyo of the important han

4

of Mito. (Nariaki bore the same name as the shogunal house because Mito was a "related" domain.) Totman conveys a nice
sense of the cautious and measured pace of Bakufu action and
of the political balancing of the various forces within the country by the fine tuning of personal relations. Robert Sakai treats
Shimazu Nariakira, daimyo of the great southern domain of
Satsuma, and his relationship to Abe Masahiro. He describes
the kind of control the Bakufu could exercise over a distant han,
the kind of autonomy possessed by that han, and the process by
which Satsuma became involved in national politics. Sakai's
study also defines the setting of Satsuma's domestic politics,
from which emerged so many of the Restoration leaders. George
Wilson traces the career of Hashimoto Sanai, an important retainer of the daimyo of another related domain, that of Fukui.
Sanai was a scholar of traditional learning, and a student of
Western studies as well, who rose to act in politics as a representative of his han. In contrast to most studies which see the
opening of Japan as the central issue in the purge of 1858, Wilson shows by an examination of Sanai's involvement that the
central question was the shogunal succession dispute. Having
supported the wrong side in this dispute, Sanai was one of those
executed in the purge.

Reading these papers on Tokugawa personalities, and especially in the case of high-ranking officials, we are struck by the
problem of the "public personality" in Japanese history. All
daimyo and their ranking retainers were morally concerned with
the welfare of their domains, and virtually all were models of
decorum and propriety. Even the public face of a Tsunayoshi
becomes a living caricature of these necessary virtues. All retainers, at least, are manly and brave. They are presented in official biographies as both samurai warriors and Confucian officials. Japanese biographers were too fond of personal detail for
any work to be wholly devoid of life. Yet so stiff are the usual
eulogistic portraits that John Hall asks "whether living biography is at all possible for Japanese who lived prior to modern
times and whose spheres of activity were political rather than
philosophical or literary." The same phenomenon of the public

personality in Japan is described by Edwin O. Reischauer in *Ennin's Travels in T'ang China.* Ennin has just returned to Japan:

> He is standing on the threshold of a dazzling career as the lead-ing cleric of Japan, extravagantly honored by the court and devotedly venerated by his fellow monks. The persecuted pil-grim is about to become the triumphant church father. The faithful diarist, whose picture of himself reveals in clear detail a strong and determined but still humble figure, is about to have his portrait painted in the heroic proportions and brilliant colors used by the court chroniclers and biographers to transform liv-ing men into the huge but lifeless figures of official history.[1]

Part of the explanation for the lifelessness of official biogra-phies lies in the Confucian canons of history by which they were written. These demanded the recording of those aspects of life that would serve as a moral mirror for posterity, not the details that would make them come alive. Tokugawa biography is thus a blood relative of the praise-and-blame biographies of statesmen heroes and villains appended to the official histories of Chinese dynasties. Diaries may take us a step beyond the cardboard-figure stereotypes of the official histories into the real matters of official life. Yet even diaries of the premodern era do not go much beyond that. An observer like Ennin was a rare bird. Most officials' perceptions of themselves were perceptions of their role activities.

This raises a second point. The man himself, when he attained office, assumed the character required by the role. He became the office. We speak of game playing or of the persona of the self. Yet the Japanese official, with far greater ease, donned the mask of his office and wore it until it became a part of the linea-ments of his own face. Or so it seemed. If Japanese have a special facility for role playing or, what is not quite the same thing, a special facility for identifying with a role, can this be explained in terms of Ruth Benedict's strictures regarding Japanese per-

[1] Edwin O. Reischauer, *Ennin's Travels in T'ang China* (New York, 1955), pp. 301–302.

sonality? Benedict described Japan as a "shame-culture" with a "situation-centered ethic."[2] The ability to take cues sensitively from a situation and to act in terms of one's position in an organization seems to fit in well with what we mean by role playing. In Tokugawa times (and *The Chrysanthemum and the Sword* certainly fits Tokugawa Japan better than it fits Japan today), role playing was further supported by an ethic which held that a man was true to his own moral essence when he selflessly fulfilled the demands of his station or role. This is quite different from the modern Westerner (and from the educated, Westernized Japanese of the modern era) who worries lest the requirements of a role make him untrue to his inner self.

The strength of the public personality must not blind us to the fact that it was but a facet of the total personality of a public figure. As more becomes known of the Japanese personality and of its historical evolution (and as more becomes known of the historical evolution of personality in general), it will become necessary to see public figures in a more complete developmental perspective. The Japanese proverb holds that "the soul of the child of three lasts for the rest of his life" (*mitsugo no tamashii hyaku made*). Not only the ambition of a public figure, but how he relates to others, his unconscious attitude toward authority, and so on, are, we assume, formed at an early age. It also will be necessary to see the adult official in terms of the idea of self formed during late adolescence. What did it mean for a Meiji official, for example, to have been a *sonnō jōi* fanatic? Was fanaticism merely a small and discardable aspect of a larger political identity? Or was it a vital component in the makeup of the leaders that later generations speak of as "the men of the Meiji era"? Finally, it will be necessary to see the effects on the public personality of the existential problems of the adult—of family concerns, of worries about security, of declining sexual powers, and the prospect of retirement, old age, and death. The process by which the reform bureaucrat of twenty-five does or does not become the conservative of sixty is not one that can be

---

[2] Ruth Benedict, *The Chrysanthemum and the Sword* (Boston, 1946), pp. 222–227.

explained in terms of role alone. Each age has its problems of identity.

In 1853 Perry opened Japan and in 1868 the Meiji Restoration occurred. The intervening fifteen years was a time when colors changed, political activists styled themselves as madmen, and the common people acted in strange ways. In the midst of foreign threats, rebellions, assassinations, battles, innovations in military technology, and complex political negotiations, the old system was destroyed. Once the new Meiji government was established, the pace of change was immensely stepped up. Japan entered its century of progress, development, wars, imperialism, and renewed growth.

Three papers in this volume deal with Meiji statesmen. Kido Kōin and Ōkubo Toshimichi, about whom I have written, are so famous as the key figures of the first decade of the Meiji that it is easy to forget that they lived most of their lives during the Tokugawa era. Mutsu Munemitsu and Itō Miyoji, treated by Marius Jansen and George Akita, were born in 1844 and 1857. Coming from areas other than Chōshū and Satsuma, both were in a sense outsiders in the Meiji government. Both men played their most significant role during the 1880's and 1890's, Mutsu as the foreign minister who obtained the revision of the unequal treaties and Itō as a member of Itō Hirobumi's braintrust. All three papers attempt to go behind the official figures to ask what they were really like. In the Meiji period new kinds of materials become available—better diaries, collections of letters, the criticisms of a political opposition with a less reverential attitude toward authority, and even comments by relatives on the early lives of the statesmen—and new canons of history enter as well. This makes possible a different kind of biography. Reading these accounts we note how different these men were from the politicians of the Tokugawa era, and we wonder whether they would seem as different as they do if we had the same kind of materials for the earlier period.

Three papers in this volume deal with twentieth-century figures. Kayahara Kazan, the most long lived (1870–1950), was a journalist. As described by Akira Iriye, Kayahara studied other nations in order to define what it meant to be Japanese and in order to say how Japan should relate to the world. His solution to these problems is a part of the intellectual history of modern Japan. Peter Duus writes of Nagai Ryūtarō (1881–1934), a politician who made the transition from the somewhat liberal party politics of the 1920's to the one party of the militarist era. Duus dissects Nagai's thought, showing elements of continuity throughout the two periods. Howard S. Hibbett analyzes the life and writings of Akutagawa Ryūnosuke, one of the greatest of modern Japanese writers, who committed suicide in 1927. Hibbett develops the theme of "negative identity" and what it meant to Akutagawa as a writer. All three of these men were a part of the same world. Yet they are so different that we are made aware of its growing complexity and diversity.

One of the questions raised by the lives of those who lived during this century of hectic transformation is about the meaning of generational change. The foreign impact on Japan in the early 1850's produced large shifts in the polity in the 1860's. This led during the 1870's to large-scale institutional changes and to a massive influx of foreign culture. Parallel to these changes and necessary to them were changes in personality. The youth styles of samurai, for example, changed from the rather docile warriors (*hanshi*) of the 1850's to the activist patriots (*shishi*) of the 1860's and then to the enlightened gentlemen (*kaika no hito*) of the 1870's and early 1880's. It is harder to define the changes that occurred among urban commoners, to say nothing of peasants, but in a period when entrepreneurs such as Yasuda and Furukawa were striking out in new directions, changes certainly must have occurred.

While the *shishi* were in some instances becoming Western-style gentlemen, a transitional generation of younger boys managed for a time to combine what they admired in both styles— dressing like *shishi* (or at least like samurai) and studying the West. William Eliot Griffis writes of his students in the year of the Restoration:

> What a sight for a schoolmaster! . . . They are all dressed in the native costume of loose coats, with long and bag-like sleeves; kilts, like petticoats, open at the upper side; with shaven mid-

scalps, and top-knots like gun-hammers. Men and boys carry slates and copy books in their hands, and common cheap glass ink bottles slung by pieces of twine to their girdles. Hands and faces are smeared with the black fluid; but, strangest of all, each has two of the murderous-looking swords, one long and the other short, stuck in his belt. Symbols of the soldier rather than the scholar are these; but the samurai are both.[3]

Arthur Lloyd wrote of his students at an only slightly later period:

When I came to Japan it was the fashion for a student to ape the ways of a *Ronin* or masterless *samurai*. If you asked them what they were after, it was "civilization." Everything Japanese was looked upon as barbarian, everything Western was "civilized," and, as such, to be drunk in, whatever it might be. The ardent youth was all of one mind in its desire for acquiring the supposed higher culture of the West. . . . The fashion did not last for long, though the fever was pretty severe whilst it raged.[4]

Observing historical change in European society, Ortega y Gasset argued that the world "changes with every generation for the very reason that the previous generation has done something in the world, has left it somewhat different from the way it found it."[5] Such a logic of generations is even more compelling in modern Japan where so rapid has been the tempo of change that the gap between parents and children may be equal to five or six European generations. Moving on from the early Meiji period, our generational images associated with the Civilization and Enlightenment movement are replaced by those of the idealistic or romantic youth involved in the People's Rights Movement. We think of the youthful Nakae Chōmin, or of the hero of the novel *Strange Encounters with Elegant Females*, the popular novel of the middle Meiji period, a youth infatuated with Japan's parliamentary destiny. The images again change during the years of the Sino- and Russo-Japanese wars. Lloyd writes,

[3] William E. Griffis, *The Mikado's Empire* (New York, 1876), p. 370.
[4] Arthur Lloyd, *Every-Day Japan* (London, 1909), p. 269.
[5] Jose Ortega y Gasset, *Man and Crisis* (New York, 1958), p. 51.

10

Introduction

The Russo-Japanese war put a stop for a while to all political strife. Since the conclusion of peace there has come over Japan a great wave of money-making, which has swept off with it Tory and Liberal alike, and turned all the intellectual classes into the votaries of Daikoku, the god of the money-bags . . . . A dozen years ago I could always lay my hand on half a score of my students whose dream it was to be Cabinet Ministers and thrill audiences of intelligent legislators with their persuasive rhetoric. Six years ago the dream was of conning-towers and bridges, of ramparts and batteries; to-day they say that their country demands from them another kind of sacrifice. It demands that they shall make themselves rich, and they take most kindly to the sacrifice.[6]

After the turn of the century there also appeared the literary youth, the philosophic youth, and the anguished youth (*hanmon seinen*) who read German philosophy and *The Sorrows of Young Werther*, and suffered from weltschmerz. In the 1920's, students once again became politicized, this time in a leftist direction. And then there appeared in succession what the Japanese, who make a great deal of generational differences, call the "before-war," "wartime," and "postwar" generations, categories that in popular interpretations are used to explain phenomena ranging from attitudes toward the emperor to food preferences.

The examination of the inner process by which each generation creates and accepts certain images of itself is also one of the areas in which the historian and psychologist can meet most fruitfully. We know little of the early childhood of most historical figures. At best we have only sketchy biographical materials and a handful of anecdotes. Of the events that occurred during their early development, we usually have no inkling of what internally was most significant to them. Even an Erik Erikson trained through long years of clinical psychoanalysis tells us of the *kind of thing* that *must have been* important, rather than what it was; he writes, "We must view the scant data on Luther's upbringing, sometimes surer of the forces than of the facts."[7] In

[6] Lloyd, *Every-Day Japan*, p. 98.
[7] Erik H. Erikson, *Young Man Luther* (New York, 1958), p. 58.

11

contrast to this he writes at a later point of the relation between the history of society and the development of the self:

> We say that tradition "molds" the individual, "channels" his drives. But the social process does not mold a new being merely to housebreak him; it molds generations in order to be re-molded, to be reinvigorated, by them. Therefore society can never afford merely to suppress drives or to guide their sub-limination. It must also support the primary function of every individual ego, which is to transform instinctual energy into patterns of action, into character, into style—in short, into an identity with a core of integrity which is to be derived from and also contributed to the tradition.[8]

Style, the sense of integrity, and the patterning of actions, chang-ing over generations, become the links between the workings of internal forces in the personality and history. These are also variables for which copious historical materials exist, for in the largest sense "style" is defined by the entire body of man's ac-tions, feelings, and thoughts.

This is not to say, of course, that all elements in a given youth style are of profound significance, either for the individual or history. Yet many elements of generational styles—the rebel-liousness of this generation or the complacency of that one— are significant and cannot be dismissed as matters of fashion. Often the "styles" reveal vital aspects of family relationships and have great social consequences. Thus Arthur Lloyd, reflect-ing back on his first years in Japan, wrote as follows on the stu-dent strikes of the early Meiji era:

> If one considers the comparative precocity of the Japanese youth, as well as the wild and lawless traditions which students of twenty years ago had inherited from their predecessors, and adds thereto the further consideration that twenty years ago parental authority was at its lowest in Japan, for the reason that the go-ahead sons were conscious of knowing a great deal more than their old-fashioned, old world parents, . . . it will not be wondered at that in those early days strikes sometimes took

[8] *Ibid.*, p. 254.

place which bore a striking testimony to the power of organization which is innate in the Japanese . . . . But I am talking of events which took place many years ago. Things are very much changed now . . . . The go-ahead student of twenty years ago is the go-ahead parent of today, and has succeeded in reestablishing over his children that parental authority which for the time slipped from the grasp of his old world father.[9]

Even matters of dress were affected by the attitude toward parental authority. In place of the ink-smeared, *shishi*-like students of the early Meiji, Lloyd found his students in the 1890's to be "clean, orderly, and well-dressed, with habits and methods of work which would pass muster anywhere."[10] Reading this passage we are struck by the parallel between the early Meiji period and Japan's second "opening" after World War II. In 1945, too, the collapse of the old regime and the rejection of political authority were coupled with a radical rejection of parental authority, and with this came a new cultural openness, a questioning of old values, and doctrinal experimentation. The present generation of students are the heirs of this second opening. One wonders if parental authority will be reestablished in the 1970's as it was in the 1890's.

In spite of the hectic pace of generational change in modern Japan, and of its high visibility, we are struck also by the degree of continuity in Japanese personality. How is it, we ask, that the basic pattern of personality is still recognizably the same in spite of generational changes? In the first place, it seems clear that generational change is less fundamental than what happens during the first decade and a half of life. A second point is that much of the content of generational change does not affect child rearing and the next generation. A third point is that many men who went through university, say, in the twenties, were not caught up in these generational currents that in retrospect seem to mark the age, and those who were affected usually had sloughed off much of the effect by the time they became parents.

[9] Lloyd, *Every-Day Japan*, pp. 272–273.
[10] *Ibid.*, pp. 269–270.

Another point is that our images of generational change are drawn mainly from university youth. The comparable images for farm and city youths who did not go on to higher education probably changed at a much slower pace. And what of women? We recall photographs showing different styles of dress. We think of the emergence of a writer like Higuchi Ichiyō, of the suffragettes, or of the "Engels-girls" who (along with the Marx boys) were involved in the radical movements of the twenties. We think of *moga*, of whatever the Takarazuka all-girl revues have meant to a generation of young girls, and of the "business *gāru"* of the present day. But with the exception of those few who were caught up in literary or political movements, most of whose members were male, generational differences seem fewer among women, and the differences are even less marked among those with less education. In sum, although generational change was only one of a number of changes affecting the home environment, it is possible to reconcile rather dramatic changes in generational images with family situations that changed very slowly.

Not only has change in personality been slow in the modern era, but there are considerable continuities between modern and premodern Japan. In the opening paper in this volume John Pelzel points out similarities between the social and personality characteristics of the gods in Japan's ancient myth cycles and those of present-day Japanese. There is more resonance between the novels of a Kawabata or Tanizaki and Heian literature than can be explained by conscious imitation alone. The work of Japanese scholars such as Hori Jirō on the rural *gemeinschaft* suggests the historical setting in which basic values and beliefs, child-rearing practices, and certain patterns of interpersonal relations and group behavior could be continued over time, only tangentially affected by changes, say, in the polity. Ruth Benedict, George DeVos, and others have suggested some of the psychological mechanisms that undergird these continuities. Their findings have been based on the recent period but can be projected back, in part at least, to earlier periods. More work and thinking about this problem is sorely needed. More work is needed, too, both by historians and social scientists, to show the relationship between core personality and generational changes. Only when a more comprehensive view of Japanese personality is developed will psychology become a practical tool for historical interpretation. We shall consider a few examples of aspects of Japanese personality that an adequate theory must encompass.

One such aspect is the relation between the individual and his group. We suggested earlier that there are similarities between the *shishi* of the Restoration movement, the ultranationalist young officers of the thirties, and the radical students of the sixties. Here we would add merely that these do not represent abnormal types of groups, but rather the extreme form of the normal group. This can be characterized by saying that the claims that the group makes on its members are great, and the ability of the members to resist these claims is small.

One claim of the group is for efficiency or hard work in achieving its goals. It is the achievement that is required, even if obtained by more hard work and less efficiency. A lack of achievement is seen as a consequence of insufficient effort. The ability of the group to make this claim is certainly one of the reasons why, in economic life or in sports, team members who are not stars as individuals will out-perform other groups as a group.

Another claim of the group is for time. Whatever the formal function of the group, it also provides for the social life of the member, for aid and comfort at a time of crisis, for leisure, and even at times for vacations or for collective travel to a hot spring or beach resort. A Japanese may nominally belong to several groups, but the demands are sufficiently great as to preclude real membership in more than one—his liege group as it were. Professor Nakane Chie, a Tokyo University anthropologist, subtitled her recent book on human relations in Japan "The Theory of a Society Made Up of Singular Groups" (*Tan'itsu shakai no riron*). In it she describes how negative most Japanese feel about attachments to multiple groups, and how an unswerving attachment to a single group is viewed almost as a kind of moral purity (*keppeki*). Those in one's group are "ours" (*uchi no mono*), those who are not are "outsiders" (*yoso no mono*).[11] Describing the same phenomenon in intellectual circles, Professor Maruyama Masao compared these tight academic groupings to octopus pots and saw them as producing an "octopus-pot culture" (*tako tsubo bunka*).[12]

Another claim of the group is for conformity or even uniformity. As the often quoted Japanese proverb has it, "the nail that sticks will be driven in." My observation of Japanese academic groups—which might or might not be typical—is that the group members are frequently very different kinds of people but that they take on a kind of surface homogeneity while interacting in the group. Nakane Chie, however, feels that the members of a given group actually come to resemble one another, because of the demand for conformity, because those who do not fit in with the group will drop out, and because a given group will attract similar personality types.[13]

One Japanese reaction to the demand for group conformity is critical. In the modern era in the most Westernized sectors of Japanese culture, great value has been placed on being an individual; this has led some to speak of the tyranny of the group that demands the sacrifice of individuality. A Japanese psychiatrist put this strongly saying that "just as a man cannot measure his physical weight in water, so we Japanese do not feel our moral weight in groups."[14]

Yet another appraisal is possible. Inui Takashi, in an article entitled "Psychoanalysis in the Context of Japanese Culture," contrasts the middle-aged American woman who confesses to her psychiatrist to relieve her isolation of self to the Japanese whose self is not yet differentiated from his family (*ie to mibunka na jiga*) or group, and who therefore cannot be treated as a self-contained entity.[15] (Of course, one notes a certain conflu-

---

[11] Nakane Chie, *Tate shakai no ningen kankei* (Tokyo, 1967), pp. 49, 55–56.
[12] Maruyama Masao, *Nihon no shisō* (Tokyo, 1961), p. 64.
[13] Nakane, *Tate shakai*, pp. 171–172.
[14] Nada Inada and Hoshi Shin'ichi, "Seishin bunseki to Nihonjin," *Shisō no kagaku*, 3:12 (1966).
[15] Inui Takashi, "Nihon bunka no naka no seishin bunseki," *Shisō no kagaku*, 3:18 (1966).

ence between this point of view and recent American tendencies to stress the family context of mental problems.) Can we not say that such an undifferentiated individual is incomplete without his group and takes on moral weight in the group—conscious of himself as a group representative vis-à-vis other groups? The positive side of the Japanese group is the support, the warmth, and the sense of belonging that it gives to its members. Robert Lifton notes that even in Westernized intellectuals who espouse the idea of selfhood, "one can frequently detect an even more profound craving for renewed group life, for solidarity, even for the chance to melt completely into a small group, a professional organization, a mass movement, and even at the cost of nearly all self assertion. Those most concerned with selfhood have often told me . . . that their moments of greatest happiness come when they feel themselves, in a spiritual sense, completely merged with groups of young comrades."[16]

What kind of a self does the Japanese group require? This is a hard question for there are many kinds of Japanese groups and self, or nonself, as a metaphysical entity is often quite different from ego in the psychological sense of the term. On the whole, however, it would appear that the Japanese group requires a weaker, or at least a less obtrusive, self. Talking about the success of psychoanalysis (which he dislikes) in the United States, Mishima Yukio has written,

> The Americans . . . are quite certain of the existence of their "conscience," if of nothing else. Whether this conscience is satisfied, shines with pride, or is wounded or shattered, it remains always the conscience—just as a regimental flag is still the regimental flag even when it is shot to tatters. Possibly the question of whether or not the conscience actually exists has never presented itself to the Americans.[17]

[16] Robert Lifton, "Youth and History: Individual Change in Postwar Japan," in *Daedalus,* winter 1962, p. 182. In Kyoto I once overheard a conversation in a second-hand book store between the proprietress and a friend. The proprietress told her friend that she was going with a religious group on a bus trip to such and such a mountain. The friend asked if it was not dangerous on the mountain roads. The proprietress replied, "If we all die together, then it's all right, isn't it?"
[17] Mishima Yukio, "A Famous Japanese Judges the U.S. Giant," *Life,* Sept. 11, 1964, p. 84.

Mishima concludes that Americans "sometimes tend to over-exist." Certainly in the West the self is taken for granted. Theology posits the irreducible individual soul. In the philosophy of a more secular age in Descartes' *cogito ergo sum* the self is built into the conjugated verb. As Walt Whitman put it, "One's-self must never give way—that is the final substance—that out of all else is sure." Or more simply, "One's-self I sing, a simple separate person. . . ."[18]

In contrast to Americans, Mishima continued,

> The Japanese nurtured as they are on Buddhism, have the curious conviction that existence is a transitory and basically unessential phenomenon, a shifting process which changes with each moment, a relative state as opposed to nothingness. . . . I am certain this thinking persists even in the minds of the young people dancing the twist in Tokyo today.[19]

Mishima suggests that the self in Japan is like the stage assistant in a Kabuki play who, dressed entirely in black, "may appear scarcely more than a shadow" and goes out of existence by turning his back to the audience.

Edwin McClellan has pointed out that even modern Japanese writers feel that plot is mechanical and that fleeting poetic moments are more real, and they are often critical of the sustained personalities in Western novels as forced and unreal. Natsume Sōseki, for example, though he abandoned the simple lyricism of the early *Kusamakura*, saw Joseph Conrad as a writer of adventure stories.[20] A major theme, certainly, in Western literature is the hero with a moral flaw who faces a crisis and emerges morally reintegrated. *The Short Happy Life of Francis Mac-Comber* comes to mind. This almost never happens to the protagonists in Japanese novels, in spite of the fact that Japanese writers have drawn heavily on Western models. The heroes of Natsume Sōseki's novels, though morally superior to those of

---

[18] Walt Whitman, *Leaves of Grass* (New York, 1931), pp. 1, 454.
[19] Mishima, "A Famous Japanese," p. 84.
[20] Edwin McClellan, *Two Japanese Novelists: Sōseki and Tōson* (Chicago, 1969), pp. 92–93. Also, personal communication.

the so-called I-novels, are typical in the hopelessness of their fate. And when moral integration of the self does occur, as in Ōe Kenzaburō's *A Personal Affair,* it has a false, tacked-on-at-the-last-minute quality. The Japanese view of self also relates to the virtual absence of tragedy as a genre in Japanese literature. This view of self also seems to relate to the negative identity of Akutagawa that Howard Hibbett has analyzed in his article. All of this is not to say that the same range of personality types cannot be found in Japan and in the West. There are many "Japanese themes" in modern Western literature. But the modalities seem dramatically different.

It can be argued that literature is an untrustworthy guide to personality. Literary circles in Japan are at a far remove from government, business, the village, or the school. The aimlessness and paralysis of will so often portrayed in literature contrasts with the dynamism and purposiveness of other sectors of society. But I would argue—putting leaders aside for the moment—that even the members of dynamic organizations display the same tendency to dissolve self into the group. The willingness to work hard and the desire for career advancements are there in abundance, but they are directed toward group ends and achieved without open self-assertiveness. Individual ends are attainable only by making a maximum contribution to the collectivity. Patterns of seniority and lifetime employment are designed to minimize the kind of competition that would disrupt work group harmony.

The type of personality that can function in such groups is formed by child-rearing practices that encourage dependence. Ezra and Suzanne Vogel have argued persuasively that both healthy Japanese children and mature Japanese are dependent to a degree that in the West would be considered unhealthy and immature.[21] Lifton argues that it is the continuity in the family connection that gives balance to Japanese college youth floundering in a sea of competing and shifting identities.[22] Doi Takeo,

[21] Ezra F. and Suzanne H. Vogel, "Family Security, Personal Immaturity, and Emotional Health in a Japanese Sample," *Marriage and Family Living,* 23, no. 2:161–166 (May 1961).
[22] Lifton, "Youth," p. 178.

a Japanese psychiatrist, has erected a theory of Japanese personality using the idea of *amaeru*, man's desire to be the dependent and passive object of love. He goes so far as to say that this is basic not only in Japan but in all human beings, but is largely hidden and distorted in the West by the cultural emphasis on individualism.[23]

Along with child-rearing practices that encourage dependence, the Japanese child is taught that virtue consists of acting selflessly for his group (though the term *muga* is somewhat out of fashion today). He learns to be *enryo*, not to push the self. He learns not to be importunate (*shitsukoi*), not to push or probe at the self of another. The result is a pattern of social relations in which there is a great sensitivity toward the emotional mood of the other person or group, coupled with an extreme reticence to express self or to query others directly. Japanese literature abounds in passages such as "Katsuko stood on the doorstep and looked forlornly at Kishimoto. Not a word passed between them, but each knew what the other felt."[24] In life each often wonders what the other feels, but is unable to ask. In literature the mood is often communicated by a description of nature rather than by words. And, as Mishima pointed out, the ethic or behavioral cues that fitted such a pattern of social relations were linked traditionally to a philosophy in which self must be extinguished in order to arrive at truth.

Another aspect of Japanese personality that an adequate theory must deal with is the mechanism of shame. Following Ruth Benedict, Japan is often described as a "shame-culture"—though this view has been modified in recent years by DeVos and others. Working during the war and trying to explain Japanese wartime behavior, Benedict quite naturally stressed the coercive aspects of Japanese society. Recently there is a greater tendency among social scientists to stress the positive side of shame, that is, to stress the positive sanctions at work in a situation-centered ethic and not merely the negative, or op-

23 Doi Takeo, "Seishin bunseki to Nihonteki seikaku," *Shisō no kagaku*, 11:6–7 (1969).
24 McClellan, *Two Japanese Novelists*, p. 96.

pressive. As John Pelzel puts it in his paper in this volume, "It is . . . the habit of . . . Japanese . . . to engage for the most part in proper acts, impelled thereto by positive sanctions . . . to gain and earn consideration for themselves as sentient beings, as well as to give that consideration, and not merely by the fear of losing it." Many Japanese writers continue to stress the negative side of group life, but many are critical of Benedict and see themselves and their society in a new light. Doi, for example, writes that in broad terms Benedict was right: Japan is a shame-culture and the West is a guilt-culture. But he feels that Benedict's definition of shame needs to be reexamined. Doi finds in Western writings "a unique cultural prejudice" to the effect that it is shameful to be a shame-culture. Quoting various recent Japanese writings, Doi criticizes first the notion that guilt is inner and good whereas shame is more on the surface and lacks an inner dimension. He notes first that guilt without shame can produce a personality so inner-oriented that it disregards the feelings of others and bulls its way through life. He quotes the anthropologist Ishida Eijirō to the effect that the Westerner's consciousness of guilt is often quite shallow and it is the tendency to push himself that is so much stronger in the Westerner than in the Japanese. Doi notes secondly that the kind of values associated with the "guilt-personality" often produces a highly self-righteous attitude toward life. In contrast to this he notes that shame is not just a matter of face or appearances (*taimen*) but is "delicate and internal and is involved with character."[25]

Another aspect of the question of shame—the direction of change in Japanese personality—is also touched on by Doi. He points out that modernization in Japan has to no small extent meant Westernization. A great deal of the cultural content of modern Japan is Western. As a result, Japanese values have become somewhat less particularistic and somewhat more universalistic. At the same time in the West, though the tradition remains universalistic, the Christian consciousness of sin has

---

[25] Doi, "Seishin bunseki," pp. 2–3. The quotation about shame as delicate and internal is from Sakuta Keiichi, *Haji no bunka saikō* (Tokyo, 1967). See Part 1.

declined greatly, weakening the sense of guilt so much in fact that David Riesman found it necessary to propose the category of "other-directedness." All of this is leading, according to Doi, to a blurring of the lines between Japan as a shame-culture and the West as a guilt-culture.[26]

Certainly the preceding is true in the sense of there being similar mechanisms, both of guilt and shame, at work in both areas, and certainly the direction of change is one that will gradually narrow the differences between the two areas. Certainly, too, no Japanese who has visited the West and no Westerner who has visited Japan has found any human trait with which he was not already familiar in his own country. But the distribution and configuration of traits is different. This is clear whether we are reading a Japanese novel or viewing Japanese social organization. Both areas still have much to learn from each other. Both cultures can still learn a great deal about themselves by studying the other.

Still another facet of Japanese character that theory must take into account—one that we can only mention in passing here—is the Japanese awareness of nature. John Pelzel writes in his paper in this volume that even in Japan's ancient myths, "this world is a harmonious union of the life of man with the life of nature," and that the myths were "the first literary expression of that acute and comradely sensitivity to physical nature that has been a hallmark of the customs of Japanese life down to our own day." This sensitivity was particularly strong in the premodern Japanese tradition in painting, in poetry, and in religion. But it is also a part of modern Japanese life, not only in flower arrangement or *haiku* or the painting of bamboo that are the preserved traditional arts, but in literature or in the use of gardens in modern architecture or in a fine photographic use of nature to convey human emotion in a television drama that otherwise may be ordinary and sentimental.

This involvement with nature can be interpreted, as Robert

[26] Doi, "Seishin bunseki," p. 4. I have added to Doi's comments the point about Christian sin and Western universalism for it is implied, I feel, in his argument.

N. Bellah has put it recently, as a search for "oases of personal autonomy" away from the claims of the group.[27] Benedict wrote that "social pressures in Japan, no matter how voluntarily embraced, ask too much of the individual."[28] The openness toward nature, like the many other forms of emotional expressiveness in Japan, may be an outlet through which the psyche can obtain relief from these pressures. Another interpretation would be to see the Japanese ability to melt into nature as akin to the ability to melt into the social group. The openness and sensitivity to subtle cues in the group mood that the group member can miss only at his peril may be similar to the receptivity toward nature and the willingness to let it flow in on the self. John Pelzel writes that for the Japanese "the natural world . . . has life and will that are all but identical with those of man." The fusing of self with nature lets self see in nature moods corresponding to its own.

Leadership is yet another problem that a theory of Japanese personality must treat. It is a particularly important problem for this volume because most of the papers deal with men who were leaders in one field or another.

Most discussions of leadership by social scientists start with the characteristics of Japanese groups or organizations and then ask what kind of a man fits in best with these characteristics. Nakane Chie, in her recent book *Human Relations in a Vertically Organized Society,* discusses a number of the attributes of the Japanese leader. (1) The Japanese leader is not Napoleonic, he is not a dictator; the scope of his personal freedom is narrow. Rather, she picks Ōishi Kuranosuke, the leader of the forty-seven *rōnin,* as the typical Japanese type of leader. (2) The Japanese leader is a member of the group rather than one who stands above the group. He is held responsible for the actions of the group, both by higher authority and by the group itself. And he must be responsive to the demands of the group. If he can do this, it matters little whether he is brilliant or even especially

---

[27] Robert N. Bellah, "Continuity and Change in Japanese Society," unpublished, p. 20.
[28] Benedict, *Chrysanthemum and Sword,* p. 315.

capable, for among his followers there will be brilliant men who can do the work. In the typical Japanese group the followers will be given considerable freedom as long as they do their work. (3) To maintain harmony within the group the leader must be personally attractive. He must have confidence in his personal influence. A Japanese expression applicable to this type of leader might begin, "When they are face to face with me . . ." (*Ore no kao ni menjite* . . .). The typical leader is a parent figure (*oyabun*) and his underlings are like his children (*kobun*).[29] The leader's strength as a leader depends on his personal control over his underlings. Japanese leaders tend to be old. If a man is old but lacks *kobun*, he is treated coldly. (4) Among his *kobun* the leader is particularly dependent on his lieutenants (*kanbu*). Because of this vertical axis of dependence there is a constant though muted struggle for power between leaders and their followers. In recent years the decline of hierarchical authority has tended to tip the balance in favor of the followers or lower echelons of a group or organization. (5) "In Japanese society brilliant leaders are not those who form groups by their individual powers. Rather they are capable individuals who are fortunate enough (since their turn to be the leader is a matter of seniority) to be a leader of a group that has won out in power struggles with other groups."[30]

These are interesting generalizations. The student of recent organizational theory may object and say that some of these are characteristic of organizations in any country. Some, however, are distinctively Japanese, and some are truer for Japan than elsewhere. The greatest difficulty is that, as even the small sample of leaders covered in this volume makes clear, no one

[29] Robert Bellah writes on this point: "While great initiative and dynamic activity of a very 'masculine' sort are necessary to put together large groups . . . the leadership that excites the strongest emotion and the greatest devotion is more passive and even feminine. Symbolically this more emotionally positive type of leadership focuses on the mother at the family level and the emperor at the national level. Both stand for nurturance and benevolence rather than domination and control. Those who dominate and direct gain their legitimacy as defenders or protectors of the more feminine type of leaders." "Continuity and Change," p. 16.

[30] Nakane, *Tate shakai*, pp. 135–155.

set of generalizations is adequate to cover the different types of leaders found in Japan.

One category is that of the hereditary leader. Because this type of leader "rose to power" simply by the accident of his birth, he had no special set of personality characteristics or particular fitness for office. A similarity of upbringing may have created a certain "daimyo-type" personality in some instances. The usual generalization is that there were many able daimyo at the start of the Tokugawa period but that the blood line gradually became thin. The rise of han bureaucracies meant that incompetent figureheads could be honored and tolerated without harm. Even in the last years of the Tokugawa era, however, we are struck by the number of able men such as Nariaki, Shungaku, Nariakira, Hisamitsu, Abe Masahiro, and so on. These men stand up well to earlier figures such as Ikeda Mitsumasa. There were also many who came to office by lateral succession as adults without having been prepared for it from birth —Tsunayoshi, Yoshimune, Keiki, and many daimyo as well.

A second category of leaders are those who built their own structure of power or who rose to leadership by their own ability in a situation of flux. These are the strongest leaders—Hideyoshi or Ieyasu, the Restoration leaders such as Kido or Ōkubo, perhaps a Hara Kei, and the founders of modern economic enterprises such as Iwasaki, Matsushita, or Ibuka. If not loved like Saigō Takamori, they are looked up to as great men. They wore in Japanese eyes that peculiar aureole that "founders" have— whether they be founders of religious, political, or economic organizations. As men who began organizations of one sort or another all were organization men in some sense of the term, but many of the usual generalizations about leaders do not fit them in a simple way.

A third type of leader described by papers in this volume might be called the ideological-charismatic leader, the leader who attracts a following by embodying the morality of a particular ideological position. Yoshida Shōin may be the best example of this as a pure type. Ōshio Heihachirō, a teacher of the most spiritual variety of Confucianism, led his followers in rebellion against the ills of his society. Akutagawa Ryūnosuke, in a very different way, was also a creative thinker and provided his followers with a moral example of rebellion against life itself. Nagai Ryūtarō is another possibility for this category. In his vision of a different society and his oratorical appeal, he seems to fit. Yet as Peter Duus points out, Nagai's prudence and loyalty vis-à-vis his party make him more organizational and less charismatic.

Another kind of leader—they are too important to be dismissed as subleaders—is represented by Mutsu Munemitsu and Itō Miyoji. They began respectively as protégés of Kido and Itō Hirobumi. They were picked up and used because of their intelligence, talents, and astuteness. Neither seems to have been particularly attractive (if anything, the opposite is true), but both became fairly powerful figures in their own right.

A final category of leadership, one not well represented in this volume, is the typical modern leader who gradually rises to the top in a bureaucratic organization, be it public or private. Is such a man typical of what we have described as the modal Japanese personality? In some ways he had to be or else he would have been rejected by his group. In most instances he had to accept lifetime employment, the practice of seniority, and the muting of competition in the interest of face-to-face harmony. Yet I find myself in disagreement with most Japanese academic writers in that I find even the typical leader of this type likely to be an unusually disciplined personality in terms of Japanese norms. The desire for success is strong in most Japanese. Only a few can attain it. Those who do must exhibit drive to an exceptional degree. On entering a bureaucratic organization the new employee works hard for the first time since studying for the college entrance examinations. All who enter a company or government ministry will advance at the same pace; but after the first few years, as differences in ability become known, they will advance on different "tracks." Some posts lie on inside tracks that lead to the top and some do not. To get these posts requires considerable ability and unrelenting effort. The fact that the aspirant for a top post must compete without appearing to compete makes the competition no less fierce, but it makes the competitors more self-disciplined. The seesaw of power between leaders and their subordinates described by Nakane results in no small part from an attempt by the underlings to have this or that policy adopted, and the adoption of a policy usually means the promotion to policy-superintending posts of those who espoused it. The all-pervasive authority of the traditional boss—who could ask his *kobun* to help out in his garden on their day off—is disappearing rapidly. But a more functionally specific authority is still strong in Japan today. The type of man who gains such authority may be disciplined to the point of being colorless, but he is not an average Japanese personality.

There are certain questions relating to personality that can be asked in any society. Is the person the first child, the in-between child, the baby of the family, or an only child? Was his father alive when he was young? What was the social status of his parents? Were his parents easygoing or strict? Even in very simple societies variables such as these produce a variety of recognizable personality types. Japan is not a simple society. Even in premodern times Japan had a society and culture which were comparable to those of the West in their complexity and sophistication. The range and complexity of personalities was therefore extensive. On top of this traditional complexity Japan has assimilated much of Western tradition during the past century. Although some mothers still raise their children with the mother-in-law looking over their shoulder, others do it with a Japanese translation of Dr. Spock in one hand. The range of variation, accordingly, grows ever larger.

Considering the potential richness of the subject and the impressive development of the Japanese university system, studies of personality are grossly underdeveloped in Japan. Following the German tradition, psychology as an academic undertaking has meant largely experimental psychology. Other social sciences until after World War II were also Germanic and abstract or when they were concrete, as in the school of Yanagita Kunio, they involved matters other than personality. The complete works of Freud were translated into Japanese by about 1920, but the general reaction to them was either indifferent or unfavorable. Even today most Japanese psychiatrists seem to feel that Freud is a mixture of the universal and the culture-bound. Doi, for example, argues that just as Freud built on positions that had been suggested by Nietzsche, so psychoanalysis in Japan must build on the insights suggested by Natsume Sōseki.[31] In the 1930's, Japanese medicine followed German medicine into a stance strongly opposed to psychoanalysis. Since the war, psychoanalysis has become somewhat more popular. Along with it there have developed vigorous departments of cultural anthropology and social psychology in Japanese universities. Yet relative to other fields, the study of personality is still at an early phase of development in Japan.

For the future, the historian and social scientist must cooperate in working out a theory of personality. The historian can test theory. The social scientist can provide the historian with tools that will be helpful in understanding the particular. Convergent studies are indicated. But for the moment it is perhaps more valuable for the historian to study this or that man in his historical setting, drawing on theory when it seems useful. This is the course taken in this book.

[31] Doi, "Seishin bunseki," p. 5.

HUMAN NATURE
IN THE JAPANESE MYTHS

John C. Pelzel

What follows is an attempt to describe one traditional Japanese literary view of human nature, that pictured in the myth portions of the *Kojiki* and *Nihongi*. Though the quality seen in man is the main interest here, it has seemed desirable to describe also the myths' view of his context—the nature of the world and of mankind's role in it.

These sources constitute only one of the models that the basic literary tradition made available to later generations of Japanese. Buddhist and lay Chinese conceptions were in time absorbed, and in recent centuries ideas from the West, and we must assume that throughout history the native talent reworked the body of perceptions it had before it in varying ways. Nevertheless, the myths are the earliest repositories of this tradition, and in spite of many additions to Japanese eschatological literature and numerous fluctuations of fashion, the myths have not been rewritten, nor have they ceased to be well known and viewed with at least some measure of respect by even moderately well-educated Japanese. They are thus the most persistent, and at least one of the basic, sources of native literary views on these matters.

The behavioral relevance of such a model is an interesting problem. One may wish to argue that a society's basic literature offers cognitive limits and patterns according to which the native mind tends to build up its understanding of the world and of man. As values, the views of prestigious literature may be accepted by native individuals as proper judgments and can even affect the choices through which, in part, they form their own personalities. Nevertheless, and critical as the question of behavioral relevance undoubtedly is in many contexts, it is beyond the scope of the present paper, which will confine itself to the attempt to discern the mythic model itself.

What the *Kojiki* and the *Nihongi* have to say about the cosmos and man was not set out in any self-conscious or reasoned statement. These books are art forms, a mixture of narrative legend and poetry. But in this they are characteristic of the main form of the Japanese literary tradition, which in this respect contrasts so sharply with the Chinese corpus as to merit a reminder.

The bulk of the respected literature of China has been a formal ethics, identified with individual professional philosophers, and a history deliberately written to illustrate the conclusions of the philosophers. Chinese literature is thus rational and intellectualized, as well as didactic. Its thrust, moreover, is such as to counsel agnosticism about the nature of the cosmos, earthly pragmatism about the role of man therein, and disinterest in most aspects of human nature except the moral. Japanese literature, by way of contrast, has from its beginnings in the myths taken forms—such as poetry, fiction, and the drama—which are best suited to an approach by intuition and imagination rather than reason. This literature has been much given, moreover, to questioning and picturing the place of individual men in a cosmos that includes, but that goes far beyond, earthly society. Certainly, then, what the Chinese and the Japanese sources have to say about man differ not alone in the traits of personality they discern or emphasize, but even more basically in the approach to the human condition that they illustrate. Chinese literature had faith in conscious moral will and exhorted man to be what he should be in one overwhelmingly important segment of life. Japanese literature instead had faith in intuition and described men in terms of the whole existence they were seen to lead.

The context and the events of life are thus basic to the interpretation of the Japanese myths, and their narrative accordingly deserves to be recapitulated here. In details, the stories of the two books under consideration vary slightly, but both were well known and had roughly equal prestige.[1] The retelling that follows attempts to combine important elements from both tales, noting the textual divergence only when this seems to have a particular significance.

The myths fall into several cycles, most centering on certain major figures and events, and roughly sequent to one another in terms of myth chronology. We may broadly divide this chronol-

---

[1] One man, Ō no Yasumaro, was the key amanuensis for both books, which were completed in 712 A.D. (the *Kojiki*) and in 720 (the *Nihongi.*) Neither book is represented as other than a compilation from then-extant sources, not now identifiable but apparently consisting primarily of the archives of various noble families (including the imperial family) and oral traditions and documents, many of the latter having themselves been written down from oral tradition. Both compilations were made at imperial order, at a time when the throne was coming into a position to assert the cultural supremacy of the centralized state over the feudalism or tribalism of the noble families and at a time when Chinese influence over the lives and thought of the upper class was rapidly increasing.

The *Kojiki* is said to be the transcript of a record dictated to Yasumaro by one Hieda no Are, a person famous for the ability to memorize, though twenty-five years after he (or she) had been set to the task of committing at least some part of the extant sources to memory. The *Nihongi* is represented as having been compiled entirely from then-existent documents by Yasumaro and Prince Toneri. The forms of the books we have are consistent with the origins imputed to them. The *Kojiki* is a smoothly flowing narrative in colloquial Japanese (though transliterated by Chinese characters used phonetically), whereas the *Nihongi* is written in the Chinese language itself, which was used then for all official documents, and includes quotations as well as numerous variants from the differing sources said to have been used.

The question has been raised of whether the *Kojiki* we have is not a much later forgery. In evidence against this view, the book shows very few of those Chinese influences which were at the time of its reputed compilation only becoming known in Japan, but which were soon to become an inseparable part of the intellectual furniture of later generations of Japanese. Moreover, the *Kojiki* also is said to preserve many archaic Japanese linguistic usages which were not known to later generations. Thus, most authorities believe the *Kojiki* to be what it pretends to be. Probably equally authentic, the *Nihongi*, however, contains many more usages and ideas derived from the continent, and thus represents a further stage of that cultural fusion which was becoming fashionable during the generation and a half that the compilers say separated the original of these texts.

The English translations used and quoted here are, for the *Kojiki*, Basil Hall Chamberlain's "Kojiki, Records of Ancient Matters," *Transactions of the Asiatic Society of Japan*, supplement to vol. 10 (1882), and for the *Nihongi*, W. G. Aston's *Nihongi, Chronicles of Japan from the Earliest Times to* A.D. 697, supplement to Transactions and Proceedings of the Japan Society (London, 1896). The Japanese text of the *Kojiki* used is that of Kurano Kenji, ed., *Kojiki taisei*, vol. 6: *Hombun-hen* (Tokyo, 1957).

ogy into three myth eras, namely, Before the Creation of the Earth, the Creation of the Earth, and the Ordering of the Earth.

THE ERA BEFORE THE CREATION OF THE EARTH

This first segment of the myths is extremely brief and, in contrast with what follows, aesthetically unrewarding. The story starts with heaven already in existence,[2] though we are told virtually nothing about it until the third and final era, and with the earth still a formless thing, floating about below heaven "medusalike," "like drifting oil." The first precursor of creation was the growth of a "thing like a reed shoot," which in its turn gave rise to three or four (varying with the source) deities described as "single," that is, each existing alone, at a different time, without discernible relation to the others, and, it may be added, without our learning anything about them other than their names.[3] These were followed by four or five generations, each of which comprised a pair of gods, one male and one female, described as "brother and sister." The last such pair, Izanagi (the brother) and Izanami, were the creator gods par excellence.

THE CREATION OF THE EARTH

With this segment, the story comes to life. The creator siblings stood on the "floating bridge of heaven," stirred the formlessness below with the "heavenly jewel spear," and watched the brine dripping from its point curdle into an island, Onogoro. Descending to it, they erected there the "pillar of the center of the land" and proceeded to the work of creation.

In part, they created as their exuviae, articles of their clothing, and so forth turned into progeny. But in part they created through normal mammalian sexual reproduction, which is given

[2] The *Nihongi* states baldly that heaven emerged before earth as a "united body" out of an original chaos, "like an egg which was of obscurely defined limits and contained germs," but all commentators consider this a Sinified exegesis.

[3] The *Kojiki* lists three "single gods" in existence in heaven prior to the appearance of the reed shoot, but none is given any prominence.

by far the greater attention in this cycle. As it turns out, they must discover or invent sexual reproduction, and they perform a ritual to accompany it, a marriage rite, as well.

Izanagi, as though casting about for a method of creation, asked his sister how her body was formed. She replied that in one place it was "not complete." Noting that his own body at one point had "something left over," he then proposed, "How would it be if we were to fill in the place on your body that is not complete with the spot on mine where something is left over, and so give birth to the land?" She replied simply, "That would be good."

Izanagi likewise devised a ritual, which consisted in their circumambulating the pillar of the center of the land from opposite directions, he from the left and she from the right; on meeting on the other side, they would "perform the acts of the honeymoon chamber."[4] On the first attempt, however, the sister exclaimed first, on the far side of the pillar, "What a fine, lovely youth!" a forwardness which her brother considered a breach of the proper male-female relationship. He therefore had them perform the circumambulation again and exclaim on one another's loveliness in the proper sequence. As a result of the breach of etiquette that had occurred, however, one of their children was born deformed.[5]

By sexual reproduction and something approaching parthenogenesis, therefore, the siblings created a large number of deities, many identifiable with the seas, islands, rivers, mountains, and vegetation of Japan and others (for example, the Sun Goddess) deities who came later to occupy key positions in heaven or in the process by which the created earth was put into order.

Only the *Kojiki* and certain variants cited by the compilers of

[4] The text of the *Kojiki* is slightly less euphemistic than that of the *Nihongi*. The term here translated *acts* of the honeymoon chamber is glossed by Kurano, p. 53, as having meant "to exchange glances and consummate a marriage."

[5] The *Kojiki* and a variant cited in the *Nihongi*, but not the text of the *Nihongi* itself, state that Izanagi and Izanami were commanded to their task of creating the earth by the "heavenly deities" and took counsel with them to discover, through their divination, the breach that had produced the deformed child. I have omitted these evidences of a complete and guiding heaven, however, for it is not shown as deeply involved in the creation of earth.

the *Nihongi,* but not the text of the *Nihongi* itself, tell a version of the common Old World tale of Orpheus and Eurydice in hades. According to the Japanese version, Izanami was badly burned by the birth of the Fire God and died, going to the "world of darkness." Mourning for her and wishing to persuade her to come back and continue the unfinished work of creation, Izanagi followed her, but when he met her he violated her order not to look at her and saw her in the corruption of her body. Frightened, he fled toward the upper world while she, in shame, sent avenging deities after him. He was able to trick them, however, and in the end took leave of his sister-wife at the Even Pass of Hades in enmity, she threatening to strangle earthly people, and he boasting that he could easily replace such losses, building "1,500 parturition huts a day." Back on earth, according to the *Kojiki,* he then saw other deities created from his exuviae, and according to both books he retired to a life of perpetual quiet on the islands of Japan.

THE ORDERING OF THE EARTH

Much the longest and most circumstantial, this segment of the myths consists of several cycles depicting the events whereby the created earth was ordered into the particular life forms we know. Not only is it richer in detail than what goes before, there also is repeated variation between the two main texts, and numerous variants are cited by the compilers of the *Nihongi.*

The story begins with a cycle depicting the relations in heaven between the Sun Goddess, now ruling there on the authority of her parent(s), and her younger brother Susanoo (the meaning of whose name we do not know). Susanoo had from birth been a selfish, cruel, and unruly god, whose very presence "withered mountains and dried up rivers and seas" and encouraged the "sound of bad deities to be like flies in the fifth moon." His parent(s) therefore had ordered him to proceed to the nether world (or the sea) to be its ruler where he could not harm the things of earth, but instead, at the start of this cycle, he had risen up to heaven.

His rising made so fierce a commotion it alerted and alarmed his sister, who wondered if he came "with good intentions" or to rob her of her kingdom. Fearing the latter, she dressed and armed herself like a man, gave a battle cry, and went to question him on the "redness of his heart," i.e., his sincerity. He protested his innocence, saying he had only wished to bid his sister good-bye before leaving to take up his own realm far away. To test the purity of his intentions, however, brother and sister engaged in an ordeal which amounted to a symbolic act of incest. She chewed up his sword and spat out its pieces as children, while he did likewise with the jewels of her regalia. They then exchanged children, those treated as hers and as inheritors of her authority and ancestors of the imperial family being the sons her brother spat out from her regalia.

The result of the ordeal was accepted as vindication of his intentions, and he remained a visitor in heaven. However, he continued to perform acts which were aggressive and destructive—breaking down the dikes around his sister's rice fields, letting a piebald colt loose in her fields at harvest time, defecating on the floor of her palace, and so forth. The Sun Goddess did not protest these acts, however, in each case finding an excuse for them that was acceptable to her. For example, she decided that in tearing down the dikes among her fields he had been moved by a helpful intent, impractical as it was in actuality, merely to increase the area that could be planted to rice, and she imagined that what looked like excrement on her floor was really nothing but vomit that he had brought up during an otherwise forgivable bout of drunkenness.

Eventually, however, Susanoo broke a hole in her roof while she was weaving, and threw in the corpse of a piebald colt flayed backwards. She (or her maids) was so startled that she jumped up and wounded herself (or themselves) on the shuttle. Indignant at this personal outrage and harm, she withdrew into a cave, locked the door, and so reduced heaven to darkness. Thereupon, the *Kojiki* adds, the "voices of the myriad [evil?] deities were like the flies in the fifth moon as they swarmed, and myriad portents of woe all arose."

The heavenly deities met together in a riverbed and consulted on how to end this intolerable situation. They collected a number of objects and performed various rituals, but they also did things to pique the Sun Goddess's curiosity and vanity. Having birds fill the air with song, they also had a goddess perform a noisy dance so lewd ("pulling out the nipples of her breasts and pushing down her skirt-string to her private parts") that they all laughed. Hearing the sounds of apparent revelry outside and wondering how the deities could make merry with herself absent and the world dark, the Sun Goddess stuck her head out to see what was happening. A mirror was immediately pushed up in front of her face, and she was told that it was a "deity more illustrious than" herself. Quite upset, she came out further until she could be grasped and was implored by the deities not to deprive them of herself again. The heavenly deities then took upon themselves the judgement of Susanoo. Fining him for the pollution he had caused, they banished him from heaven, in effect voting for the continued rule of the Sun Goddess.

In the next cycle, Susanoo descended to earth, at a spot known historically as Izumo, and after saving the daughter of a pair of "earthly deities" from a monstrous dragon, produced from her a progeny that was to rule earth for a period, the principal descendant being the so-called "Master of the Land." Susanoo himself then proceeded to the nether world he had for so long avoided.

At this point, the sources vary considerably. It is clear from all that the earth was still untamed. As one variant says, "This central land of reed-plains had always been waste and wild. The very rocks, trees, and herbs were all given to violence." The text of the *Nihongi* notes that "earth had numerous deities which buzzed like flies. There were also trees and herbs, all of which could speak." This subcelestial world had to be "constructed . . . for the sake of the visible race of man as well as for beasts . . . in order to do away with the calamities [that occur to] birds, beasts, and creeping things," and all texts make it clear that the progeny of the Sun Goddess, who were eventually to rule Japan, did not want to take on so noisome a place until it had been made habitable.

However, the *Kojiki* and several of the variants cited by the compilers of the *Nihongi* have most of this taming task performed by the Master of the Land, earth-born scion of Susanoo, before the Sun Goddess's emissaries descended, and tell a number of tales in which he exerted his humanizing influence on earth. The *Nihongi* itself, in contrast, gives very little space to Susanoo's progeny and has the humanizing work performed by ministers of the Sun Goddess and the heavenly deities, thus implying the dereliction of Susanoo's line. It is in this that the text of the *Nihongi* perhaps most clearly edits the record in a way ennobling to the imperial family, which claimed descent from the Sun Goddess. The tales told of the Master of the Land by the *Kojiki* and the variants add much that is of cultural interest, however, and because they also were available to all readers of the myths they will be recapitulated here.

In one, the Master of the Land is pictured as at first the despised servant of his eighty lusty, aggressive, and selfish brothers, relegated by them to carrying their baggage while they go in pursuit of a desirable female. On the way, they met a hare which had lost its fur. The elder brothers, as a cruel joke, told it to bathe in sea water, but when it did and the water dried, its skin cracked and put it in great pain. The Master of the Land, feeling pity for it, told it to roll in pollen, which formed a soothing cloak, and the hare in gratitude promised him the hand of the princess. Angered because she therefore accepted him rather than themselves, the eighty brothers twice killed the Master of the Land, once by striking him with a searing hot stone and once by catching him in the fork of a split tree, but each time his own mother brought him back to life.

Going to the nether world, the Master of the Land married his half-sister, the daughter of his father, Susanoo. His cruel parent then submitted him to several tortures. Once confined in a pit of snakes and once in a house filled with centipedes and wasps, the son was in each case saved by a scarf, given him in secret by his wife, which served to ward off these loathsome creatures. Again, Susanoo shot an arrow into the moor and sent the Master of the Land to fetch it, but then set fire to the moor grass to kill him. The Master of the Land again was saved, this time by a mouse that showed him a hole in which to hide while the fire passed overhead and then showed him the location of the arrow, which he therefore was able to return to his father as ordered. In the end, Susanoo fell asleep while the Master of the Land was performing the filial task of picking lice out of his hair, which the son therefore tied to the rafters and, stealing his father's sword, bow and arrows, and lute, fled with his own wife. Starting up, Susanoo was delayed long enough by his hair's entanglement that the refugees were able to get past the Even Pass of Hades. Thereupon Susanoo, giving the accolade to success, called to the Master of the Land that he must become the ruler of the earth and put his eighty unruly elder brothers to death, which he did.

The *Kojiki* continues its special attention to the progeny of Susanoo, competitors-to-be of the imperial line, by picturing a series of love affairs the Master of the Land had with several women on earth after he had returned to it in the company of his wife. He took up again with the princess he had earlier won from his eighty elder brothers. Again, telling of his courtship of another girl, the myth is able to paint the type of scene that was to be popular in Heian literature at least three centuries later. The Master of the Land is shown standing all night outside her bedroom, rattling her locked door and imploring her to let him in, while she replies that she is "like a drooping plant, my heart . . . a bird on a sandbank," and that she will not let him in until the next night, when she promises that his "arms white as rope of paper-mulberry bark shall softly pat [my] breast soft as the melting snow."

Predictably, the wife of the Master of the Land became jealous and must have threatened to leave him, for he sang that if she indeed left, her "weeping shall . . . rise as the mist of the morning shower." She, trying then to appeal to his sympathy, offered him a drink and sang "[Thou], being a man, probably hast on the various island headlands that thou seest, and on every beach, . . .

a wife like the young herbs. But as for me, alas! being a woman, I have no man except thee. . . ." In spite of this appeal, the *Kojiki* ends this cycle of amorous tales by listing the numerous progeny the Master of the Land subsequently had with still other girls.

The same sources that tell the story of Susanoo's progeny on earth, moreover, ascribe to the Master of the Land a series of the humanizing tasks. It is said that "for the sake of the visible race of man as well as for beasts, [he and his helper] determined the method of healing diseases," and also that they, "in order to do away with the calamities of birds, beasts, and creeping things, established means for their prevention and control." Again, it is noted that whereas formerly "the very rocks, trees, and herbs were all given to violence," the Master of the Land has "now reduced them to submission, and there is none that is not compliant . . . . It is I, and I alone, who now govern this land."

In any event, there begins here the cycle of tales according to which, with only slight variations, all sources agree that in spite of the Master of the Land's ministrations the earth was still not a suitable place, and tell of the steps by which the Sun Goddess's descendants take over its control. Japan "is still painfully uproarious," "violent and savage earthly deities are numerous," and rocks and vegetation still have the power of speech. In sum, "that country . . . is a tumbledown land, hideous to look on," and the Sun Goddess's progeny refuse to descend to it as they are ordered until things have been put right there.

In consequence, when the Sun Goddess decided that the son her brother spat out from her regalia (or, in other versions, when another god decided that her grandson through that son) shall rule the earth, a congress of heavenly deities has first to be convened to decide which of the gods should be sent to make the land fit for the divine children. The emissaries so dispatched, it turned out, were not faithful, but instead curried favor with the ruling Master of the Land, settled down with earthly goddesses, and did not even report back to heaven. Ultimately, however, a pair of emissaires was found who asked the Master of the Land to stand down in favor of the heavenly line. Consulting his own son, the incumbent ruler decided not to resist the intercession and "became concealed" forever in the shrine of Izumo, still one of the principal spots of state Shinto worship. In all versions, Ninigi no mikoto, grandson of the Sun Goddess, is the first of the heavenly line to descend and rule the earth, after the emissaries who received the submission of the Master of the Land pacified it and made it a fit place to live.

Among the heavenly grandchild's first acts on earth was his mating with a beautiful girl. The *Kojiki* and some variants also say that he refused to mate as well with this girl's ugly elder sister, and that because of this act of uncharity the emperors of Japan were doomed to be mortal. In all versions, Ninigi no mikoto made his wife pregnant in only one night and therefore expressed doubts that he could possibly be the father. Piqued, and submitting herself to an ordeal to prove his paternity, she set fire to her parturition hut and the children born therein were unharmed. At his death, the heavenly grandchild was the first of the long line of early emperors who were buried in the great *kurgans,* many of which are still known in western and central Japan.

In a final cycle, the two sons born to Ninigi no mikoto proved to have gifts for fishing and the sea, and hunting and the land. They decided to exchange tools and occupations for awhile, but soon became bored and the fisherman elder brother asked for his hooks back. The clumsy younger brother, however, had lost them, and though he made offers of restitution nothing would satisfy the overbearing elder brother except the return of the very hooks lost. The younger brother was in despair, but eventually made his way to the palace of the Sea God, at the bottom of the sea. Marrying the Sea God's daughter and recovering the lost hooks, he returned to land with his wife and a jewel that gave him control of the tide, which he used to make his elder brother liege to him. One of the sons (or, according to a variant, one of the grandsons) of the younger brother and the daughter of the Sea God came to be known as Jimmu Tennō, taken by traditional Japanese historiography to have been the founder of the imperial Japanese family.

At this point, what the Japanese considered to be the mythic portion of the tales ends. Though much of what follows in the *Kojiki* and *Nihongi* still smacks more of legend than of history, it is perhaps permissible to abandon the story here and turn to the attempt to analyze the myths.

Cosmology

On the whole, the cosmos pictured by the myth-makers is the earth the Japanese knew, and only the earth they knew. The features of the realm called "the land" are of course those of the Japanese islands, often given the place names they still had in historical times, and only one or two remarks indicate even an awareness of other regions of the globe, including those parts of the nearby continent known to Japanese long before the dates at which the present texts of the *Kojiki* and *Nihongi* were compiled.

The homogeneity and familiarity of the mythic cosmos go far beyond this, however. Realms other than earth are indeed pictured—heaven, nether world(s), and a land beneath the sea—but only in the tale describing Izanami's dark and physiologically corrupted hades is any of these shown as at all different from man's own world. Certainly the High Plain of Heaven is nothing but the mold from which the earth was cast—a land of familiar vegetation, rivers, and mountains; of villagers subsisting by irrigated rice agriculture and making their clothing in weaving halls; of government by a ruler who is little more than the executive of consensuses reached in town meetings; of a religion of familiar ritual and pollution taboos; and of gods who feel the same joys and pains, and exhibit the same aptitudes, as individual men on earth do.

If the forms of the cosmos are thus almost everywhere the same, so too are the processes at work in it, those that men find in their own experiences to be natural. Most features of the environment, and most gods, are born by normal mammalian reproduction, discovered as even human children left to themselves can discover it. Most behavior conforms either to cultural conventions quite like those of men or to individual motivations understandable to the human reader.

41

There are some events that do not have this familiarity—the aboriginal generation of something "like a reed shoot," the creation of certain beings by parthenogenesis, the resurrection of the Master of the Land, the "concealment" of some deities, the primeval mobility of plants and rocks, whatever force it may be that renders ordeals effective, and so forth. Yet many of these instances need not be considered unnatural. If immortality is natural for gods, then so is their "concealment," which it is clear is only the process by which they change from one form of life to another. Izanami's is the only such case in which the alter life included physical change, but she continued to be active, even though in hades. In other examples, because the deity in question reappears later leading a normal life in heaven or the nether world, one must conclude that "concealment" amounted to no more than a physical transportation from one to another location. In still other instances, the "hidden" god in fact remains alive in this world, as the Master of the Land continues to farm his rice fields and to live with a retinue in his palace-shrine. He has merely, as the result of a spirit change, quite literally "hidden himself" from the eyes of others, and taken on a role that no longer obtrudes itself on them. In the same vein, there is no suggestion, in the telling of the ordeal of Susanoo, that its efficacy needs to be guarded by supernatural, rather than human, means. It can be considered to be a form of the promise, a transaction between men, accepted or rejected in terms of the probity, the will, and the faith in one another of its human participants.

Other exceptions, unfamiliar to human experience as they may be, are presented as being irrelevant to men. The noisiness and aggression of plants and rocks was the state of affairs of antiquity, but had been corrected by the time the heavenly deities and their descendants came to occupy earth. Clearly also, the myth-makers treat the distinction between mammalian birth and parthenogenesis as immaterial. Even though the myths seem to have been compiled in part as a political apologia for the temporal supremacy of the imperial family, the two sources differ without comment on the form of birth, and the source of authority, of even the Sun Goddess. One has her created parthenogenetically and sent to rule heaven by her father alone;

the other makes her the result of the mating of the creator siblings, and her rule take its legitimacy from the order of both
these primal gods.

The earthly condition as men know it is thus presented by the
myths as all but universal and, in any event, the only context
men need seriously consider. Moreover, once the heavenly dynasty has taken possession of the world, there is little evidence
that other regions of the cosmos can any longer even have much
effect on men's realm. In the past, it is true, the gods came from
heaven, and all Japanese are their genealogical descendants.
The main political emphasis of the myths was to establish the
biological tie between the ruler of heaven and the rulers of
earth, but the descent of noble Japanese families from other
deities was also, within that context, accepted. By the beginning
of recorded history, at the latest, very large segments—if indeed not all—of the Japanese people may well have been considered genealogically related to the gods, presumably through
some form of adoption to the aristocratic lines if not biological-
ly.[6] Nevertheless, the myths tend to assure us that these physical
links now have been broken, and give no evidence that the two
realms are any longer in a position to affect each other very
substantially.

Similarly, the main impression a reader receives of the nether
world(s) is that it is significant only for those beings who must
be excluded from the normal community—whether because of
the kind of polluting physical accident that maimed Izanami, or
for the qualities of personality that made Susanoo a source of
constant trouble for those around him. There is here no suggestion that normal gods or men need expect this exile. Moreover,
though hades can to a certain extent affect this world—as is
clear from Izanami's threat to destroy earth's inhabitants—its
impact also can be nullified from earth, for Izanagi maintains
that he can easily repair her ravages. All things considered, the
nether world(s) is merely a distant island, much like the major
islands on which men and the gods live, where those who are

---

[6] At least this is one interpretation that can be made of the evidence on the
family system of the day. See Ariga Kizaemon, "Nihon kodai kazoku," in Tanabe
Juri, ed., *Shakaigaku taikei*, vol. 1: *Kazoku* (Tokyo, 1948), pp. 103–150.

beyond the social pale can live out their lives without harming their fellows.

In sum, the Japanese myths show few of the workings of a "metaphysical" imagination, and give a resounding priority and value to things of this world. Except for a very few, and surely Sinified, exegeses, there is no suggestion of impersonal or unearthly processes, such as the Yin-Yang, karma, or even the absolute law of God, which have made much in the continental Asian cosmologies an engine amoral to and/or beyond the understanding of man.

Similarly, there is no hint that such cosmic forces as do exist can overpower life as man proposes to live it. The gods do not have arbitrary powers; an earth-nurturing Izanagi can counteract an earth-threatening Izanami, and the heavenly deities were able to take control of earth only with the agreement of its previous masters. Even the imagery of the myths shows us little to fear or to marvel at. The only monsters appear in Izanami's hades—but not in that of Susanoo—and in the form of the eight-headed eight-tailed dragon, a brief nightmare, easily destroyed. The godly captiousness of so humanistic a mythology as that of Greece—Zeus of the thunderbolt or Hera of the jealous eye—have no counterparts in the Japanese stories, where gods and events pursue a gentle and sociable, an almost homely, course. Only the Sun Goddess's younger brother acts arbitrarily, and he is banished for behavior that conforms more to that of the American Peck's Bad Boy than to that of a devil.

The moral of the myths thus seems to be that life for men can be expected to follow courses that are almost wholly intelligible and actionable in earthly and human terms. More, one can expect them to run along a fairly even way, in sight of neither the abyss of frustration nor the mountain of miracle. One need not fear terror or hope for ecstasy of any ultimate proportions.

THE HUMAN WORLD

It is tempting to say that the myths thus show the world to be "good," and indeed in one very important sense they do. Nevertheless, it is a kind of "good" for which the English adjective is not an apt translation.

Except for those who are physically maimed, there is no different world with which to contrast our own. For the generality of men and gods, even the "nonworld" of death is not clearly pictured, individuals either disappearing from the narrative without explanation, being exiled to other worlds much like ours, or "concealing" themselves in a new form of our life. We may wish to assume that the strict pollution taboos we know surrounded death in early Japan led the myth-makers to avoid mention of any different kind of life after death; their silence then would not indicate that they also refused to admit of mortality. Certainly much later Japanese literature seems bemused by a fear of death. Yet such an interpretation is also arbitrary, and it seems as economical to conclude that the myth-makers quite simply denied death as a final or different state, that they saw life, essentially as we know it on earth, universal in time as it is in space. The preoccupation of later Japanese literature with the waste of death can be seen as a natural reaction of a people with the myth-fed faith in the hopefulness and permanency of life, who subsequently have had to take cognizance of the imported South Asian heresy—that life is pain, and its end to be sought.

If there are no states other than those of our world and our life, we must conclude that at this point in Japanese history the idea of fundamental value alternatives—of "good" and "evil" as an elemental dualism—did not exist. On this basis, it is meaningless to characterize the mythic view of the things of our experience as merely "good." Far more basically, they "are," and are compatible with one another.

So existential a view does not, of course, preclude evaluation. The myths do judge a great many things positively or negatively, and together with the verbal judgment justify appropriately cathetic behavior—avoidance or expiation of the ritually unclean, joyous mating with the beautiful girl, and so forth. There is no sense, however, of that massive concentration of "evil" at one point and time, and of "good" at another, which is so char-

45

acteristic of Chinese thought and of the theory of the dynastic cycle on the continent. Instead, what is evaluated in the myths are particular states, individual events, and beings, which one runs into only at random. We shall do well, therefore, to interpret things so evaluated simply as items in the "is-ness" of life which are appreciably above or below the mean and average, rather than as things foreign to life. Even the "evil" Izanami and Susanoo are merely banished to realms where they can live out more fully the particular characteristics that make them "evil" for most men. "Evil" thus is not destroyed. Indeed, to the extent that we are correct in our general understanding of this philosophy, the denial or destruction of evil, its removal from the cosmos of what "is," would be inconceivable. One can think only to isolate its harmful effects from the rest of life.

It is congruent with this kind of evaluation, clewed as it is only to the standards of life, that the judgments of particular things handed down in the myths recognize no priority among all the possible types of "good" and "bad." Rather than subordinating other cathexes to a metaphysical, or a moral, or any other single kind of good, the texts name what is valued in each case differently, isolating verbally now one, now another, kind of standard. Sometimes they call it by the catchall, as well as moral, terms "good" and "evil," but as often they call it "lucky" or "unlucky," "bright" or "dark," "clean" or "dirty," "beautiful" or "ugly," "goodhearted" or "evilhearted," and so forth. It seems most useful to interpret such terminology as the expression of a catholic and on the whole unbiased appreciation of the many kinds of value a thing can have to the lives of men, and thus basically to an appreciation of things in terms of their facilitation or inhibition of human life.

It is not strange to find in this world, where life is the only criterion of value, that the state of being is equivalent to the possession of spirit, that impersonal or will-less forces do not exist. Gods and men of course are spirit, but one of the most nearly central, and unique, elements of the myth story records that at an early date plants and what we call "inorganic" matter also had identical attributes of life and spirit. For many plants

46

and features of the topography we are given the genealogy, facts of birth, and names that personify them. For all, we are assured that they once possessed the powers of speech, movement, and violence.

Their use of these attributes was as troublesome to life for men as was Susanoo's behavior. The heroes of the Japanese myths therefore remedied this defect. Like many another cultural charter, therefore, the myths of Japan also celebrated the heroes of the significant process by which an aboriginal earth was made fit for men, and in the celebration validated a line of rulers and a system of rule.

Yet how enormously different are the Japanese and, for example, the Chinese myths in this regard! In the Chinese myths, physical nature is pictured as only a passive entity. It is troublesome for man because he still, at that early date, lacked the cultural artifacts to exploit its inertness for his own benefit. The continental heroes were therefore inventors of artifacts and custom—of ditches to drain the swamps, of plows to tear the grass-matted soil, of techniques for growing grain. The Chinese view thus assumed an absolute gulf of nature between man and even beasts, let alone the "lower" orders of life. Man adores man, and only man.

In the Japanese myths, in contrast, human culture much as it persisted well down into historical times is taken as already given, its origins of no interest, its celebration of no utility. The natural world has life and will that are all but identical with those of man, save that like Susanoo they often use these to antisocial ends. The task of the culture heroes was to make nature civil, removing from it the troublesome qualities of speech, mobility, and violence.

We must note that there is no suggestion that in doing so the heroes reduced physical nature to a lifeless and spiritless state, or made it into an order unworthy of man's attention. The myths are filled with an appreciation of the flora and topographic features of the islands of Japan, and the message of the hero tale is that this world is a harmonious union of the life of man with the life of nature. One sees here, in other words, the first literary expression of that acute and comradely sensitivity to physical nature that has been a hallmark of the customs of Japanese life down to our own day. One feels that as early as the time at which the myths were told the Japanese genius already had avoided Rilke's "mistake of drawing too sharp distinctions."[7] This view persists, so that it is not strange for even a contemporary Japanese novelist to say of his heroine "Looking around her garden, a little gone to seed [after a week's absence], . . . she felt that each of its plants and trees, each in its own language, was speaking to her."[8]

HUMAN NATURE

There is as yet, in the myths, as little evidence of what Gilbert Murray called a "failure of nerve" about man's capacity to achieve a satisfactory fate in this world as there was among the early Greeks. Nor need there be. The universe conforms to worldly and human experience, and provides no more justification to the fatalist than it does to the Pollyanna. Events oscillate fairly evenly about a mean that for man as a whole is life sustaining, and thus encourage neither pessimism nor optimism. In time, Buddhist and continental imports, with their visions of other worlds and idealized goals, would prepare the soil for those clichés about the "transiency" of life, "regret" for the unrequited, and *akirame* ("giving up") the unattainable that were to be so characteristic of later Japanese literature. But one senses that in the mythic view it is the fate of mankind to succeed, with reasonable effort, in grappling with the very material problems of daily life, as indeed it is his unconsciously accepted goal.

Individual fates do differ, some men attaining more, others fewer, of those earthly experiences and attributes that are "good" or "bad" because they are above or below the mean. There is as yet, however, no hint of Buddhist or Chinese explanations of these differences in terms of karma or "hidden good and evil."

[7] Ranier Maria Rilke, *Duino Elegies,* tr. and ed., J. B. Leishman and Stephen Spender (New York, 1939), "First Elegy," line 81.
[8] Osaragi Jirō, *Munakata kyōdai,* (Tokyo, 1952), pp. 184–185.

There is no picture of differences in individual fate so thorough-going as to impress one with the contrast between misery and blessedness.

We thus sense no ontological gulfs dividing men or gods into fundamentally different types. This is, of course, congruent with the myth's view of the descent of all men from the gods. The most basic element of man's nature is his spirit—that bit of the godhead dwelling in each Japanese, derived from one primal common source, and thus in the most basic sense alike in all men. The myth-makers even extend their universalism in a way that is cross-culturally quite rare, for to them mankind shares his descent from the gods, and his nature as spirit, with all other things of this world. The way was thus open not only for that sense of kinship with nature which has continued to charac-terize the Japanese, but also for such modifications of imported concepts as the doctrine which allowed Buddhahood even to what continentals considered "lower" orders.[9]

It is also true that later, as Japanese came to have contact with other peoples, for whom a kindred descent from the gods could not be claimed, they were forced into that pervasive ethnocen-trism so characteristic of many isolated tribal peoples—an ethnocentrism that cannot accord even human status to others. In somewhat the same vein, the emphasis in the myths on man's nature as spirit would lead Japanese thinkers, from Shōtoku Taishi to men of our own day, into almost compulsive attempts to try to define what it is that best describes the "Japanese spirit." It even seems possible to argue that the stress on success in at-taining worldly "goods" inevitably validated that hierarchialism which has been so characteristic of Japanese social relations; he who succeeds knows no reason for tempering his satisfaction or for querying its rightness, just as he who falls behind finds no legitimation for his resentment. The man who succeeds is pat-ently, and in a most pervasive sense, "better" than the failure.

The assumptions of the myths about man's fate and nature thus would conduce to particularisms that other peoples and

[9] See Nakamura Hajime, *Ways of Thinking of Eastern Peoples* (Honolulu, 1964), chap. 34, especially pp. 356–360.

times would find corrosive or petty. But the compilers of the myths wrote as if they were unaware of these possibilities, and we as well must admit the real universalisms at home here.

It is against this background of a common nature and fate for all created things that the myths were able effectively to concentrate their attention on individuality. Each actor has particular characteristics—of beauty or strength, of skill, of sociability, and so forth. We remember clearly the sympathy of the Master of the Land for the naked hare and his elder brothers' cruel prankishness, the quickness of hand of the god who seized the Sun Goddess from her cave, the hunter and fisher sons of Ninigi no mikoto, the womanly pique of the Sun Goddess when she imagined that her neighbors could enjoy themselves even in her absence, Susanoo's irascibility. These texts do not, it is true, draw so full and unique a picture of each character as the best modern fiction does. But the Sun Goddess and her brother come close enough, and as Kroeber has pointed out, the later literature of Japan approached that of the West more closely than most in this respect.[10] The actors in the myths are pictured much as we think of the members of our own family or closest friends—alike, but in ways so fundamental as seldom to arouse awareness, all our interest being concentrated on the quite individual quirks by which each person is stereotyped for identification by his intimates.

It was above all the emotions of the actors that excited the interest of the myth-makers, and it thus seems possible to say that at the individual level human nature was defined heavily in emotional terms. The principal emotions portrayed, moreover, fall into two opposing sets—love for the other person and love for oneself. Susanoo concentrates into his character most of the extreme examples of the latter, but love for others is described repeatedly, for numerous actors, and in a variety of forms. One can only conclude that in the mythic view love for others is the more common quality of mankind, as it is unhesitatingly, with no apparent *arrière-pensées* at all, judged "good."

A quite uncomplex sexual love reappears again and again, and

[10] A. L. Kroeber, "The Novel in Asia and Europe," *University of California Publications in Semitic Philology*, 11:233–241. (1951).

in terms that forced the Victorian sensibilities of Chamberlain to render whole passages of the *Kojiki* into Latin. These are all cases, be it noted, of physical attraction at first sight, with immediate pleasurable copulation as their straightforward aim. To generalize the myth phraseology, when a boy and girl meet and are pleased with each other, almost his first remark is the simple "Let's go to bed. How about it?," and very few refusals are recorded.

In this picture of sexual love, mutuality is obviously the standard. There is no suggestion of brutal initiatives, of sadism or rape, of neurosis, and if a person refuses it is simply because he finds the other unattractive. The myths even make it clear that it is improper to deny a person who proposes love his or her pleasure merely because the attraction is not reciprocated, for the emperors of Japan are not immortal, it is said, because the Sun Goddess's grandson would not sleep with one goddess whom he found ugly. The aim of love is not merely to gain pleasure but, as important, to give it.

At no point do the myths picture sexual love as in conflict with social "goods," or as conditioned by the requirements of society. Kinsmen are not shown as having anything to do with one another's marriages, let alone love affairs, and there is no suggestion that the community need judge sexual relations. This emphasis on the absolute goodness and individual autonomy in judgment of the bond of pleasurable love is carried even to the point of an uncritical portrayal of what we, and at least historical generations of Japanese, were to consider brother-sister incest. The creator deities are of course full brother and sister. Though the relationship between the Sun Goddess and her brother may be considered to have been masked by the only symbolic form of their incest, the Master of the Land married his half-sister without attracting the myth-makers' condemnation. As late as the reign of the Emperor Ingyō, what the traditional Japanese view treats as history records the union of Crown Prince Karu with his full sister, and though they are punished by the exile of one (or both) of them, their relationship is described with some sympathy as a case of a true love.[11]

[11] Aston, *Nihongi*, pp. 323–325.

It seems quite clear that this presentation of sexual love as something that does, and should, well naturally and undenied from the hearts of two people has remained the basic norm of the Japanese people to our time. In Heian literature, upper-class manners are shown as more complex, and in the upper class of the Tokugawa some currency was given to the imported Chinese convention that sexual love is legitimate only when harnessed, through the arranged marriage, to the machine of family politics. But by and large, the view of the myths that sexual love is an unconditional good, subject only to the mutual wills of those who share it, has continued to exert a strong appeal in the literature and the daily customs of the Japanese. *Yobai*, the visit of a youth to his girl's bedroom, is first acted out by the Master of the Land, and the curiously aroused mutuality (if not the constraint) of the modern *geisha* and her customer would not seem out of place if described in the myths. Even where the family-haunted conventions of China at last reduced the Japanese spirit, the values first celebrated in the myths have tempered them, for in Japan the principals play a far larger role in the marriage arrangement, just as their wishes help account for the great prevalence even into modern times of the *naien* or common-law marriage.

Sexual love, however, is only one of a variety of gentle loves that characterize the relation of men or gods in the story. In a real sense, one can argue that it is love between individuals that begets all communal and societal morality. The Master of the Land, it will be recalled, helped the hare; he likewise determined the methods of healing diseases "for the sake of the visible race of man as well as for beasts." The bond between parents and children is never pictured as other than one of love, and the unilateral social obligation of filial piety that was so obtrusive in Chinese thought about this key bond never put down deep roots in Japan. Above all, the mechanism through which harmony is achieved and maintained within the social community can only be described as the working out of a steady mutuality among not merely the rights but, more important, the sensibilities of its members.

52

No doubt the formal social institutions of the village of the gods—the town meeting with its decisions reached by consensus, the obvious limitation on the ability of the Sun Goddess to make important decisions arbitrarily—were such as externally to constrain the individual to cooperation with his fellows, without any necessary commitment of his will to this end. No doubt also the form of the myths, as a creation of art rather than of reason, inhibited their statement of social duty in terms of abstract moral principles, and the absence of such statements is not evidence that these principles were not also operative. Nevertheless, even in later ages Japanese were not attracted to the Chinese habit of trying to produce moral behavior through conscious obedience to abstract principles. Moreover, in *giri*— a duty to a specific person—and in the compulsions ascribed to *ninjō*, as in the legal importance given confession, the Japanese have shown an interest in morality as a matter of the emotional commitment of the individual to others. It seems not inappropriate, therefore, to interpret the myths in the same terms, as a portrayal of morality achieved, or denied, in the personal relations of individuals.

Where behavior takes the form shown by Susanoo it is "evil." He makes loud noises that frighten others and acts impulsively, without the warning that would at least save their being startled. He tricks people, promising to be considerate but breaking his word, perhaps with intent to do so from the outset. He does not shrink from inflicting physical harm on others or from harming them through their possessions. Yet there is no suggestion that his behavior results from either long plotting or a perverted pleasure in harm for its own sake, as there is little evidence that he aims through his actions to gain any special material rights for himself. In other words, he is either a complete egoist or an emotional cripple. Needing only to express himself, he makes the freedom to do so his goal, so that in the end he admires his son for having exploited the same freedom to thwart him. He cannot, or will not, empathize with the pain his actions bring to others. He shows no capacity whatsoever to give, or to receive, consideration.

The quality of the Sun Goddess is not morally upright in any self-conscious sense. Rather, she shows understanding of how to mold herself with the people around her in a harmony that still does not deny the individuality of each. It seems no accident that she is typically termed "bright," a sign perhaps more of her humane than her astral attributes. She does not obtrude herself markedly on the lives of others, on the whole seeming to live and let live. When she acts as heaven's chatelaine, she asks more than she orders the behavior of others, letting herself be guided in major things by the consensus of the gods and gaining her ends by persuasion. She overlooks or forgives small errors and accepts their consequences, willing to give her brother and her recreant messengers to earth every benefit of the doubt. Yet she is not cowardly, and when she suspects her brother of evil she is willing to fight if need be. Nor does she lose the sense of the inner borders of her own individuality, for when her brother has clearly violated her trust she withdraws from society, sick at a world in which she can no longer maintain a minimal dignity. She is lured out of this withdrawal only by the firm evidence that her fellow gods are lonely without her, and are willing to act to change that world back to the one of reciprocal emotional trust that alone she can abide.

It thus does not seem amiss to say that morality lies in the total sympathy of one person for another, in the desire to give, not humanitarian "rights," but human fulfillment, even as he receives the same common and essential gift. In a real sense, morality derives from the forms of love.

Against this background, we should perhaps restate the myth's evaluation even of sexual love. It is not merely that they show no sense of "wrongness" attaching to this act and thus reduce it to the level of the behavior of the human animal. Instead, wherever man and woman want one another it is a "good" to take and give this pleasure, and perhaps even the most nearly idealistic of all rapports. One needs some such interpretation to explain the enduring romanticism of the Japanese literary treatment of this relation.

The emphasis given here to morality as emotional rapport between individuals comports poorly with the frequent contemporary view that Japan's is a "shame culture." If such a culture is one in which improper behavior is frequently prevented or punished by the negative reactions of other persons, the description of Japan in these terms is apt. As every Japanese child soon learns, if he errs in propriety or fails in an effort, he will be "laughed at," and ridicule, however gently applied by Western or Chinese standards, is unbearable. Likewise, if he sins deeply or repeatedly against others, he will be "abandoned," emotional as well as material support being withdrawn from him.

Nevertheless, it is nonsense to squeeze one's description of morality down to only negative sanctions against improper behavior. It is surely as much the habit of modern Japanese as it was that of their ancestors as portrayed in the myths to engage for the most part in proper acts, impelled thereto by positive sanctions—again, in the myths, to gain and earn consideration for themselves as sentient beings, as well as to give that consideration, and not merely by the fear of losing it.

The myths make it seem as clearly partial to claim that the main sanctions, whether negative or positive, are those imposed by other persons. Susanoo is not judged in terms of whether he did objective good or evil, and not even according to the opinion of the other gods on his actions. He was judged rather according to his own intentions—his will or "heart"—to do good or evil to others. The point of his ordeal is that it seemed to confirm his profession that his heart was "clean," and his sister was willing for a long time thereafter to forbear from judging what was in fact his disruptive behavior. She overlooked the harm he caused the fields as due to his ignorance of the field economy. She assumed that he was drunk when he vomited behind her chair; the seat of the moral will lies in that part of the mind that is given a vacation in drunkenness, and even today Japanese law and custom consider it not only forgivable, but "good," that an individual give himself this holiday occasionally.

Susanoo ultimately was judged "evil" only when the Sun Goddess and her neighbors came to understand that he either wanted to visit evil upon them or was incapable in his own heart of distinguishing good from evil, crimes so polluting that he must pay an expiatory fine and be banished. The basic sanction to morality is thus the individual's own conscience, his compassion that not only, as Mencius put it, "cannot bear to see the sufferings of others," but wishes them joy.

Much of this view of the matter is still built deeply into the Japanese legal system. Its emphasis is not on whether an objective crime has or has not been committed, and not on restoring equity or punishing the offender, but on gaining from him that self-realization and repentence that is the true meaning of the confession so sought at every legal level.[12] The myths seem already to have contributed to this system the view that social evil is the failure, as good is the common success, of the individual will to be compassionate with others.

[12] Arthur von Mehren, ed., *Law in Japan* (Cambridge, Mass., 1963), pp. 426–427.

IKEDA MITSUMASA
AND THE BIZEN FLOOD OF 1654

John W. Hall

Exemplary in his words and deeds, Ikeda Shintarō Mitsumasa
need not have felt shame even before the superior men of old.
Deeply humble, he devotedly practiced frugality in his own
life. Before all else he put the task of benefiting his people and
perfecting the conditions of his domain.[1]

With these words of high praise Matsudaira Sadanobu, shogunal regent (*hosa*) of the late eighteenth century, placed Mitsumasa, founder of the Okayama branch of the Ikeda house,
among the "Four Superior Lords" of the 1630's.[2] The judgment
is hardly one to be taken literally. Mitsumasa had entered Okayama in 1632, when he was only twenty-three. He was not to hit
stride as an administrator for another ten or more years. But a
daimyo who in his day had given as conspicuous support to Confucian studies as Mitsumasa was bound to have a good press
from the Confucian-educated historians of a later day. His reputation, inflated as were so many of those among the daimyo who
figured as "dynastic founders," had been perpetuated without
skeptical reflection by his successors and admirers in Okayama
and Edo. Mitsumasa has come down in history as a "good" founding daimyo and is accepted as such by contemporary historians.[3]

* For a key to persons mentioned by abbreviated title see p. 83.

[1] Quoted from Matsudaira Sadanobu's *Denshin roku*, in Nagayama Usaburō,
ed., *Ikeda Mitsumasa Kō den*, 2 vols. (Tokyo, 1932), 2: 1443.

[2] "*Kan'ei no shi-kunshi.*" The other three were Tokugawa Yorinobu of Kii
(1602–1671), Abe Tadaaki of Oshi in Musashi (1602–1675), and Itakura
Shigenori of Karasuyama (1616–1673). Mitsumasa also has been placed among
the "Three Wise Lords (*Sankenkō*)," along with Hoshina Masayuki of Aizu
(1611–1672) and Tokugawa Mitsukuni of Mito (1628–1700).

[3] This is the burden of Nagayama's biography cited in footnote 1 and also that
of Taniguchi Sumio, *Ikeda Mitsumasa* (Tokyo, 1961).

Yet for all that has been written about him, Mitsumasa the man in history remains a shadowy figure, a person, one suspects, who could hardly be explained by the stereotyped and idealized picture biographers have given us of him.

This confronts us with the question of whether living biography is at all possible for Japanese who lived prior to modern times and whose spheres of activity were political rather than philosophical or literary. There have been a few exceptions— giants like Hideyoshi or Ieyasu. But aside from such men, the lives of Japan's premodern political greats, despite the rash of biographies that have appeared in recent years, have remained almost totally void of their personal thoughts and actions. Japanese history as currently related by its own historians is almost entirely lacking in evidence of personal involvement by great figures of history. We must ask whether this is the fault of historians who have ignored the individual in history in favor of a preoccupation with trends and public institutions, or whether there is inherent in the historical traces which Japanese men in high places have left behind them a paucity of the intimate details on which "life-writing" can rest.[4]

There have been times, of course, in the recent course of Japanese historiographical development when the past was conceived of as being primarily the work of individuals, a style of interpretation reflected in English by early historians like James Murdoch. But this is not what we are talking about. The assumption that events were the creatures of persons in high places, the assigning of character stereotypes to prominent individuals to explain away the complexities of the age in which they lived, is old style historiography and rightly has been abandoned. Along with this must go the still prevalent tendency to accept flattering official biographies at face value. Stereo-

---

[4] The difference between sterile "biography by formula" and the kind of living biography I have in mind is brought out by Paul Murray Kendall's word "life-writing." See his *The Art of Biography* (New York, 1965), pp. 1–28. The question of whether biography as the revelation of the inner man is at all possible is a matter of ultimates. A provocative statement of the problem was presented by Professor Harry Harootunian at the 1968 meeting of the American Historical Association in a paper entitled "Japanese History, Personality, and the Problem of Biography."

types, whether imaginary or fabricated, remain historical falsifications.

Yet the solution is not to ignore and certainly not to deny the individual's role in Japanese history.[5] If the earlier historians were too ready to believe the myths which had been built up around the great figures of the past, the current generation of historians has been too little inclined to dig for the evidence that would make living persons of these men. The historian of Japan undoubtedly is handicapped in this endeavor, for biographical materials are scarce. Letters are few and generally unrevealing of thoughts and motivations. Contemporary biography was written by formula, whether in praise or in blame. The cult of the individual seemingly was alien to Japanese culture. Autobiography was unheard of until modern times. Arai Hakuseki, that rare exception, was in fact more scholar than statesman. Traditional Japanese society and the political process it fostered clearly played down the spheres of individual action and the individual's expression of his own identity. Public life placed unusual emphasis on the leader's "role-playing" function, accentuating for those at the top their symbolic and ceremonial importance.[6] Decisions emerged from group or family consultation, for which the leader served as ultimate legitimizer not as ultimately responsible initiator. The task of finding the individual behind the haze of consensus and ritualism is frequently next to impossible.

But materials do exist from which living biographies can be written. And I suspect the Japanese historian has not been sufficiently diligent in uncovering and exploiting them. He has by and large left to the historical novelist the exercise of the kind of imagination by which the bones of biographical fact can be

[5] I realize that emphasis on "life-writing" places the burden of my inquiry on the *individual* rather than his *role*. The latter has been the issue of considerable debate among Japanese historians, particularly as it applies to recent political events. See Horigome Yōzō, *Rekishi to ningen* (Tokyo, 1965), particularly pp. 196–240.

[6] The same observation is made about traditional ideas of the "society-personality relationship" in Chinese history by my colleague Arthur Wright. See his unpublished paper, "Reflections in Biography and Personality, Western and Chinese" (Yale University, 1967).

fleshed out with a sense of the probable. The historian's forte
has remained works of the "life-and-times" variety, works which
generally are light on the life and heavy on the times of their
subjects.

Among the men who presumably were in positions of political
influence in Tokugawa Japan, the daimyo have fared particularly poorly at the hands of modern biographers.[7] Once the era of
great wars and territorial consolidation was past, daimyo appear
largely as figureheads and pious stereotypes. It is possible that
the evidence is too meager to permit anything else. There are,
to be sure, official diaries (records of official transactions) and
collections of sayings and remembrances about these men. But
the first tell almost nothing about the person, and the second
are highly unreliable and almost wholly eulogistic. It may be
that the individual daimyo, particularly after the middle of the
seventeenth century, did not count for much—that he was little
more than a figurehead, the ritual apex of the institutional structure over which he had little personal control. Admittedly there
was a distinct routinization of the lives of daimyo once the
Tokugawa political system had been stabilized. But one is made
uneasy by the ease with which some historians have dismissed
the daimyo as men of no consequence. The fact that many
daimyo appear to take on individual characteristics in the more
certain light of the later half of the nineteenth century, especially as they are illuminated in the writings of the first Westerners
to enter Japan after 1854, should urge caution on the historian
who would dismiss them all as puppets or boobs.

Ikeda Mitsumasa served as daimyo in the transitional era between the busy period of territorial consolidation and the later
years of increasing administrative routinization. Institutions
were still in their formative stage, as the daimyo of each locality
worked out their particular solutions to local problems of governance. Mitsumasa as a consequence has been associated with a

7 This situation has been changed somewhat in recent years by the publication
of a series of biographies of leading daimyo in Kodama Kōta and Kimura Motoi,
eds., *Daimyō retsuden,* 8 vols. (Tokyo, 1966–).

large number of administrative and legal changes in his domain. Yet, as viewed by the institutional historian, the problems he faced and the solutions he offered were neither unusual nor unconventional, and one is tempted to question whether a good deal of the protestation of brilliant leadership attributed to him was not, as in the case of so many others, a matter of pious exaggeration.

Fortunately for us, there is a private diary (*Nikki*) covering the thirty-two years of Mitsumasa's public life from 1637 to 1669.[8] Can this perhaps help to resolve the conflicting images of Mitsumasa as a historical figure? The *Diary*, to be sure, is little more than a calendar of events in which Mitsumasa jotted down matters of official business which came to his attention. It is not a personal record. Little of him as an individual is disclosed, and there is almost nothing to suggest the thoughts and motivations behind his acts. Yet the existence of a diary indicates some degree of personal awareness on Mitsumasa's part. And, if nothing else, in sheer volume and care with details, it reveals that Mitsumasa was an alert and careful administrator, meticulously interested in the details of his domain's affairs. The *Diary*, thus, offers the possibility of linking Mitsumasa the man and the historical events of his time and place. And this is particularly so for the climactic "year of troubles" (1654), when Mitsumasa was obliged to face the consequences of a disastrous flood in his home province of Bizen. The diary becomes especially full at this point and its entries more than usually indicative of his personal involvement in the affairs of his domain.

Ikeda Mitsumasa was born in Okayama in 1609, the first son of Ikeda Toshitaka, heir to the vast domain of over one million *koku* which had been accumulated by Terumasa and centered

---

[8] The original, belonging to the Ikeda family, presently is deposited in the Okayama Museum of Art. A printed edition prepared by Professors Fujii Shun, Mizuno Kyōichirō, and Taniguchi Sumio was published in 1967 by Okayama Tosho Shuppan K. K. The main text contains 585 printed pages. Passages translated from the *Diary* will be identified by date, *i.e.*, year/month/day. In extended passages, omissions from a single day's entry will be indicated by ellipses (. . . .). Omission of entire entries will be indicated by asterisks.

on the great castle of Himeji in the province of Harima. Toshi-taka had entered Okayama castle in 1603 as chief administrator of the province of Bizen, one of the parts of the Ikeda holdings. In 1613, when Terumasa died, Toshitaka returned to Himeji with his son Mitsumasa to take command of the main Ikeda domain.

Mitsumasa as a boy was groomed to inherit one of the largest domains in all Japan, but this high promise was not fulfilled. To its great distress, the Ikeda house was shortly divided into two separate lines and reduced to a combined total of less than 650,000 *koku.* Toshitaka's untimely death in 1616, at the age of thirty-two, began the Ikeda decline. On the pretext that Mitsumasa was not of age to inherit Himeji, he was transferred by the shogunate to the relatively undesirable domain of Tottori and reduced to a holding of 320,000 *koku.* Ikeda Tadao, Mitsumasa's uncle, retained an independent status as daimyo of Okayama. When Tadao died in 1632, his son and heir being a minor, the shogunate ruled that the son could not remain in Okayama which, despite being assessed at only 315,000 *koku,* was considered strategically too important. The two branches of the Ikeda house consequently were ordered to exchange domains between Okayama and Tottori. Mitsumasa thus returned to Okayama in 1632, at the age of twenty-three. From this time to the Restoration, the two Ikeda lines were to remain at Oka-yama and Tottori; 1632 became the date at which the two domains were stabilized. The Okayama han of historical times came into existence with Mitsumasa's transfer, and Mitsumasa became in essence the real "founder" of the Okayama domain.

Not that the domain was unstructured or Mitsumasa's officers without experience. Mitsumasa entered a territory that had been reduced to a peaceful and reasonably prosperous condition under two short generations of Ikeda administrators. He brought with him a well-organized band of followers—men who had served in Himeji and Tottori—who quickly took command of the province and established administrative control. In short order the daimyo's retainers were allotted fiefs in the country-side and assigned residences in the castle town; basic laws from

Toshitaka's time were revised or reiterated. Mitsumasa accustomed himself to what appeared to be an easy routine.[9]

On the eighth day of the tenth month, 1637, Mitsumasa began his diary. What prompted him to do so, we do not know. He was something of a scholar and ultimately would have several works of philosophical commentary to his credit. But the diary was not a literary or intellectual endeavor. The first entry was singularly unexceptional:

> 10/8: Memorandum from Heki Buzen and Haga Naizō-no-suke. [They submitted] a report on the investigation of criminals.[10]

That is all; yet the entry was in some ways portentous in its expression of Mitsumasa's continuing concern over security and proper behavior. Entries in the early pages of the diary were sporadic and largely Bakufu-oriented. It is hard to determine what motivated the selection of subjects. There was a momentary flurry of interest in anti-Christian measures following the Shimabara revolt. Mitsumasa does not even report the birth in 1638 of his first son, the future Tsunamasa, though he makes a good deal of the recognition given the child by the shogun in 1642.

The year 1642, when Mitsumasa was thirty-three, emerges in the pages of the diary as something of an early turning point. The volume of entries noticeably increases, and there is evidence of a deepening concern with domain affairs. In the sixth month, Mitsumasa established the office of executive elder (*shioki-karō*), designating three out of six of his chief retainers to serve publicly as administrative officers of the domain.[11] They were obliged to swear a special oath of loyalty to Mitsumasa

[9] The history of the consolidation of the province of Bizen into the Okayama domain is covered in my *Government and Local Power in Japan, 500 to 1700* (Princeton, 1967), pp. 296 ff.

[10] Heki was an elder (*karō*) enfeoffed at 14,000 *koku;* Haga was a group captain (*kumi-gashira*) receiving 2,000 *koku.* I have followed the practice of the *Diary* in omitting the title *kami* (governor) in territorial titles, *i.e.,* Buzen, not Buzen-no-kami.

[11] These were Igi Nagato (33,000 *koku*), Ikeda Dewa (32,000 *koku*), and Ikeda Iga (22,000 *koku*).

which committed them to work in concert and not to divulge official secrets. Having done this, Mitsumasa called together the remaining retainers and informed them that the three *shioki* would carry the daimyo's full authority.

Through his three executive officers, Mitsumasa began to take more interest in domain policy. One of the first tasks assigned them was to conduct a thorough review of the laws and procedures of the domain. Many lengthy entries in 1642 are taken up with admonitions to the new officers. For instance,

> 1642/9/19: I told the three elders, for weighty problems not to make independent decisions. . . . For example, supposing a person goes to Dewa with a housing request, and supposing Dewa turns down the request because there is no vacancy. Then supposing a person later goes to Nagato, and, there being a vacancy, his request is granted. Then the person who had gone to Dewa would believe that there had been discrimination. For this reason, the three of you should compare notes before starting your office days and complete your business conjointly.

The next few years appear in the diary as quiet ones marked by deepening involvement with the shogunal establishment. Mitsumasa, having conceived the idea of setting up a branch of the Tōshōgu (the shrine to Ieyasu) in Okayama, obtained permission to do so in 1643. The shrine, raised on Maruyama to the east of Okayama castle, was completed within the year and dedicated with great ceremony. Meanwhile, Mitsumasa had been obliged to assist in construction at Edo castle, his heir was received by the shogun, his brothers were given minor grants in Bitchū and Harima, and his second daughter, Teruko, was adopted by the shogun Iemitsu and then betrothed to the Ichijō family of Miyako, one of the court nobility. In 1648, Mitsumasa received the singular honor of being requested to remain in Edo as guardian for the shogun's heir, the future Ietsuna, while the shogun was absent on his progress to Nikkō. Teruko's wedding took place in 1649, and Mitsumasa was honored by a special shogunal audience as a consequence. Teruko also was

64

granted an audience before leaving Edo for Miyako. There she was a guest for several days in Nijō castle before she "entered the Ichijō house."

Although the diary says little about it, these were the years in which Kumazawa Banzan (1619–1691) served most actively in Bizen.[12] Originally employed by Mitsumasa as a Confucian advisor in 1634, Banzan left his service in 1638. Rehired in 1646, he quickly rose to high office, receiving 300 *koku* in fief in 1647, and another 3000 *koku* in 1650. It seems fairly evident that Mitsumasa relied heavily on his services and his advice at this time. Perhaps due to Banzan's Confucian promptings, the diary now took on certain tones of moral admonition toward the Okayama administrative staff. It is significant that Mitsumasa adopted through Banzan the doctrines of the Wang Yang-ming school of Confucianism. Later termed Ō-gaku, it was at this time referred to as Shingaku and was distinguished from the officially recognized Shushigaku school by its emphasis on individual conscience and action. A spate of entries at this time concerned with military preparations may stem from Banzan's influence as well. A lengthy lecture on military spirit to the housemen in 1648 stresses the need to keep in martial trim. "One must be prepared at all times to be able to enter the field with a half day's notice."

Iemitsu died in 1651, and was succeeded as shogun by Ietsuna. Mitsumasa's concern over establishing the proper relationship to the new Tokugawa head is revealed in the diary:

4/23: At the castle, Sanuki read the departed shogun's final injunction.[13]

Same day: Along with Sagami made inquiry of Sakai Sanuki on procedures for [the signing of] the new oath.

4/24: An answer from Sanuki to the previous inquiry. We are told to consult with Abe Bungo and Matsudaira Izumi.

❊ ❊ ❊

5/10: Signed the oath at Bungo's residence.

[12] See the chapter "Banzan to Eichū" in Nagayama, *Ikeda Mitsumasa Kōden*, pp. 1137–1175.

[13] Sanuki is Sakai Sanuki-no-kami Tadakatsu, *tairō* from 1638 to 1656 under the shoguns Iemitsu and Ietsuna. For a key to the identity of persons mentioned informally in the diary, see the note at the end of the article.

Mitsumasa was again legitimized by the shogunate. But between him and the shogunal high council certain strains had begun to show. On the sixth day of the fifth month, when paying farewell respects to the Great Councillor, Sakai, he was warned about his adherence to Shingaku. Mitsumasa left Edo on the eighth and arrived on the twenty-first in Miyako, where he met with Lord Ichijō and Itakura Suō-no-kami.[14] Itakura also warned Mitsumasa of the Bakufu's criticism of his brand of Confucianism. In this way subtle pressures were applied to Mitsumasa to abandon Shingaku for the official Shushigaku doctrine. Unfortunately, Mitsumasa does not record his reactions to this pressure. He did not panic, that is certain, and he did not abandon Shingaku until 1658, after the relationship with Banzan had cooled for other reasons.

During the early 1650's, Mitsumasa's diary shows his attention turning increasingly to Bizen and to the economic troubles facing his domain. Toward the end of 1652, the district magistrates (*kōri bugyō*) were called in and exhorted to pay closer attention to rural administration and to see to the reliability of village officials. In the last month of 1652, the problem of debts incurred by the Ikeda housemen became a major issue. Mitsumasa called in all the group captains (*kumi-gashira*) and instructed them to inquire into the financial difficulties of the men under their command. Then, in consultation with the *shioki*, he announced the following plan. Each indebted retainer should

1. Plan on setting aside 2 percent of his annual rice stipend for five years.
2. Calculate the value [of the rice thus saved], assuming the price of rice to be 25 *momme* [per *koku*].
3. Figure in the number of males and females in his household.
4. Make an estimated budget for all household expenses.
5. Make a plan for repayment of the borrowed money.
6. On the preceding basis, explain in detail his household finances to his group captain.
7. [Understand that] those who find it impossible to make ends meet on this basis will be rusticated.

14 Itakura was Kyōto deputy (*shoshidai*).

The problem of samurai indebtedness was to continue to be worrisome. The *Diary* began the year 1653 with the usual description of New Year's celebrations, but quickly turned to more serious matters:

> 1/2: [After visits to family temples and the granting of new appointments], in the statements by those who borrowed money from [merchants in] Miyako, some request a change of fiefs and others report that they cannot pay back their debts even if they were to put aside 2 percent of their rice income. . . . For those who have asked for a change of fief because of the poor quality of their present holdings, the group captains should investigate conditions [in these fiefs] over the past several years.

❋ ❋ ❋

> 1/18: Those who accompany us to Edo and whose fiefs do not yield 38 percent in dues, will uniformly receive a supplementary grant to bring their incomes up to a 38 percent yield. . . .[15]

❋ ❋ ❋

> 2/22: Because Shimōsa has five portions of his fief which have poor yields—the fact that the yield from these locations has been poor for over twenty years has been reported in writing to Iga—and no matter what he does he cannot make ends meet, therefore these five pieces will be absorbed into the domain's granary lands and in their place he will receive payments in granary rice.

The fateful year 1654 began with Mitsumasa in Edo. Members of the Ikeda staff celebrated New Year's Day with the usual festivities:

> New Year's Day: Three cups in honor of the emperor; burned incense; Iyō also was present.[16] Thereafter the Ceremony of Investigation (*kakubutsu*); read a portion of the *Classic of Filial*

---

[15] The average, and hence normal, return on land in Bizen domain was considered to be *mitsu-hachibu* or 38 percent on the assessment figure. The figure was itself an arbitrary one, so that the annual return was normally less than 38 percent of the actual yield.

[16] Iyō was Mitsumasa's son and heir, Iyō-no-kami Tsunamasa.

Piety. . . . Visited Lady Fukushoin with Iyō;[17] after which, celebration in the inner chamber. In the outer offices, celebration for all who are in attendance in Edo. Passed wine cups to Shukei, Shirōbei, Iori. . . . Then to Iyō's apartments for the Tachi-sankon ceremony. Iyō began. After that, the first riding of the horse; the first shooting of the bow.

1/2: At after half past the sixth hour went to the shogun's castle; Iyō-no-kami accompanied. Gathered in the Tenjō-no-ma [here a description of the ceremony before the shogun].[18] Afterward celebrated with Daizen, Satsuma, Uesugi, and Iyō. . . . After returning to the residence went out to pay respects; visited thirty-six places [*i.e.*, other daimyo].

1/3: Thirty places.

1/4: Twenty-seven places.

1/5: Entertainment at Iyō's.

1/11: Ceremony with armor . . . .

1/13: Lord Bungo called in Shōzaemon and gave the following instructions: "Regarding Christians, you have been continuously instructed by Lord Daiyuin.[19] The same policy remains in force. Now with the change of shogun you are instructed to renew the notice boards. This is to be acted on throughout the provinces." He received a copy of the correct wording of the notice board.

1/14: Sent word to Okayama. Gave instructions to Iga and Wakasa to rewrite the notice boards.[20]

Same day: Went to Uta's residence and discussed the problem of financial assistance to Lord Ichijō, a request for 1,000 *ryō* having come through Itakura Suō-no-kami . . . .

That same evening: Lord Uta came and said he had spoken to Sanuki, who had said that 1,000 *ryō* was far too much and that he himself thought 20 *kan* should be enough. I replied that 30 *kan* seemed about right.[21] He agreed that Ichijō should not need more. Court nobles will spend as much as they have. . . .

---

[17] Lady Fukushoin was Mitsumasa's mother.

[18] Tenjō-no-ma is one of the public chambers in Edo castle.

[19] *I.e.*, the shogun Iemitsu.

[20] Heki Wakasa succeeded his father, Buzen, in 1653 as executive elder.

[21] In theory, 1 *kan* silver (1,000 *momme*) was the equivalent of just over 16 *ryō* (1 *ryō*=60 *momme*). Hence 30 *kan* was roughly 500 *ryō* or half of what Ichijō had requested.

He would prefer the smaller amount, but either 20 or 30 should be permissible . . . .

1/17: Sent instructions to give 30 *kan* of silver to Lord Ichijō [there follows, a copy of the letter to Itakura explaining the preceding].

For the next six months Mitsumasa's diary was filled chiefly with personnel matters. Then in the seventh month he began his preparations for return to Okayama.

7/18: Visited Lords Sanuki and Uta to request permission to depart [for Bizen] . . . .

Same day: For the year up to now, expenditures were nearly 300 *kan* over income.

7/19: Departed Edo.

7/26: At Okazaki, having received word of a flood in Bizen, sent Narumi Hanjūrō to Bizen. Sent message to Edo that the *rōjū* should be informed . . . . With Hanjūrō the following [message to the elders in Bizen]:

I can do nothing from here. There may be those among my housemen who lack rice. Take care of them. Prepare maps to record the extent of damage to the castle and its environs.

8/2: Arrived at Lord Ichijō's . . . . At Suō's a communication from Sanuki [saying that] when Shintarō arrives in Miyako he should be set straight regarding his Shingaku learnings.[22] Even if he himself cannot abandon it, he should be told that the doctrine should not be spread among his retainers. He showed me the communication.

✿　✿　✿

8/3: Left Fushimi by boat.

Mitsumasa arrived back in Okayama on the fifth. The devastation he confronted is not described in his diary. From other official sources, however, we learn that a downpour had lasted from the nineteenth to the twenty-second of the previous month. The Asahi River, which runs through the town of Okayama, had risen nearly twenty feet. Parts of the main castle had been

[22] Mitsumasa generally referred to himself by his youthful name of Shintarō and continued to sign his correspondence with it.

flooded, and some of the outer rampart walls had crumbled. Over three thousand houses had been swept away or damaged. Broken down by social categories, these were as follows: houses of officers, 439; lower samurai, 573; townspeople, 443; farmers, 2,284. Fields producing 11,664 *koku* had been ruined. Persons killed at the time of the flood numbered 156. Those who later died of famine came to 3,684. In addition, many bridges, canals, irrigation ditches, and reservoirs had been damaged.[23] The scene obviously made a deep impression on Mitsumasa, who took the disaster as a personal tragedy. His diary now became much fuller, and every day had lengthy entries describing his efforts to meet the crisis.

8/6: Sent Yamagoshi to Edo with my respects.
Reviewed the entire band of retainers . . . . After that, with the elders, group captains, and department heads, I reviewed [the favorable events that had transpired in Edo and then expressed regret over the hardship caused to high and low by the recent flood].

8/7: Shin Zusho named commissioner in charge of repairs to the three bridges [across the Asahi River].

8/8: Called in Iga, Wakasa, Ikkaku, Geki, and Kanzaemon and spoke to them: This year's drought and flood are the greatest disaster to befall my tenure [as daimyo]. I have thought about this and concluded thus: Because we are governed by heaven, this territory has been put in my trust at a fortunate time. It is for the salvation of the people. Because of my faults, heaven has visited on me a disaster to the people. I see it as an admonition from above, and am grateful. I am convinced of the need for reform.

In this time [of trouble], I believe it is improper for me to visit the ancestral graves. For this month Iga and Wakasa will remain on duty in the castle without time off. Even when they return home [to sleep], they should not relax. They should inquire fully into all domain matters. So as not to become overburdened, Iga will handle matters dealing with the castle, the

[23] For an extended documentary history of the flood, see the chapter "Shōō san-nen no Bizen kōzui," in Nagayama, *Ikeda Mitsumasa Kō den*, pp. 583–604.

retainers, the town, and the environs of Okayama. Wakasa will handle the problems of the countryside.

If rice from other provinces arrives, let it enter [our ports]. Because of the scarcity of rice in the castle, rice stored in Osaka should be brought up to Okayama speedily.

Because there will be widespread need for relief, the rice and silver in the castle should be distributed throughout the domain. Insufficiencies will be made up by making silver loans . . . .

8/10: [An investigation ordered of persons suffering from want in the retainer-held fiefs (*kyūsho*).[24] An admonition given to the district magistrates.]

8/11: Elders, group captains, and department heads called in . . . . Samurai both of high and low status down to townsmen and farmers will be forgiven all the wrongs heard about them and anything that transpired before today . . . . From this day let us change our hearts from the very bottom. Each one of us must forget past weaknesses and be reborn. . . .

[Because of the persistent difficulties with the collection of land dues in the fiefs and granary lands, the following reform of the tax system is announced.] From this summer on, both in granary lands and fiefs, a standard tax rate (*mononari narashi*) will be adopted . . . .[25]

We must avail ourselves of the wisdom of the entire domain. Consequently, a suggestion box will be set up. All, from the elders to those of lowest status, should write recommendations anonymously and place them in the box. . . .

Same day: [General instructions regarding use of maid servants.]

8/14: [Procedures outlined for coordinating the inspection of the domain's rice lands.]

8/15: [Instructions given to fief holders to have their rice harvested early a little at a time.]

---

[24] The Ikeda domain still assigned fiefs to its upper retainer staff. For the manner in which this was done and later modified, see my *Government and Local Power in Japan*, pp. 404–406.

[25] This decision to standardize the tax rate throughout the domain was a major innovation which effectively eliminated the independent authority of the upper-level Ikeda housemen over the lands and persons of the cultivators of their fiefs. The Okayama domain did not actually reduce all retainers to stipendiary status, for a fictional form of enfeoffment was continued, but all land taxes were henceforth collected through the daimyo's field administration.

8/16: [Punishments announced for several rural administrators and village officials.]

8/17: Called in district magistrates and commissioners of construction [and went over reasons for lack of progress on reconstruction].

Same day: Ordered rice [stored] in Osaka to be brought up immediately by oared boats . . . .

8/18: . . . Talked to each of the ten district magistrates individually [admonishing them to be evenhanded] . . . . I told them that I believed that not even one person in our domain should suffer from starvation . . . .

Same day: Memorandum to the group captains and department heads. Retainers whose residences were damaged by the flood will be assisted. [Here follow instructions on procedures for transfer of residence from the castle town to the country and for making silver loans.]

Gave word that townsmen should be instructed to write up the damage to their houses and that their statements should be collected ward by ward . . . .

8/19: [The elders were called in and lectured on their behavior, reminded of their position in the Ikeda establishment and that they must serve as models for those beneath them. Later each was called in separately and his character analyzed by Mitsumasa. Ikeda Dewa was singled out for criticism.]

Same day: [Personnel matters.]

8/22: [Same as above.]

8/23: The problem of destitute persons. Relief rice has been provided up to the fifteenth of the month. Ikkaku and Geki asked what to do beyond this. Gave the order that relief rice be given from now to the middle of next month. . . . For males, 2 *go;* for females and boys under fourteen, 1 *go* [per day].

Same day: [Ikeda Dewa submitted an explanation and apology for conduct which had received criticism by Mitsumasa. He also presented an oath of good behavior.]

8/24: Instructions to the district magistrates. There are replies from them on questions concerning household labor service, the postponement of taxes until spring, and whether taxes should be paid up within a year. [Here follow seventeen separate replies.]

8/25: Called in all the elders [and went over my decisions

regarding the points raised by the district magistrates' statements]. They all concurred. Statement to the twenty district magistrates:

1. From this year on, taxes will be collected within the year.
2. Previous tax delinquencies will be excused.
3. Spring loan rice and "cattle silver" owed by cultivators of both granary and fief land can be repaid during the coming spring . . . . [The next twelve items deal with relief rice rations, preservation of lesser cereals and greens for food use, control of *sake* brewing, facilitation of transportation, abolition of barriers, determination of the tax rate, and collection of tax rice.]

8/25: [Several items dealing with transport barriers, relief boat service, the tax rate in the domain, and so forth.]

8/26: To the cadastral inspectors (*kemi no mono*). Because the thirty groups established earlier have proved insufficient another fifteen groups are created.

8/29: Settlement of the matter of Ikeda Sado's retainers. [Here a list of stipendiary grants to five retainers.]

9/1, 9/2, 9/4, 9/5: [Minor personnel matters noted.]

9/8: Because of the reports that there are many destitute people in the environs of Okayama, some of whom have died, Ikkaku and Geki were sent to investigate. Geki reported some four or five persons on the day he went out. Ikkaku reported about ten. Later it was determined that there were some sixty or seventy. Therefore, the two men were informed as follows: Make a shelter for those who cannot stand or walk; place them in it and nourish them. [A warning follows to watch out for fakes and not to let them enter the shelter.]

9/11, 9/15, 9/17: [Personnel matters noted.]

9/19: The two elders, Shirōzaemon, Kan'uemon, Kanzaemon, Geki, Ikkaku, and Moku reported. Expenses for the Works Office and for the relief of starving persons are estimated to run about 1,000 *kan*. I ordered Iga and Wakasa to make inquiry in Osaka and Sakai for silver loans.

9/17: [sic] Nagura Gozaemon returned from Edo with permission from the *rōjū* to repair the castle wall.

9/20: Called in all elders and spoke to them: The inspection of the crop has been completed from one end of the domain to the other end and the land stewards have been ordered to calculate the [possible] rate of taxation. But this is something that cannot be hurried. I put it to the group as to whether we should not [adopt a figure of] 10 percent for the fiefs. They agreed. I therefore told Iga and Wakasa to report this to the group captains.[26]

Same day: Spoke to Dewa, Nagato, Iga, Wakasa, and explained it was wrong for the personnel groups not to have subcaptains. One person should be assigned to each group. [Here follow various admonitions on the personal conduct of the daimyo's retainers.]

9/23: On the occasion of the funeral services for the emperor, I sent Hida to Miyako and Gemba to Edo.

9/25: [Various reports on misconduct among villagers.] Ordered jails built in each district and persons who commit crimes imprisoned. Gave the granary superintendents [prizes of] ten bales of rice each for five years of good service. . . .

9/26, 9/27, 9/29: [Personnel matters and criminal judgments.]

Same day: Gave orders for the assignment of persons from the town to the reconstruction of Kyōbashi Bridge . . . .

10/3: [A prize of five pieces of silver given for heroism in saving lives during the flood.]

10/6: Memorandum sent to all elders, group captains, department heads [regarding household debts of retainers, household management, and sumptuary regulations; an oath to exercise frugality was demanded of all retainers]. . . .

From now on the group captains (*kumi-gashira*) will be called company captains (*ban-gashira*). A captain will be assigned to each company . . . .

10/7, 10/9: [Personnel matters.]

10/14: Baba Jirozaemon appointed chief of the kitchen.

Same day: Emi Jimbei returned from Miyako. He reported the acquisition of a loan of 550 *kan* of silver. Gave instructions that this be used to cover 140 *kan* of retainer debts, the rest to be brought to Okayama.

Same day: A courier arrived from Edo. He brought a message declaring a general amnesty for those convicted of small crimes because of the emperor's funeral. Also due to Lord Uta's

[26] This meant that retainers would receive about one quarter of the expected return (38 percent) from their enfeoffment figures.

efforts, the *rōjū* agreed that the usual gifts of local products need not be sent except to the shogun . . . .

10/18: Instructions to the fifty-four [newly appointed] intendants (*daikan*). Each is assigned to about 10,000 *koku* . . . . Gave orders that each should receive thirty bales [as supplementary salary].

11/20: Three jailed persons released. . . . This day gave orders for silver to be given for [the rehabilitation of] townsmen's houses after the flood. Altogether about 10 *kan*.

Same day: Furuta and Kishi ordered into rustication because of their inability to make ends meet.

10/23: [Settlement of an inheritance.]

10/24: Instructions to the fifty-four intendants:

1. Intendants will normally remain in the rural districts during the year and will attend to business.

2. They should immerse themselves in [the affairs of the] villages under their jurisdiction, making sure that their concern penetrates to the lesser cultivators and treats granary and fief lands in an equal manner.

3. In all matters, if villagers present arguments, they should investigate personally and then consult with the district magistrate.

4. The tax registers should be promptly and carefully investigated.

5. If there are cultivators who cannot pay their taxes, the district magistrate should be consulted. After a careful investigation, and if there are unavoidable difficulties, these should be exempted immediately from the lossage fee (*kason*) . . . . Undue pressure to collect the tax should not be applied.

6. [On treatment of wrong-doers.]

7. The existence of any excessive exaction of taxes should be strictly investigated, for it has been reported that holders of fiefs are guilty of such practice . . . .

8. Land may be bought or sold only after cause has been presented to the intendant and an investigation made.

9. Regarding the special service (*yokoyaku*) required beyond the yearly rice tax, [because there have been abuses] a careful inspection should be made of the service registers so that the abuses are corrected . . . .

10. Inquiry should be made into the character of the village

heads to determine whether each is honest or dishonest.

11. The existence of cultivators who have more land than is necessary for their livelihood should be reported.

12. When investigating a village, it is imperative to go to it. Business should not be conducted from another village.

13. When traveling to the intendant's office, porters and horses for transportation may be employed on a daily basis. Grounds keepers should not be requisitioned. Cleaning service and firewood should be provided by the village. Beyond this, further requisitions are not permitted.

The above articles are to be strictly obeyed.

Sent in writing to the *daikan*, tenth month, twenty-fourth day.

10/25: With regard to working out a uniform income for the various fiefs, I asked Yuasa Mimbu to have the intendants balance those whose fiefs have not produced enough rice against those which have an excess.

10/26, 11/1: [Personnel matters noted.]

11/3: Sent Kajita Seizaemon to Edo to make a request of the shogun through Higashi-no-maru.[27] The details are recorded elsewhere. In general, however, the request was for 2,500 *kan*, or if possible 3,000 *kan*, to be paid back at the rate of 300 *kan* per year for ten years.

Same day: The three works commissioners reported: For the work of sand clearance in the adjoining districts, more day laborers than expected turned out. Even some blind women appeared. I replied that this was excellent and that the work was well suited for such persons.

Same day: Spoke to the entire group of elders: Because of the flood, the tax return for the entire domain is 16 percent. [As this creates a burden on those with small salaries, it is proposed to give supplementary rice stipends. This will require 1,200 *kan* from the money which is being borrowed from Edo.][28]

11/5: [Made sure the intendants each received the injunctions of the previous day.]

---

27 This is Lady Tenjuin, Mitsumasa's mother-in-law, influential in the shogun's court because she was a daughter of the second shogun, Hidetada.

28 This meant that even the stipendiary retainers would receive less than half their normal income. The details of how supplementary stipends were awarded are not revealed in the diary.

Same day: [Report on the "cutting of the front hair" for six of Mitsumasa's retainers.]

11/8: [Note on rustication of several retainers.]

Same day: Instructions to the district magistrates:

1. As the intendants already have been admonished, you are not to go about making arbitrary decisions on the assumption that farmers are [all] bad and deceitful and that [only] you have ability. To be insincere in one's handling of people is to teach deceit to the people . . . .

2. It is argued that the exhaustion of our domain results from [adverse] weather conditions over the past few years. This is undeniable, but if you would make a careful investigation of the conditions in the villages since our entry into Bizen, noting the absence of farmers [from some land] and the increase or decrease of farmers, you would be able to determine whether or not the problem [might] result from our management.

3. District magistrates should go personally into the districts and thoroughly observe the economic conditions and the state of affairs among the villagers, spring, summer, and fall. They also should investigate carefully the condition of fields of good, medium, and poor quality and methods of taxation . . . .

4. It is reported that most of the starving people have small landholdings and large families. But it is seldom that among the starving there are those who were born with small holdings. In most cases, [the trouble lies] in having sold [the best] land and having retained only the poor . . . . [Once the family runs into tax difficulties], the ablebodied ones go off to work as servants [in samurai houses], leaving only the aged and women and children behind. Thus, the entire family becomes destitute. Its fields, even in good years, are like wasteland.

5. With respect to providing assistance for buying back farm lands . . . , where possible the district magistrate and the intendant, using their sense of compassion, should urge farmers to use some of their relief rice to buy back land. Or in the villages, where there is land of poor quality [and hence abandoned] or land which is a burden to its owners, the tax rate should be lowered on it and then it should be distributed, depending on household numbers, to destitute families.

6. Where there are orphans who have no family connections, the district magistrate and intendant should treat them with

kindness and [attempt to] find a place for them. Those who cannot be placed in homes should be supported by the entire village .... If the village cannot carry this burden, this care should be considered as part of the labor service requirement.

7. Village heads and group heads have been ordered to inquire into the condition of destitute persons.[29] They report that most of these are knaves and rascals. Although it is true that there are cases in which persons have obtained relief rice several times [over], nonetheless these are people who are looking for relief because they have sold their land. Even before selling, they did not have enough to make ends meet.

8. The village group heads at this time are by and large in the bad habit of reporting that the lesser farmers are dishonest ..., and because of this, the district magistrates think that it is difficult to improve conditions. However, if you will pursue all matters conscientiously and personally look into the smallest details, you will discover that this is not [necessarily] the case. [Here follows a criticism of the village group heads.] You are directed to make written reports on the honesty and dishonesty of the village group heads.

9. Everyone is of the opinion that village heads should be appointed from among those who cultivate large landholdings. But you are directed to pick out even those with small landholdings, if they are honest, and appoint them as village heads ....

10. In the case of those with more land than they can cultivate . . . or those for whom the tax assessment is incorrect ..., a small amount of relief is insufficient .... Yet they are not given extra relief for fear of creating a precedent .... It goes without saying that they too should receive relief ....

11/9: Memorandum to all elders:

1. Regarding mountains, forests, bamboo, and trees in the

---

[29] Village heads, called *shōya*, were responsible for a single village, or sometimes a portion of an exceptionally large village. Group heads (*ō-jōya*) were placed over clusters of ten or twenty villages and served in an intermediary position between the intendants and the village heads. Both *shōya* and *ō-jōya* tended to come from prosperous village families, often of former samurai status. Hence they sided with the samurai administration in trying to exact as much from the cultivators as possible and tried to retain a privileged social position. Mitsumasa's reform of rural administration was as much directed toward the upper levels of the *hyakushō* as toward the excesses of samurai officials. Note especially his effort to break the hold of established families as seen in Item 9 of this memorandum.

fiefs, these will be administered as heretofore. However, the district magistrates must be consulted before cutting . . . .[30]

2. The mountains and rivers tax in the fiefs will be absorbed by the domain.

3. Reclaimed land will become the property of the domain, the one exception being the land individually cultivated by those samurai currently resident in the countryside.

Instructions to the district magistrates: [Details on the handling of relief rice, loans to villagers, cattle silver, tax arrears, and so forth].

Same day: [Details on temple construction in Kojima District.]

11/10: Morning, entertained twenty district magistrates in the castle. Thereafter had Kyūbei read the instructions of the day before yesterday and had particulars explained orally one at a time. Following this, the statements in the suggestion boxes of the several districts were placed before the magistrates . . . .

By the time of this entry, Mitsumasa had been back in Okayama for just over three months. The main lines of activity and major policy changes occasioned by the flood were essentially determined. The diary did not report all that had been decided within the domain headquarters, but it showed Mitsumasa to have been enormously active and directly involved in the strategy of reconstruction and rehabilitation. Relief was rushed to those in need. Loans were solicited to cover extraordinary expenses. Basic changes were made in the administrative system, especially in village administration. Most important of all, Mitsumasa, on the pretext of bringing a sense of unity to the domain and as a way of making the resources of the domain equally available to all within it, had intruded into the last remaining sphere of independence possessed by his retainers. He had reduced all territory, whether already under the daimyo's direct control or whether held in fief, to one uniform administrative command. His constant admonition to the intendants, land inspectors, and district magistrates to go into the villages, to observe the conditions of the countryside, and to work out uniform

[30] This is another example of the imposition of a uniform field administration over both fief and granary land.

policies was calculated to assert a centralized field administration over all of Bizen.

In the first months after the flood, Mitsumasa had given prime attention to the relief of the farming population. But toward the end of the year, he turned with somewhat more sympathy to his samurai retainers. They had been neglected, or treated rather arbitrarily: Their stipends had been cut; those who held fiefs found their authority withdrawn from the villages; many were in deep financial trouble. So it is natural that as the end of the year approached and the prospect of the New Year's festivities made all the more poignant the suffering which was everywhere visible, Mitsumasa should think of the welfare and the morale of his housemen. Yet he did not compromise the basic policy of centralized control. Relief was given, but on a temporary basis:

12/25: Gave to each of the company captains a falcon's goose.[31] Took this occasion to speak to each one individually, explaining that I understood that there may well be men of low rank in their companies who are having difficulty even in finding enough rice to eat. I [explained] that they should help these men as they saw fit . . . .

* * *

12/30: Informed Wakasa the review of personnel for tomorrow should be as in previous years. It should begin at five in the morning.

There are a few among our samurai who do not have enough rice to eat; gave instructions that they should immediately be given the opportunity to borrow rice.

New Year's Day brought good weather. Seven hundred and nineteen Ikeda retainers gathered for the review. Mitsumasa performed the usual ceremonies and then took the occasion to go before his assembled housemen. After commenting on the struggles they had all endured, he turned to the subject which must have been foremost on his retainers' minds.

Some of you may be thinking, "Our Lord is only concerned about taking care of the farmers. It is as though the samurai

[31] *Taka no kari, i.e.*, a goose brought down by one of the daimyo's falcons.

did not exist." But [to think] this is the height of short-sighted-
ness. Do you not know the reason that the samurai have suffered this year and last is because the farmers have been unable
to fulfill their proper function? It is the people who [through
their labors] support the lord, his retainers, and the townsmen.
Do you not believe that the people are [the economic] treasures
[of our domain]?

And again, he turned the blame for the plight of the farmers
on the arbitrary exactions made by fiefholders in previous years.

With these entries Mitsumasa closed what was to him the
darkest year of his life. The troubles faced by him and his staff
in Okayama were not over by any means, and the diary continues for several more months to be devoted almost completely
to matters of relief and rehabilitation.

Mitsumasa kept his diary until 1669. The volume of entries
continued high through 1660, tapering off somewhat thereafter.
The content remained the same. Administrative policies, assignment to official posts, the affairs of samurai retainers, relations with the shogunate were at the forefront of his attention.
To the end, little is shown of the inner man, but a great deal is
revealed about the daimyo as administrator and public figure.

The diary shows a man of obvious seriousness and energy with
a firm sense of command and purpose, intensely dedicated to the
good governance of his domain. He knew his higher officers in-
timately and used them well. Nor was he afraid to prod or to
criticize. The staff system established in 1642 gave him an executive machinery which was flexible and effective. His elders
were prestigious members of the retainer band, each one with
over 10,000 *koku* in territory. To use them not simply as charismatic advisors but as executive officers was a major bureaucratic
innovation which did much to enhance the central authority of
his domain. Below the level of executive elder, the system of
company captains and department heads meant that at a moment's notice Mitsumasa could assemble a group of officers who
could carry out his commands or convey his sentiments to the
rest of the Ikeda houseband.

Mitsumasa obviously was firmly in command of his housemen; he was a man who paid close attention to appointments to office and to the definition of official duties. The bureaucracy had not taken its final form when he entered Bizen, and opportunities were still available to improve the structure. The thrust of his policy was constantly to increase central authority at the expense of local and private interests. Nor was Mitsumasa satisfied with simply giving orders and assuming that results would follow. He kept at his men be they elders, village heads, or district magistrates, writing patiently in his diary the small details of what was expected of each officer. He was attuned to the particular weaknesses of each group of officials. At the time of the flood, as we have seen, he first took the blame for the disaster on himself, then turned it on his retainers.

Confucian theory never was used blindly by Mitsumasa. It was certainly in keeping with Confucian concepts that the cultivators be protected, but Mitsumasa was well aware of the practical necessity of supporting the villagers simply in order to strengthen the economic base of his domain. It was common sense that the farmers be given first priority. His housemen were captive under his command and could somehow survive the crisis. The farmers, however, had to be treated with consideration and nursed back to health. It was here, then, that the daimyo's personal authority and the welfare of the villagers coincided to the detriment of samurai independence. Theory served to support what in fact was a very practical move toward domain centralization.

One would wish for more background on the fateful decision that terminated the free administration of fiefs by retainers and converted the Ikeda houseband to stipendiary status. Here was a major turning point in domain management, one that had been adopted by many other daimyo by this time but that many of the Tozama lords were never to undertake. From the point of view of the institutional historian, the adoption of *mononari narashi* in Bizen could hardly be considered an unexpected turn of events. Yet it did not happen automatically or inevitably. Its adoption brings Mitsumasa, the man, and the flow of events in Bizen together in intimate interrelationship. The new policy was logical. Perhaps it was contemplated before 1654, perhaps it was resisted by the retainers. Clearly Mitsumasa as leader seized the occasion to bring it about, and the diary gives the evidence to show how at least one daimyo found himself in a position to make history. In this sense the diary serves to extricate Mitsumasa from the leveling process whereby historians have tended to reduce historical figures to stereotypes or pawns in the hands of impersonal forces.

Key to Persons Mentioned by Abbreviated Title

Bungo: Abe Tadaaki, shogunal senior councillor (*rōjū*), 1633–1651.

Dewa: Ikeda Dewa, executive elder (*shioki-karō*), 1642–1652; 32,000 *koku*.

Daizen: Mōri Tsunahiro, daimyo of Hagi.

Geki: Kamizaka Geki, Ikeda assistant finance officer (*urahan*); 500 *koku*, later 1,500 *koku*.

Gemba: Ikoma Gemba, Ikeda chamberlain (*koshō-gashira*); 1,000 *koku*.

Hida: Dohi Hida, Ikeda company captain (*ban-gashira*); 4,200 *koku*.

Iga: Ikeda Iga, executive elder (*karō*), 1642–1668; 22,000 *koku*.

Ikkaku: Kobori Ikkaku, Ikeda chamberlain (*koshō-gashira*); 100 *koku*.

Iori: Mizuno Iori, until 1653, captain of the Musket Guard (*teppō-gashira*) at 1,000 *koku*. In 1653, appointed Edo elder (*Edo karō*) with a stipend of 3,000 *koku* in granary rice (see *Diary*, 1653/5/16).

Iyō: Ikeda Tsunamasa, Mitsumasa's first son.

Izu: Matsudaira Nobutsuna, shogunal senior councillor (*rōjō*), 1633–1662.

Izumi: Matsudaira Norikazu, shogunal senior councillor (*rōjū*), 1642–1654.

Kan'uemon: Kanie Kan'uemon, Ikeda commissioner of construction (*fushin-bugyō*), 1645–1655; 300 *koku*.

Kanzaemon: Kitayama Kanzaemon, Ikeda chief of finance (*kanjō-gashira*), 1642–1667; 350 *koku*.

Kyūbei: Morikawa Kyūbei, became Ikeda assistant finance officer (*urahan*) in 1657; 500 *koku*.

Moku: Andō Moku, Ikeda assistant finance officer (*urahan*), 1650–1657; 500 *koku*.

Nagato: Igi Nagato, Ikeda elder (*karō*); 33,000 *koku*. Executive elder, 1642–1652.

Sagami: Ikeda Mitsunaka, daimyo of Tottori.

Samon: Ikeda officer in Edo, unidentified.

Sanuki: Sakai Tadakatsu, shogunal great councillor (*tairō*), 1638–1656.

Shimōsa: Ikeda Shimōsa, elder (*karō*), 1635–1657, 14,000 *koku*.

Shirōbei: unidentified.

Shirōzaemon: Nakamura Shirōzaemon, Ikeda commissioner of construction (*fushin-bugyō*), 1626–1662.

Shōzaemon: Nose Shōzaemon, Ikeda Edo deputy (*rusui*).

Shukei: unidentified.

Suō: Itakura Shigemune, shogunal Kyoto deputy (*shoshidai*), 1619–1654.

Tabei: unidentified.

Uta: Sakai Tadakiyo, shogunal chief councillor (*rōjū*), 1653–1666.

Wakasa: Heki Wakasa, Ikeda executive elder (*shioki-karō*), 1642–1677; 14,000 *koku*.

TOKUGAWA TSUNAYOSHI, THE GENROKU SHOGUN

Donald H. Shively

The shogun Tsunayoshi was clearly one of the more bizarre figures in Japanese history. Some of his eccentricities were so extreme that it has been suggested that he was "half mad." That is probably an unjust diagnosis, but it does explain why he usually is not taken seriously.[1] The peculiarities of his personality and of some of his actions distract attention from the contributions he made to the development of Tokugawa government and intellectual life.

Tsunayoshi (1646–1709), the fifth in a line of fifteen shogun, was a man of strong convictions. Throughout his twenty-nine-year rule, he was an arbitrary despot, greatly feared, like his father Iemitsu and his great-grandfather Ieyasu. In addition he attempted to play the role, later performed more successfully by the eighth shogun Yoshimune, of the humanitarian sage-king with the mission of edifying the populace through the encouragement of Confucian studies and the propagation of ethics. But

NOTE: I should like to express my appreciation to Professor Hiramatsu Yoshirō of Nagoya University for reading and discussing portions of the *Tokugawa jikki* with me, an experience which interested me in attempting this paper on Tsunayoshi. I wish also to thank Assistant Professor Nakano Yoshio of Kyoto Sangyo University for aid in locating some of the materials used in this study. My colleague, Professor Albert Craig, read the paper and made many helpful suggestions.

[1] There is as yet no biography of Tsunayoshi. The modern historical writings which give the fullest attention to him are the following: Kurita Mototsugu, *Edo jidai* (Tokyo, 1937), part 1, vol. 9 of *Nihonshi taikei;* Nakamura Kōya, *Genroku jidai kan* (Tokyo, 1919); Tokutomi Iichirō, *Genroku jidai* (Tokyo, 1925), part 1, vol. 17 of *Kinsei Nihon kokumin shi;* Shigeno Yasutsugu, "Tokugawa Tsunayoshi (Jōken'in) jiseki," in *Shigeno Hakase shigaku rombun shū* (Tokyo, 1939), 3:21–36; Yūzankaku, ed., *Isetsu Nihonshi* (Tokyo, 1932) (Jimbutsu hen 7), 6:205–248.

unlike the policies of these three great shogun, which were revered and emulated by their successors, some of Tsunayoshi's measures misfired and were repudiated by the next ruler. He failed, though not because of unfavorable political conditions, for his was a time of peace and prosperity, when the authority of the Bakufu was at its height. Nor did Tsunayoshi lack talent, for he had a quick mind and he was the most scholarly of all the shogun. His intentions were good. There were, however, fatal flaws in his personality, the most serious of which was lack of judgment and moderation. He was inclined to go to extremes, with the result that his good intentions often miscarried. His personal failings prevented him from being a great ruler, but there are, nevertheless, grounds for considering him to be an important one. I say this for two reasons.

First, he contributed to the century-long transformation by which the early Tokugawa state, dominated by a psychology of military strategic considerations, gradually turned into a more civil-minded warrior bureaucracy infused with ethical and humanitarian ideas. And because the state was the dominant force in the society, this contributed in turn to the diffusion of education and ethical concerns to all classes. Although this process evolved slowly throughout the Tokugawa period, the most conspicuous changes came in the decades around 1700 and were specifically implemented by Tsunayoshi.

Second, Tsunayoshi's rule (1680–1709), bracketing the Genroku year-period (1688–1704), is acclaimed as the golden age of the Tokugawa, a time of commercial development and affluence, of the first flowering of the arts of the commoners in the cities, an age which produced many of the leading literary and intellectual figures of the Tokugawa period. The Genroku was also a time of extravagance and indulgence in pleasure, not only by the wealthy merchants, who set new standards of luxury, but by daimyo and *hatamoto* (bannermen) as well. It was, in fact, the most "swinging" period in Japanese history—until the late 1960's, which newspapers and magazines have dubbed the "Genroku of the Shōwa era."

Procedures in the Bakufu were well enough established by Tsunayoshi's time that the government could operate with a figurehead shogun, as it had under his predecessor, Ietsuna. On the other hand, the despotic power of the shogun was so great that if he showed the slightest vigor or personal initiative, many would rush to follow his lead. The 260-odd daimyo were personal vassals, frequently summoned to Edo castle to do obeisance and humble themselves before the shogun. Over 5,000 *hatamoto* and 17,000 *gokenin* (housemen) were his direct vassals. He controlled the granting (by the emperor) of all court rank and titles and all important Buddhist offices and titles.

Tsunayoshi had a vigorous interest in ruling and, being a severe and sometimes capricious despot, he was held in dread. It followed that his tastes and style should make an impression on the country. Of course, the relationship between the ruler and his times appears in more subtle ways. A strong ruler, although able to shape his society to some extent, is at the same time fundamentally a product of it. There appears to be, in any case, some resonance between Tsunayoshi and the spirit of the Genroku period.

It is difficult to discover much about the personality of any of the Tokugawa shogun. There are almost no personal papers or diaries and only a few letters. Contemporary chroniclers treated the several strong shogun in stilted phrases and with great respect, giving us little feel for the men. The other shogun were not men of ability and took little part in government, and they usually were rather secluded even from the leading ministers. Consequently, they did not give the historians much to record. Moreover, the historians were scholars of the Confucian classics who used the Chinese style of history writing as their model of expression. The elevated language used to describe the activities of the Tokugawa shogun was similar to that used in the reverential treatment of the emperor in Chinese and Japanese histories. It is a rare instance when we are given sufficient personal detail to detect beneath the honorific language any foibles or unusual predilections. And there is a paucity of popular history and anecdotal material, because it was prohibited to include in stories or plays anything about the affairs of the Tokugawa or other important families.

In the treatment of Tsunayoshi, however, there are some striking exceptions. In some accounts written shortly after his death, we find far more personal information in the way of critical comment, rumor, and satire than in the case of any other shogun. The official chronicle of the Tokugawa shogun, the *Tokugawa jikki* (compiled between 1809 and 1849), gives a detailed and plodding day-by-day account of occurrences within the Bakufu during the rule of each shogun. One of the major sources used by the authors of the *Tokugawa jikki* in compiling the account of Tsunayoshi's rule was the *Kembyō jitsuroku* (*True Record of Tsunayoshi*), a contemporary account written by Ogyū Sorai (1666–1728) and Hattori Nankaku (1683–1759). Tsunayoshi's activities are recorded in the *Tokugawa jikki* without comment in the same manner as those of other shogun. However, following the section on each reign is a supplement (*furoku*) in which there are observations and anecdotes concerning the ruler from a variety of sources. Although the comments concerning Tsunayoshi are often laudatory, there are a few which contain implied criticism.[2]

In contrast to this unprecedented, if pale, criticism, several other works contain extremely severe criticism. The best of these is the *Sannō gaiki* (*Unofficial History of Three Rulers*), an account of Tsunayoshi and his two successors. It is written in Chinese, in a terse and incisive style well suited to the evaluation of Tsunayoshi's various actions and personal characteristics. It records some extraordinary rumors and scandals concerning Tsunayoshi, and by deft comment or by lack of comment implies that the stories may be true. The remarkable skill in the choice of expression gives support to the attribution that the author was the Confucian scholar, Dazai Shundai (1680–1747).

[2] The *Tokugawa jikki* is published in Kuroita Katsumi, ed., (*Shintei zōho*) *Kokushi taikei* (Tokyo, 1929–1935), vols. 38–47. The section on Tsunayoshi's reign runs from 42:353 to 43:752, the *furoku* comprising 43:727–752. The *Kembyō jitsuroku* is extant only in manuscript copies. It was completed in 1714, but minor revisions were made in 1717.

The *Sannō gaiki* circulated as a private document, and was not printed until after the fall of the Tokugawa regime.[3] Another instance of the unusual treatment of this shogun is Chikamatsu's satire on Tsunayoshi, in a play performed only five years after his death.[4]

That such accounts were written and survive probably can be attributed to two factors. One was that Tsunayoshi's eccentricities were so well known and the scandals connected with his name so sensational that they could hardly go unmarked. The other was that Tsunayoshi had no direct heir to protect his name and reputation in history. He was succeeded by his nephew, Ienobu, whom he had taken most reluctantly as his successor. When Ienobu became shogun, he at once set about reversing some of Tsunayoshi's most cherished policies. Because of these circumstances we have been provided with some colorful accounts of Tsunayoshi, but we still are left without sufficient reliable information to formulate a clear picture of his personality. The difficulty is, in good part, the abnormality of our subject.

Tsunayoshi's strengths and weaknesses were shaped to a considerable degree by his mother, Otama, to whom his upbringing and education were entrusted. An affectionate and intelligent woman, she continued to influence his policies until her death, late in his reign, and her name is associated with some of the measures for which he was criticized.

She was of extremely humble birth, the daughter of a green grocer in Kyoto. When Otama's father died, her mother went to serve in the house of Honjō Tarōbei Munetoshi, a retainer in the household of the Nijō family of the court nobility. In due course

[3] *Sannō gaiki* was published by *Gajikanga Shoya*, Tokyo, in 1880.

[4] The puppet play by Chikamatsu Monzaemon (1653–1725), *Sagami Nyūdō sembiki inu* (1714), is analyzed in D. H. Shively, "Chikamatsu's Satire on the Dog Shogun," *Harvard Journal of Asiatic Studies,* 18:159–180 (1955). The best examples of the popular works which contain rumors concerning Tsunayoshi are *Nikkō Kantan makura, Tōeizan tsuya monogatari,* and *Gokoku onna taiheiki* (or *Yanagisawa sōdō*). The first was written in the decade after Tsunayoshi's death, and the other two are evidently elaborations of the stories. Because of the unreliability of these accounts, they have not been used for this paper. The first and third, which have been published, can be found in *Kinsei jitsuroku zensho* (Tokyo, 1928–1929), vols. 1 and 8 respectively.

she bore him a son, Munesuke, and eventually became his second wife.[5] Otama grew up to be a beautiful girl, and she was sent to Edo to serve as a lady in waiting in the women's quarters (*ōoku*) of the shogun's castle. She came to Iemitsu's attention and, when she was nineteen (1646), she bore him a son, later to be named Tsunayoshi. When Iemitsu died five years later, she became a lay nun, as was customary, took the name Keishōin, and devoted herself to the guidance of her son.

According to one story, Iemitsu recognized the young boy's precociousness and instructed Otama to see to it that his son received the good education for which he himself had not had time. Because Iemitsu had two older sons, the possibility of Tsunayoshi's becoming shogun was remote. Iemitsu evidently was concerned that should such an intelligent and willful boy develop an interest in politics and scheming, he might become a problem to the heir, Ietsuna, who lacked ability and energy.[6] It was the course of prudence, therefore, to direct Tsunayoshi's energies into scholarship.

Little is known of Tsunayoshi's boyhood. Two months before his father's death in 1651, he was assigned lands scattered through six provinces, with an assessed yield of 150,000 *koku*. He was living with his mother in a mansion in Edo. Two years later when he was only seven, his *gembuku* ("manhood") ceremony was held, and his child name, Tokumatsu, was replaced by Tsunayoshi. At fifteen he was appointed daimyo of Tatebayashi castle in Kōzuke, and his lands were increased to 250,000 *koku*, but he continued, for the most part, to live in mansions in Edo and to be carefully tutored in Confucian studies. When he was eighteen, he received his official wife, a high-born lady of the

[5] It is not known how old Otama was when she and her mother went to Honjō's house. One account says that her family was so poor that she began to serve Honjō before her husband died. It also has been said that Honjō did not adopt Otama until she rose to fame. Kurita, *Edo jidai*, pp. 428–430; Saiki Kazuma, "Tokugawa shōgun seibo narabi ni saishō kō," in Nihon Rekishi Gakkai, ed., *Rekishi to jimbutsu* (Tokyo, 1964), pp. 429–430.

[6] Iemitsu is quoted as having said that care must be taken to train Tsunayoshi in humility in order that he should not fail to behave properly toward his elder brothers. *Tokugawa jikki*, 43:727a; *Buya shokudan* (preface, 1709), in Kokushi Kenkyūkai, ed., *Kokushi sōsho* (Tokyo, 1917), ser. 2, pp. 86–87.

court nobility, following the customary arrangement for members of the Tokugawa family. The girl, Nobuko, was the thirteen-year-old daughter of the former minister of the left, Takatsukasa Norihira, and younger sister of the imperial regent (*sesshō* and later *kampaku*) Fusasuke.

Tsunayoshi's oldest half brother Ietsuna had become shogun in 1651 at the age of ten. He was a sickly boy, and he was weak-willed and ineffectual as a ruler. He was served well, however, by a succession of able chief ministers, led by his uncle Hoshina Masayuki (1611–1672) as regent. The government proceeded with tolerable efficiency until the latter half of his reign when, under Sakai Tadakiyo (1623–1681), who became great council-lor (*tairō*) in 1666, the administration became lax and there were rumors of bribery and corruption.

In the fourth month of 1680, Ietsuna fell ill. The nomination of his successor became an issue among the senior councillors (*rōjū*). Tsunayoshi's other older brother, Tsunashige, daimyo of Kōfu, had gone insane and committed suicide in 1677. As Ietsuna had no children, Tsunayoshi, as Iemitsu's only surviving son, seemed the logical choice. Tadakiyo, so the story goes, said that Ietsuna did not favor Tsunayoshi but wanted to invite an imperial prince, Arisugawa-no-miya Yukihito, from Kyoto, following the precedent of the Kamakura Bakufu, which used Kyoto princes as puppet shogun from 1252 to 1333. This proposal was opposed by Hotta Masatoshi (1634–1684), who had become a senior councillor only the previous year. In the fifth month, on either the fifth or sixth day, Ietsuna's condition became critical. In the middle of the night, Tsunayoshi was urgently summoned to the castle, where he was met by Masatoshi, who led him to Ietsuna's bed. Ietsuna adopted him on the spot, making him his heir. On the seventh, Tsunayoshi moved into the Ninomaru (second enceinte) of Edo castle, and the next day Ietsuna's death was announced. Two months later Tsunayoshi moved into the Hommaru (main enceinte) and the next month received the title of shogun from the emperor. Before the end of the year Tadakiyo was dismissed as *tairō*. This account of the succession dispute is recorded in the *Tokugawa jikki,* which states that the story is undocumented but implies that it is true.[7] We cannot be certain, of course, whether Ietsuna, when he adopted Tsunayoshi, was still competent or, for that matter, still alive. In any event, Hotta Masatoshi emerged from the change of regime with great power.

Tsunayoshi, at the age of thirty-four, and his minister, Masatoshi, embarked at once on a program of strict and ethical administration. They reasserted the power of the Bakufu as it had been in the days of Iemitsu by a number of swift and severe judicial decisions. The most dramatic was the handling of the Echigo quarrel (*Echigo sōdō*) of the Takada han. This was the domain of Matsudaira Echigo-no-kami Mitsunaga, a great-grandson of Ieyasu, and it was assessed at 260,000 *koku*. A dispute had persisted for several years between two of the senior retainers (*karō*). Tadakiyo had had the case investigated in 1679 by an inspector general (*ōmetsuke*), who rendered the judgment that both retainers should be punished by being put into the custody of other daimyo (*daimyō azuke*). Two years later, because of unrest in the domain, Tsunayoshi reopened the case. Summoning the parties to Edo castle, he had Masatoshi question them for one day, and then, sitting in judgment personally, the shogun handed down his decision on the following day. He sentenced one of the retainers and his son to *seppuku* and sent the other retainer into exile on Hachijō-jima. Twenty others were banished or put into the custody of daimyo. But the part of his judgment that astonished the country was that he expropriated the entire domain and put the daimyo and his son into daimyo custody for negligence in permitting such a quarrel to arise. The inspector general, whose decision was overturned, was exiled for faulty judgment. Tsunayoshi was praised for his handling of this extremely complicated case which, it was said, he skillfully untangled and settled decisively.

---

[7] 42:354b–355a. There are a variety of theories concerning Tadakiyo's motives in attempting to install an imperial prince as shogun, if indeed the story is true. See Kurita, *Edo jidai*, pp. 427–428. Tadakiyo's descendants held high office in the Bakufu later in the Tokugawa period, which would indicate that his proposal was interpreted as bad judgment rather than as disloyalty to the Tokugawa house.

This was the last time that a Tokugawa shogun sat in direct judgment of a case.[8]

Throughout his reign Tsunayoshi adhered to a policy of strict and clear rewards and punishments in the manner approved by the Chinese Legalist tradition. During his rule more than thirty-three daimyo lost their domains and the holdings of thirteen daimyo were reduced as punishment, the losses and reductions totalling 2.2 million *koku*.[9] More than one hundred *hatamoto* and countless *gokenin* lost their fiefs or stipends. The *Tokugawa jikki* says that from the viewpoint of its day (more than a century later), the judgments might seem too severe, but this policy was adopted to make it clear that the indecisiveness of the previous regime had been replaced by a return to strong control and authority. It was like a fresh wind blowing through the land.[10]

Another perspective on Tsunayoshi is provided by a German physician, Engelbert Kaempfer, who made the journey from Dejima to Edo once in 1691 and again in 1692 with the Dutch mission to perform obeisance before the shogun. He speaks of "Tsinajos" as "a Prince of great prudence and conduct, and heir to the virtues and good qualities of his predecessors, and withal eminent for his singular clemency and mildness, though a strict maintainer of the Laws of the Country."[11]

---

[8] Kurita, *Edo jidai*, pp. 435–436.

[9] *Ibid.*, pp. 477–483. The amount of land seized by Tsunayoshi was approximately double the amount taken under his predecessor Ietsuna, but it was considerably less than the lands confiscated by Iemitsu. (The three reigns were of approximately the same length.) The amount taken by Tsunayoshi was greater than the confiscations in the remaining century and a half of the Tokugawa period.

[10] 43:733a.

[11] Engelbert Kaempfer, *The History of Japan, Together with a Description of the Kingdom of Siam, 1690–92,* tr., J. G. Scheuchzer (Glasgow, 1906), 3:336. In an earlier passage, Kaempfer wrote, "Tsinajos hath the character of a severe, but just and prudent Monarch. He inherited from his ancestors along with the Crown, an absolute and unlimited Power over all his Subjects, from the meanest extraction up to the highest rank. Even the greatest Princes, and Lords of the Empire, are so far his vassals, that he can disgrace, exile and deprive them of their lives and dominions, as he pleases, or as he thinks, the peace and welfare of the Empire requires, or their crimes deserve" (1:129).

Tsunayoshi must have been a formidable figure to face. There is evidence of this in the *Sannō gaiki*:

> Tsunayoshi's majestic judgments made all the daimyo fearful, and even when it was not cold, they shivered. The Sendai lord, [Date] Tsunamura, once told someone: "When I had audiences with Ietsuna long ago, I always looked at his face. But in the case of the present shogun, I do not dare to look at his face. Whenever I have an audience, I lower my head involuntarily."[12]

Hotta Masatoshi was a vigorous, straightforward administrator, so strict, we are told, that even Tsunayoshi was in awe of him. His inflexibility made enemies and was in the end his undoing. His own cousin, Inaba Masayasu, a junior councillor (*wakadoshiyori*), stabbed him in Edo castle in 1684.[13] The shock of Masatoshi's murder affected Tsunayoshi deeply. The senior councillors' offices were moved away from the area of the shogun's chambers, and thereafter Tsunayoshi met only rarely with the councillors. He used his own trusted retainers, the most important of whom held the post of grand chamberlain (*soba yōnin*), for communication with the councils.[14] The *tairō* and senior council declined in importance and lost initiative as the executive positions of the Bakufu, not regaining substantial power again for a century. As the shogun became more sequestered, his chamberlains and attendants were entrusted with more responsibility and power. Tsunayoshi was left without an able minister from among the experienced *fudai* daimyo families to caution him against unwise policies or admonish him about his personal weaknesses and eccentricities. Increasingly, Tsunayoshi came to be looked on by his contemporaries as a tyrant, an idiosyncratic, bad ruler. Yet in some accounts there is praise of Tsunayoshi as an idealistic sage-ruler. We shall examine these two views and then consider in what respects they might be reconciled.

---

[12] *Sannō gaiki*, pp. 1b–2a.
[13] Kurita, *Edo jidai*, pp. 440–441; *Tokugawa jikki*, 42:520b–523a.
[14] Conrad Totman, *Politics in the Tokugawa Bakufu, 1600–1843* (Cambridge, Mass., 1967), p. 101.

TSUNAYOSHI AS TYRANT

The most unpopular of Tsunayoshi's measures were the innumerable laws for the protection of animals, birds, and fish, known as the *shōrui awaremi no rei* (laws of compassion for living things). The first laws, which began to appear about 1685, were to prevent mistreatment of dogs and other animals. They began mildly enough, with instructions that dogs and cats need no longer be leashed when the shogun was proceeding through the city.[15] Subsequent regulations required that stray dogs be fed by the neighborhood and sick or injured dogs be taken to dog doctors. As the laws became more strict, townsmen and farmers who were guilty of wounding or killing a dog were sometimes crucified or beheaded. Samurai also were severely punished. There were instances of a lower samurai being exiled for failure to care for a puppy abandoned by his gate, for not stopping a dog fight, or for injuring a dog which barked at him. One samurai who killed a dog which had bitten him was ordered to commit *seppuku*. Dogs, emboldened by this impunity, became increasingly troublesome and, as a consequence, some met with foul play. The Bakufu then ordered that a dog census be kept, which would record a description of each dog, its sex and color and dates of birth and death. As the number of dogs rapidly increased, the government had to establish large compounds in Edo to house unwanted dogs at Kitami, Yotsuya, Ōkubo, and Nakano. The latter two, which covered over 150 acres (185,000 *tsubo*), accommodated 48,748 dogs in 1698. A special tax was levied on the people of Edo to provide food for these compounds.[16]

It was popularly believed that dogs were given such special treatment because of a superstitious belief of the shogun's. His only son had died in 1683, and when he failed to have another

---

[15] *Tokugawa jikki*, 42:553. The date is 1685/7, but there is reference to earlier notices on the subject.

[16] Kurita, *Edo jidai*, pp. 605–612; Nakamura, *Genroku jidai kan*, pp. 127–141; *Sannō gaiki*, p. 2.

son despite all prayers and incantations, the abbot Ryūkō (1649–1724), a special favorite and confidant, is said to have suggested that this was retribution for having killed in a previous life, and that the ban might be removed by showing compassion toward living things in this life. Dogs should be given special treatment because the shogun was born in the zodiacal year of the dog. Tsunayoshi was nicknamed Inu Kubō, "the Dog Shogun." It happened that his two favorite ministers, Makino Narisada (1634–1712) and Yanagisawa Yoshiyasu (1658–1714) also were born in the year of the dog, so they were privately referred to as "the Three Dogs." The people would have suffered less, notes one historian, if the three had been born in the year of animals not native to Japan such as the dragon or the tiger.[17]

The dog laws were the most extreme aspect of a broader policy to protect all living things. Falconry was abolished at the Bakufu, and those officials who fed and trained the birds were assigned to other duties. Fowl, shellfish, and shrimp were not to be served in the castle except to entertain nobles from the imperial court. It was prohibited to sell live birds and fish or to keep them as pets. Hunting and fishing were greatly curtailed. Boar and deer that damaged crops might be driven off only with noisemakers. It was forbidden to brand horses or to bob their tails and, for a time, they could not be used as beasts of burden. There were severe penalties for the violation of these laws, many persons being jailed or even exiled for killing birds. Although shogunal law applied only in territories under direct Bakufu control, the daimyo were expected to follow Edo's policies in their domains. That most of them solemnly issued and enforced laws to protect animals and birds indicates the power of the Bakufu during this period.[18]

Tsunayoshi pursued his policy by punishing offenders with undiminished determination, despite the great suffering that

[17] Kurita, *Edo jidai*, p. 607.

[18] When Kaempfer passed through Kurume in Kyushu in 1692, he learned that a reward of silver coins was offered "to any body that would discover the accomplices of a murder lately committed upon a dog. Many a poor man hath been severely punish'd in this country, under the present Emperor's [Shogun's] reign, purely for the sake of dogs." Kaempfer, *History of Japan*, 3:205.

was caused to human beings. The campaign increased in intensity until his death twenty-four years after the first of the laws appeared. He left a testament for his heir that this one policy should be carried on as a filial duty through his reign and should continue for one hundred years. But Ienobu was concerned about the "hundreds of thousands" who had been punished for violating these laws, and the thousands who were still in jail—not to mention nine offenders who had died while awaiting their day in court and whose corpses were pickled in brine so that they might still be formally sentenced! Ienobu reported to Tsunayoshi's bier even before the funeral took place that he must repeal the laws.[19] He issued a general amnesty for 8,831 prisoners and exiles, many of whom were undergoing punishment for violating these "laws of compassion."[20]

In his pursuit of this policy, Tsunayoshi failed as a Confucian ruler on several counts. The most obvious was the severity of the punishments. Another, made much of in Chikamatsu's satire, was giving to beasts food that was needed by men. Chikamatsu referred to Mencius's admonition to King Hui: "Your dogs and swine eat the food of men, and you do not make any restrictive arrangements," which Mencius said was "leading on beasts to devour men."[21]

Tsunayoshi's reputation suffered also from the excessive manner in which he indulged his sexual proclivities and the air of scandal that emanated from his affairs with handsome boys as well as women. Homosexuality was still common, perhaps even customary, among military aristocrats in the seventeenth century, and it could not have been considered remarkable that the shogun preferred boys to women. His father Iemitsu had a similar preference. His great-grandfather Ieyasu, though he produced eleven sons and six daughters by his thirteen wives and concubines, and had six additional acknowledged concubines as well, had more than his share of boys.[22] What was unusual

[19] Miyazaki Michio, (*Teihon*) *Oritaku shiba no ki shakugi* (1964), pp. 224–225.
[20] *Ibid.*, p. 245.
[21] Shively, "Chikamatsu's Satire," pp. 164–165.
[22] Saiki, "Tokugawa shogun," pp. 421–426.

was the degree of Tsunayoshi's indulgence; he appointed a large number of youths of all classes to posts as attendants, and he promoted eleven or more of them to daimyo.[23]

Another scandal was that some of his favorites rose to be leading officials. The most spectacular case was that of Yanagisawa Yoshiyasu. The son of a samurai of only 150 *koku*, and twelve years Tsunayoshi's junior, Yoshiyasu became Tsunayoshi's disciple in Confucian studies and went with him to Edo castle and became an attendant (*konando*) in 1680. In 1688, he rose to daimyo rank, became a grand chamberlain, and for the remaining twenty years of Tsunayoshi's rule he was the most powerful minister. He received successive increases in income until in 1703 he was given the Kōfu domain, assessed at 150,000 *koku*.[24] He was evidently clever in anticipating and pandering to Tsunayoshi's whims. He does, however, seem to have been in addition intelligent, well-educated, and an able administrator.

The *Sannō gaiki,* in its terse Chinese style, states bluntly,

> The ruler liked sex with males. From among the sons of *tozama* daimyo and *hatamoto* down to soldiers and housemen, no matter how humble, if they were handsome, he appointed them as attendants. [The text lists the names of nineteen daimyo or daimyo's sons.] They were all selected because of sex. There were only a few who were not appointed attendant because of sex [three names listed]. Both Yanagisawa Yoshiyasu and Kuroda Naoshige pleased him with love from the time they were young pages, and finally they were promoted to daimyo. . . . Others who pleased with sexual love and received stipend and rank are too numerous to count.[25]

There is record of at least 130 of these youths, and it was rumored that a special official was appointed in 1693 to select

23 *Tokugawa jikki,* 43:733b.
24 The yield of the Kōfu domain was actually in excess of 200,000 *koku*. In 1701, Yoshiyasu was given permission to use the Tokugawa clan name of Matsudaira, and the shogun gave him the character "Yoshi" from his name. (Hitherto Yoshiyasu's name had been Yasuaki.) He was also given the privilege of minting coins in Kōfu. His two younger sons were made daimyo. Kurita, *Edo jidai,* 1:443–444; *Sannō gaiki,* p. 8b.
25 *Sannō gaiki,* p. 3.

handsome boys.[26] The favorites were jealously guarded from the possibility of other liaisons by being confined like the concubines in the women's quarters.[27] Tsunayoshi was extremely generous in giving his favorite youths fiefs, advancements in rank, increases in stipends, and gifts and honors.[28] He did violence to the traditions of hereditary social status and privileges by making daimyo's sons, and even young *tozama* daimyo, serve as pages in company with boys of all social backgrounds from samurai down to commoners and budding *nō* actors.[29]

Tsunayoshi's preference for boys and his indiscriminate promotion of them did not set a good example for the daimyo. According to the *Sannō gaiki*, "Many *tozama* daimyo imitated him like stupid children. The Lord of Nakatsu [Ogasawara] Nagatane loved a fellow called Akimoto and made him his leading minister, whereupon the administration of the domain fell into disorder. . . ."[30]

There is less information concerning Tsunayoshi's relations with women. In addition to his official wife, he had three rec-

---

[26] Kurita, *Edo jidai*, p. 437.

[27] The most prized youths were kept in a dormitory at the residence of Yanagisawa Yoshiyasu according to the *Sannō gaiki* (pp. 4b–5a): "The ruler liked youths. They were promoted, for the most part, because of sex. Of several tens of attendants, twenty-odd were favored, and they were kept at the residence of the Lord of Kawagoe [Yoshiyasu]. Some had wives, others not. They were under regulations concerning their travel to the castle every day, their return from the castle, their rising, eating, studying, and so forth. There were four men in charge of watching them. They waited for an evening call. . . . Whether they were at the castle or not, they could not look around [to flirt] or talk on the street. Even their fathers and brothers could rarely see them or correspond with them. Twenty-two or twenty-three boys from daimyo families became such attendants, and three were sons of court nobles. Sons of *hatamoto* and *gokenin*, even if lowly, were summoned if they were beautiful."

[28] *Tokugawa jikki*, 43:733b. Some youths who later displeased him, including some who had been made daimyo, were stripped of their rank and sent into exile or put into the custody of daimyo. There were several youths who caught his eye but who, fearful of the risks that went with an appointment, declined the offer. They too were exiled.

[29] The *Tokugawa jikki*, 43:739b, lists the names of forty-seven attendants who were of daimyo background or who were made daimyo, and it notes that the next shogun, Ienobu, returned them all to their "original status."

[30] *Sannō gaiki*, p. 3a. In 1698, Nagatane was instructed to retire in favor of his younger brother, and the domain was cut from 80,000 to 40,000 *koku* for "negligence." *Tokugawa jikki*, 43:733a; Arai Hakuseki, (*Shinhen*) *Hankampu* (Tokyo, 1967), 3:16.

ognized concubines, well below the average number for a Tokugawa shogun. Two were from the lower court nobility, reputed to be beautiful and talented women, and with his consort they formed a small Heian-kyō harem from the years before he became shogun, but these unions produced no children. The other concubine, Oden, was the favorite.[31] She bore him his only children, a daughter Tsuruhime in 1677, who married the heir of Kii, Tokugawa Tsunanori, and a son Tokumatsu (given the same childhood name as Tsunayoshi), born in 1679, who died when he was only four.

Tsunayoshi's practice of paying frequent visits to the mansions of his favorite ministers was quite unprecedented and led to gossip. It was rumored that Makino Narisada made both his wife and his daughter available to Tsunayoshi and that, as a consequence, the daughter's husband committed suicide and the daughter herself suddenly fell ill and died.[32]

The most extraordinary story of all concerned the boy Yoshisato, born in 1687 to Yanagisawa Yoshiyasu's wife or mistress. It was rumored that Tsunayoshi was the father. This story is used to explain Yoshiyasu's appointment to daimyo the next year and his rapid rise thereafter. The story also is used to explain Tsunayoshi's numerous visits to Yoshiyasu's mansion

---

[31] Saiki, "Tokugawa shogun," pp. 431–433. Tsunayoshi appears to have been devoted to Oden and is said to have treated her as if she had the status of his consort. The *Sannō gaiki* (p. 1b) announces that this was the beginning of the ascendancy of women favorites at the shogun's court. In 1698, one of the leading genre painters of the day, Hanabusa Itchō (1652–1724), or Fujiwara Chōko as he was called at that time, published a book of illustrations (*ehon*) entitled *Hyakunin jōrō* (*A Hundred Noble Ladies*), in which he included a drawing illustrating the current rumor that Tsunayoshi frequently took Oden boating in the Fukiage garden of the castle. Tsunayoshi is shown poling the boat himself and reciting *nō* while she accompanies him on the hand-drum. The artist was arrested and banished to an island where he remained eleven years until Tsunayoshi's death. Shirai Kyōji and Takayanagi Mitsutoshi, *Nihon itsuwa daijiten* (Tokyo, 1967), 6:2256–2257. The picture alludes to the T'ang dynasty story of the Emperor Hsuan-tsung boating with Yang Kuei-fei. See, for example, Tu Fu's poem, "Ai chiang t'ou," *A Concordance to the Poems of Tu Fu*, Harvard-Yenching Institute Sinological Index Series, supplement no. 14 (Peking, 1940), p. 43, no. 20.

[32] *Sannō gaiki*, p. 3a; *Isetsu Nihonshi*, 6:355–361. Tsunayoshi visited Narisada's residence thirty-two times, but the first visit (1688) was the year after the alleged scandal. Kurita, *Edo jidai*, 1:442–443.

(fifty-eight are recorded between 1691 and 1708) and the special favors that were shown the boy. The shogun, having lost his heir, would have liked to adopt Yoshisato as his successor, but the scandal would have been too great. Years later, in 1704, Tsunayoshi found himself with no choice but to adopt his nephew, Tsunatoyo, daimyo of Kōfu (who succeeded him five years later as Ienobu), and he was moved to Edo, opening up the Kōfu domain. This was given to Yoshiyasu despite the tradition that it should be held by a Tokugawa and that it was improper to grant it to a retainer. The story was that Tsunayoshi had promised Yoshisato, who would eventually succeed to this domain, that it would be increased to one million *koku*, and that it would include Suruga and other provinces in the original homeland of the Tokugawa. If Tsunayoshi were to retire and move to Sumpu, in Suruga, following the precedent of Ieyasu, holding court as the retired shogun (*ōgosho*), he would, in effect, be creating a private state for himself and his secret son. The story continues that Tsunayoshi's consort Takatsukasa, hearing of this outrageous plot, stabbed Tsunayoshi to death and then killed herself. Her death was announced one month after Tsunayoshi's. According to one satirical poem, Tsunayoshi's death left Yoshisato 850,000 *koku* short.[33] There is no reliable evidence for these accounts, but that such scurrilous rumors circulated illustrates the degree of infamy he had attained in his own day.

One of Tsunayoshi's great enthusiasms was *nō* drama. In addition to watching the stately, dignified performances, he liked to dance himself. Sakai Tadakiyo, who was dismissed as *tairō* in the first year, presumed to admonish him that it was not proper for the shogun himself to perform *nō*.[34] Undaunted, Tsunayoshi began in 1681 to perform at formal occasions at Edo

---

[33] *Sannō gaiki*, pp. 3b and 8b; *Isetsu Nihonshi*, 6:337–353; Kurita, *Edo jidai*, pp. 444–445; Naitō Chisō, *Tokugawa jūgodai shi* (Tokyo, 1958), 3:1445. Isaac Titsingh, the chief agent of the Dutch post at Dejima (1779–1780 and 1781–1783), records that Tsunayoshi was stabbed by his consort because he planned to adopt Yoshisato as his heir and she feared that this would result in revolution. Titsingh did not record the rumor that Tsunayoshi was Yoshisato's father. Titsingh, *Illustrations of Japan*, tr., Frederic Shoberl (London, 1822), pp. 30–32.

[34] Kurita, *Edo jidai*, pp. 450–451.

castle.[35] After Hotta Masatoshi's assassination in 1684, the last restraint was removed, and Tsunayoshi began to perform frequently. Later that year he invited the heads of the three main branches of the Tokugawa (*gosanke*), senior councillors, and other important officials to witness his performances. In 1686, there was a memorable program, when the most honored daimyo in Japan each performed a dance, including Maeda Tsunanori, lord of Kaga, as well as the heads of the *gosanke* and their heirs. Among the performers was the redoubtable Mitsukuni of Mito, dancing in *Ama*.[36] During the following decade formal performances increased in number. The *Tokugawa jikki* records fourteen in 1696 alone.

Nō performers, as professional entertainers, traditionally were regarded as of the lowest social class, and were, in theory, outcastes. Tsunayoshi, however, favored handsome and talented young performers and musicians and appointed them *gokenin* and made them pages at the castle.[37]

Because one of the easier ways to gain favor with the shogun was through proficiency in *nō* dancing, *nō* became popular at daimyo mansions. We are told that there was none among his attendants or even among the daimyo and officials who did not take part.[38] One historian refers to Tsunayoshi's years as the "era of dancing."[39]

---

[35] *Tokugawa jikki*, 42:401a.

[36] *Ibid.*, 42:572b. Later in 1686 there was a large audience at the castle when all the daimyo then in Edo and their heirs, as well as the higher *hatamoto* and many officials, were invited to a banquet and a performance of *nō*. The shogun himself danced *Kantan, Funa Benkei, Shōjō*, and *Midare. Ibid.*, 42:580.

[37] The *Tokugawa jikki* records that during the six years, 1685 to 1690, the shogun appointed as pages ten *nō* actors, two *kyōgen* actors, two reciters, a flutist, and four drummers. In 1696, eight more actors were appointed and thirteen others were put on stipend, but evidently they were not appointed to posts at the castle. Nakamura, *Genroku jidai kan*, pp. 95–97. The *Tokugawa jikki* records that "because of his excessive liking [for *nō*], he summoned members of the troupes and frequently appointed them to fine posts. Hence, many people would practice hand gestures and foot movements day and night so that there was [as in the *Shu-ching*] 'drinking and singing in the chambers and constant dancing in the palace'" (43:752a).

[38] *Tokugawa jikki*, 43:751b.

[39] Nakamura, *Genroku jidai kan*, p. 91. The *Sannō gaiki* states (p. 3b), "The ruler liked *sarugaku* [*nō*]. The daimyo and those of lower rank followed his example. The sounds of *nō* recitation were heard far and wide and filled the castle

The *Sannō gaiki* claims that only five of the daimyo preferred *gagaku* to *nō*.[40] This implies criticism of Tsunayoshi, for the stricter Confucian scholars in the Tokugawa period condemned *nō* as "licentious music," and they said that only *gagaku*, the staid music and dance form of the imperial court since Nara times, was appropriate for the shogun's castle.[41]

According to traditional historians, one of the most serious threats to a ruling dynasty was that the ruler might come under the influence of the women's quarters. Mothers, consorts, and concubines who meddle in the affairs of state and wheedle appointments for their relatives were thought to undermine the dynasty. Tsunayoshi's favors to his wife and concubines were relatively minor, but there is no question that he was excessively willing to please his mother Keishōin. Her relatives were most generously treated. Honjō Munesuke, her younger half brother (her mother's son by Honjō), was made daimyo of Kasama (Hitachi) at 70,000 *koku*. Her stepfather's older son and Munesuke's younger son (the older son being his heir) were both given daimyo domains. The *Sannō gaiki* warns that "since the beginning of the country [the Tokugawa regime?], never had maternal relatives been so successful. Han Yuan-ti enfeoffed the Wang family and made five marquises.[42] Wise men judged this a mistake. When in our Japan three were made lords from one family of maternal relatives, is it possible to say that it is not a

---

towns. Retainers and their sons vied with each other in studying it, and in that way sought to be appointed to office. Even samurai, to say nothing of those of lower rank, were not ashamed to act in the same way as *sarugaku* actors."

[40] The five daimyo were Ikeda Tsunamasa of Bizen, Yamauchi Toyomasa of Tosa, Sōma Masatane of Nakamura, Tamura Takeaki of Ichinoseki, and Nambu Naomasa of Hachinohe. *Sannō gaiki,* p. 3b.

[41] *Nō* was criticized as "licentious music" by Arai Hakuseki in *Shintei no an* in *Arai Hakuseki zenshū* (Tokyo, 1907), 6:264-265, and by the reputed author of the *Sannō gaiki,* Dazai Shundai, in *Keizairoku,* in *Nihon keizai sōsho* (Tokyo, 1914), 6:49.

[42] The author's point is that appointments for relatives of Emperor Yuan-ti's consort led to the undermining of the former Han dynasty. Actually, Yuan-ti appointed only his consort's father, Wang Chin, but Yuan-ti's successor, Cheng-ti (r. 32-6 B.C.), appointed five of Wang Chin's sons marquises in one day. The son of one of these marquises was the usurper Wang Mang. *Han shu,* 98:5a, in *Erh-shih-ssu shih* (Shanghai; Ssu-pu ts'ung-k'an ed.).

mistake?"[43] Keishōin's distant relatives also were given appointments and advances, but this favoritism probably was less damaging in practice than it sounded in principle to scholars trained in the history of the Han dynasty.[44]

Tsunayoshi also responded generously to his mother's numerous requests for the support of Buddhist temples but, according to the *Kembyō jitsuroku,* she did not try to influence him about great matters of state.[45] Perhaps there is no evidence of her meddling in major decisions, but her influence on Tsunayoshi seems to have been pervasive. Her name is linked with the laws of compassion and government sponsorship of scholarship. She was also influential through her domination of the women's quarters.

In his desire to honor his mother, Tsunayoshi had the emperor give her the Junior First court rank in 1702. It was unprecedented for any woman of the shogunal house to attain such an honor before her death, not to mention a woman of such humble birth.[46]

It was Tokugawa policy to respect and patronize Buddhism. The first three shogun utilized able monks as advisors. The Tendai monk, Tenkai (1536–1643), who served all three shogun, proposed the Nikkō mausoleum for Ieyasu and the Tōeizan Kan'eiji at Ueno in Edo to safeguard the Bakufu from the northeast, the unlucky direction. Kan'eiji was conceived of as a counterpart of the headquarters of the Tendai sect on Mount Hiei, outside Kyoto, and hence was called the Eastern Hiei (Tōei). Like the main temple, it had an imperial prince as its abbot. He served a special purpose for the Bakufu, since he was on hand for use as a replacement for the emperor in case of difficulty between the Bakufu and the imperial court. The early shogun con-

---

[43] *Sannō gaiki,* p. 3b.

[44] Among the distant relatives of Keishōin who benefited were the Rokkaku, Ōzawa, Kondō, Tomita, Okitsu, Toda, Mori, and Sano. But Tsunayoshi, being fair-minded, or at least Legalist-minded, punished relatives who committed offenses, as he did Rokkaku Hiroharu in 1696. *Tokugawa jikki,* 43:747b; *Kurita,* p. 429.

[45] *Ibid.,* 43:731a.

[46] Junior First (*ju-ichi*) was also the highest rank that Tsunayoshi held during his lifetime. He was made Senior First on his death.

tinued to build up this and other temples, such as the Jōdo temple Zōjōji in the Shiba district, which would serve the Bakufu in religious and ceremonial functions.

Tsunayoshi's support of Buddhism, however, went far beyond that of any other Tokugawa shogun. When Keishōin was a girl in Kyoto, according to one story, a Shingon monk, Ryōken (1611–1687), read her physiognomy and predicted that she would reach a noble position. Later, just before the birth of Tsunayoshi, she summoned Ryōken (then the abbot of the Chisokuin in Edo) to perform incantations to ensure a safe delivery. Ryōken predicted that she would bear a son and that he would reach the noblest and highest position. Because these two predictions came true, Keishōin ever afterwards had the greatest faith in him. At her request, Tsunayoshi established a new temple for Ryōken in 1681, the Gokokuji (Temple to Protect the Country) at Ōtsuka, dedicated to the prosperity of the Bakufu.[47] She often visited the temple, and the abbot was frequently at the castle.

In 1686, on Ryōken's recommendation the monk Ryūkō was summoned from Yamato to head the Chisokuin.[48] After Ryōken's death the next year, Ryūkō took his place as the most favored monk. The Chisokuin was rebuilt in an extravagantly ornate style at a new site just beyond the Kanda Bridge, northeast of the castle where it would protect the unlucky quarter. It was most unusual to have a large temple so close to the castle, because after the Meireki fire of 1657 which burned out the central part of the city, most of the temples had been relocated in the outskirts. This nearby location was obviously for the convenience of Tsunayoshi and his mother. The shogun visited the temple twenty times, and Ryūkō frequented the castle.[49] During the following years elaborate new structures were built at both the Gokokuji and the Gojiin (as the Chisokuin was renamed)

---

[47] *Tokugawa jikki*, 42:400a.

[48] *Ibid.*, 42:572.

[49] Kurita, *Edo jidai*, pp. 587–589. In 1695, the Chisokuin was renamed Gojiin, and Ryūkō was given the title of Daisōjō as head of the New Shingon Sect (founded 1288). The Gojiin did not survive long. It burned in 1717 and was not rebuilt, its name being given instead to the Gokokuji.

and at other Edo temples.[50] Large sums were given for construction and repairs of many temples and Shinto shrines in other parts of the country.[51] It is alleged that the generous and continual donations of land and money to temples was a major drain on the treasury, which had become seriously depleted in the 1690's. Whereas the endowment and repair of temples by earlier shogun had, for the most part, been calculated to have political utility to the regime, much of Tsunayoshi's giving stemmed from his or his mother's personal interest in patronizing favorite monks.

Confucian chroniclers were not sympathetic to such squandering of resources on Buddhism. They considered Tsunayoshi superstitious. The *Sannō gaiki* says, "The ruler liked incantations and exorcism. He worshipped at shrines. A great number of Buddhist monks and fortunetellers were summoned and recommended their methods to him. He built Buddhist temples and repaired tombs far and near without end."[52] This book also records that he once made a decision by going to a shrine and drawing lots instead of consulting a trained fortuneteller.[53] He appears, like his mother, to have been prey to all types of religious practitioners. It is said that he had more faith in the spells of Buddhist priests like Ryūkō than in treatment by physicians.

Another of the shogun's unusual superstitions was his awe of

[50] A number of renowned Shingon and Tendai monks from the Kyoto area were summoned to Edo to establish temples or to devote themselves to prayers for the regime. The Komponchūdō, the main building at Kan'eiji, was completed in 1698 with the involuntary assistance of the Shimazu family. The Bakufu granted 25,000 *ryō* for the dedication ceremony, and an imperial messenger arrived with a tablet bearing the name of the hall in the emperor's calligraphy. On 9/6, as people were crowding toward the temple to witness the arrival of the tablet, a fire broke out in the residential quarter and spread across Ueno, destroying most of the temple area except for the new building. *Tokugawa jikki*, 43:344; *Sannō gaiki*, pp. 5b–6a.

[51] During a period of only nine years, from 1688 to 1696, over fifty shrines and temples outside of Edo received donations for construction or repairs, including the Shinto shrines Ise, Nikkō, Kunō, Atsuta, Kasuga, Iwashimizu, Fushimi, Atago, Tsurugaoka, Hakone, and Sengen, and the Buddhist temples Tōdaiji, Kōyasan, Hōraiji, Daijuji, and Serada Chōrakuji, in the amount of 30 ingots of gold, 164,000 *ryō*, over 2,800 *kamme* of silver, and 21,300 *koku* of rice. Kurita, *Edo jidai*, p. 590.

[52] *Sannō gaiki*, p. 3b.

[53] *Tokugawa jikki*, 43:727b.

the spirit of Ieyasu. For this reason he took great pains to be on good terms with the abbot-prince Kōben (1669–1716), who performed the ancestral ceremonies at Nikkō. According to the *Sannō gaiki,* he was in a state of anxiety on the days of these rites. "When a letter was received saying that the rites were completed without incident, he rejoiced, and his melancholy was dispelled. Had he heard that there had been wind or rain or perhaps some untoward incident and that it had not been possible to complete the rites, he would have been fearful."[54]

His anxiety about natural phenomena seems to have exceeded contemporary prevailing ideas about such matters. It was, of course, in the Chinese imperial tradition that the ruler should concern himself with the meaning behind unusual phenomena. Tsunayoshi was terrified of earthquakes and thunderstorms.[55] In 1682, when a comet appeared, he reflected on his own behavior and was praised for this act by his minister Hotta Masatoshi.[56] As the *Kembyō jitsuroku* informs us,

> He was particularly fearful and reverential about natural calamities. When there was some minor phenomenon of nature, he would reflect upon himself and remonstrate with himself. About 1686, he ordered Hayashi Daigaku-no-kami Nobuatsu to compile a record of natural phenomena in Japan and China in ancient and recent times, which could be used to caution the ruler. The book was entitled *Ryōchō saihenkō,* and he always kept it in readiness at his side.[57]

It is difficult in this case to judge whether he was being a good Chinese ruler, or whether, compared to contemporary attitudes, he merely was being superstitious.

During the last six years of Tsunayoshi's reign, there was an unusual succession of natural disasters, as if heaven were passing judgment on the moral competence of the ruler. On 1703/ 11/22, Edo and the surrounding provinces were struck by the worst earthquake since 1649. In addition to severe damage to

[54] *Sannō gaiki,* p. 4a.
[55] *Tokugawa jikki,* 43:746b.
[56] *Ibid.,* 43:745b.
[57] *Ibid.,* 43:741.

the castle walls and the large temples, fire broke out in Edo, and 37,000 people lost their lives.[58] A week later another fire destroyed much of the east and northeast parts of the city, and 3,000 more persons were killed. Because the earthquake was the most severe disaster in a long time, in 1704/3 the era-name was changed from Genroku to Hōei.[59] The *Tokugawa jikki* records that in that month, despite earlier prohibitions, "false rumors" continued to circulate concerning the earthquake and that they were being made into plays and satirical poems. Offenders were to be arrested.[60]

The same year Tsunayoshi's only daughter, aged twenty-seven, died childless. His mother died the next year, and Tsunayoshi observed mourning for three years.

On 1707/11/23, there was a great eruption of Mount Fuji, forming the small outcrop on its slope which now spoils the symmetry of the cone.[61] Eruptions and tremors continued for five days. Ashes fell several inches thick on the four surrounding provinces. This devastated crops over a large area and necessitated great expense to remove the volcanic ash so that the fields could be tilled again. The sky over Edo was black, as ashes continued to fall for over two weeks. It was the worst calamity in several hundred years, according to the *Sannō gaiki*.[62]

Tsunayoshi summoned learned monks to question them about these portents. The Jōdo monk Yūten (1637–1718), of Denzū-in, replied that although sand belonged on the earth, now it was falling from the sky. This was an unfavorable sign. Neither was it favorable, he continued, to kill men for the sake of birds and beasts. Tsunayoshi was not pleased, but he summoned Yūten the next day and rewarded him for his frankness.[63]

The *Tokugawa jikki* reports that the next year, Hōei 5 (1708), was another year of successive natural disasters. On New Year's

---

[58] *Ibid.*, 43:520; Naitō, *Tokugawa jūgodai shi*, 3:1401–1402; *Sannō gaiki*, p. 6a.

[59] *Sannō gaiki*, p. 6a.

[60] *Tokugawa jikki*, 43:534b–535a.

[61] This outcrop is called Hōeizan, named for the year-period.

[62] *Sannō gaiki*, p. 6b; Miyazaki, *Oritaku shiba no ki shakugi*, pp. 199–202.

[63] Naitō, *Tokugawa jūgodai shi*, 3:1438.

Day there was an unusually heavy rain, causing floods. In the third and fourth months "white hair" grew on the ground throughout the provinces. In the third month there was a great fire in Kyoto which destroyed the palaces of the emperor and the retired emperor and burned a considerable part of the city. An epidemic of measles struck all classes, causing many deaths. Mount Fuji erupted again. In the sixth month the Kyoto and Osaka area was struck by a typhoon, causing severe flooding and loss of crops. At the end of the year there was a great fire at Osaka which burned for two days.[64]

In the twelfth month Ienobu, Tsunayoshi's heir, contracted measles and as the year ended Tsunayoshi too came down with the disease. By the tenth day of the new year he was dead.[65]

Of the policies followed by Tsunayoshi, the two which brought the most resentment against him by his contemporaries and by the regime which followed were his laws of compassion and his debasement of the currency. The development of commerce in the last decades of the seventeenth century found the country without sufficient coinage in circulation. The mounting expenses of the Bakufu since the middle of the century had depleted the gold reserves until they were completely exhausted in Tsunayoshi's time. His extravagance and the unfavorable balance of trade with the Osaka-Kyoto area made the situation critical. There was not sufficient gold available to mint an adequate supply of new coins of good quality. It was decided in 1695 to issue new coins, decreasing the quality of metal in the gold, silver, and copper coins, and to recall the old money. Successively more extreme debasements resulted in loss of confidence in the currency and in considerable economic dislocation,

[64] *Tokugawa jikki,* 43:649–719; Miyazaki, *Oritaku shiba no ki shakugi,* pp. 200–203.
[65] There is difference of opinion as to whether the disease was measles or smallpox. Miyazaki, *Oritaku shiba no ki shakugi,* p. 206. Tsunayoshi was confident of his knowledge of medicine, for he had read medical texts, and he refused to follow his physicians' advice to take *ginseng* and other medicinal herbs, and instead gave the instructions himself. He had improved enough by the ninth to have a celebration and accept congratulations from the *gosanke* and other daimyo on his return to health. There was another banquet the next day, but during the party Tsunayoshi suddenly was taken ill and died within a few hours. *Tokugawa jikki,* 43:722b–723a.

which included disorder in the monetary market. The most serious consequence, however, was inflation caused by depreciation of the value of coins vis-à-vis many commodities. In 1708, a large copper coin was issued with a face value of ten of the old one-*mon* coins, but it circulated, in practice, at only 2.5 or 3 *mon*. Tsunayoshi's last year, the second year of successive disasters, ended, according to the *Tokugawa jikki*, with the artisans and merchants complaining about this coin, while the officials demanded daily that it be used by everyone.[66]

This debasement of the currency was the first in Japanese history. It offended the conviction of Arai Hakuseki (1657–1725) and other scholars that metals were the "bones" of the nation and that tampering with their quality weakened the country.[67] The debasement was proposed by Ogiwara Shigehide (1656–1713) and when his plan was accepted, he was appointed finance commissioner (*kanjō bugyō*) to carry it through. He was greatly resented not only because of this policy but also for enriching himself in the process, for accepting bribes, and for other financial irregularities. In 1707, he levied 450,000 *ryō* on various domains and fiefs for the expenses of removing volcanic ash in the provinces around Mount Fuji, but he is said to have diverted most of the funds into the general account of the Bakufu. It is not clear how directly Tsunayoshi was involved in Ogiwara's measures, but their unpopularity and the stench of corruption made Tsunayoshi's last days even darker.

An enumeration of the many acts for which Tsunayoshi has been criticized reads like a catalog of the faults of the last bad ruler of a Chinese dynasty. He is depicted as a tyrant who favored beasts more than men, who meted out cruel and harsh punishments, who made sycophants his chief ministers and gave free rein to corrupt officials. His palace was the scene of moral depravity, the ruler intent on strange sexual pleasures, entertainments, and banqueting, with a mania for performing

[66] Miyazaki, *Oritaku shiba no ki shakugi*, p. 204.

[67] A policy of debasement could be a useful response to the demand for more currency but, if inflation and its undesirable consequences were to be prevented, it had to be moderate or, ideally, only to the point of eliminating the existing deflationary pressure. (Personal communication from Professor Kozo Yamamura.)

dances in front of his retainers. He was driven by superstition, and he was under the influence of a woman. He was extravagant, wasting the substance of the realm on lavish gifts to unworthy favorites and to Buddhist monks, for whom he built great temples. He adulterated the coinage. During the final years of his rule, heaven condemned his lack of virtue by causing strange natural phenomena and by visiting disasters on the country.

TSUNAYOSHI AS SAGE-KING

Tsunayoshi began his rule as a reformer. The reassertion of Bakufu authority, Hotta Masatoshi's attention to orderly administration, and the personal involvement of the shogun as the judge in the Echigo case gave promise of a renaissance of strong, ethical government. His aspiration, according to some contemporary accounts, was to be a model of the just king who brought moral order to the people through the clarity of his decisions. His aim was to enlighten and civilize all the people by teaching humaneness (as we shall see) and Confucian ethics, by encouraging scholarship and the arts, and by setting in order the ethical fabric of human and supernatural relationships by scrupulous observance of the rites and ceremonies related to his ancestors, the emperor, and the sages and deities of Confucianism, Buddhism, and Shinto. Toward all of these objectives he took the lead himself by posing as an exemplar to guide the people. His ideal was to be a sage-king. This vision was based on his education in Confucian classics and Chinese histories, which taught him the principles of governing and the rules of personal conduct that had distinguished wise rulers of the past.

Tsunayoshi's intentions went far beyond orderly government. He had a vision of raising the people to a new standard of ethical conduct. He considered that the society of his time had not yet emerged from a barbarous age. From the outbreak of the Ōnin War in 1467, Japan had been torn for more than a century by continual factional struggles and regional campaigns which embroiled almost all of the country, culminating in the massive battles of the last decades of the sixteenth century and the Korean campaign. The legacy of the long period of warfare, with its killing, pillaging, and destruction of property, was a military class raised on violence. Following the restoration of peace in 1615, the process of taming the warriors for peacetime living and reorienting their goals toward administrative service had proceeded for two or three generations by the time Tsunayoshi became shogun. Although the behavior of daimyo and samurai had undergone a major transformation, there were still frequent incidents when, on matters of honor and shame, tempers flared and swords flashed even in the daimyo mansions and the shogun's castle.

There was still violence in the town, robberies and senseless killings on street corners at night (*tsujigiri*). Gangs of bravados —rival groups of *gokenin, rōnin,* and commoners—known as *kabukimono* or *yakko,* emerged from time to time to terrorize the people or hold gang wars. Tsunayoshi moved decisively against them in 1684; he rounded up two hundred members of *gokenin* and *rōnin* gangs, executing eleven and banishing the others. Two years later he acted against the *chōnin* groups, and from that time on gangs were not a problem.[68]

Tsunayoshi put into effect a considerable number of measures which showed his humaneness and concern for the unfortunate. Because of the many deaths among prisoners awaiting trial at the Edo jail in Kodemma-chō, he improved health conditions by erecting better ventilated buildings, and he provided five baths a month, additional clothing, and other necessities for the inmates.[69] He built compounds and shelters for outcastes and for the sick and homeless. He ordered that those who fell ill while traveling were to be given medicine and nursed back to health at the post towns instead of being turned out as they usually were. He issued a law to protect servants from exploitation by landlords and agents. In prohibiting infanticide and the abandoning of babies, he also directed that those who could not raise their offspring might appeal to the authorities.[70]

[68] Kurita, *Edo jidai,* p. 598; *Tokugawa jikki,* 42:586b.
[69] Kurita, *Edo jidai,* p. 503; *Tokugawa jikki,* 43:751a.
[70] Kurita, *Edo jidai,* p. 503.

Probably, the infamous laws of compassion for animals should be interpreted as part of this program—for their avowed purpose was to teach humaneness by making the prople considerate of all living things. As these laws increased in their demands, however, the punishments also became more severe in an attempt to enforce perfect observance. The rationale of the entire program to teach humaneness is explained in the *Kembyō jitsuroku:*

> The old practices of the warring states period became the way of the samurai and officials; brutality was regarded as valor, high spirits were considered good conduct, and there were many actions which were not benevolent and which violated the fundamental principles of humanity. . . . [It was essential that Tsunayoshi, therefore] admonish the slightest unbenevolent act in order to try to perfect the benevolent spirit of the common people.[71]

The purpose behind the laws of compassion also was explained in an obscurely worded order which was issued in 1694 to officials serving at the castle:

> You should keep in mind that [the laws of] compassion for living things are only due to the mercy of the shogun. But beyond this mercy, the shogun has a more profound intention. Even if he were not to issue orders concerning compassion, you officials should have in mind that people should become benevolent and that their intentions should become gentle. You should tell this to those under your command and those in your units, and you should pass it on so that it will be known by everyone down to the servants.[72]

The intention of the order seems to have been to say in a subtle way that the following message should be passed along informally to everyone at the castle: The shogun has issued these laws, not out of superstition or any crazy notion, but to

---

[71] *Ibid.*, p. 605.
[72] *Gotōke reijō*, Law #508, in Ishii Ryōsuke, *Kinsei hōsei shiryō sōsho* (Tokyo, 1959), 2:248.

teach benevolence. The wording also indicates that it should not be thought of as simply Buddhist mercy; rather it was Confucian benevolence.

A fundamental ingredient of the program of establishing a great peace was to inculcate ethical ideas and encourage moral behavior through education and exhortation. The resources for moral teaching came mainly from Confucianism and Buddhism, and it was therefore government policy to support both doctrines.

The Tokugawa first recognized Confucian learning as a specialty distinct from the general competence of Gozan monks in Chinese studies by the appointment of Hayashi Razan (Dō-shun) (1583–1657) as an official Confucian scholar. He lectured to Ieyasu on Confucian texts, but he was not an intellectual advisor with the status of the monks Tenkai and Sūden (1569–1633). He was more a textual specialist, chronicler, and researcher in Sino-Japanese history and law. Razan's position rose in Iemitsu's time, when he and his brother Eiki were given the title of *hōin* (originally a title for Buddhist monks), but his stipend did not rise above 900 *koku*. The Hayashi were granted land at Shinobu-ga-oka (Ueno) to establish a library (1630). The lord of Owari, Tokugawa Yoshinao, built a Confucius Hall for them (1632) and presented them with statues of Confucius and his four disciples and the paraphernalia for the Sekiten Ceremony.[73] These rites, which had fallen into disuse at the imperial court in the late fifteenth century, were revived in 1633 by the Hayashi, and Iemitsu himself went to worship at the temple. With the death of the monk Sūden that year, the Hayashi took over the revision of the *Buke shohatto* (laws of the military houses) and the handling of foreign relations documents, in addition to the large compilation projects assigned to them from time to time.[74]

[73] The Sekiten or Shakuten Ceremony originally was celebrated at the Daigakuryō of the court before portraits of Confucius and the Ten Disciples in the second and eighth months to honor Confucian learning. The ritual usually included a lecture on a Confucian canon. Kondō Masaharu, "Seidō to Shōheizaka Gakumonjo," *Kinsei Nihon no jukagu* (Tokyo, 1939), pp. 199–205.

[74] Kurita, *Edo jidai*, p. 566. Among these projects were the compilation of the genealogy *Kan'ei shoka keizuden* and the chronicle *Honchō hennenroku*, which later developed into the *Honchō tsugan*.

The patronage of the Hayashi family increased under Ietsuna, but Tsunayoshi exceeded all Tokugawa shogun in his support of Confucianism. In 1690, he had a large Confucian temple built at Yushima on a site closer to the castle to replace the Shinobu-ga-oka establishment. He personally wrote the calligraphy for the tablet to be hung in the hall. The slope below the temple was renamed Shōheizaka, after Confucius's birthplace. In 1691, the Hayashi family head, Nobuatsu (Hōkō, Shunjō) (1644–1732), was given the Ritsuryō title of *daigaku-no-kami* (head of the university) and granted a stipend of 3,500 *koku*. Official Confucian scholars were no longer required to shave their heads and were freed at last from being categorized with Buddhist monks. The Hayashi school and temple was endowed with lands and was transformed, in effect, from a family endeavor to an official establishment of the Bakufu and the center of education in the country.[75]

It was part of Tsunayoshi's educational program to sponsor the study of the Confucian classics within his own circle and among his officials and other daimyo and *hatamoto*. As a youth he had developed a scholar's love for textual exegesis. He had before him the examples of two relatives who were daimyo-scholars, his uncle Hoshina Masayuki of Aizu, regent to Ietsuna, and another grandson of Ieyasu, Tokugawa Mitsukuni of Mito. As his competence increased, he aspired to act the part of the Confucian master by lecturing to his retainers. He had not been shogun more than a few months before he had Hayashi Nobuatsu begin trimonthly lectures on the *Great Learning*. In the eighth month of 1690, he himself began to lecture to the senior councillors and other officials on the *Great Learning* which, with the *Classic of Filial Piety*, were his favorite texts.[76] Thereafter month after month he lectured on the *Four Books*, summoning daimyo, *hatamoto*, Confucian scholars, monks, and Shinto priests to make up his captive audiences. When an imperial envoy or an envoy from a Kyoto temple came to the castle, he entertained him with a lecture. When he visited the Edo mansions of daimyo,

[75] Katō Toranosuke, "Tsunayoshi to jugaku," *Kinsei Nihon no jugaku*, pp. 35–52; Kurita, *Edo jidai*, pp. 565-566; *Tokugawa jikki*, 43:736–737.
[76] *Tokugawa jikki*, 43:82b and 43:735b.

he would give a lecture and then listen to lectures by the host, his retainers, and scholars of the domain.[77] He gave a prodigious series of lectures on the *Book of Changes,* extending from 1693 to 1700, a total of 240 sessions! It was from these activities that Tsunayoshi got his other nickname, Shomotsu Kubō, the "Book Shogun."

The *Kembyō jitsuroku* praises his accomplishments by saying that since early times the rulers of China and Japan had listened to the lectures of Confucian scholars, but it was without precedent for the ruler himself to give a series of lectures. (Wu-ti of Liao and Shōtoku Taishi of Japan did lecture, it is true, but merely on Buddhist sutras.)[78]

The purpose of such Confucian studies, of course, was to cultivate one's self and thus develop the qualities necessary to regulate the family, rule the country, and bring peace to the world. Ostensibly, Tsunayoshi's efforts had the further purpose of setting an example for others, of encouraging daimyo and officials to study Confucian teachings. There is an anecdote relating that the monk Yūten once expressed his concern to Keishōin that Tsunayoshi was taxing his health by adding his scholarly efforts to his burdens as ruler. She is said to have replied, "This is not something for you to speak about. The shogun engages in scholarship in order to lead the country to good teachings. He does it for the country and not for himself. I should like you to tell your branch temples and your followers that since the shogun does not begrudge shortening his life by devoting himself to scholarship in order to encourage all the people to do good works, the people of your religion should also strive harder." The monk flushed.[79]

Keishōin's protestations may only deepen our suspicion that Tsunayoshi's mania for lectures and discussions on Confucianism may have been more to play at scholarship than for intellectual or ethical enrichment of himself and others. It is natural that his activities should have the effect of encouraging a fashion (if not

[77] Kurita, *Edo jidai,* pp. 430–433.
[78] *Tokugawa jikki,* 43:422b–423a and 735a.
[79] Kurita, *Edo jidai,* pp. 438–439; *Tokugawa jikki,* 43:736a.

the popularity) of attempting to puzzle out Confucian texts. The *Kembyō jitsuroku* says that thanks to Tsunayoshi's example, "The various daimyo who came [to Edo] in alternate attendance carried volumes of the classics on their persons. Samurai who guarded the castle attended lectures . . . . The entire country inclined toward peace."[80] Some would, of course, be quick to follow his lead simply because he was the shogun, but many of those subjected to his formal lectures at the castle must have been bored to distraction. As the shogun Yoshimune later said in reference to Tsunayoshi's efforts, "to use political authority to make people engage in scholarship will not be of any benefit."[81]

Tsunayoshi also set an example by striving to live the Confucian ethical code, at least in the observance of the cardinal virtues of filial piety and loyalty. He was filial to the extreme toward his mother and, of course, toward his deceased father and other ancestors. His attentions to his mother read like a story of one of the paragons of filial piety. The year he became shogun he built the Sannomaru (third enceinte) of Edo castle as a residence for her, and accorded her the treatment of a shogunal consort-dowager.[82] He sent a messenger daily to inquire of her welfare and frequently called on her himself. To entertain her he painted and performed dances, and he took her with him to visit at his ministers' homes. He served her tea with his own hands, and when she dined at the main castle, he placed her tray stand before her.[83] He had the regulations concerning mourning made more elaborate to lengthen the period of mourning as an honor to her in preparation for the time when she would pass away.

His reverence for his ancestors was without precedent. When he went to worship them at Kan'eiji or Zōjōji or when he dispatched a proxy, he first purified himself, bathed, and put on clean clothes. His manner at such times was one of awe and

[80] *Tokugawa jikki*, 43:729b.
[81] *Isetsu Nihonshi*, 6:207.
[82] *Tokugawa jikki*, 42:388.
[83] Kurita, *Edo jidai*, pp. 433–434.

trepidation, we are told, as if he were actually face to face with his ancestors. On the eve of the rites, he sat up all night to read over and over the *Classic of Filial Piety.*[84]

The notion that the role of the military ruler and his government was more than simply to maintain order and collect taxes, and included taking responsibility for the edification of the people, had not been fully acted out until the time of Tsunayoshi. Tokugawa laws of 1650 and 1655 provided for punishment of unfilial children, and the *Buke shohatto* of 1663 also contained an article on the subject. Tsunayoshi's version of the *Buke shohatto* (1683) introduces the expression *loyalty and filial piety* in the first article.

In 1682, Tsunayoshi issued a number of *kōsatsu*, proclamations written on wooden placards to be posted throughout the entire country. The first of these, which was known as the "Loyalty and Filial Piety Placard" (*chūkō-satsu*), began as follows:

> Strive in loyalty and filial piety, and be benevolent and forbearing in relations between husband and wife, older and younger brother, and toward all relatives, servants, and employees. Do not be luxurious, and in housing, clothing, food, and drink, be frugal. Do not harbor bad feelings or lie or say unreasonable and unfair words for your personal gain or to harm people. Strive in your respective productive activities. If there are thieves or those who commit evil acts, report them. There invariably will be a reward. It is prohibited to gamble. Do not engage in quarrels and fights . . . .[85]

Tsunayoshi's concern for reforming the morality of the people was evident in his instructions the same year to the highest judicial officials. In making decisions on lawsuits, he told them, they should be concerned not merely with evaluating the merits of the case at hand, but even more with how their judgment could improve the morals of the people.[86] He issued sumptuary laws in far greater number and detail than had earlier shogun,

[84] *Tokugawa jikki,* 43:730a and 735b; Kurita, *Edo jidai,* p. 434.
[85] *Tokugawa jikki,* 42:449.
[86] Kurita, *Edo jidai,* p. 571.

because proper dress, consumption, and behavior in conformity with status were considered essential parts of moral conduct.[87] Private and unlicensed prostitutes were banned, and it was forbidden to employ waitresses in teahouses, as they frequently served as prostitutes.[88] There were still many daimyo and *hatamoto* who frequented the Yoshiwara quarter, including such imposing lords as Tokugawa Mitsukuni, Ii Naooki (1656–1717) of Hikone, and Matsudaira Yorisada (1664–1744) of Moriyama. Tsunayoshi assigned disguised detectives to tail them. During his years some twenty daimyo were disciplined for visiting the Yoshiwara.[89]

A more positive method for the improvement of morality inaugurated by Tsunayoshi was to commend and publicize instances of exemplary conduct. In 1681, he gave the first award for filial piety in the Tokugawa period to Goroēmon, a farmer of Suruga. He was commended not only for filiality but for assistance to neighbors in distress. He was summoned to Edo, and despite his protestations that he had not done anything out of the ordinary, he was given a vermillion-seal document confirming in perpetuity the land he cultivated with a yield of 90 *koku*. He was given, in addition, a cash reward by Great Councillor Hotta Masatoshi and Senior Councillor Abe Masatake. Hayashi Nobuatsu was directed to write Goroēmon's biography and to have it published.[90] From this time on there were frequent citations of this type. By the Kansei period, a little more than a century later, the Bakufu had given awards to 7,469 individuals, and the deeds of many of them were recorded in a collection, the *Kōgiroku* (*Record of Filiality*).[91]

Tsunayoshi's demonstration of "loyalty" toward the emperor consisted of various measures he took to increase the income and raise the dignity of the imperial house. He increased the lands of the emperor from 20,000 *koku* to 30,000, and those of

[87] D. H. Shively, "Sumptuary Regulation and Status in Early Tokugawa Japan," *Harvard Journal of Asiatic Studies* (1964–1965), 25:123–164.

[88] *Tokugawa jikki*, 42:460 and 42:468.

[89] *Isetsu Nihonshi*, 6:208.

[90] *Tokugawa jikki*, 42:440 and 43:733b.

[91] Kurita, *Edo jidai*, pp. 572–573; *Nihon itsuwa daijiten*, 1:433.

the retired emperor by 10,000 *koku*. He provided a subsidy to make possible the revival in 1694 of the Aoi Festival of Kamo Shrine, which had not been celebrated for two centuries, and in 1687 of the Daijōe ceremony at the court, the first rice-tasting of an emperor's reign, which had not been observed for a century or more.[92] As a consequence of the weakness of the imperial court through the feudal period, the tombs of former emperors had been neglected and many were no longer marked. Tsunayoshi ordered that they be sought out, restored, and marked off with fences.[93] There was also a new cordiality in relations with the court, in the exchange of collections of poetry and gifts. Before receiving an imperial envoy, Tsunayoshi always purified himself and changed into clean clothes. Through these actions, minor though they were, Tsunayoshi showed more formal respect and more generosity toward the imperial house than perhaps any other Tokugawa shogun.

Tsunayoshi was the first great patron of arts and letters among the Tokugawa shogun. The most dubious example was his patronage of *nō*, which was encouraged, it was claimed, for its edifying value. The *Kembyō jitsuroku* explains that in an age when there were still remains of the turbulent spirit of warfare, the enjoyment of *nō* drama, and in particular participation in the performance, would be beneficial in making men's hearts peaceful. This reasoning was based on the Confucian idea that the ruler should regulate the country through rites and music.[94] No matter what we may think of this rationalization, the effect was to divert some daimyo and samurai from whatever else they might have been inclined to do to perfecting their *nō* dancing.

Of greater benefit was Tsunayoshi's support of many scholars in a wide variety of fields. In addition to the Hayashi family, he patronized other Confucian scholars, especially Kinoshita Jun'an (1621–1698), but also he frequently called on Ogyū Sorai and

[92] Kurita, *Edo jidai*, pp. 516–518; *Tokugawa jikki*, 43:730a and 731a.
[93] Of the seventy-eight emperors' tombs identified, new fences were needed for sixty-six. The tombs of twenty-two emperors could not be found. *Tokugawa jikki*, 43:365b–367a and 731b; Kurita, *Edo jidai*, pp. 516–518.
[94] *Tokugawa jikki*, 43:751b–752a; Nakamura, *Genroku jidai kan*, p. 87.

Shimura Sanzaemon, who were in Yoshiyasu's employ, for lectures, discussions, and for special projects.[95]

Among the innovations made by Tsunayoshi was the involvement of the Bakufu on a much larger and broader scale in the subsidizing of different kinds of scholarship. Among the scholars he appointed to new posts, all of which became permanent offices at the Bakufu, were the following:

Yasui Shunkai (1639–1715), a student of astronomy whose observations had revealed errors in the Chinese calendar, then used in Japan, and proposed a revised calendar which was adopted by the Bakufu as the Jōkyō calendar in 1684. Yasui was appointed the Bakufu astronomer (*temmonkata*), a position which became hereditary in his family.[96]

Kitamura Kigin (1624–1705), pioneer *kokugaku* scholar, who wrote the first great commentaries on Heian literature and poetry. He was invited from Kyoto in 1689 to take a post as a scholar of Japanese poetry (*kagaku-kata*) and to lecture the shogun on Japanese poetry and history.[97]

Yoshikawa (Kikkawa) Koretari (1616–1694), founder of Yoshikawa Shinto, was appointed in 1682 as Shintoist (*shintō-kata*), a position which remained in his family until the Restoration.[98]

Sumiyoshi Gukei (1631–1705), an artist in the Yamato style, was appointed an official painter in 1685, a post which was carried on by his family until the end of the Tokugawa period. Hitherto only painters of the Kanō School had been appointed by the Bakufu.[99]

Tsunayoshi was evidently interested in a wide range of subjects and enjoyed listening to lectures by Buddhist monks, Shin-

---

[95] Ogyū and Shimura were directed to punctuate and publish those of the twenty-one histories which had not yet been printed in Japan, and also to prepare and publish with commentary an official edition of the *Four Books*. *Tokugawa jikki*, 43:738a. Hayashi Nobuatsu, Kinoshita Jun'an, and Hitomi Chikudō edited the *Mikawa-ki* and compiled a large work on the exploits of the various daimyo and *hatamoto* families, the *Butoku taiseiki*. *Ibid.*, 43:737b.

[96] *Ibid.*, 42:528 and 43:749b.

[97] *Ibid.*, 43:62 and 43:749b–750a.

[98] *Ibid.*, 43:750a.

[99] *Ibid.*, 42:542 and 43:750a. Tsunayoshi also added a fourth branch of the Kanō family to the roster of painters appointed to stipends from the Bakufu.

to priests, scholars of Japanese literature, and physicians.[100] He fancied himself an authority on medicine and liked discussions with physicians, frequently disagreeing with treatments they proposed and dismissing a good number for incompetence.[101] On Dr. Kaempfer's visits to Edo castle, the shogun put many questions to him about Western medicine and medical practice, and requested that some medicine be procured for him from Batavia.[102].

Tsunayoshi's support of Confucian studies and institutions, and also of Buddhism, contributed to the moral education of all classes. He also gave instruction to the people directly through laws designed to teach humanitarian attitudes and considera-tion for the unfortunate. He exercised his judicial function to give clarity and authority to the government as a moral example. All of these were policies considered to have edifying value. Tsunayoshi, in short, did play the role of the sage-king. The quality of his performance was another matter, for it is only too evident how inconsistent and ill-considered the execution of many of his policies was.

TSUNAYOSHI'S PERSONALITY AND HIS TIMES

The contrasting evaluations of Tsunayoshi are best repre-sented by two nearly contemporary accounts of his reign. The critical *Sannō gaiki* was written by an independent scholar more than a decade after the shogun's death, when changes in the

[100] In addition to the countless lectures and discussions on Confucian studies, the shogun often listened to lectures by Buddhist monks of many different sects and discussions among Buddhist monks. For example, a group of nineteen dis-tinguished Zen monks was summoned to the castle in 1693. The *Tokugawa jikki* records that he heard lectures on texts of Japanese literature (*Tsurezure gusa,* the "Momiji" chapter of the *Genji monogatari,* the *Shinkokinshū,* the "Age of the Gods" chapter of the *Kojiki*), on ceremonials of the imperial court, on the pronunciation of (contemporary?) Chinese, and on acupuncture. *Tokugawa jikki,* 43:739. Tsunayoshi also employed six *rōnin* Confucian scholars and four from daimyo service, and had them discuss Confucian books by his bedside when he retired in order that he might fall asleep listening to their conversation. *Ibid.,* 43:749b.
[101] *Tokugawa jikki,* 43:749.
[102] Kaempfer, *History of Japan,* 3:92–93 and 174–175.

lines of succession permitted him to write (if not to publish) his views with considerable candor. The *Kembyō jitsuroku,* on the other hand, was written by scholars in Yoshiyasu's employ. They were expected to present the shogun in a good light which would, in turn, reflect on their patron. Tsunayoshi is depicted in this work as a conscientious and sagelike ruler, and this was probably how he saw himself. He issued humane legislation, carried out reforms, encouraged and rewarded ethical behavior, supported scholarship, and gave lectures. Like a sage who teaches by moral example, he was peerless in filial piety and meticulous in ritual observances, he studied texts, and he performed "music." This was his "public face," the side of Tsunayoshi and the interpretation of his intentions that followed the formal specifications and became the official record.

However, his image as a wise ruler is blemished by the harsh punishments he imposed and by his spendthrift ways. His private life was even more difficult to reconcile with his pose as a moral exemplar; sexual indulgence and willful handling of attendants and retainers showed scant concern for ethical conduct or social proprieties. Although his personal life could be considered to some extent a separate "private face" which he showed in the inner rooms of the castle as a release from the demands of his office, it was not always strictly private. Did he not see something incongruous in his own conduct if, on a visit to a daimyo's mansion, he delivered a lecture on the *Classic of Filial Piety,* performed an edifying *nō* dance, and then bedded down with the daimyo's son or wife? The Tsunayoshi of the *Sannō gaiki* is a parody of the sage-king.

Perhaps we can understand Tsunayoshi better if we engage in some speculation concerning his upbringing and the shaping of his personality. We can imagine that he was watched over by a doting mother, pampered by a host of servants, and surrounded by a circle of young attendants who admired him and deferred to him as a son of the great shogun Iemitsu. A spoiled boyhood led to lack of self-discipline as an adult. Perhaps his fear of thunder and his superstitiousness stemmed from the neglect of training in martial arts and spartan spirit. Rarely reprimanded, he grew up without learning to examine himself critically or to restrain his impulses.

Tsunayoshi was a bookish youth, tutored by Confucian scholars and praised for his precociousness. He was not trained to be a man of political affairs; quite the contrary, he was given a pedantic education, with the intention of removing him from the political arena. He gained a knowledge of history and state-craft from Chinese classical texts and neo-Confucian writings, which cast all events in a moralistic framework. And in his se-cluded quarters he had little opportunity to learn about the practical world of his times or about how to understand and use men.

At thirty-four he brought to the office of shogun a conception of kingship which was the more dangerous for its perfectionism. He was self-righteous in his theoretical knowledge and he would not be swayed from his course by advice. His priggishness de-terred able men from coming forward to serve him. Insulated from reality by his mother and his fawning ministers, he could perform acts which were subjectively virtuous without knowing the objective consequences. He was strict about matters of minor importance, being excessively fastidious in ethical and ritual observances, demanding perfection of everyone around him, never forgiving minor lapses or faults in others. Quick-tempered, arbitrary, and vested with despotic powers, but out of contact with reality, he quickly strayed from a course of moderation in both personal conduct and government policy.

Despite the obvious shortcomings of Tsunayoshi's prepara-tion for his office and his faults of temperament, his efforts did have the effect of accelerating the "civilizing" trend in govern-ment and society of his times. He also made a direct contribu-tion by his support of scholarship, by institution building, and by subsidizing scholars and research projects on a much larger scale than had been conceived heretofore. These actions, emu-lated by an ever increasing number of daimyo, gave impetus to the appointment of scholars and the founding of schools in all parts of the country.

Tokugawa Tsunayoshi

Throughout the first half of the Tokugawa period there was a gradual transformation of the Tokugawa regime from a government which subordinated all else to military security and preparedness to one whose main concern was the housekeeping operations of a secure administration staffed by Confucian-educated bureaucrats of civilian mentality. For the samurai, this meant a shift of emphasis from training in military arts (*bu*) to education—the literary and civil arts (*bun*). The secular tendencies of the seventeenth century gradually gained momentum to culminate in a burst of literary and scholarly activity in Tsunayoshi's time. Many factors, of course, contributed to these developments now that the country was unified and at peace: codification of precedents, growing complexity of administration, and a more involved fiscal organization. These processes were the cumulation of the activities of a variety of men, but having at the top a "Book Shogun" reinforced the actions of men throughout the government structure. Tsunayoshi did more to enhance the status of Confucian studies than any other shogun. He also spread Confucian ethics throughout society by a variety of means and, to judge from the popular literature of the day, these values were diffused much more widely than in earlier decades. We should not be distracted by the modern view of the "feudal" nature of Confucian ethics from recognizing the positive contribution made by these social values as a civilizing influence on the people of the seventeenth century, who were emerging from a much ruder and more violent age.

The shogun's indifference to military sports and training, evidenced not only by his own lack of participation but also by his elimination of some military posts in the Bakufu, hastened the shift in emphasis among the Bakufu samurai from military to intellectual accomplishments. Tsunayoshi's successor found that he could not conduct a military inspection because the weapons and standards in the armory had been so long neglected. A decade after Tsunayoshi, Yoshimune launched a campaign to reemphasize falconry, horsemanship, and swimming, as well as training in weapons, in an attempt to rally the martial spirit and skill of the samurai class.

The name of Tsunayoshi's era, the Genroku, calls to mind not so much staid developments as the spectacular efflorescence of the new culture among commoners in the cities, a culture represented by the short stories of Saikaku, the plays of Chikamatsu, the *kabuki* styles of Sakata Tōjūrō and Ichikawa Danjūrō, the prints and genre painting of Hishikawa Moronobu, new styles of weaving and dyeing, and the splendors of the Yoshiwara and other entertainment quarters. Tsunayoshi was indifferent to these developments. Perhaps he was even displeased with them, considering them presumptuous and vulgar. He certainly did not encourage or support them. Yet he inadvertently contributed to the development of plebian life and culture by his extravagant spending and by debasing the currency, both of which increased the amount of money in circulation, caused inflation, and fed the economic boom. His personal life set a peculiar example of extravagance and reckless improvidence, indulgence in *nō* dancing and in sex, absorption in parlor pastimes to the neglect of his family calling as head of the military class. He abandoned the way of the samurai. His relaxation of personal discipline and his impulsive, free-living ways echoed the spirit of the Genroku era.

ŌKURA NAGATSUNE
AND THE TECHNOLOGISTS

Thomas C. Smith

Although Ōkura Nagatsune was not rich, highborn, powerful, or a genius, he is interesting to history as a representative of a numerous class of Tokugawa writers who may be called *technologists*. The technologists were mostly obscure men—farmers, merchants and small manufacturers—who never held high office and generally lived out their lives in villages and small towns. All had some education and therefore some acquaintance with the classics, but none was concerned primarily with the great problems of government and society that so engaged Confucianists. Instead, they were concerned almost exclusively with material problems, practical and earthy ones such as keeping silkworms free of their own droppings and improving the yield of oil from rape seed, in the solution of which they saw the means of economic progress and human betterment. By these concepts, though they had no names for them, they unmistakably meant a broadly shared increase in what we would now call national income.

Such notions hardly could have been more at odds with the ideas of orthodox Confucianists, who were far from thinking economic welfare an end in itself and indeed were suspicious of too much of it as bad for morals. In any case, they thought it flowed uniquely from the quality of government, never from mere technic, independent of politics. Unorthodox as they may have been, however, the ideas of the technologists, to judge from the number of books that were published expressing them, were widely held among educated commoners by the early nineteenth century. This paper seeks to describe the characteristic

127

features of this literature and to suggest its meaning for the history of the Tokugawa period. Unfortunately, the literature is highly technical, widely scattered, and for the most part available only in original editions, for which reasons the observations here are based on a very limited sampling. This sampling consists of a careful reading of four important books by Ōkura (the most prolific and lucid of the technologists),.and a half dozen major eighteenth- and nineteenth-century works on sericulture,[1] and on a skimming of eight or ten books representing such diverse fields as forestry, mining, and sugar manufacture.

Very little is known about the lives of the technologists. More is known about Ōkura Nagatsune's than most, yet only the barest outline can be pieced together from the few letters that survive and occasional autobiographical asides in his technical writing.[2] Nagatsune was born in a substantial farm family in north-central Kyushu in 1768. His grandfather, whom he clearly admired, was an expert cotton-grower and took great pains to train the servants in this demanding specialty. The house name *wataya*—"cotton shop"—suggests that the family was probably engaged in buying, selling, and processing as well as growing cotton;[3] but this business, along with the family's prosperity, seems to have disappeared with the grandfather's death, when Nagatsune was eleven. Shortly afterward, Nagatsune and his father went to work for a relative who was in the business of manufacturing wax from the juice of the lacquer tree, an important domestic industry in Kyushu, and Nagatsune continued in this employment so long as he lived in the village.[4]

In his early teens, according to a friend who knew him later, Nagatsune (who had already learned to read and write, essential skills in a commercial household), developed the ambition to be a scholar. This brought him into conflict with his father.

---

[1] All cited hereafter (except *Seikatsu roku*) in Saigusa Hiroto, ed., *Nihon kagaku* (Tokyo, 1944), 11: 203–241.
[2] The letters are reprinted in Hayakawa Kōtarō, *Ōkura Nagatsune* (Tokyo, 1943), pp. 289–394.
[3] *Mempo yōmu, Kagaku kōten*, 11: 252–253.
[4] Tamura Eitarō, *Ōkura Nagatsune* (Tokyo, 1944), p. 5.

Books were not only useless to a farmer but positively harmful, the father insisted; they led to pride, to dissatisfaction with farming, and, eventually, to economic ruin. He forbade Nagatsune to study and, on discovering the boy going secretly to the village schoolmaster for instruction, cautioned the teacher against helping him. This episode appears to have changed Nagatsune's life. In obedience to his father's wishes, he gave up the classics but found a way of compensating: "Even if I could not study the classics and thus learn the secrets of ruling a country, I refused to spend my life doing nothing of value; so I concentrated my ambition on learning the art of farming and studied it for many years."[5]

Indeed, he studied it until the end of his life, though just when he began is uncertain. Possibly it was to advance his studies that he left home at twenty-four and spent the next five years traveling in Kyushu, stopping now and then to work at paper-making and sugar-refining, no doubt learning something about local farming practices in the process. Whether he made notes of his observations this early is uncertain, but it is possible. Miyazaki Antei, the first and greatest of the technologists, whose classic *General Treatise on Agriculture* published in 1697 was still being read, had made travel, observation, and note-taking established methods for students of farming.[6]

At twenty-nine, Nagatsune's travels took him to Osaka, where he lived for many years, working first as a calligraphy teacher and later by selling lacquer-tree seedlings imported from Kyushu. An advertisement in the back of one of his books stated that, although most seedlings sold in Osaka were imported from Shikoku, Nagatsune now offered to send the Kyushu variety to buyers anywhere on request.[7] This business allowed him to continue his study of farming by taking him to villages all over the Kinai, where the most advanced and highly commercialized farming in the country was to be seen. By this time he was observing systematically; wherever he went, he asked questions of

[5] *Ibid.*, p. 6.
[6] *Ibid.*, pp. 8–10; Miyazaki Antei, *Nōgyō zensho* (Tokyo, 1936), 376 pp.
[7] For text, Tamura, *Ōkura*, p. 13.

skilled farmers about local soils, seeds, fertilizers, irrigation, and tools, taking down what they had to say and making detailed sketches of plants, tools, and operations.[8]

Nagatsune published his first book in 1802, about twenty years after leaving home. It dealt with cultivation of the lacquer tree and wax-making, the subjects he knew best; its title, *Farm Family Profits* (*Nōka-eki*), sounded what was to be a major theme of nearly all of his work. The books kept coming after that; he never seemed to write himself out. His last book, if it was not posthumous, appeared when he would have been eighty-eight. Not counting five unpublished manuscripts, there were twenty-eight books in all: one on ethics, two dictionaries, two on nutrition, two on government policy, one on education, and all the rest on the technology of farming and farm by-employments. The agricultural writings, which covered a great range of subjects, were among the best of their kind for clarity of language and range and pertinence of detail. They eventually brought him a certain amount of recognition, including employment as an advisor to the Bakufu and several han, which encouraged him to give up his seedling business and move to Edo, where he lived for many years, traveling through the Kantō and the northeast and continuing to write books until his death about 1856.[9]

Nagatsune's motives as a writer were undeniably strong and probably mixed. It seems likely that he was not insensible to the possible financial rewards of writing, and he used his books to advertise his seedling business. He himself insisted that he was moved by the wish to make a difference in the world through scholarship, a very Confucian desire, which was probably real enough despite its sententious expression.[10] He also may have been moved by the hope of official preferment. In his first book he expressed the hope that officials would read it and spread its ideas, and when preferment came he seemed to welcome it.

[8] *Mempo*, pp. 253, 261; *Nōgu benri ron*, *Kagaku kōten*, 11:45.
[9] Tamura, *Ōkura*, pp. 23–26.
[10] *Nōgu*, p. 49; *Mempo*, p. 253; Tamura, *Ōkura*, p. 5.

However, as strong as any other motive was an interest in agricultural reform itself. He passionately wanted to improve existing farming methods, which he regarded as generally lamentable, and every page he wrote testified to this wish. It explains why he addressed himself to farmers rather than officials, discussed mainly seeds, fertilizers, and farm tools rather than government policy, and why he consciously wrote in language farmers could understand, knowing it would strike some as inelegant. That he also hoped for recognition and financial gain from his efforts does not detract from the sincerity of his interest and may account for its passion .What, after all, is more compelling than a noble cause grounded in self-interest?

As to the meaning of agricultural progress, though he did not use the term himself, Nagatsune never had the slightest doubt. It consisted in substituting more for less efficient methods of farming—substituting methods that either increased yields, reduced costs, or took less skill or strength than those supplanted. Whenever he recommended a technic or tool, it was one or a combination of these grounds. Thus the *eburi*, a light hoe for raking up soil around the roots of plants, he claimed not only did a better and cleaner job than the heavier *kuwa* but could be wielded with ease by a ten-year-old girl. Often he calculated the superiority of one method over another rather precisely, taking care to put the calculation in terms familiar to farmers. The *kusakezuri*, a specially designed weeder, permitted work to be done in two hours that normally required a full day; the *tenowokuwa* made it possible for a woman to make in the same time as many furrows in a field as two men working with spades.[11]

Some technics offered a constellation of advantages. In recommending a potato planter consisting of a spiked wheel run along the ground at the end of a handle in order to drill holes for the seed, Nagatsune noted (1) that it was faster than making holes by hand and also made straighter and more evenly spaced rows, (2) that it facilitated weeding, and that it economized both (3) seed and (4) land.[12] Efficient methods sometimes en-

---

[11] *Nōgu*, pp. 53, 79, 88, 90.
[12] Called *imoueguruma; ibid.*, pp. 91–92.

tailed disadvantages, however, and he implied that in such cases no invariable rule concerning efficacy could be laid down. The balance could be struck only by the individual farmer taking particular local conditions into account.[13] In Bingo Province, for example, powdered sardine was used almost exclusively as a fertilizer because it was relatively cheap in this Inland Sea region and because its rapid effect shortened the growing season, minimizing the danger of crop damage from fall typhoons. This enabled Bingo farmers to average some 60 *kamme* of cotton per *tan* of land compared to 40 in the Kinai, where the cultivation of cotton was highly developed with more varied fertilization. On the other hand, exclusive use of sardine fertilizer resulted in an inferior fiber that brought less in the market than Kinai cotton. The lower price apparently was offset in Bingo by surer and larger yields; elsewhere it might not be—depending on the local cost of sardines and the degree of vulnerability to typhoon.[14]

In his travels, Nagatsune met many skeptics who were quick to point out that the superiority of a method was no guarantee at all of peasant acceptance. Peasants were wedded to received methods, whereas anything novel contained an element of risk.[15] Nagatsune admitted this difficulty; he frequently stated that peasants could never see for themselves the inefficiency of inherited methods.[16] But they could be shown, and once shown, they would no more reject a superior method than a sick man would refuse the help of a doctor.[17] The metaphor is suggestive: Farming was like an illness that could be cured by proper treatment, and Nagatsune fancied himself the doctor.

There were two ways, he said, to show farmers the superiority of a new method. Both were the opposite of exhortation and command, the chief resort of government. In trying to promote

[13] Tamura, *Ōkura*, p. 245; *Mempo*, p. 261.

[14] *Ibid.*, *Mempo* p. 286.

[15] *Nōgu*, pp. 129–130.

[16] "Peasants are simple and prejudiced. No matter how much you instruct them, they are not easily persuaded to grow a crop they have no experience with." *Mempo*, p. 252.

[17] Ōkura used the rapid spread of the *semba-koki* to illustrate this principle. *Nōgu*, p. 131.

improved methods, he said, the government typically called the peasants together in their villages where they were made to listen to the reading of a document stating the lord's wish that they farm this way or that, or plant this or that new crop. They typically listened respectfully and did nothing, which was predictable. Peasants would never try what they had not seen for themselves merely on the advice of a remote if majestic authority.[18] But send an expert into the village, give him several *tan* of land to work with the new method, and the peasants would come to observe; if he got good results, they would adopt the method of their own accord. Why? Because they had seen it, and seen that it worked. The key to developing a country's economy "in this age when everyone is out for a profit," he said, lay in the "profit to the farm household" (*nōka no eki.*)[19]

The other way was to persuade village leaders of the superiority of a method, and let them teach and persuade others by example, which would presumably be the more influential because of their local standing.[20] How such men were to be persuaded in the first place, Nagatsune did not say; but he clearly thought they could be reached through the written word without concrete demonstration—presumably because they were better educated, in a stronger economic position to take risks, and more accessible to abstract ideas than ordinary peasants. He and other technologists wrote for this class of men and saw them as potential leaders of reform. "What I pray for," one of them wrote in expressing hope for the improvement of sericulture, "is that the skilled of the world will teach the unskilled, and the unskilled will learn from them."[21]

Nagatsune hoped that "the leading men (*osataru hito*) of

[18] Arthur Young, the English agricultural reformer and a near contemporary of Nagatsune, thought that farmers could not be induced to try a new crop without payment of a bounty to cover the possible loss from the experiment. He thought not "one farmer in twenty thousand will [otherwise] venture the attempt. A certain premium for every acre is the only thing, which, I apprehend, will ever spread the culture." *The Farmer's Letters to the People of England* (London, 1768), pp. 214–215.

[19] Tamura, *Ōkura*, p. 34.

[20] *Nōgu*, p. 52.

[21] Baba Shigehisa, *Kaiko yōiku tekagami*, in Inosaka Tadaichi, ed., *Sansō kōten shūsei* (Ueda, 1927), pp. 60–61.

villages will experiment with specialized tools so that they will see for themselves their advantages and will then teach others to use them."[22]

If the question had been put to Nagatsune, "You say that agricultural progress depends on the adoption of more efficient methods. But where do these improved methods come from and what assures that they will keep coming?" he could have answered the first part of the question but possibly not the second. He certainly would have pointed out, first, the importance of invention, using the modern word *hatsumei* and meaning the same thing by it that we do now—the discovery, inadvertently or by study and experiment, of any method that was new in some important respect.[23] And he could have illustrated such discoveries without being able to account for them, though he would have had some ideas on this subject too.

In his book on farm tools, he credited a farmer near Osaka named Imamiyamura Kyūzaemon with inventing a new plow, called a *nichōgake,* with two parallel blades. The two blades permitted rows of a growing crop to be straddled and the rows between to be plowed, which made it easier to plant a winter crop while the summer crop was still ripening, giving both crops a longer growing season. This was difficult without the new plow, which Nagatsune said would turn eight times as much land in a day as could be turned with a spade, because of the overlapping of the peaks of labor at the harvest and the planting. This plow had a special advantage in the Kinai where winter wheat overlapped summer cotton, a particularly labor-intensive crop, and where consequently it was often necessary to avoid the overlap by removing cotton plants from the fields before they had finished blooming, with a consequent loss of yield and an adverse effect on the color and quality of the cotton.[24]

[22] *Nōgu,* p. 521.
[23] *Mempo,* p. 278. In *Nōgu benri ron,* Nagatsune included a biography of an inventor and correspondent of his named Kōraku Matsuuemon, who made important innovations in hydraulic engineering. For other references to invention, see Ta Tomonao, "Yosan suchi," mss. (National Diet Library), vol. 2, unpaginated; and *Yosan kensetsu* and *Shinsen yosan hisho* in Inosaka, ed., *Sansō kōten,* pp. 90, 322.
[24] *Nōgu,* p. 96.

It was not necessary for an invention to be attributed to a particular person. In the same book, Nagatsune cited at least one anonymous invention, the *sembakoki* (or *mugikoki*, as he called it), one of the most important farm tools developed in the Tokugawa period. It consisted of a waist-high frame fitted with bamboo or iron teeth through which stalks of rice or other cereal were pulled to strip away the heads of grain. According to Nagatsune, it was ten times faster than the older method of pulling the stalks with one hand between two sticks held in the other like chopsticks, which was slow and wasteful of grain and could not be used by children and old people, requiring as it did great skill and arm strength. Because labor was always short at the harvest, the new thresher, by easing the shortage, reduced the danger of loss from bad weather and made it easier to plant a winter crop hard on the fall harvest.[25]

Whether invention was potentially an endless process in which new discoveries forever succeeded one another was a question Nagatsune never seriously entertained. His first reaction might have been to dismiss it. Practically, he might have argued, there already existed an inexhaustible store of "inventions" not widely or universally known. This was the result of centuries of adaptation of farming—of tools, seed, crops, tillage —to local conditions of climate and soil. These adaptations varied endlessly, with the result that although the spade was used everywhere, for example, its size, design, and heft differed almost from village to village.[26] Because this kind of micro-adaptation suffused all aspects of farming, the country constituted a vast network of local agricultural experiment stations —not Nagatsune's words, of course, but a concept he would have understood—and in any one of the stations there were likely to be inventions that could be applied advantageously elsewhere. The problem was to seek these out and spread knowledge of them, the object of Nagatsune's endless travels and voluminous publications. Such adaptations were to be found in backward as well as advanced regions, and scarcely any ele-

[25] *Ibid.*, pp. 130–132.

[26] Nagatsune stated that, in general, the same *kuwa* was not used beyond a radius of 3 *ri* or 7 1/3 miles, which he attributed mainly to local differences in soil. *Nōgu*, p. 66.

ment of technology could be safely overlooked. What seemed clumsy to an observer might be perfectly suited to the problems of a particular agriculture. Consequently, Nagatsune explained, he included in his book on tools many sketches of implements the value of which outside their own localities was unknown to him, and he exhorted readers to try out any tool that looked useful.[27]

It was obvious to him that enormous improvements in agriculture could be made through the diffusion of the innumerable "inventions" that existed. Miyazaki Antei had described the most advanced methods of cotton cultivation a century ago, and those methods, Nagatsune said, were backward compared to methods now in use. Even so, cotton was still grown properly in only half a dozen provinces; elsewhere it was poorly fertilized or grown on the wrong kind of soil, though the right kind was available.[28] In parts of the country all farming operations were done with a few basic tools, whereas in the Kinai specialized tools were used, with a substantial gain in efficiency, for weeding, mulching, fertilizing, furrowing, aerating, raking, transplanting, thinning—even different spades were used for different soils.[29] Again, in the southwest, whale oil was commonly used to great effect against *inamushi*, whereas in the northeast crop losses from this insect were enormous.[30]

Still the question remained, in theory at least, of what would happen when all existing technics had been perfectly diffused. Would agricultural improvements come to a halt, or would new and more efficient technics appear and keep appearing? Possibly Nagatsune would have come down on the optimistic side of this question. He obviously believed that farm technology was not stable and never could be, for no element of it could be applied in precisely the same way on two farms. Each farmer

[27] *Ibid.*, p. 5.

[28] *Mempo*, pp. 251–253.

[29] *Nōgu*, p. 52. Nagatsune described the significance of tool design graphically: "If tools are ill-adapted to their uses, even a strong young man working with them wastes a vast amount of strength (*chikara*) and effort (*rō*) and yet gets poor yields; whereas efficient tools can be used by a delicate young girl and yet give good results at the harvest." *Ibid.*, p. 49.

[30] Hayakawa, *Ōkura*, pp. 75–86.

had to adapt each technical element to the unique combination
of soil, climate, and terrain on his farm, trying first this and then
that to get the best results. For this reason, contrary to the usual
opinion, said Nagatsune, farming was the most subtle and demanding of all occupations, and there was all the difference in
the world between the intelligent and the stupid farmer. The
intelligent farmer by making constant adjustments and observing their results would make "discoveries" or "inventions" (hatsumei).[31] Other technologists also seem to have believed that
there would always be intelligent farmers who would improve
on the most advanced technics. The author of an indescribably
detailed book on sericulture, who clearly thought his book represented the best knowledge of the time, explained,

> What is written here is for persons without experience and
> by no means explains everything. The reader should keep firm-
> ly in mind the distinctive coloring of the worm upon sleeping
> and waking as explained earlier. Then with a few years of ex-
> perience at raising worms he will master the technic, and there
> will be no such thing as failure. Moreover, in this way the num-
> ber of experts (kōsha) will increase, and they will discover
> (hatsumei) excellent new methods, and the people who may
> be considered treasures of their localities will become numer-
> ous.[32]

Nagatsune gave an example of the kind of "inventions" an
intelligent farmer might make. If he had on his farm both sandy
and heavy soil, he would note that cotton grew more luxuriantly
in the latter, but that, because the plants had to be placed farther apart, the yield from a given area of land was less than with

[31] *Mempo*, pp. 261, 278; Tamura, *Ōkura*, p. 245.
[32] Ta Tomonao, "Yosan suchi," vol. 2, unpaginated. Most writers stressed the
need for adaptability on the part of the farmer, as no rule of thumb for fertilization, planting dates, and so on applied equally to any two places. For a statement of the principle by a village headman in the mid-Tokugawa, see Nomura
Noboru, ed., *Kinsei shomin shiryō* (Osaka, 1955), p. 187. The writer cited in the
text claimed women made poor sericulturalists because, though they could learn
a routine by rote, they were nonplused by any change in weather requiring
adaptation. The reason, he said, was that "Although there are women who are
naturally intelligent, their understanding is inferior to that of even a stupid man.
. . ." "Yosan suchi," vol. 1, unpaginated.

the former. He might therefore try mixing the two—by no means an improbable idea, given the constant working of grass, leaves, and ashes, and other matter into the soil, and the practice of transferring soil from river bottoms to hillside terraces—thereby discovering how to improve the yield of either soil alone.[33]

Nagatsune seemed to believe that by virtue of the need for constant adaptation to local conditions, farming of necessity entailed experimentation and discovery. This process was presumably what had produced the present stock of technics and might go on indefinitely. But this is inference; neither he nor any technologist explicitly raised the problem of sustaining the process of invention. For them, the real problem was the diffusion of existing technics. They were quite familiar with the idea of experiment in the limited, but important, sense of deliberately trying alternative methods and comparing results.[34] Although he does not give all the details we would wish, the author of the oldest extant Japanese book on sericulture, published in Edo in 1712, appears to describe just this process when he recounts, "One year I tried various kinds of eggs and also early, middle, and late cocoons, and by this means discovered the reason that the worms' sequence of sleeping and waking is sometimes delayed."[35]

It was characteristic of the work of writers like Nagatsune that they described in great detail the technology they sought to disseminate. On the subject of fertilizing cotton, for example, Nagatsune tells the reader, among other things, the kinds of fertilizers—dried sardines, oil cakes, urine, night soil, manure, ashes, river muck—to be used at particular stages of growth; the proportions of water to fertilizer in making liquid fertilizer; how the proportions should be varied with growth of the plant;

---

[33] *Mempo*, p. 278.

[34] Arthur Young used the term *experiment* to mean merely try or test. Thus, for example, it was an experiment to grow parsley on a farm for the first time for use in feeding sheep; and when Young speaks of knowing something "experimentally," he means knowing from having tried it oneself. *Farmer's Letters*, pp. 219, 220, 224, 234, 236, 241, 244, and especially 246.

[35] Baba Shigehisa, *Kaiko yōiku tekagami*, p. 60.

the advantages and disadvantages of fast-acting fertilizer; how close to the stem to drill holes for fertilization; what types of fertilizer to avoid in certain kinds of soil; the appropriate quantity and probable cost of fertilizer per *tan* of land.[36] His book on tools contained drawings, with measurements, for each part of each tool, so they could be made easily by a village carpenter or blacksmith; usually he also gave information on where a tool could be purchased and the probable price. A passage from a book on sericulture will illustrate this attention to detail.

> After three morning feedings on the third day following the emergence of the larvae from the eggs and their placement in trays, the now young worms should be moved to new trays, being placed in them with twice as much space as before. This is called *hekikoku*. Then, after the transfer, the center part of the leaves of the mulberry should be prepared for feeding, taking care to chop them cross-hatch. One must be careful not to use leaf too close to the stem at this time; such leaf is tough and the young worms cannot eat it well and therefore become thin. But if the tender center part is fed them, the worms grow fat and their sleeping and waking will be regular, so that they sleep and wake in unison. In feeding the worms from this time until the first sleep, it is necessary to pick and chop the mulberry leaves separately for each of eight feedings. For if the worms are fed with leaves left from even the previous feeding, the leaves will have dried out, and the worms will be unable to feed sufficiently and will starve.[37]

Or, to cite another example,

> In choosing cotton seed, pick a bush of medium height with luxuriant shrubbery and no dead branches, and take cotton bolls in full bloom with heavy fibers from a branch three or four branches from the bottom. This should be done when half the bolls on the tree have opened. The choice of the seed is extremely important and should be done by the family head and not entrusted to servants. In buying seed from other districts, examine it in the palm of the hand. Good seeds have a slightly

[36] *Mempo*, pp. 270–276.
[37] Ta Tomonao, "Yosan suchi," vol. 1, unpaginated.

black look, bad ones a reddish hue. Also knead the seed with the fingers. Round seeds generally are poor; pointed seeds generally are good. For storage, remove the seed from the surrounding cotton and dry it in the sun. Then take it out from time to time to expose it to the sun in order to keep it absolutely free of moisture.[38]

Passages like this, on nearly every page of every book, suggest the enormous importance these writers attached to the technical mastery of the operation of farming. Indeed it would hardly be an exaggeration to say that, in their view, success depended on this mastery alone. If it were achieved, success was assured, if not, nothing would help. Other factors tended to be ignored or rejected outright. Virtually no mention was made of frugality or industry in the farmer, qualities that orthodox Confucian writers harped on (to the neglect of technical skill), clearly not because these virtues were thought unimportant by the technologists but because they were taken for granted. Nor was mention made of the rate of taxation, the quality of justice, and other political and administrative factors that Confucian writers regarded as crucial, again not because they were deemed insignificant but because the technologists and their readers could do nothing about such matters anyway.

However, the technologists vehemently attacked religion and the idea of fate in its effect on farming. Results were determined by skill, they insisted, not luck or divine help, and they insisted no doubt because contrary beliefs were widespread. Passages like this one from a book on sericulture by an egg-grower in Shinshū are typical:

It is true that luck is not wholly absent from sericulture, yet in the final analysis results depend on skill. There are good and bad years depending on weather, but one man gets better results than another because of his methods. Let two men be equally lucky, one will succeed and the other fail by reason of differences in skill. Even in good growing years when everyone prospers, yields nevertheless vary with skill. Although everyone

[38] *Mempo*, p. 18.

is the same distance from heaven, it is plain that there are differences in ability (*jinriki*). People who do not recognize this fact stupidly pray to the Buddha and *kami*, or they blame the eggs for their bad results and envy the success of others. The Buddha and *kami* may help ever so much, but if one's sericultural methods are slipshod (*orosoka*), one is not going to get good results. But if one's methods are made sound by inquiring tirelessly about methods from experts, one will get good results even in bad years.[39]

Some sericultural writers seem to exclude the possibility of failure with proper methods. "Success with silkworms is not a matter of luck but depends entirely on skill."[40] "People who know [the five errors to avoid] will not have one bad year of cocoon production in a hundred."[41] "If one takes this book out before the worms hatch and thereafter reads the [appropriate section] every day and further follows the methods outlined, he will never suffer failure."[42]

Amid such assertions, however, others of a different kind occasionally creep in. The author of an influential book on sericulture, first published in 1803 and translated into French in 1884, quoted a number of Chinese sayings on sericulture of dubious value, such as that burying silkworm dung on the northeast of a house would assure the prosperity of the family's sericulture.[43] In the middle of a sober technical discussion of the feeding of silkworms, another work pauses to warn against raising more worms than one can feed, on the ground that this condemns part of the worms to starvation, an offense against nature (*shizen*) punishable by the ruin of the family and the sickness and death of its head.[44] Or, again, an author deduces the love of the silkworm for warmth from the fact that these

[39] *Yosan kyōkōroku*, p. 409.
[40] Ta Tomonao, "Yosan suchi," vol. 1, unpaginated.
[41] Narita Jūhyōe, *Yosan kensetsu*, p. 299.
[42] *Shinsen yosan hisho*, pp. 70–71. This book, published in 1801, was a revision of a book (or manuscript) completed in 1757, and the language of this passage is almost word for word the same as a passage of *Kaiko yōiku tekagami* published in 1712, p. 25.
[43] *Yosan hiroku*, in Inosaka, ed., *Sansō kōten*, pp. 9–10, 232.
[44] Ta Tomonao, "Yosan suchi," vol. 1, unpaginated.

insects originated from the ear of a horse and therefore shared its *yō,* or male, sun-loving character.[45]

The welfare of farm families was the principal objective of improved farming in Nagatsune's view. Indeed, he thought that one without the other was impossible, for farm families would change their ways only when they saw an advantage for themselves. In recommending particular reforms he was careful to point out advantages that would appeal to them—higher yields, lower costs, higher prices, full employment.[46] From some of the reforms he advocated farmers alone could benefit, such as improved tools that eased the physical strain of farm work, or leather shoes to keep the farmer's feet warm as he went about his chores in cold winter weather. "If anyone sees this book and discovers in it methods which prove profitable," Nagatsune wrote in a treatise called *Hōkaroku furoku,* "my many years of collecting information will not have been wasted."[47] Moreover he was primarily interested in economic advantages. When he spoke of "profits," he meant monetary profits. This is evident from his writing mainly about cash crops and cottage industries, from his concern with yields and costs, and from his extensive citation of prices. Even when apparently talking of other benefits, he was likely to have monetary profits in mind, as whenever he spoke of saving labor, which easily translated into lower wage bills or (alternatively) larger family earnings from by-employments with the labor saved.

Great stress was laid by Nagatsune and the sericultural writers on the long-run significance of small increases in output or savings in costs.

> Cotton seeds selected in this way [by suspension in water to pick the heaviest] may be sown sparingly, one-half *kamme* per *tan* of land being used instead of the normal *kamme* and a half; and because of their superiority these seeds will root well, grow vigorously, and require little thinning.[48]

[45] *Yosan chawa,* in Inosaka, ed., Sansō kōten, p. 95.
[46] *Nōgu,* pp. 52, 63, 72, 75, 79; *Mempo,* pp. 266, 267, 270, 276–277; *Seiyuroku,* in Kagaku kōten, 11:316, 332–335.
[47] Tamura, *Ōkura,* p. 240.
[48] *Mempo,* p. 270.

The costs eliminated by better tools amount to a substantial benefit (*eki*) over a year's time, quite aside from the improvement in crops they bring.[49]

Tsuranuki [leather footgear worn in winter by Kinai peasants] have other advantages over straw sandals. One can go into the fields earlier in the morning and work better because they keep the feet warm and supple, and they eliminate the need for hot water to wash the feet daily. These are not great advantages in a single day, but day after day over a lifetime they become significant.[50]

The utmost care should be taken not to let a single silkworm die: Every worm represents a potential profit.[51]

Farm family profits—to use Nagatsune's phrase—were the primary aim of all technologists. An example is the author of *Yosan suchi*, who was raised in a sericultural family and relates the background of his influential book. Dissatisfied with the prevailing methods of sericulture, he read all the Chinese and Japanese books he could get on the subject and put their wisdom to the test; then he traveled about the country studying the methods of others; finally, he experimented with ideas of his own and made several "discoveries" (*hatsumei*). After all this, he states none too modestly, he understood sericulture thoroughly and, thinking it a shame to use his knowledge to benefit a single family, decided to share it as widely as possible with others. He points out how important the decision might be, for "Families which raise silkworms earn half of their income from this source, so that those who are successful year after year become wealthy; those who fail are impoverished."[52]

Again and again, in different ways, this theme recurs in writings on sericulture. One author called sericulture "an occupation which creates wealth" (*tomeru waza*) because from egg to silk filament takes only a little more than a month; therefore, where sericulture flourished, wealth accumulated in every

[49] *Nōgu*, p. 52.
[50] *Ibid.*, pp. 100–101.
[51] Ta Tomonao, "Yosan suchi," vol. 1, unpaginated.
[52] *Ibid.* "I was able," the author writes, "to discover things that are in no modern or ancient book on sericulture."

household. A single family known to this author in Jōshū had an income of 376 *ryō* (worth about 400 *koku* of rice at the time of writing) in ordinary years (*reinen*) from raising eggs; small operators (*koie*) in the same district made one tenth that on average.[53] Another writer pointed out that sustained success with silkworms would permit a family "to multiply its wealth a hundredfold," and he offered an edifying example. There was a young boy in his district who lost his father, and the boy and his mother were so poor that they could not afford to light a fire morning or evening. Then the boy began raising silkworms, inquiring of expert growers throughout the neighborhood about method, working night and day to improve his technic. After five or six years he became expert himself and his profits began to increase; he invested them in farmland and forests and in time became the wealthiest man in the region. Thus, said the author, was *toku* (virtue, in this case filial piety) rewarded by *toku* (profit).[54]

Despite such dramatic illustrations of the efficacy of proper method, however, it is clear that the technologists were more interested in general improvement than in the enrichment of a few gifted or lucky farmers. Nagatsune spoke of ameliorating the labor of the "masses" (*banmin*) by improving farm implements; he and others hoped exceptional men in each village would instruct the ordinary men around them in better farming. One of the writers cited in the previous paragraph thought sericulture could increase the income of tens of thousands of little people (*saimin*), and declared that his book was intended "to make sericulture easy" and "to prevent the novice from falling into error."[55] Technologists conventionally apologized for their literary style, pointing out that they wrote so that, with the aid of phonetic signs alongside the characters and illustrations, even women and children could understand.[56]

---

[53] Narita Jūhyōe, *Yosan kensetsu*, pp. 319, 326–330.
[54] *Yosan hisho*, pp. 216, 289.
[55] *Yosan kensetsu*, p. 299.
[56] *Ibid.*, p. 297; *Kaiko yōiku tekagami*, p. 25; *Yosan hiroku*, p. 196. Although humble about their literary accomplishments, technologists were far from modest about their technical knowledge. The following is typical: "The text contains

In aiming at improving the income of numberless farm families, these writers came very close to a crude notion of economic development. "If everyone will follow this book," says the preface to a sericultural manual published in 1810, "not only will it enrich [*fūki*] individual families, but the wealth of heaven and earth [*tenchi*] will increase [*fueru*] like the sea coming in at full tide. Tomorrow we see the results of what we do today...." Very often the technologists used the word "*kaihatsu*"—development —to describe the spread of an industry or technic over an entire district. Sometimes they implied *kaihatsu* without using the word, citing examples that make the meaning unmistakable.[57]

Narita Jūhyōe, a practicing Ōmi sericulturalist, estimated that the production of silk yarn had doubled between the beginning of the Tokugawa period and the early eighteenth century, then quadrupled between that time and the date of writing in 1813. Nor, evidently, was this at the cost of other production. Sericulture, many writers pointed out, could be carried on entirely with female labor so as not to displace male labor from farming. Narita said that in all parts of the country the prosperity of sericultural villages was obvious to anyone. He thought that the production of many other commodities had developed (*kaihatsu*) in the same way as silk yarn in the last one hundred or even fifty years. He illustrated from his own province, where a certain kind of weaving had been invented in the Meiwa era (1764– 1777) and half a century later, "ten thousand" families made their living by it.[58]

The technologists were not alone in grasping, albeit crudely, the idea of economic development; officials and orthodox Confucians were familiar enough with the idea of an increase in output from a given population.[59] But they had a very different notion of the benefit that ought to accrue from such development. For most of them its significance lay mainly in the increase

---

many mistakes in characters, *kana*, and composition; but concerning the principles (*kotowari*) of sericulture, there is no doubt of its usefulness in all of the many provinces." *Teisei yosan hisho*, Inosaka, ed., *Sansō kōten*, p. 193.

[57] *Shinsen yosan hisho*, p. 63.

[58] *Yosan kensetsu*, pp. 211, 325, 343.

[59] Fujita Teiichirō, *Kinsei keizai shisō no kenkyū* (Tokyo, 1966), pp. 31–60.

in government revenue or an improvement of a fief's balance of payments; any increase in popular welfare was incidental.[60] For the technologists, the aim of development was clearly "to enrich" farm families and its effect on government finance was secondary. Indeed the latter subject was rarely mentioned. It is true that they occasionally used the word *kokueki,* a term meaning "benefit to the nation" that was popular with officials; but the term was a vague one and it is by no means clear that, in using it, the technologists meant the interests of government rather than those of the people of the country or, where the stress was on government, that they meant increased revenue rather than the general political benefits that might be expected to flow from a prosperous population. The municipalist Narita, who used the term frequently, went out of his way to explain that by *kokueki* he did not mean increased government income, which entailed increasing taxation and was therefore like gambling in a family (taking from one to give to another), thereby implying that true *kokueki* was an increase in total welfare.[61]

This stress on private interest to the neglect of the government was natural. The technologists wrote for the edification of farmers and other producers whose exertions and innovations they saw as the mainspring of economic progress, the only kind they were concerned with. They were convinced, judging from Nagatsune's explicit statements and the implicit assumptions of others, that farmers and artisans could be moved only by self-interest. Moreover, as practical men of affairs, they did not question the propriety of this egotism but accepted it as a datum, part of human nature. This view, if I read it correctly, was radically un-Confucian, for if there was any proposition that united Confucians, it was that the social good required the curbing of selfish interests and could not conceivably be built on them.

A considerable audience for technological information and

---

[60] Not everyone took this view. Chiku Keisō in *Kakinoki dan* wrote, "People who nowadays advocate profiting the nation (*kokueki*) strive only for the lord's profit. But if one would enrich a country, the best method is to make the people prosperous first." *Nihon keizai taiten,* 15:132.

[61] *Yosan kensetsu,* p. 324.

views on the propriety of selfishness emerged only in the eighteenth century with the spread of commercial farming and farm by-employments. These developments spread literacy, put cash in the hands of farmers for buying books, and gave them a new appreciation of the importance of increasing yields and cutting costs. How pure the appreciation could be on farms only partly commercial is shown by the notes on agriculture of a farmer in Kishū about 1700. It is clear that the author is speaking of an agriculture devoted mainly to the cultivation of cereals, one with no major cash crops such as cotton, indigo, or sugar. Yet, astonishingly, he not only lists and quantifies the costs and income of a typical farm for a year, but also calculates the cost of producing one *koku* of rice, breaking the cost into seventeen inputs, including the labor of separate operations (planting, weeding, harvesting) and the cost of wear and tear on tools.[62] This is the commercial mind with a vengeance.

The author of these notes, being literate and a village headman, was no ordinary peasant. But he comes very early; later there were many farmers with such attitudes scattered about the country who could be reached through books. One book on sericulture had a first printing of 3,000 copies, and many books went through several editions.[63] The spread of literacy through rural Japan, without which the technical literature on farming could not have flourished, is a fascinating story not yet fully known;[64] clearly it was linked to closer ties between town and country and increased rural income. Rural schools usually were locally supported, and it is impossible to believe that this voluntary expenditure on education was at the expense of other forms of consumption, given the general austerity of rural life. At any rate, by the late eighteenth century, villages without several literate members were rare enough that Nagatsune could complain of farmers reading tales and stories rather than his books.

The developments that produced the audience—commercial

[62] *Saizōki*, in *Kinsei chihō keizai shiryō*, 2:414.

[63] Inosaka, ed., *Sansō kōten*, p. 7; several books carried the word *revised* in their title, such as *Shinsen yosan hisho* and *Teisei yosan hisho*.

[64] Ronald P. Dore, *Education in Tokugawa Japan* (Berkeley, 1965), pp. 252–290.

farming, by-employments, rising income, literacy—produced the technologists themselves. Few came from the samurai or official class or even from castle towns; almost to a man they were from villages and small towns, where they were commercial farmers or merchants of the kind thrown up by the eighteenth-century changes in agriculture and the growth of rural industry. Miyazaki Antei was a farmer and, as his far-flung travels, citation of Chinese books, and surname suggest, a man of some means, education, and status.[65] Nagatsune's grandfather was a cotton-grower and merchant; he had relatives who were wax-makers on a sufficient scale to hire labor. He himself became a seedling merchant. Nearly all of the writers on sericulture were sericulturalists, egg-growers, or silk merchants, and several were at the same time village teachers and doctors.[66] Commercial occupations operating in highly competitive markets where profit margins were narrow, where the difference between 18 and 25 percent oil yield from rape seed was the difference between bankruptcy and prosperity, for example, inevitably turned some men's attention to improving technology.[67]

The travel that the more commercial of these occupations required of their followers also underlined the importance of technology, permitting the observation of local technical differences and their economic consequences. Significantly, nearly all writers on technology tell of extensive travels either in the course of business or for study.[68] One is struck, moreover, by how easily these men, who were commoners and without office, seemed to have moved about the country; they speak matter of factly of going from one province or region to another. Rarely do they mention going from fief to fief—as if these jurisdictions did not exist. Such apparent ease of movement did not exist until the eighteenth century. It was the result partly of improved transport and partly of the relaxation of administrative barriers through the routine issuance and acceptance of passports, in

[65] *Nōgyō zensho*, p. 6.
[66] Inosaka, ed., *Sansō kōten*, pp. 5–13.
[67] *Seiyuroku*, p. 316.
[68] *Nōgyō zensho*, pp. 24–28.

order to facilitate the movement of labor required by the geographically uneven growth of industry and trade.[69] Travel did
not become legally or administratively free; but by the late
eighteenth century no severe restrictions were put on the movement of individuals as opposed to families, who were the units
responsible for the cultivation of land, as can be seen from the
very high percentage of legal residents of villages who actually
lived and worked elsewhere.[70]

The eighteenth-century improvement of the mails, largely
through the development of private postal companies, also facilitated the work of technologists, who depended on them to
reach readers and to communicate with one another. Because
technologists were widely scattered about the country, the mails
must have been crucial to morale as well as to the substance of
their work. Nagatsune knew farmers interested in agricultural
improvement all over central Japan, no doubt partly from his
travels but also from acquaintances made through the mails. In
his book on tools he made a plea for readers to send him sketches
of any implement they found he had overlooked.[71] The preface
of the *Shinsen yosan hisho* reveals what appears to have been a
three-cornered correspondence among sericulturalists, for the
two authors of the preface lived in different provinces from each
other and from the author of the text. How the three communicated does not appear; but the preface states that the book's author, after finishing the manuscript, had sent it to the preface
writers, asking each for criticism in the light of the sericultural
practices of his own district.[72]

Two other factors help explain the rise of the technologists in
the eighteenth century. It was one thing to improve one's own

[69] Oka Mitsuo, *Hōken sonraku no kenkyū* (Tokyo, 1962), pp. 152–153, 158.
Twice serious efforts were made to return to their villages rural migrants to Edo
and other cities, but even the more severe of these, in 1843, applied only to
migrants who were without passports issued by their village headman. Kōda
Shigetomo, "Edo no chōnin no jinkō," *Shakai keizai shigaku*, 8, no. 1 (April
1938): 13.

[70] Katada Seiji, "Nōgyō hiyatoi no hen shitsu katei," *Chihōshi kenkyū*, p. 23;
Hayami Akira, "Shinshū Yokouchi-mura no chōki jinkō tōkei," *Mita gakkai
zasshi*, 59, no. 1 (1966):70.

[71] *Nōgu*, p. 5.

[72] *Shinsen yosan hisho*, p. 63.

farming or sericulture, another to collect and collate information at great effort, and possibly expense, for the benefit of others. This civic spirit probably was partly due to the Confucian notion, which went with the spread of education, that the highest function of knowledge was public service, together with the inability of most technologists to hold public office. The other factor was the availability of technical books in Chinese as models, without which this particular substitute for office might not have occurred to anyone. However, the technologists do not appear to have been greatly indebted to Chinese authors for their technology. They constantly cited their own observations and experience, rarely the Chinese; and when they did cite the Chinese, it was generally to establish the originality of their own views or the inappropriateness of Chinese experience to Japanese conditions.[73] Nagatsune did not mention China in the four books I am most familiar with; and, except in historical passages, the Chinese were only passingly mentioned by the sericulturalists. The one extended discussion of Chinese practice by any of the sericulturalists to the best of my knowledge was a passage discussing the fact that silkworms normally slept three times in China and four times in Japan, and attributing this difference to environment. The proof was as follows: Three-sleep worms occasionally occurred in Japan as a result of mutation (*hensei*), and they were typically small and yielded silk of inferior quality. Some years ago the author bred eggs from a number of three-sleep worms, discovering that in the second and third generations they slept four times and made excellent cocoons; but in following generations they reverted to three sleeps and again gave poor thread. "Hence, it is clear that our country is suited to four-sleep worms, and people should not be misled by a liking for novel things and Chinese books into thinking that three-sleep worms are profitable."[74]

How much influence the technologists may have had on prac-

---

[73] Boastful statements were fairly common; for example, "No one in China or Japan has previously explained these five prohibitions in such a way as to make sericulture easy [as is done in this book]." *Yosan kensetsu*, p. 299.

[74] Ta Tomonao, "Yosan suchi," vol. 3, unpaginated.

tice is a matter of conjecture. Technology made slow but cumulatively important progress during the Tokugawa period; few branches failed to see significant if less than revolutionary innovations, and the best existing technics were greatly extended geographically, sometimes with powerful effects. In the course of the eighteenth century, for example, the so-called *taka* loom, until then confined to Kyoto, displaced the simpler, smaller, and less versatile *izari* loom all over the country, increasing output and quality and variety of textiles.[75] If technological progress cannot be attributed to the technologists, it is at least certain that it could not have occurred without the commercial interest in technology these writers reflect.[76] Any influence on practice they may have had very likely continued beyond the Tokugawa period. Improvements in agriculture in the generation after 1868, the magnitude of which is debatable, came largely from the better dissemination of Tokugawa technology through the efforts of private reformers who may have been influenced by their Tokugawa precursors.[77] The latter's books continued to circulate and to be reprinted after the Restoration, whereas new and better ones accumulated slowly. Private agricultural reformers, as well as the government officials who around 1900 became the chief agents of reform, may have found inspiration in the dedicated lives of men like Nagatsune.

But, surprisingly, politics was the sphere in which the technologists were perhaps most important. Although they said virtually nothing explicitly political, they gave expression to views

[75] Sampei Kōko, *Nihon kigyō shi* (Tokyo, 1961), pp. 197–210.

[76] The case of Russia underlines the importance to technological improvement in agriculture of a numerous class of commercially oriented farmers. During the latter half of the eighteenth and the first half of the nineteenth centuries, there appears to have been no significant general improvement in Russian agriculture, despite the proliferation of societies among the nobility for the improvement of farming. One of the reasons for this would seem to be that the Russian serf was largely cut off from the market by lordly exploitation. Jerome Blum, *Lord and Peasant in Russia* (New York, 1964), pp. 404–413; and Michael Confino, *Domaines et seigneurs en Russie vers la fin du XVIII siècle* (Paris, 1963).

[77] Shūjirō Sawada, "Innovation in Japanese Agriculture, 1880–1935," in William Lockwood, ed., *The State and Economic Enterprise in Japan* (Princeton, N. J., 1965), pp. 338–344; Ronald P. Dore, "Agricultural Improvements in Japan, 1870–1900," *Economic Development and Cultural Change*, 9, no. 1, part 2 (October 1960):69–91.

radically subversive of a political system based on a hierarchy of inherited classes, status, occupations, and economic rewards thought to represent a natural moral order. This order was profoundly disturbed by the economic and technological change which altered occupations and status, and most of the political writing of the period attacked such change as arising from moral turpitude, as the assertion of selfish interests and ambitions over the public good, which had to be suppressed at all costs. The technologists, on the other hand, applauded it. They exhorted peasants to make themselves prosperous and indeed rich, and the richer the better, by improving their farming, expanding income from by-employments, and exploiting market opportunities.[78] How antagonistic this advice was to the orthodox conception of society can be seen by a glance at agrarian legislation in any part of the country; everywhere it was mainly concerned with suppressing the engrossment of land, high rural wages, the diversion of agricultural land and labor from staple to cash crops and from farming to trade and industry, and "luxurious" habits among the peasants—all manifestations of the very kind of economic individualism encouraged by the technologists.[79]

Not only were the technologists saying, by implication, that men with enough intelligence and enterprise to alter their status and style of life might ignore the limitations placed on them by birth; they were also saying, in effect, that the pursuit of private interest by enough people would change society for the better, adding to the sum of human welfare, and therefore that the good

[78] A village headman in Kawachi Province writing about the beginning of the eighteenth century warned that, for villagers, attempting to become too rich would almost inevitably lead to ruin, and he gave many examples from his village to prove his point. These were mainly of families who had tried to engage in long-distance trade with Nagasaki and the northern provinces. But his point was that there were great dangers in overextending oneself, not that there was anything wrong with such ventures if successful. Nomura Noboru, ed., *Shomin shiryō*, pp. 194–195.

[79] For example, *Akita kenshi. Shiryō kinsei* (Akita, 1963), 2:852–853; Oka, *Hōken sonraku*, pp. 152 ff.; Takeyasu Shigeji, *Kinsei tochi seisaku no kenkyū* (Osaka, 1962), pp. 58–67; Ishii Ryōsuke, ed., *Hampōshu Tokushima han* (Tokyo, 1960), p. 921.

of society was not uniquely determined by the moral quality of the ruler but might in part well up from the blindly selfish strivings of the masses. It is not surprising that these implications were not drawn out, for they were directly contrary to the ideas of the ruling samurai class, namely, that the egotism of ordinary men could be held in check and kept from ruining society only by the constant example, admonition, and resolute power of the rulers. Almost certainly the technologists were largely unaware of the full implications of what they wrote.

But every society, even Japanese, has its cranks, and the technologists can be said to have been politically important only insofar as their ideals were shared by others. Fortunately the evidence, though circumstantial, suggests a tentative answer. The technologists spoke for a large number of people. First, they were not abstruse, precious, or even speculative thinkers. They were practical men who addressed themselves to the most con- concrete and widespread problems imaginable. Second, they wrote for a fairly large readership, considering the limitations of literacy. Third, they came from a numerous class of commercial farmers and rural merchants and manufacturers whose concerns they seem to have reflected, and these men were leaders in their own communities. Finally, in the increasingly commercial environment of the countryside, a considerable proportion of the peasants sought to maximize returns and enlarge their holdings and income at the expense of neighbors. One has only to glance at a few surviving land registers in districts not cut off from market influences by distance or geography to see that land was continually changing hands by purchase and foreclosure,[80] and to confirm observations to this effect by contemporaries.[81] This competitiveness of the rural population helps to account for its extraordinary responsiveness after the Restoration to the op-

[80] Hasegawa Shinzō, "Kinsei kōki minami Kantō nōson no kōzō," *Shichō*, no. 99, pp. 62–68; Takeyasu, *Tochi seisaku*, p. 57; Imai Rintarō and Yagi Akihiro, *Hōken shakai no nōson kōzō* (Tokyo, 1955), pp. 50–54; Inoue Kazuo, ed., *Mikawa no kuni Hoi chihō shūmon nimbetsu aratame-chō* (Toyohashi, 1961), pp. 557 ff.

[81] Takeyasu, *Tochi seisaku*, pp. 48–49, 60, 62, 67.

portunities of industrialization, public education, and freedom of residence and occupation.[82] Altogether, therefore, the technologists appear to have reflected aspirations and strivings that were widely shared, and if Ōkura Nagatsune had historical importance, it was as a spokesman not of novel but of commonplace ideas.

How commonplace has by no means been shown, but if they were as widespread as seems likely, though never expressed as an ideology, they help to explain the transition from Tokugawa to Meiji society. Great historical structures are not brought down until the popular beliefs and behavior supporting them are deeply eroded, and this necessarily long process is not always accompanied by the beating of ideological gongs. Unless some such process was at work in Tokugawa Japan, the Restoration and its social consequences become nearly unintelligible, and we are thrown back on statements about special Japanese qualities of leadership and popular response that pose greater problems of understanding than any they solve.

[82] The following paragraph is from the jottings of a village headman in the early eighteenth century: "Because this is an era of rising costs, if one does not work as hard as he can and get the greatest possible yield from his crops, he will be unable to maintain his family (*ie*) and to nourish his wife and children. Therefore *let him pray that his children will surpass others* (*hito ni kosu*) and thereby make their way through life." (Italics mine.) *Saizōki,* p. 399.

ŌSHIO HEIHACHIRŌ (1793–1837)
Tetsuo Najita

Ōshio Heihachirō was a political sage (*seija*) in late Tokugawa Japan. He was, however, a sage of a particular sort; in many ways he was a saint bent on attacking political and economic corruption—indeed, conceptual corruptions of all sorts—and offering a paradise of justice for the common folk. He had no God, no Western Paradise. Yet he taught the Confucian truism of sageliness in the "hearts" of all that made men potentially extraordinary, far beyond their function and status in society. He believed that men had the capacity to realize immortality in the active rectification of injustice as defined in the tradition of Ōyōmei (Wang Yang-ming, 1472–1529). For Ōshio, the sage was neither a scholar writing erudite commentaries nor a recluse reflecting on the tragic and ephemeral nature of things but the iconoclastic rebel. Driving dogmatism (found in every page of his lectures) replaced eloquence and suppleness of style. Fearless protest and activism displaced conventional loyalism, as he rebelled against the very regime (the Bakufu) to which he and his ancestors had sworn fealty on the grounds that the realization of justice for the people and the restoration of humane imperial rule (*chūkō*) constituted inseparable parts of a single moral imperative.

Little need be said as to why he would be viewed with mixed feelings by advocates of the status quo or with more than a touch of admiration by late Tokugawa loyalists such as Fujita Tōko of Mito, Yoshida Shōin of Chōshū, and Kasuga Sen'an of Kyoto, as well as by men of varying shades of thought in the modern era, nationalists and Marxists alike, disenchanted with the injustices spawned by industrial organization. Ōshio was a sage in his day, a hero for later generations—not a hero in Hook's sense of the decisive personality impinging on the flow of history, but an idealized personality with a set of ethical precepts enticing even to men in the modern era.[1]

Little is known of Ōshio's childhood. His parents died when he was seven. Subsequently he was cared for briefly by his grandfather and then by a foster father, one Asai Chūrin, a minor bureaucrat in Owari. Due to uncertainties regarding Ōshio's upbringing, some believed he had been adopted into the Ōshio family. Ōshio, however, denied this story about his adoption and traced his ancestors to a vassal house of the Imagawa and later Tokugawa families in the late sixteenth century. According to Ōshio, his ancestors were assigned a post in Osaka as servitors of the Tokugawa house, a post which he claimed as his rightful inheritance. Ōshio served for some twenty years in the East Osaka magistracy in the Temman district as police censor (*gimmi yoriki*), a low-ranking post in the over-all Bakufu structure but an important one for the actual administration of Osaka. Between 1820 and 1830, Ōshio gained wide fame (along with his great skill in lancemanship) for being the most effective police censor in Osaka, cleaning out corruption in Buddhist churches, secret religious groups (presumably Christian), and a number of prostitution rings.

Despite the reputation Ōshio had as a bureaucrat, his image in subsequent history has been that of a social iconoclast. In 1818 (at about age twenty-five), Ōshio married a wealthy farmer's adopted daughter (Yū), a person of inferior status in Tokugawa society. He also arranged a marriage between his only son (Kakunosuke, whom he adopted around 1829) and his father-in-law's natural daughter. Moreover, his school, which he named Senshindō, was attended by students from all classes, including small merchants and farmers of varying economic status. Of

---

[1] See Kōda Shigetomo, *Ōshio Heihachirō* (Tokyo, 1910), p. 5; Shisō no Kagaku Kenkyūkai, ed., *Meiji ishin* (Tokyo, 1966), p. 137; Inoue Tetsujirō, *Nihon Yōmei gakuha no tetsugaku* (Tokyo, 1910), pp. 440–446; Miyake Setsurei, *Ōyōmei* (Tokyo, 1893), pp. 128–130; Tatebe Tongo, *Riku Shōzan* (Tokyo, 1897), pp. 199–240; Fukushima Kashizō, ed., *Kinsei Nihon no jugaku* (Tokyo, 1939), pp. 811–813; Rekishigaku Kenkyūkai, ed., *Meiji ishinshi kenkyū kōza* (Tokyo, 1959), 1:137–146; and Abe Makoto, "Ōshio Heihachirō," in Hayashi Motoi, ed., *Nihon jimbutsushi taikei* (Tokyo, 1959), 4:267–304.

fifty students known to have frequented his school in the mid–1830's, at least twenty were from these lower social groups. These have been cited as indications of a divergent pattern of behavior in Ōshio's career. On the other hand, however, Ōshio adopted his son from a fellow samurai's family and it was to him that he passed on, in 1830, the post in the bureaucracy held traditionally by Ōshio's family. Indeed, by his own admission, Ōshio set out to serve in the bureaucracy to embellish his family name, and although after 1830 he devoted his entire time to teaching and scholarship, he at no point renounced his genealogy. It would seem, therefore, that up through the early 1830's, he had not turned to study the ideas of Ōyōmei in protest against the Bakufu and its rules governing social status, but that it was his immersion in those ideas that pointed him in the end toward rebellion.

It is not certain precisely when Ōshio developed an interest in Ōyōmei, or where and under whom he received formal training in Confucian studies. Some claim he studied in Edo, but others point to his activities in Osaka, which make this impossible. Regardless, his knowledge of the Ōyōmei tradition was considerable. From the late 1820's, even while still serving as a bureaucrat, he had begun to give private lectures on the subject. In 1834, he published his famous lectures, *Senshindō satsuki*, which established his reputation as the foremost spokesman for Ōyōmei studies in Western Japan. It was on the basis of the ideas articulated in those lectures that, three years later, he launched his rebellion in Osaka against the Bakufu—known as *Ōshio no ran, Tempō no ran*—along with his adopted son Kakunosuke and some twenty devoted followers.[2]

[2] These are some of the salient biographical data on Ōshio Heihachirō (known also as Chūsai, Kōso, and Shiki). They are far from adequate and virtually preclude writing an analysis of him from the point of view of his social background or private life. Despite this thinness of data, much has been written on him. Since Inoue Senjirō wrote *Ōshiō Heihachirō genkōroku* in 1879, describing Ōshio as forerunner of the Liberal Democratic Movement, a steady stream of literature has appeared. Major critics such as Miyake Setsurei and Tokutomi Sohō commented and made assessments of him in the late nineteenth century, Miyake in glowing language, Tokutomi with decidedly less enthusiasm. In 1910, Inoue Tetsujirō discussed Ōshio at length in his well-known work, *Nihon Yōmei gakuha no tetsugaku*, and in that same year, Kōda Shigetomo published what

As a scholar in the Tokugawa Ōyōmei tradition, Ōshio is thought of as one of the principal figures who brought that tradition to its fullest development. Although preceded by such hallowed names as Nakae Tōju, Kumazawa Banzan, and Miwa Shissai,[3] Ōshio gave to that tradition of thought the unmistakably radical reading of action as public rather than private or familial, which had not been seen in such clear terms before him.[4] He is often assessed in this light with Satō Issai (1772–1859), who taught a comparable message. But unlike Satō, who taught the ideas of Ōyōmei behind the screen of lecturing for the Bakufu on orthodox Shushigaku (school of Chu Hsi), Ōshio made plain his primary allegiance to Ōyōmei thought despite full knowl-

---

is still the standard biography of Ōshio. In 1914, Mori Ōgai published his historical novel, *Ōshio Heihachirō*, recounting in colorful detail the last two days in Ōshio's life. In 1920, Ishizaki Tōkoku published his biography *Ōshio Heihachirō*, with the aim of making Ōshio a hero for the participants in the Rice Riots of 1917–1918. During the 1920's and 1930's, Ōshio received much attention from nationalistic writers and critics such as Nakano Seigō, and he also was taken up by historians in the context of what has turned out to be an ongoing debate regarding the "progressive" and "feudal" nature of late Tokugawa society. Scholars such as Sano Manabu, Horie Hideichi, Hattori Shisō, and Inoue Kiyoshi viewed Ōshio as a radical critic of the Bakufu in the sense of having pioneered the strategy of a lower-class alliance against the feudal order. Horie, for example, saw the critical period of Japan's modern transformation as beginning with Ōshio's rebellion and ending with the Chichibu riots of 1884. Recent studies have stressed other dimensions of Ōshio. Okamoto Ryōichi, in his short yet excellent study (Osaka, 1956), has emphasized the nonrevolutionary characteristics of Ōshio's ideology and style of action; Abe Makoto has emphasized Ōshio's this-worldly asceticism and related it to the rise of capitalism in Japan. An excellent discussion of these views is Okamoto Ryōichi's "Toshi uchikowashi—Ōshio sōdō o chūshin ni" in Rekishigaku Kenkyūkai, ed., *Meiji ishinshi kenkyū kōza*, 1:137–146. Abe Makoto's views are summarized in his "Ōshio Heihachirō," 4:267–304.

I have restricted the scope of this paper to analyzing the relationship between Ōyōmei thought and political activism in late Tokugawa as seen in Ōshio. Accordingly, I have relied primarily on Ōshio's lectures, *Senshindō satsuki* (Iwanami edition of 1940, with notes by Yamada Jun; a good version is in the third volume of Inoue Tetsujirō's *Yōmei gakuha*, 3 vols. [Tokyo, 1935] and a new publication is forthcoming under the editorship of Shimada Kenji), and also on the "summons" with which he launched his rebellion in 1937. "Ōshio Heihachirō gekibun," included in Kondō Heijō, ed., *Shiseki shūran*, vol. 98, (Tokyo, 1881–1885).

[3] Nakae Tōju (1608–1648), Kumazawa Banzan (1619–1691), Miwa Shissai (1669–1744). Inoue Tetsujirō, ed., *Yōmei gakuha;* also Inoue, *Nihon Yōmei gakuha no tetsugaku*. Miwa is generally considered to be the last great teacher of Ōyōmei prior to Ōshio and Satō Issai in the early 1800's.

[4] See, for example, Sagara Tōru, *Kinsei no jugaku shisō* (Tokyo, 1956), pp. 211–220.

edge of the Bakufu's official opposition to such heterodox ideas. Indeed, he denounced teaching Ōyōmei thought under the guise of Shushigaku as blatant hypocrisy and had no part of it. Moreover, whereas Satō kept a safe distance from current events—perhaps to protect his lecture podium, which was one of the most influential in the country—Ōshio refused to be content with teaching and scholarship and, instead, acted out his ideas in the political realm. Thus, Ōshio can be seen as being more consistent to the activist principle in Ōyōmei thought than Satō and, in this sense, is more revered in the pantheon of Ōyōmei scholars. As Miyake Setsurei said years later (1890), Ōshio was more consistent in his activism than the great master Wang Yang-ming himself—high tribute indeed for one who died leading an abortive, and in many respects, miserable, rebellion.[5]

Despite Ōshio's reputation as a scholar and thinker, he was far more a teacher; but his samurai background made him rely heavily on passion and zeal rather than on analytical finesse and subtlety of insight. His lectures were accompanied by the frequent use of the whip on his students for laxity in the pursuit of sagely studies, excessive concern with scholarly commentary, poetry, aesthetics, and indulging in the vulgar activities of reading novels, drinking in excess, and courting wicked women.[6] The rules Ōshio set down for his students were puritanical and indicated a disposition of mind that favored passionate repetition over systematic and sustained exposition. His lectures were terse, repetitive, aphoristic—for the modern reader, excessively cryptic. One searches in vain for extended treatments of philosophic ideas associated with the Ōyōmei tradition. Yet in the redundant structure of his lectures, there is discernible a clustering of ideas around a set of potent words, phrases, and images.

The constant governing Ōshio's ideas was the a priori assumption that the essence of all things, animate and inanimate, was identical with absolute spirit. Referred to as *taikyo*, this absolute possessed these usual definitional characteristics: It was uni-

[5] Shimada Kenji, *Shushigaku to Yōmeigaku* (Tokyo, 1967), p. 129 and *passim*; also, the highly readable work of Sugiura Mimpei, *Ishin zen'ya no bungaku* (Tokyo, 1967), pp. 71–94.
[6] Ōshio, *Senshin*, pp. 11–12.

versal, prior to heaven, to things, and to sensations; it was therefore the "creative force" of "heaven, earth, the ten thousand
things."[7] Moreover, it "admitted no opposites (*mono to taina-
shi*)" and, reminiscent of classic Buddhist thinking, negated all
(*mukyoku*) and thereby included all and was transcendent of
form, time, history, and change.[8]

Because the rest of his ideas followed from this premise,
Ōshio could not accept, even provisionally, any form of dualism.
He rejected with particular vehemence the various categories of
distinctions used by scholars of Shushigaku. Indeed, Ōshio made
a special point of denying that these categories represented the
essential ideas of Chu Hsi, stressing instead Chu Hsi's concept
of ultimate source of ideal—*taikyoku*—which scholars had mutilated with superficial analyses. By arguing in this manner,
Ōshio could place Chu Hsi within the idealistic scheme of
thought supported in the Ōyōmei tradition and turn him against
those purporting to teach his ideas.[9] As is well known, however,
Chu Hsi's ideas were ambiguous, having in them monistic and
dualistic features, with the latter not being insignificant by any
means. Among other things, the interplay between reason and
matter in Chu Hsi had special prominence in explaining reality
as "dynamic" rather than "impermanent," hence illusory as
claimed in Buddhism. Similarly the provisional distinction between self and things also was important in conceptualizing a
basis of objectivity (referred to as *kakubutsu kyūri* or *kyokei
kyūri*) from which to examine things and attain self-realization.

Although these tenets were directly attributable to Chu Hsi's
writings, Ōshio rejected them as unrepresentative of Chu Hsi and
labeled them as false distinctions, the source of self-deception
itself, which subseqeunt scholars had raised uncritically to
the level of high dogma. The argument for making distinctions,
he warned, obscured the real nature of things and hence of
the self, because it involved the imposition of artificial concep-

---

[7] Ōshio, *Senshin*, pp. 53, 81–82, 309–312. See also Inoue, *Nihon Yōmei gakuha
no tetsugaku*, pp. 411–534; Okamoto, *Ōshio Heihachirō*, pp. 46–60, and Abe,
"Ōshio Heihachirō," 4:267–304.

[8] Ōshio, *Senshin*, pp. 40–50, 297–312.

[9] *Ibid.*, especially: pp. 356–368.

tual barriers based on sensate perception. The essence of reality was prior to the senses and thus, he noted in pungent language, "it should be absolutely clear that it [absolute spirit] cannot be perceived by scholars with their specialized knowledge."[10] To Ōshio, therefore, essence—"principle"—in things was either absolute or it was not. The argument that all things stemmed from an absolute principle yet that distinctions could be made among them was contradictory. But more important, Ōshio saw grave consequences stemming from this contradictory view of reality. He saw it giving rise to selfish judgments of value as to good and evil, the superiority of one form compared to the next, the superiority of one thing over another, one person or groups of persons over others. For Ōshio, then, social injustice itself was traceable to these dualistic schemes of analysis used in Shushigaku which had nothing reliable to say about the internal workings of things.[11]

One a priori assumption regarding the nature of the universe was followed by yet another. Absolute spirit was equated with moral truth and goodness (*sei, makoto*) in the Confucian sense. Thus, because absolute spirit transcended conventional distinctions between good and evil, superior and inferior, it was pure goodness itself. The "original nature" of all things, he repeatedly insisted, was "only goodness," pure "as the spirit of a newborn child."[12] The classic imagery of "recovering" quiet innocence should not confuse us, however. For Ōshio, absolute goodness stood for universal ideal to which all could "reidentify" (rendered *kitaikyo,* literally "to return to the absolute"). This key concept of reidentification linked the two sets of a priori assumptions about the real nature of things as absolute ideal and as moral goodness. And it linked them in a manner that attributed to men the active potential for grasping the essence of absolute in self, of perceiving that "men are fundamentally one with heaven, their essences one with moral truth."[13]

[10] Ōshio's language; *Kesshite gakusha bunjo no koto ni arazaran koto danjite shirubeshi*[!]. *Ibid.*, p. 312.
[11] *Ibid.*, pp. 41–50.
[12] *Ibid.*, pp. 121, 175.
[13] *Ibid.*, p. 309; also pp. 43, 242, 329.

It should be noted, however, that Ōshio's imputation of the spiritual absolute in men (and things) did not give them an independence of "will" either to guide history or to place "conditions" on the absolute. On the contrary, that spirit in men made them "natural" servitors of heaven's "imperative," "dictate," or "command"—all these terms seem appropriate in rendering *mei*. Reidentification with absolute truth, therefore, meant ipso facto "to have already heard the command (*sude ni mei o kikeri*) from which the five relations and the one hundred acts follow."[14]

Despite the conservative connotations implicit in the relationship between reidentification and Confucian ethical action, there was in it a generalizing potential of considerable significance. Because deception, as already suggested, stemmed from fallacious distinctions made by the viewer and did not inhere in things, it followed that reidentification must imply ridding the mind of categories of distinctions, focusing, in short, on "self-clarification (*chiryōchi*)." But clarification of the self also meant, by virtue of the essential unity of things, clarification of all things. Self-clarification, in other words, did not denote introspective meditation but the active obliteration of distinctions between internal and external, so that things once presumed to have been external to self were now one with the self. In opening the floodgates of the self to the universe, the self once presumed internal was now "nonself" or "without self."[15] Thus, introspection became a meaningless category of action. By the same token, all thoughts, attitudes, feelings, and actions outside the self were rendered meaningless as external events.

In this fashion, the idea of reidentification encompassed not only self-realization but the clarification of society. Individual action and social events were conceptualized within an all-inclusive frame of reference. On one half of the coin, therefore, all the good in the universe, either as abstraction or as concrete fact, was indistinguishable from goodness in the self. But on the other half, passion, suffering, ignorance, and injustice, regardless

---

[14] *Ibid.*, pp. 84, 115, 119, 157, 164–167, 291–292.
[15] *Mushin, mukyoku, mu ni itaru*, etc. *Ibid.*, pp. 146–147, 177–180, 217–227, 295–299.

of magnitude and locus in society, were likewise indistinguishable from self. As Ōshio described this latter, "the evil words and actions of men are within us," and "punishment meted out to an evil man is pain inflicted on the spirit of the sage."[16] Thus, men sincerely concerned with the pursuit of knowledge could not observe and select desirable things and attitudes and reject others as unrelated to self. Stated simply, a person who perceives and merely condemns evil as separate from the self admits the existence of those blemishes in his heart. Although not committing the act himself, he departs from the principle of goodness in self. Because that which is personal and that which is social are identical and coincidental, "self-clarification means public action," and "the way of the sage is [always] in the public realm alone."[17]

In short, Ōshio used the concept of reidentification to mean action by which to dissolve self into nonself so that every relentless attack aimed at expunging evil from the self was by its very nature an utterly public act. He did not intend this to mean action to clarify self in contrast to others, nor certainly self as against political structure. Yet he advocated a broadly applicable principle of selfless action in society that is often not adequately stressed in discussions of this mode of thinking.

Commitment to public action, however, makes little sense without a conception of evil. Ōshio's treatment of this problem can be confusing, for he used evil in at least two different ways. On numerous occasions, he identified it in common-sense language as a "given," virtually as "natural" pain and suffering in the lives of men in society. On as many other occasions, he interpreted evil in a more logically consistent fashion in the context of his premise of a single absolute and, hence, viewed evil as not inherent in men and things. Although Ōshio did not indicate that he sorted out the differences of meaning, it was the latter definition of evil that he used in his notion of public action.

In light of Ōshio's premise of absolute spirit as goodness, evil

16 *Ibid.*, pp. 112–113.
17 Ōshio's words: *seija no michi wa shikō nomi*; and *mei nareba sunawachi kō. Ibid.*, pp. 206 and 306; also pp. 69–88. One's action in society, he also wrote, should be "as if one is mad (*kyōja no gotoki*)," p. 231.

by definition was impermanent. It was not a theoretical constant as in the Buddhist notion of impermanence or the unpredictable flux of things. To admit it as a constant would have been synonymous with accepting a contradictory universal. Thus, for Ōshio, goodness was permanent, innate in men and things, hence not of man's creation; evil was impermanent, not essential to men and things, hence of man's doing (or lack of doing). Quite aside from whether or not this adequately explained the nature of evil and corruption, it went hand in glove with his definition of public action. Patterns of evil were not inevitable and permanent fixtures in the human condition, and, for this reason, they could be "rectified"—perhaps "conquered" comes closer to his quality of thinking—through action in society. It was within this frame of reference that he used the Chinese character understood by scholars of Shushigaku as "making distinctions" (the *kaku* of *kakubutsu*) to read consistently "rectification" of evil (*kaku* read as *tadasu* as in *fusei o tadasu*).[18]

The logic of overcoming evil was part of a broader pattern of reasoning aimed at dissolving all theoretical contradictions and dialectical categories of formal thought. Thus, he swept aside such classic categories as the following: form and formlessness (*yūkei* and *mukei*), active and passive (*dō* and *sei*), essence and function (*tai* and *yō*), positive and negative (*u* and *mu*), reason and matter (*ri* and *ki*), knowledge and action (*chi* and *gyō*), and, above all for Ōshio, past and present (*ko* and *kon*) and life and death (*sei* and *shi*).

Time, or the contradiction of past and present, like evil, was impermanent and hence not a valid counterpoise to the timeless absolute. Time could be "rectified" into timelessness, making each moment potentially "absolute." There was no place in Ōshio's thinking for a "historical perspective," a notion of cumulative development in time, but only a series of moments in which, simultaneous with the rectification of evil, "a day becomes a hundred years."[19] In the conquest of time, moreover,

---

[18] *Ibid.*, pp. 95–96, 123–124, 138, 198, 235, 242. See also Inoue, *Nihon Yōmei gakuha no tetsugaku*, pp. 475–503.
[19] Ōshio, *Senshin*, pp. 164–167; also pp. 42–53, 90–91.

the distinction between life and death would be dissolved. In that moment when man rectifies evil and time, he becomes a sage, one with the sages of the past and with the absolute in all things. He becomes indestructible; his spirit "survives the seasons."[20] The "ordinary man," by contrast, fears death, hence cannot transcend it; he dies with his form. Again and again, Ōshio lectured his students, in a language strongly reminiscent of Zen Buddhism, to be imperturbable in the face of death, for immortality could be realized in the total sacrifice of self to the conquest of evil and time.[21]

It is not at all surprising that Ōshio should be attracted to the idea of conquering time and death with death. This had deep roots in the idealized medieval tradition of the samurai. And Ōshio was still a samurai even after committing himself fully to "scholarship." Indeed, he might be thought of as a samurai with a philosophy rather than a philosopher with spartan virtues. What needs to be stressed, however, is that for Ōshio, loyalty to the lord, either in personalized or institutionalized form, was being superseded by loyalty to absolute moral truth, which dictated action in and for society. His iconoclasm stemmed from that commitment. The quality of his vigor was no doubt conditioned by his samurai spirit, but the direction and nature of his actions were shaped by his ideology.

The strength of Ōshio's iconoclasm is plain enough. Through the intellectual framework denying the validity of all conceptual distinctions, he could reject much in society in relatively sweeping fashion, unfettered by considerations of service to fief or status or kin. Of greatest significance in this regard was his rejection of formalized social, political, and economic distinctions between men. In place of these distinctions he imposed the criterion of the original goodness of men. "The fundamental spirit of the ordinary man," he wrote, "is no different from that of the sage . . . , [that of] the wretched man identical with the aristocrat."[22] Irrespective of genealogy or geographical location,

---

[20] *Ibid.*, pp. 50–54, 84, 157, 248.
[21] *Shisu to iedomo nanzo* [!]. *Ibid.*, pp. 115, 298–301, 313–318, 320.
[22] *Ibid.*, pp. 41–48, 250, 329.

all men had the spirit enabling them to "reidentify" with the absolute and "transform their personalities (*kishitsuhenka*)" into sages. At the same time that "ordinary men" could transform themselves into sages, "aristocrats" could sink to the level of "ordinary men." Thus, "A prince who knows goodness but does not act [against evil] becomes lowly. A lowly man who knows what is not proper and refrains from acting can become a prince. Let us not, therefore, merely rely on princes or despise the lowly."[23]

For Ōshio it was ordinary men with high rank and wealth that were despicable, not ordinary men of low birth. The former, in his view, ought to know and act humanely. Yet, posturing as learned men and mouthing the principle of goodness, they continued to spin out "the evils of undeveloped scholarship" and led wretched lives, enhancing only their power and material comfort, not the cause of justice in society. One should be sympathetic to men of low birth, on the other hand, for their anguish was genuine.[24] Victimized by the scholarship and politics of oppressive "distinctions," they were unaware of the innate qualities of the sage in themselves. However, because they were not afflicted with the pretentions of rank, education, and wealth, they could become sages, lacking status but having the virtues of a king as with Confucius.

Even as he spoke of the potential of lowly men to become sages, Ōshio retained a fierce sense of elitism. Implicit throughout his lectures is the theme that only a few will actually become sages. And because most will not realize their sagely potential on their own, the sage must act as a salvational figure, a saint, for whom public action is "to save the people" (*kyūmin*, the characters on Ōshio's banner of revolt). Egalitarianism and elitism were utterly congruous in Ōshio's ethics of action.

The weakness of Ōshio's ethics, however, was not in its elitism. It lay in that same iconoclasm that denied conceptual distinctions. If this iconoclasm provided Ōshio with a framework ac-

[23] *Ibid.*, p. 136.
[24] Ōshio used the classic phrase drawn from Mencius to express this: *tami o miru itashimu ga gotoshi. Ibid.*, p. 127. See also pp. 304, 363–368.

tively to deny social reality, it denied him an ideology for sustained protest and revolt. Dialectics in time and between self and external things had no place in Ōshio's conception of the absolute nature of self in a discrete moment. His iconoclasm, therefore, veered toward radical mysticism, pointed less toward practical and theoretical considerations of revolt, more toward realizing immortality as a sage, as a "great hero."[25]

Although the relationship between philosophical assumptions and action outlined so far explains Ōshio's general conceptual framework, it does not tell us concretely how he launched his criticism. This dimension needs to be spelled out in assessing Ōshio's political personality.

Ōshio mainly used historical analogy to argue against the Bakufu and orthodox Shushigaku. But this was dressed in interesting cloth. With scrupulous consistency, Ōshio avoided mention of the Bakufu or the Hayashi house that directed the teaching of Shushigaku in Edo. Moreover, he avoided romantic discussion of heroes in Japanese history. Among Japanese thinkers, he mentioned only Nakae Tōju (1608–1648, one of the earliest proponents of Ōyōmei studies in Japan), and this in the descriptive context of a pilgrimage to his gravesite. On the other hand, he made extensive and provocative use of Chinese historical data drawn especially from late Ming and early Ch'ing to set up a historical "model" by which to cast, by analogy, damaging light on Bakufu thought and politics.

Ōshio left little room for doubt that in his view the quintessence of timeless truth in Confucianism from the ancient sages on was best captured in more recent times by thinkers such as Lu Hsiang-shan (1139–1192, referred to in Japanese as Riku Shōzan) and, above all, Wang Yang-ming. More important, he felt strongly that the intellectual tradition of these great men had reached its height in the late Ming, not because it subsequently dominated the intellectual life of China, but because the splendor of that legacy was brought into fullest view during that tragic time. Reminding his students that bureaucratic cen-

[25] *Ibid.*, pp. 298–300.

sorship could not blemish or obscure that tradition, he exhorted them to listen to him with undivided attention[26] as he described ideology and action in the careers of the great loyalists of the late Ming (eleven of whom he discussed in some detail, about thirty others in composite form).[27]

These loyalists were without exception heroes, as great sages as the ancients. All were either disciples of Wang Yang-ming or students of that school of thought. Fearless of those above them in government and deeply affectionate toward the people, their sole aim was to bring truth and justice to the empire. To them, as he described it, "the fate of society and of their lives was one."[28] Committing their lives in this fashion, they openly criticized high ministers, even the emperor, and defied petty bureaucratic procedures—including confiscating imperial tax money— to help the weak and poor. Yet, although critical of despotic bureaucratism and facing exile and public beatings, they continued to teach the ethic of universal truth and imperial justice (*ōdō*). Thus, they were fiercely loyal to the legitimate Ming dynasty and gave their lives in the desperate struggle against the invaders from Manchuria. The convergence of these outstanding characteristics in this group of men at this time, he argued, was not accidental. It was attributable to the ideology

---

[26] *Shōshi kore o kike* [!]. *Ibid.*, p. 200.

[27] Many of Ōshio's heroes do not appear in standard biographical dictionaries. Of those that do, the following might be mentioned. Forerunners of the late Ming loyalists: Tsou Tung-k'uo (1491–1562, referred to as Sū Tōkaku); Ou-yang Nan-yeh (1496–1554, referred to as Ōyō Nanya); Lo Nien-an (1504–1564, referred to as Ra Nen'an); Wang Lung-hsi (1498–1583, referred to as Ō Ryūkei); and Wang Hsin-chai (1483–1540, referred to as Ō Shinsai). Of the late Ming loyalists, Ōshio emphasized the following: Lu Shan-chi (1575–1636, referred to as Roku Zenkei); Huang Tao-chou (1585–1646, referred to as Kō Dōshū); Liu Tsung-chou (1578–1645, referred to as Ryū Sūshū); Tsai Yu-te (1586–1644, referred to as Sai Yūtoku); Meng Hua-li (1545–1597, referred to as Mō Kari); Sun Ch'in-feng (1584–1675, referred to as Son Kihō); Huang Tsung-hsi (1610–1695, referred to as Kō Sūgi); and Li Yung (1627–1705, referred to as Ri Yō). It should be noted that in discussing the loyalism of these men, Ōshio overlooked their complicated intellectual fabric. For example, he left unmentioned the critique of the introspective tradition of Wang Yang-ming by some of them, such as Liu Tsung-chou. And the fact that these men were seriously interested in developing techniques of empirical historical research and in mathematics went undiscussed. See *Ibid.*, pp. 198–208.

[28] *Ibid.*, pp. 204.

of reidentification with the absolute, and it explained the heroic quality of the late Ming as contrasted to the humiliating end of the Sung.[29]

The evaluation of late Ming loyalism as the culmination of the Confucian tradition carried with it an obvious implication. That fine tradition was ruthlessly betrayed by the Ch'ing dynasty with bureaucratism and false orthodoxy. The loyalists were publicly persecuted, the best of them brutally executed by drowning and hanging. Their writings, moreover, were systematically censored. And intelligent men sharing the sympathies of the loyalists had to develop deceptive scholarly techniques and compile arid tomes that pretended to comment on the teachings of Chu Hsi.[30] Ōshio's technique of spicing his lectures with references to the fate of loyalism in early Ch'ing was not intended as an exercise in empirical historical research. It was obviously pointed at the Bakufu as a polemical argument, so that when he wrote the character "Ch'ing," "Bakufu" could just as easily have been inserted in its place. Indeed, this implication was so plain that when Ōshio asked Satō Issai to pass on his lectures to the head of the Hayashi house after perusing them, Satō refused in monumentally evasive language.[31]

Argument from analogy was a convenient device to use. Historical distortions could be glossed over to retain an effective polemical stance. But it was convenient in another sense as well, for it begged the question of who were the analogous counterparts of the Ming loyalists in Japan. Here, through the use of strident and insistent language, Ōshio conveyed his belief that the loyalist sage in Japan had yet to appear. There is no doubt that he had deep sympathy for the defenders of the Kemmu Restoration of 1333, a fact that welded his friendship with the historian Rai San'yō. But these men did not have the ideology that Ōshio believed *sine qua non* for true loyalism. Thus, within his structure of analogy, Ming loyalism was made to mesh, not with the achievements of historical figures, but with the mission

[29] Ōshio's words: *Sōmatsu to ōi ni hansuru mono wa nanzo ya. Kore mata ani ryōchi no kyo . . . ni arazaran ya* [!]. *Ibid.*, p. 206.

[30] *Ibid.*, pp. 200–208, 281, 302–304, 341, 363–368, etc.

[31] *Ibid.*, as an addendum to Ōshio's lectures, pp. 419–420.

of Ōshio Heihachirō as a potential sage. His unmistakably religious sense of mission stemmed from this conviction. And in
viewing himself as the embodiment of the sagely virtues of
Ming loyalism, he took on the garb of an angry Maitreya, the
savior potential, promising "to save the people from the hell
of the past and . . . establish paradise before their very eyes."[32]

Ōshio wrote the preceding words in the "summons" (*gekibun*) with which he launched his rebellion. They mark the end
of criticism by analogy, the beginning of armed rectification of
injustice. For the historian, however, they also point to a problem
of deeper significance: They throw light on the fascinating
process in which "action" shaped Ōyōmei thought in a concrete
historical situation. Like abstract thought, concrete action was
universal, so that the particular contours within which action
took place were stripped conceptually of their distinctive characteristics. Precisely for this reason, we find Ōshio imposing on
the Japanese emperor (as son of heaven) a quality of unim-
peachable moral purity. Ōshio's summons provides clear evidence of his unwitting modification of abstract ideas in terms of
particular historical circumstance, thus giving, in this process
of "corruption," a political significance to his ideas of universal
moral truth that went beyond his immediate concern of rectifying evil.

Ōshio addressed the summons to the "people and farmers"
(*tami hyakushō domo*) in the four surrounding areas of Osaka—
Settsu, Kawachi, Izumi, and Harima—to outline for them the
purpose and strategy of his rebellion.[33] Now openly referring to
the Tokugawa shogunate (for example, as Tōshōgūkun),[34] Ōshio
blamed it for failing to bring just and moral government to the
people. Despite nearly two and a half centuries of ostensive
peace under its aegis, there was only increasing chaos. Morally
decadent and arrogant bureaucrats ran the country by accept-

---

[32] Ōshio, "Ōshio Heihachirō gekibun," printed in 1837 and included in Kondō,
ed., *Shiseki shūran*. See also Inoue Senjirō, *Ōshio Heihachirō genkōroku*, and
Abe, "Ōshio Heihachirō," 4:267–304, especially pp. 267, 299–304.
[33] "Ōshio gekibun" (unpaginated).
[34] *Ibid.*

ing bribes and listening to the petty advice of women in the inner chambers. Leaving utterly unattended the condition of abject famine among the people, they drank fine *sake* and lived the life of pleasure with rich merchants, "men of the theater," and wicked women. Indeed, these men were no better than common robbers who stole "lunches" from little children. Thus, with the full cooperation of the giant merchant houses of Osaka, they hoarded the supply of rice and channeled the bulk of it to Edo while contemptuously ignoring the spread of famine in the capital area. The situation dictated action on behalf of the people who supported the life of the upper classes, yet lacked adequate channels to express their anguish. "For those of us viewing that agony from the shadows of the grasses," he noted, there was only one course to take: "Respect heaven's command and carry out its wrath."[35]

Although couching his language for peasant uprising in classic Confucian rhetoric, Ōshio directly linked that uprising to the aim of "imperial restoration" in Japan, thus giving to the active consequences of his thought a peculiarly Japanese flavor. Rebellion against the Bakufu "to save the people" was equated with "restoring the moral government of Emperor Jimmu"—and, indeed, of the goddess Amaterasu. In introducing this formula, however, he faced the uncomfortable fact that there was no real "golden age" of imperial justice in Japan, at least not within historical memory, hence his references to mythical figures. But because the Bakufu was not a "dynasty," imperial justice could not occur under its aegis. The Bakufu, in short, was not legitimate and had used intellectual chicanery, the scholarship of deceptive distinctions, to buttress its selfish interests and obfuscate its betrayal of the emperor, a betrayal which had become especially outrageous since Ashikaga Takauji's villainous destruction of the Kemmu Restoration. Until the emperor exercised his rightful power to mete out justice, there could not be peace and harmony in the land.[36]

The erosion of the Chinese historical "model" is readily appar-

---

[35] *Temmei o tatematsuri, tembatsu itasu sōrō. Ibid.*
[36] *Ibid.*

ent in Ōshio's plea for restoration. As a "given" in Japanese history, there was only one dynasty (or the myth of it), not dynasties linked by moral criteria. Yet this dynasty to be "restored" had neither power nor a structure of government to "defend," as had been the case with the Ming loyalists. Ōshio, however, could not speak of the actual weakness of emperors in Japan in terms of moral turpitude. Nor could he admit the impossibility of true justice under a son of heaven (imperial justice, *ōdō*) for Japan. Restoration meant establishing justice for the first time for an emperor without a government. The "model" had become a captive of history, which ideology aimed at transcending.

Perhaps of greater importance for the historian was the potent relationship between emperor and people that Ōshio drew. Famine, ignorance, endemic suffering among the fundamentally good people, and the humiliating house exile of the emperor were part of a single manifestation, as indicated in the Bakufu's refusal to send rice to the Kyoto court with the same arrogant contempt with which it treated lowly men. In heaven's eyes, therefore, the suffering of the people was one and the same with the anguish of the betrayed emperor. It followed that the termination of suffering among the people would be realized in "restoration," in the moral fusion of the two most abused segments of society. Yet this unity must be preceded by the destruction of the intervening network of injustice; thus Heaven's dictate to the sage to lead an armed uprising.[37] In Ōshio's reasoning we see the main ingredients of a political attitude which, in the context of a sharper awareness of history and of technological and other impacts from the West, would recur in similar configurations throughout much of the modern era as justification for "restoration" and just political change vis-à-vis the power structure intervening between emperor and people.

For Ōshio, however, those items had not fallen into place as components of a unified strategy, an item readily apparent even to Yoshida Shōin, who was not a strategist of much renown himself. As best as can be made out, Ōshio's over-all plan, if it

[37] *Ibid.*

can be called that, was to have his vanguard of some twenty men set fire to Osaka as a signal to farmers in the countryside to rush to join his rebellion. In other words, although he appealed primarily to farmers who would provide him with manpower, he planned to trigger the rebellion itself within the city where there was money.

Thus, he dispatched a few of his men into the country to "bribe" men of talent, without regard to status or degree of literacy, to join his rebellion. Moreover, to stir the potentially radical instincts of poor farmers, he encouraged them in his summons to burn and destroy, without fearing the punishment of law, records of personal indebtedness and registrations of all kinds deposited at local offices and village councils.[38] Similarly, he urged them "to kill without hesitation and exception" all officials in their area knowing of Ōshio's revolt.[39] While encouraging these actions, he threatened literate men in the village (priests, doctors, and the "wealthy and elderly") with ruthless punishment for failure to relate the contents of his summons to the illiterate.[40]

While sending his plea to farmers, he laid concrete plans in early October 1836 to trigger the revolt in Osaka by setting fire to the houses of large merchants, confiscating their wealth, and turning a popular peasant army against the centers of Bakufu power. Partly to conceal this plan, Ōshio sent carefully worded appeals to the Osaka magistracy and to giant merchant houses— for example, Kōnoike, Mitsui, Tennōjiya, Hiranoya—to use their authority and wealth to distribute rice among the poor. Meanwhile, however, he proceeded to sell his library to purchase a cannon and some rifles (probably no more than a dozen), hired a specialist on gunnery to train his "vanguard," and collected several hundred swords to distribute along with money to the poor.

Having this general strategy in mind, he promised "the people and farmers" that his revolt would not be a sporadic and momen-

---

[38] *Nengū . . . shokiroku chōmenrui wa subete hikiyaburi yakisute mōsubeshi sōrō. Ibid.*
[39] *Muenryo . . . banjin o nokorazu uchikoroshi mōsubeshi sōrō. Ibid.*
[40] *Ibid.*

tarily destructive "peasant uprising (*ikki*)." It would be sustained until justice was fully realized for the people. Yet, clearly, it was not a belief in the strength of his strategy that made him speak of sustained revolt. Rather it was the conviction that his revolt was based on principle (*dōri*) and on heaven's will, as contrasted, he noted, to those of rebels in the past such as Taira no Masakado and Akechi Mitsuhide who wanted only power.[41] Within this framework, even had he had more time, his rebellion would not have been more effective.

Clearly, Ōshio's structure of ethical ideas could permit him to relate thought to action, but not action to strategic organization. This was fatal to his cause. He did not attempt to ally himself with a lord of a han, for seeking out a friendly patron was a course of action repugnant to his ethics. Furthermore, he did not seriously consider establishing a coalition of farmers and lowly merchants. Even the thought of cultivating a network of secret societies (as in China) was foreign to him. Indeed, during his period of bureaucratic service in Osaka, he had shown only contempt for religious organizations, Buddhist as well as secret "Christian" groups,[42] so that, even while plotting his rebellion, he made no attempt to seek their support. His rebellion was fated to end miserably.

The fires he set on February 19, 1837, raged for two days through one fourth of Osaka, primarily the section occupied by the large merchant houses. But his peasant army did not materialize. The wealth of large merchants he "confiscated" was of such magnitude that it could not be carried away by his vanguard. The volume of silver at Kōnoike alone was prohibitive for this sort of confiscation.[43] The hundreds of swords he had distributed to the townsfolk were used, in a way reminiscent of actions of some Parisians in 1848, to sack silk and *sake* shops rather than to support fully the battle against Bakufu troops. Not having a spontaneous army, he was no match for the Bakufu forces. Despite gunfire and much fury, he did not inflict a single serious casualty on them. The flow of free *sake* came to an abrupt

[41] *Ibid.*
[42] Kōda, *Ōshio*, pp. 44–83.
[43] According to Kōda (*Ōshio* p. 258), 40,000 *ryō* or 160 *kamme*.

halt, ending, for some, two days of festivity. An epidemic followed the fires. And the men who had set out"to save the people" were systematically hunted down and killed or brought to trial in Edo, where only one lived through torture to hear the verdict. Ōshio himself was discovered a month later (March 27) in his hideaway at the home of a friendly merchant between Osaka and Kobe. There he took his life and that of his seriously injured son by sword and by flame, the latter to prevent subsequent mutilation.[44]

If this violent end of Ōshio was miserable, it was consistent with the ethics he taught. For in that final sacrifice to the cause of justice for the people, he became one with loyalist sages of late Ming and with all sages in the Confucian tradition since time immemorial.

The self-destructive implications of Ōshio's thinking were perhaps best understood by the historian Rai San'yō, Ōshio's friend and senior by twelve years. He would have written an introduction for Ōshio's lectures, had not death intervened, because he admired his single-minded and humanitarian dedication to country. Rai, however, accepted the need to rely on reason. He was a poet and a writer of historical prose, he once told Ōshio, because he believed in rational observation and selection (making "distinctions," in Ōshio's view).[45] Although left unmentioned, this view of Rai's probably also explained his fondness for fine drink and exquisite painting. Having this dramatically different philosophy and style of life, Rai easily detected the flaw in Ōshio's belligerent ideology. During a visit sometime in 1833, Rai posted a poem in Ōshio's study. In it Rai first praised Ōshio as the true "child of Yōmei" and then added "I fear only that you will bring misfortune on your extraordinary talent; I pray you sheath your sword after polishing it; Observe [this] poem I leave on the wall."[46] With only slight reworking, these words might well be taken as Ōshio's epitaph in history.

44 Kōda, *Ōshio*, pp. 200–347. See also, Mori Ōgai's colorful account in *Ōshio Heihachirō*.
45 Ōshio, *Senshin*, p. 455.
46 *Ibid.*, p. 469.

However accurate Rai's imagery, it also can obscure Ōshio's significance in late Tokugawa history. Ōshio's significance lies in the intellectual process he went through in advocating engagement in social reality in terms of a set of abstract humanitarian ideas outside the flow of history. In identifying these ideas as absolute constants, he disengaged himself from historical values governing status and commitments of loyalty to lord and kin. The imperative of public action, in turn, dictated reengagement with historical reality in the light of moral values that plainly contradicted the system of knowledge and of social stratification used by the Bakufu. And out of this reengagement, we see a provocative mode of iconoclastic political action emerging from within the samurai elite itself. Simultaneously, we see a groping for a language of political criticism, which gave to Ōyōmei thought a force of its own within a particular historical sequence. In more refined and sophisticated form, it would be used repeatedly by subsequent generations against men in power.

In this language, oppression of "the people and farmers" and rejection of the emperor (son of heaven) in history were expressed as inseparable halves of a single injustice that required resolution or rectification through "restoration." On one hand, the plea of justice for the people was couched in the language of Confucian egalitarianism, the ideal of innate goodness in all men that Ōshio constantly reiterated. If this egalitarianism had strong elitist overtones in the ideal of the "sage," it was, at the same time, the theoretical base on which to "level" society and to judge men other than by genealogy and social function. On the other hand, this egalitarianism was given political content through identification with the romantic idea of realizing justice through restoration, so that the imperial institution itself was being reshaped into a symbol of egalitarianism, the symbol of the collective agony of the people (later its collective glory). And because restoration had yet to be achieved, it also took on apocalyptic coloration despite the conservative implication of the rhetoric. As already mentioned, this did not imply for Ōshio secularizing the Buddhist paradise into a "city of God" on earth,

176

or directing the course of history either in developmental or dialectical fashion toward a secular utopia. It meant for him rectifying evil in a moment and creating a timeless order of justice. Yet, through the notion of total restoration, he had begun to formulate a framework within which to present the case for humane treatment of the oppressed people—primarily farmers for him but not necessarily so for later advocates of restorationism.

It was in the juxtaposition of these images of downtrodden masses and betrayed emperor (expressed in the Imperial Charter Oath of 1868 as "the union of high and low") that Ōshio's philosophical idealism took on political significance. Egalitarianism and imperial justice were both swaddled in the conceptual clothing of absolute moral ideal, gaining the appearance of unchallengeable principles. Thus, an explosive tie was being forged between transcendent ideal and history (later nation). In this relationship, the moral ideal was not being conceptualized as a theory to buttress the status quo or to liberate the individual in the light of a transcendent identity, but to anchor the plea for just transformation in history. It might be suggestive to mention in this connection that the greatest interest in Ōyōmei thought in the modern era came in that period (ca. 1885–1905) when political critics and thinkers were most concerned with unraveling the complex relationship between nationalism and idealism.

Obviously, Ōshio was not alone in shaping the rhetoric of loyalism, and he should be considered in the context of a broader reinforcing development in late Tokugawa history. Yet, perhaps more than others, he provides clear insights into the intellectual connection between the Ōyōmei mode of thought and the samurai psychology of protest ("the spirit of loyalism"). This relationship, moreover, would tend to reaffirm the point of view that sees late Tokugawa loyalism being generated mainly from within the Confucian debate over the proper means by which to grasp moral principle, and less from the reaction to Confucianism in all forms on grounds of distinctive history as articulated by Motoori Morinaga, Hirata Atsutane, and others of the School of National Studies (Kokugaku). At no point do we see Ōshio addressing himself to these proponents of distinctive history. For him, engagement in social reality followed from timeless ethical premises, particularly those held in Ming loyalism. Commitment to those ideas and public action in particular history were not thought of as contradictory, as they would have seemed to those in National Studies. However, in Ōshio's complicated blending of the decidedly antihistorical notion of timeless loyalism with the images inherited from particular history, we see the basis of interconnection between his loyalism and that of National Studies. It was most probably on a basis of that sort that Japanese loyalists of a later day would combine fervent commitment to national history with deep sympathy (and active support) for the rebels of late Ch'ing.

One further general observation might be offered in considering the relationship between Ōyōmei thought and loyalism as seen in Ōshio. The absence of a conscious strategy to forge an alliance between farmers and merchants precludes assessing him primarily in terms of his impact on the immediate political and social environment. It is true that farmers and townsfolk idolized Ōshio for many years after his death, referring to him reverently as "Heihachirō sama," usually in the context of casting opprobrium on Bakufu officials in Osaka. It is also true that leaders of uprisings in Bingo, Echigo, and Settsu within a six-month period after Ōshio's rebellion regarded themselves as "disciples" and "supporters" of Ōshio—thus prolonging the myth that Ōshio had not died. These data, however intriguing, cannot obscure the fact that Ōshio's radicalism did not provide a basis for coordinating his potential followers into a unified structure of protest.[47] Thus, the image entertained by some (especially those searching for an indigenous dialectical process leading to political change) of the Bakufu being shaken at its foundation by Ōshio's rebellion can be misleading. The Bakufu was no doubt concerned, and it made certain during the trial to condemn Ōshio and his men as common criminals and to erase all political significance from the uprising. The Bakufu's con-

[47] This position also has been argued by Okamoto Ryōichi in his *Ōshio Heihachirō*, pp. 110–147.

cern, however, should not be equated with its being structurally challenged in a fundamental sense.

Characterizations that claim such an impact miss the obvious. Ōshio was not a conscious social revolutionary, a point noted by Mori Ōgai in the addendum of his novel, *Ōshio Heihachirō* (1914). His philosophy, Mori observed, could produce neither humane nor "frightening" socialism—the latter no doubt referring to anarchism of the late Meiji. Rather, Ōshio was primarily a religious figure who acted out of moral, not political, impulses. His religiosity, however, was not the secular asceticism underlying the rise of capitalism in Japan, as suggested by some.[48] His internalization of evil was part of a philosophical definition of self as nonself, and this did not have economic implications of the sort discussed by Weber or by Bellah. His religiosity was pointed more generally in the direction of romantic and idealistic nationalism of the modern era. As already noted, he was one of the earliest articulators of the myth of spiritual union between people and emperor as absolute moral virtue. And this political phenomenon does not fall easily within such categories as feudal, antifeudal, progressive, and reactionary.

These, then, are some of the interpretive implications that seem to emerge from an examination of Ōshio Heihachirō. There were in him certain classic characteristics of the hero in Japanese history. Like many others in that catalogue of revered names, he staked his life on an indisputably just cause and went down in defeat and death at the hands of a corrupt bureaucracy and ambitious politicians. But unlike other heroes, he was a belligerent saint, a saint without God or a community of chosen who nonetheless preached immortality in the sacrifice of self in moral public action.

[48] For example, Abe, "Ōshio Heihachirō," 4:281–282. See also, Rekishigaku Kenkyūkai, ed., *Meiji ishinshi kenkyū kōza*, 1:137–146.

179

POLITICAL RECONCILIATION IN THE TOKUGAWA BAKUFU: ABE MASAHIRO AND TOKUGAWA NARIAKI, 1844–1852

Conrad Totman

To be effective, a politician must have a style and employ techniques appropriate to the political system within which he is working. In the Tokugawa system, skill in compromise, a sense of pragmatic caution, and finesse in exploiting elements of status respect and personal obligation were particularly important to a politician. The utility of these skills was evident in Abe Masahiro's handling of Tokugawa Nariaki between 1844 and 1853. As the real leader of the Bakufu, Abe had ample need of Nariaki's cooperation because the latter, as head of the great domain of Mito,[1] was the most influential daimyo in Japan, and his good will was crucial to the success of Abe's administration.

Several factors made it difficult for Abe to deal with Nariaki. First, Mito was one of the *sanke* or "three houses," the three most important Tokugawa-related domains, and the nature of the Bakufu-*sanke* relationship created difficulties for Abe. Some difficulty was inevitable between Bakufu and *sanke* han because they constituted separate but interacting polities, and inescapably policies that benefited one might be harmful, or at least might be regarded as harmful, to the other. In the early Tokugawa period, disagreements springing from such conflicts of interest usually had been subject to comparatively forthright resolution because the leaders of Bakufu and han were ordi-

NOTE: Abbreviations:—*DNIS, Dai Nihon ishin shiryō; ISK, Ishin shiryō kōyō; KNK, Kinsei Nihon kokuminshi; TYK, Tokugawa Yoshinobu kōden.*

[1] The term "Mito lord" is here applied to Nariaki even though after mid–1844 his son Yoshiatsu was the daimyo. In the thought of most of those with whom we are dealing here, Nariaki remained the real lord of Mito.

narily shogun and daimyo respectively, and their formal status and authority relationships coincided with their power relationship: As Table 1 indicates, on all formal counts of status and power a shogun was superior to a *sanke* lord. In terms of author-

Table 1 STATUS RELATIONSHIPS OF TOKUGAWA SHOGUN, TOKUGAWA NARIAKI, AND ABE MASAHIRO

Characteristic	Shogun	Nariaki	Abe
Court rank:[a]	Junior, first rank	Junior, third rank	Junior, fourth rank, lower class
Principal court title:[a]	Minister of the left (sadaijin)	Imperial advisor (sangi)	Chamberlain (jijū)
Other court titles:[a]	Provisional major councillor (gondainagon)	Provisional middle councillor (gonchūnagon)	—
	Great commander of the right imperial bodyguard (ukonoe taishō)	Middle commander of the left imperial bodyguard (sakonoe chūjō)	—
Honorary castle chamber:	—	First (ōrōka)	Fourth (teikannoma)
Putative yield of domain:[b]	Edo: 6,720,000 koku	Mito: 350,000 koku	Fukuyama: 100,000 koku
Vassal force:[c]	35,000	5,000	1,500
Daimyo category:[d]	—	Most honored kinsman of shogun (sanke)	Vassal of shogun (fudai)

[a] Court rank and title relationships are clearly indicated in *Dokushi biyō*, pp. 536–537. Shogunal titles were not completely standardized; those given seemed most common.

[b] The domainal figure for a shogun's domain is house land (*chokuryō*) plus liege vassal (*hatamoto* and *gokenin*) fiefs in the nineteenth century.

[c] The vassal force figure for shogun is the crude estimate of nineteenth-century liege vassals and their retainers given in my *Politics in the Tokugawa Bakufu* pp. 50, 282. The figures for Mito and Fukuyama are rough estimations solely for comparative purposes.

[d] Mito was not only a *sanke* house; it was also the one *sanke* house that had cultivated the convenient myth that the Mito daimyo had a unique and customary role as special advisor to the shogun (*fuku shōgun*).

ity the shogun, as head of the Tokugawa house of which the *sanke* were but junior branches, as liege lord of all the daimyo, and as the emperor's sanctioned military protector, had authority over *sanke* daimyo sufficient to justify the orders he issued them. He convincingly could combine coercion with charges of disloyalty and of conduct unbecoming a junior member of the Tokugawa house.

By the latter half of the Tokugawa period, however, the Bakufu decision-making process had changed considerably, and often the real leader of the Edo government (that is, the man whose active support was essential to convert consequential proposals into policy) was not the shogun but one of his highest vassal officials, the chief of the council of *rōjū*, or *rōjū shuseki*. Because this chief councillor could invoke the shogun's authority in support of his policies, he was able to exercise the Bakufu's institutional authority and use its power to support his programs.[2] However, his own political position was much more vulnerable than that of a shogun: The shogun had no peers and could not be deposed; the chief councillor was but one of several senior councillors, any of whom could assume the *shuseki* role and all of whom were appointed and legitimately could be replaced. A man holding the office of chief councillor thus could exercise great institutional authority, but he did so from a very insecure position.

A chief councillor was particularly disadvantaged when dealing with a *sanke* lord. As Table 1 indicates, his formal personal status was in all ways inferior to that of a *sanke* daimyo. To give orders to such a man meant dictating to a status superior, and because the Tokugawa social ideal was a single diffuse status hierarchy, this could be done effectively only by exercising the greatest tact. The problems arising from this incongruity of status and authority were compounded by the weakness of a chief councillor's political position. Because of his vulnerability he welcomed *sanke* support. But this support could be liability as much as asset for he also needed the support of regular Bakufu officials. Customarily holders of higher Bakufu offices, by tradition *fudai* (vassal) daimyo, were distrustful of any *sanke* lord who seemed to encroach on their monopoly of administrative functions and so tended to resent any official who seemed to rely too heavily on *sanke* advice or support. In sum, the disparities between his personal status, his position in the Bakufu,

---

[2] A *rōjū shuseki* also, of course, had certain traditional authority by virtue of his membership in the council of *rōjū*. George Sansom (*A History of Japan* [Stanford, Calif., 1963], 3.22) lists the *rōjū* authority as specified by Iemitsu in 1634.

and the authority accruing therefrom hampered a chief councillor's efforts to maintain a satisfactory relationship with a *sanke* lord.

The difficulty Abe thus faced, because of his political position and formal relationship to Nariaki, was compounded by particulars of the two men's lives. Nariaki was born in 1800, Abe was born in 1819. Nariaki had become daimyo in 1829; Abe succeeded to his title at Fukuyama in 1836, became a senior councillor in 1843, and rose to head the council in 1845. In both age and experience, then, Abe was decidedly junior to Nariaki. Moreover, the two men were very dissimilar in temperament. Whereas Abe was a cautious leader who evidently saw no mortal weaknesses in the political order and who preferred to avoid unrest and to resolve conflicts by compromise, Nariaki was a highly articulate, strongly opinionated man who saw his society as being in a state of advanced decay and facing an insidious foreign menace, and he found inactivity intolerable and policy compromise abhorrent.

Abe's efforts to deal effectively with Nariaki were also troubled by the fact that managing the Mito lord was only one aspect of his broader attempt to resolve several problems, solutions to which were not always mutually compatible. His most important task, perhaps, was to reduce the extraordinarily high tensions existing between the Bakufu and Mito. To be of value to the Bakufu, however, this task had to be so handled as to contribute to tranquillity within Mito itself. At the same time Abe had to cope with the increasingly frequent foreign requests for provisions, trade, and even diplomatic intercourse, and most of those who faced the question believed that whatever diplomatic policy were pursued must be accompanied by coastal defense preparations. Finally, because regardless of the policies he pursued Abe could do nothing should he fall from office, he had to do his best to preserve his base of power and mollify or thwart any dangerous rivals.

In terms of Abe's policy toward Nariaki, this all added up to a program of restrained courtship. This courtship was essential for Edo-Mito relations because the most vigorous and influential group of Mito vassals fervently supported Nariaki, and Edo could secure this group's good will only by winning Nariaki's favor. Edo's wooing had to be restrained, however, because after mid-1844 Mito was governed by a faction antipathetic to Nariaki, and reckless courting of the Mito lord would only contribute to more unrest and possibly open violence in the han.

For Abe's defense effort, Nariaki's support was invaluable because the Mito lord was strongly committed to defense preparations and because his views commanded the respect of many great daimyo whose support was essential to the success of any major military program. However, for Abe's own political survival, Nariaki's support was almost as much threat as blessing because some important members of Bakufu officialdom regarded him as an outsider threatening their realm of authority. If Abe were to be unseated, it would be by a faction of such officials supporting one of their own, and there was scarcely a better way to generate such a faction than by seeming to foster a threat to the prerogatives of its leading members.

Under the best of circumstances, it is apparent, Abe and Nariaki were not likely to find cooperation easy, and in 1844, when Abe's rise to power at Edo initiated their political relationship, they were already in direct conflict because Abe had just played an instrumental role in stripping Nariaki of his office and casting him into humiliating confinement. It was from this difficult starting point and under these unpromising conditions that Abe succeeded, in part by utilizing the political techniques mentioned at the outset, in healing the harshest and most dangerous quarrel that the Tokugawa family had known in a century. This success assured that the family was unified when confronted by the arrival of Commodore Perry in 1853.

Two Years of Inactivity: 1844/5–1846/5[3]

A decade of growing estrangement between Edo and Mito culminated in 1844/5 when the Bakufu abruptly ordered Nari-

[3] Dates are given here by lunar months and days. "Int.," as in 1852/int.2/19, identifies an intercalary month.

aki to come to Edo, retire as daimyo, and move into strict house arrest at his secondary mansion in the Komagome District. For some time Bakufu leaders had resented his tendency to criticize their governance, offer unsolicited advice, and pursue policies at Mito that created unrest in the han and seemed to them to damage Bakufu prestige.[4] When a factional change at Edo in late 1843 and 1844 weakened support for him within the Bakufu, he was forced from power and his policies repudiated. Yoshiatsu, the twelve-year-old heir, succeeded, but lest the lad prove a loyal disciple of his father, the Bakufu ordered three daimyo from cadet branches of Mito to form a regency (*sanrenji*). Of the three, Matsudaira Yoritane of Takamatsu was dominant, with the lesser daimyo of Moriyama and Fuchū playing supporting roles. In the ensuing purge, dozens of Nariaki's supporters, including Toda Tadakata and Fujita Tōko, were dismissed and, of the active han officials, only Yūki Toraju, who had turned against Nariaki, remained in office.[5]

At the age of forty-four, Nariaki thus was deprived of his position and relegated to close confinement, and Abe Masahiro was directly involved in his downfall. He had carried out the interrogation that set the stage for Nariaki's summons to Edo, and his seal had accompanied that of chief councillor Doi Toshitsura on the summons itself. From this early date in their political relationship Abe was committed, if only as Doi's supporter, to a policy toward the Mito lord that could hardly have been better conceived to assure their permanent estrangement.

For two years after helping to confine Nariaki, Abe showed no interest in altering the situation.[6] Until well into 1845, he was

---

[4] The causes of Nariaki's fall are explored at some length in *TYK*, 1:59–65, and *KNK*, 28:501–508. Material on this matter also can be found in *DNIS*, 1, no. 6:379–389, and in Watanabe Shūjirō, *Abe Masahiro jiseki*, (Tokyo, 1910), 2:412.

[5] *TYK*, 1:66–69; *KNK*, 28:456–508. In his *Itsuji shiho* (*Bakumatsu ishin shiryō sōsho* [Tokyo, 1968], 4:9–10), Matsudaira Yoshinaga suggests personal aspects of Yūki's conflict with Nariaki.

[6] From the first, Nariaki's loyal vassals were unwilling to leave their lord in detention and lobbied vigorously to ease his condition. Evidently in response to their pressure and concurrent unrest at Mito, the Bakufu in late 1844 modified his punishment to a less onerous form of house arrest. This gesture ended the worst of his humiliation and reduced the furor in Mito, but it did not change

busy consolidating his own position as Doi's successor, and during the next year or so, after Abe's central role in affairs became apparent. Nariaki wrote several letters to him that could only reinforce his conviction that the best place for the Mito lord was in confinement.

Nariaki began to write to Abe in the latter part of 1845, initially to criticize Edo's handling of foreign affairs,[7] and then to complain about the Mito regency, but the new chief councillor chose to ignore these criticisms and complaints.[8] The tenor of their relationship was evident in correspondence of 1846/2, when Abe made his first gesture of confidence toward the Mito lord. Early in the month Nariaki asked that the *sanke* lords be shown recent Bakufu correspondence with the Dutch. He wrote in a direct manner, making no particular effort at graciousness, asking bluntly to be shown the documents. He criticized the Bakufu for abandoning in 1842 the *uchi harai* ("shell and repel") policy of driving away all foreign vessels that approached the shore. He advised Abe to bring Ezo under direct Bakufu control and in closing made only a perfunctory apology for the frankness of his letter.[9]

Abe's reply was gracious and conciliatory. In the cover letter accompanying the diplomatic papers, he addressed Nariaki in an extremely formal, elegant, and respectful manner. He made the necessary comments on the weather and Nariaki's health,

---

the complexion of politics at either Mito or Edo because it was accompanied by an order enjoining him from participating in han politics and reaffirming Bakufu support for the regency. *Ishin shi*, 2:64.

[7] Two issues seem particularly to have vexed Nariaki: Bakufu indecision regarding a Dutch request of 1844 for broader commercial contacts and Abe's handling of a shipwreck incident. In 1845/3, an American vessel returned some shipwrecked Japanese sailors to Uraga, and although Bakufu regulations then in force forbade it (*KNK*, 28:229–230), Abe instructed his Uraga *bugyō* that "an interpreter is to warn [the foreigners] that as an expedient for this occasion only, the castaways are to be received at Uraga" (*KNK*, 29:195–196). After these incidents, Nariaki began to express his displeasure with Bakufu policy. Abe limited his replies to formal acknowledgment of the letters. *KNK*, 30:221–239.

[8] Indeed, when in 1845/12 Nariaki wrote a letter to Abe denouncing the regency and asking Abe to admonish it for being severe on his supporters, Abe refused, and instead nine more of Nariaki's supporters were placed in confinement and Yūki Toraju was promoted. *KNK*, 30:280–291; *TYK*, 1: 70.

[9] *DNIS*, 1, no. 1:92–95.

some brief comments on the enclosed papers, and a closing laudatory passage acknowledging the excellence of Nariaki's opinions and expressing his own desire to let the Mito lord know of his admiration.[10]

The laudatory tone did not, of course, deceive Nariaki about his own ineffectiveness, and his frustration was reflected in two critical letters he wrote to Abe after seeing the Dutch correspondence. In his letter of 1846/2/18, Nariaki elaborated his ideas on foreign policy, stressing the need to make samurai aware of the perfidious Dutch menace in order that their élan be stirred and their devotion to military strength intensified, confident that "knowing one's enemy and oneself, in a hundred battles there will be no danger." This being so, he argued, the *uchi harai* law ought to be reasserted and the Dutch so informed, as this would deter them. And should it not do so, a war fought thus would be far less damaging than a war fought as a last resort after heaping concession on concession.

Nariaki spelled out a series of policy recommendations that included again his earlier proposals that the Bakufu assume control of Ezo and let daimyo cast cannon and build naval vessels. He again leveled criticisms at the Bakufu, asserting that "the termination of the *uchi harai* law was extremely regrettable," and, in a blunt attack on a decision Abe had made a year earlier, arguing that "foreign vessels are to be informed that even castaways shall not be received." He attacked Abe for replying to the Dutch letter in Chinese rather than Japanese written style and, in his rather more testy letter of 2/29, attributed the blunders in handling the Dutch to Bakufu failure to consult with the *sanke* daimyo. He complained that "in previous years the Bakufu from time to time consulted [us] on political matters . . . [but] since Mizuno Tadakuni rose to high office, there has been no consultation and the *sanke* are treated like *tozama* [outside] daimyo." This theme he repeated three times in the course of the letter, finally apologizing for raising the issue and observing acidly that his advice at that point was of little use in the Dutch affair any-

---

10 *Ibid.*, 1, no. 1:95–96.

way, but that he hoped in the future such a development would not recur.[11]

To these letters of uninvited criticism and advice Abe made no reply and, as winter passed to spring, there was no noticeable change in his attitude toward Nariaki despite the continuing agitation of Mito vassals.[12]

For Nariaki, the years since his confinement had shown a very small yield indeed, but from Abe's vantage point things looked rather more agreeable. The damage already had been done; his relationship to Nariaki could hardly worsen, and even if it did the Mito lord was in no position really to trouble him. Nariaki's views on *uchi harai* made cooperation on foreign policy rather awkward,[13] and his concept of the *sanke* role at Edo was not very welcome, but the Mito lord's letters had made it clear that the two agreed on the importance of improving coastal defenses, and this agreement could become the key to an improvement of Edo-Mito relations should Abe choose to utilize it.

ABE, NARIAKI, AND THE FOREIGN INCIDENT OF 1846

In mid-1846, Abe was confronted by simultaneous French and American requests for commercial contacts, the French in the

---

[11] *Ibid.*, 1, no. 1:97–100, 103, 120–122.

[12] *TYK*, 1:70; *DNIS*, 1, no. 1: 265–268, 282–289.

[13] This is not to say that Abe opposed *uchi harai* in principle; to the contrary, he probably favored it, but when the principle threatened to lead to conflict, he preferred compromise. Abe's foreign policy views were neither clear nor fixed. In part they may have been shaped by his prior Confucian training, but by the 1840's they were shaped as much by his political affiliations and the course of events. Thus, as Bakufu leader of the anti-Mizuno faction in 1844–1845, he led the final stages of the purge of Mizuno's followers, some of whom were men such as Takashima Shūhan, men familiar with Dutch learning and Western military technology (*KNK*, 29:158–184), who warned that a direct confrontation with the Western powers would be disastrous and that Western military techniques should be adopted. By the late 1840's and 1850's, however, Abe was more and more listening to the advice of these men or their spiritual heirs. At the time of the Morrison debate in 1838, Abe had opposed repeal of the *uchi harai* law (Watanabe, *Abe Masahiro jiseki*, 1:72–73). He opposed the Dutch request of 1844, and as late as 1846/4/28, a year after letting castaways land at Uraga just outside Edo Bay, he in effect instructed the daimyo of Kawagoe, in a clearly qualified way, to apply *uchi harai* to any foreign ships that entered Edo Bay itself. (*DNIS*, 1, no. 1:446). But in the dilemma two months later, he made

Ryukyus and the Americans in Edo Bay itself. Although both requests came to naught, they thoroughly alarmed the Bakufu and embarrassed Abe. He began to regard Nariaki as a desirable political ally, particularly as a staunch supporter of the defense program that he had initiated, and so his handling of Nariaki began to change.

Initially Abe's response to the French request for Ryukyuan trade only complicated his relations with Nariaki because it heightened the latter's distrust of him. Abe had instructed Shimazu Narioki of Satsuma to handle the French request peacefully, even if it led to trading with France in the Ryukyus, but he insisted that these Bakufu instructions be kept secret.[14] Nariaki evidently grew suspicious when he received no official notice of a Bakufu decision in the matter,[15] and in a letter to Abe on 1846/6/17, he discoursed at length and in a critical tone on the importance of forbidding trade even in the Ryukyus, of reviving the *uchi harai* law to stop the constant approach of foreign ships, and of undertaking vigorous defense preparations, especially the construction of large warships.[16]

Abe recognized the danger in his situation. His secret agreement with Shimazu left him exposed to serious criticism. Many Bakufu officials were unhappy with his concessive policy, and it might in the end ruin his relations with Shogun Ieyoshi. He scarcely could afford to let Nariaki criticize him without reply, and so he conceded a measure in his handling of the Mito lord. For the first time since rising to power, on 1846/7/8 he sent him a long explanatory letter couched in a conciliatory—and evasive —style. After the usual epistolary formalities he agreed to let Nariaki see the correspondence with the American Commodore James Biddle, whose request for commercial and diplomatic contacts directly with the Bakufu had been summarily rejected, and he then proceeded to deal with Nariaki's complaints. Abe wrote, in part,

---

massive concessions in the Ryukyus, and in succeeding years he never agreed to Nariaki's requests for the revival of *uchi harai.*

[14] *DNIS,* 1, no. 2:1–9, 30:30–45.

[15] *KNK,* 30:256.

[16] *DNIS,* 1, no. 2:303–307.

Failure to reissue the notice of 1825 in its original form as an order to "shell and repel with no second thought" is really bad for the future of Japan. . . . Certainly [the foreign encroachment] justifies reissuing this *uchi harai* law, but at present one can scarcely say that our coastal defense preparations are fully completed. There would be occasions when enforcing the law would invite conflict, and in the event we reissued the *uchi harai* order and the foreigners retaliated, it would be a hopeless contest, and there would be no worse disgrace for Japan. Therefore, starting at Uraga Bay . . . we shall prepare our defenses . . . and when we can fight effectively, we shall revive the law. This matter is now under discussion.

On the matter of warships, I have read your earlier memorials on the topic, and indeed I agree with you. Japanese cargo ships and the like, which even have to be rowed in high seas, certainly are unable to fight the foreign ships. . . . Recently a French vessel that came to the Ryukyus requested a trade agreement, but it would be most difficult for Japan ever to permit this. Affairs in the Ryukyus have been entrusted to Shimazu Narioki, and in this present matter he is exercising the greatest wisdom in handling affairs. In fact, the shogun directly instructed him to preserve the *kokutai*, to exercise restraint and adaptability, and in no case to leave seeds of future trouble. However, [because the Ryukyus are particularly defenseless and we have no adequate vessels], if we do not first construct warships, we cannot expect in the future to defend ourselves and fight freely. Therefore, we are now considering permitting the construction of seaworthy vessels along the coast at Uraga, Nagasaki, Matsumae, and Satsuma, and after Bakufu vessels have been built, depending on the situation, we may permit others also to build such ships.

Regarding the provisions requested by the foreigners who came to Uraga Bay, your arguments [against providing such provisions] are entirely reasonable. . . . However, the Uraga magistrate [*bugyō*] inquired if he should provide food, fuel, and water on request, and he was instructed that if strongly asked, he should provide fuel and water, but that it would be difficult to provide food. Nevertheless, if the crewmen faced starvation and vigorous requests were made, he was to provide some foodstuffs.[17]

Thus, although agreeing on the desirability of reviving the *uchi harai* law, Abe made it dependent on effective defense preparation. Although agreeing with Nariaki's advice on the construction of warships, he indicated that if the Bakufu decided to build them at all, their use in the foreseeable future would remain subject to Bakufu control. On the Ryukyus matter, he equivocated as best he could and tried to deflect Nariaki's attention by discussion of the warship proposal. And even as he agreed that it was important not to allow foreigners to trade, he indicated that he would permit them to obtain necessary provisions. And lest Nariaki be distrustful, he promised in closing to show him all records of such transactions.

It was hardly a reply whose policy content would cheer him, but Nariaki recognized immediately that in replying at all Abe had made a political concession. He then tried to extract further concessions in a series of letters to both Abe and Lady Anenokōji, probably the most influential lady in the shogun's household.[18] Failing to make headway, he finally modified his own position in a letter of 1846/8/6, addressed directly to Ieyoshi and sent by way of Anenokōji. He explained the modification thus:

> [Because of the foreigners' military power], Japan in her present state is far too weak simply to proclaim the *uchi harai* edict. Therefore, starting in places like Uraga, both the Bakufu and those daimyo with coastal domains should prepare defenses vigorously. Also for protection against the foreigners, the Bakufu should allow daimyo, beginning with the *sanke* lords, to construct warships. Ordering these things as soon as possible and announcing with unyielding resolution that internal preparations are to be advanced rapidly, diligent efforts will be made and then the *uchi harai* policy can be applied effectively.[19]

[17] *Ibid.*, 1, no. 2:308–312.
[18] *Ibid.*, 1, no. 2:313–38, 487–495, 498–499, 557–562.
[19] *Ibid.*, 1, no. 2:500.

This shift in priorities brought Nariaki much closer to Abe's view, despite their obvious disagreement on arming daimyo, and six days later the chief councillor in effect informed him of this by reporting that Ieyoshi approved his opinions on coastal defense and by inviting him to continue expressing them. In the same letter, however, Abe parried another of Nariaki's requests by arguing that because of the need for prompt decisions, Bakufu officials could not possibly consult directly with the great related daimyo.[20]

In the months following Biddle's visit, Abe put great effort into defense preparations, and this program undoubtedly helped to mollify the Mito lord despite Abe's reluctance to adopt his more extreme proposals.[21] Then as a New Year's gesture on 1846/12/28, Abe ordered Nariaki's vassals Toda and Fujita released from strict house arrest. When he informed Mito of their release, he ordered that they not be readmitted to han office, but even so Nariaki could hardly resent the action, and his acknowledgment of Abe's gesture was couched in terms of gratitude and respect absent from earlier communications.[22]

The foreign incident of 1846 had given Abe reason to welcome Nariaki's support, and in this new situation both men compromised other points—Abe his refusal to discuss policy with Nariaki and the latter his insistence on immediate *uchi harai*—and so their relationship began to change from total hostility to

[20] *Ibid.*, 1, no. 2:555–556.

[21] Abe's defense policy was essentially an intense application of well-sanctioned techniques. He ordered the han to carry out the defensive enterprises, whereas the Bakufu functioned primarily as a coordinating agent and reservoir of funds should they be necessary. And in keeping with tradition, he concentrated most of his endeavors in the Kantō region. Thus, during 1846/7, he ordered Asano of Hiroshima to add his great strength to that of Kawagoe and Oshi, already active in the coastal defense work near Edo. In following months Abe kept in touch with the work of these daimyo as they dispatched troops, opened up training areas and billets, laid up military stores, built modest breastworks, and carried out various studies of more elaborate work to be done at selected points. With each passing month he received reports and opinions on defense needs and progress made. *ISK*, 1:27–53, cites documents relating to defense activities during this period.

[22] *DNIS*, 1, no. 3:557–558, 559–560. Besides Toda and Fujita, Imai Korenori also was released at this time. Shibusawa attributes their release in part to Abe's sympathy for their plight and in part to pressure emanating from the shogunal household as a result of agitation by Nariaki's vassals. *TYK*, 1:71.

limited cooperation. Cooperation could not for long be limited to the issue of coastal defense, however, because of the eclectic nature of Nariaki's interests and the interconnections of Abe's problems. Following the line implied in his release of Toda and Fujita, Abe departed in mid-1847 from his policy of the previous three years and began again to interfere in the internal affairs of Mito han.

MAJOR STEPS TOWARD RECONCILIATION: 1847/5–1849/6

In three successive spurts of Bakufu interference at Mito during 1847, 1848, and 1849, Abe tried to solidify his ties to Nariaki, improve the broader Mito-Edo relationship, and still ensure tranquillity in the han. During early 1847, while devoting his energies to coastal defense,[23] he still adhered to his policy of nonintervention at Mito, but in 1847/5, after Nariaki had asked him to make Mito leaders invigorate the han military program, Abe wrote what was to be his last defense of nonintervention.

> In the matter of military drill at Mito, you are entirely correct in arguing that it is quite unacceptable in these critical days for a situation to persist in which one cannot even carry on a daily training program. I gather that you want us to intercede in this matter of military training as well as in other things, but how would it be if we senior councillors were to issue a formal statement when there had been no inquiry through regular administrative channels? Rather, you should first approach Yoritane to seek a private settlement. Then, if necessary, we

[23] On 1847/1/22, an inspection report by Bakufu officials indicated that more coastal batteries were still needed along the Edo Bay coastline, that warships for coastal defense must be constructed, that more troops were needed at Uraga, and that han carrying the defense burden needed more financial assistance, perhaps as much as 3,500 ryō per year (*DNIS*, 1, no. 3:741–748). In his 1847 effort, Abe ordered further changes in the Edo Bay defense setup, instructing Hikone and Aizu to assist Oshi and Kawagoe in the construction of coastal batteries in the area. During the following several months, leaders of these han received detailed instructions from Edo, studied their problems, made specific policy recommendations to the Bakufu, started sending more troops and building batteries and breastworks, and submitted to periodic inspections of their work by Bakufu officials. *ISK*, 1:60–92, cites documents relating to defense activities during this period.

can justifiably intervene. . . . [As for the ill treatment of your doctors], a senior councillor order is unsuitable there also. . . . In one way or another arrange a compromise with Yoritane and get his agreement and that of the Mito elders. The Bakufu will then not take notice of the matter, and so an official inquiry will be unnecessary and you should be able to arrange matters as you wish.[24]

Abe thus indicated his reluctance to inject himself directly and openly into Mito affairs on the side of Nariaki, but his letter also revealed both his preference for the latter's policies and the inadequacy of his own nonintervention policy. Nariaki's emphasis on han military preparation had suggested a direct connection between Mito affairs and the Bakufu defense program, and during the following months Abe initiated a discreet investigation of Mito government in which Bakufu investigators accumulated substantial testimony critical of regency leadership and strongly in Nariaki's favor.[25]

Then in 1847/7, even as the investigation progressed, a fortuitous dynastic misfortune provided Abe with an opportunity to put Nariaki yet more deeply in his debt. The lord of the Tokugawa branch house of Hitotsubashi died without a successor, and the field of desirable and eligible replacements was so limited that Nariaki's seventh child, Yoshinobu, became a major candidate.[26] Backed by some of Nariaki's supporters in Mito, by Abe and his followers at Edo, by some ladies in the shogun's household, and personally favored by Ieyoshi, the ten-year-old lad was named to head the Hitotsubashi house on 1847/8/25, becoming thereby a very possible successor to Ieyoshi's heir and sole surviving son, the childless twenty-three-year-old Iesada. Nariaki's gratitude showed clearly through the ritual protests in his letter accepting the Bakufu request that he give the boy to Hitotsubashi.[27]

24 *DNIS*, 1, no. 5:360–363, 364–365.
25 *Ibid.*, 1, no. 6:377–389.
26 Yoshinobu (Keiki) was then known by his childhood name of Shichirōmaro. In 1867/2, the Bakufu announced that his adult name would be pronounced Yoshihisa, but the pronunciations Yoshinobu and Keiki have been more commonly used by historians. *ISK*, 7:54.
27 *TYK*, 1:73–94; 5:56–57, 88–89.

Yoshinobu's appointment upset the men in control at Mito almost as much as it gratified Nariaki. They interpreted it as further evidence of Abe's wooing of Nariaki, and at Mito both Abe and Nariaki were severely criticized.[28]

The fears hidden in this bellicosity were soon justified: the investigation of Mito had gone poorly for the regency, and on 1847/9/22 Abe made a thorough personal inquiry into the alleged abuses of han elder [*karō*] Yūki Toraju, found his conduct unsatisfactory, and, abandoning his aloof position of four months before, advised the han to remove him from office.[29] On the same day Abe permitted Toda and Fujita to end their self-enforced inactivity and advised the han to release several political prisoners.[30]

At the same time, however, Abe again forbade these men to become active in han politics, and for months thereafter he made no further concessions. By placing Yoshinobu at Hitotsubashi, he had put Nariaki in the position of moral debtor and, having the political advantage, he was satisfied to alleviate the harshest of the penalties that Nariaki's followers still endured. He had no desire to let the group regain power and again create turmoil. As though to make this position plain, shortly before the New Year the Bakufu expressed its gratitude to Yoritane for his work in keeping Mito stable.[31]

---

[28] Watanabe, *Abe Masahiro jiseki*, 2:417.

[29] A contemporaneous incident seems to have compounded Abe's discontent with the Mito leadership. Even as the investigation was in progress, on 1847/7/12 Abe had instructed the *sanke* to enhance their own military preparedness, "for the *sanke* lords serve as guides for other daimyo in every sort of affair." In none of the three was there a favorable response, however, and in Mito leaders suppressed the instructions entirely. News of this suppression later reached Abe and undoubtedly helped to undermine his confidence in the regency. *DNIS*, 1, no. 6:453–457.

[30] *ISK*, 1:106, 112. Imai reportedly died of illness on 1847/9/23. Self-enforced inactivity was the state that Toda and Fujita had enjoyed after their release from strict house arrest in 1846/12. The nuances of political restraint rarely have been more thoroughly developed than in Tokugawa Japan.

[31] *ISK*, 1:119. The gains Abe made in his courting of Nariaki during the latter half of 1847 were partly offset by a renewal of Nariaki's discontent with his foreign policy. A Korean embassy was invited to visit Osaka, and this aroused Nariaki's suspicions of Bakufu weakness and foreign plots, and led him to reiterate his criticisms of the Bakufu, the repeal of *uchi harai*, and the admission of foreigners to the Ryukyus. Again he urged Abe to consult with the daimyo,

The winter passed and late in 1848/3 Yoshiatsu's hair was cut to classic *bushi* lines. Within a month rumors were circulating that the regency soon would be discontinued and the government of Mito turned over to the young daimyo. The ingratiating effect of this rumor, as well as gestures of good will that the Bakufu made toward Hitotsubashi Yoshinobu at this time, probably were responsible for an uncommonly mellow letter that Nariaki sent to Abe.[32]

> On the second day of the month, for the first time since entering the Hitotsubashi mansion, Yoshinobu came to visit me and we talked together about various matters. I heard that since his move to Hitotsubashi the shogun has become closer to him and given him many gifts. I am utterly unworthy of all this; he is indeed fortunate. Perhaps because he now goes to the castle frequently, his deportment is much improved, and this pleases me greatly. I also have heard that since his first visit to the castle you too have assisted him in many ways, and I am profoundly grateful for this, because, as you can see, he is such a country bumpkin. I rely especially on this guidance that you are giving him.[33]

Undoubtedly these kind words were welcome to Abe, but he still was unready to end the regency and let Nariaki or his supporters manage Mito affairs. Instead, he intensified his attempts to heal the breach within the han. On 1848/6/1, Yoshiatsu was formally summoned to Edo castle and warned about alleged abuses by the Mito government since the regency's establishment.[34] However, when shortly thereafter Yoshiatsu suggested,

---

and again Abe tried to quiet him, this time by citing historical precedents, assuring him that the Koreans were peaceful, and indicating that he had shown the Mito lord's comments to Ieyoshi, but insisting that it was difficult to change policy abruptly. *DNIS*, 1, no. 7:360–388.

[32] *TYK*, 1:93, *ISK*, 1:143. On 1848/3/16, Ieyoshi visited Yoshinobu at his Hitotsubashi mansion and on 5/2, with Bakufu permission, Yoshinobu called on Nariaki at his Komagome mansion.

[33] *KNK*, 30:342–343. At about this time Nariaki also made a rare statement of confidence in Abe in a letter to Takahashi Taichirō, the vassal who had lobbied most effectively on his behalf all these years. Watanabe, *Abe Masahiro jiseki*, 2:419.

[34] *ISK*, 1:149.

perhaps at Nariaki's urging,[35] that the regency be dissolved, Abe disapproved, explaining his position in some detail.

He wrote Yoshiatsu: "I have discussed this matter in detail with my colleagues . . . and it seemed to us that it would be difficult right now to issue a notice dissolving the regency. But as you are gradually growing older, and especially now that your childhood hair has been cut, the regency will not remain indefinitely." He then gave the sixteen-year-old boy a fatherly Confucian lecture on good governance:

> [As you know], you should be especially diligent in pursuit of the civil and military arts and also, of course, in the discharge of filial duties. And in governing Mito, you should show absolutely no partiality in meting out rewards and punishments. You should feel compassion for your people and on all matters issue instructions accordingly. To have factional divisions among your vassals is a matter of the greatest concern, for with factions there can be no good government. You should consider matters carefully, and sincerely set an example for others. Because the administration of your house is widely regarded as a model for the daimyo, we wish you to be most diligent.

Abe extolled Nariaki, explicitly pointing out,

> From the beginning of his administration, he made special efforts to nourish his fief, reformed ostentatious manners, and thoroughly invigorated study of the civil and military arts, and in 1843 he was given exceptional commendation by the shogun. For years he has labored mightily on defense against foreigners and has prepared coastal defenses on his lands, and his exertions in these matters have been entirely appropriate.

Since Nariaki's day, Abe went on, Mito administration reportedly had been lax, and although that situation did not warrant extensive administrative changes, it was not desirable. "At present the regents and elders are giving the utmost attention and taking the greatest trouble in these matters, but gradually as you grow older, you will not be able simply to delegate all

[35] *KNK*, 30:338.

matters to them." Therefore, Abe concluded, Yoshiatsu ought not always to rely on the word of his regents and elders, but should use his own mind and heart in making decisions.[36]

In short, the regency was to remain, and Yoshiatsu was to continue to cooperate with the existing leadership, despite deficiencies in its record. However, Abe had praised Nariaki as never before, had spelled out very directly his preference for Nariaki's policies, and had suggested Yoshiatsu's responsibility for seeing that these preferences were reflected in Mito policy.

In his letters Abe did his best to avoid offending the Mito leaders, but understandably they had not appreciated his active intervention during 1847 and 1848, and gradually they found allies among Bakufu officials and advisory daimyo who for reasons of their own were dissatisfied with Abe's leadership.

Abe's moves during 1847 had stimulated dissident activities, and by early 1848 there had appeared at Edo a full-fledged anti-Abe faction headed by senior councillor Aoyama Tadanaga.[37] During the first half of 1848, Aoyama's group acquired more reason to resist as Abe pushed on with his defense effort and made further moves to attract Nariaki.[38] Although Abe left the regency intact in 1848/6, his mounting pressure dismayed Yori-

---

[36] *Ibid.*, 30:338–340. It is perhaps indicative of Abe's tortuous path that in discussing Nariaki's past he dismissed lightly the events of 1844 and instead cited the praise given Nariaki in 1843 by Mizuno Tadakuni, whom he had punished two years later.

[37] During 1847, Aoyama allegedly cooperated with Yoritane and certain lesser Bakufu officials to unseat Abe, but the latter was able to override their opposition and continue his programs (Watanabe, *Abe Masahiro jiseki*, 1:55–57; Nakamura Katsumaro, *Ii tairō to kaikō* (Tokyo, 1921), pp. 104–105, 132, 155–156). Born in 1807, the son of a highly regarded *rōjū*, Aoyama was Abe's senior by twelve years, had held office longer than he, and had been deprived of a regular promotion to *rōjū* in 1843 when Abe had bypassed him. Previously Abe had been his subordinate when Aoyama was the chief *jisha bugyō*, and apparently their relationship even then had not been good. Presumably Aoyama was not pleased to find himself subordinate to the man who once had been his underling and who had risen to high office with inordinate speed.

[38] During 1848, Abe gradually broadened the scope of the Bakufu program of military strength, involving some *tozama* daimyo, keeping pressure on the *sanke*, following closely the activities of the four han charged with Edo defense work, adding forces at Uraga, and instructing certain han to construct more than one hundred canon for coastal deployment by the Bakufu. *ISK*, 1:95–150, cites documents relating to defense activities during this period. The order for cannon is cited on page 114.

tane, his supporters, and their factional allies at Edo and at last brought the anti-Abe movement to a climax. Aoyama made the classic protest of a Bakufu high official: After a few days of official "illness," he informed the shogun early in 1848/7 of his wish to resign. Ieyoshi properly refused to permit this, but, perhaps at Abe's suggestion, he did agree to let Aoyama rest for awhile, thus quietly deflecting the latter's attempt to sway him into restraining Abe, and the pressure on Mito continued. In response, on 1848/8/6, Yoritane and his two colleagues in the regency admonished Nariaki directly for stirring up trouble in the han, and the latter immediately sent letters to Yoritane and Abe defending his own behavior. Abe apparently believed that the Mito leaders dared thus openly attack Nariaki (and by implication himself) and also foster ill will between Yoshiatsu and the Bakufu because of their ties to Aoyama, and at last during 1848/9 he evidently induced Aoyama again to offer his resignation and the shogun that time to accept it.[39]

Although Aoyama's fall robbed Abe's enemies of their legitimate leader and left them ineffective, for several months after this clash there seems to have been a distinct decline in the vigor with which Abe pushed his programs.[40] It is difficult to tell whether this reflects the chastening effect on him of the recent contention at Edo, or whether it merely reflects the cyclic and deliberate quality in his approach to both the Mito and foreign problems. In any case, it was a winter of uncommon quietude at Edo. Late in the year the Bakufu began to prepare for the eventual marriages of both Yoshiatsu and Yoshinobu, and after

[39] *Ibid.*, 1:157. Information on the conflict between Aoyama and Abe is very scarce. My sources (Watanabe and *KNK*, primarily) seem eventually to trace back to a few comments made by Takahashi Taichirō in his memoirs, *Enkinkō*. Takahashi was not, of course, a disinterested observer, but his incessant lobbying on Nariaki's behalf during these years kept him uncommonly well informed about Edo affairs.

[40] There seems to have been a perceptible slowing of Abe's defense program after the intensive effort of early 1847, in part perhaps because the foreign danger lost its immediacy as the scare of 1846 receded in memory. But the tempo probably slowed as well because the limited programs that had been undertaken were being completed and because earlier enthusiasm waned, among the han as finances grew strained, at Edo as the political cost began to mount. *ISK*, 1:154–193, cites documents pertaining to the defense effort during the period 1848/7–1849/3.

that the next politically significant act in regard to Mito was the termination of the regency in 1849/3.[41] At that time the Bakufu also canceled the order proscribing Nariaki's involvement in han affairs.

In a rather lengthy letter, the senior councillors formally notified Nariaki that "because Yoshiatsu has grown older, the regency has today been ordered abolished . . . and the shogun has expressed his wish that henceforth the order proscribing your political activity be canceled." Then, after pointing out the shogun's concern that Nariaki help Yoshiatsu, the councillors dwelt at length on the dangers of factionalism. "It is necessary to be as just and broadminded as possible. In general, the failure to preserve harmony among your vassals during recent years was due to a tendency to go to extremes in handling affairs. Therefore, we wish you to give matters earnest solicitude and not to fail to discuss them with others." The councillors informed Nariaki that Toda and Fujita were to remain out of politics and acknowledged that many others of Nariaki's men were still in confinement. They refused to release all these men at once, but observed that "it will be appropriate as the years pass gradually to extend compassion to them." They admonished Nariaki to exercise restraint in his selection of personnel:

> It cannot be denied that, as in the unexpected case of Yūki Toraju which you mentioned previously, one who is thought to be entirely loyal may at that very time be sullying one's judgment. Consequently one should forbear from recommending for office only his sympathizers. In any case, when one employs procedures that create factions, from first to last he is most unlikely to enjoy even a moment of harmony. After all, as there is no vassal who desires the collapse of his lord's house, it is of utmost importance that you manage affairs with an earnest impartiality and thus assure the shogun's peace of mind.[42]

[41] *Ibid.*, 1:168, 174, 191. The arranging of a shogunal hunting expedition in 1849/2 provided opportunity for ceremonial exchanges with Nariaki and probably fostered an environment favorable to the actions of the next month. *KNK*, 30:356–361.

[42] *KNK*, 30:352–355.

Abe thus had granted Nariaki's faction one of its greatest wishes. But he had done it in such a way as to assure that the existing leadership in the han could not be thrown out and that Nariaki's men could not take office.[43]

During the next three months Abe felt compelled to make a few more moves in his quest for a stable and reasonably harmonious settlement at Mito. More of Nariaki's followers were released from confinement, and in 1849/6 when the Mito lord asked him to make further personnel changes, Abe instructed Yoshiatsu to reappoint as elder a vassal who, Abe hoped, would bridge the factional chasm. At the same time he tried to amalgamate the groups of major vassals advising Yoshiatsu at his Koishikawa mansion and Nariaki at Komagome by instructing Yoshiatsu's officials to keep the Komagome group informed of their policy decisions. However, Abe refused to order the dismissal of those high han officials whom Nariaki had denounced, asserting that the latter had not demonstrated their shortcomings. He added, by way of keeping Nariaki's courage up, that he would be willing to consider the matter again at the end of the year.[44]

Between 1847 and 1849, the chief councillor had actively interfered in Mito affairs. He had ousted Yūki Toraju, had ended many of the disabilities of Nariaki's men, had urged Yoshiatsu to emulate his father, had criticized and finally abolished the regency, had allowed Nariaki—in principle—to assume a political role, and then had tried to stimulate the development of a han leadership that would heal the factional division. Although he carefully had kept Nariaki and his followers from returning to undisputed control, the anti-Nariaki forces nevertheless had found his policies unacceptable, had tried to resist at Edo, and had been defeated.

Abe's attempt to avoid further factionalism at Mito served, however, to prevent Nariaki from shaping policy within the han. Mito leadership was not really unified, the han did not con-

[43] *Ibid.*, 30:366; *TYK*, 1:96–98.
[44] *ISK*, 1:196, 211, 212; *TYK*, 1:98–99; *KNK*, 30:289–290.

tribute as much to the Bakufu defense effort as Abe wished, and so the chief councillor still had reason to seek further changes there.

RECONCILIATION COMPLETED: 1851/3–1852/12

The final adjustment of the Abe-Nariaki relationship in 1851–1852 followed a period of well over a year, from the latter part of 1849 until early in 1851, during which Abe refrained from further political interference at Mito. The inaction of this period probably stemmed from the difficulty he experienced in reconciling his several policies. Thus, his earlier actions had much improved his relationship with Nariaki: The latter was supporting his defense effort at Edo, and there was no likelihood of any Bakufu rival wooing the Mito lord from him. However, these same actions had precipitated serious countermoves, and though Abe had weathered the storm of 1848, he could reasonably assume that further moves on Nariaki's behalf would only generate more resistance. This was particularly likely after mid–1849 when Abe again revitalized his coastal defense effort despite the discontent it generated.[45]

[45] During this period Abe at last began to pressure the Bakufu elite *ban* forces and liege vassals in general (*hatamoto* and *gokenin*) into intensified military training. And more pressure was brought to bear on the han. By late 1849, a flood of reports informed Abe of the great enterprises being launched by many, many han. Within this flow of verbal rearmament was a core of real effort. In the han guns and cannon were cast, men were trained, and castles were repaired. An increasing number of han obtained permission from the Bakufu to train troops in Edo and to increase their garrisons there, and *bushi* began to take a revived interest in improved military techniques, both conventional and Western. Documents pertaining to the defense effort of 1849/4–1850/3 are cited in *ISK*, 1:208–249.

The defense effort was being undertaken with the resources at hand, and in many cases these soon proved inadequate for they were not accompanied by any changes in *bushi* consumption habits. The defense program was probably a significant factor in the financial disruption at this time of such han as Himeji, Kawagoe, Mito, Tottori, and Tsushima, and may have been a factor in Kii, Ōgaki, and Owari. In Kawagoe, long burdened with special Kantō coastal defense obligations, the problem became very serious and required considerable remedial attention. The Bakufu moved to assist a number of han, usually with loans and grants of money or land as opportunity and need dictated. Documents concerning han difficulties are cited extensively in *ISK*, vol. 1, for the years 1847–1852. *KNK*, 29:331–338.

Abe Masahiro and Tokugawa Nariaki, 1844–1852

During 1850, Abe was able to play family politics with unusual success, allowing two of Nariaki's children to enter major *tozama* families. But the time had passed when he could expect Nariaki to be very grateful for such actions, and in any case these were not plums comparable to the Hitotsubashi appointment of 1847.[46] Whatever good will these moves may have brought Abe was in all likelihood offset by Nariaki's dismay at the worsening economic condition of the han, and Abe's decision finally to intervene again at Mito probably sprang from the hope that political changes would improve the han situation, thereby gratifying Nariaki, reducing tensions within the han, and making it more cooperative, more defense-oriented, and a better model for the other daimyo.[47]

In 1851/3, after an extraordinary interval of sixteen months, Nariaki again wrote Abe to complain of his inability to influence Yoshiatsu and to ask therefore that Abe again help him to change some Mito officials. Abe refused the request but Nariaki persisted, arguing that in the last two years the Bakufu had instructed him to attend to Mito affairs, that he was trying to do so, but that he was concerned because of the tension between himself and Yoshiatsu, because certain "bad men" might engage in desperate activities, and particularly because of rumors of a

[46] In 1847/8, Abe had selected Yoshinobu to be lord of Hitotsubashi. Three months later another of Nariaki's sons, whom the Bakufu had permitted Hamada han to adopt, succeeded to his title there, and in 1848/8 yet another son went to Oshi. Both han were close to the Bakufu and were supporting Abe's defense effort, and these adoptions thus strengthened the Abe-Nariaki defense work association. In 1850/2, the Bakufu allowed the Morioka daimyo to marry a daughter of Nariaki, and in 1850/8, a son of Nariaki was adopted by Tottori. These two were *tozama* domains, and these acts suggest that Abe hoped through Nariaki to draw other daimyo into fuller support of his policies. During 1850, the Bakufu also executed the several ceremonial steps required for the adoption by the shogun of a girl from Kyoto and announcement of her eventual presentation to Yoshiatsu as bride. *TYK*, 1:8–12, 101–102; Watanabe, *Abe Masahirō jiseki*, 2:416; *ISK*, 1:69, 117, 156, 241–288, 310–330.

[47] By 1850/4, the Mito economic situation was serious: Han warehouses were empty, and to ease the crisis, the Bakufu granted the han an immediate loan of 10,000 *ryō*. But financial problems still plagued the house, and by 1851/1 rice prices were inflated so much that the han was giving relief to commoners so that they could feed themselves. Mito was not alone in its trouble, but a crisis of this sort in one of the *sanke* involved the dignity of the Bakufu, and this may have convinced Abe that major changes were needed. *ISK*, 1:253, 290, 295.

poisoning plot. He concluded by arguing that if the "bad men" were removed from office, he and Yoshiatsu could work together harmoniously.[48]

On 1851/4/6, Abe replied, informing Nariaki that the Bakufu was not prepared to order extensive personnel changes, but that he would advise Mito officials first to dismiss two high officials known for their intransigence and then to make office changes in consultation with the Mito lord. He added that henceforth Nariaki was not to involve the Bakufu in Mito affairs. Despite his simultaneous instructions to a Mito elder, however, only a few adjustments were made at the time, hardly enough to satisfy Nariaki, and in 1851/6 the latter again complained to him, reiterating the arguments of his previous letters.[49]

Nonetheless Abe believed that he had done enough. He choose to act no further, and the year passed with only the ritual preparatory to Yoshiatsu's marriage occupying the stage of Mito-Edo relations. But the new year proved Abe's estimate to have been correct. By 1852, the years of pressure and Nariaki's gradual reemergence had apparently demoralized the remnants of the anti-Nariaki faction so completely that even without Abe's intervention Nariaki was able to influence han personnel policies. When further personnel changes were made at Mito, they seem to have been largely a result of Nariaki's restored influence. Despite Yoshiatsu's dismay and without overt pressure from Abe, leaders in the anti-Nariaki faction were removed at last from leading positions. In 1852/int. 2, the Mito government permitted Toda and Fujita again to hold han office, and by the time the personnel changes had run their course in the autumn, scores of han vassals had fallen from or entered office.[50] As many wished, Nariaki was the effective leader, Yoshiatsu was his puppet, and

----

[48] *KNK*, 30:371–375. Probably Nariaki's influence at Mito was rather greater than he cared to have Abe believe. He was not in full control, but even in late 1849, han leaders had pardoned another group of his vassals after he had complained to Abe about han affairs, although Abe seems to have done nothing about the complaint. *TYK*, 1:101; *ISK*, 1:220, 229, 231.

[49] *KNK*, 30:375–379; *TYK*, 1:102; *ISK*, 1:305.

[50] *KNK*, 30:380–382, 385; *TYK*, 1:102; *ISK*, 1:320, 328, 331, 343, 344, 379.

the Bakufu under Abe was content to keep only a distant eye on Mito affairs.

Preparation for the wedding of Yoshiatsu in 1852/11 provided Abe with an opportunity to put the final touch on the reconciliation. On 11/22, Ieyoshi summoned Nariaki to the castle to discuss the ceremony. The full significance of this was grasped at once: Nariaki could again go to the castle. Since that grim day in 1844 when he had been summarily dispatched to Komagome, he had been denied access to the headquarters of his family founder. On this day of triumph he made his way to the castle, met Ieyoshi in state, and returned to his Komagome mansion. And that night the mansion was a scene of the wildest rejoicing with songs and *sake,* food in abundance, dancing, and poetry recitation.[51] The years of isolation had ended.

The New Year of 1853 found Abe Masahiro in fine fettle. He had less reason than the Komagome group for rejoicing, but he could still fairly find satisfaction in the situation. In 1851, he had begun with great apparent reluctance to end the factional deadlock at Mito by easing more men out of han office and letting Nariaki's followers back in. By 1853, the process was complete, and Nariaki's men were as fully in charge of the han as they had been a decade before. But far from being in office despite Bakufu animosity, they were now there only because the shogun's chief councillor had on several occasions actively interfered in the han on their behalf. The relationship between Edo and Mito leadership was better than it had been for at least a decade, and perhaps for over two decades. Although bitterness still existed between factions in the han, it had not erupted into violence despite a total leadership reversal. The faction now in charge at Mito was the one more inclined to support Abe's long-range military preparedness program. Through Nariaki, its leader, Abe had extended his influence among the daimyo further than it ever before had been, and these selfsame ties to Nariaki also assured Abe that this most prestigious and respected related

---

[51] *TYK,* 1:102–105; *ISK,* 1:384, 387.

lord of his day would not become an ally of a rival within the Bakufu. And by minimizing his own role in the final adjustments in the han, Abe was able to avoid the worst of the displeasure of those at Mito and Edo who opposed his ties to Nariaki and the latter's return to power. Two years and dramatic events were to intervene before Abe again faced a major factional challenge to his power.

CONCLUSION

I have treated Abe's rehabilitation of Nariaki as a three-phase development. From Nariaki's incarceration in 1844 until the foreign problem of 1846, Abe made no effort to change Nariaki's political situation and left the anti-Nariaki group in control at Mito. During the next three years, to mid–1849, he actively courted Nariaki and made substantial changes at Mito, ending most disabilities of the Mito lord and his followers and modifying the han leadership to give them a share in policy making. Within two years thereafter, however, it was apparent that this arrangement was unsatisfactory, and Abe then made the few moves necessary to precipitate a final period of adjustment during which Nariaki and his supporters were able to oust the rival faction and reestablish complete control over the han.

On many occasions during this eight-year exercise in political maneuver Abe had demonstrated his skill in compromise, sense of pragmatic caution, and finesse in exploiting elements of status respect and personal obligation. Frequently he adopted positions carefully fashioned to appease both Nariaki and his rivals, and when this was not possible, he did his best to make his decisions palatable to the injured party. He had used many dimensions of his position, such as his control of ceremonial affairs, legal pardons, Tokugawa marriages and adoptions, and gestures of familial solidarity or kindness, in order to reap as much political gain as possible with the slightest expenditure of policy substance or power position.[52] Whenever he made moves that

[52] The *Zoku Tokugawa jikki* (Tokyo, 1906), vol. 3, is almost totally silent about the matters covered in this essay. However, it does contain a number of

had substantive dimensions, he did so only after accounting, as far as possible, for the ramifications of these moves. And after making the moves, he allowed months and even years to elapse in order to gauge the consequences of his action before making further major adjustments.

All this is not to suggest for even a moment that in 1852 Abe completed a policy that he had devised in 1845 or 1846 and meticulously followed thereafter. Almost certainly he had no intention in 1845 of seeing repudiated his work of the year before in helping to depose and confine Nariaki, and in later years it is likely that he would have preferred factional balance at Mito to total revival of Nariaki's domination, but his constant efforts to deal with his several problems relentlessly led to the 1852 outcome.

I have not intended to argue that Abe formulated his policies alone and was impervious to the pressures of opinion that flowed about him. Certainly he responded to these pressures; Nariaki's opinions, those of other Bakufu officials, of consequential *fudai* daimyo, and of his own vassals, and the wishes of men and women close to the shogun all counted. But accommodation of impinging pressures and adoption of useful ideas are in the nature of politics. What marks Abe as an able politician in his handling of Mito is that one can discern in all this adjusting a reasonably clear and consistent line of policy, a line that helped Abe resolve the problems he faced.

Abe took a superlatively cautious approach to politics, and one might suggest that as a consequence his political methods hardly deserve commendation. Yet in terms of his own family position, the position of his political colleagues, and the position of the Tokugawa house—whose welfare he was charged to protect—it can be argued that these were nearly optimal techniques, permitting change while minimizing political discord. To say it differently, they contained both adaptive and stabilizing dimensions that were well suited for coping not only with the Mito

---

entries for these years that suggest the role of ceremony, marriage, and so on in Bakufu dealings with Mito, and I would interpret these as indications of Abe's skill.

problem, but also with the slow incremental domestic problems, such as fiscal inelasticity and widespread status incongruence, that the regime had to resolve if it were long to endure.[53]

[53] By the rubric "status incongruence," I refer to the manifold tensions evident in most ranks of society—samurai, urban commoners, and villagers—as a result of long-range structural changes that gradually had created or magnified a variety of changes in social relationships. Status incongruence is discussed by Andrzej Malewski in Reinhard Bendix and Seymour Lipset, eds., *Class, Status, and Power,* 2nd. ed. (New York, 1966). It is a broader concept than status deprivation as discussed in Everett Hagen's *On the Theory of Social Change* (Homewood, Ill., 1962). Hagen discusses the disruption of Tokugawa Japan primarily in terms of the frustrations of lower-ranking samurai.

SHIMAZU NARIAKIRA AND THE EMERGENCE OF NATIONAL LEADERSHIP IN SATSUMA

Robert K. Sakai

Soon after the conclusion of the Opium War and the signing of the first treaty settlements with China, the Western powers began pressing aggressively for similar treaty arrangements with the Ryukyu Kingdom. Hitherto the affairs of the kingdom had not been of direct concern to the Tokugawa Bakufu; it was left to the government of Satsuma to keep watch over these southern islands as a detached part of its jurisdiction. The coming of foreign warships to the Ryukyu Islands with demands for treaties, however, immediately affected the Bakufu and its responsibilities for national defense. If the Westerners secured a base in Ryukyu, their next target would be Japan proper.

This study is concerned primarily with the effect of the Ryukyu crisis on Bakufu-Satsuma relations and on the interaction between personalities and policy within Satsuma. Though Ryukyu was an area of Satsuma responsibility, the foreign problem there was national in scope. Satsuma was the most powerful of the *tozama* domains, which were considered to be hostile to the Bakufu, but the Ryukyu crisis called for close cooperation between these two political units. If it was difficult for the Bakufu leaders to depart from the traditional practice of deciding all matters of national importance within its own councils, it was even more difficult for some of the Satsuma leaders to lay aside their suspicions and work with the Bakufu toward

NOTE: The author is indebted to the University Research Council, University of Hawaii, for financial support, and to Mrs. Kazuko Yamada for her able research assistance.

209

a policy which sacrificed a measure of han autonomy and self-interest for the national good. The man who most clearly perceived the crisis in national terms was Shimazu Nariakira (1825–1858), but his views were contrary to those of his father, the daimyo of Satsuma.

NATURE OF THE RYUKYU CRISIS

With the beginning of the nineteenth century, an increasing number of Western ships began to appear in the Ryukyu archipelago. Trading ships and whaling vessels in nearby waters, often caught by severe storms, found friendly refuge in the islands. From these incidents the Ryukyuans gained a reputation among Westerners as humane and kindly people. The idea of establishing formal treaty relations with the Ryukyu Kingdom naturally occurred to many.[1]

The Ryukyu government was glad to provide supplies to ships in distress, and they asked no compensation. By declining payment for their goods and services, they wished to make clear that trade was not desired. In response to Western suggestions for treaty relations, the Ryukyu position was that their island economy could not support foreign trade, that their people were content with Confucian, Buddhist, and local religious beliefs and did not wish to be exposed to Christianity, and that future complications could be prevented by minimizing foreign contacts.[2] In short, the Ryukyu officials supported the Tokugawa seclusion policy (though it was never mentioned in these terms to foreigners), and they believed that it served their self-interest. The kindness of the Ryukyuans toward foreigners stemmed not only from their good nature but also from necessity, for the kingdom was stripped of weapons as a result of Satsuma's control policy.[3] Because unwelcome foreigners could not be re-

[1] For a survey of Western contacts with Ryukyu, see Kagoshima-ken, ed. and pub., *Kagoshima kenshi* (Tokyo, 1940), 2:781–812, hereafter *Kenshi;* and George H. Kerr, *Okinawa, the History of an Island People* (Rutland, Vt., and Tokyo, 1958), chap. 6.

[2] These arguments were made repeatedly in the negotiations discussed here.

[3] For a description of the control system, see the author's "The Ryukyu (Liu-ch'iu) Islands as a Fief of Satsuma," in John K. Fairbank, ed., *The Chinese*

pelled by force, the alternative was to provide them with minimum needs and speed them on with Ryukyuan blessings.

The Ryukyuans probably were aware of the dangers of Western contact. An incident which should have dispelled complacency occurred at Tokara Island in 1824, when the crew of a British whaler landed to take on food and water. These supplies always had been furnished willingly, but when the British tried to run off with cattle and horses, they were attacked by the islanders and one of the crew was slain.[4] The shock of this incident motivated the stern Bakufu order of 1825 to drive off foreigners from Japanese waters "without a second thought" (*ninen naku*).

The possibilities for a treaty with Ryukyu were explored tentatively by the British in 1819 and in 1832, but it was not until the French arrived on the *Alcmène* in 1844 that a serious effort was made to conclude an agreement with the kingdom.[5] The French treaty proposal sought to establish friendly diplomatic relations, trade between the two countries, and the right of missionaries to propagate Christianity in the islands.

The French officials, unable to dent the stubbornness of the king's ministers, who rejected the proposal, retired from the islands with a promise to return with a naval fleet in order to obtain a more positive response. Before they left, however, they put ashore a French missionary (Théodore Augustin Forcade) and his Chinese interpreter, and then hastily sailed out before the exasperated Ryukyuans could return the men to the ship. These unwelcome strangers were left behind to study the local language in order to serve as interpreters when the French navy returned.

World Order (Cambridge, Mass., 1968); and for its motivations, "The Satsuma-Ryukyu Trade and the Tokugawa Seclusion Policy," *Journal of Asian Studies*, 23:391–403 (1964).

[4] Kunimitsu-sha, ed. and pub., *Terakuni-kō kankyū roku* (Tokyo, 1899), p. 43, hereafter *Kankyū roku*. The incident also is described in Watanabe Shūjirō, *Abe Masahiro jiseki* (Tokyo, 1910), 1:83–84; *Kenshi*, 2:783; and in Kōshaku Shimazu-ke Hensanjo, ed., *Sappan kaigun shi* (Tokyo, 1928), 1:356, hereafter *Kaigun shi*.

[5] Satsuma's report to the Bakufu on this incident is in *Shimazu Hisamitsu-kō jikki* (Tokyo, 1910), 1:1a-3a, hereafter *Jikki*. See also *Kankyū roku*, pp. 41–45; *Kaigun shi*, 1:393–406; *Kenshi*, 2:787–788.

The mission of the *Alcmène* touched off a lively rivalry between France and Great Britain as to which country would
obtain prior treaty rights with Ryukyu. Their aggressiveness
frightened not only the Ryukyu officials but also the authorities
in Satsuma and Edo. On one occasion Forcade, who was on
Okinawa, the main island of the Ryukyu chain, confided to local
officials that the British planned to establish a trading base on
the island so that they could extend their commercial activities
more readily toward Japan and Korea. He argued that if the
Ryukyu king agreed to the French treaty, France would exert
her influence to ward off British pressures on Ryukyu.[6]

As promised, the French returned with four vessels arriving
successively on the eleventh, twelfth, and thirteenth of the fifth
month, 1846.[7] There were some 1,500 men on board these ships,
and they were permitted by their officers to go ashore freely
and roam the streets of Naha, Shuri, and other communities.
Some rode on horses borrowed from the local people. Others
went to work mapping the terrain of the island or charting the
coastal waters. The presence of so many men was an obvious
show of force to help advance the diplomatic talks.

This second round of negotiations by the French in 1846 began with a banquet for Ryukyu officials on board the commander's ship. The commander's talk, however, about recent
developments in Europe, the advantages of signing a treaty
with France, and the gravity of rejecting the French proposal,
dulled the appetite of his guests. Two days later, a French
delegation marched directly to the chambers of the king's ministers to demand a response to their treaty proposal. Threats and
displays of violent temper proved of no avail, however; the royal
officials refused to sign a treaty.[8] This unpleasant encounter
promptly was reported by special messenger ship to Satsuma,

[6] *Kaigun shi*, 1:407–408; *Kankyū roku*, pp. 46–47.
[7] In this text, Japanese dates are retained as found in the documents except
for the year, which has been converted to the Christian year. Nariakira's report
to the Bakufu is in Shimazu Nariakira Monjo Kankō Kai, ed., *Shimazu Nariakira
monjo* (Tokyo, 1959), 1:42–44, hereafter *Monjo*. See also *Kenshi*, 2:792–794;
Kaigun shi 1:411–412.
[8] *Monjo*, 1:42–43.

and from there the report was sent to Edo, where the Ryukyu problem immediately became a major issue.

Besides the direct pressures applied by warships and diplomatic confrontation, Westerners reminded the Ryukyuans of their impotence by carrying out surveys in disregard of local sensibilities. The British were as culpable as the French in this infringement of Ryukyu sovereignty. In 1843, the crew of the *Samarang,* with the help of local recruits, spent twenty-one days charting the reefs and shoals of the islands of Miyako, Yaeyama, and Yonaguni as well as surveying the land from village to village. For this breach of etiquette, the local government lodged an official protest with the British consul at Foochow.[9] When British warships appeared twice in 1845, in the fifth and seventh months, they were asked not to sound territorial waters. The British complied, for their primary mission was to investigate French activities and intentions in the islands.[10] In 1847, however, both French and British ships carried out mapping and charting missions without local permission.[11]

Perhaps the most irritating problem posed by the Westerners was their practice of abandoning missionaries, sometimes with their families, on Ryukyuan soil, forcing the islanders to take care of them despite the strict ban against Christianity. For example the Frenchman Forcade was replaced after two years by others. The most annoying personality, however, was the British missionary, Bernard Jean Bettelheim, who came with his wife and two infants in 1846 and stayed until the arrival of Commodore Perry in 1853.[12] Bettelheim was a German Jew converted to Christianity, and a religious fanatic who never quite succeeded in being ordained. Perhaps this accounted for the zeal which made him relish preaching loudly at street corners or bursting into the privacy of homes to distribute forbidden

[9] *Kaigun shi,* 1:388, 410–411.
[10] *Kankyū roku,* p. 49; *Kaigun shi,* 1:410–411; Watanabe, *Abe Masahiro jiseki,* 1:87–88.
[11] *Kaigun shi,* 1:424–425.
[12] Kerr, *Okinawa,* pp. 279–296, gives a good description of Bettelheim. See also Watanabe, *Abe Masahiro jiseki,* 1:87–88; *Kankyū roku,* p. 50; *Kenshi,* 2:791–792.

religious tracts. These activities were highly embarrassing to the local people, who were liable to severe punishment if they showed the slightest interest in the foreign religion. Bettelheim was a complete failure as a missionary, but he succeeded in instilling fear among the local officials and obtaining material from them by invoking the might of the British navy and government. At one point his arrogant behavior provoked a physical attack, and he was struck momentarily unconscious, a fact which he proudly reported to his superiors. From the Ryukyuan point of view, his continued presence was a constant worry, for another such incident might provide the opportunity for British naval intervention.

ABE MASAHIRO DELEGATES POWER TO SHIMAZU NARIAKIRA

The Bakufu did not have direct channels of information on matters concerning the southern archipelago. Reports reached the Tokugawa officials after they had been filtered through the Satsuma offices in Kagoshima and Edo. The vagaries of weather and the dangers of ocean travel often delayed the receipt of information at Edo for several weeks. If the Bakufu wished to check on the accuracy of reports submitted by Satsuma, the results of the investigation could not be expected for several months. Under the circumstances, Bakufu officials had little choice but to accept these reports at face value.

The aggressiveness of the French in 1846 alarmed the Satsuma daimyo sufficiently to cause him to report the situation to the shogun with a request for an appropriate course of action. It was not easy for Shimazu Narioki, lord of Satsuma, to make this request, for he regarded the Ryukyu Kingdom as part of his own domain, from which he wished to exclude Bakufu interference. The daimyo particularly feared that if the Bakufu officials became very interested in Ryukyu, Satsuma's long-standing illicit trade with that country might be exposed.

The man whose responsibility it was to make the report on the Ryukyu situation was Zusho Shōzaemon, Narioki's most trusted advisor.[13] Zusho was also the architect of Satsuma's highly successful Tempō reforms, and through his economic interests he undoubtedly was involved in promoting the Satsuma-Ryukyu trade, which brought in contraband goods in competition with the Bakufu's own trade monopoly conducted at Nagasaki. Because of this background Zusho could see the commercial advantages of the French treaty proposal.

It was not until early summer of 1846, after France's second round of diplomatic jousting at Okinawa, that Zusho submitted his report to Abe Masahiro, chief councillor of the Bakufu.[14] His account stressed two factors: the grave danger confronting Ryukyu and Japan unless some trade were allowed the French, and the active military measures being undertaken by Satsuma to counteract the danger. Zusho also met with the shogun. The latter was startled to learn what had happened earlier in 1824 at Tokara Island.[15] Clearly, the foreigners were rough; Japan might suffer the recent fate of China unless some of their demands were met. As for Satsuma's military measures, Zusho reported that the previous year seven hundred samurai had been sent to defend the southern islands, although at the moment only six hundred remained. These warriors could not withstand a full-scale assault, so he recommended a compromise of Japan's exclusion policy to "prevent an invasion of the homeland."[16]

Zusho, of course, made no mention of the tremendous economic advantage to Satsuma if Ryukyu were permitted to trade with France while the rest of Japan remained bound by the *sakoku* ("closed country") policy. The Bakufu could not know at this time that Zusho's report on the number of samurai sent

[13] Zusho Shōzaemon (1775–1848) began his career in 1790 as Lord Shimazu Shigehide's (1745–1833) tea-server. In 1827, he was given full responsibility for directing han financial reforms, a task to which he devoted the remainder of his life. He attained the rank of *karō* (han councillor) in 1833. The most recent and authoritative study of Zusho Shōzaemon is by Haraguchi Torao, *Bakumatsu no Satsuma* (Tokyo, 1966).

[14] The report was submitted on Int. 5/25. *Kaigun shi*, 1:413–415; *Jikki*, 1:1a–3a.

[15] *Kaigun shi*, 1:418.

[16] *Ibid.*, 1:413. Watanabe, *Abe Masahiro jiseki*, 1:89, 91, states that Satsuma warriors set sail from Yamakawa, but immediately turned around and returned.

to Ryukyu was false, or that instead of the large force which had been gathered at Yamakawa to deceive Bakufu agents, only a token force of about 150 samurai was sent south.

Abe Masahiro, who had been in charge of military defense before his appointment as chief councillor, understood the implications of the Ryukyu crisis.[17] Western pressure on the exposed southern kingdom could be a prelude to future demands on Japan proper. The French proposal for a treaty with Ryukyu ran counter to Japan's seclusion policy and her strict proscription of Christianity. Should these two pillars of the Tokugawa control system be maintained at all cost, or should they be compromised with the excuse that the Ryukyu Kingdom was beyond the pale of Japan?

Immediately after receiving Zusho's report, Abe conferred briefly with his specialist on foreign affairs, Tsutsui Masanori, whose official position was that of *ōmetsuke* (inspector general), and the following day he secretly sent Tsutsui to obtain the views of Shimazu Nariakira.[18] This was a bold and unprecedented act, for Nariakira was next in line to succeed the daimyo of Satsuma, and Satsuma was the most powerful of the traditionally hostile *tozama* han. Such problems always had been deliberated by members of the Bakufu without reference to the views of outsiders.

Besides the fact that Nariakira's knowledge of Ryukyu was exceptional, for Satsuma controlled that kingdom, he was generally acknowledged by his peers as unsurpassed in intelligence and political acumen.[19] Besides, Abe trusted him as a friend, and he knew Nariakira's concern to be nationwide in scope

---

[17] Watanabe, *Abe Masahiro jiseki*, 1:78.

[18] *Kaigun shi*, 1:415; Watanabe, *Abe Masahiro jiseki*, 1:87.

[19] Ida Yoshihara, "Sappan ni okeru yōgaku: Tamasato bunko shozō yōgaku kankei shoseki kō," *Kadai Shigaku*, 12 (1964), indicates the broad range of Nariakira's interests. Ōkubo Toshiaki, "Meiji Ishin to Kyūshū," *Fukuoka UNESCO* 3:65 (1966), stresses that Nariakira "keenly felt a sense of international crisis" as a result of his confrontation with the Ryukyu problem. On this point an admirable study of the effect of the Ryukyu crisis, especially on the two protagonists, Nariakira and Zusho, is given by Mori Toshihiko, *Meiji Ishin seijishi josetsu* (Tokyo, 1967), pp. 45–62. See also Ikeda Toshihiko, *Shimazu Nariakira-kō den* (Tokyo, 1954).

rather than seeking advantage for his han alone. For Nariakira, the defense of Japan against Western aggression could not be piecemeal, and the security of each han was dependent on the military alertness of the whole country.

In his discussion with Tsutsui, Nariakira essentially agreed with Zusho Shōzaemon's analysis concerning the danger of an unyielding seclusion policy without adequate thought to the military problem. He recommended that the French be allowed some trade. In the meantime Japan should look to her defenses and stimulate the samurai spirit, which had grown lax over the long period of the Tokugawa peace. He pointed out that Japan was not in sole control of Ryukyu's foreign relations, for the kingdom was in a *yang* (the positive element in Chinese cosmology) relationship to China and a *yin* (the passive element) relationship to Japan, openly acknowledging the sovereignty of China on the one hand, while secretly being bound to Japan on the other. Thus, if any unyielding policy were adopted in Ryukyu, the foreigners might turn to China as a way of forcing Ryukyu to terms. In that event, Japan might not have a voice in the final decision. It would be wise, therefore, to give silent assent to Ryukyu for limited trade with the French, but to deny them the right to propagate Christianity.[20]

Tsutsui returned at once to Abe and gave his strong endorsement to Nariakira's views. The Bakufu's silent assent to trade at Ryukyu was a convenient way of avoiding a direct break in the seclusion policy, yet such a decision should be kept secret, for within the Bakufu itself there were many who would fiercely oppose a departure from past practice. Abe accepted Nariakira's recommendations and he notified the shogun Ieyoshi. As a result, on 1846/int. 5/27, Lord Narioki and his son, Nariakira, received secret instructions from the Bakufu ordering Nariakira to hasten back to Satsuma and take charge of problems caused by intruding foreign ships.[21] On the first day of the sixth month, Narioki and Nariakira were warmly received by the shogun himself, who said, "The Ryukyu matter I completely entrust to

[20] *Kaigun shi,* 1:415–416.
[21] *Ibid.,* 1:416.

you. You must adopt a mild or militant policy in accordance with your judgment of the circumstances. You must give careful thought so as not to occasion future grief or loss of national prestige." As an expression of the shogun's appreciation and special favor, he presented them with a fine horse.[22] The Bakufu had given Satsuma virtually a blank check for foreign negotiations at Ryukyu.

On the fifth, Abe Masahiro had a private meeting with Nariakira at the former's residence. Tsutsui and Kawaji Toshiakira, another of Abe's assistants, were also present. The councillor noted that the shogun had accepted Nariakira's opinions on Ryukyu and was relying on him not to bring injury to the country. "Because Ryukyu is an outside han," he said, "the Bakufu will not press its will and interfere. It will not be necessary to ask about discretionary measures." Abe added that force should be used if France resorted to coercive action, but "the issue of trade may be conceded." This concession, however, should be extended only to France and not to any other country. "Exert yourself to keep the problem small and do not allow it to enlarge."[23] After this meeting Abe invited the han councillors to his residence and repeated the Bakufu instructions in a written statement. He assured them that Bakufu orders were not required for dealing with the Ryukyu problem, and the adoption of appropriate measures would be left to the discretion of the han lord.[24]

On the same day, Tsutsui and Shimosone Kinzaburō were sent to the Satsuma residence to inform Nariakira of a heated discussion which had taken place among Bakufu officials. Three Bakufu magistrates had taken exception to Abe's view that Ryukyu must be allowed to follow China's lead in trading with the West.[25] If Ryukyu were allowed to trade with France, the

---

[22] *Ibid.*, 416–418, for texts of instructions by the Bakufu and shogun.
[23] *Ibid.*, 1:418.
[24] *Ibid.*, 1:419.
[25] The three magistrates (*san bugyō*) were the magistrates of temples and shrines (*jisha bugyō*), of Edo City (*machi bugyō*), and of finances (*kanjō bugyō*).

magistrates had protested, Bakufu profits from the commerce at Nagasaki would be affected. Abe had countered that if the Ryukyu Kingdom became involved in war, eventually Japan herself would not be able to avoid disaster. Therefore, Satsuma should be given a free hand to take appropriate steps without a formal order, for it would be difficult for the Bakufu to give consent openly to foreign trade. Tsutsui and Shimosone stated that if trade with France were allowed, she should be told clearly that this trade must be limited because of Ryukyu's scant resources. Moreover, other countries should be notified that they should not consider the trade agreement with France to be a useful precedent.[26] Nariakira was in complete agreement with this advice. He departed for Edo three days later and arrived in Kagoshima on 1846/6/25.

NARIAKIRA'S DIFFICULTIES IN SATSUMA

Nariakira had been ordered to go to Satsuma and deal with the foreign problem in Ryukyu in a way that would reduce the threat to Japan and at the same time preserve the political structure of the country. With these general instructions, the Bakufu had given him a free hand to devise the specific measures. Because Ryukyu was an "outer han" the Bakufu would not raise an issue about a little trade with the French. But Nariakira promised to take energetic military measures to prevent foreign demands from escalating.

Being perhaps the most enlightened leader of his time, Nariakira was aware of the commercial opportunities of his carte blanche orders, but he also was better informed than most contemporaries of the pitfalls of trading with industrially advanced, militarily powerful Western countries. He was a realist who recognized that some trade concession must be made to minimize Western aggressiveness, but such commercial contacts

---

[26] *Ibid.*, 1:419. *Kankyū roku*, pp. 51–57, gives an account of these meetings. See also Watanabe, *Abe Masahiro jiseki*, 1:90.

must be accompanied by an all-out effort on the part of Japan to meet the military and economic challenge.[27]

It is of interest to note that, immediately on his arrival in Kagoshima, he ordered Ichiki Masuemon (later known as Ichiki Shirō) to assist in the negotiations at Okinawa, with instructions to give in on the trade issue if necessary.[28] When it was learned that the French had departed without obtaining this concession from the Ryukyu ministers, Nariakira did not press for trade arrangements. His realistic approach is revealed in his letter to Nariaki of Mito written on 1847/6/23, a few months after he had departed from Kagoshima.[29]

In this letter he outlined his strategy of minimal concessions. First of all, he informed Nariaki that no trade had been granted yet, and should the French return, their request would be denied again. Second, if the French refused to be put off, Ryukyu would suggest that some trade might be allowed at Foochow as Ryukyu herself was too small a country to support trade. Third, if the French considered this inadequate, some trade might be permitted in one of the smaller islands such as Miyakojima or Yaeyama. Finally, if the foreigners still demanded better terms, trade might be allowed in Naha, but they would not be permitted to establish a trading post, and in such an event the commercial regulations should be so strictly enforced as to discourage Western notions about expanding their commercial opportunities.

Nariakira feared that a trade concession would lead to demands for land and buildings for use by trading companies and for the right to station agents there year-round. Permanent residence by foreigners would increase their adverse influence on the local people. Such a base on Okinawa also might increase foreign interest in trading with Japan. Unfortunately the Satsuma representatives would not be able to argue directly against their coming to Japan, for Satsuma's control over Ryukyu was

[27] For a discussion of this aspect of Nariakira's ideas and policies, see the author's "Introduction of Western Culture to Satsuma," *Report of the Second Kyushu International Cultural Conference* (Fukuoka, 1968), pp. 24–31.

[28] *Monjo*, 1:42–44.

[29] *Ibid.*, 1:71–74.

a carefully guarded secret, and Satsuma officials disguised themselves as local officials or officials from Tokara Island. Nariakira suspected that the foreigners knew the true nature of Satsuma-Ryukyu relations, but they had not raised any questions about it. In any case it was easier to deal with the Westerners as if Ryukyu were not an integral part of Japan, for agreements reached in Okinawa would not thereby seriously affect the Tokugawa seclusion policy.

Finally, Nariakira requested Nariaki to use his good offices to secure financial assistance for the lord of Fukuoka and the lord of Saga, who were eager to strengthen the defenses of Nagasaki. Such aid for the defense of Nagasaki also would benefit Ryukyu, other islands, and the coastal areas of the country. Nariakira always considered defense in national terms. In other communications with Nariaki, he discussed the foreign threats to Matsumae (Hokkaido), the Kurile Islands, and the Bonin Islands, and at times expressed even greater concern for the security of these frontier areas than for Ryukyu. He frequently urged Nariaki to give constructive advice on defense matters to the Bakufu officials.[30]

Nariakira laid great stress on attaining military readiness for impending Western challenges. His efforts were concentrated, however, on home defense rather than defense of the southern islands. When queried by impatient samurai as to when he would send troops to Okinawa to engage the French, he explained the impracticality of such action. His argument was that Satsuma had no real navy to compare with the French fleet. Moreover, even if samurai were transported successfully to Ryukyu, they would be inadequate for the defense of the kingdom, and the local people would not appreciate the presence of Satsuma warriors and the dubious protection they provided.[31]

In Satsuma, on the other hand, Nariakira worked energetically to improve han defenses. He went up and down the coast supervising the selection of fortification sites, inspecting troops,

---

[30] Nariakira's concern for national defense is seen particularly in *ibid.*, 1:36, 73, 124–126, 132–134, 204–205, 215–218, 221–223, 236–239, 248–251.
[31] *Kankyū roku*, p. 58; *Kaigun shi*, 1:41.

and exhorting them to give their utmost effort and devotion in the face of unprecedented national danger. Among the problems he encountered in Satsuma was the existence of rival schools of military arts, each with its own "experts" on foreign techniques of warfare. Nariakira himself was a close student of foreign weapons, and he no doubt saw through the superficiality of some of the experts.

His task was not made easier by the fact that his presence in Satsuma was largely due to his selection by the Bakufu. This, combined with the fact that he was almost a stranger in Satsuma, his previous trip having been an eight-month sojourn in 1834, made him suspect for some people.[32] Nariakira had spent most of his life in Edo, where he had acquired the sophistication of the aristocrats in the capital city. Moreover, his dynamic presence and broad-gauged reform program no doubt constituted a threat to the routine and security of some local officials prone to rural provincialism.

The staunchest opposition to Nariakira came from the all-powerful Zusho Shōzaemon, the trusted advisor of the daimyo and, earlier, of Narioki's grandfather, Shimazu Shigehide. Nariakira's cosmopolitan outlook and enterprising spirit reminded Zusho of his former master, Shigehide. The latter's great interest in Dutch studies and scientific projects had contributed to an alarming deterioration of the han's financial position, and it had been Zusho's task over the past twenty years to remedy the situation. Having worked so hard to accumulate a substantial savings for the han treasury, Zusho did not appreciate Nariakira's ambitious and costly program for a military build-up.[33]

Neither the daimyo Narioki, nor his chief minister Zusho, shared to the same degree Nariakira's concern for national defense, and they were in no way eager to relieve the Bakufu of its foreign menace. These men had been struggling with desperate han problems, many of which derived from the restrictive policies of the Bakufu. They had effected the recovery of

[32] Ikeda, *Shimazu Nariakira-kō den*, pp. 82–83.
[33] Haraguchi, *Bakumatsu no Satsuma*, pp. 161–162; Mori, *Meiji Ishin seijishi josetsu*, pp. 59–62.

Satsuma from her economic ills despite Bakufu policies and even in violation of Tokugawa regulations. They were naturally wary of the Bakufu, and their interest in preserving han autonomy was deeply rooted. This provincialism of Zusho and Narioki could not suddenly be transformed by the Ryukyu crisis into a patriotic concern which placed the nation over the han. For them, the han came first; cooperation with the Bakufu was incidental and reluctantly given.

Another formidable obstacle for Nariakira and his efforts to rouse the han to meet the foreign danger was the ambitious Yura, mother of Nariakira's half-brother, Hisamitsu. She used her charm over the daimyo to promote the interests of her son over those of Nariakira, the legitimate heir apparent. Zusho, Yura, and Narioki thus formed the nucleus around which rallied other powerful han bureaucrats who felt threatened by the energy and intelligence of Nariakira.[34]

Nariakira had come to Kagoshima on 1846/6/25. On 1847/3/8, his father, for whom he had been serving as deputy, arrived from Edo.[35] Nariakira's position in the han thereby became untenable, and a week later he departed for Edo. After his departure, it became increasingly clear that the authority formerly vested in him was being shifted to his half-brother, Hisamitsu.

The return of Narioki just eight months after Nariakira had been sent to Satsuma was bitterly criticized by Nariaki of Mito. In a letter to Abe Masahiro, he charged that the daimyo's trip was unnecessary, wasteful, and selfishly motivated.[36] Nariaki perhaps was alarmed that Nariakira's policy of military preparedness would be replaced by a han-oriented commercial policy which would give Satsuma special and exclusive advantages in Ryukyu. He raised the question with Abe as to when Narioki would retire as daimyo of Satsuma.

The departure of Nariakira was followed by the rapid elevation of Hisamitsu. He was placed in charge of a newly created office of military service in the tenth month, 1847. In 1848, he

---

[34] Haraguchi, *Bakumatsu no Satsuma*, pp. 160–163.
[35] *Kaigun shi*, 1:424.
[36] *Monjo*, 1:45–46.

was appointed *jitō* (steward) of Chosa-gō, with responsibility to act for the daimyo in all military matters. About the same time he was named to the post of *karō* (han councillor), a rank which, according to the instructions accompanying the appointment, placed him at the top of the social scale, for he was ordered on ceremonial occasions to "sit at a place higher than that of *jōdai* [deputy in charge of the castle]." Still another order placed him in charge of the han whenever the daimyo was away. It was apparent that he was being groomed to be the next daimyo.[37]

DOMESTIC POLITICAL CRISIS IN SATSUMA, 1849

Nariakira's return to Edo reflected his estrangement from the Narioki-Zusho faction, which was endeavoring to isolate him from han affairs. He no longer received official reports and communications concerning Satsuma and Ryukyu. As a consequence, he was forced to rely primarily on his own correspondents to keep him informed about such matters as Satsuma officials and their missions to Ryukyu, the arrival of foreign ships and the behavior of foreigners in the islands, the state of military preparations in the han, the rivalry among the different schools of gunnery, and the various rumors concerning the han and the kingdom.[38]

Abe and the shogun were disturbed by the removal of Nariakira from responsibility over the Ryukyu problem, for their policy was predicated on their trust in him, not Narioki or Zusho. The latter already had revealed themselves to be not completely reliable on matters concerning Ryukyu. They had not reported the 1844 arrival of the *Alcmène* until two years after the event. When the gravity of the French demands made it impossible for them to conceal the situation from the Bakufu, they had sought to convey the impression that the foreigners would soon be brought under control by Satsuma. In his report, Zusho had been misleading, to say the least, when he announced that seven

[37] *Jikki,* 1:3a–5a.
[38] See especially *Monjo,* 1:74–83, 98–101, 106–120, 129–132.

hundred samurai had been dispatched from Satsuma to defend Ryukyu. In fact, only 150 men had been sent. When confronted with the discrepancy a year later, Narioki made the excuse in a letter to Abe (1847/8/15) that bad weather had prevented the departure of the originally intended larger expedition.[39]

The policies of the Narioki-Zusho leadership caused Nariakira much anxiety as well. Not only were his own qualifications and ideas set aside, but the lack of candor of his father and Zusho in reporting to the Bakufu also reflected on Nariakira's credibility, as he was the legitimate heir apparent of Satsuma. The breakdown of relations between the Bakufu and Satsuma would seriously affect the country's ability to respond to Western threats. Moreover, Nariakira worried over the inadequate defense measures at home and the inept handling of the Ryukyu situation, which might even drive the Ryukyuans from Satsuma into the arms of the Westerners.

Nariakira's countermeasures were to establish his own information network in Satsuma and to rely on his friend, Lord Date of Uwajima, to explain his predicament to the Bakufu. He depended particularly on Yamaguchi Sadayasu and Shimazu Hisataka for information from home,[40] at the same time stressing repeatedly the need for utmost secrecy and caution.[41] He instructed them as to who was trustworthy and who was not. After reading his letters, he said, they should burn them. A special watch should be kept on Zusho's activities with particular attention to the goods being brought into the han. He reported that the Bakufu spies were ferreting out information about Zusho and the secret would soon be out.

It appears that Nariakira had decided at about this time to divulge the facts of the Satsuma-Ryukyu smuggling traffic, perhaps in order to do so before the Bakufu found out for itself. Such a bold course of action risked exposing the han to the awesome wrath of the Bakufu but, on the other hand, if Naria-

---

[39] *Kaigun shi*, 1:425–426.

[40] Yamaguchi Sadayasu at this time served in the humble but strategic post of chief tea-server (*sukiya kashira*). Shimazu Hisataka was a councillor with the post of deputy in charge of the castle (*jōdai karō*).

[41] *Monjo*, 1:68–70, 74–87, 90–93, 98–120.

kira did not report the situation, the consequences for Satsuma might be even more dire. He entrusted this delicate task to Lord Date, who secured Abe Masahiro's sympathetic understanding of Nariakira's dilemma. In his letter to Date (1848/8/27), Nariakira thanked him for obtaining Abe's assurance that he would overlook minor irregularities and not take Satsuma to court as long as the Ryukyu problem could be solved satisfactorily.[42] The latter condition would seem to have implied that Abe would now work to install Nariakira as daimyo in order to ensure a proper Ryukyu policy.

A change of policy for Ryukyu required the removal of the Narioki-Zusho faction from power in Satsuma. The first step was to get rid of Zusho, on whom Narioki relied heavily, and the next was to obtain the resignation of the daimyo. Zusho was most vulnerable to charges of violating the Tokugawa restrictions on trade. The Abe-Nariakira agreement, however, was to avoid implicating Narioki. Punishment of the daimyo would arouse serious disunity in the han and virtually destroy any opportunity for Nariakira to carry out effective leadership.

Late in 1848, four months after Nariakira's cryptic letter of appreciation to Date, Zusho unsuspectingly met with Abe to report on han matters. During the meeting, the latter's line of questioning suddenly made Zusho realize that the chief councillor was aware of the terrible truth about the Satsuma-Ryukyu trade. Devoted and loyal to his lord to the last, Zusho sought to assume full responsibility for the illicit trade by committing suicide on 1848/12/18.[43] The Bakufu did not make a public issue of the case, though Zusho's family was stripped of honors and material wealth and his son was forced to change his family name and retire from his post in the han government.

Grave unrest prevailed in the han for the next several months. Many of Zusho's adherents, who did not suspect that their leader had been betrayed by Nariakira, continued in positions of influence, and many charges of corruption surfaced against them. After twenty years of tight control by the powerful Zusho, many

[42] *Ibid.*, 2:123–124.
[43] *Ibid.*, 1:135–136; Haraguchi, *Bakumatsu no Satsuma*, pp. 159–170.

now looked for a change of regime, and these elements became increasingly impatient with the seeming disinclination of Narioki to retire. They also were obsessed with the fear that Narioki's consort, Yura, was actively conspiring to bring harm to Nariakira and his offspring in order to obtain the succession of her own son, Hisamitsu.[44]

Concerned with the situation at home, Nariakira urgently asked Ijūin Kanenao, Yamaguchi Sadayasu, and Yoshii Taiyu (letters of 1849/1/29) for information about developments in Satsuma, the activities of the Zusho faction, the state of unrest among the people, and the nature of rumors circulating in the domain.[45] Whether intended or not, his remark to Yoshii that plans should be made to break the power of the "evil woman" (Yura) conveyed the sense of a conspiracy against her. He urged great precautions for secrecy, and in his letter to Yoshii the names of their political adversaries were written in the western alphabet to confound possibly hostile readers. In the Zusho affair, he confided, Lord Kuroda of Fukuoka had worked hard and Lord Abe had acted his role magnificently. As for his father, Nariakira reported that he would be retiring as soon as he had participated in the ceremonies involving the impending visit of the Ryukyu envoys to Edo. Narioki's desire for an honorary promotion in the imperial court, however, seemed out of reach, and how gracefully he would be allowed to retire would depend on the successful removal of the Englishman Bettelheim from Ryukyu. This information may have been intended to restrain Nariakira's impatient supporters from taking drastic action.

By summer, emotions in Satsuma had reached crisis proportions, as evidenced by reports of strong religious movements of the Ikkō sect, which culminated in an uprising in Kawanabe-gō. In their frustration, Nariakira's admirers believed that Yura was casting a curse on his family, causing the death of his children one by one. To counter such imprecations they asked for articles of clothing from Nariakira and his sons, or paper images of them,

[44] Haraguchi, *Bakumatsu no Satsuma*, pp. 170–171.
[45] *Monjo*, 1:135–143.

to be used for prayers and purification rites in their behalf. Inoue expressed his belief that the time to get rid of the han villains had arrived. He meant by this not an assassination plot but a determination to consult with Kuroda of Fukuoka in order to enlist the aid of the Bakufu against the "evil" incumbents in the han government.[46]

Toward the close of the year, Narioki became aware of a plot against the lives of Yura, Hisamitsu, and Shimazu Shōsō (who had been closely associated with Zusho). In a great fit of anger, he ordered the arrest of forty Nariakira adherents. Over a period of several weeks, beginning on 1849/12/6, several of the ringleaders were ordered to commit suicide. Moreover, afterward some of the bodies were exhumed and crucified, and one was further mutilated. Other Nariakira adherents were exiled, deprived of their samurai status, or demoted.[47] Among the chief victims were high-ranking officials, well known in Edo circles, and therefore this cruel event could not go unnoticed by the Bakufu.

Three of the intended victims managed to escape to Fukuoka, where they were given protection by Lord Kuroda, granduncle and admirer of Nariakira. From these refugees he learned the full details of the so-called Yura uprising, and he reported the desperate situation in Satsuma to the Bakufu.[48] The following year, 1850, Nariakira, Kuroda, Date, and Abe laid elaborate plans to force the retirement of Narioki.

THE COALITION AGAINST NARIOKI AND THE SUCCESSION OF NARIAKIRA

The violence of the political strife within Satsuma emphasized for Narioki's opponents the urgent necessity for his retire-

---

[46] *Ibid.*, 1:143–157.

[47] Haraguchi, *Bakumatsu no Satsuma*, pp. 170–174; *Kenshi*, 2:279–290.

[48] The reports by Satsuma men to Kuroda are found in *Shimazu-ke kokuji ōshō shiryō*, vol. 14. This is a collection of twenty volumes of unpublished manuscript copy which was kindly made available to me by the University of Kagoshima Library. As pagination is missing, identification of material will be by volume and dates of documents. Nariakira's disclaimer of foreknowledge of the assassination plot against Yura, Hisamitsu, and Shimazu Shōsō is in *ibid.*, vol. 11, letter dated third year of Kaei (1850), Nariakira to Date, as copied by Tsutsui. See also Nariakira's letter to Ijūin Kanenao in *Monjo*, 1:359–360.

ment. His ouster, however, was extremely difficult to achieve, for the slightest suggestion of insult to the daimyo might cause an already tense situation to worsen. Nariakira was anxious to avoid exacerbating the problem. If he were to succeed as an effective leader, he needed the unified and loyal support of his clansmen. To secure this support his image as a wise and strong moral force had to be maintained. A display of eagerness to succeed his father would make him vulnerable to the charge of being unfilial and selfish. At the same time, Nariakira could not ignore the perilous situation confronting the country, a situation in which his own han must necessarily play a leading role. Therefore, he worked quietly behind the scenes with powerful supporters to hasten his father's retirement.

Normally the Bakufu would not have been much concerned with the disciplinary problems of a han. Chief Councillor Abe and the shogun, however, were displeased with Narioki's attitude on the Ryukyu problem, and they were happy to cooperate in the conspiracy to retire him. Even after Zusho's suicide, Narioki continued to withhold vital information about Ryukyu from the Bakufu. He continued to protect han interests by misrepresenting the facts. His report to the Bakufu in the summer of 1850, for example, announced that the French missionary (Pierre Marie Le Turdu) had departed, and though the Englishman Bettelheim still remained in Okinawa, the people there were unconcerned, as he was interested only in administering medical help to the blind and the outcastes.[49]

The Bakufu was kept informed of the inaccuracies of Narioki's reports through Nariakira's friends. In his letter to Date Munenari, Nariakira indicated that the Bettelheim problem was by no means negligible.[50] Ryukyu officials had requested China to have Bettelheim withdrawn; Bettelheim, in turn, threatened to reveal to China the fact that Ryukyu was actually submissive to Japan. These facts had not been reported by Narioki. He had also neglected to mention the arrival of another British ship with an official request for treaty relations. The British had announced their intention to return for further negotiations.

[49] *Monjo*, 2:9–11.
[50] *Ibid.*, 2:2–9; Watanabe, *Abe Masahiro jiseki*, 1:104.

Nariakira surmised that the suppression of such important information was due to the daimyo's fear that if the new problems came to light, the Bakufu might cancel the forthcoming mission from Ryukyu to Edo, an event which always enhanced the prestige of the lord of Satsuma. Narioki also was aware in reporting on the Bettelheim affair that the situation affected the possibility of his garnering further honors.

While publicly taking the part of the dutiful, loyal, and obedient son, Nariakira plotted strategy with Lord Date of Uwajima and Lord Kuroda of Fukuoka. Their ideas were carried by the latter two to Abe Masahiro. Abe then put their plan into action by instructing his chief advisor, Tsutsui, to put pressure on Narioki's representative, Yoshitoshi Chū. Yoshitoshi, for his part, sought to shield his lord from direct confrontation with the lords of the opposition camp. By late fall of 1850, the coalition for Nariakira had unleashed their campaign by openly suggesting that Narioki retire without further delay.

Although an agreement had been reached informally between Abe and Narioki at the time of Zusho's death that the daimyo would retire soon after completion of the Ryukyu mission to Edo, both Narioki and his retainers sought to postpone the retirement. Yoshitoshi fended off Kuroda and others of the Nariakira camp from seeing Narioki by pointing out that such pressure would be interpreted as improperly inspired by the daimyo's son.[51] Similarly, direct orders from the Bakufu would be taken by Satsuma samurai as an affront to their lord. Tsutsui, carefully avoiding phraseology which would imply that he was transmitting Abe Masahiro's orders, revealed to Yoshitoshi on about 11/5 that from his conversation with Abe he gathered that the latter was dissatisfied with the way Narioki had escorted the Ryukyu envoys. Though Abe did not say specifically what the source of the dissatisfaction was, he had said that he could not guarantee no reprimand if his colleagues in the Bakufu found out about Narioki's behavior. Therefore, it was highly de-

---

[51] *Shimazu-ke kokuji ōshō shiryō*, vol. 11, Kuroda's letter to Date reporting his conversation with Yoshitoshi, 1850/10/11.

sirable, said Tsutsui, that Yoshitoshi urge his lord to retire before his illustrious achievements were besmirched. Yoshitoshi countered, saying that a hasty retirement by Narioki would be misinterpreted by the people of Ryukyu as a sign of improper management of the foreign problem by Satsuma and by the supporters of the recent culprits in the Yura uprising as a vindication of their cause.[52]

This inconclusive skirmishing between Tsutsui and Yoshitoshi was highly unsatisfactory for Nariakira. If matters were allowed to drift, there could be another uprising within the han. Moreover, the Ryukyu problem was becoming critical. The exploitative policy instituted by Zusho had made, according to Nariakira, the allegiance of the Ryukyu people problematical at the very moment that the British were wooing them for their friendship. It was urgent to win back the favor of the islanders for Satsuma.

Two days after the Tsutsui-Yoshitoshi encounter, Nariakira outlined for Date the next steps that should be taken.[53] Tsutsui must be instructed by Abe to speak with Yoshitoshi more bluntly and forcefully. They must refute the Narioki camp's argument that retirement now would be a vindication of the recent rebels; Tsutsui must say to Yoshitoshi that Abe's displeasure with Narioki had nothing to do with his disposition of the recent would-be assassins. Narioki's vulnerable point was his Ryukyu policy, for which Abe had spared him public rebuke at the time of Zusho's suicide. There was always the threat that other officials of the Bakufu would learn about Narioki's complicity with Zusho, and the daimyo should be made aware that others had been informed of Narioki's earlier agreement to retire. Narioki should be told that he was to retire without delay or risk official disgrace. Nariakira also anticipated that Yoshitoshi would not be so blunt in speaking with his lord, but would try to gloss over the situation. To avoid this, a written statement urging retirement should be given to Yoshitoshi for transmittal with the

[52] *Ibid.*, vol. 11, Tsutsui's report to Date on his conversation with Yoshitoshi, 1850/11/5.

[53] *Ibid.*, vol. 11, Nariakira to Date, 1850/11/7.

promise that Lord Date would be seeing Narioki directly for a response to the statement.

Nariakira also alerted Date that his father contemplated staying in Satsuma after his retirement so that he could continue issuing orders. In such an event Nariakira's policies for Ryukyu would be of no avail. Adequate measures must be taken to prevent his father from residing in the han after his retirement.

The pressure mounted by Nariakira's coalition of han lords and Bakufu officials produced the desired result. On the twenty-seventh of the same month, Nariakira wrote a long letter to Date thanking him for his unstinting efforts toward securing the retirement of his father.[54] He had just learned from Lord Kuroda that Narioki was prepared to submit a petition to the Bakufu requesting permission to retire. There were still some precautionary measures to be taken to ensure the elimination of the influence of the Narioki faction, but members of Nariakira's coalition felt a great sense of relief.

On 12/3, Narioki was called before the shogun, who praised him for past services and presented him with a prized set of tea utensils, the implication being that the set was a retirement gift. Narioki took the hint, and a month later he requested that Nariakira be named his successor. On 1851/2/3, at the age of forty-three, Nariakira became daimyo of Satsuma.[55]

CONCLUSION

In the mid–1840's, the Western powers had made Ryukyu into a mutual problem for the Bakufu and Satsuma. This mutuality, however, did not necessarily evoke a unified response or common policy. The strong-willed daimyo Narioki and the equally determined Zusho continued to regard Ryukyu as a closed preserve for the han, to be controlled without interference from the Bakufu. Nariakira, in contrast, foresaw the danger to the larger political entity, the nation, of which Satsuma was but a minor part. The Bakufu needed the support of the power-

---

[54] *Ibid.*, vol. 11, Nariakira to Date, 1850/11/27.
[55] Ikeda, *Shimazu Nariakira-kō den*, p. 118.

ful southern han as much as the han required the understanding and cooperation of the central government.

It is hard to conceive how this working relationship could have been attained without the persuasive personality of Nariakira or the moderate and pragmatic character of Abe Masahiro. For all of Nariakira's intelligence, however, his effectiveness in helping to formulate Japan's foreign policy at this critical juncture would have been greatly minimized had his opponents succeeded in keeping him from his inheritance of han leadership. Although he secured Abe's support for his own succession, Nariakira's political acumen and patience can be measured better by his careful and firm behind-the-scenes maneuvers to retire his father in a manner that preserved his moral integrity in the eyes of his Satsuma followers. He fully appreciated the political necessity of maintaining the image of traditional virtue if he were to rally his people to the challenge of a new era.

THE BAKUMATSU INTELLECTUAL IN ACTION: HASHIMOTO SANAI IN THE POLITICAL CRISIS OF 1858

George M. Wilson

All will agree that 1858 marks a turning point in late Tokugawa history, and few have doubted that foreign policy was the pivotal issue governing the course of events in that critical year. My aim is to challenge this latter view through an examination of the role played by Hashimoto Sanai, intellectual and politician from the large collateral han of Fukui.

In 1858, the Bakufu, led by the *tairō* or great councillor, Ii Naosuke, put its seal to a new commercial treaty with the United States, effectively terminating the traditional Tokugawa seclusion policy that Commodore Perry had breached several years earlier. At the same time, the Bakufu moved to silence domestic opposition to the open-country policy (*kaikoku*) which the treaty represented. The treaty's opponents, however, were not the only ones to suffer the *tairō's* wrath in what is called the Ansei purge. Some who actively supported the treaty also met their end, one of these being Hashimoto Sanai. As the Scottish historian Murdoch put it with characteristic élan,

> It is sometimes assumed that the severity of the Tairō on this occasion was in a measure justified by the necessity of crushing a factious opposition to his comparatively liberal and advanced notions of foreign policy. It is to be remembered, however, that Ii looked upon the reopening of Japan as an unfortunate necessity, a mere tentative temporary measure that might be revoked when the nation was strong enough to trust to its armaments. But Hashimoto Sanai was of the opinion that the reopening of the Empire would be quite as advantageous to

234

his own countrymen as it would be to the foreigners then clamouring for a footing in the ports. And yet Hashimoto was among the Tairō's victims on this occasion. It is indeed difficult to pardon Ii of Hikone for the enormity of ending the life of this brilliant young statesman of 25 by the hands of the public executioner.[1]

If politics in 1858 turned on the foreign issue, and if Sanai in fact favored the American treaty, then what did he do to deserve the death penalty? The answer implicit in Murdoch's harangue is that Ii Naosuke was a bully who overreacted. But the record of Sanai's activity makes another answer plausible: The view from Fukui suggests that the crisis actually turned on the more arcane domestic problem of choosing a successor to the weakling shogun Iesada. Sanai and his lord, Matsudaira Shungaku, had disagreed sharply with Ii on this issue. They and their allies attempted to win the succession for Hitotsubashi Yoshinobu as a means toward the end of widening the base of political leadership in the *bakuhan* system. Their efforts precipitated a fierce clash of opinion with the traditionalists around Ii who were determined to cling to custom at this time of foreign crisis. Ii triumphed in the short run, but his purge of the Hitotsubashi forces destroyed the potential for meaningful long-term reform of the Tokugawa political system in order to meet the security threat which the advancing Western nations posed not only to the Bakufu but to Japan as a whole.

In the caste system of Tokugawa Japan, Sanai was born (on April 19, 1834) to an irregular status. For several generations his forebears had been physicians in the service of the lord of Fukui at an annual stipend of 25 *koku*.[2] A physician was a valu-

---

[1] James Murdoch, *A History of Japan*, vol. 3: *The Tokugawa Epoch, 1652–1868*, rev. and ed., Joseph H. Longford (London, 1926), pp. 694–695.

[2] Details of Sanai's genealogy appear in Yamaguchi Muneyuki, *Hashimoto Sanai* (*Jimbutsu sōsho*, no. 84; Tokyo, 1962), pp. 4–5, 298–301. Yamaguchi's is the only postwar biography of Sanai. A 25-*koku* stipend was above average even for samurai in Fukui at this time. See Kanai Madoka, "Fukui, the Domain of a Tokugawa Collateral *Daimyō*: Its Tradition and Transition," Paper no. 2, Rutgers-Japan Conference (April 1967), pp. 28–30.

able professional, but like a merchant or artisan he dispensed a service and therefore did not enjoy samurai status (*shibun*). Sanai's father, Gen'ya, had become one of the more illustrious doctors in the family line: He studied Dutch medicine and helped pioneer its introduction in Fukui, eventually earning the privilege of attending the daimyo personally.[3]

Chronologies tell us that Sanai displayed impressive scholarly talents from an early age.[4] Until 1849, his training was of the conventional Confucian sort, with special concentration on *kimongaku* (the branch of Japanese neo-Confucianism named for Yamazaki Ansai), but in that year his father sent him off to Osaka to learn Western-style medicine at Ogata Kōan's school. Returning to Fukui in 1852, he took over most of his ailing father's practice (including vaccination of a populace that had been ravaged by smallpox in previous decades) and when his father died in November 1852, he succeeded to the family headship and the yearly 25-*koku* stipend. Not yet twenty, he was responsible for a medical practice and a family consisting of his mother, two younger brothers, and a sister.

But as one of the han's most promising young intellects, Sanai was sent to Edo early in 1854 to study at the school of Sugita Seikei. There he branched out: In addition to medicine, he studied physics and chemistry, mathematics, and military science, and his reading included materials written in English and German as well as Dutch. He achieved samurai status late in 1855 as a reward for excellent academic performance.

Sanai's period of study in Edo also brought him into contact with the political intrigues then beginning to embroil the Bakufu and some of the larger han. He met a number of samurai from Mito and took an interest in factional divisions there. He heard of a plot to poison "Suifu rōkō," the old lord of Mito, Tokugawa Nariaki, the most controversial personality of the time.[5] The

[3] Shiga Tadashi, *Keigaku Hashimoto Sanai*, 3rd ed. rev. (Tokyo, 1938), p. 8.
[4] At six, he began to study the Chinese classics; he wrote commentaries on the *Sankuochih* at nine, and five years later entered the school of Yoshida Tōkō, the leading han Confucianist. Shiga, *Keigaku Hashimoto Sanai*, pp. 305–306; Yamaguchi, *Hashimoto Sanai*, pp. 305–307.
[5] "Mito hanshi bō yori sensei e no himitsu sho," August or September 1856, *Hashimoto Keigaku zenshū* (Tokyo, 1943), 1:179–180; hereafter cited as *HKZ*.

celebrated Mito scholar Fujita Tōko and also Saigō Takamori of Satsuma became acquainted with Sanai. On one occasion he wrote to a colleague in Fukui that Sakuma Shōzan had been arrested and jailed because "one of his students" (Sanai did not know the name; it was Yoshida Shōin) had tried to stow away aboard a ship in Perry's fleet.[6]

It appears that Sanai's name first came to the attention of a high-level han leader through the coincidental intercession of Fujita Tōko. Suzuki Chikara, Matsudaira Shungaku's chief minister in Edo, supposedly complained to Tōko that there were no men of ability in Fukui. To this Tōko replied that if a han had men of the caliber of Hashimoto Sanai, who might be young but was certainly able, then its fate was in good hands.[7]

In the summer of 1856, Sanai returned to Fukui as instructor in charge of Dutch studies at the new han academy, the Meidō-kan, and by February 1857, he had become the school's headmaster. During the seven months of his tenure in this post he expressed most of his best known ideas about education in general and Western studies (*yōgaku*) in particular. His educational philosophy amounts to a set of exhortations in support of a new and more utilitarian curriculum.

First, the purpose of education was to find and cultivate men of talent (*jinzai*). Such men, trained in practical studies (*jitsu-gaku*), would be able to handle the complex affairs of society and government. He encouraged the study of mathematics and other utilitarian subjects, complaining that standard neo-Confucian training lacked relevance. Among Confucian scholars of earlier generations, only Kumazawa Banzan, Arai Hakuseki, and Rai San'yō commanded his admiration. Most Confucianists of his own day, said Sanai, had simply mastered "the art of parroting" sages of the past and were unfit to deal with current problems.[8]

Second, Sanai advocated the introduction of navigation, sur-

---

[6] Sanai to Kasahara Ryōsaku, May 5, 1854, *HKZ*, 1:64.
[7] Nishimura Fuminori, *Hashimoto Sanai* (Tokyo, 1909), p. 27; Shiga Tadashi, *Idai naru seinen Hashimoto Sanai* (Tokyo, 1928), p. 48.
[8] "Gakusei ni kansuru iken sasshi," *HKZ*, 1:257–258.

veying, chemistry, and similar subjects in preparation for rapid expansion of domestic and international commerce. As he saw it, Japan needed to develop extensive reciprocal trade relations with other countries if national wealth and power were to grow.[9]

Third, acquiring knowledge about the modern West was a vital step in the direction of building Japan's strength. The rationale for Western studies, however, was not admiration of the West for its own sake. The object was "to adopt [Western] techniques in order to supplement our own talents."[10] Sanai ordered caution in selecting *yōgaku* students. Things Western should not obscure the importance of the Japanese tradition nor cause students to ridicule Japan's backwardness. Out of some 1,800 students at the Meidōkan, only 30 could enroll in the new department of Western studies (*yōsho shūgakujo*) which Sanai established in May 1857. And students outside the department were not to examine Western-language materials without special permission.[11]

Sanai's most famous statement about the West adequately sums up his utilitarian approach: "We shall take the machines and techniques from them, but we have our own ethics and morals."[12] This resembles Sakuma Shōzan's much better known call for Western techniques and Eastern ethics, and like Shōzan he prefigures post-Restoration thinkers who often wondered how, if Westernization proceeded to its logical limit, the result-

[9] "Sensei no gaikoku bōeki setsu," *HKZ*, 1:348–349. An English translation appears in Kanai, "Fukui," pp. 39–40.

[10] "Gakumonjo jiken ni tsuki sensei no furei gen'an," *HKZ*, 1:244.

[11] "Gakumonjo jiken," *HKZ*, 1:245, 247.

[12] Numata Jirō, "Acceptance and Rejection of Elements of European Culture in Japan," *Cahiers d'histoire mondiale*, 3, no. 1:241 (1956). In Japanese this quotation appears so often as an epitome of Sanai's views that there is no value in citing more than one recent example: Ozawa Eiichi, *Kindai Nihon shigakushi no kenkyū, Bakumatsu hen* (Tokyo, 1966), p. 10. In point of fact, nowhere in *HKZ* or any other published source of Sanai's writings is such a statement to be found; there is no doubt, however, that it is a modern corruption of a complicated *sōrōbun* passage in a letter from Sanai to Murata Ujihisa, dated December 7, 1857: "If we [continue to] proclaim our own way of benevolence and righteousness (*jingi no michi*) and our own doctrine of loyalty and filial piety (*chūkō no oshie*), and if we begin to take the skills of machinery and techniques from them, . . . it will come to the point when they must be very careful of us" (*HKZ*, 1:471–472).

ant Westernized nation could also remain Japanese. Sanai was no less aware than the men of Meiji who issued the *Imperial Rescript on Education* that during a period of innovation, traditional values could act as a kind of social cement to preserve unity and stability.

In the intellectual history of his time, Sanai acted as a synthesizer of two main schools of thought. On the one hand, he represented the *yōgaku* tradition, in which he received his medical training; to the student of *yōgaku*, Western ways appeared both reasonable and practical.[13] On the other hand, however, Sanai had absorbed the ideas of the increasingly prominent Mito school, which condemned Westerners as barbarians and generally placed little value on Western studies except at the level of improving military hardware. To straddle these two apparently contradictory intellectual traditions was not so hard as it might seem. For both, the natural political unit had come to be Japan as a whole; the congeries of disparate polities of the *bakuhan* system was unnatural. For both, the major objective was to preserve Japan's security, and all practical means to that end should be explored.

Sanai accepted the Mito doctrine of *sonnō jōi* (revere the emperor and repel the barbarian). His educational policy as headmaster of the Meidōkan bore an intentional resemblance to that of the Kōdōkan, Tokugawa Nariaki's academy at Mito. Sanai once stated that Fujita Tōko was the most impressive figure he had ever known,[14] and he declared that Mito stood highest among han, setting a standard for all the others.[15]

[13] As a *yōgakusha*, Sanai was unusually well equipped for his time. He could read Dutch, English, and German, whereas some *yōgakusha*—Yokoi Shōnan, for instance—did not read any Western language. On the other hand, Sanai was neither a devoted scholar nor an enthusiastic disseminator of information about the West. Asked to act as an editor for a Dutch-Japanese lexicon, he declined on grounds that he lacked the detailed knowledge an editor should have and that a dictionary was not a practical necessity at the time. Sanai to Nakane Yukie, May 12, 1856, and Sanai to Kasahara Ryōsaku and Ōiwa Shuichi, May 13, 1856, *HKZ*, 1:100–102. This is a far different attitude from that attributed to a publicist like Sakuma Shōzan, who wanted to spread knowledge of the West to Japanese in all walks of life. See Maruyama Masao, "Bakumatsu ni okeru shiza no henkaku: Sakuma Shōzan no baai," *Tembō*, no. 77:13–41 (May 1965).

[14] Sanai to Nakane Yukie, May 12, 1856, *HKZ*, 1:97.

[15] Sanai to Kuwayama Jūbee, September 4, 1856, *HKZ*, 1:176–177.

But Sanai suffered from none of the irrational xenophobia that gripped so many followers of *mitogaku*. Foreigners were not "barbarians," and to try literally to "repel" them was undesirable as well as impossible. Toward individual Westerners, such as Townsend Harris and his interpreter, Heusken, he could be generous in his praise. "For just the two of them to endure the waves of great oceans and courageously enter the metropolis [Edo] is heroic behavior, and although they are foreigners we must really be extremely impressed with them. . . . It is pointless to view them as barbarians."[16]

Nor did Sanai's support of *kaikoku* spring simply from the realization that Japan could no longer sustain the seclusion policy. He took the positive stand that opening the country would lead to new opportunities for Japan to exploit and therefore contribute to national security. In an informal debate with a Hitotsubashi retainer, Hiraoka Enshirō, Sanai defended foreign trade as the best basis for building "a rich country and a strong army" (*fukoku kyōhei*), and he also urged tolerance toward Christianity as well as acceptance of foreign residents in Japanese communities.[17]

His service in the Meidōkan forms an important chapter in Fukui educational history, but Sanai was too valuable an asset to leave at the han academy indefinitely at a time when the political atmosphere in Edo was so heated. His knowledge of the West and his exposure to a broad spectrum of ideas and personalities within Japan made him a logical choice for advisor on han policy, and Matsudaira Shungaku soon ordered him to come to Edo, responding to requests to do so from Nakane Yukie, chief Fukui minister in Edo after Suzuki Chikara's death. Sanai arrived on October 7, 1857. His tasks were to draft memorials

---

[16] Sanai to Murata Ujihisa, December 7, 1857, *HKZ*, 1:471.

[17] *Sakumu kiji*, Nihon shiseki kyōkai, eds., (Tokyo, 1968), 3:290–291. Sanai was free of that thorough distrust of Christianity as the "evil religion" (*jashūmon*) which marked the thinking of his idol, Fujita Tōko. In one of his infrequent references to Christianity, Sanai and an acquaintance agreed that there was much to be admired in its doctrines, but that it was not entirely a good idea to bring it into Japan. "Ansei heishin (sannen) nikki," *HKZ*, 1:129–130.

and letters for the daimyo and to keep close track of the fast-changing political situation in the shogun's capital.[18]

When Perry made his first appearance in 1853, Shungaku had advocated rebuffing the American's demands that Japan open its doors, and his response to chief councillor Abe Masahiro's solicitation of daimyo opinion was so hawkish as to seem an echo of Tokugawa Nariaki's.[19] By 1856, however, Shungaku's position had changed. Under the moderating influence of Shimazu Nariakira of Satsuma and Yamauchi Toyoshige of Tosa, he forswore his earlier xenophobic attitude and came to support the idea of opening the country.[20]

The problem of finding a successor to the shogun had also germinated in 1853, the very year that Tokugawa Iesada assumed the office, for he was in poor health even then. Fully mature when he took office, Iesada had no children and his physical condition was infirm, to say the least. He may have been a victim of epilepsy, although contemporary reports do not tell enough to confirm such a diagnosis. "The shogun is ill," wrote Sanai. "It is most difficult for him to sit up straight for even half an hour, and he continuously has the shakes and bends. It is very hard for him to speak clearly."[21]

There were two candidates to succeed Iesada. One was the seventh son of Tokugawa Nariaki of Mito, Yoshinobu, adopted lord of the house of Hitotsubashi. The other was Iesada's first cousin, Tokugawa Yoshitomi, child daimyo of the great house of Kii. As early as the summer of 1853, Matsudaira Shungaku suggested to chief councillor Abe that Hitotsubashi Yoshinobu was the better choice, perhaps because he was Nariaki's son and

---

[18] *Sakumu kiji*, 2:145.

[19] Shungaku's reply to Abe is translated by W. G. Beasley, *Select Documents on Japanese Foreign Policy, 1853–1858* (London, 1955), pp. 114–117; for Nariaki's response, see pp. 102–107.

[20] Shungaku already had swung to a *kaikoku* position by the time Sanai returned to Edo in October 1857, so it is incorrect to say that Sanai was the cause of his lord's change of heart, as is held, *inter alios*, by Tōyama Shigeki, *Meiji ishin* (*Iwanami zensho*, no. 128; Tokyo, 1951), p. 98, n. 6, and by Inoue Kiyoshi, *Nihon gendaishi I: Meiji ishin* (Tokyo, 1951), p. 113, n. 5.

[21] Sanai to Murata Ujihisa, October 13, 1857, *HKZ*, 1:378.

at the time Shungaku stood opposed to opening the country. But even after changing his mind on the foreign question, Shungaku continued to support Hitotsubashi, assuring potential allies such as senior councillor Matsudaira Tadakata that the young man's character was not the same as his father Nariaki's; that is, Hitotsubashi supported *kaikoku*.[22]

The senior councillors (*rōjū*), who made up the bakufu's governing board, were all *fudai* (hereditary) daimyo and tended to back Kii rather than Hitotsubashi. So did the members of the Antechamber, which was the only regularly significant advisory assembly of daimyo and consisted in the main of prominent *fudai*, headed by Ii Naosuke, lord of Hikone, the largest *fudai* han in Japan. *Fudai* support for Kii stemmed from the conviction that as a child he could be expected to provide no personal leadership and to remain firmly under the control of the senior councillors. Just the opposite might happen if Hitotsubashi Yoshinobu became shogunal heir: He was fully grown, and his father was the outspoken Tokugawa Nariaki, who had labored for years to bring *shimpan* (collateral) and *tozama* (outside lord) voices into the Bakufu's inner councils.[23]

[22] Shungaku to Matsudaira Tadakata, December 2, 1857, *Sakumu kiji*, 2:207.

[23] The daimyo, over 250 in number, came to Edo according to the specifications of the *sankin kōtai* system and were divided into seven chambers for purposes of attendance at Edo castle. Only three of these chambers contributed in any significant way to the political process, and even their contributions were indirect, because in the mature Bakufu the senior councillors had full control of policy making. The most prestigious of the chambers was the Great Corridor (*ōrōka*), which in 1855 included four *tozama* and seven *shimpan* (headed by the *sanke* or Three Houses of Mito, Owari, and Kii). The most effective politically was the Antechamber (*tamarinoma*), which had seven *fudai* and three *shimpan* members in 1855. Some of the largest *tozama* were members of the Great Hall (*ōbiroma*), but because they were *tozama* they had no recognized privilege of advising Bakufu leaders. Nor did the *shimpan* of the Great Corridor have such a privilege, but being direct relatives of the shogun they could be sure that their opinions were treated with respect. Because the senior councillors were themselves *fudai*, they depended to a degree on the good will and approval of their fellow *fudai* in the Antechamber, making that body the most influential of the seven chambers. For elaboration on this system of chambers, which despite its ungainliness functioned for over two centuries with relative effectiveness to permit articulation of differing political interests, see Conrad D. Totman, *Politics in the Tokugawa Bakufu, 1600–1843* (Cambridge, Mass., 1967), pp. 35–36, 165–167.

Abe Masahiro, chief of the senior councillors since 1845, sympathized with the idea of naming Hitotsubashi heir to the shogun. He took this position, an unusual one for a *fudai* daimyo, because of his commitment to a policy of national unity in the face of the foreign threat. Abe hoped that by choosing Hitotsubashi he could bring all daimyo together in a common effort to protect Japan's security, but his attitude drew the disfavor of his fellow *fudai*. Faced with heavy pressure from both sides, he resigned as chief councillor in November 1855, turning that post over to Hotta Masayoshi in a move widely interpreted as a concession to *fudai* interests. In the summer of 1856, Townsend Harris arrived and began to urge the Bakufu to inaugurate trade relations between Japan and the United States. This new pressure from abroad, coupled with Abe's death in August 1857, brought a renewal of the sharp dispute between the "ins"—the *fudai* daimyo who traditionally had decided Bakufu policy—and the "outs"—great *shimpan* and *tozama* lords who sought a place in the decision-making process.

Step by step, Harris persuaded the senior councillors that the Bakufu should recognize him as an official consular representative of the United States government, that as consul he was worthy of an audience with the shogun, and that the Bakufu must sign a commercial treaty with America lest the British and French come fresh from their depredations in China to demand a more onerous treaty of their own. In the year and a half that it took Harris to accomplish these goals, Matsudaira Shungaku enlisted much new support for his campaign to have Hitotsubashi named shogunal heir. His allies included, or were soon to include, several of the greatest *tozama* daimyo, such as Shimazu of Satsuma and Yamauchi of Tosa, Date Munenari of Uwajima, Hachisuka Narihiro of Tokushima, and Nabeshima Narimasa of Hizen, as well as Tokugawa Yoshikumi of the great *shimpan* house of Owari. Hitotsubashi supporters even emerged among the *fudai*, such as Itakura of Annaka (*not* a member of the Antechamber), and among important *hatamoto* (bannermen) officials of the Bakufu, including finance commissioner Kawaji

Toshiakira and defense officer Iwase Tadanari, the latter being one of the chief negotiatiors with Harris.[24]

The Hitotsubashi supporters did not think of themselves as possessors of an alternative to the *bakuhan* system; they were not revolutionaries.[25] Their hope was to strengthen the Bakufu so that it could more effectively perform its major function of defending all of Japan from external danger.

There were only two legitimate ways for the reformers to proceed.[26] One was cumbersome and unlikely to bring success: to win over influential *fudai* and gradually, through them, get the attention of the senior councillors, who might act to change the system but probably would not because to do so could jeopardize vested *fudai* interests. The other way was to bypass the senior councillors altogether and nominate a strong personality as shogun, for the shogun was, after all, the Bakufu's top officer. This is what the Hitotsubashi backers wanted to do. They argued that it was bad for Japan to have a weak and unimpressive shogun meeting foreign envoys such as Harris. What the office needed was a mature (*nenchō*), intelligent (*eimei*), and popular (*jimbō*) figure like Hitotsubashi, and they made these three criteria their campaign slogan.[27]

By nominating Hitotsubashi, Shungaku and his allies did not intend primarily to impress foreigners but rather to legitimize a host of reforms in both domestic and foreign policy. The leaders of the Hitotsubashi group never formally spelled out the extent of these reforms, but Sanai set forth the main directions of the

[24] Kawaji and Iwase favored having a strong shogun because it would mean more decisive leadership than they could expect from the recalcitrant senior councillors. See Sakata Yoshio, *Meiji ishin shi* (Tokyo, 1960), p. 104.

[25] Postwar biographers of Sanai and Matsudaira Shungaku are adamant in their insistence that the Hitotsubashi group basically was loyal and committed to the *bakuhan* system and had no revolutionary intentions vis-à-vis the Bakufu. See Yamaguchi, *Hashimoto Sanai*, pp. 92–99; and Kawabata Tahei, *Matsudaira Shungaku* (*Jimbutsu sōsho*, no. 138; Tokyo, 1967), pp. 94–95.

[26] See Edwin Borden Lee, "The Political Career of Ii Naosuke" (Ph.D. dissertation, Columbia University, 1960), p. 51.

[27] Shungaku sent a memorial to the senior councillors on December 2, 1857, calling for a man with the qualifications of maturity, intelligence, and popularity; *Sakumu kiji*, 2:205. By the time the movement got to Kyoto in the spring of 1858, merely to mention these three criteria as desirable in a shogun was to indicate a preference for Hitotsubashi.

reform effort in a remarkable letter, dated January 12, 1858, to his colleague Murata Ujihisa, the man who had succeeded him as headmaster of the Meidōkan in Fukui. Sanai called for nothing less than a new way of looking at Japan. He asked that his countrymen "see all of Japan as one family"—in effect, as a nation-state in a world of competing nation-states.[28]

Sanai proposed that national political leadership under the shogun be concentrated in four posts, each a "chief ministership" (*saishō*). There would be three chief ministers for domestic affairs: his own lord, Matsudaira Shungaku; Shimazu Nariakira, lord of Satsuma; and Tokugawa Nariaki of Mito. They would undertake new policies, including systematic encouragement of production and trade within Japan, colonization and development of Ezo (Hokkaido), and employment of men of talent, both high and low in status, in the many offices of the Bakufu.[29]

Turning to the international front, Sanai prescribed that the fourth chief minister should be Nabeshima Narimasa, lord of Hizen, who would oversee the conduct of Japanese foreign policy. Sanai's principal interest in this sphere was to promote the idea of alliance between Japan and Russia in order to fend off Great Britain. He reasoned that a colossal struggle for world leadership was in the making, and that for the time being the winner must be either Britain or Russia. "Britain is vicious and greedy," he wrote, "whereas Russia is rough and stern. But I think that popularity will come to Russia." Japan, meanwhile, had to work hard just to remain independent. "For Japan to survive is unlikely," he continued, "unless we annex Korea and parts of Manchuria and the Maritime Provinces; or perhaps parts of the American or Indian continents." This would be difficult because Britain already held India and the Russians were laying hands on the Maritime Provinces.

> Our strength is insufficient and it would be hopeless for us to challenge the military forces of the West in a prolonged war, so we must instead find an ally. . . . Britain and Russia are the two

[28] *HKZ*, 1:555.
[29] *HKZ*, 1:554–555.

great powers, and because they cannot coexist . . . it is clear
that they will soon clash. Britain may well seize the initiative
and strike at Russia, asking us for a leasehold at Hakodate on
Ezo. When that happens, shall we resolutely deny the British,
or shall we follow them? This is the policy issue to be decided.
I think that we shall definitely want to follow Russia, because
Russia is trustworthy and is our neighbor. . . . If we have Russian backing, even should we lose [in a war with Britain], not
everything would be destroyed.

To prepare for such a war, Sanai recommended that Japan rely
on the United States for defense in the East and hire American
and Russian advisors to initiate military reforms.[30]

Sanai's plans were ambitious and even visionary. His attempt
to surmount the problem of the Bakufu's limited national sovereignty by investing all control in a new quadripartite council
under the shogun's prescriptive authority foreshadows the con-
ciliar schemes of the mid-1860's, although it fails to indicate
what would become of the han with their traditional prerogatives of internal autonomy. Sanai's international program called
for trade and alliances to preserve Japanese security while building up wealth and military power at home, and these were to be
the primary goals of the Meiji government (although, of course,
its leaders eventually chose to make an alliance with Great
Britain rather than Russia).

But in his own time Sanai's hopes for reform depended on the
outcome of the two burning policy issues—treaty relations and
shogunal succession. And of these the succession issue was para-
mount. Sanai himself acknowledged that the reforms could not
materialize unless Hitotsubashi became heir to the shogun, for
his succession was needed to symbolize the drive for national
unity and to provide a mandate for change. "There can be no
other policy," Sanai stated emphatically, for solving domestic
and foreign problems.[31]

At the beginning of 1858, neither the treaty nor the succession
issue seemed likely to be settled with dispatch. Daimyo opinion

[30] *HKZ,* 1:552–554.
[31] Sanai to Murata Ujihisa, November 22, 1857, *HKZ,* 1:441.

on the treaty remained sharply divided. Most daimyo recognized that the Bakufu could not undo what it had already done in the Perry Convention of 1854 and subsequent pacts with the Dutch and Russians, but they resisted the full commercial relations and other new departures which Harris demanded. And on the matter of shogunal succession no consensus developed. By and large, the *fudai* held to their commitment to Kii, whereas important *shimpan* and *tozama* rallied around Hitotsubashi. Faced with this impasse on both issues, chief councillor Hotta Masayoshi made a choice and decided to implement it by a dramatic step: To placate Harris he would go to the old imperial city of Kyoto and secure the court's permission to sign the commercial treaty.

Why did Hotta elect to try to resolve the treaty issue first? One answer is that he did so because it seemed easier to handle than the succession question, on which opinions were perhaps more rigid.[32] And it is true that even a hardened *jōi* champion like Tokugawa Nariaki had reconciled himself to some form of *kaikoku*. But just as plausible is the explanation that Hotta regarded the treaty as the more immediate of the two issues. Harris was pressing hard; the British and French were busily tidying up their war against the Ch'ing government in China, and they might decide to visit Japan soon. Hotta had dealt with little else but the foreign question since Harris's arrival in 1856, and his reputation was that of a minister for foreign affairs. His popular nickname was "the daimyo hung up on the Dutch" (*rampeki daimyō*), and people said that he was "touched by the West."[33]

But why did Hotta feel that he needed to go to Kyoto? Why should the court's permission be necessary before the Bakufu signed a treaty with a foreign government? For two and a half centuries the Bakufu had conducted foreign policy without seriously considering the court's opinion. What had happened to change the situation?

For three decades, ever since the appearance of Aizawa Sei-

---

[32] See Lee, "Political Career of Ii Naosuke," p. 66.

[33] Konishi Shirō, *Kaikoku to jōi*, vol. 19 of *Nihon no rekishi* (Tokyo, 1966), p. 77.

shisai's pathfinding *Shinron* (*New Proposal*) in 1825, Mito scholars and others influenced by Mito writings had called for all Japanese to "revere the emperor and repel the barbarians" (*sonnō jōi*).[34] This meant only that the people should unite against the foreign menace; rejection of Bakufu leadership was in no way implicit in the original use of the slogan. By the time Perry arrived in 1853, even an important *fudai* daimyo like Ii Naosuke could respond to Abe's request for daimyo opinion by suggesting that he consult the emperor.[35] Five years later many more daimyo were counseling Hotta to seek court opinion before acting on the treaty. Matsudaira Shungaku was one of those who did so, as indicated in his memorial of January 10, 1858.[36]

Hotta was therefore under no constraint to obtain the emperor's sanction to sign the treaty, but he did believe that this was the most direct method for silencing criticism of the Bakufu and getting the issue resolved. Confident of success, he allowed his representatives to agree with Harris, on February 18, 1858, that within sixty days the government would sign the commercial treaty.

Plainly Hotta expected no trouble at court. Bakufu negotiators made light of the nobles and even the emperor. Harris recorded their comments: "Kyoto is comparatively a poor place. . . . It is merely a city of priests and temples. . . . (They spoke almost contemptuously of the Mikado, and roared with laughter when I quoted some remarks concerning the veneration in which he is held by the Japanese. They say he has neither money,

---

[34] The late Mito school's first use of the two phrases *sonnō jōi* together was not in Aizawa's *Shinron* but in the "Kōdōkan ki" of 1838; see Motoyama Yukihiko, *Meiji shisō no keisei* (Tokyo, 1969), p. 20.

[35] See Beasley, *Japanese Foreign Policy*, p. 119.

[36] *Ibid.*, p. 180. In *The Japanese Imperial Institution in the Tokugawa Period* (New York, 1968), p. 241, Herschel Webb contends that Shungaku called for the court to be consulted on the issue of shogunal succession; this he never did publicly. The matter of succession was a Tokugawa family concern, but one on which even he, a close collateral, could not speak out too vocally. Shungaku would not have imagined announcing publicly that the court should intervene in a family matter, even though he himself regarded it, as did all supporters of the Hitotsubashi cause, as a grave issue of public policy, because it could lead to a restructuring of the Bakufu.

political power, nor anything else that is valued in Japan. He is a mere cipher.)"[37]

When informed of Hotta's plan to go to Kyoto, Harris tried to follow the reasoning behind such a move: "I at last discovered that they wished to delay the signing of the Treaty until [Hotta] could proceed as 'Ambassador to the Spiritual Emperor' at Kyoto and get his approval; that the moment that approval was received the *Daimyo* must withdraw their opposition." To Harris this seemed to open at least the possibility of failure. "Having concluded this extraordinary conversation, I asked them what they would do if the Mikado refused his assent. They replied in a prompt and decided manner, that the Government had *determined not to receive any objections from the Mikado.*" Perplexed, as he might well be, Harris asked "what is the use then of delaying the Treaty for what appears to be a mere ceremony. They replied that it is this solemn ceremony that gave value to it; and, as I understood, it being known that the Mikado [had been] thus gravely appealed to, his decision would be final, and that all excitement would subside at once."[38]

Three months later, however, on May 15, the negotiators reported evil tidings to Harris: Hotta had failed in his mission; the emperor refused to permit signing of the treaty without further consultation, and the "city of priests and temples" was in turmoil:

> The matters at Miako are more difficult than words can express. The throne of the Tykoon has existed in full power for 300 years. During that period only three embassies have been sent to Miako, and heretofore they have only remained ten days. . . . A conspiracy exists at Miako to murder Hotta. . . . The population of Miako and the adjacent districts are in a state of great excitement. The Mikado said, "When you have got the consent of the *Daimyo*, I will give my consent."[39]

[37] Townsend Harris, *The Complete Journal of Townsend Harris*, rev. ed., Mario E. Cosenza, ed. (Rutland, Vt., 1959), p. 518.
[38] *Ibid.*, pp. 538–539.
[39] *Ibid.*, p. 560.

The court's refusal to give Hotta the permission he sought is only comprehensible in view of three factors: the xenophobia and gross ignorance of world conditions which all the nobles apparently shared; jealousies and rivalries within the court; and the energetic activity at court on the part of the Hitotsubashi forces. The leading figure in this activity was Hashimoto Sanai.

Matsudaira Shungaku sent Sanai to Kyoto with instructions to lobby for an imperial decree favoring Hitotsubashi as shogunal heir. Some historians, notably Kawakita Nobuo, insist that Sanai's original orders were to assist Hotta in getting the court's permission to sign the Harris treaty,[40] but there are at least two reasons for doubting this. First, scarcely anyone could have conceived that Hotta would fail in his mission. Never before had the court denied a Bakufu request. So why should it be necessary to send an envoy to Kyoto in order to lobby for a sure thing?

Second, Sanai contrived an elaborate cover story to mask his true purpose for going to Kyoto. Shungaku's instructions, for instance, tell him to proceed not to Kyoto but to Osaka in order "to examine original [Western] sources on navigation."[41] Sanai himself wrote a letter to Saigō Takamori, who was also in Edo, informing Saigō that he would be "going home" for a month or so—that is, to Fukui. And shortly after his arrival in Kyoto, Sanai wrote to Nakane Yukie explaining that there were several pretexts for his visit to the imperial city: He was planning to collect rare specimens of calligraphy from famous court nobles, or he intended to search for private family records.[42] He also took an alias, calling himself Momonoi Iori.[43]

If Sanai were going to Kyoto to help Hotta, why should he engage in all this subterfuge? To a man the senior councillors

[40] Kawakita Nobuo, *Bakumatsu no seisō* (*Kōdansha gendai shinsho,* no. 149; Tokyo, 1968), pp. 37–39.

[41] *Sakumu kiji,* 2:388–389; "Sensei jōhan no jirei," March 9, 1858, *HKZ,* 1:650.

[42] Sanai to Saigō Kichibee (Takamori), March 11, 1858, *HKZ,* 1:651; Sanai to Nakane Yukie, March 22, 1858, *HKZ,* 1:670.

[43] He also called himself Momonoi Ryōtarō. The court nobles and their retainers whom he met in Kyoto always referred to Sanai by these pseudonyms in correspondence. Momonoi was the surname of Sanai's paternal ancestors.

supported the Harris treaty, so if Sanai was acting on that issue he could scarcely arouse their antipathy. On the succession question, however, the situation was different. Most if not all of the senior councillors were known to support Kii. Hotta's own position was unclear, but the Hitotsubashi camp had to assume that he inclined toward Kii, as did almost all *fudai*.[44] Furthermore, the shogun himself, or his closest relatives and advisors, traditionally decided the succession. For the agent of a *shimpan* daimyo not immediately connected with the issue to go to the court and lobby on behalf of a candidate whom the senior councillors did not favor was an extraordinary action contrary to hallowed practice and therefore perhaps fraught with danger.

What Sanai found in Kyoto dismayed him from the outset. The court itself, structured as a government but having performed no significant governmental functions for many centuries, was hard enough to understand.[45] Kōmei, on the throne since 1846, was a mature and perceptive emperor whose sympathies, however, ran decidedly against opening the country. His chief officers, such as the *kampaku* (first minister), Kujō Hisatada, and the *taikō* (former *kampaku*), Takatsukasa Masamichi, often clashed on personal grounds.[46] Some nobles were influential not so much as a result of the offices they held but because of impressive personal qualities. Sanjō Sanetsumu and Konoe Tadahiro, for example, were much admired. So was Prince Awata, assigned to the abbacy of the Shōren'in; he was a man so vigorous and skilled in the martial arts—most unusual for a court noble—that the Bakufu had kept a sharp eye on his activities.[47]

---

[44] In *Bakumatsu shi gaisetsu* (Tokyo, 1930), p. 176, Inobe Shigeo asserts that before going to Kyoto Hotta favored Kii. Ii Naosuke had the same impression, which he communicated by letter to his man in Kyoto, Nagano Shuzen, during Hotta's campaign to get imperial approval for the Harris treaty. See Sakata, *Meiji ishin shi*, pp. 111–112.

[45] Webb, *Japanese Imperial Institution*, pp. 78–99 and 128–131, gives an excellent overview of the offices and personnel making up the imperial court.

[46] Murdoch, *History of Japan*, 3:677–678; see also "Sensei yori Kyōto no keisei nado o hōzuru Edotei e no missho," April 12, 1858, *HKZ*, 1:729.

[47] See Nezu Masashi, "Kōmei tennō to Nakagawa no miya," in Tōyama Shigeki, ed., *Ishin no gunzō*, vol. 10 of *Jimbutsu/Nihon no rekishi* (Tokyo, 1965), pp. 39–40.

The emperor and high-ranking nobles enjoyed the luxury that their plentiful incomes afforded, but the majority of lesser court families lived more modestly, and all of the nobles, from the emperor down, felt that the Bakufu did not provide for them in a manner commensurate with their stature as an aristocratic elite. Hotta Masayoshi sought to trade on the nobles' genteel poverty by bribing them, a normal practice whenever the Bakufu wanted something from the court. He brought large sums to Kyoto as "gifts," hoping that this largesse would assure speedy issuance of imperial sanction for the treaty. Similarly, Matsudaira Shungaku supplied Sanai with ample funds to smooth his way into the good graces of the aristocrats.[48]

Preceding Sanai to Kyoto were letters from Shimazu Nariakira to Sanjō Sanetsumu and Konoe Tadahiro, and Sanai carried with him a letter to Sanjō from Yamauchi Toyoshige. These letters implored Sanjō to support the Hitotsubashi cause.[49] Sanai himself set out to reinforce the point. On March 23, bearing landscape sketches, fancy *fusuma* paper, and 1,000 pieces of gold, he visited Sanjō.[50] He saw a number of other nobles as well, in particular Prince Awata and Takatsukasa Masamichi. But his relationship with Sanjō typifies his method of dealing with the nobles and their attitude toward the critical issues of the day.

Sanai tried to explain to Sanjō that Japan was facing great danger. The nations of the West possessed highly refined techniques and institutions that had enabled them to swallow up other lands, and Japan needed desperately to learn Western methods as a means of self-preservation.[51] For all this Sanjō showed no enthusiasm. He was disinterested in foreign barbar-

---

[48] See Webb, *Japanese Imperial Institution*, pp. 97–99, on the relative affluence of the nobles. A tabulation of the monetary gifts which Sanai bestowed on various people at court, mostly retainers of prominent nobles, is given in his account of the trip, "Shuppan shojiki," in Yamaguchi Muneyuki, ed., *Zenshū mishū Hashimoto Sanai kankei no shiryō kenkyū* (Kurume, 1965), pp. 71–80.

[49] Shimazu Nariakira to Konoe Tadahiro and Sanjō Sanetsumu, February 19, 1858, *HKZ*, 1:636–637.

[50] "Sensei yori Kyōto no keisei nado o hōzuru Edotei e no missho," *HKZ*, 1:724.

[51] "Sensei yori Sanjō Sanetsumu e no teisho hikae," late March or early April 1858, *HKZ*, 1:691–696.

ians and remained serenely confident of the superiority of Japan, the "divine land" (*shinshū*).

But when Sanai changed the subject to argue that in such straits Japan required an energetic figure like Hitotsubashi Yoshinobu as shogun, Sanjō "clapped his hands for joy" and promised all the help he could offer.[52] Sanai encountered the same kind of response from other nobles with whom he consulted.[53]

By the end of April, the Hitotsubashi lobby had gained the backing of almost every leading noble at court, but the price turned out to be heavy. Despite his commitment to opening the country, Sanai stopped trying to persuade the nobles that Hotta should receive imperial sanction for the American treaty. He found it necessary to jettison the whole argument that foreign trade was desirable, for he had to cater to the xenophobia of the nobles in order to hold their support for Hitotsubashi. This he could do in good conscience only because he knew that the treaty was absolutely unavoidable anyway and the important thing was to revamp the Bakufu before it went into effect, a task requiring that Hitotsubashi become heir to the shogun.

Sanai's successful effort to gain court support for Hitotsubashi therefore had the unintended corollary of dooming Hotta's campaign for imperial approval of the treaty. As time passed it became clear that Hotta had won only a single important ally at court, Kujō Hisatada, the *kampaku*. Hotta got Kujō's support largely because of the efforts of a confidential agent, Nagano Shuzen, whom Ii Naosuke had dispatched to Kyoto in order to work on Kujō's retainer, Shimada Sakon. But the *kampaku* was virtually alone in favoring the treaty. And on April 6, and again

[52] "Sensei yori Kyōto no keisei nado o hōzuru Edotei e no missho," *HKZ*, 1:725.

[53] Sanai generally approached the nobles through their retainers, and he used whatever connections he possibly could, whether matrimonial, professional, or geographical. For instance, he converted Takatsukasa Masamichi to the Hitotsubashi cause in large measure through the help of his tutor, Mikuni Daigaku, the son of a prosperous merchant from Wakasa near Fukui, who was an acquaintance of Nakane Yukie. Shungaku himself wrote a letter to Mikuni urging that he persuade Takatsukasa to support Hitotsubashi. Shungaku to Mikuni Daigaku, May 1,1858, *HKZ*, 1:774-775.

on May 3, Hotta received formal notification from the emperor directing him to ask for daimyo opinion on the whole subject and then report back to the throne.[54]

The court's intransigent xenophobia left Sanai deeply frustrated, not only because he so strongly disagreed with it but also because he had to play down his own *kaikoku* convictions in order to keep court opinion on his side of the shogunal succession debate. His correspondence makes abundantly clear how impatient he grew with the situation in Kyoto. The day after he arrived, on March 22, he wrote to Nakane that "Confucian students" (*shoseihai* or *juseihai*) were keeping people in the imperial capital in a needless state of agitation by spreading rumors that Hotta had brought news of impending war with the "barbarians."[55] A few days later he complained that Kyoto was "a vulgar place, disorderly and hard to bear." Referring to Sanjō's obstinate unwillingness to acknowledge the challenge of Western technological superiority, Sanai lamented that Sanjō was, after all, a court noble, unable to escape old-fashioned attitudes. Some of the nobles were clever speakers and nice stylists, to be sure, but not one of them had the "real talent and practical knowledge" (*shinsai jitsugaku*) to handle the important affairs of the realm. No wonder power had long ago passed from Kyoto to Kamakura! If it ever returned to the court, he joked, the "barbarians" (*iteki*) were certain to overwhelm Japan in no time.[56]

Despite his frustration, Sanai seemed to have achieved his primary goal in Kyoto. It appeared that Hotta would get an imperial message recommending that the succession issue be settled in favor of Hitotsubashi. Mikuni Daigaku, a subordinate

---

[54] See Yamaguchi, *Hashimoto Sanai*, p. 150; for a translation of the second imperial reply, see Beasley, *Japanese Foreign Policy*, pp. 180–181.

[55] *HKZ*, 1:670. Sanai was referring to Yanagawa Seigan, Umeda Umpin, and Rai Mikisaburō, *rōnin* who did much to inspire the anti-Bakufu *sonnō jōi* movement in its initial Kyoto phase. On March 28, Sanai gave Yanagawa 100 pieces of gold, evidently hoping to silence him. See "Shuppan shojiki," in Yamaguchi, *Zenshū mishū*, p. 75.

[56] Sanai to Kawaji Saemon no jō (Toshiakira), March 26, 1858, *HKZ*, 1:687; "Sensei yori Kyōto no keisei nado o hōzuru Edotei e no missho," *HKZ*, 1:727; "Sensei yori Edo hantei Nakane Yukie e no missho," April 12, 1858, *HKZ*, 1:718; "Sensei yori Kyōto no keisei nado o hōzuru Edotei e no missho," *HKZ*, 1:727; "Sensei yori Edo hantei Nakane Yukie e no missho," *HKZ*, 1:719.

of *taikō* Takatsukasa Masamichi, wrote to Nakane Yukie on May 5 to report that an imperial instruction would reach Hotta soon. It would tell him that in such grave times resolution of the succession issue was an urgent necessity and that "intelligence, popularity, and maturity" were the criteria to be sought in the heir.[57]

But it did not happen that way. Instead Hotta received an imperial message declaring only that the succession was a matter of considerable gravity which demanded quick settlement.[58] Not a single word appeared about maturity, intelligence, or popularity. At the last moment Ii Naosuke's agent, Nagano Shuzen, had persuaded Kujō Hisatada, who as *kampaku* actually issued the emperor's statements, to remove the key phrase from the final draft of the imperial message.

Hotta himself was dumfounded by the exclusion. By then he had become convinced that only the naming of Hitotsubashi could induce the court to approve the treaty.[59] Because they liked and trusted the daimyo supporting Hitotsubashi, the nobles apparently felt that they could accept a treaty concluded under Hitotsubashi auspices. That Hotta should believe this serves to underscore the importance of Sanai's mission to Kyoto. The chief councillor went back to Edo determined to win the succession for Hitotsubashi Yoshinobu.

Sanai was also preparing to return to Edo. So confident was he that the court had formally communicated its preference for Hitotsubashi that he took a leisurely tour south through Uji, Nara, and the Hōryūji, pausing often to reflect on the many shrines, monasteries, and other monuments of early Japanese civilization in that historic area.[60] It appears that not until his

---

[57] *HKZ*, 1:809. Another source holds that court officials came to Hotta on May 5 and told him that the imperial will favored the three criteria which denoted Hitotsubashi; see Yamaguchi, *Hashimoto Sanai*, p. 180.

[58] "Saijō ikken ni tsuki densō yori Hotta Bitchū no kami e no tasshi," May 8, 1858, *HKZ*, 1:840.

[59] Hotta argued in favor of Hitotsubashi in his reply to the imperial instruction telling him to settle the issue quickly; "Den gi ryōsō jisan no chokujō ni taisuru Hotta Bitchū no kami no shomen," May 9, 1858, *HKZ*, 1:840–842.

[60] The entries for May 9–10 in "Shuppan shojiki," in Yamaguchi, *Zenshū mishū*, pp. 77–78, show that Sanai gave himself up wholly to relaxation during his trip. He records his liking for the deer at the Kasuga Shrine, his admiration

arrival in Edo on May 23 did he learn the truth: Kujō arbitrarily had excised the words "intelligence, popularity, and maturity" and thereby vitiated Sanai's success in Kyoto.

Events moved rapidly during the next few months. On June 4, 1858, three days after Hotta's return to Edo, Ii Naosuke became *tairō*, superseding Hotta in authority. At least one of the senior councillors, Matsudaira Tadakata, had actively encouraged Ii to take the appointment as great councillor, and the rest evidently acquiesced.[61] On July 29, Ii permitted the Bakufu negotiating team to sign the Treaty of Amity and Commerce with the United States, although he had not yet gone back to the court to seek its opinion again, as the emperor's message of May 3 to Hotta had requested. Gradually the *tairō* proceeded to demote leading pro-Hitotsubashi Bakufu officials. On August 2, he dismissed Hotta from the board of senior councillors. The following day, August 3, Matsudaira Shungaku, Tokugawa Nariaki, and Tokugawa Yoshikumi of Owari paid an irregular visit to Edo castle and practically besieged Ii in an eleventh-hour effort to persuade him to name Hitotsubashi as heir to the shogun; failing this, they hoped to convince Ii that if he did name Kii, he should appoint Shungaku as regent. They also attacked the great councillor for having "violated the imperial will" (*ichoku*) in agreeing to sign the Harris treaty.[62] None of this moved Ii Naosuke. On August 4, he publicly announced the choice of Kii as successor. And on August 13, in retaliation for their unauthorized call at the castle, he placed Shungaku and

---

of the Great Buddha at the Tōdaiji, and similar trivial bits of information. As Yamaguchi Muneyuki sees it (*Hashimoto Sanai*, p. 181), "It was precisely because he believed the movement had succeeded that he could have such a period of leisure amidst the pressures of business."

[61] Kawakita, *Bakumatsu no seisō*, p. 43, holds that Tadakata maneuvered to secure Ii's appointment as *tairō* simply in order to counter Hotta until he himself could take over as chief councillor.

[62] The story of what happened during the "irregular visit to the castle" (*fuji tojō*) is likely never to be fully clarified. There is a simple account, confined to the debate over the treaty, in *Ishin shi*, Ishin shiryō hensankai, ed. (Tokyo, 1940), 2:493–497. The story from the Fukui side appears in *Sakumu kiji*, 4:259–270. In English, see Conrad D. Totman, "The Struggle for Control of the Shogunate (1853–1858)," *Papers on Japan* (Harvard University, East Asian Research Center, 1961), 1:87–88, n. 94.

his colleagues under house arrest and stripped Shungaku and Tokugawa Yoshikumi of their titles as daimyo.

By these decisive strokes Ii eliminated the Hitotsubashi group's chances of success through legitimate political action. And Hashimoto Sanai's brief career as a politician was over. He and Nakane Yukie contemplated suicide for having brought their lord to the point of enforced retirement, but Shungaku dissuaded them, asking his trusted retainers "not to desert" him.[63] Barely a week after Ii had punished Shungaku, Sanai ordered Kondō Ryōsuke, whom he had left in charge of affairs in Kyoto, to desist from all activity there.[64] On November 27, 1858, officers representing the Edo city magistrates called at the Fukui residence at Tokiwabashi and placed Sanai under arrest. For the next year he was held prisoner within the mansion grounds, and he underwent periodic interrogation, first at the city magistrates' office and then, in 1859, at the offices of the *hyōjōsho,* the Bakufu's highest tribunal.

Sanai's attitude under questioning was generally one of guileless candor. Occasionally he was disingenuous, as, for example, in responding to a query about his pseudonym Momonoi. His acquaintances in Kyoto were so numerous, he said, that had he used his real name he would have gotten no work done.[65] But on the whole he answered frankly. He even admitted quite freely that he had acted on Shungaku's orders. For this he was criticized by some who held that a samurai's first duty was to protect his lord by claiming to have acted on individual initiative, but Sanai believed that if he explained the true situation the officials would see the light, realize that the Hitotsubashi group had only the Bakufu's best interests at heart, and release Shungaku from house arrest.[66]

Because of his faith in the essential altruism of the Hitotsubashi cause, Sanai was shocked when, on October 27, 1859, he was removed to the prison at Demma-chō. On the morning of

[63] Yamaguchi, *Hashimoto Sanai*, p. 211; Shungaku to Sanai, August 13, 1858, *HKZ*, 2:1009.

[64] Sanai to Kondō Ryōsuke, August 22, 1858, *HKZ*, 2:1018.

[65] "Hyōjōsho nite torishirabe ōtō," August 1, 1859, *HKZ*, 2:1162.

[66] See Yamaguchi, *Hashimoto Sanai*, pp. 232–233.

November 1 he heard his sentence. It listed the charges against him at some length, coming to the point only with the very last word: "The former lord of Echizen [Shungaku], wanting to establish Lord Hitotsubashi as shogunal heir, sent you to Kyoto in order to arrange affairs at the imperial palace. . . . You should have remonstrated with your lord that this was no matter to be taken lightly. . . . You acted without respect for the Bakufu's will. Because of the insolence of these circumstances, the penalty is death."[67] Later that same morning Sanai was taken to the execution ground with two other men involved in the activity at Kyoto. One was Rai Mikisaburō, a well-known tippler who was the son of the historian Rai San'yō and belonged to the group of xenophobic "Confucian students" who had so upset Sanai in Kyoto. The other was Iiizumi Kinai, the obscure retainer of an unimportant *hatamoto* official. All three were put to the sword, and just three weeks later their prison mate at Demma-chō, Yoshida Shōin, met the same fate.

The crisis of 1858 involved two major issues, of which one (the treaty) was indisputably a question of public policy, whereas the other (shogunal succession) had public policy implications but was technically a Tokugawa family affair. We have seen that Sanai and his superiors placed the succession movement ahead of the treaty issue. They assumed that *kaikoku* was inescapable. Their primary concern, as a matter of long-term policy, was to bring about a reform of the Bakufu so that it could function more effectively as a national government. It was in support of this aim that they enlisted the aid of the imperial court.

At court in Kyoto during the spring of 1858, Sanai had tried to convince influential nobles that opening the country was beneficial as well as unavoidable. They proved disinterested, and he knew why: They were stuffy and provincial aristocrats ignorant of political realities. But knowing this did not deter him from fanning enthusiasm for Hitotsubashi's candidacy among the Kyoto elite. Despite his contempt for their political sagacity,

[67] "Sensei shokei no mōshiwatashijō," *HKZ*, 2:1174–1175.

he intended to use whatever help he could get in order to ensure Hitotsubashi's nomination as heir, for this was the key to achieving political reform.

After Sanai's failure in Kyoto, Matsudaira Shungaku again tried to capitalize on the court's prestige when he charged Ii Naosuke with "violation of the imperial will" for signing the Harris treaty. Much has been made of this charge as a mere device in a power struggle, a stick to beat Ii, inasmuch as the Hitotsubashi backers were themselves known to favor *kaikoku*. But Shungaku and his allies were not protesting chiefly against the signing of the treaty: They objected to Ii's pending announcement of Kii as heir to the shogun. This decision, said Shungaku, also violated the imperial will because it ran counter to the court's clear preference for Hitotsubashi.[68] And in this sense Shungaku's accusation against Ii did amount to a convenient political device, for the Hitotsubashi forces were willing to use anything, including the emperor and his court, in their contest with Ii over the succession. As Fujita Shōzō has remarked, the modern Japanese state based on the "emperor system" could only have been built by men who were liberated from faith in the emperor.[69]

For the *tairō*, too, the crisis of 1858 appears to have turned on the succession rather than the foreign issue.[70] He knew that his opponents approved of the treaty. What angered him was their action in promoting Hitotsubashi's candidacy at the imperial court. This defied Tokugawa custom by involving the throne in a partisan issue. More importantly, it threatened to undermine the Bakufu's very authority over the daimyo by questioning the validity of its decisions. It cannot have pleased Ii to hear

---

[68] *Sakumu kiji*, 4:105. But the Hitotsubashi forces did not flinch from assailing Ii with the charge of signing the treaty against imperial wishes. *Sakumu kiji*, 4:71–72, records a letter dated July 2, 1858, from Shungaku to Tokugawa Nariaki, saying that if the Bakufu signed the treaty without imperial sanction, it would call down such wrath from the daimyo that only the appointment of a strong shogun (that is, Hitotsubashi) could overcome the charge of violating the imperial will and reassert Bakufu authority. Again, of course, this points up the primacy of the succession issue in the minds of the Hitotsubashi group.

[69] Fujita Shōzō, *Ishin no seishin* (Tokyo, 1967), p. 26.

[70] This is the explicit interpretation of Tokinoya Masaru, "Ii Naosuke to Hashimoto Sanai," in Tōyama, ed., *Ishin no gunzō*, p. 35.

Shungaku inquire of him rhetorically, "If the shogun does not heed the imperial will, are the daimyo likely to obey the Baku-fu's orders?"[71]

The *tairō's* man in Kyoto, Nagano Shuzen, summed up his lord's belief that the traditional way of doing things was sacrosanct and that what the reformers proposed was alien:

> The peace and order of the realm are due to the dignity and virtue of the great shogunal family, not just to the relative intelligence [of an individual shogun]. This is the custom of our empire, different from that of other countries. If, despite this, we now reject the one closer in blood [Kii] and choose the one who is intelligent [Hitotsubashi], it is foreign-style and not the custom of our empire, which must be to respect the direct line of descent.[72]

And Ii expressed his own attitude very clearly in a letter to Nagano written during the heat of the intrigues at Kyoto. Affirming that the issue of succession was a critical one, he asserted that there was no recourse but to name Kii heir. "To nominate a lord because of his intelligence is to have inferiors choose their superior and is entirely the Chinese style. What is worse, never before has the selection been made for reasons of personal gain. That is the ultimate in perfidy."[73]

The Ansei purge was Ii's answer to his critics. He dealt firmly if mercifully with the leading daimyo and Bakufu officials who had ranged themselves against him, but the purge soon widened and grew more cruel. The *tairō* scattered his myrmidons across Japan seeking all who were even slightly associated with the Hitotsubashi cause. In Kyoto, Nagano Shuzen and senior councillor Manabe Akikatsu arrested and jailed not only the "Confucian students" but also the retainers of court nobles. Nor were the aristocrats themselves immune: Sanjō Sanetsumu, Takatsu-kasa Masamichi, and Konoe Tadahiro had to resign their positions under duress. As far away as Chōshū, Yoshida Shōin went to jail, was handed over to Bakufu authorities, and found him-

---

[71] *Sakumu kiji,* 4:260.
[72] Quoted in *Ishin shi,* 2:443.
[73] Quoted *ibid.,* 2:442–443.

self behind bars again in Edo. There was a grim thoroughness about this purge, even though it touched only about one hundred persons.[74]

Whether the failure of political reform in 1858 was an avertible misfortune, an accident of Ii's personality and those of Sanai and the other antagonists, is something one can judge only in a speculative way. Japanese historians, accustomed to thinking of history as a process whose motive force is conflict, tend to argue that the reformers necessarily had to fail, that they were too committed to the system they wanted to reform and were beating their heads against the stone wall of Bakufu traditionalism: Only the overthrow of the "feudal" system could make possible the changes that followed the Meiji Restoration. Yet it is worth questioning the conclusion that failure was inevitable. The Tokugawa system had been flexible enough to last two and a half centuries.[75] In the late 1850's, it had at least the capability for effective reform. And it was Ii Naosuke as much as the reformers who departed from normal political practice, although he did so, to be sure, in the hope of preserving the traditional system of *fudai* hegemony over policy making. While in Kyoto, Hotta Masayoshi had come around to the Hitotsubashi cause. Hotta was chief councillor and the board of senior councillors ordinarily would have done his bidding had he asked support for Hitotsubashi.[76] But Ii, whose ancestors on

[74] Kawabata, *Matsudaira Shungaku*, p. 159; see also Edwin B. Lee, "Ii Naosuke's Attempt to Save the Tokugawa Shogunate," *Studies on Asia*, 8:27 (1967).

[75] See Totman, *Politics in the Tokugawa Bakufu*, p. 255–256, for a discussion of Bakufu administrative flexibility.

[76] By the mid-nineteenth century, the senior councillors had long held unquestioned authority to decide issues of public policy. But on an issue that, despite its public implications, was technically a family matter, such as shogunal succession, the Great Interior (*ōoku*) had considerable, if mysterious, influence. The Great Interior consisted of women who were the immediate relatives of the shogun or their attendants and servants. Politics there were byzantine indeed; for a discussion, see Totman, *Politics in the Tokugawa Bakufu*, pp. 103–108. In 1858, the ladies of the Great Interior were opposed to any son of Tokugawa Nariaki, their *bête noire*. Therefore their support, for what it was worth, went to the backers of Kii; see Shibusawa Eiichi, *Tokugawa Yoshinobu kō den* (*Tōyō bunko*, no. 88; Tokyo, 1967), 1:138. Lacking adequate information, one must conclude provisionally that the Great Interior was an important but not decisive factor in settling a question of shogunal succession.

five previous occasions had exercised the office of great councillor largely as a powerless regency, had himself appointed to the post and then took the highly irregular course of eliminating all his opposition through the use of house arrest, incarceration, and even the executioner's blade. The very abnormality of his actions made him a constant target, and his assassination in 1860 can have come as no surprise. As Conrad Totman notes, "The Ii role as great councillor was one of ineffectiveness which has been concealed by the deceptive career of Ii Naosuke. . . . For two centuries the Ii family's high office had conveyed no power. Ii Naosuke then tried to violate the house tradition and be powerful. He paid with his life."[77]

Despite their failure, the reformers deserve attention as politicians whose objectives and methods resemble those of the leaders who were to come after the Restoration. More than Ii and his coterie of traditionalists, they displayed the qualities of rationality and achievement orientation that we commonly associate with Meiji leadership. Hashimoto Sanai illustrates this point very well. One of the darlings of prewar nationalist writers because he died at Ii's command just as Yoshida Shōin did, Sanai was indeed a proponent of *sonnō jōi*—but so was everyone else. What mattered was not the fact but the content of one's particular commitment to *sonnō jōi*.[78] For Shōin, it came to involve the overthrow of the Bakufu. For Ii, it connoted maintaining the

[77] Totman, *Politics in the Tokugawa Bakufu*, pp. 164–165.

[78] Excellent as illustrations of prewar exaltation of Sanai as a *sonnō jōi* loyalist are the articles about him by Hiraizumi Kiyoshi, *Bushidō no fukkatsu* (Tokyo, 1933), pp. 11–57. Postwar writers do not deny that Sanai believed in *sonnō jōi* but emphasize his overriding commitment to the *bakuhan* system, however strongly he wished to reform it; see Yamaguchi, *Hashimoto Sanai*, pp. 239–297. Ichii Saburō puts Sanai together with Yoshida Shōin as one who had a "self-conscious sense of *jōi*" (*jikakuteki jōi ishiki*), which involved opening the country as a necessary security measure; he was therefore different from the fanatics who accepted *jōi* on faith (*shinkōteki jōi ishiki*) and demanded literal "repulsion of the barbarians"; Ichii Saburō, "Ishin henkaku no shisō: Chōshū sonjōha no shisōteki keifu," in Shisō no kagaku kenkyūkai, ed. *Kyōdō kenkyū Meiji ishin* (Tokyo, 1967), p. 129. Nakazawa Morito argues rather implausibly that Sanai's views led in the direction of Asian union against Western imperialism, a direction quite different from that of the *sonnō jōi* Meiji leaders who, he says, committed aggression in Asia in order to follow the example of Western imperialism; Nakazawa Morito, "Hashimoto Sanai," in Naramoto Tatsuya, ed., *Ishin no shishi*, vol. 10 of *Nihonshi no jimbutsuzō* (Tokyo, 1967), pp. 57–59.

status quo at any cost. For Sanai, it meant reform of the political system.

Of these three concepts of *sonnō jōi*, the one identified with Shōin conforms to what happened in the Meiji Restoration, when the Bakufu was in fact overthrown. But in 1858, Sanai was much closer than an isolated idealist like Shōin to the pragmatic spirit of reform that motivated the makers of the Meiji state. Nor was Sanai so tradition-bound as Ii Naosuke, despite his commitment to the framework of the *bakuhan* system. A shrewd politician adept at persuasion and manipulation of institutions, Sanai was as alert as anyone to the menace of the West. But he responded by defining specific new policies to implement the goal of achieving a wealthy and powerful nation rather than by playing traditional roles to the hilt, as Ii and his followers did in their ultimately unsuccessful attempt to preserve the status quo.[79] Sanai represents an early manifestation of nationalist ideas put into political action in a Japan that, for better or worse, came to typify the rise of modern nationalism in the non-Western world.

[79] The distinction I am drawing here is one that has been employed in general comparisons of the Japanese and Chinese responses to Western impact in the nineteenth century: Japanese behavior is characterized as primarily directed toward goal attainment (achievement orientation), whereas Chinese behavior was aimed chiefly at system maintenance (status orientation). See Robert N. Bellah, *Tokugawa Religion* (Glencoe, Ill., 1957), pp. 188–192; and Edwin O. Reischauer, "Modernization in Nineteenth-Century China and Japan," *Japan Quarterly*, 10:303–304 (July–Sept. 1963).

KIDO KŌIN AND ŌKUBO TOSHIMICHI: A PSYCHOHISTORICAL ANALYSIS

Albert M. Craig

The Meiji leaders were a lively and diverse group. Saigō Takamori, a huge man with a size 19½ neck, was sufficiently a man of destiny to sit in exile on a lonely island and sift political intelligence without losing a sense of involvement.[1] Takamori's brother, Tsugumichi, later naval minister, was a practical joker: He once sent a group of colleagues off on a rabbit hunt on an island where there were no rabbits.[2] Itō Hirobumi, the consummate politician and constitutionalist of the 1880's, is described by one scholar as the master of "the art of the possible."[3] He is reputed to be the author of the lines, "Asleep with one's head in the lap of a beauty, one awakens at dawn to resume the mantle of empire," that many middle Meiji bureaucrats took as their ideal.[4] Yet early photographs reveal a brash youth with massive jaw and two swords who, against hopeless odds, began the Chōshū civil war in 1865.

Kuroda Kiyotaka was a dipsomaniac who murdered his wife and was sent off to develop Hokkaido to get him out of the capital. The sketch of Gotō Shōjirō in Sansom's *The Western World and Japan* shows a fat face, a white mustache, and long sideburns, looking very much like a fuddy-duddy, small-town band-

---

[1] Ryūsaku Tsunoda, William Theodore de Bary, and Donald Keene, *Sources of the Japanese Tradition* (New York, 1958), p. 654. The uniform of Saigō is preserved in the Yasukuni Shrine Museum.

[2] Kurihara Kōta, *Hakushaku Itō Miyoji* (Tokyo, 1938), 1:112–113.

[3] George Akita, *Foundations of Constitutional Government in Modern Japan, 1868–1900* (Cambridge, Mass. 1967), p. 107.

[4] This is often quoted. See, for example, Oka Yoshitake, *Kindai Nihon no seijika* (Tokyo, 1960), p. 43.

master. Yet at the time of the Richardson assassination, he leaped from his horse and decapitated the fleeing assailant with a single stroke, "a feat," as Sansom puts it, that cannot "be performed without practice."[5] Yamagata Aritomo, army minister and prime minister, hoped as a youth to become a master spearman. He once defeated all comers at a famous school of spearmanship while visiting in Yanagawa han. Even in later life he continued his practice on a great fig tree situated outside his bedroom; eventually the tree died from his thrusts.[6] When asked what sort of a man he had been, the young mistress of Yamagata's later life could only reply, "Oh, how afraid I was" (or "How fearsome he was," *aa kowakatta*).[7]

The Meiji leaders were not a uniform group acting facelessly behind the anonymous figure of the Meiji emperor. True, political individuality in the Western sense of the term was minimized by the façade of "personal rule by the emperor (*goshin-sei*)," by the continuation into the Meiji of the Tokugawa practice of secrecy in government affairs, and by the lack of strong public opinion to reflect policy debates and identify this man with that policy. The seeming facelessness of the Meiji leaders stems largely from the fact that little has been written about them in English and that modern Japanese scholarship tends to overlook personality as a dimension of history.[8]

This paper will treat Kido and Ōkubo, the two most powerful and creative of the early Meiji leaders. What were the stages in their development? What kind of men were they? What kind of leaders were they? In dealing with these problems, I shall at times raise questions for which I have only partial answers in the hope that others will be stimulated to pursue similar lines of inquiry. In particular, in the past few years our grasp of Japanese personality has been greatly extended by the writings of DeVos,

[5] George B. Sansom, *The Western World and Japan* (New York, 1951), p. 317.
[6] Oka Yoshitake, *Yamagata Aritomo* (Tokyo, 1958), p. 1.
[7] Roger Hackett, personal communication.
[8] In general, in Japan psychologists have ignored history, and historians are uninterested in the insights of psychology. An exception that comes to mind is Kuwabara Takeo's work on Nakae Chōmin. There are also, of course, popular writers who write of great men (*jimbutsu*) in history.

Wagatsuma, Vogel, Lifton, and Doi. The time has come to use their concepts in historical contexts, even if it means putting forth conjectures that, for lack of data, we cannot prove conclusively.[9]

FAMILY LIFE

Our theoretical understanding of Japanese psychology begins with Ruth Benedict's *The Chrysanthemum and the Sword*. Benedict demonstrates the "fit" between shame, Japan's particularistic ethic, and the patterns of social obligations and expectations in Japan. Simply put, one consideration regarding an action is whether it is right or wrong. If the value "controlling" the action is universal, the act is always right or always wrong. If the value is particular, the act may be right sometimes and wrong other times; the question is one of appropriateness of time, place, and person. Both types of values become internalized. If a desire is merely inappropriate to a situation, it usually will be suppressed. There is no need to bury it in the unconscious, no reason not to admit that such a desire could exist within oneself. Thus suppression is the mechanism associated with shame. By and large Benedict's analysis is still compelling; the lack of a universal ethic, the relative lack of sexual guilt, contribute in Japan to the formation of personalities in which shame is relatively more important than in the West.

Furthermore, there is an obvious correlation between the shame orientation, the weakness of self, and the depth and sensitivity of individual involvement in the group. The Japanese genius for effective work group cooperation, for the formation of groups stronger than their individual members, is partially illuminated by Benedict's analysis.

[9] This article is an offshoot of my current research on the establishment of the Meiji government. I am especially indebted to Professor Yukihiko Motoyama who, with deep devotion to scholarship and good-natured patience, compelled me to read endless volumes of the letters and diaries of early Meiji leaders. I also have profited immensely from our many discussions of Meiji history. I appreciate suggestions received from Robert Bellah, George DeVos, John Dower, Howard Hibbett, Kate and Yoshiyuki Nakai, Donald Shively, Benjamin Schwartz, Ezra Vogel, and from my wife.

But Freud said that civilization was built on repression. Is it possible, following the shame hypothesis, that Japan's is not? Fortunately or unfortunately, depending on one's bias in the matter, Japan is no exception to the rule. There is much in Japan that shame does not explain: the guilt in Sōseki's *Kokoro,* the thinly veiled Oedipal and Electra relations in Kawabata's *Thousand Cranes,* the burning desire for career success in Japan's business world, or the drive and will power of the Meiji innovators—men who were in no sense simply reacting to situational cues as to what was or was not appropriate.

The guilt hypothesis starts with the fact that there are incest taboos in Japan as elsewhere. These are particularistic in that they apply only to certain persons, but universalistic in regard to time and place. Sexual feelings toward the mother are never appropriate, and Japanese children, especially boys, tend to have exceptionally warm, close relations with their mothers. The sexual feelings that appear in this relationship must be repressed—hidden in the unconscious—and not admitted to. What is repressed becomes a kind of dam behind which energies build up. These energies subsequently seek other channels through which to press out against the world. The drive from these energies is often directed toward worldly success that will partially pay back the debt owed the parent, that will expiate the parent-centered guilt.

The nature of guilt in Japan and its relation to expiation and achievement has been powerfully demonstrated by George DeVos in "The Relation of Guilt toward Parents to Achievement and Arranged Marriage among the Japanese." Hiroshi Wagatsuma has discussed the Oedipal complex in a Japanese setting in "A Psychoanalytic Study of Ishiwara Shintarō's Early Novels and Their Implications for the Understanding of Japanese Male Psychology." Ezra Vogel in *Japan's New Middle Class* has defined a family context that fits the hypotheses of DeVos and Wagatsuma. The problem for this paper, however, is how these hypotheses apply to late Tokugawa samurai. There are no studies of guilt in Tokugawa society. There are no studies of child rearing in samurai families that will answer even the most elementary questions. Moreover, there is little data in the hagiological bibliographies of the Meiji leaders of a kind needed for a satisfactory study. We shall begin the exploration here with what is known of the childhood experiences of Ōkubo and Kido.

A preliminary consideration is family size. Within the samurai class there was a wide range of modalities, with varying patterns of family relations. A high-ranking samurai might live in a huge compound containing maids, servants, and rear vassals, as well as the three-generation family. The social relationships within such an establishment were diffuse. A child might see servants more than his mother (the daimyo pattern). His father might be away much of the time in the castle or in Edo. Lower sumurai and soldiers, on the other hand, were poor and without servants. The father and other family members often worked at home and family relationships were of an intensity approximating those in artisan households—except for specifically samurai patterns of dignity, honor, or discipline.

Both Kido and Ōkubo were born into the lower strata of upper samurai ranks.[10] Kido's family had a servant; Ōkubo's probably did not, except perhaps during periods of official favor. Judging from their biographies, servants did not play a significant role in their early lives. They were raised in small families with close ties among the members. Kido's family was much wealthier than Ōkubo's.

Chōshū samurai were better off than Satsuma samurai with an identical stipend, and the earned income of Kido's father was far greater than his stipend.[11] Kido lived in a large house fairly

[10] Words like upper and lower do not help much. In 1827, the population of Kagoshima was 72,000. Of this, 72 percent were *bushi*: 1 percent were upper, 22 percent were *heishi*, and 49 percent were *sotsu*. As a *heishi*, Ōkubo was in the upper 23 percent of the castle town population. Breaking this down further, of the 4,004 upper and *heishi* houses, 3,094 were in Ōkubo's stratum. Assuming four members in the average family, then only 5 percent of the Kagoshima population were of higher rank than Ōkubo's. But as the vast majority of Satsuma samurai were *gōshi* or rear vassals living outside of Kagoshima, Ōkubo's status as a *heishi* eligible for the han officialdom was high indeed—even though no *heishi* received a stipend greater than 150 *koku*. See *Kagoshima kenshi*, (Tokyo, 1940) 2:3–52; and Tamamuro Taijō, *Saigō Takamori* (Tokyo, 1960), pp. 3–8.

[11] Satsuma *chigyō daka* were expressed in unhulled rice; the *daka* of most han in hulled rice was worth twice as much. Tamamuro, *Saigō*, p. 6.

near the Hagi castle. (It was apparently finer than that of Taka-
sugi's family, who received a stipend of 150 *koku*.)[12] Ōkubo lived
in a district some distance from the Kagoshima castle town. He
was not as poor as Saigō, who in winter had to share a quilt with
his three brothers, but he was poor enough.[13] At least once during Kido's childhood his father was away for a protracted period
accompanying the Chōshū daimyo in Edo. Once during Ōkubo's
childhood he was boarded for a time with a paternal aunt while
his father lived at the official residence for administrators of
Ryukyu affairs.

Ōkubo, an only son, was born in 1830; he had one older and
three younger sisters. We know little of his mother save that she
was tall, thin, refined, and a woman of few words. Biographies,
searching for the genetic roots of greatness, pass over the mother
to the maternal grandfather, a Dutch-style doctor of considerable reputation in Kagoshima. This doctor, though he disliked
children in general, is said to have been fond of Ōkubo. He died
when Ōkubo was eight.[14] Ōkubo's father was short, broad, robust,
white-skinned, and every inch a Satsuma samurai. Not particularly lettered, he was known for his openness and breadth of
character. Ōkubo, we are told, inherited these characteristics.
The father studied Wang Yang-ming philosophy and pursued
Zen for many years with the aid of a famous, local Zen priest. He
liked company. He went out of his way to make the friends of
his son feel welcome at his home. He was by all accounts extremely permissive toward Ōkubo, holding that "One need not
severely censure a boy for being wild; only cowardice and mean-
ness cannot be tolerated."[15]

Psychologists today feel that a certain amount of open aggression in children is not unhealthy. In samurai society, too, a kind
of boisterous mischief seems to have been expected of boys.
Though Ōkubo was thin, tall, and quiet, like his mother, he was
stubborn and, like the young Fukuzawa, given to pranks, which

[12] Ōe Shinobu, *Kido Kōin* (Tokyo, 1968), p. 13.
[13] Tamamuro, *Saigō*, p. 4.
[14] Katsuda Magoya, *Ōkubo Toshimichi tsūden*, (Tokyo, 1922), 1:13–16;
Kagoshima-ken kyōikukai, *Kōto sensei itsuwa* (Kagoshima, 1938), p. 20.
[15] *Itsuwa*, p. 20. For description of father, see Katsuda, *Tsūden*, 1:8–13.

both his official biography and his sisters recounted with relish. He diverted the hot water at a spa, causing the mixed bathers to leap out to avoid the cold. He overfed an innkeeper, a friend of his family, who paid a visit at his home. He threw rocks into the Kagoshima volcano, ignoring the protests of some who felt the god who lived inside the volcano would be angered.[16] As an only son Ōkubo must have been very well treated.

When Ōkubo was twenty his father was exiled in connection with a dispute over the succession of the daimyo. Ōkubo's sisters cried as the family saw him off at the pier. Ōkubo reproved them, saying, "Are you not samurai women?"[17] Early every morning during the five years of his father's exile, Ōkubo went to pray at a local shrine for his release. During those years Ōkubo bore the responsibility of caring for his family, and for a time his mother was ill. In the *Collected Works* of Ōkubo, the first entry is a letter borrowing money.[18] Before his mother died, she asked him to care for his sisters. He did and they remembered him with great warmth and only a little awe after his death.[19] In the early Meiji years the demands of official life pulled Ōkubo away from his own family to some extent, but as a father Ōkubo was very much like his own father. He never scolded his sons. His second son wrote later that home was always the most enjoyable place.[20] When Ōkubo was consulted by his two older sons about what to specialize in at Tokyo University, Ōkubo told them to study what they liked best.[21] All in all our impression of Ōkubo as a family man, easygoing, warm-hearted, and even humorous, is one hundred and eighty degrees removed from our impression of him as a statesman.[22] There is little mention of Ōkubo's wife in his biography, letters, or in the reminiscences of his sisters.

[16] Katsuda, *Tsūden*, 1:18–19; *Itsuwa*, pp. 8–9.
[17] *Itsuwa*, p. 23.
[18] *Ōkubo Toshimichi monjo* (Tokyo, 1927), 1:1.
[19] *Itsuwa*, pp. 453, 467.
[20] *Ibid.*, pp. 452. Before going to the office in the morning and between visitors, Ōkubo would play with his children. *Ibid.*, p. 450.
[21] *Ibid.*, pp. 455–456. In general, Ōkubo paid a great deal of attention to his children's studies.
[22] I first felt that this was a contrast between the private and public Ōkubo. Yet there is some evidence that he also was kind to his direct bureaucratic underlings. See Masumi Junnosuke, *Nihon seitō shiron* (Tokyo, 1965), 1:51. Also

Kido was born in 1833 into the Wada family, a hereditary samurai physician of Chōshū. His father was not a scholar but had studied Dutch medicine. The family stipend was 20 *koku*, but his main source of income was his medical practice. Kido's biography suggests that the father was clever with money. How frugal he was we do not know, but when he died he left behind an extraordinary amount of money and properties. None of the adjectives used to describe Kido's father—man of the world, witty, adroit, excellent bedside manner, no sharp corners—is particularly suggestive of samurai character.[23]

Wada family relations were complex. Kido's grandfather was an adopted son, his father was an adopted son, and before Kido was born, his father adopted as his heir another promising young doctor. Kido's father was fifty-four when Kido was born. Kido's mother was the daughter of a Chōshū rear vassal, a soldier of very low rank, and was the second wife of Kido's father. Kido's father already had two daughters by his earlier wife. His adopted heir first married the eldest of the daughters and, when she died, the other. As they grew up Kido and his younger sister Haru frequently quarreled with their older half sisters.[24]

The situation became even more complex when, at the age of eight, Kido was adopted out as the heir of the neighboring Katsura house; this was a slightly higher-ranking family than Kido's own: In comparison to Wada's 20 *koku*, the Katsura had 150, and Kido had 90 after the death of the Katsura family head. The head of the Katsura house died twenty days after Kido was adopted. His adoptive mother died nine months later. Kido then returned to the Wada house to be raised by his own mother

---

Itsuwa, p. 286. Probably the contrast is between his informal and formal posture. Yoshiyuki Nakai comments that there is an assumption in Japan that one who is social outside his home (with a good *sotozura* or outer face) is likely to have a bad face (*uchizura*) at home, and vice versa.

[23] *Shōgiku Kido kōden* (Tokyo, 1927), 1:3; Ōe, *Kido Kōin*, pp. 12–15. Ōe points out the importance in late Tokugawa history of doctors' sons, Ōmura Masujirō, Kusaka Genzui, Hashimoto Sanai, etc. Was this an openness to the West stemming from Dutch studies, or was it an attitude of professionalism that cut across the grain of what we imagine as the samurai ethic?

[24] *Shōgiku*, 1:2–5; Tsumaki Chūta, *Kido Shōgiku-kō itsuji* (Tokyo, 1932), pp. 1–3.

and father. But his position in his own family was ambiguous. He was exceedingly lucky while still a boy to enjoy the income and status of the head of a middle-ranking samurai family; but on the other hand, he was a guest in his own home. Though he was his father's only son, he constantly had to defer to his brother-in-law. He was neither his father's heir nor was he slated to become a physician. Rather, he was destined to become a "real" samurai, and he was constantly enjoined to measure up as the head of the Katsura house.[25]

In his relations with his parents, the complexities of his situation seem to have had few negative effects. When Kido was thirteen his mother became ill while his father was away in Edo with the daimyo. Kido stayed by her side day and night, but to no avail. After her death his grief was so extreme that he contemplated becoming a monk. Two months later his older half-sister died, and Kido himself became ill. He was still abed the following year when his father returned from Edo and doctored him back to health. When Kido was seventeen his father died. During his illness Kido went every day to the local shrine to pray for his recovery. After his father's death, Kido wrote a long letter to his brother-in-law in order to establish their relation on a better footing than had existed in the past. Kido also spoke to his younger sister, stressing that she should forget the past quarrels and obey her older half-sister as the wife of the new family head. In 1854, the Wada family head died. Kido mourned his death and expressed regrets that he had been away in Edo and unable to help care for him. At this time Kido wrote to his younger sister, enjoining her to obey her half-sister more than ever.[26]

Kido observed the proprieties; he was by all accounts a filial youth. Yet there are some indications of tension between the young son and the old father. At sixteen Kido wanted to travel to eastern Japan to improve his fencing skills and see something of the world. His father opposed the plan and he was unable to go. A year after his father's death Kido got permission from the Chōshū government and went off at his own expense.[27] Another

[25] *Shōgiku,* 1:5–6.
[26] *Ibid.,* 1:9, 13, 14.
[27] *Ibid.,* 1:10–16; Ōe, *Kido Kōin,* p. 17.

possible indication can be seen in the terms of the will drawn up by Kido's father in 1849, in which Kido was left 10 *kamme* of silver. This was a considerable amount; the income from it was probably greater than the stipend of the Wada house. (Kido's sister was left 7 *kamme;* his brother-in-law, 50 *kamme* plus properties.) In the will Kido's father stipulated that Kido was to receive "only the interest" from this amount "until he marries." "While young it will not do if he thoughtlessly wastes it," so the principal was to "be set aside and kept for him until he becomes more responsible."[28]

Kido's own family life in later years also was not simple. His early marriage to a Chōshū girl soon ended in divorce. In 1862, while active in national politics in Kyoto, he began a romance with a geisha. When hunted by Bakufu troops in 1864, she cared for him, saving his life. He then fled to a rural town in Tajima where he lived some months in disguise, tending a small shop, before returning to Chōshū. In 1868, the geisha was adopted into a samurai family of suitable rank and formally married to Kido. Even after 1868, Kido's nonofficial life was considerably less family-centered than that of Ōkubo.[29] Kido had no children. As he was sickly and it was his duty to preserve the house of Katsura, he adopted at the age of sixteen the ten-year-old son of his older sister as his heir. This child was lazy and lacked manliness so Kido switched to another son. The second heir died in the fighting between Chōshū and Bakufu troops in Kyoto in 1864. As his third heir Kido chose the second son of his younger sister—who died in 1882 on board ship while returning from study in England. Eventually the family was carried on by a fourth nephew (educated at Amherst College), who became Kido's heir in 1884, seven years after his death.[30]

Another aspect of the childhood of Ōkubo and Kido was their relationship to society outside the family, especially to other children. A boy wins or loses a thousand times before he is thir-

---

[28] *Shōgiku*, 1:10–13. The will also may be interpreted as fatherly concern for a teen-age boy. The question is how Kido reacted to it.

[29] *Ibid.*, 1:409–445; Ōe, *Kido Kōin*, pp. 145–146.

[30] *Shōgiku*, 1:6–7; Sidney D. Brown, "Kido Takayoshi and the Meiji Restoration: A Political Biography, 1833–1877" (Ph.D. dissertation, University of Wisconsin, 1952–1953), pp. 10–18.

teen. Ōkubo was probably a winner. Together with Saigō Taka-mori and another youth, he was one of the "three warrior boys" of neighborhood renown.[31] All biographies stress his closeness to Saigō; the two were apparently in and out of each other's homes as children. Ōkubo's sisters say that even at seventeen (and twenty) Ōkubo (and Saigō) were set apart with an authority that made them respected and feared by the younger boys in their district such as Tōgō Heihachirō, Saigō Tsugumichi, or Ōyama Iwao.[32] Thus Ōkubo does seem to have been one of the leaders of the district teen-age society. On the other hand, it must have been difficult to have Saigō as a best friend. The historical Saigō is the most potent personality in Japanese history. Even as a youth he was immensely popular, physically powerful, and a natural leader. It was Saigō, not Ōkubo, who became the group leader (*nise gashira*) in the local youth organization.[33]

Ōkubo's formal schooling took the normal course for a Kagoshima samurai boy. He studied jujitsu, fencing, and spearmanship, though for a time at the age of fifteen or sixteen he became sickly and had to give up "sports."[34] Like his father, he did Zen with the priest Musan. He began his study of letters with members of his family and then went on to a private school. As the heir of a house of sufficient rank, he was eligible, like Kido, to attend the han academy. His morning lessons at the academy centered on the Chinese classics, which were interpreted in the orthodox Chu Hsi fashion.

But formal schooling was probably less important to the shaping of Ōkubo than was the district youth organization (*gōjū*) at which he spent the rest of his day and some evenings as well. This unique Satsuma institution was designed to take boys from their homes at the age of six or seven, subject them to the discipline of their peers and seniors, and mold them into samurai. Moral training was central. Its members always wore their two

---

[31] Shirayanagi Shūko, *Ōkubo Toshimichi* (Tokyo, 1943), pp. 69–70.
[32] *Itsuwa*, p. 11.
[33] Ivan Hall, "Mori Arinori" (Ph.D. dissertation, Harvard University, 1969), p. 61. Seniority meant a great deal. Perhaps Saigō became the leader simply because he was three years older than Ōkubo.
[34] Katsuda, *Tsūden*, 1:17.

swords. They comported themselves with dignity and learned to be prickly about their honor. They stressed etiquette, propriety, and purity (*renchi*). Younger boys studied together, wrestled and fenced, played war games, flew kites, and swam in the nearby river. Older boys continued their studies, quizzed each other on how they would behave in complex hypothetical situations involving their duty or honor, and gathered together to read and discuss through the night the *Military Record of Sekigahara,* the tale of the forty-seven *rōnin,* or other heroic literature. They also participated in han ceremonies.

At eighteen, Ōkubo wrote in his diary of a procession of the Kagoshima *gōjū* to Myōen temple the night before the anniversary of Satsuma's defeat at Sekigahara. The previous day was spent in preparation, having the family armor repaired and borrowing the necessary accouterments. As the youths departed, "The moon was faintly shining, the helmets and armor were reflected in the frost, just as if we were waiting upon a battlefield. Our spirits soared."[35] While mingling with others at the temple, Ōkubo was insulted by another youth. His honor impugned, he went the next morning to call him to account. Ōkubo discovered, however, that a misunderstanding had occurred; he therefore said the correct things and left.[36]

The usual interpretation of the *gōjū* is as a training institution for Satsuma's vertically organized, late feudal society. It made boys into samurai. Younger boys (age seven to thirteen) were instructed by boys in the older group (age fourteen to twenty-two), toward whom they used honorific language. The older group in turn was under the loose supervision of a committee of "old boys." If a child misbehaved at home, his parents could compel obedience by threatening to tell his *gōjū*. Ruth Benedict found the Japanese family less a place of refuge and more open to the pressures of the larger society: It would be surprising if the *gōjū* had not been open to similar pressures. Yet I would

---

[35] *Itsuwa,* pp. 14–16. For other descriptions of the *gōjū*, see Matsumoto Hikosaburō, *Gōjū kyōiku no kenkyū* (Tokyo, 1932); *Kagoshima ken kyōikushi,* vol. 1 (Kagoshima, 1960); *Kagoshima kenshi,* 2:912–916; Tamamuro, *Saigō,* pp. 4–6; Hall, "Mori Arinori," pp. 51–73.
[36] *Itsuwa,* p. 16.

like to stress the degree to which the *gōjū* were horizontal, fraternal organizations, sheltering youth from the pressures of a vertical patriarchal society. Of the youth organizations of Sparta, Norman O. Brown has written, "The energy which builds fraternal organization is in rebellion against the family and the father; it is youthful energy."[37] Countervailing the vertical pressures of Satsuma society, the *gōjū* were largely self-governing. Their elaborate rules were drawn up mostly by the members. They were exclusive groups with fraternitylike secrets known only to the members. The members were committed to aid as well as discipline each other. They compelled obedience—an obstreperous member would be subjected to the equivalent of *mura hachibu*—but in a spirit of fraternal equality. For Ōkubo there was a hiatus, but for many it was a short step from the emotional education of the *gōjū* to the horizontal, fraternal *sonnō* (honor the emperor) groups active in the Restoration. *To a certain degree,* the Restoration can be seen not as the triumph of hierarchical han, but as the victory of rebellious fraternal bands that captured the han for their own idealistic purposes.

We know less of the formative years of Kido's childhood. There was no *gōjū* in Chōshū; a boy's life centered more on family, schools, or informal neighborhood relationships. Kido went to several small schools for tutoring before entering the han academy, where the course of studies centered on the Confucian classics. Some scholarship students lived in the academy dormitory, but Kido commuted from home. Kido was no slouch at his studies but neither did he excel. He won two small prizes for poetry, early tokens of the literary ability apparent in his letters later in life. At one point, in his mid-teens, Kido asked his father to buy for him the works of Rai San'yō, a nationalistic historian.[38] This reflected a budding interest in politics or, at least, the influence of a teacher interested in political questions. Kido was not particularly good at sports either. He attended the Naitō school of fencing, but was not among the two students from that school selected for advanced training in Edo on han

[37] Norman O. Brown, *Love's Body* (New York, 1966), p. 13.
[38] *Shōgiku,* 1:9.

scholarships. All in all Kido was very much what Japanese call a *botchan*, a boy of good family, without great virtues or special vices, raised carefully without a knowledge of privation or hardship.[39]

A turning point came in 1849, when at the age of seventeen Kido entered the school of Yoshida Shōin, age twenty. The teaching at the school centered on the military classics of the Yamaga school and on Mencius. Shōin was not yet a revolutionary but already had a transformative influence on his juniors. It was his school that created in Chōshū the fraternal ideological groups. What the *gōjū* and *sonnō* groups did in two steps in Satsuma, it combined in one. The tie between Kido and Shōin continued for years until the death of the latter. Professor Shinobu Ōe characterizes it nicely as a relationship between "an older brother and a slightly unworthy younger brother."[40] When Shōin was decapitated in 1859, Kido was one of the four who went to retrieve his body. As one of the first students and oldest members of Shōin's school, Kido to a considerable extent inherited leadership of the group.

A second turning point came in 1852, when Kido received permission from Chōshū to study swordmanship in Edo for three years, using his own funds. This was the start of what became a fairly long period of residence outside of the han. Away from his family, Kido blossomed out in many directions and rapidly became more mature. Within a year of his arrival in Edo, he was made the head student (*jukugashira*) at the Saitō fencing academy.[41] Shōin met Kido in Edo in 1853, and wrote, "I met with Shōgorō [Kido] after a year's separation. Is this a case of 'a change in residence changing the man?' He has become a person to look up to. I felt a certain misgiving about my own development."[42]

But fencing was the least significant part of his life in Edo. He studied at the school of Egawa Tarōzaemon, who taught him Western military techniques. It was doubtless the influence of

[39] Ōe, *Kido Kōin*, p. 15.
[40] *Ibid.*, p. 16.
[41] *Ibid.*, p. 18.
[42] *Shōgiku*, 1:35.

Egawa that led Kido to propose that peasants be recruited as soldiers when the "black ships" of Perry came in 1853. Kido joined a team surveying what is now Tokyo Bay, and studied cannonry with Nakashima Saburōsuke. He did guard duty with the Chōshū Edo contingent at Sagami Bay during the crises of 1853 and 1854. He joined a group at the Chōshū compound in Edo reading Dutch texts. He later traveled to Nagasaki to study Western shipbuilding; it was Kido's memorial to Chōshū that led to its attempt to build a Western-style schooner in 1856.[43]

In short, to the universalism of Mencius and the political teachings that he had learned with Shōin, Kido added the openness of Dutch studies, the cosmopolitan air of Edo, the more powerful military technology of the West, and a wide range of contacts with samurai of other han. At a time of impending crisis, these new types of learning were to become critical. When he received his first official appointment in 1858 at the age of twenty-five, he was already a man of considerable views, resolution, and open intellectuality.

The biographies of both men are highly laudatory. We are not told of childhood difficulties except those that were overcome by exceptional fortitude. We know little of their feelings. To understand their early years we must assume some things we do not know. Reasonable conjectures distort less than omissions.

Probably the boy heroes of samurai society were treated fairly permissively: To be an *otoko* was good and to be an heir, better. A wildness was encouraged as a sign of masculinity. Also, in contrast to modern Japanese society, there was no constant demand for academic performance. The lack of traumas associated with entrance examinations and the absence of "education-mamas" must have made this facet of boyhood fairly relaxed. Yet there was discipline, too. Large areas of life that in modern society are less formal were conducted in an almost ceremonial fashion. Certain things were not done. Certain proprieties had to be observed. How parents, together with teachers and peers, taught the rules, how they disciplined waywardness, is unclear. Did they encourage dependence and then

[43] Ōe, *Kido Kōin*, pp. 18, 19, 26–42.

278

use this dependence for discipline? Did samurai mothers sleep by the side of their children, envelop them in the same warmth, encourage the same *amae* as mothers in modern Japan? Whatever the case, the rules were strict and children doubtless felt some hostility toward parental authority. Combined with this resentment of authority was the Oedipal hostility toward the father (if evidence from more recent times may be read back), —and feelings of guilt over early aggressive behavior toward the mother. (One wonders if samurai boys were permitted to throw tantrums and hit their mothers like some boys in more recent generations.)

At the same time the stress on filial piety and the sanctions upholding it were incomparably stronger than in Japan today. Not to be filial was not to be human. No child could admit that he felt hostility toward a parent; such feelings had to be buried deeply, becoming a focus for guilt in the personality. My feeling is that the DeVos thesis of parent-centered guilt probably applies even more powerfully to Tokugawa society than to Japan today, though the possibilities for expiation by achievement were limited by ascription until after 1853.[44]

A second point is that the samurai father was more central than the middle-class father today. He was at home more. He had a stronger position in the home, and the wife a somewhat weaker position. He was a direct role model for his sons, with a life style that his sons could imitate. On most points he contrasts with Ezra Vogel's present-day middle-class fathers who are absent most of their children's waking hours and guests "on the periphery of the intimate circle of mother and children."[45] In Tokugawa Japan, most samurai boys probably worked through and out of dependence on the mother earlier and more easily than in Japan today.

In terms of these perspectives, Ōkubo seems simpler than

[44] If all societies have guilt, does it explain anything about any one society or any one individual to say that it or he has? The answer, obviously, is that what counts is how the guilt is handled in the personality. For a discussion of guilt in Japan, I refer the reader to the writings of DeVos. My concern here is merely to point out the likelihood of greater repression of hostility toward parents in Tokugawa than in modern Japanese society.

[45] Ezra Vogel, *Japan's New Middle Class* (Berkeley, 1963), p. 212.

Kido. We cannot specify the form or context of his repressions, but they doubtless began from an early age. We do not know what the key experiences were in his relations to his parents. When Ōkubo's father went off on Satsuma business, we do not know if Ōkubo, close to his mother, was pleased to see him leave and afraid of his pleasure, or whether he felt guilt at having caused his father to leave. But judging from the strength and relentlessness of his drive to achieve fame in later years, it is clear that something very powerful was working within him. Ōkubo's father was more easygoing, more open, more likable, and less busy, perhaps, than Kido's. Ōkubo, as his father's son and heir, early established a basic identification with him that was never seriously shaken. In his early teens Ōkubo found a social identity apart from his family in the *gōjū*. On coming of age, Ōkubo joined his father in the Satsuma officialdom; in time he replaced his father or, in a sense, became his father as a han official. Twice his bureaucratic career—and thus his identity— was threatened. Both times he made strenuous and calculating efforts to regain the lost status. By and large it was when Ōkubo was twenty, at the time of his father's exile, that he put aside the easy way of youth and became a responsible adult. His early morning pilgrimages to the shrine to pray for his father's return, his dutiful care of his family, his steady concern with politics and his career thereafter all suggest a kind of expiation. This seems to parallel expiation by turning over a new leaf in the study by DeVos. Likewise in his care for his sisters after his mother's death, we find a successful performance of the never-ending task of overcoming guilt.

Judging from his character later in life, as well as from his childhood situation, Kido's personality seems more complex. We lack the evidence to say what the configurations in his early life meant. From the few accounts remaining about his family life, Kido seems to have been closer to his mother. Her death caused a profound reaction in him. Did he blame his absent father for her illness and death? Or were his sickness and his expressed desire to become a Buddhist monk ways of expiating a guilt that he felt in his own relation to her? Kido was not his father's heir. Did he resent, we wonder, his father's adoption of an heir? Giving away a child for adoption often occurred in samurai families and adopting *yōshi* was even more common a practice in medical families. Yet the fact that his father's heir had been adopted before he was born and that this was common practice did not necessarily make it less painful for Kido. Kido was not fated to be a doctor. Could he help but resent the time his father spent with the heir and their professional closeness? How much time did the old father give to the son of his second marriage? How much was he engrossed in the adult world of his professional practice? Ernest Jones in his study of Sigmund Freud suggests that Freud had a more difficult time than most in resolving his Oedipal conflicts because of the fact that his mother was much younger than his father, making Oedipal fantasies more plausible. The same question, at least, can be raised in the case of Kido.

Once free from his family, Kido transcended an unsatisfactory childhood and developed a political-intellectual identity. The years to 1868 were doubtless the best in Kido's life, filled as they were with adventure, romance, and power. Yet the hostilities and resentments of childhood and, probably, some sense of guilt continued. In his later relations with women as well as in his early strong attachment to his mother, Kido seems less mature than Ōkubo.[46] Kido's handling of guilt was often self-destructive.

[46] The whole question of how upbringing and schooling affected the samurai attitude toward sex is complex. For one, there was the samurai male pride. Afraid of becoming vulnerable, they probably tended to avoid emotional intimacy. I wonder if Wagatsuma's strictures on phallic character do not apply as much to samurai as to present-day Japanese. In one sense, Kido seems closer to the norm than Ōkubo. Are we to connect his early attachment to the mother and his later pursuit of variety—a sort of Japanese Don Juan complex—or are we to say that the enjoyment of variety was merely the standard pattern of samurai, and particularly of *shishi*, behavior? Or, if it was normal, was it because of certain kinds of relations with mothers? Any psychologizing about individual cases needs a frame of reference that is at present still sketchy. Ōkubo may have had one mistress in addition to his wife (Masakazu Iwata, *Ōkubo Toshimichi, The Bismarck of Japan* [Berkeley, 1964], p. 252). Yet one Japanese writer describes Ōkubo (with eight boys and one girl) and Saigō (with six children) as ascetically inclined "*onna kirai.*" See Kamishima Jirō, *Kindai Nihon no seishin kōzo* (Tokyo, 1961), p. 277. There is more of a problem here than the simple one of cultural perception. For in Satsuma and elsewhere, there was during the Tokugawa a streak of puritanism that cropped out at times. Ivan Hall traces

Only at intervals after 1868 were the energies from his repressions effectively turned outward into a drive for self-validation through effective political action. He frequently felt despair and futility. Success did not mean what it ought to have meant. Ōkubo, in contrast, became his own man to a greater extent, and his drive for power was not marred (or graced) by self-questioning or doubts.

KIDO AND ŌKUBO AS DOMAIN LEADERS

Both Kido and Ōkubo had qualities demanded of leaders anywhere. They were intelligent, forceful, and prudent. They knew when to act and when to bide their time. They had good personal relationships with other influential persons in their domains. They were as well-educated as was deemed necessary in their society. They were of a social status such that their early career achievements did not brand them as upstarts.

The common pattern in the rise of both men to top positions of leadership in their respective han was that they straddled the two key groups in their han: the regular han bureaucracy and the loyalist (*sonnō*) clique. As members of the establishment bureaucracy, initially of its lower echelons, they were trusted by the authorities. They were needed by the han government

---

Mori Arinori's adult emphasis on monogamy back to the sexual asceticism of the *gōjū*, citing a code that Mori drew up for himself at the age of seventeen that included "rooting out the sexual passion." Hall, "Mori Arinori," pp. 73–75. In Kagoshima it was apparently a point of honor for young *gōjū* boys never to talk to girls. Ōkubo's grandfather had a "riding cow" that the neighborhood boys liked to borrow. He got around them by naming his maid "Oushi." When the boys came to ask for the cow, he sent out the maid, forcing the boys to turn away. Katsuda, *Tsūden*, 1:14–15. Fukuzawa's advocacy of monogamy also comes to mind. On the other hand, most Satsuma samurai apparently overcame this ascetic bias. The British diplomat, Sir Ernest Satow, while a language student, was promised an *"onna gochisō"* by a Satsuma samurai. This term has a distinctly nonpuritanical ring. On another occasion Satow visited a *jorōya* disguised as a Satsuma brave. If Satow, with his Christian upbringing, could throw himself into the current of the times, the weaker asceticism of a samurai boyhood did not have much of a chance. (On May 23, 1867, Satow confided to his diary, "We pass through a street full of houses with at least twenty *jorō* in each, and I feel a desire to share myself amongst them all." "Diary," Public Record Office 735, PRO 30–33–15–1.)

to control and recruit talent from the many intense but able young men in the extremist clique. But they also were needed by that clique as a voice in the han bureaucracy. This double leverage enabled them to play an increasingly influential role in both groups. When external circumstances led Chōshū and Satsuma to adopt versions of the extremists' policies as the han policies, Kido and Ōkubo became the leading decision makers in their han.

The early ups and downs of Ōkubo's official career corresponded with cycles of daimyo clique politics in Satsuma. He entered the bureaucracy at the age of seventeen or eighteen as a junior archivist. His father was important enough in the han officialdom to be a member of the clique supporting Nariakira as the heir of the daimyo. When Nariakira's candidacy was defeated, those of higher rank than his father were ordered to perform *harakiri,* and his father was exiled. Ōkubo lost his official post for having served his father as a messenger and was ordered into domiciliary confinement. Several years later the daimyo died, Nariakira became daimyo, and in 1854 Ōkubo and his father were pardoned. Ōkubo again entered the bureaucracy, advancing steadily until 1858 when, at twenty-eight, he held a fairly responsible, middle-grade post. Then misfortune struck again: Nariakira died, and Ōkubo, Saigō, and others in his clique were purged.[47]

His dismissal aroused in Ōkubo a sense of desperation. In 1859, he cast his lot with forty young loyalists who plotted to leave Satsuma, attack Bakufu positions, and demonstrate in sacrificial deaths their loyalty to the emperor. This was one of many such plots during the pre-Restoration period. We are left with the feeling that the tale of the forty-seven *rōnin* and other military romances had as deep an influence on young samurai as did their formal schooling in the classics. Ōkubo became the leader of the moderate wing of this *sonnō* group (one is reminded of ex-bureaucrats becoming the leaders of political parties after 1900). To forestall their action Hisamitsu, the father of the daimyo, wrote asking the group to aid him in carrying out

---

[47] Katsuda, *Tsūden,* sections, 1, 2.

the will of Nariakira. Ōkubo saw this letter, which listed his name along with others and addressed the group as "spirited and loyal warriors (*seichūshi*)," as an opening through which to regain his lost position. He was willing, therefore, to be impressed with the "sincerity" of Hisamitsu, and he persuaded his fellow loyalists to give up their scheme. "If you insist on leaving, first kill me and then go," he said to his comrades at one point in the confrontation.[48] It was after this incident, some historians say, that Ōkubo learned to play the game of *go* in order to get close to Hisamitsu.[49]

In 1860, Ōkubo was granted an audience with Hisamitsu and reappointed to the bureaucracy. Ōkubo joined the top circle of han policy makers in 1861, when Satsuma entered national politics.[50] The following year, at the age of thirty-two, he was appointed to a still higher office. The new office had attached to it a pikeman who accompanied the holder to and from the castle each day as an honor guard of sorts. According to his sisters, Ōkubo took side streets on his way to the castle in order not to flaunt his new status.[51]

Chōshū was the stormy petrel of the pre-Restoration (1853–1868) period. Kido's colorful career reflects the more convulsive pattern of its politics. After his years of travel and study in eastern Japan, Kido entered the Chōshū officialdom in 1858. From this time Kido's policy, like Ōkubo's, was practical: He advocated political action within the framework of han policy. He disagreed with the radical activism of his teacher, Yoshida Shōin. After the assassination of the Bakufu leader Ii, Kido participated in the Chōshū decision of 1861 to enter national politics. In 1862, he led the loyalist faction in the han bureaucracy, pushing for a more radical policy. When this policy was countered by the military actions of Satsuma and Aizu in Kyoto, Kido counseled restraint. When he was overruled, he joined the military expedition to Kyoto in 1864. The expedition met defeat

[48] *Itsuwa*, pp. 47–48.
[49] Ikeda Kiyoshi, "Meiji ishin ni okeru taisei no kōsō," in Mitani and Shinohara, eds., *Kindai Nihon no seiji shidō* (Tokyo, 1965), p. 80.
[50] Katsuda, *Tsūden*, secton 3, 4.
[51] *Itsuwa*, pp. 26–27.

and was scattered; Kido hid with his geisha, and then fled in disguise. He returned to Chōshū after its civil war in 1865 to become a leader in the top decision-making group. By 1868, he was the premier spokesman for the military power of his domain.

Were Kido and Ōkubo rebels? Was their participation in fraternal *sonnō* cliques a form of rebellion against authority? We shall approach this question by comparing their childhood attitudes to authority in the family and their later attitudes to han authority. The father was the authority figure in the family, the daimyo in the han. Psychologically, there is no doubt that the daimyo was the father figure in the han: Like the father, he was benevolent, stern, paternalistic, and somewhat aloof from the ruck of small affairs. Yet it sounds better in terms of Japanese society to say, reversing the image, that the father was the daimyo figure in the home (*ie no tonosama*). As Robert Bellah has put it, "the family is the polity writ small."[52] Loyalty was ranked higher than filial piety and was learned as filial piety toward the father. No one thought of calling the daimyo the "father-mother official," as the district magistrate was called in China.

Erik Erikson has written, "In some phases of his life cycle man needs . . . a new ideological orientation as surely and as sorely as he must have air and food."[53] When the seventeen-year-old Kido went to school with Yoshida Shōin, his hunger was fed. He gained a wider sociopolitical identity in the han and in Japan, an identity which had for him a cosmic setting and significance. From this new orientation he wrote to Shōin in 1854, discussing the need for changes in han policy: "Though I am under the command of the present daimyo, my house has been enfeoffed by the House of Mōri [the daimyo] for two hundred years, so in fact I am a vassal of the Mōri ancestors. Even if my ideas go against the will of the present lord, can I bear to remain silent!"[54] There is a nice parallel between this passage and Kido's position in his own home, where his filial duty was not owed to

[52] Robert N. Bellah, *Tokugawa Religion* (Glencoe, Ill., 1957), p. 18.
[53] Erik Erikson, *Young Man Luther* (New York, 1958), p. 22.
[54] *Kido Kōin monjo* (Tokyo, 1929), 1:22.

his present father but to the ancestors of the "fatherless" Katsura house into which he had been adopted. Without accepting a point-to-point relation between authority in the family and authority in the state, we may ask, Was there not enough ambiguity in Kido's relation to his father to make it easier for him to embrace an ambiguous position toward han authority? We may, of course, further query whether there is not always enough ambiguity for this to occur if circumstances warrant it. The circumstances, in Kido's case, were the influence of Shōin and his free position outside of the han government until 1858.

In the case of Ōkubo, we have no such clear statement rejecting daimyo authority. Except in the sense in which everyone in Japan was *sonnō*, we may even wonder at Ōkubo's espousal of the loyalist cause. Ōkubo was three years older than Kido. As an official he was ten years older than Kido; he had gained his identity in the pre-Perry era of the late 1840's when he first joined the han bureaucracy. The knowledge of the necessary complexity of government, of the attractiveness of power, of what he was, probably insulated him from the simplistic, dedifferentiating *sonnō* doctrines. He joined the *sonnō* movement in 1858, not in the process of forming his self-identity, but when that identity was threatened. There is even some evidence that he joined as a ploy to regain his lost position.[55] This was still rebellion of a sort against the rule of Hisamitsu, but not rebellion against his father or *his* daimyo (Nariakira). It was not the spontaneous combustion of youth and ideology seen in younger Kagoshima samurai who went directly from the *gōjū to* the loyalist movement.[56]

After assuming power in their han, Kido and Ōkubo resolved the ambiguity between rebellion in fact and loyalty in theory and reasserted han authority in the name of the daimyo and emperor. Thus, in 1862, Kido wrote that "we must resolve to stand alone" and to make "Chōshū into an independent country

[55] Mōri Toshihiko, *Meiji ishin seijishi josetsu* (Tokyo, 1967), pp. 99–100.
[56] This is not to say that all of the hot-headed, self-destructive, ideologues were young. Arima Shinshichi, the leader of the extremist *sonnō* faction, who advocated action by *shishi* to kill the traitors at the side of the emperor, was five years older than Ōkubo. See Ikeda, "Meiji ishin," p. 79.

(*ichi tenchi*)."[57] In 1864, he wrote, "The various matters must be decided by the will of the daimyo (*goshindan*)," and it would not do for the "lower ranks to take power into their own hands as at present"[58] (for "lower ranks" read "the more radical of the *sonnō* extremists"). And writing to Itō in 1867, Kido came out even more bluntly for hierarchical authority: "What is wrong with Chōshū is that the tail wags the dog."[59]

The attitude of Ōkubo and the leadership in Satsuma toward daimyo authority was essentially the same. In 1866, the Satsuma leaders in Kyoto sent a letter to the Bakufu representatives in Kyoto refusing to contribute troops to the second Bakufu expedition against Chōshū on the grounds that it was immoral. Ōkubo was summoned before the Bakufu officials but refused to change his position. The Bakufu then rejected the Satsuma letter on the grounds that it lacked the daimyo's signature, so Ōkubo and the others prepared a letter with the "signature" of the daimyo. The Bakufu asked how they could get the signature so quickly when the trip to Satsuma took weeks. The reply of the Satsuma representatives was, in effect, we are the will of the daimyo.[60] Both Ōkubo and Kido resolved their earlier ambiguity toward the daimyo by assuming the mantle of his authority. Ōkubo wore the mantle with greater ease.

Were Kido and Ōkubo, rebels in this limited sense, a new kind of man? Did they have a different view of their own society? If so, where did the view come from?

The standard view of Tokugawa society was that the genius of Ieyasu had come close to duplicating in Japan the ideal society of the Confucian sages. If not rule by goodness alone, it was at least a *hōken* system, paternalistic and benevolent. China had deviated in the direction of a centralized bureaucratic state (*gunken*). Japan had the four classes, the rule by an educated military aristocracy, the ownership of all land by the lord, char-

---

[57] *Kido monjo*, 1:285–286.
[58] *Ibid.*, 2:2–3.
[59] *Ibid.*, 2:352.
[60] Tanaka Sōgorō, *Shidōsha to shite no Saigō Nanshū* (Tokyo, 1938), pp. 212–216.

acteristic of the early Chou.[61] There was tension in Tokugawa Japan between ascription and a Confucian emphasis on men of ability, but there was tension in the Chou too. One function of moral ideology is to keep up the body tone of a society by maintaining tension between the real and the ideal.

At the top of this polity was Japan's single dynasty emperor. The single mandate which the imperial family had received from Heaven was taken as evidence of a virtue incomparably greater than that of China's multifarious "short" dynasties. One source of this effulgent virtue was that the emperor was a *kami*, with a lineage extending back to the Sun Goddess.

Using the criteria of R. N. Bellah, this view of society was in most respects religiously "archaic."[62] That is, (1) the polity was headed by a divine king; (2) the religious institutions (Shinto and Confucian) were not differentiated from the polity—Buddhist temples were separate but were subordinate to political authority; (3) society was viewed as a part of the natural order; and (4) the world view was monistic, there was no religious "other" (except in Buddhism, which in its Tokugawa form offered no alternative to Tokugawa society).

Perry's arrival in 1853 triggered changes that by 1858 had split the emperor from the shogun, depriving the latter of his legitimacy. This provided an excuse for political action at many other levels in the society. In these actions were joined a variety of motivations, as I have suggested in treating Kido and Ōkubo. Yet we are amazed to discover in reading the letters of Kido and Ōkubo that until after the Restoration—when the momentum of events forced them into action—they had no idea of a society different from the Tokugawa society. Ōkubo wrote in 1866 that up until now there had been a "despotic system," and this must be replaced by "public opinion (*tenka no kōron*)," but all he meant by public opinion was the establishment of a council of han to replace the Bakufu.[63] The *sonnō* movement of *baku-*

---

[61] For a treatment of this subject in its full complexity, see Asai Kiyoshi, *Meiji ishin to gunken shisō* (Tokyo, 1939), chap. 1.

[62] Robert N. Bellah, "Religious Evolution," *American Sociological Review*, 29, no. 3:364–367 (June 1964).

[63] *Ōkubo monjo*, 2:442.

matsu Japan saw the emperor at the head of a *hōken* system. Kido wrote in December of 1867 advocating that neutral Bizen be invited to join the new government so that it would be fair and impartial and not appear to be dominated by Satsuma and Chōshū.[64] But apart from abstract moral principles, such letters included no discussion about how society should be organized.

Yet on another level, a fundamental change occurred in their view of society. This developed out of their experience as han decision makers. Before 1853, for at least a century there had been men like Ōkubo and Kido who rose to become lower- or middle-grade officials. At a time of financial crisis such a man, a Murata Seifū, might make major decisions in a han, especially if the daimyo and elders were inept. The decisions they took made them aware that parts of the Tokugawa system were not "natural." Bureaucratic consciousness does not jibe with the "archaic" view of society as natural. On the other hand, the scope of official decisions before 1853 was limited, and the sage's model of the ideal society was fairly abstract. There was room for a good deal of bureaucratic tinkering without infringing on the ideal forms of the society.

After 1853, the shell of seclusion was cracked from without, opening the way for internal change. Ōkubo and Kido became officials at a time of flux. They had to make decisions affecting every aspect of life. As a consequence most of their sage society became denaturalized.[65] Society became an existential organization—structured by the vectors of many human wills. Anything that had to be changed to attain their political ends could be changed by the application of the necessary force and persuasion. The translations of Fukuzawa, conversations with foreigners, travel abroad, gave them the new blueprints, and they set about after 1868 and 1873 to put them into effect.

Their political ends, of course, were defined largely by tradition. But it was a truncated tradition (the *kokutai*) cut loose

---

[64] *Kido monjo*, 2:356.

[65] The context is slightly different and the quotation is not footnoted, but Ōkubo is said to have commented in 1873 on human nature as follows: "What is natural is not necessarily right (*tadashii*). Man fulfills his potential only by correcting and training his nature (*tensei*)." Shirayanagi, *Ōkubo Toshimichi*, p. 34.

from the Confucian sage society. And even the *kokutai* was not Mito-minted and ready-made. Nadav Safran has described how Nasser smashed the Muslim Brotherhood on the one hand while using Islam to gain legitimacy on the other.[66] In Japan, too, the *kokugaku* movement was discouraged even while the Meiji leaders made great efforts to define and redefine the emperor tradition to fit their political ends. Too often interpretations of the period suggest that the *kokutai* was the active force and men passive, when the opposite is equally true.

Thus, to answer the question posed earlier, Kido at twenty and Ōkubo at twenty-three were not new men in 1853, not culturally, socially, or in their personalities. Had Perry not come they no doubt would have ended their lives as minor bureaucrats. And by 1853, the identities of both were largely formed: Ōkubo as an official and Kido as an intellectual-political figure in his domain. Kido had already been in Edo for two years when Perry arrived in Japan. The five years of study remaining before him were primarily career training, not an intellectual moratorium in the sense in which Erik Erikson uses that term.

The question of what Ōkubo and Kido would do with what they were was still open in 1853. They were ready to be caught up in the action. By 1868, they had undergone experiences without parallel in previous generations. They had changed from youths who could work within the old order to "men of Meiji" who could create a new one. Their potential that in a Tokugawa setting would have meant one thing came to mean something vastly different. In their relation to their society, if not in terms of personality, they had become new men. The acting out of rebellion, especially for Kido, was a necessary part of the transformation.

KIDO AND ŌKUBO AS MEIJI LEADERS

As a country becomes modern, faces change. Photographs from the *bakumatsu* or early Meiji periods show peasants with

---

[66] Nadav Safran, *Egypt in Search for Political Community* (Cambridge, Mass., 1961), 255.

a kind of inert stolidity that the psychic changes of modernization have long since erased. Similarly, there are few samurai
faces on a Tokyo bus today. The self-control and the chip-on-
the-shoulder combination of pride and fierceness have been replaced by something more civil.

In appearance, Ōkubo the statesman was almost a dandy. His
clothes were usually Western and fashionably cut. His chin was
bare, but his thick mustache flowed out toward the sides of his
face to join his bushy, black sidewhiskers. In most photographs
Ōkubo looks sensitive or even literary—a Japanese Victorian author. Only in a few do we note the erect posture, the piercing
eyes, or any inclination of the toughness that his contemporaries
remarked on. Ōkubo, we are told, spent considerable time each
day on his grooming, believing in Confucian fashion that the
outer and inner man should match.[67]

Kido had a fairly modern look even in the early Meiji years.
Perhaps many late Tokugawa statesmen looked the same.
His jaw was determined, yet his face was composed with the
thoughtfulness of a man who dealt with complex issues. Clean-
shaven, he seems less typed by the specific fashions of the mid-
nineteenth century than Ōkubo. Rather handsome, he wore the
white shirt, bow tie, and suits that were the uniform of the Meiji
statesman after 1873.

Looks, however, are deceiving. Ōkubo as an adult was highly
integrated, single-minded, and political. He had few distrac-
tions. He could compromise when compromise was the only
alternative, even compromise principle. He wrote in 1873, "endure shame, give up what is right," but achieve our goals.[68] Basically Ōkubo saw himself not as a compromiser but as a doer,
as one who drives others to accomplishment. Kido, in contrast,
was less single-mindedly political, less steadfast. He worked for
this or that goal, but in the end looked back and saw himself
with some dissatisfaction as a go-between, not as a principal.
We shall turn first to Ōkubo.

Ōkubo's diary and letters reveal a man with a steely and im-

---

[67] *Itsuwa*, p. 458.
[68] Katsuda, *Tsūden*, 3:119.

placable will. The diary is a laconic record of the day's transactions. His letters are tough and forceful but lack color. Only rarely does he bother to search for an image—as he did in 1869 when he wrote to Iwakura: "To think that what exists today is peace is no different than thinking it fortunate that the fire under the floorboards has not yet burned through."[69] Ōkubo's usual style was to present a terse message followed by a lengthy exhortation. Do not waver, do not give in to outside influences, do not forget the course of action we agreed on only this morning, he would write to Iwakura. And when the latter failed to carry out Ōkubo's instructions, Ōkubo would scold him with a combination of abuse and the honorific: "Your honorable actions are senseless (*muchakucha de gozaru*)."[70] In a single letter written to his fellow samurai of Satsuma in 1869, Ōkubo used over thirty expressions meaning to "put forth an effort" or "make a selfless effort." Even his view of the Restoration was heroic, moral, and strenuous.[71]

All of Ōkubo's contemporaries recognized the force of his character. Iwakura said of him, "Ōkubo has no talent and no learning; his virtue is that he is firm and unmoving."[72] Sasaki Takayuki, an intimate of Iwakura who never understood that Ōkubo "ran" Iwakura and not the contrary, wrote in his diary, "Ōkubo is unlettered (*monmō*) and unable to justify his positions. Soejima has a knowledge of history and supplies him with arguments."[73] Ōkuma, who opposed Ōkubo until 1873 and then joined his clique, spoke of him as follows:

> Ōkubo was persevering and did not reveal his feelings. He would listen to the explanation of another with few words and deep silences. Then if he answered "all right," he would in the end put the decision into effect. He would not deviate. He would

[69] *Ibid.*, 3:162.
[70] *Ibid.*, 4:318.
[71] Expressions such as *"funzen gojinryoku ni kettei," "watakushi o sari," "shi o ki su," "shii o sashihasamazu," "onore o wasure," "ikko no chikara o tsukushi,"* etc. *Ibid.*, 3:348–358.
[72] Sasaki Takayuki, *Meiji seijō to shin Takayuki* (Tokyo, 1928), p. 226.
[73] *Ibid.*, p. 227.

carry through even if it meant overcoming a hundred obstacles. Heroes are persevering but are often seen by the public as wily plotters. Ōkubo frequently was criticized in these terms.[74]

The effect of Ōkubo's personality on his associates was overpowering and at times even numbing. Itō described Ōkubo's dignity (*igen*) as "a kind of natural phenomenon," unlike that of other men.[75] Fukuchi Gen'ichirō, who accompanied him on the Iwakura Mission, wrote that coming together with Ōkubo was "like meeting an iceberg in the Arctic ocean," and "all of my friends felt the same way."[76] Yamamoto Gombei observed, "Overwhelmed by his dignity, we were struck silent and became smaller."[77] The first Assembly of Local Officials was held in 1875. When Kido was in charge the meeting was in an uproar. Kido wrote to a friend in Yamaguchi, "I feel as if I have fallen into hell . . . . The world is a depressing place, but I am holding on for the sake of the people."[78] But, as one observer wrote, "when Ōkubo entered the hall it became quiet like dust settling when water is scattered. Ōkubo gave a few words of explanation and even those that did not understand pretended that they did."[79] There are also many stories about Ōkubo as home minister: How conversation and laughter stopped when he arrived, and the whole Ministry settled down to work, quiet like a cemetery at night. Or, that even when he entered the Council of State (Dajōkan), his fellow statesmen would "lower their voices and adjust their dress."[80]

Did Ōkubo enjoy the power he wielded? Certainly he displayed none of the exuberance of style that we associate with a Roosevelt or a Kennedy. He was always polite in his use of language, formal in dress, and completely serious in behavior.

[74] Masumi, *Nihon seitō shiron*, 1:47.
[75] *Itsuwa*, p. 434.
[76] Ikeda, "Meiji ishin," p. 69; Masumi, *Nihon seitō shiron*, 1:48.
[77] *Itsuwa*, pp. 295, 434.
[78] *Kido monjo*, 4:177.
[79] Masumi, *Nihon seitō shiron*, 1:49.
[80] Shirayanagi, *Ōkubo Toshimichi*, p. 25. Masumi, *Nihon seitō shiron*, 1:48. I am left with the impression that to some extent Ōkubo played up to his reputation. He would have been less than human if he had not.

His office, when he was home minister, was described admiringly by one official as "sacred (*shinsei*)" in atmosphere.[81] Ōkubo was burdened with a sense of mission. Power was his means. In a certain sense he acted not merely in national politics but in a cosmic setting. In 1868, he was "overwhelmed with gratitude and choked with tears" on receiving *sake* from the emperor.[82] He made his first pilgrimage to Ise in 1869. In his diary he described his feelings: "It was as if the spirit of the god moved within my body and my heart was cleansed; for the first time I understood why Japan stands at the head of all nations."[83] And the depths of his religious feelings toward Japan were related to his sense of family. In 1869, he wrote in his diary: "For base-born me to serve closely the jeweled throne, holding friendly conversations with the emperor, receiving this enormous gift (*on*) is, if I reflect on it, like a dream. My descendants should ponder deeply on this." In 1876, he wrote, "I would not have dreamed that the emperor would ever visit my home. It goes without saying that this honor (*menboku*) will last till I die. Even to my children and grandchildren this obligation (*on*) must not be forgotten."[84] Such passages suggest that in his service to the nation there was a sense of his debt to his own parents as well.

Ōkubo's personal life was austere. He liked simple, light foods.

[81] *Itsuwa*, pp. 295, 296.

[82] *Ōkubo Toshimichi nikki* (Tokyo, 1927), 1:458.

[83] *Ibid.*, 2:33. Ōkubo urged Hisamitsu to repair shrines as a part of *sonnō* in the mid-1860's. *Itsuwa*, pp. 69–72. He also made many other pilgrimages to temples and shrines to give thanks after 1868. These are recorded in his diary.

[84] *Ōkubo nikki*, 2:61, 488. Ōkubo's everyday attitude to the emperor was practical. "Up until now the emperor has lived within the jeweled curtains as a being different from other men. . . . So inordinate is the people's respect for him that the emperor has come to think of himself as more lofty and awful than is appropriate to his station . . . until finally he has become estranged from the people." Ōkubo's solution, in January of 1868, was to get the emperor down out of "the clouds," to establish his "heavenly calling" as the "father-mother" of the people, and to set up so strong a government that "the entire populace will tremble when an order is issued." *Ōkubo monjo*, 2:192–194. Sasaki records that during the Ōkubo era, "the emperor was treated as if he were a child and no attention was paid to anything he might say." Sasaki, *Meiji seijō*, p. 405. But at the edges of Ōkubo's practical outlook—like a frame—was a symbolic or religious dimension.

He liked good tea. He had a favorite tobacco.[85] But he was not a typical Meiji statesman. He drank rarely. He did not frequent geisha houses. Apart from his family, and possibly one mistress, he was little involved with women. Probably Ōkubo was unskilled with women. Among the poems in his collected works are eight love poems; they presumably date from the pre-Meiji era, though the object of his affection is unknown. The sentiments they express are straightforward and ardent, but not particularly subtle. A few of the titles are "Thwarted Love," "Unvoiced Love," and "Expressing Love."[86] Ōkubo's only recreation was *go*, which he played regularly with friends or with a woman expert named Otaka. At times when he lost he would become angry and kick over the *go* board. In less intimate company this was apparently not the case: According to Ōkuma, he would make a wry face but not lose his temper until he got home. Losing put him in a bad humor and "even his footsteps from the hallway sounded differently when he had been defeated at the game."[87] For some in Japan, *go* is a Way (*michi*) to be played with imperturbability and self-possession. For Ōkubo, politics was the Way and *go*, a game.

Ōkubo's single-minded dedication to the Meiji state is reflected clearly in his thought; he had little intellectual life apart from policy formation. His thinking was tied to doing, to the definition of goals and the selection of the means to achieve them. Because of this his ideas have a practical, both-feet-on-the-ground quality. They are marked by a caution and moderation that fits our conception of his personality. In the early Meiji years, he was concerned almost wholly with the consolidation of the central government. The terms in which he saw that structure were more Confucian than Western. More often than not he was opposed to those favoring strong programs of Westernization, though even more opposed to "feudal conservatives." This was not opposition to Westernization per se but rather his

[85] *Itsuwa*, pp. 459, 460.
[86] *Ōkubo monjo*, 9:340–344.
[87] Masumi, *Nihon seitō shiron*, 1:48.

sense of priorities. (Ōkubo's personal life was quite Western in some ways: "He had bread and dark tea for breakfast, usually wore Western dress at home, lit a stove in the winter, and rarely entered the Japanese rooms in his house."[88])

A turning point came in 1873. Political consolidation had been accomplished. Ōkubo had been profoundly impressed by his experience abroad—he told a friend in 1872 that "old men like himself could not handle what the future required."[89] He returned to Japan in 1873, joining Itō, Ōkuma, and other Westernizers, to implement his new vision. The result was a program of social and economic change. Here, too, Ōkubo was always practical. He was critical, for example, of those who opposed state-run industries on laissez-faire grounds. "These industries are absolutely necessary," he argued, "even though they go against the laws of political economy." Japan was "something different (*ibutsu*)" and needed "different laws (*hensoku*)" to make it develop.[90] Political disturbances prevented Ōkubo's playing a direct role in economic development. A final turning point came early in 1878 when, the Satsuma Rebellion quelled, Ōkubo told Itō that he could now join him in progressive developments.[91] A few months later Ōkubo was assassinated by samurai dissidents from Kaga and Shimane.

Kido had more human weaknesses than Ōkubo. He was good at games and elegant amusements. He drank to excess in the company of friends. According to his diary, in one month in 1868, he drank with friends and geisha and then went on to spend the night at a "geisha house" eleven times—and this may have been an incomplete record.[92] Kido became involved in complicated affairs with women. Once he wrote a poem on the cloth in which a geisha friend wrapped her samisen plectrum; this was pur-

---

[88] Satō Seisaburō, "Ōkubo Toshimichi," in Kamishima Jirō, ed., *Kenryoku no shisō* (Tokyo, 1965), p. 39.

[89] Oka Yoshitake, *Kindai Nihon seijishi* (Tokyo, 1962), p. 137.

[90] Satō, Ōkubo Toshimichi," p. 39.

[91] Katsuda, *Tsūden*, 3:735, 736.

[92] This slackened considerably after 1869. For one such entry, see *Kido nikki*, 1:8.

chased by a conservative critic who took it to the High Court (Danjōdai), demanding that Kido be impeached.[93]

Kido enjoyed conversation, talking with friends or, as on the Iwakura Mission, with younger officials. Some praised him for this. Matsudaira Shungaku, the lord of Echizen, wrote, "Ōkubo was a totally uninteresting man, but anyone could communicate with Kido; he was good at listening."[94] Others condemned him for talking out of school. Sasaki Takayuki, an associate of Iwakura, wrote,

> Kido has not yet displayed the ability for which he is renowned. He is, in short, a planner with good insights, but also drafts policies that cannot be carried out. He gets lost in details. ... It is said, too, that he discusses government affairs with outsiders. He has literary talent. He writes his opinions on events since the Restoration and shows them to people; he therefore appears in a good light to those who are not in on things. To posterity, too, he will appear several times better than his actual worth.[95]

Algernon B. Mitford wrote, after a conversation with Kido in 1872,

> Through the heat of the afternoon we remained chatting over every conceivable matter grave and gay, but chiefly discussing politics and the application of European principles of government to Japan. Of all subjects this is the favourite among this improvement-seeking class.[96]

I have come across no such records of conversations between foreigners and Ōkubo, though there must have been many during his travels.

Kido's letters are lively and filled with colorful images. Facing the arrogant han in 1869, Kido wrote, "We are surrounded on four sides by many little Bakufu." In a moment of frustration he

---

[93] Masumi, *Nihon seitō shiron*, 1:48.
[94] *Ibid.*, 1:47.
[95] Sasaki, *Meiji seijō*, p. 226.
[96] Akita, *Constitutional Government in Modern Japan*, p. 7.

wrote, "It is better to talk to sticks and stones than to memorialize the court." Discussing the proper tempo of change in 1870, he argued, "We can not go forward like a white horse running." And when pulled back into the government in 1875 by Ōkubo, without being given any real power, Kido described his situation as that of "a country bumpkin in a city whorehouse."[97]

Kido would display his affection for Inoue Kaoru at times in humorous letters. In one he joked, "I hear that these days you eat a Western breakfast of two eggs, butter, and bread. This is unfortunate. For someone weak like me it would be all right; but if you do it, any woman worthy of the name in Japan will have to watch out. Therefore I humbly advise you . . . as the course of compassion . . . to return to a diet of rice and tea." In another letter in 1875, Kido signed off, from the lowly "Hanshichi" to "my older brother, the Hsuan emperor of the present day [a T'ang emperor famous for his attachment to the beauty, Yang Kuei-fei]."[98] Even writing to Ōkubo at a moment of crisis, Kido once signed a letter "Excited Kido."[99]

The emotionally expressive side of Kido also appears in his attitude toward Chōshū. He wrote in his diary in the summer of 1868 that some in Chōshū were saying that "while working for the court I have forgotten my country"; but in fact he was working only "to put at ease the spirits of those samurai who have died" fighting against the Bakufu and "to repay the daimyo" of Chōshū. Kido described how one night he "bowed from afar to the two lords [of the house of Mōri] and cried." He lamented that some did not understand the purity of his intentions. Kido asked the court for permission to fight in the battles in northeastern Japan: "If I died in battle they would understand [my sincerity]," he wrote, but permission was denied. Kido went on, "I am only human [I can only stand so much], I cannot control my heart. I am aware that I tend to be overly emotional. I had two friends who knew me, now both are dead. One once told me he

[97] *Kido monjo*, 3:240, 3:389, 4:99, 7:259.
[98] *Ibid.*, 4:130, 6:141.
[99] *Ōkubo Toshimichi kankei monjo* (Tokyo, 1966), 2:386.

feared I would fail because of emotion." Three years later the daimyo domains were made into prefectures and the daimyo into governors. Kido wrote that such was his debt to the "governor-lord" of Chōshū that "he choked with emotion to see him bow and receive the order like the others."[100] In contrast to this, Ōkubo had lost his han to Saigō after 1868 and was an upstart traitor in the eyes of Hisamitsu and many of the Satsuma samurai. Whatever his feelings may have been, he did not commit them to paper.

Kido was more of an intellectual than Ōkubo. His mind played with concepts and their possible applications. Just as he earlier had been caught up in *sonnō* ideas, so after the Restoration he was far more open to new ideas from the West than was Ōkubo. He was the first to see the need for a centralized bureaucratic system. Having a vision of a new polity quite at odds with the existing Japanese society gave him greater objectivity—but often at a two-step remove from reality and so less geared to practical questions of policy than the less far-ranging thought of Ōkubo.

Kido agreed with Ōkubo that power in Japan should be centralized at the top. But he gave first priority to mobilizing the energies of the people and to deepening the base of government to include them. This would strengthen Japan. In 1868, he argued for the equality of all people (*jimmin byōdō no sei*). In 1870, he characterized Japan's backwardness by saying, "Eight out of ten officials still think the people exist for the government, not the government for the people." He argued the need for representative assemblies rather than despotic government by two or three persons. Until the time of his death he maintained the Mencius-like concept that government was for the people and should look to their welfare. In 1876, he lamented that the people were suffering, that "central authority" alone was growing stronger, and that the "prefectures are like slaves" of the central government. In 1877, he rejoiced when the land tax was cut, the result, he felt, of his petitions of December 1876.[101]

---

[100] *Kido nikki,* 1:56, 57, 2:72.
[101] *Kido monjo,* 8:78, 4:161, 6:413; *Kido nikki,* 3:476–477.

Yet the "stupid masses (*gumin*)" were not ready for parliamentary government. They were unenlightened and lacked patriotism: "They think the government is Korean or Chinese and not theirs." Caught in the dilemma of all authoritarian modernizers, Kido felt he must "cause the people to be free." Kido's freedom had an objective intent, linking individual freedom with love of country and national independence. This was to be achieved by education; he wanted Fukuzawa's writings used as texts in schools. He wanted nongovernmental newspapers, though he did not like it when such newspapers criticized the government. He continually stressed the need for universal principles, which he contrasted with the parochial inadequacy of Japan's *bushidō*.[102]

For the "protector of the people (*minshu*)"—as Kido once signed a letter—freedom meant, ultimately, freedom to act as one ought to act, in support of the program of an enlightened central government. The purpose of assemblies was not primarily to voice local interests, but to obtain local cooperation and consensus in carrying out government policy. When local representatives behaved otherwise, Kido fumed and became authoritarian. In 1868, he excoriated representatives sent to the first assembly as ridden with cliques of conservatives, *jōi* advocates, *kaikoku* supporters, those favoring the Tokugawa, and those too lazy to have any fixed position.[103]

After 1873, in reaction to the peoples' rights movement, samurai rebellions, and his own experiences abroad, Kido became more cautious. He wrote bitterly in 1875 of popular rights groups that "act because they are dissatisfied, not because they are truly patriotic and concerned for the people." In the same year he vetoed a suggestion that Fukuzawa sit on a committee to draft a constitution: "The ideas of scholars often are at odds with the actual situation"; for the time being, he wrote, "we have no choice but to use despotism." He also spoke of the unexpectedness of the French Revolution, warning that Japan must not sacrifice order as it moved from despotism toward freedom. In

[102] *Kido monjo,* 3:21, 3:320, 4:100.
[103] *Ibid.,* 6:97, 3:186.

1876, he became even clearer: "I have a cold heart at the Turkish Revolution. Nothing is so terrible as a change in the times and in human affections. Even in the remote countryside children talk of the limits of the emperor's authority. . . . The people must first know the limits of their own authority."[104]

Summing up Kido as an early Meiji statesman, his failings were several. He was a "difficult" person. He was overly sensitive to slights and subject to mercurial emotional fluctuations.[105] Iwakura said of him, "Kido has foresight, but his shortcoming is that he sulks and gives vent to his dissatisfaction. He does not discuss matters openly but rather speaks of his frustrations in private conversations with men not involved in affairs."[106] Some of such criticisms can be discounted as views of a Chōshū politician by opposing cliques.[107] Yet Kido's diary confirms the fact of his worries, jealousies, and suspicions.

Another shortcoming was a weakness of will. If Ōkubo's letters are gray slag mountains of will, Kido's are vivid but irresolute. His sense of crisis was no less than Ōkubo's and at times he could be forceful, but he spoke less of determination, steadfastness, and putting forth an effort. Thus, in 1868, he wrote with a sigh that this life "is a floating world." In 1871, he wrote again: "Nothing goes as it should. One can say this is the usual state of affairs in this floating world, but I am tired of it. My ideas are not carried out. I would like to quit the government and be free." A week after this he wrote to Itō that "my role in the government for years has been that of an arranger." Kido compared himself to a "madam" seeking "to match a customer with a whore." "I have endured that which is difficult to endure, but not a single day of it has been pleasurable."[108]

After 1873, Kido was plagued intermittently by illness. This further weakened his resolve. In 1873, even before accepting the post of minister of education, Kido already was talking of re-

104 *Ibid.*, 7:126, 6:299, 7:29–30, 49.
105 Masumi, *Nihon seitō shiron*, 1:46.
106 Sasaki, *Meiji seijō*, p. 226.
107 Itō too felt that Kido was "narrow." See *Itsuwa*, p. 435.
108 *Kido monjo*, 3:170, 4:373, 4:275.

signing.[109] Early in 1876, Kido wrote to Inoue: "I have no further hopes in this world . . . and would like to live out the rest of my life quietly."[110] According to a friend, Kido frequently said during this period that "only death will cure my sickness."

Kido's positive contributions to the Meiji government are also impressive. He was prudent, consistently so, supporting Ōkubo against Saigō in 1873, opposing the Taiwan expedition in 1874, and opposing the government's Korean policy in 1876. Kido was effective as a clique leader. He was open and easy with his subordinates, without pretensions or arrogance.[111] A general from Chōshū described him, saying, "Kido knew he was intelligent but did not feel he was wise. He therefore liked to listen to others and to learn from them. Whether young or old, senior officials or junior employees, he would sound out their opinions, encouraging them to speak freely."[112]

Kido's most important contribution to the Meiji state was that he combined in his leadership an attitude of cooperation and a measure of self-abnegation. Kido was aware that the existence of the government depended on Satsuma-Chōshū cooperation. When sick in 1873, Kido wrote asking Itō to aid Ōkubo: "Whether in office or abroad Ōkubo is serious and hardworking, his character is upright and true; with one or two good men to help him, the affairs of government will go well."[113] Ōkubo also was well aware of the need for cooperation, but he was stiff-necked and not very good at yielding to others. He felt that his policies were right and those who opposed him were deficient in devotion to the Meiji government. One of the few occasions on which he did step down was in June of 1871 before the abolition of the han. Afterward he wrote in his diary (whether in disgust or wry

[109] *Ibid.*, 5:157.
[110] *Ibid.*, 6:396.
[111] Masumi, *Nihon seitō shiron*, 1:51–52.
[112] *Ibid.*, 1:47.
[113] *Kido monjo*, 5:81. Kido and Ōkubo each recognized the worth of the other. Ōkubo wrote in March of 1868 that the urgent need of the government was for good men, mentioning Kido in this context. *Ōkubo monjo*, 2:235. Kido wrote in November of 1868 that "Ōkubo is the only person in the government worth talking to." *Kido monjo*, 3:180–181. Ōkubo also made negative comments about Kido.

humor his bald account does not reveal), "I proposed to Kido that [I step down and enter a ministry and that] he and Saigō be the two councillors of state. To a certain extent I was making a show of humility. Kido, however, agreed [with my proposal, not recognizing it as humility]."[114] In the first decade after the Restoration much of the cooperation had to come from Kido's side.

Even granting that part of what Kido wrote was a rationalization of Ōkubo's greater strength, we must admit that he usually put the interests of the government or of Japan higher than those of his own clique. Thus, when unhappy that some resented his actions in the government, he wrote in October of 1868, "It would be unworthy to pretend to be ill and resign. I continue working with my heart facing Heaven and Earth." In November of 1870, Kido wrote to Ōkubo pledging that Chōshū and others "will follow the lead of Satsuma" until dispositions were arrived at for dealing with foreign affairs. In 1873, Kido wrote to a friend that he felt "great dissatisfaction," yet he "was holding back his feelings" for the sake of "the best interests of the government and the well-being of the people." In 1874, he wrote to another of his attempt to maintain a façade of unity in the government: "The officials of the Home and Education Ministries are privately very much in opposition to the Taiwan expedition and protest to me. But I hold in the great opposition which I also have in my heart and equivocate. In this floating world is there such a hell!" In February of 1875, Kido wrote in a letter that he "could not avoid his duty as a *Nihonjin*," but that, were it not for the press of affairs, he was "sick of officials" and would resign. Later in the same year the question of sending an envoy to Korea reemerged. Kido wanted to go himself, fearing that Kuroda of Satsuma might provoke a war. Inoue Kaoru advised him that "it would be better if Chōshū men do not bear the responsibility." They were to let Satsuma men do it and then, if they failed, "use this to regain power at the court." According to his diary, Kido rejected his friend's advice, putting national interest first. In 1876, Kido wrote to Inoue lamenting that "at present everything goes more or less according to the Satsuma argu-

114 *Ōkubo nikki*, 2:173.

ments," but in spite of this, Kido held his peace "for the sake of the nation and the people." In short, during the critical period when the Meiji government might easily have been split down the middle, Kido acted to preserve its unity—even when that unity centered on the policies of Ōkubo. Not until he was on his deathbed at the time of the 1877 Rebellion did Kido write to Iwakura asking that he might die in battle against the Satsuma rebels.[115]

A final virtue of Kido as a statesman, and of Ōkubo too, is that they were honest. Having honest officials at the top of a government is no guarantee, even in a Confucian nation, that lower officials will be honest. But certainly having dishonest officials at the top, in any nation, will produce corruption all along the line. What a contrast it makes with the leadership of so many developing nations today that Kido had no wealth when he died and Ōkubo's family needed a special bequest from the emperor to pay for his funeral expenses.[116]

CONCLUSION

To further pursue the point made in the opening of this essay —that the Meiji leaders were distinct individuals and differences between them counted—we might ask what the consequences would have been had Ōkubo and Kido been assassinated in 1867. This was not improbable: Assassination was the constant random factor in Restoration history. My feeling is that a different combination of men could have led to a somewhat different working out of events, for the new leadership had

---

[115] *Kido monjo,* 3:171, *Ōkubo kankei monjo,* 2:391; *Kido monjo,* 5:94, 5:240, 6:42; *Kido nikki,* 3:272, 6:394–397, 7:296 (also see 289–290).

[116] Kido bought a fine house in Kyoto before his death, but apparently had to go into debt to do it (Motoyama Yukihiko, personal communication). As for Ōkubo, "Ōkubo devoted considerable energy to public works, using money freely. It is said that at the time of his death he had only the paltry sum of a few hundred yen." His family received 7,000 yen for funeral expenses. His eldest son and heir was awarded 30,000 yen by the Meiji government. Itō said that Ōkubo had no money and 8,000 yen of debts when he died. Takasaki Seifū commented that Ōkubo had several thousand yen of debts, not to rich merchants but to friends. See Katsuda, *Tsūden,* 3:794.

to come from Satsuma, Chōshū, Tosa, or Saga, and their human resources were finite.

First, who apart from Ōkubo was capable of handling Saigō? Had Saigō broken with the new government earlier, say in 1869 or 1870, the commanders of the victorious government army would have been difficult to control. If Satsuma had led them in rebellion before 1871 the result would have been chaos. On the other hand, if Saigō, Itagaki, and other army commanders had been brought into the government and given a greater voice in policy making, then its course would have been different—slower paced and more favorable to samurai.

Second, could Satsuma-Chōshū cooperation have been maintained without Kido and Ōkubo? Imagine Ōkuma, Itō, Inoue, Shibuzawa, and the other proponents of rapid Westernization trying to carry out their policies during the early years without the protection of Kido. Imagine the actions of the "Satsuma reactionaries" without the steadying influence of Ōkubo. As it was, many thought that the government would split and Satsuma would war with Chōshū. Certainly Itō and Yamagata were too junior in 1868 to play the role they took up after 1878.

Third, without Kido and Ōkubo, could the coalition in favor of a war with Korea have been defeated in 1873? It is not likely. Even with them it was touch and go. Without them the issue might have come up even earlier. Would a samurai expedition to Korea have involved Japan in a war with China or have provoked troubles with the Western powers?

Contrary-to-fact hypothetical questions can be misleading. The course of a government is not like the limbs of a "decision tree" that branch off in one direction or another. There were constants in the early Meiji situation, such as the unequal treaties and the powers, that would have acted to correct "wrong" decisions. There were also constant factors within Japan that would have confronted any government leaders. The long-term effects of not having Ōkubo and Kido may have been small. Yet in a government that most Japanese historians label "absolutistic," the question of who is at the top is one that matters.

Ōkubo gained such power within the new government that

the period from 1873 to 1878 is sometimes called the "Ōkubo dictatorship (*dokusai*)" by Japanese historians. Why was it that Ōkubo fitted better the requirements of the Meiji state than did Kido? Why his greater power?

Some of the reasons for this are not simply matters of personality. One reason was Ōkubo's relationship to Iwakura, the only able noble in the new government. This relationship predated the Restoration. Kido had a similar tie to Sanjō, the other noble in a top position under the emperor. Sanjō, however, was weak and ineffective. As a consequence, though for a time Kido's voice was equal to Ōkubo's in the decision-making councils of government, it was the Ōkubo-Iwakura axis that monopolized the decision-ratifying prerogative of the emperor.

Another vitally important function of Ōkubo in the early Meiji government was the management of Satsuma and Saigō. Resisting all centralizing reforms, Satsuma with its 40 percent samurai population was like a time bomb, ticking away. Whether it would explode or not was up to Saigō. When making policy decisions Ōkubo had to balance government needs against Satsuma intransigence and his own tie to Saigō. He had to consider also the relations between the Satsuma clique in Tokyo and Satsuma leaders in the han. He had to prevent the explosion until the central government was strong enough to contain it. This responsibility alone would have made him a key figure in the government. Kido had no comparable responsibility. All Chōshū men of ability entered the new government. There was insufficient leadership left in the han to form an effective opposition. Several flare-ups occurred, but they were easily crushed.

A third objective factor was Kido's bouts of illness, especially after 1873. I sense some degree of incongruity between Kido's effectiveness in the Chōshū years and the querulousness that his associates noted after 1873. How much it was illness that sapped his vitality and his will to power, we cannot say. Nor can we tell whether illness produced the change in his personality, or merely permitted latent aspects to come to the surface.

Yet, in the balance, character probably counted for more than did particular relationships. Sickness apart, even if their positions had been reversed and Kido had been linked with Iwakura and Saigō, I feel that Ōkubo would have emerged as the more central figure. For all of Ōkubo's energies were absorbed in government, whereas Kido spent his energies and emotions in a variety of different directions: on government, on friends, on women, on drinking, on ideas, and even on self-expression. At a time when the framework of government still had to be built, when there was a handful of slogans defining government goals but no consensus on programs, it was the tougher, more disciplined leader who was needed. Admired and feared but never loved, it was Ōkubo (and after him Itō and Yamagata) who fit the prescription.

Man recreates himself at each stage of his life, yet in the mature Kido and Ōkubo we see clearly the influence of their earlier lives. Kido's intellectuality and political concerns go back to the atmosphere of Yoshida Shōin's school and his later Western learning. Kido's social abilities and the pattern of his pleasures probably were formed during his student years of traveling in Japan and through his wide contacts with samurai of other han. Ōkubo's narrower concern with political matters stemmed from his earlier and more complete vocational commitment to the life of a Satsuma official. The only interruptions in this career were the two occasions on which he was dismissed. Each interruption pushed him into a deeper involvement with national questions, the first time through Nariakira and the second time as a leader of the sonnō clique.

Casting back even further, to their early family years, we only can conjecture. Certainly as children they were not "statesmen in the egg." Rather than seeing them as exceptional children going on to extraordinary careers, I would guess that both represented modalities within the normal range of samurai children. What made them statesmen was not a special drive or ambition though they had both in abundance, but the way in which later events channeled their early potential. At the same time, however, there is an important sense in which the child continued on in the man.

Ōkubo's upbringing was freer and more permissive than the

average. Probably this made it easier for him to resolve successfully the early Oedipal ties. Thus, as a youth he could devote all
of his energies to the Spartan training of the *gōjū,* preparing for
his future vocation. Behind Ōkubo as a Meiji official was Ōkubo
the han official, and behind the han official was Ōkubo the son
of the father—a column of strength stretching back in time.

The evidence is sparser in the case of Kido. His relationship
with his older half-sisters and the adopted Wada heir, together
with the fact of his own adoption, made his childhood more
complicated than most. His closeness to his mother and the advanced age of his father may also have made the resolution of
family ties more difficult. Had Kido gone directly from family
to han bureaucracy he might have failed. He needed time away
from home. Once away, he was remarkably successful in slicing
through the complications of his family milieu and in developing
a sense of himself. But it was not as single-minded a one as that
of Ōkubo. Rather, it would appear that his multiple emotional
ties to domain, daimyo, women, friends, and associates which
injured his effectiveness as a politician were necessary to him
as a person. But that this identity was not deeply rooted in
family was also significant. For there seems to exist a resonance
between the ambiguities of his early life and the irresolution
within him even as he stood near the pinnacle of power in the
Meiji state.

MUTSU MUNEMITSU
Marius B. Jansen

The leaders of the Meiji period have received a good deal of
attention from Western historians of Japan. Their remarkable
staying power, versatility, and success made it natural to focus
on them. Respectful biographers conveniently had compiled
official lives studded with documentation, and often supplemented these with printed sources of many kinds. As a result
the genrō have become inviting subjects for seminar and dissertation study also. Unfortunately the materials and the biographies usually focus on the public, political, and patriotic,
and their users find it hard to see through the reverential aura
of wisdom and insight that distinguishes their subjects. In effect
we are asked to believe that the Meiji leaders never thought
about themselves, but only of their country.

The account of Inoue's visit to Ōkuma in 1914 is a case in
point. The purpose of the visit, and most of the conversation,
concerned future politics and promises, but the recollections of
the two elderly men about their earlier days must have contained much of interest for any historian. We know them as
able, arrogant, and forceful. Yet the official *Life* gives only a
mild exchange of compliments; how well we remember, Inoue
remarks, your great services in earlier days! Not at all, Ōkuma
replies (no doubt remembering how he was thrown out of the
government), you gentlemen were the ones who really made
things work. And then they both catch themselves to remember
to credit everything to the august virtue of the Meiji emperor,
without which nothing could have been done by anyone.[1] We
can only be sure that they thought, and probably said, a good
bit more than this.

[1] *Segai Inoue Kō den* (Tokyo, 1933–1934), 5:352.

A serious drawback of much of this literature is that it treats only the public personality. And because the top Meiji leaders were a small group of men who interacted on all important issues and occasions, the reader is led time and again to the same council chambers. Although the individual under discussion usually fares best in his own biographer's account, the area of disagreement remains limited in scope. As a result we get too few flashes of the character and personalities of a group that seems to have had its full share of life and color.[2]

Mutsu Munemitsu provides an interesting exception. He was sufficiently highly placed to participate in some key decisions of the 1890's, but because of his Tokugawa background and personal inclination he remained an outsider. Without the opportunity to build a personal power base, he had to rely on the backing of better grounded Meiji leaders, and he increased his maneuverability by maintaining earlier connections with Tosa party politicians. He was supremely confident in the personal abilities that were his only asset, contemptuous of some of his rivals, and secretly condescending toward his sponsors. And though so many of his contemporaries professed to think only of emperor and country, Mutsu was contemptuous of cant and preferred a frank discussion of drawbacks and advantages of policies unhampered by such conformity. He was quite free from self-righteous posturing and willing to admit that he thought of himself. He liked power, he wanted more, and he

---

[2] Indeed, rather too much of it in the case of Kuroda Kiyotaka, who seems to have been moderately popular through a willing display of human frailties. He apparently struck his wife a fatal blow in a fit of drunken rage, after which the Meiji Emperor would have no part of him in posts close to the court. See Tsuda Shigemaro's editing of Sasaki Takayuki, *Meiji Seijō to shin Takayuki* (Tokyo, 1928), p. 725. Itō, we know from many accounts, vaunted himself as one of the three great statesmen of the age (with Bismarck and Li Hung-chang, according to Sasaki, p. 727), and he also had a penchant for practical jokes. Dr. Baelz, who prescribed medicine to the Meiji Emperor and his statesmen, once answered a sick call from Itō. As he came forward respectfully in the darkened room muttering his concern, he stopped short on seeing the blonde curls and naked shoulder of what was clearly a young woman in bed with the marquis. His honor touched, he said "Sir! It is contrary to all principles of respect for my profession that you should ask me here to treat you while you are in bed with a woman!" Itō burst into laughter and displayed his bedfellow, especially ordered from Mme. Tussaud's waxworks. I owe this anecdote to Fred Notehelfer, and he to Lloyd C. Griscom, *Diplomatically Speaking* (Boston, 1940), pp. 235–236.

plotted his course with that in mind. About all, he was a realist, aware of what it was he himself and his country had to do and put up with in order to achieve greatness.

Mutsu is known chiefly as the foreign minister who finally succeeded in the revision of the unequal treaties and who served during the Sino-Japanese War. He left for his countrymen a remarkable and personal account of that war and its diplomacy, *Kenkenroku*. His youth in Restoration Japan and his remarkable political career, that included both prison and power, have received much less attention. *Gaimushō* publications issued in connection with the recent dedication of a statue commemorating the seventieth anniversary of Mutsu's death make it timely to examine this Meiji statesman again.[3] I propose here a brief examination of Mutsu's background and youth and of his career pattern in the Meiji government, with particular attention to subsequent actions and reflections that illumine his view of himself and his contemporaries.

Mutsu's youth brought him schooling in all the hazards of political life in late Tokugawa Japan. His han was the Tokugawa domain of Kii, with its castle town at Wakayama. As one of the

---

[3] *Mutsu Munemitsu Haku,* issued by the "Society to Commemorate the Seventieth Anniversary of the Death of Count Mutsu Munemitsu" in 1968, contains Mutsu's autobiography, a detailed chronology, and some letters and other writings not previously printed. Mutsu's son, Hirokichi, edited a more substantial volume of his father's writings under the title *Hakushaku Mutsu Munemitsu ikō* in 1929. This volume includes *Kenkenroku,* of which there are a number of other editions. There are a number of biographies; one of the first, by Sakazaki Bin (1898) sold for 50 *sen* but remains valuable. Watanabe Ikujirō's biography appeared in 1934, and provided, with the Sakazaki, important support for Shinobu Seizaburō's convenient biography (*Mutsu Munemitsu*) in 1938. Shinobu's larger study of diplomacy, *Mutsu gaikō* (1935), remains a standard work. And in 1962, Tektjeng Lie completed a Harvard dissertation entitled "Mutsu Munemitsu: 1844–1897, Portrait of a Machiavelli" (162 pp.). Mr. Lie provides excellent detail organized around his contention that hatred—against han, Bakufu, and *hambatsu*—was the driving force in Mutsu's life and career. I have some difficulty with this thesis, however, for it seems to do justice neither to Machiavelli nor to Mutsu's rationality. Hagihara Nobutoshi is now at work on the revision of a biography he published serially in the *Mainichi Shimbun* from June 1967 to December 1968. I have profited from his comments on this essay, and particularly from two of his essays, "Mutsu Munemitsu," pp. 123–151, in Kamishima Jirō, ed., *Kenryoku no shisō* (vol. 10 of *Gendai Nihon shisōshi taikei*) (Tokyo, 1965), and "Reibun shūji no jutsu: Mutsu Munemitsu no seijigaku," in *Kikan geijutsu,* (Tokyo, 1968), no. 7:34–39.

three houses central to the shogunal line, Kii was intermittently involved in Bakufu politics, as successors to a childless shogun normally were taken from Kii. It was such a succession problem, and its solution through the selection of a young Kii daimyo by the shogunal minister Ii Naosuke in 1858, that activated Tokugawa politics and introduced the turbulent decade that brought an end to Tokugawa rule. For Tokugawa traditionalists, the integrity of the succession order transcended the foreign threat; for reform-minded daimyo, the priority of the foreign threat made it more important that the next shogun be mature and able than that he be from Kii.

Mutsu's family, Date, had entered Tokugawa service after their transfer from Sendai in the seventeenth century. His father, Date Munehiro, was a powerful and influential bureaucrat, a recognized leader of the "home" faction of samurai who competed with the "Edo" faction for control of domain politics.[4] The father had risen through a series of posts that brought him the direction of han finances and an income of 800 *koku*. In 1852, with the death of the retired daimyo who stood as sponsor to Mutsu's clique, the Edo faction had its chance. Its success was climaxed by the selection of the young daimyo as shogunal heir in 1858 and his succession as Shogun Iemochi in 1860. But Mutsu's father was in disgrace long before that. Charged with financial irregularities, he was imprisoned and his family, including the eight-year-old boy, banished from the castle town.

Mutsu was an only son, but technically a younger son, for his father had adopted an heir prior to his birth—hence his freedom to select a family name, for which he reached back to his family's seventeenth-century affiliation, and a course of action. He left Kii and headed for Edo, where he supported himself with minor jobs and began his education.

He soon was absorbing a practical training in politics that must have been most useful. During the years of attempted reconciliation between Bakufu and Court, his family's fortunes

---

[4] The tangled course of those politics seems to bear out the analysis of han cliques politics made by Conrad Totman in *Politics in the Tokugawa Bakufu 1600–1843* (Cambridge, Mass., 1967), pp. 176–178.

improved again. The father, who had once studied *kokugaku,* emerged from prison in 1861 a firm loyalist, and took his family to Kyoto, where he was granted a small stipend by the han. The growing problems Iemochi faced with loyalists made a Kyoto connection through Date useful for the Kii men in power. As the loyalist and *kōbu gattai* influence grew in Wakayama, Date Munehiro and his adopted heir began to come into their own again, and they even secured the imprisonment of their old enemies. But not for long. When the Bakufu swung against Chōshū loyalists after 1864, the political climate in Wakayama became unfriendly again, and when the Kii daimyo was charged with responsibility to subdue Chōshū, it became hostile. Mutsu's father and brother were soon back in custody, and he a *rōnin.*

He was well prepared for this. He had returned to Edo in the 1860's as the family fortune improved and had made the acquaintance of people like Aizawa Seishisai, Kido Kōin, and Itagaki Taisuke. The years of peak loyalist activity—1862–1864 —saw him in Kyoto, in the retinue of loyalist nobles like Anenokōji and Nakayama. And when Katsu Kaishū, the Bakufu's naval commissioner, set up a school of naval training in Hyōgo, Mutsu was among those who signed up. Now his companions included Sakamoto Ryōma and the others from Tosa, and many Satsuma men, including Itō Sukenori, who would one day lead the Japanese fleet to victory in the battle of the Yellow Sea. And when the Bakufu, in its final stage, turned against the innovators, dismissed Katsu, and tried to discipline Chōshū, Mutsu was able to follow Sakamoto Ryōma first to Satsuma protection, and finally to Nagasaki for membership in the commercial-military enterprise, the Kaientai, that Sakamoto established there in 1865. All of this provided fine credentials for service in the early Meiji government. Mutsu registered himself as a Tosa samurai, and it was Gotō Shōjirō who stood sponsor for him in the Restoration government. The same Tosa connections provided dangerous entrée for political plotting in 1877 and useful opportunities for political maneuver in the 1890's.

Yet the upper-class samurai from Kii was always there, and this probably helped make Mutsu a loner among his *rōnin*

companions. His early trips to Edo included study with Confucianists like Yasui Sokken, and his writings are studded with
references to the Chinese classics and experience. He was particularly fond of reading the *Tso Chuan,* and professed to find
it of considerable value in making foreign policy decisions. Consequently, many of the *rōnin* must have seemed rather crude to
him. Of Sakamoto Ryōma, for instance, he felt obliged to con-
cede in 1880 that "this man was in origin a swashbuckler and
unlettered," before going on to praise him. His Kii origins also
must have made him seem suspicious to his anti-Bakufu companions, especially when, as in the Kaientai's dispute with Kii over
the sinking of a ship, tempers shortened and violence seemed
near. Even earlier, in the Hyōgo school, Katsu noted that Mutsu
was thoroughly unpopular. He was much too bright for most of
his companions, who were a rough lot. Sakamoto Ryōma was sufficiently afraid that one of the group might murder Mutsu to ask
his friends in Echizen to take care of him for a time. Yet on occasion, perhaps to compensate, Mutsu shared to the full the
temper of his companions, particularly their wrath at the murder
of Sakamoto in 1867. He took the lead in an attempt to take
vengeance on a man named Miura Taitarō, from Kii, who was
suspected of the murder.[5]

As they approached seniority, most of the Restoration leaders
were thoroughly bemused by their youthful deeds and heroism.
Not so Mutsu. By 1897, the year of his death, the Restoration
rōnin were the subject of much adulation, and Mutsu after all
qualified for a full share. But it is interesting to find him, in an
article he published under a pseudonym in *Sekai no Nippon*
entitled "The Influence of *Rōnin* in Early and Recent Times,"
quite cool and impartial. The *rōnin,* he agrees, were an important political element, chiefly because Satsuma and Chōshū
support made it impossible for the Bakufu to suppress them. And
then, he notes, the same Satsuma and Chōshū men became the

[5] For Mutsu on Sakamoto, *Hakushaku Mutsu Munemitsu ikō,* p. 35. For
Katsu's recollections, Shinobu, *Mutsu Munemitsu,* pp. 32–33. The *Iroha* incident
is described in M. B. Jansen, *Sakamoto Ryōma and the Meiji Restoration* (Princeton, N. J., 1961), pp. 273–274. The incident with Miura is described in Hirao
Michio, *Kaientai shimatsu ki* (Tokyo, 1941), p. 278.

objects of a new *rōnin*like group who produced the political party movement. Itagaki's use of liberalism, he thought, ought to
be compared to the Sat-Chō use of loyalism, each a convenient
weapon with which to attack a selfish governmental monopoly.
But this granted, there was nothing particularly noble about any
of it. "It seems to me," he ended, "that with the exception of a
very few, the Restoration *rōnin* were not a particularly admirable group of men. In the same way, there is no reason to think
particularly highly of the political party types of the present."
It was rather the case, he went on, that each group expressed
something of the needs of its time and conveyed in consequence
an inevitable force. The *rōnin* were ultimately successful in
overthrowing the Bakufu, and the party people would share
more governmental power in the long run. It was a hopeless
cause to try to devise permanent barriers to such developments.[6]

Although Mutsu did not emerge from Restoration politics en-
thralled by the nobility of his *rōnin* contemporaries, he had even
less reason to think well of his feudal superiors. Osatake Takeshi
and others have considered it possible, perhaps even probable,
that it was Mutsu who wrote "Hanron," an incomplete pamphlet
associated with Sakamoto Ryōma.[7] In this the author, giving
what he says are the opinions of an "old friend of his" (presumably Sakamoto), argues that neither surface Westernization
nor blind traditionalism will serve Japan's needs. What is needed
is the ability to sense the spirit of the age and revise both the
national and fief governments. Daimyo and other irresponsible
incompetents must go, and instead a system of indirect repre-
sentation in which retainers select their superiors through a
series of elections should be instituted.

And there is no doubt about Mutsu's authorship in 1867 of a
"Plan for Commercial Law" that developed out of his knowledge of the Nagasaki shipping companies of Thomas Glover
and others. His argument here was designed to increase the
strength and income of the Kaientai, and he proposed more

---

[6] "Kokin rōnin no seiryoku," in *Mutsu Munemitsu Haku*, pp. 122–129.
[7] "Hanron" is discussed in Jansen, *Sakamoto*, pp. 339–342; for the Kaientai
ibid, pp. 223–270, and for Mutsu's document, p. 310.

freight operations, competition through establishing limited liability companies in other major Japanese ports, and the development of a company-owned fleet instead of reliance on commercial carriers. The Kaientai also was instrumental in military preparations for the fall of the shogunate through its purchase of Western guns for Satsuma and Chōshū armies, and in time it received the official sanction and support of the Tosa han administration. Thus it would have been difficult to improve the schooling and the contacts of the young, but haughty, Kii *rōnin* on the eve of Restoration.

He had learned at first hand about the deficiences of Bakufu politics, he had learned about loyalism in Kyoto, about Satsuma, Chōshū, and the West in Nagasaki, and he was naturalized as a Tosa samurai. His own experience and ambition kept him from putting full confidence in any one of the dimensions of this experience, except perhaps in his affection for Sakamoto Ryōma. But what he later praised about him was the kind of quality that would distinguish his own career. "Ryōma," he wrote, "used to say that every man should hold to his determination, and work out a way of realizing it. He should never let setbacks discourage him, and if he stuck with his purpose something would be gained, even if he died without having realized his ambition."[8] Mutsu took this to heart, and himself instructed his son Hirokichi in part, "Never surrender to failure. Concentrate, when your plans miscarry, all your efforts on how to salvage them." And, a bit later and significantly in the same injunction, "Do not deal with people on a basis of equality. If you cannot patronize them, let them patronize you."[9]

Before specialized patterns of career developed in Meiji Japan, there was a limit to the ways a man could achieve political power. The inside track was restricted to men from Satsuma and

---

[8] *Hakushaku Mutsu Munemitsu ikō*, p. 35.

[9] Lie, "Mutsu Munemitsu," frontispiece. Mutsu Hirokichi, "Chichi Mutsu Munemitsu o kataru," in *Mutsu Munemitsu Haku*, also quotes these, but only in part, providing the former but not the latter phrase. I have not seen the original scroll.

Chōshū, with a very few from the court.[10] Others could have recourse to the patronage and backing of those within this charmed circle, for its members were quick to recognize and reward unusual ability or special skills. Alternatively, some found it possible to develop and deliver additional support that was needed by the Satsuma-Chōshū monopolists. The Tosa and Saga leaders brought this kind of leverage with them in their political careers.

The first decade of the Meiji period saw Mutsu consider and utilize each of these means. He was, we know from his son, single-mindedly and intensely political in his concerns and approach. The injunctions cited previously included an admonition against relaxing or daydreaming. Whether resting or traveling, whenever it was impossible to do anything else, "fix your mind's attention on one single problem. Later, when you meet that problem in actuality, you will be much the better for having worked it out." And he lived up to this himself. "My father occupied himself constantly with political problems, whether he was traveling abroad, in prison, or stricken by illness. He never rested."[11] And he was ambitious. Many young samurai aspired to office in early Meiji, but none with more intensity than Mutsu. This contributed to his restlessness as he saw favoritism come into play where Satsuma and Chōshū men were involved. Because his own patronage was on the Chōshū side, it was particularly the Satsuma presence, and especially the favor accorded Ōkuma Shigenobu, that rankled in him.

These emotions were the more important and explosive in the first decades of Meiji, before a hierarchy developed. Minister Mori Arinori, in Washington, could talk back to government leader Kido Kōin in 1872, and Mutsu argued with his finance

[10] The broader "elites," of course, required wider recruitment than the restrictions noted here for the inner power group. See the conclusions of Silberman in *Modern Japanese Leadership: Transition and Change*, ed. Bernard S. Silberman and H. D. Harootunian (Tuscon, Arizona, 1966), p. 411–423. For the inner circle, see Roger F. Hackett, "Political Modernization and the Meiji *Genrō*," in Robert E. Ward, ed., *Political Development of Modern Japan* (Princeton, N. J., 1968), p. 65–97.

[11] "Chichi . . . o kataru," *Mutsu Munemitsu Haku*, pp. 154, 156.

superior Yuri Kimimasa. The men were young and they felt themselves equal. Mutsu, one suspects, felt himself superior. As Hara Kei, who edited Mutsu's small autobiography, put it, "After the battle at Fushimi-Toba, the count's old friends were widely scattered. Some were leading parties of troops against Kōyasan, others on the San'indō; but only the count understood the situation."[12]

The future count responded to this understanding by going immediately to see Ernest Satow, who took him to Sir Harry Parkes, with a plan for formal announcement of the new government's proposition to take over foreign relations.[13] He then went to Iwakura Tomomi with the same plan, and impressed him sufficiently to be named *Gaikoku jimu-kyoku goyō kakari*. Mutsu, now twenty-five, was in what he proudly called "my first position of trust," a full colleague of Itō, Godai, Terajima, and others charged with the critical management of relations with the imperialist giants. Formally he came into office still a Tosa man, as the nominee of Gotō Shōjirō.

But these auspices were not as good as they needed to be, for in the frequent reorganizations of the next few months it developed that Mutsu's colleagues from Satsuma and Chōshū, and even Ōkuma, rose faster than he did. Within a few months Mutsu resigned with a memorandum pleading his unworthiness, a paper that should, his biographers agree, be read as irony designed to complain about official favoritism. He was dissuaded for a time, however, and played a useful role in the negotiations for the transfer of the *Stonewall* from American to Japanese government hands. For this he had to raise funds for payment from Osaka merchants. Early in 1869 we find him writing an enthusiastic endorsement of the Himeji daimyo's request that he be permitted to surrender his han and that it be combined with Hyōgo; all fiefs, Mutsu argued, should be centralized. But the official road proved rocky. A short stay in the finance office was terminated after violent disagreements with Yuri Kimimasa.

[12] *Mutsu Munemitsu Haku*, p. 3.
[13] E. Satow, *A Diplomat in Japan* (Philadelphia, 1921), p. 307, however, says that his talk with Mutsu came before Fushimi-Toba.

There followed service under Gotō, then in several governor-ships under Itō's wing. When Itō moved into the central gov-ernment in the summer of 1869 and recommended Mutsu for a post in Hokkaidō, however, Mutsu decided to try his fortune by developing a local power base in Wakayama instead.

Mutsu was not the only one to return to his domain. Itagaki Taisuke headed for Tosa in 1869, and he and a number of others set out to try modernization in one fief. For Mutsu the decision to change his registration back to Kii from Tosa represented a need for an independent power base, one he was later to try to use.

The Kii administration had tried to lure its prominent *rōnin* back in the hope that he would intercede with an imperial gov-ernment that did not trust Tokugawa domains. Mutsu had at first refused to help, but he later relented enough to keep Kii from having to pay a huge "gift" it had felt obliged to offer the suspicious central government. He refused a merit award of 1,000 *koku* the domain offered him, but he permitted them to settle a 200 *koku* retirement income on his father.

Wakayama had begun a series of reforms under the leader-ship of Tsuda Izuru. "We were determined," Tsuda later re-called, "to make our han the pioneer in reform for all Japan."[14] Hayashi Tadasu was the resident expert in international law, and Hoshi Tōru taught English to, among others, Mutsu. But the principal need seemed one for military reform, in which Torio Koyata served as advisor. The military humiliations that had been incurred during the unfortunate Tokugawa war against Chōshū now led to a conscription system, a search for German military instructors, and sweeping changes in the class and administrative structure. The han budget was published to show the extent of the crisis and justify slashes made in samurai sti-pends. Commoners, among them a pharmacist and a brewer, were put in important administrative posts. Mutsu himself was sent abroad in 1870 and 1871. Before going he checked his plans with Gotō Shōjirō and Iwakura Tomomi and received encour-agement for what he was to do. He was in Europe during the

---

[14] Quoted in Shinobu, *Mutsu Munemitsu*, p. 70.

Franco-Prussian War, and headed for Germany to hire military instructors and equipment. He then returned to Kii, where he soon headed the han government. But the abolition of the fiefs and establishment of prefectures in 1871 brought a stop to all of this before the program bore fruit or the Germans arrived. When it was called off, some of the Kii leaders wanted to use their new troops on the Meiji government, but they were overruled. Mutsu's views prevailed, and he was rewarded with the governorship of Kanagawa.

In the next few years Mutsu was close to Kido Kōin, and particularly resentful of the Satsuma influence and favoritism. As these were also years of rising influence for Ōkubo Toshimichi, he found much to distress him. While the Iwakura mission was abroad, Mutsu was in the Land Tax Office, and there he drew up a long and vigorous memorandum arguing for the free sale of land and the use of assessed value as the basis for a predictable, publicly verifiable government income. He was very much afraid of the plans for war with Korea, and saw them as a sure road to even greater Satsuma power. He did what he could to get Sanjō to hold the line and hasten the recall of the Iwakura ambassadors. On their return, he made clear to Kido his displeasure with Ōkuma Shigenobu, who had been promoted to head the Finance Ministry over him. In the struggle that split the government after the decision was made against war with Korea—the attack on Iwakura, the withdrawal of Saigō, and the resignation of Itagaki, Gotō, Etō Shimpei and the others— Mutsu thought he saw the dissolution of the Satsuma-Chōshū monopoly of governmental positions. "I was never in favor of war with Korea," he wrote in his autobiography in discussing his resignation, "and I did not disagree with the officials of the government on that point, but the political situation of the time was such that I thought it would be wiser for me to work outside the government than to stay in the government, and so I asked to be relieved of my office."[15]

At the same time Mutsu wrote a long essay, *Nipponjin,* which

---

[15] *Hakushaku Mutsu Munemitsu ikō,* p. 14.

he presented to Kido.[16] His theme was a simple one. Japan was all of Japan and Japanese lived everywhere in Japan; however great the merit and contributions of the four han that had led in the Restoration, they went too far if they arrogated to themselves all the benefits of the new structure. The chief sources of public discontent and distrust lay in the confusion between public and private, the personal appropriation of party and office, and the partiality and favoritism that led to discrimination in the case of all the high officials, all the military leaders, most of the officials, and even most of the students sent abroad. Furthermore, within the ranks of the two great han, bitter rivalry and jealousy lay behind outward cooperation, with the result that policies were endangered and trust declined. Mutsu could be sure of his audience in Kido, who soon resigned himself. In 1875, the Osaka Conference and talk of governmental reorganization drew Kido back, and he in turn persuaded Mutsu to return to serve in the *Genrōin*. Here he served as secretary general, but the post, like the institution itself, proved to be a dead end instead of a road to power.

Then came the Satsuma rebellion and the crisis of the Meiji government. Mutsu saw this as an opportunity. Already, in his *Genrōin* post, he had been charged with responsibility in preparation of constitutional proposals. Constitutional government had come to America, to France, in fact to most countries, as a result of the sort of dissension that wracked Japan, and he saw no reason why the disorder should not force the government to change its policies in order to get greater support. One form of leverage existed in the Wakayama troops he had helped to organize a few years earlier. He now proposed making them available against Saigō, and offered to lead them. He also urged that Gotō Shōjirō be brought back into the government. The government hesitated, then refused. Others would recruit the Wakayama troops. Torio Koyata warned that it would be dangerous to trust Mutsu with his own regional force. Ōkubo listened to Sasaki Takayuki's warnings against both Gotō and Mutsu, and

---

[16] Text in *ibid.*, pp. 101–111.

sent Sasaki, who was Mutsu's colleague in the *Genrōin,* to Kōchi to report on dissidence there.

He did not have long to wait. In 1878, Mutsu became involved in a complex plot with Tosa groups centering on Hayashi Yūzō. He himself was to lead the Wakayama troops. A group of activists under Ōe Taku would assassinate a group of government leaders including Torio Koyata and Ōkubo. Arms would come from the Osaka arsenal, ammunition from Wakayama, and more would be purchased in Shanghai. Mutsu's initial, and only, contribution was to make available the *Genrōin* communication facilities after private wire services were closed for the duration of the emergency. The government's military success against Saigō, and the plotters' failure to get the arms in Shanghai, doomed the enterprise.

Mutsu's role eventually came to light, and he was arrested in June of 1878 and sentenced to a prison term of five years. The sentence was more than he expected, but it also made admission of his motives. He had, "while an official of the *Genrōin,* knowledge of the plot of Hayashi Yūzō and Ōe Taku to raise troops and overthrow the government, he knew of the plans for the assassination of important government leaders, and he planned to utilize the disorder these men provoked to carry out plans to reform the government." There is an interesting and philosophical letter from Mutsu to his wife, reminding her how his father had maintained his determination and holding out the prospect of a "happy reunion in a few years if fate ordains it."[17]

The prison years provided Mutsu with the time for reflection on political matters he later spoke to his son about. He was held, first in Yamagata, where his health worsened, and after Itō became alarmed for his well-being, he was moved to Miyagi. He was treated with leniency and he read a great deal. A world history by Taylor, not further identified, convinced him of the fact that the society of nations was a jungle. And then he turned

[17] The plot is well described by Shinobu, *Mutsu Munemitsu,* pp. 143–175. Sentence as quoted without comment, in Mutsu's autobiography, *Mutsu Munemitsu Haku,* p. 16; letter to wife, *ibid.,* pp. 86–87. For Sasaki's warnings, activities, and report, *Meiji Seijō to shin Takayuki,* pp. 367–397.

to Jeremy Bentham, whose *Principles of Moral Ethics and Legislation* he set about translating. Bentham's thought remained basic to Mutsu's outlook, and in his writings he quoted him sufficiently frequently to make it worth his while to abbreviate references to the first of the three characters used for his name, *Ben shi iwaku* ("Master Ben says . . . ."). His reading included the Chinese classics, especially the *Tso Chuan,* as well.[18]

Mutsu regained his freedom in January 1883. By then his old Tosa friends had built up the *jiyūminken* movement to great strength, and they expected to find an articulate and brilliant associate in Mutsu. Everywhere there were welcoming meetings for him, and the Tokyo papers wrote of one in Wakayama that it was almost as though a daimyo (*kokuō*) had returned to his province. A special meeting was convened for him in the Wakayama prefectural assembly hall, the stage draped with banners reading *Mutsu Munemitsu Banzai.*

But Mutsu had decided that he needed to go abroad again to see and study. A subsidy was provided by Inoue, Shibusawa, and especially Itō, who was just back from his study of European constitutions and with whom Mutsu had been careful to maintain connections. In April 1884, he headed for London, and then to Vienna. There he spent most of his time in reading and study under the direction of Stein. Minister to Austria-Hungary Saionji wrote approvingly to Itō about his diligence. He returned to Japan in February of 1886.[19]

Mutsu returned with all the authority of a man who knew the

---

[18] He later published his translation under the title *Rigaku seishū.* The preface is included in *Mutsu Munemitsu Haku,* pp. 96–97. Hagihara, "Reibun shūji no jutsu," pp. 36–38, discusses Mutsu's debt to Bentham and relates it to a prior enthusiasm for Ogyū Sorai and for the *Tso Chuan.* His essay is particularly important for its discussions of Mutsu's prison writings. Mutsu was assisted in his translation of Bentham by Hoshi Tōru. Hoshi had been sponsored by Mutsu and Inoue for the study of law in England from 1874 to 1877, and became the first Japanese to satisfy the requirements for Barrister at Law. During his stay in England he became a follower of Bentham. Nakamura Kikuo, *Meiji teki ningenzō: Hoshi Tōru to kindai Nihon seiji* (Tokyo, 1957), pp. 33–41.

[19] For Mutsu and Itō, *Mutsu Munemitsu Haku* reprints a letter dated 1877 which expresses consternation at reports of Itō's illness, and assurances of his high regard and filial obligation to him. See also Shinobu, *Mutsu Munemitsu,* p. 179. Saionji wrote of Mutsu's great drive and ability and suggested that if Itō did not secure his services immediately on his return home, it would be a great loss for both parties. Letter in *ibid.,* pp. 182–183.

West and knew himself. He had never been an ideologue; still less now. In prison he had written a Benthamite piece arguing that abstract talk of rights and right had no relevance without consideration of the institutional structure of the country concerned.[20] Now he had further knowledge of the need for united effort to accomplish the vast changes that were necessary to bring Japan into a status of equality with the West. Thus, when the Wakayama prefectural assembly convened to hear Mutsu on his return, its members may have expected political views and perhaps leadership, but what they got was a discussion of how much there was to be done before Japan would be able to revise its treaties with the West. Japan needed both the sources and the products of Western industrialization, Mutsu warned, the intangible and the tangible. It was not enough to build railroads, set up telegraph lines, and build Western-style buildings, though this had to be done too. And all this would cost money; government and people would have to sacrifice, for "we are going to have to pay for civilization with our pennies." Moreover, equal treaties would require unrestricted residence and travel for Westerners, and that in turn meant that the whole country, not just the ports, would have to be modernized. Yet at present that was still unthinkable. A foreign traveler would soon find himself unable to find a proper house, bread to eat, bed to sleep or chair to sit on, or even a glass in which to drink his beer![21]

Consequently Mutsu was little interested in the pleas of his old associates that he rejoin the political party movement at a time when it seemed to be picking up enthusiasm again with treaty revision as a principal issue. His explanation is remarkably candid.

> The reasons I decided to be a statesman inside the government were as follows. It was not because I thought that the popular parties were just unprofitable, harmful, or unstable as-

[20] "Mempeki dokugo" (Monologue while Facing the Wall), in *Hakushaku Mutsu Munemitsu ikō*, p. 23.
[21] Part of the speech is provided by Sakazaki, pp. 102–105. The author, writing twelve years later, feels compelled to add an editorial: "Ah! To think that the condition of the empire was so low then! From today's perspective it is almost like recalling a dream" (p. 106).

sociations. On the contrary, I thought that if they were care-fully nurtured they would become powerful elements in our country's political world in the future. But when I reflected on my past career, and remembered that I already had served a long sentence of imprisonment for political crimes, I did not have much desire to stand in opposition to the government again. I felt that if I had a choice, I would prefer to offer my services to the government instead.[22]

In Meiji terms, this is a remarkable statement. There is no language about service to throne and country, but simply an honest preference for being in power over being out of power. Presumably there were things Mutsu felt needed doing, but his instinct and expression remained, as they had been, cool, de-liberate, and reasoned.

Mutsu's decision to cut himself off from the parties was re-sented by the party leaders, but of course it made him more acceptable to the government. His foreign exposure and ex-perience made him a logical candidate for the diplomatic serv-ice, and in 1887 he was posted to Washington as minister. While there he negotiated a new and equal treaty with Mexico, one he hoped would become a model for others with European coun-tries later. He liked it abroad, and when recalled in 1889, came close to staying in the United States. It took the promise of a cabinet ministry to bring him back.[23] Even then his progress

[22] From the autobiography, in *Mutsu Munemitsu Haku*, p. 17. Hagihara, "Mutsu Munemitsu," in *Kenryoku no shisō*, p. 142, rightly adds the reminder that when Mutsu returned to action his old associates of early Meiji were in control of the government.

[23] Mutsu writes that his appointment came about as a result of another chapter in his long rivalry with Ōkuma, who had just been appointed foreign minister over Mutsu's protests. He tendered his resignation immediately, and Ōkuma, feeling that an immediate defection of that quality would look bad, promised him Washington. Evidently the distance made it bearable. Autobiography, *Mutsu Munemitsu Haku*, p. 18. Hagihara's essay in *Kenryoku no shisō* is set in the context of a meeting Mutsu had with Baba Tatsui in Atlantic City in 1888, and contrasts Mutsu's decision for government service to Baba's choice of exile. Mutsu's report to Ōkuma on the meeting can be found in Hagihara, *Baba Tatsui* (Tokyo, 1967), pp. 309–311. But Mutsu clearly did not consider that he had capitulated to the government. He wrote his son in 1890 that he would remain a government official only if he received a satisfactory offer. If that failed he would stand for the Diet, and if neither course succeeded he would remain in America. Hagihara, in *Kenryoku no shisō*, p. 142.

was slow. By the time of his return he found that Yamagata had given his cabinet post to someone else. Furious, he refused to take his baggage through customs and announced he was returning to the United States. But his friends, especially Inoue, put him up in the Rokumeikan and worked mightily to humor him. Soon a resignation opened the Ministry of Agriculture and Commerce for Mutsu after all, and he served through the Yamagata and into the Matsukata cabinet. Here his old ties with the Tosa group were of some use again in the compromises that characterized the first Diet sessions. Mutsu's position on this was straightforward. Politics, he once wrote Inoue, was an art, and not a science, and the important thing was to make the constitution work.[24] He recognized that the government held the better cards for the early contests, and refused suggestions that he accept the Diet seat to which he had been elected from Wakayama and stand for speaker of the Lower House.

As cabinet member he tried to bring some unity and order to a political scene in which the group of notables was also a group of equals. George Akita has described Mutsu's unsuccessful efforts to develop an institution to centralize decisions and announcements and make the ministers pull together.[25] Information and decisions were to be cleared through a single bureau, appropriately headed by its designer. But it did not work. A number of his colleagues rejected his interference indignantly, and Mutsu decided to utilize the Matsukata election interference of 1892 to resign his post. There followed a period of service in the Privy Council before his final opportunity as foreign minister under Itō. Mutsu had contracted tuberculosis at the time of the Restoration, and throughout his career he was dogged by ill health. He was forced to resign his Foreign Ministry post shortly after the conclusion of the war with China, and died in 1897, still hoping for the health and premiership that had been denied him.

[24] "Seiji naru mono wa, jutsu (aato) nari, gaku (saiensu) ni arazu." Letter provided as appendix to Hagihara essay in *Kenryoku no shisō*, pp. 152–155.

[25] George Akita, *Foundations of Constitutional Government in Modern Japan, 1868–1900* (Cambridge, Mass., 1967), pp. 93–96.

Mutsu's period as foreign minister is the best-documented part of his life, and he contributed importantly to this with his apologia for the Triple Intervention in *Kenkenroku*. His work was distinguished by the same confidence, calculation, and realism he had shown in his earlier career. His tactics in securing treaty reform combined toughness toward domestic critics with a moderate stance abroad that was firm on the essentials of national equality. He forced Itō to suppress the Diet and showed his personal contempt of the new anti-foreignism, and thereby established his good faith with foreign powers. On the Korean issue and the China war, he made a cool determination of the national interest, and when he was ready, quietly ordered Minister Ōtori to "commence active movement on some pretext, taking care to do what is least liable to criticism in the eyes of the world."[26] And when the Triple Intervention proved the government had miscalculated the European reaction to the cession of Liaotung, Mutsu reluctantly agreed on the necessity to give up this Manchurian foothold.[27] The torrent of public and private abuse he received for his inability to defy Germany, France, and Russia left him with few illusions about himself or his contemporaries.

It is interesting, however, to reflect on Mutsu as a Meiji type, albeit perhaps somewhat more liberated than most contemporaries in the government because he was an outsider. A confident appraisal will have to await the scrutiny of the full body of his personal correspondence, but the evidence at hand in the writing Mutsu did under his own name in *Kenkenroku* and under various pseudonyms is sufficient to permit some suggestions. Certainly he was sufficiently well-grounded in his own tradition, and sufficiently aware through personal experience of its limita-

[26] For a discussion of the sequence in which this instruction fell, see Hilary Conroy, *The Japanese Seizure of Korea: 1868–1910* (Philadelphia, 1960), p. 254. See also the preliminary "Notes on the Sino-Japanese Conflict 1894/5: Tokyo's Decision for War," by Eric Klestadt, in *Nihon gaikōshi kenkyū: Meiji jidai* (Tokyo, 1957), 6 pp.

[27] See, most recently, Frank W. Inklé, "The Triple Intervention: Japan's Lesson in the Diplomacy of Imperialism," *Monumenta Nipponica* (Tokyo, 1967), 22, nos. 1–2:122–130.

tions, to free him from the uncertainties about identity and mission that plagued so many of the next generation.

Mutsu was proud of his country and of himself, but he was no ideologue. Although he was close to the group that fashioned the modern imperial institution for its countrymen, he was not the captive of this creation. References to emperor and ages past are remarkably few in his writing; a bow is made in that direction in the early pages of *Nipponjin*, but it is submerged in its emphasis on fairness for all Japanese. Pride is inherently comparative, of course, and Mutsu's letters from abroad include notes of satisfaction that Japanese were considered more progressive and hardworking than other Asians.[28] *Kenkenroku* recalls with satisfaction the reversals in world opinion of China and Japan that followed the military contest between the two. But its principal emphasis is a cold-blooded evaluation of national interest, and not jingoism.

Mutsu had little use for the chauvinists, and his discussion of the enthusiasm for national mission and duty—*meigi* and *meibun*—does not give these slogans much substance. "I never thought there was any reason for internal reform in Korea beyond our political interest," he wrote, "and I thought that there was little use in trying to see ourselves as a chivalrous, crusading army. Our political interest was what mattered, and nothing was to be sacrificed to it."[29] In contrast, he noted, the idealists with their talk of mission were a nuisance to government planning and a danger to its execution, for once successes began to mount they were joined by jingoists who demanded the fall of Peking and the cession of province after province. In this Mutsu was a typical Meiji leader, with a clear view of the political purposes of force, and he and his associates were probably safer neighbors than their successors, who combined the language of the idealists with the extravagant goals of the jingoists.

The irony of Mutsu's pursuit by the jingoists lay in the fact that until the Sino-Japanese War Mutsu, like his fellows in the government, was often concerned by what seemed a deficiency

[28] 1885 letter from St. Petersburg, *Mutsu Munemitsu Haku*, p. 89.
[29] *Kenkenroku*, in *Hakushaku Mutsu Munemitsu ikō*, p. 322.

in national identification and pride among the Japanese, and one suspects he must have felt his countrymen had passed from apathy to arrogance without experiencing confidence. Thus in a discussion of bravery that he wrote in 1880, while still in prison, he expressed his alarm over the low state of respect for the military and discussed ways in which this might be rectified. He urged increases in pay, efforts to build public esteem and pride, the encouragement of competitive and martial sports, and utilization of the theater. Once the contest was joined, monetary rewards for bravery could be added. Only fifteen years later, in *Kenkenroku,* he was critical of the jingoes who charged that the civilians had thrown away what the soldiers had won by their bravery.[30]

Thanks to his penchant for writing under pseudonyms, Mutsu's evaluation of his own contributions is not hidden behind the protestations of unworthiness and dependence on the emperor's virtue that characterize the official biographies. He was not only willing to take credit where due, but outraged if he did not receive it. This was particularly the case when Hatoyama Kazuo, a Waseda academic and a political and Foreign Office protégé of Ōkuma, wrote in *Taiyō* of January 1897 that Mutsu's treaty revision success had been built on the victory over China and the previous efforts of Soejima, Inoue, and Ōkuma. Mutsu answered in the *Sekai no Nippon* of the following month under the byline "A Foreigner in Tokyo." He began with modest assurances that as a foreigner he knew little about the inner workings of the Japanese government; he knew it only from the newspapers, though in "the course of some twenty years' residence in your country" he had developed a great and sincere admiration for Japan's accomplishments. But there were certain thoughts about the matter, seen from the perspective of a foreigner, that might be of interest to the reader. Hatoyama's arguments were then demolished. The treaty with the British was worked out before the war with China, and the English, who expected the Japanese to lose, almost held it up in dis-

---

[30] "Fukudo dokugo," in *Hakushaku Mutsu Munemitsu ikō,* pp. 55–97. *Kenkenroku,* in *ibid.,* p. 555.

pleasure. The argument about the contributions of previous drafts was even more nonsensical. Actually they contained concessions to the foreigners that could well, the foreign writer suggests, have made it a great deal more difficult for Foreign Minister Mutsu. "I am sure," he ended pleasantly, "that Dr. Hatoyama is a scholar who should be respected, but I could not resist correcting his argument with the facts . . . ."[31]

Everything that has been said would prepare one for unfavorable comments on Ōkuma, and these abound in two pieces published under pseudonyms in *Sekai no Nippon* in 1896 and 1897.[32] The first is not a formal attack, though it summarizes, under headings of finance, Hokkaidō colonization, and treaty revision, issues on which Itō and Ōkuma differed sharply. But the second, ostensibly undertaken to clear Ōkuma of the "common error" that he is a nobody who arrived at his position through laziness and luck, actually does little more than add elements of calculation and opportunism to the explanation. Its story begins in Restoration days, when Ōkuma did nothing except make contacts and talk in Nagasaki while others were risking their lives. Sakamoto Ryōma is quoted with approval as saying of him that he was better at argument than action. But when the early government sought support from important han there was absolutely no one worth considering in Saga, with the result that Ōkuma and Soejima, the young students who had

---

[31] "Hatoyama Hakushi no Nichi-Doku jōyaku hyōron o yomu," in *Mutsu Munemitsu Haku,* pp. 112–121, and *Hakushaku Mutsu Munemitsu ikō,* pp. 592–600. Hatoyama replied, and Mutsu in turn blasted his response. Printed in *ibid,* pp. 617–626. Hatoyama (father of the Seiyūkai and postwar Hatoyama Ichirō) was trained in law at Columbia and Yale, taught at the Imperial University, entered the *Kaishintō* and *Shimpotō,* was speaker of the lower house, a Foreign Office *jikan* in the Kenseitō under Ōkuma, and head of Waseda, thus an Ōkuma man all the way until he shifted to the Seiyūkai shortly before his death in 1911. Biography in *Shinsen dai jimmei jiten* (Tokyo, Heibonsha, 1942), 5:139–140.

[32] "Itō Ōkuma seiken idō no rekishi," pp. 567–576, and "Ōkuma Haku shusshin shimatsu," pp. 627–655, in *Hakushaku Mutsu Munemitsu ikō.* The pseudonyms are all different, and obscure, with the exception of the Ōkuma piece which is signed "Hizen Ryūzōji" for the pre-Tokugawa daimyo family. Matsukata, inevitably, fares little better than Ōkuma. In "Matsukata Haku shusshin shimatsu" (*ibid,* pp. 577–585), Mutsu dismisses him as a cipher in Restoration times who grew to power and influence as a mediator between Satsuma and Chōshū interests.

met so many of the Restoration figures in Nagasaki, seemed appropriate. Then came a series of successful tours in office through careful attention to the Satsuma, and especially Ōkubo, patronage. Ōkuma's shift from mild opposition to war with Korea to enthusiastic support of war for Formosa illustrated his opportunism, and the qualities that made him useful to the Satsuma men. Then, with the exit of Ōkubo and Kido, and the revelation of his mistaken financial policies, his light began to dim; when he tried to recoup his strength by exploiting the Hokkaidō issue, Itō seized the opportunity to get him fired. In the 1880's, Ōkuma added a foreign policy failure to his treasury errors, and only the ability to manipulate popular disappointment over the retrocession of Liaotung, together with Matsukata's need for a party offset to the Tosa men, made it possible for him to return to the center of the stage.

In personal evaluations of his colleagues which Mutsu wrote on another occasion, Ōkuma came out slightly better. He was, it seems, willing to listen to people, although he felt obliged to show his superior intelligence and wisdom. His *Sekijitsudan,* suffering from the need to justify himself, confused chronology and issues badly. Also, Mutsu contrasted Ōkuma's recent speech to the Diet with an earlier speech by Foreign Minister Mutsu. It comes as no surprise that Mutsu's was the superior performance, despite the fact that it had to be delivered to a hostile house, whereas Ōkuma's audience was a friendly one. Nevertheless, Ōkuma had undoubted ability and intelligence, and he did give his visitors an opportunity to speak their mind.[33]

This kind of frankness and venom makes one suspect that there must be, or certainly must have been, a wealth of interest in closer study of the Meiji leaders if it were only possible to get past their biographers and relatives and at their persons. Mutsu left further indications of this in pieces he wrote about his associates, again under pseudonyms. Perhaps it helped to know that he was incurably ill. In his description of "The Gen-

[33] "Sho genrō danwa no shūheki," in *Mutsu Munemitsu Haku,* pp. 130–138, and *Hakushaku Mutsu Munemitsu ikō,* pp. 609–616. This was published in *Sekai no Nippon* in May 1897.

rō's Conversation Habits," cited previously, there is just enough to make one wish for more.

Itō, alas, comes through as a crashing bore. He loves to talk, and no one gets away without hearing the heroic tales of the old days—how he and Inoue got back to Shimonoseki just in time to mediate an end to the war with the foreigners. It is very interesting the first time, and not without its value, especially for the young, but there is no one who does not tire of it, especially when forced to hear it for the fourth or fifth time. And Itō never permits his visitor to get a word in edgewise. Itagaki suffers from the same problem. There is no escape from his account of the great days in the Restoration wars and of his leadership in the reform program in Tosa in 1869. His friends have heard it all, and many times. But, like Itō, he talks by preference about the past.

Inoue is very different. He speaks of the past rarely, he does not speculate about the future, and he concentrates on present problems. He likes to talk, but he is bound to details and practicality, with the result that his larger purpose is often unclear. Yamagata has the reputation of saying little or nothing. Actually it is more his manner of speaking, for he seems to conserve, husband, and weigh his words. There are never any personal details. The listener has to provide the second half of what Yamagata suggests; as a result he is really too cryptic, and often fails to make his point clear.

Gotō Shōjirō has the reputation of being an inveterate boaster, one who can bore people half to death. But Mutsu thinks this undeserved. He is much more sparing in his tales of the old days, despite his central role in the shogun's resignation. Unlike the other old men, he recollects only when asked to do so. Indeed, in a separate evaluation, Mutsu made it clear that Gotō was a great favorite of his.[34] Despite a failure in almost everything he attempted, he writes, Gotō remained cheerful, affable, able, was more Irish than English, and there will not be many more of his kind. Again, Gotō's honesty and forthrightness, his will-

[34] "Gotō Haku," in *Mutsu Munemitsu Haku,* pp. 139–152, dictated a month before Mutsu's death.

ingness to approach issues without any cant about imperial reverence and national gain or loss, show he is not a product of the Meiji political world. He almost seems to fit better into Chinese politics of the periods that followed the fall of the Han or T'ang dynasties.

Fittingly, Mutsu included an evaluation of Mutsu, perhaps to protect his pseudonym. He did not come off badly. He described himself as very able, but rather too argumentative. He listened carefully to people, but did so only to score debater's points over them. He was also too careful, too insistent on playing his cards close to his chest. As a result he did not really ingratiate himself with people who never knew quite where they stood with him. In this we recognize the warnings that Katsu Kaishū had for his young follower in the Kobe naval school a third of a century earlier; he was too smart, too calculating, too superior. Perhaps, also, the Wakayama upper samurai, the man who probably would have been a central figure in his local and Bakufu politics without the Restoration, could not refrain from judging his associates and, in fact, superiors, against that background.

It would be futile to seek theories and generalizations from the case of so particular a personality. Mutsu was able, difficult, and frequently bitter. Yet his cold, calculating determination and intelligence, his willingness to accept risks and responsibilities, and his determination to receive rewards and recognition probably put us closer to some of the mainsprings of the Meiji accomplishment than do the pious platitudes of the official biographers.

At the same time the evidence of factional and personal jealousies and recrimination this small body of evidence provides suggests an iceberg beneath the surface documentation we possess. Perhaps because the danger of being blamed for failure was so great, and the safety of obscurity so preferable, the process of selecting cabinet leaders and ministers was usually tortuous. Sasaki Takayuki's diaries contain numerous conversations in which he ranges through the list of Meiji statesmen with the emperor and with court officials who deplore their ministers' inconstancy and unwillingness to stand up under pressure; at times the emperor wished for another Ōkubo. It is striking to see how often these men lament the lack of political cohesion in Japan. We know from many sources how often the leading oligarchs feared for the success of constitutionalism in the 1890's.

In contrast, there is the ability of the government elite to reconcile itself to reabsorbing a man who had proved himself as dangerous as Mutsu, and the opportunity for a host of erstwhile "rebels" like Ōe Taku and Kataoka Kenkichi to reemerge into full civil rights and parliamentary status. If one were to accept the self-evaluation of the Meiji leaders of which we have record, their associates made error after error until they awoke in the twentieth century to find themselves the first successful political modernizers. Certainly victorious wars helped bring popular and political solidarity, although they brought other problems with them. And perhaps, in fact, the stock reminders of the emperor's grace need to be looked at as well.

THE OTHER ITŌ: A POLITICAL FAILURE
George Akita

The temperature in the heart of Tokyo in July and August 1932 averaged in the high seventies and low eighties; the humidity averaged an uncomfortable 79 to 82 percent. The dog days of summer drove even habitually neat Japanese to dishabille. Yet Itō Miyoji, age seventy-five, was foppishly and meticulously attired in Japanese dress even when the temperature soared into the nineties. Miyoji's hairline had receded considerably, and his ears were much too large for his face. His once well-formed lips were pinched in that pucker distinctive of old age. The effect of the whole was still striking, but the face was almost a caricature of what was once the handsomest in Meiji politics.[1]

Many a day and night this summer of 1932 was spent composing the epitaph for a stele in Seoul commemorating the twenty-fourth anniversary of Itō Hirobumi's death. It was natural that Miyoji was entrusted with this task. He had been as close to Itō as any man except Inoue Kaoru, who had been dead for seventeen years. Miyoji also had the reputation of being comfortable in Chinese composition and a consummate writer of drafts. He had written several touching Chinese poems expressing his great admiration and affection for Itō, but the permanent

NOTE: Work on this article was begun early in 1968 when I was a Fulbright research scholar attached to the Social Science Research Institute, Tokyo University. I am especially indebted to Mrs. Hisako Masumi for her research assistance. I am grateful to Professors Junnosuke Masumi, Hiroshi Wagatsuma, Seizaburō Satō, George Yamamoto, and Robert Stauffer, Dr. L. Takeo Doi, and Mr. James S. Yamada for reading the manuscript and making suggestions and corrections.

[1] Miyoji's surname is homophonous with that of Itō Hirobumi, though the second of the two characters in their names is different. Miyoji's contemporaries, Itō, Katsura Tarō, and Maeda among them, called him Miyoji. Maeda Renzan, *Seihen monogatari* (Tokyo, 1918), p. 230; Maeda Renzan, "Kempō no bannin: Itō Miyoji," *Chūō kōron*, 49, no. 4:191 (1934), hereafter cited *CK;* letter from Katsura to Yamagata Aritomo, dated April 17, 1898, in Baba Tsunego, "Itō Miyoji ron," *CK,* 45:209 (July 1930). This practice will be adopted.

memorial that described Itō's life and achievements for all to see was insipid.[2] It was testimony that the passage of time had not blunted the edge of his antipathy for Itō.[3]

An innovative and successful leader is one who, according to Erikson, "[lifts] his individual patienthood to the level of a universal one and [tries] to solve for all what he could not solve for one alone."[4] By this dictum, Miyoji was a double failure. Miyoji was never a creative, successful leader even though he tried to model himself after the successful and innovative Meiji genro. Moreover, to his dying day he was unable, indeed never sought, to come to grips with the inner rages that ineluctably isolated him from his subordinates, peers, and superiors.[5]

This judgment, however, must be qualified. Although there were among his own generation politicians who were successful, there was none who can be characterized as "reformist or inno-

[2] The epitaph is quoted in Kurihara Kōta, "Shintei ikōshū," *Hakushaku Itō Miyoji* (Tokyo, 1938), 2:183–186 (hereafter cited as *HIM*); this is Miyoji's "official" biography in two volumes. For Miyoji as a superlative writer of drafts, see Ishikawa Hanzan, "Batsuzoku no ōbantō," *CK*, 32:50 (July 1917). Miura Gorō, no admirer of Miyoji, said that Miyoji's draft for establishing the *Rinji Gaikō Chōsa Iinkai* was well done; Hara Keiichirō, ed., *Hara Kei nikki* (Tokyo, 1950–1951), 7:175 (May 31, 1917). Miyoji drafted important speeches and documents for Prime Minister Terauchi Masatake (Oct. 1916–Sept. 1918); *Hara nikki*, 7:134, 187 (Feb. 27, June 16, 1917). He also drafted the declaration of war against China in 1894; Kurihara, *HIM*, 1:211–214. Two examples of Miyoji's epitaph style are available. Both are very brief, are for minor figures, and cannot be used for comparison. Kurihara, "Shintei ikōshū," *HIM*, 2:206–207. For the Chinese poems to Itō, see, for example, Kurihara, *HIM*, 2:70–71, 74–75, 125, 129–130 (section on Chinese poetry). I am indebted to my colleague, Mr. Tien-yi Tao for his assistance in working with Chinese material.

[3] In December 1933, Miyoji was asked to compose the epitaph for Itō's statue, which was going to be erected near the Diet. He died after writing a rough draft. This draft was much longer and Itō's accomplishments are cited in greater detail than in the epitaph written for the stele in Seoul. See Kurihara, "Shintei ikōshū," *HIM*, 2:213–224. In the winter of the same year, however, he wrote a composition about his appointment by Itō as special ambassador to China to exchange ratifications of the Sino-Japanese peace treaty (1895). (For details of this episode, see Kurihara, *HIM*, 1:241–269.) Nearly forty years after the event, he still was bitter that Itō at first had doubts about the wisdom of choosing him as special ambassador. Kurihara, "Shintei ikōshū," *HIM*, 2:160.

[4] Erik H. Erikson, *Young Man Luther: A Study in Psychoanalysis and History* (New York, 1958), p. 67. See also Stephan R. Graubard, Preface, "Philosophers and Kings: Studies in leadership," *Daedalus*, summer 1968, p. v.

[5] Strout talks about trying to understand "emotional difficulties which the agent could, in principle, bring to self-consciousness, but which in fact he does not." Cushing Strout, "Ego Psychology and the Historian," *History and Theory*, 7, no. 3:293 (1968).

vative."[6] Miyoji was successful within certain limits. He reached the highest levels of the bureaucracy as a powerful and feared member of the Privy Council. Prime ministers "asked" for his views. This son of a Nagasaki commoner family sought wealth and became wealthy beyond the wildest dreams of his youth. And though he was unable to sustain meaningful and mature relationships with his political peers and superiors, his ties with the members of his immediate family were close and warm. He was a doting father. We catch a glimpse of him, for example, flying a kite on a Sunday afternoon with his children in spite of the crush of official business.[7] When he was chief cabinet secretary (August 1892–September 1896), he was quite strict about maintaining standards pertaining to government employment. However, a decade later, we see him badgering Hara to hire his son as an engineer in the railroad bureau and "frequently asking for favors" for his son.[8]

One of the qualifications requires further modification. Though Miyoji did attain high bureaucratic standing as privy councillor, the role he envisaged for himself in that position was a static, conservative one. He did not attempt to be innovative. He conceived of his responsibility as a guardian of political traditionalism. This role is not inconsistent with political "success." It is suggested, for example, that the conservative role played by the Privy Council in the 1930's may have been a primary check "against a pure form of fascism emerging in Japan."[9] Moreover, even a politically negative function cannot necessarily be equated with failure.[10] Miyoji, however, had still another conception of his political role. He fancied himself a latter-day

---

[6] For judgments of Hara and Katō Takaaki, two prominent prewar prime ministers, see Tetsuo Najita, *Hara Kei in the Politics of Compromise: 1905–1915* (Cambridge, Mass., 1967), pp. 21, 22, and Peter Duus, *Party Rivalry and Political Change in Taishō Japan* (Cambridge, Mass., 1968), p. 248.

[7] Maeda, "Kempō no bannin," p. 196.

[8] *Hara nikki,* 5:27–28 (Feb. 2, 1912).

[9] James Crowley, "Remarks on Political and Military History" (Paper delivered at the Conference on the Status of Studies in Modern Japanese History, Nov. 8–9, 1968, Social Science Research Council, New York), p. 16.

[10] E. E. Schattschneider talks of the "achievement" of the Republican party (1860–1932) in terms of *what was prevented.* "United States: The Functional Approach to Party Government," in Sigmund Neumann, ed., *Modern Political Parties: Approaches to Comparative Politics* (Chicago, 1956), pp. 197–198.

genro—a mysterious, powerful figure manipulating men and events from behind the scenes. But he lacked the broad and far-sighted vision, the commitment to programs and goals, the willingness to take political risks and to assume consequences, and the bigger-than-life quality that characterized an Itō or a Yamagata. What Miyoji craved was status, security, and wealth. And ironically for him, even the style of politics he tried to emulate, that of genroship, became progressively passé in the 1910's and 1920's. It is in this specific sense that Miyoji was a political failure.

BACKGROUND AND EARLY CAREER

Miyoji died a count. The committee that compiled his biography, like most biographers of famous Japanese, felt impelled to embellish his genealogy with a dignity and prestige that was undeserved. Miyoji, on his part, assisted his future biographers by leaving behind handwritten notes on which the account was based. The results sometimes verged on the ludicrous. Miyoji traced his ancestry to the Itō of Izu, a family with vassalage ties to Toyotomi Hideyoshi. After the fall of Osaka in 1615, the main family settled in Bitchū (presently a part of Okayama prefecture) as the daimyo of the Okada han (11,000 *koku*). The house split, with the antecedents of Miyoji's family finally settling in Nagasaki. But Miyoji's claim to ties to the Itō of either Izu or Bitchū is badly damaged unwittingly by the biographers themselves in their statements that "little is known of the Nagasaki Itōs before Miyoji's grandfather" and that the "details of Miyoji's childhood are vague."[11]

His father, according to his biographers, was a *machidoshiyori nembanzuki kakimonoyaku* in Nagasaki. This meant that he was a clerk dealing in some aspect of Nagasaki trade, whose salary

---

[11] Kurihara, *HIM*, 1:4–6, 10. The genealogy of the Izu Itōs does not mention the Nagasaki Itōs. Ōta Akira, *Seishi kakei daijiten* (Tokyo, 1934), 1:438–446, and *Dokushi biyō* (Tokyo, 1933), p. 491. A standard biographical source does not go beyond Miyoji's father. Shimonaka Yasaburō, *Shinsen daijimmei jiten* (Tokyo, 1937), 1:313.

sometimes may have been fattened by "extra emoluments."[12]
Maeda Renzan, who is fairly sympathetic in his treatment of
Miyoji, called him an "interpreter's son."[13]

Miyoji was born on 1857/5/7 in Sakaya-machi, Nagasaki-shi.[14]
Little is known of his tender years, but if his biography is to be
believed, he was a child prodigy in language. He is alleged to
have started his English studies under Guido F. Verbeck at the
age of seven (1864). Ōkuma Shigenobu was another pupil but
it is not certain whether their tutelages overlapped. Ōkuma was
twenty-three years old when he first started his English lessons
in 1861.[15]

Miyoji was a filial son and a generous brother. He worked in
the Hyogo prefectural government office when he was sixteen
and, though not the eldest son, he sent for his parents to live
with him in Kobe (1874). When he settled down in Tokyo in
1877, he also sent for his parents. His father (Zempei) died in
1883 (age sixty-nine) when Miyoji was twenty-five. Miyoji was
extremely close to his mother (Naka) who died in 1904 (age
eighty-one). He was highly solicitous of her welfare and was
devotedly dutiful and obedient. Miyoji's oldest sister (Mio),
who was divorced in 1894, became a member of Miyoji's family
and spent her last years in his home and died in 1929 (age
seventy-seven). Miyoji also was the faithful lover of a concubine. He had married his wife Ayae in 1875 when he was
eighteen and she was seventeen. Around 1880, Miyoji took a
concubine, Ochiyo. In twenty years, Ochiyo bore him nine sons.
Two of these sons died in infancy, Ochiyo dying at the birth of
her ninth with Miyoji at her side.[16]

---

[12] Kurihara, *HIM*, 1:6–7.

[13] Maeda, "Kempō no bannin," p. 191. His maternal grandfather is said to
have been Nagasaki's *bugyōsho tammono mekikiyaku*, a petty official who made
decisions on the quality and proper price of piece goods; Kurihara, *HIM*, 1:8.

[14] His family register gives 1857/5/9 as the date of birth. In his notes (*shuki*),
the date is 5/7. Kurihara, *HIM*, 1:1.

[15] Kurihara, *HIM*, 1:2 (biographical section), also p. 11; Watanabe Ikujirō,
Ōkuma Shigenobu (Tokyo, 1952), pp. 15–16, 396; Robert M. Spaulding, Jr.,
Imperial Japan's Higher Civil Service Examinations (Princeton, N. J., 1967),
p. 36, fn. 12. There is no mention of Miyoji in William E. Griffis, *Verbeck of
Japan* (New York, 1900).

[16] Kurihara, *HIM*, 1:8, 9–10, 33; *Suiusō nikki* (unpublished, National Diet

Miyoji called four men his *onjin* (benefactors). Two of them taught him English. His relationship with all four during his youth, moreover, followed a pattern which is of significance in understanding his personality. Miyoji's first *onjin* was the Reverend Henry Nelson Stout of the Reformed (Dutch) Church. The date of the beginning of his important association with Stout is not clear. At the very earliest, the association began in 1869 when Miyoji was twelve.[17] Stout is said to have recognized Miyoji's considerable talents and pushed him hard. Miyoji responded by progressing "remarkably" in English until he was teaching a dozen or more students when he was only barely in his teens.[18] Stout was about thirty at this time. The picture that emerges from his obituary is of a person cold, stiff, individualistic, strong-willed, self-righteous, as well as resourceful, methodical, and precise.[19] These are some of the adjectives which later were applied to Miyoji by his critics.

Miyoji's second *onjin* added another dimension to his utilitarian education: the law. Frederic M. Chruchley, an Englishman, was the editor of the *Hiogo and Osaka Herald* and a solicitor who practiced in the consular courts when Miyoji began to work for him. This was in 1873, and Miyoji was sixteen.[20] Miyoji translated from Japanese newspapers into English for Chruchley's newspaper. He also translated legal papers and interpreted for Chruchley's clients. His hours were long, often

---

Library), 1:125, 128–129, 175 (April 6, 9, and 21, 1901) (this is Miyoji's diary and it is not paginated; the pagination is mine). Because the Miyoji family register records a daughter being born on June 15, 1900, it would seem that Miyoji had another concubine. It is possible that Ayae was the mother, but she was forty-one in 1900.

[17] His biography has Miyoji studying under Stout at age nine (1866); Kurihara, *HIM*, 1:3 (biographical section). Stout, however, did not arrive in Japan until 1868 or 1869. *Japan Weekly Chronicle*, Feb. 29, 1912, p. 366 (1868); Rev. H. V. S. Peeke, "The Late Rev. Henry Stout, D.D.," *Japan Evangelist*, 21:151 (1869); William E. Griffis, *The Rutgers Graduates in Japan* (Albany, N. Y., 1886), p. 19 (1869).

[18] Kurihara, *HIM*, 1:12.

[19] Peeke, "Rev. Henry Stout," pp. 151–154.

[20] Kurihara, *HIM*, 1:22; *Chronicle and Directory of China, Japan, the Philippines, etc.* (Hong Kong, 1875), pp. 85, 352; *Japan Chronicle, Jubilee Number, 1868–1918*, "History of Kobe," p. 15; Endō Motoo and Shimomura Fujio, *Kokushi bunken kaisetsu, zoku* (Tokyo, 1965), p. 431.

from 8:00 A.M. to the dead of night. Miyoji did not mind, for he was learning the law and was becoming well-known among those in the foreign community as "Mr. Itō, the interpreter." He also was paid 30 yen a month and given his room, board, and clothing expenses. Chruchley, like Stout, was much older than Miyoji, and also had an abrasive personality and a scurrilous pen.[21] Miyoji, too, was to exhibit these traits.

Miyoji, a commoner, now had the kind of "innovational" education and training that was a basic prerequisite for lower samurai bureaucratic success in the early Meiji. Chance operated to open his way to conspicuous success. Miyoji happened to act as an interpreter for a case arising out of a conflict of rights over land use on the Hyogo waterfront. Kanda Takahira, governor of Hyogo prefecture, and the American consul were negotiating the problem. Miyoji impressed Kanda and was asked to become an interpreter for the Hyogo prefectural government. Miyoji, though flattered by the attention, wanted to remain in Chruchley's employ and to become a lawyer. However, after a tear-stained letter from his mother urging him to accept Kanda's offer, he went to work as an interpreter and translator in the Hyogo prefectural office in August 1873.[22]

Miyoji was sixteen and Kanda, his third *onjin*, was twenty-seven years older. Kanda treated Miyoji with "great affection," as if Miyoji were his own son. It happened that Miyoji was the same age as Kanda's adopted son, who was in the United States as a student. Kanda also added sheen to Miyoji's rather un-

---

[21] Chruchley had purchased the *Hiogo and Osaka Herald* in 1869. At this time, he already had been in Japan for "many years," and had worked for the *Japan Herald* of Yokohama. British embassy and consular archives in the Public Records Office, London, F.O. 262/181 R. 78 Chruchley, F. M., to Sir Harry Parkes, April 29, 1869. I am indebted to Mr. James Hoare for sharing his notes on Chruchley with me. Mr. Hoare has worked on the treaty ports in the *bakumatsu* and early Meiji periods under Professor William G. Beasley, University of London. For comments on Chruchley's writings, see the *Hiogo News*, April 6, 1870. Chruchley was once sued for libel in the British consular court at Kobe for $5,000, a princely sum. Records of the Supreme Court at Shanghai, F.O. 656/41 A. A. Annesley to Sir Edmund Hornaby, no. 10, July 10, 1875.

[22] Kurihara, *HIM*, 1:26–28, 5 (biographical section). Both his parents wrote, but he vividly remembered his mother's letter. Chruchley gave Miyoji his blessing. Miyoji continued to work part-time for him and was able to absorb more law in the process. Kurihara, *HIM*, 1:31–32.

systematic education by teaching him to read and write in the classical Chinese style.[23] More importantly, Kanda introduced him to Shizuma Kensuke, a Chōshū man and friend of Itō Hirobumi.

Miyoji quit his Hyogo post over a factional dispute and went to live at Kanda's home in Tokyo. This was in November 1876. On December 27, 1876, he was introduced to Itō by Shizuma. He impressed Itō with his ability in English and was hired on the spot as *gondairoku* (acting senior secretary) in the Kōbushō (Ministry of Public Works) on January 10, 1877, at a respectable salary of 40 yen a month. This was his first step in the national bureaucracy. Itō was thirty-five years old, Miyoji nineteen. Miyoji recalls that when Itō saw him, he remarked that Miyoji was younger than he had expected.[24] Miyoji called Itō his fourth *onjin*.

Of the four people that Miyoji remembered as his benefactors, three were considerably older than he was. All four met him when he was still in his teens. Three treated him as if he were their son. Two were foreigners and quickly left his life. Kanda Takahira, who was once a member of the Meirokusha, was essentially a scholar. He had a quiet bureaucratic career and was appointed to the House of Peers in 1890, the same year Miyoji was. He was made a baron in 1898, the day before he died at the age of sixty-eight; Miyoji was appointed a baron in 1895 at thirty-eight. Miyoji, unlike Kanda, had made a decision in 1880 to enter the life of *seiji* (politics).[25] Kanda, in short, like the two foreigners, was not competitive with Miyoji and posed no threat to him. Kanda was perhaps the only Japanese, outside of his immediate family and the concubine Ochiyo, toward whom Miyoji felt sustained warmth.[26]

When Miyoji met Itō, he already had the reputation of being quick, intelligent, and energetic. He knew some Chinese and

[23] Kurihara, *HIM*, 1:31–32; 2:167, 169.
[24] Kurihara, *HIM*, 1:34, 35–38.
[25] Komatsu Midori, *Itō kō to Yamagata kō* (Tokyo, 1936), p. 84; Kurihara, *HIM*, 1:50, 13, 19 (biographical section).
[26] Kurihara, *HIM*, 2:167–169.

this may have appealed to Itō. He had a better than average acquaintance with certain aspects of international law and equity. He probably was fluent in reading English.[27] This was the talent that Itō bought. But Miyoji possessed another quality that may have attracted Itō. At this time he was extremely handsome. Komatsu in describing him uses the terms *tanrei* and *bibō*, words designating an effeminate type of handsomeness. Komatsu adds that Miyoji was conspicuously tall.[28] The Meiji leaders grew up in a period when *chigo* (catamite) was acceptable, so it is possible that Itō might have been vulnerable to Miyoji's physical attractiveness.

Miyoji was in the Ministry of Public Works for a year and eight months (January 1877–August 1878). Itō succeeded Ōkubo Toshimichi as minister of home affairs in May 1878, and Miyoji followed Itō in August. In February 1880, he was appointed to *sōnin* rank seven, the lowest *sōnin* rank. This was his first step upward in the higher bureaucracy. He was twenty-two.[29] He literally never left Itō's side from the time he went to

[27] We have only indirect evidence of his ability. Chruchley must have been satisfied because he continued to use Miyoji even after he had left the *Hiogo and Osaka Herald.* One writer, who knew Miyoji personally, said that Miyoji read with care Henry Wheaton's *Elements of International Law* and Edmund H. T. Snell's *The Principles of Equity* when he was in Chruchley's employ (Komatsu, *Itō kō to Yamagata kō,* pp. 82–84). Any Japanese who read these two books with care was hard-working and persevering. If he understood them, he was intelligent, had control of the English language, and had a fairly good knowledge of the law. Miyoji's own evaluation is that Chruchley was "astonished by my mastery of English, my youthfulness notwithstanding." Kurihara, *HIM,* 1:23; see also 1:75, 82. Japanese tend to be generous in their judgment of his ability. See Kobayashi Tatsuo, ed., *Meiji hyakunenshi sōsho—suiusō nikki—rinji gaikō chōsa iinkai kaigi hikki nado* (Tokyo, 1966), p. 4 ("Kaidai"). Cf. Sir Francis Piggot, "New Japan," *Fortnightly Review,* 52 (new series), no. 309:377. Sir Francis called the translation of the Meiji constitution into English an "unfortunate translation" and "full of grammatical blunders."

[28] Komatsu, *Itō kō to Yamagata kō,* pp. 83, 84, 87. Miyoji, according to one typology, would be considered a beautiful man (*bidanshi*) rather than an attractive man (*kōdanshi*). Hiroshi Wagatsuma, "The Social Perception of Skin Color in Japan," *Daedalus,* spring 1967, p. 419 (also p. 411). Hara Kei also has been described as "tall for his age" and a "handsome" boy. Duus, *Party Rivalry,* p. 69.

[29] Kurihara, *HIM,* 1:41–44. Hara and Inukai Tsuyoshi (1855–1932) were both twenty-six years old when they became *sōnin.* Hara, however, entered the higher bureaucracy as quasi-*sōninkan.* Spaulding, *Civil Service Examination,* p. 55.

the Ministry of Public Works to the time he resigned as agriculture and commerce minister in April 1898. As Itō's star rose, so did Miyoji's. He began by teaching Itō English and serving as his personal valet.[30] Miyoji went on to draft policy papers of increasing importance, and there is evidence that Itō had implicit trust in his abilities because, for example, Miyoji accompanied Itō to China to conclude the Tientsin treaty (February–April 1885). Itō left all details to Miyoji, and only after they had left Yokohama for China did Itō inquire about the preparations made by Miyoji for the final talks. Miyoji also participated in the drafting of the Meiji constitution. His biographers consider this to have been his most "noteworthy achievement."[31] By 1890, Miyoji was being asked advice on state affairs by men like Itō, Yamagata, and Matsukata. Maeda may be overstating but he writes that Miyoji, around the time of the Ōtsu incident, was the "brain" of the government and that even state ministers humbled themselves to ask him for "guidance." He also is depicted as having had the coolest head and as being the soundest advisor during this incident.[32]

Itō became prime minister for the second time in August 1892. Miyoji resigned as chief secretary of the Privy Council and became chief cabinet secretary the same month. Miyoji remained in this post until September 1896.[33] This was the period in which Miyoji came into his own. His biography designates this period the "most brilliant" in his life; his contemporaries, not necessarily friendly to him, agree. Baba Tsune-

[30] Maeda, *Rekidai naikaku monogatari* (Tokyo, 1961), 1:7–10. Kurihara, *HIM*, 1:65, 69–72. Cf. Tokutomi Soho, *Waga kōyū roku* (Tokyo, 1938), p. 43.

[31] Kurihara, *HIM*, 1:65, 73–74, 78–80, 84–85, 108–119. See also Kaneko Kentarō, "Itō kō to kempō seitei jigyō," *Kokka gakkai zasshi*, vol. 24 (July 1910). Miyoji also drafted the "infamous" peace preservation law of December 1887 on his way back from Okinawa with Itō. Kurihara, *HIM*, 1:95–96, 100–103.

[32] Kurihara, *HIM*, 1:151–157; Maeda, "Kempō no bannin," pp. 194–196, and *Seihen monogatari*, pp. 229–234. The incident involved the attempted assassination of the Grand Duke Nicholas Alexandrovich, the future Nicholas II, in Ōtsu on May 11, 1891. An excellent study in English is Barbara J. Teters, "The Ōtsu Affair: The Formation of Japan's Judicial Conscience," *Studies on Asia* (to be published).

[33] Itō had resigned in August 1896. Kurihara, *HIM*, 1:175, 276.

go calls it the "golden age" for Miyoji. Ishikawa designates it the time of Miyoji's "proudest moments."[34]

Miyoji had a freedom of action unavailable to most state ministers. The chief cabinet secretary was responsible to the prime minister, and, basically, he was in charge of the cabinet's confidential documents and of handling routine cabinet business. A man of ordinary talents in this post would be but a petty bureaucrat acting as a combination messenger boy, traffic policeman, and private secretary. But a talented, aggressive, and experienced person like Miyoji could "control" the cabinet and take into his own hands the powers of the prime minister. He could do this because the prime minister could not deal personally with each ministry and solve all problems. An able and strong chief cabinet secretary also had to have the full support of the prime minister in order to act as his deputy. The prime minister was usually happy to back a strong secretary, who attracted bitterness, antipathy, and disappointment away from the prime minister to himself. The rewards for the chief cabinet secretary were great. It is said, for example, that vice ministers, bureau chiefs, or prefectural governors who needed cabinet support for their projects became sad or happy at seeing Miyoji's mood.[35]

One of Miyoji's most notable achievements as chief cabinet secretary was in bringing about a rapprochement between the Itō cabinet and the Jiyūtō in 1895. This resulted in the passage of a record-breaking budget and ninety-three bills in the ninth session of the Diet and Itagaki Taisuke's appointment as home minister in April 1896.[36] As a result, Miyoji became closely identified with the Tosa faction of the Jiyūtō, so much so that he came to be known as a *tōshi* (party elder). In this capacity, he

[34] Kurihara, *HIM*, 1:176; Baba, "Itō Miyoji ron," p. 205; "Batsuzoku no ōbantō," p. 47. See also Uzaki Rojō, "Hyōmen in noridashita Itō shi," *CK*, 32:41, 42 (July 1917).

[35] Tōyama Shigeki and Andō Shizuko, *Kindai Nihon seiji shi hikkei* (Tokyo, 1967), p. 62; Toyabe Shuntei, *Meiji jimbutsu shōkan* (Tokyo, 1902), pp. 160–166, 176, 179.

[36] For details, see George Akita, *Foundations of Constitutional Government in Modern Japan, 1868–1900* (Cambridge, Mass., 1967), pp. 117–119.

gave advice to the party and probably exerted some leadership through Itagaki. Miyoji's attitude toward the Jiyūtō is significant in the light of his later moves. He did not, despite rumors to the contrary, seek to become the president of the party. Furthermore, he did not feel that his fate was inextricably intertwined with that of the party—in the sense that he would sink or swim with it. Still, it was his support of Itagaki and the Jiyūtō that caused his angry resignation from the third Itō cabinet (January–June 1898) after only a brief tenure as agriculture and commerce minister (January–April 1898).[37]

His resignation did not remove him from stage center in politics. He continued to mediate between the Jiyūtō, Kenseitō, and Seiyūkai parties and several cabinets. He played a role in bringing about the rapprochement between the Kenseitō and the second Yamagata cabinet (November 1898–October 1900). He helped to draft the manifesto, party regulations, and the platform of the Seiyūkai. He was in part instrumental in preventing the early downfall of the first Katsura government (June 1901–January 1906) by manipulating the "moderate" faction of the Seiyūkai.[38] He was offered cabinet posts in the second Yamagata cabinet, the fourth Itō cabinet (October 1900–May 1901), and the first Katsura cabinet (June 1901–January 1906).[39] A parade of politicians marched to his residence informing him of political developments and urging him

---

[37] Kurihara, *HIM*, 1:285; Maeda, *Seihen monogatari*, p. 296; Uzaki, "Hyōmen ni noridashita," pp. 42–43; *Taiyō*, 8, no. 7:39 (June 1902); Sakai Yūkichi, in an unpublished, untitled paper on a study of documents relating to Itō Miyoji for the period 1895–1905, with particular emphasis on the period around 1898, pp. 4–5 (Mr. Sakai is with the Meiji bunko, Tokyo University, and has graciously given me a photocopy of his paper). Miyoji believed that Itō reneged on his promise to appoint Itagaki as home minister in April 1898. See Kurihara, *HIM*, 1:282–288; Komatsu, *Itō kō to Yamagata kō* p. 93; *Suiusō nikki*, 1:219 (April 27, 1901). See also Sakai's unpublished paper, pp. 9–12.

[38] Baba, "Itō Miyoji ron," pp. 210–211; Kurihara, *HIM*, 1:318–319; letter from Miyoji to Itō dated Aug. 5, 1900, quoted in Kurihara, *HIM*, 1:320–322; Maeda, *Seihen monogatari*, p. 502.

[39] Yamagata offered him the agriculture and commerce post; *Suiusō nikki*, 1:216–218 (April 27, 1901). Itō offered Miyoji the foreign, home, and communications ministries; *Suiusō nikki*, 1:143–144 (April 13, 1901); Kurihara, *HIM*, 1:344–345, 348. Katsura asked him to choose from among the home, finance, and foreign ministries; Kurihara, *HIM*, 1:357.

to accept cabinet posts. The giants of the political world like Itō, Yamagata, and Katsura called on him at his home. He exchanged cups with Matsukata, Ōyama Iwao, Saigō Tsugumichi, as well as with Katsura, Itō, Gotō Shimpei, and Yoshikawa Akimasa at a Japanese-style restaurant.[40]

At this point in life, then, Miyoji stood at a crossroad. He was indisputably talented. Unfriendly critics called him able, astute, versatile, and a person of uncommon energy and administrative ability.[41] He had served a long, hard, and rewarding apprenticeship in the bureaucracy.[42] He was being actively urged by party men, junior statesmen, and genrō to accept the most important ministries in the government. Even his enemies conceded that he was potentially one of the two greatest statesmen in Japan. Baba later asserted that if Miyoji had joined the Seiyūkai in 1900, he might have become Itō's successor ahead of Hara. Yet the only position he accepted was a sinecure—the unexciting, secure job of privy councillor.[43]

THE DECISION TO BE A GENRO

About this time, too, another promising young bureaucrat faced a decision. Katō Takaaki could "choose between continued service as a neutral, nonpartisan bureaucrat, or he could enter the new party that Itō was planning to organize."[44] In 1900, Katō put off the decision. He entered Itō's fourth cabinet as foreign minister but did not join the Seiyūkai.[45] In mid-

[40] *Suiusō nikki*, 1:84, 86, 122, 124, 126, 129–130, 143–144, 150 (March 14, 16; April 2, 4, 5, 7, 10, 13, 15, 1901).

[41] Uzaki, "Hyōmen ni noridashita," pp. 44–45; Ishikawa, "Batsuzoku no ōbantō," pp. 50–51; *Taiyō*, 6, no. 13:27 (1900); Umehara Ryūhoku, "Hoshi Tōru shi oyobi Itō Miyoji dan," *CK*, 16:2–3 (April 1901).

[42] His experience as a bureaucrat is said to have been one of the main reasons for his success as chief cabinet secretary. Toyabe, *Meiji jimbutsu shōkan*, pp. 163, 179–180.

[43] Umehara, "Hoshi Tōru shi oyobi Itō Miyoji dan," pp. 1–2; Baba, "Itō Miyoji ron," p. 209; *Suiusō nikki*, 1:218 (April 27, 1901).

[44] Duus, *Party Rivalry*, p. 55.

[45] Miyoji also did not enter the party. Kurihara, *HIM*, 1:320–321, 405, 406. Hara visited Miyoji and was told by the latter his reasons for not joining. Hara does not list the reasons, but he wrote that Miyoji's real intentions did not lie in his explanations; *Hara nikki*, 2:287 (July 30, 1900).

February 1913, Katō again faced a fork in the road. This time he elected to become a party politician.[46] There was another way in which an exbureaucrat could reach the highest political rung. Takahashi Korekiyo succeeded Hara as prime minister (November 1921–June 1922) not because he actively desired the position but because of the force of circumstance—the assassination of Hara on November 21, 1921.[47]

Miyoji, the gifted bureaucrat, deliberately rejected the world of highly competitive, visible, risky, responsible public politics which might have given him the opportunity to become a creative political leader. A noted critic wrote in 1930 that Miyoji stood "at the first rank among those [politicians] who are still alive."[48] But no one had seriously considered Miyoji as an active politician for over two decades.

Miyoji's decision to turn away from public politics was probably made in 1898. Five reasons may be suggested for this decision: (1) a fear of constant and undeflected public attacks; (2) his experience as chief cabinet secretary, which made a "mere" cabinet post unattractive; (3) the compulsion for financial security; (4) a sulky attitude toward Itō; (5) the desire for status. The denominator common to all is Miyoji's easily bruised ego.

His anger at Itō for not appointing Itagaki as home minister is usually cited as the reason for his disenchantment with politics. There are some who believe, however, that the attacks against him on the Dōjima "question" is the real cause. Miyoji came under daily attack by the newspaper *Manchōhō*, which accused him of accepting a bribe of 30,000 yen for taking action relating to the Dōjima rice exchange in Osaka.[49] As a result,

---

[46] Duus, *Party Rivalry*, pp. 59–60.
[47] *Ibid.*, p. 170.
[48] Baba, "Itō Miyoji ron," p. 202.
[49] Kurihara, *HIM*, 1:289–291; Ishikawa, "Batsuzoku no ōbantō," p. 49. He sued the newspaper in the Tokyo district court. It was a situation in which Miyoji could hardly lose. He based his suit on the law that "anyone who insults the official conduct of a government official will have committed the crime of contempt against government officials even without reference to the truth or falsity of the charge." *Itō ke monjo*, item 352/7 (Kensei shiryō shitsu, National Diet Library).

Miyoji may have felt that once he took a cabinet post and became a public figure he would be fair game for his political enemies. Perceptive journalists had noted that Miyoji could not "stand the heat." Toyabe hit true when he pointed out that though Miyoji was reputed to be a "ruffian," he did not really "possess the kind of courage to risk everything in battling a dangerous situation."[50]

Miyoji himself revealed his touchiness about public criticism. In 1898, Itō asked Miyoji to enter his third cabinet. Miyoji replied that because people were criticizing him for his "unsavory" character, he should not be appointed minister of education. Miyoji also peevishly complained in his diary about the "unreasonable" attacks the newspapers were launching against him for his supposed political activities. At the same time, it is possible to sense a kind of perverse pleasure he enjoyed in being the center of so much newspaper speculation. He wrote, "The five [Seiyūkai cabinet] ministers [Hayashi Yūzō, Suematsu Kenchō, Matsuda Masahisa, Kaneko Kentarō, Hara] do not have the confidence of the people and are undistinguished. Therefore, the public thinks [wrongly] that someone must be behind them making the strong decisions."[51]

It is evident that from about this time he was enjoying playing the genro. He gave political advice freely, recorded with obvious relish his close association with the genro, protested too loudly of his annoyance with the "daily visits of the politicians," and implied that he was much too busy with his *bonsai* collection to be bothered with incompetent politicians.[52] In

[50] Toyabe Sentarō (Shuntei), *Meiji jimbutsu hyōron* (Tokyo, 1898), pp. 203–204. He also said that although Inukai and Miyoji were equal in intelligence, Inukai was superior in courage; *ibid.*, p. 34. See also Miyake Yūjirō (Setsurei), *Yononaka* (Tokyo, 1914), p. 112.

[51] Kurihara, *HIM*, 1:285–286; *Suiusō nikki*, 1:130, 167–168, 180, 183–184, 205 (April 10, 20, 22, 23, 25, 1901). Around 1898, if a newspaper article in Tokyo discussed "machinations" or "intrigues" in high government circles, Miyoji's name was more often than not mentioned. Sakai, untitled paper, p. 1.

[52] *Suiusō nikki*, 1:41–46, 48–55, 58–60, 86 (March 3, 5, 7, 16, 1901). This role-playing was evident to Hara, who noted that though Katsura was cool toward Miyoji, Miyoji "goes out of his way to make it appear that he is an advisor to the cabinet." *Hara nikki*, 2, sequel: 11 (Oct. 21, 1902). *Suiusō nikki*, 1:167 (April 20, 1901).

this way, he sought to conjure up a vision of a latter-day Yamagata—a Yamagata who was at this time associated in the popular mind with his Chinzansō garden and its babbling brooks. Moreover, Miyoji had exercised great power as surrogate genro when he was chief cabinet secretary. He had bullied state ministers, manipulated the revered party leader Itagaki, and even "moved" Itō.[53] By his own account he also had been responsible for getting Yamagata safely through the fourteenth session of the Diet (November 1889–February 1900).[54]

"Working in the White House is the ultimate seduction. Afterwards every other passion is a tasteless encounter."[55] So wrote a former member of the Lyndon B. Johnson staff. Miyoji's power and position was greater than that of most members of the White House staff. Miyoji himself asserted that it was easy enough to become a state minister, but extremely difficult to be a chief cabinet secretary. He also reputedly told Itō in 1898 that the only position he would consider would be that of prime minister, which was one way of pricing himself out of the political market.[56] Miyoji, in short, having experienced the "ultimate seduction," preferred to enjoy the power and ego-fulfillment of behind-the-scenes manipulation in relative security to the risk of being battered in public office. And there is no doubt that there was "high recognition value" in Miyoji's role, for, as Maeda has recalled, "From 1885 to 1900 . . . , just as the shadow follows the form, Miyoji followed Itō. In every major incident Miyoji's shadow was seen, like the bat which flies at dusk and the owl which cries in the dark."[57]

The fragility of his ego also was evident in his compulsion

---

[53] Uzaki, "Hyōmen ni noridashita," p. 42; Komatsu, *Itō kō to Yamagata kō*, p. 87; Okazaki Kunisuke, "Itō shishaku no dōraku," *CK* 32:45–46 (July 1917); Fujiwara Masato, ed., *Kokumin no tomo* (Tokyo, 1967), 28b, no. 296:119 (May 16, 1896) [see also 17a, no. 264:8 (Oct. 5, 1895)]; Tokutomi, *Waga kōyū roku*, p. 37.

[54] *Suiusō nikki*, 1:225 (April 27, 1901). According to Sakai, Yamagata felt the "greatest good will" toward Miyoji during the second Yamagata cabinet (November 1898–October 1900). Untitled paper, p. 15.

[55] Jack Valenti, in the Washington *Post*, Jan. 6, 1969, p. B7. See also Patrick Anderson, *The President's Men* (New York, 1968), p. 1.

[56] Toyabe, *Meiji jimbutsu shōkan*, p. 164; Kurihara, *HIM*, 1:285.

[57] Maeda, *Seihen monogatari*, pp. 230–231.

for accumulating wealth. Miyoji once told Maeda that because of his shortness of temper, he was apt to submit his resignation at any time. Therefore, from the time he had become Itō's secretary, he made preparations to resign from the government at any moment without worries about his livelihood.[58] This was his stated reason. But a precipitous drop in the income of his family during his childhood may explain his insecurity.[59]

Later in life, Miyoji matter of factly said that he had accumulated a fortune "before I knew it," by saving part of his salary, buying land cheaply in the outskirts of Tokyo, investing in stocks, and renting out houses.[60] He did not mention that his ownership of the Tokyo *Nichi nichi shimbun* contributed sub-

---

[58] Maeda, "Kempō no bannin," p. 200.

[59] In 1865, the salary of a *nembanzuki kakimonoyaku*, the position held by his father, was 4 *kamme, 250 momme* in "silver." The official exchange rate established by the Tokugawa Bakufu was 1,000 *momme* to 1 *kamme*. In 1857, the year of Miyoji's birth, 97 to 100 *momme* of "silver" could buy 1 *koku* of rice in Osaka, depending on the type of rice. This meant that the Miyoji family had an annual stipend of approximately 42 *koku* of rice. This was not low. But, in 1867, the salary could buy only 4 to 5 *koku* of rice, for 1 *koku* in Osaka now cost from 815 to 960 *momme* (*Nagasaki sōsho [III]: Zōho Nagasaki ryakushi* [Nagasaki, 1926], 1:506; *Dokushi sōran* [Tokyo, 1966], pp. 776–777). E. S. Crawcour and Kōzō Yamamura have shown, however, that silver currency-by-weight went out of use; that it was replaced by credit instruments in Osaka, Kyoto, and Edo; and that there is no evidence that *chōgin* (monetary silver) was in use from 1787 to 1868. The consequence was to decrease the real value, or purchasing power, of Miyoji's father's stipend, which undoubtedly was fixed in nominal terms (or in credit units) ("The Tokugawa Monetary System, 1787–1868," unpublished, pp. 4–5; see also Taya Hirokichi, "Edo jidai no heisei," in Horie Yasuzo, ed., *Kinsei Nihon no keizai tō shakai* [Tokyo, 1958], pp. 145–146). This de facto inflation probably was the reason why his biographers called the stipend "very insignificant." Horie Yasuzō has shown also that at the beginning of the Tokugawa period the ratio of silver to copper in silver currency was 80:20. From 1837 to 1858, the ratio was 26:74; and from 1859 to 1865, 13:87. Therefore, even if Miyoji's father was paid not in credit units but in coins, the debasement of coinage may have reduced the family to living on whatever "extra emoluments" the job could bring ("Chōgin," in Honjō Eijirō, ed., *Nihon keizai jiten* [Tokyo, 1940], 2:1062–1063).

Bernadino de Avila Giron, a Spanish trader who lived in Nagasaki at the turn of the sixteenth century, observed perceptively that in the city no matter how high a person's rank, he was despised if he had no money. Assuming that this attitude toward money remained unchanged, the steep slide in purchasing power of the Miyoji household must have been traumatic for a bright, impressionable lad (Morinaga Taneo, *Bakumatsu no Nagasaki: Nagasaki daikan no kiroku* [Tokyo, 1966], p. 2).

[60] Maeda, "Kempō no bannin," p. 200; *Asahi seiji keizai sōsho: Sūmitsuin mondai,* quoted in Kurihara, *HIM,* 1:547.

stantially to his fortune. Miyoji acquired the newspaper without charge as part of Itō's first plan to form a political party (January 1892). Hara noted that Miyoji treated the newspaper as if it were his "private property." He recalled that when he was in the Foreign Ministry (he is probably referring to the period 1892–1895), Miyoji received a subsidy for the paper of 5,000 yen from the cabinet and 1,000 from the Foreign Ministry. He believed that the second Yamagata cabinet gave Miyoji a "substantial sum." He also wrote that the "present Katsura cabinet is naturally" giving Miyoji a large amount of money. Miyoji also used the newspaper as a club to extract money from government officials and others. Hara is again the source, and he dutifully recorded that Miyoji was receiving 5,000 yen yearly from the Imperial Household Ministry on the promise of not slandering officials in the ministry. Hara on a later occasion wrote that Miyoji blackmailed other persons in the government as well as industrialists.[61]

Miyoji was adept at keeping down expenses by questionable means. He paid his employees "extremely low" salaries and used employees paid by other companies such as the shipping firm, Nippon Yusen Kaisha. He was said to have used the private secretary's official quarters as a branch office of the newspaper and to have made the newspaper compulsory reading for bureaucrats all over Japan. His final sin was in selling the newspaper, which he had received without payment, to Katō Takaaki. This action greatly angered Inoue Kaoru.[62] His cupidity contributed to his political isolation, especially as it confirmed the stereotypes of commoners held by the ex-samurai leaders in the highest levels of politics. For example, in 1916, the position of imperial household minister was vacant. Yamagata rejected Miyoji as a candidate because "he liked money." This

[61] Maeda, "Kempō no bannin," p. 197; *Hara nikki*, 2, sequel: 189 (Sept. 30, 1904), 7:362 (March 30, 1918); 2, sequel: 10–11 (Oct. 21, 1902), 190 (Sept. 30, 1904).

[62] *Hara nikki*, 2, sequel: 11 (Oct. 21, 1902); Uzaki, "Hyōmen ni noridashita," p. 42; *Hara nikki*, 2, sequel: 196 (Nov. 7, 1904). See also *ibid.*, 2, sequel: 191 (Oct. 9, 1904). Cf. Katō's approach to the newspaper in Duus, *Party Rivalry*, pp. 57–58.

aspect of Miyoji's character weighed heavily in the mind of the ex-samurai Yamagata, for in 1918 he again said that Miyoji was "avaricious for money."[63]

Miyoji compounded his unpopularity and aggravated his isolation by using the newspaper to violently attack his political enemies. In one instance, he used the newspaper columns to assail the Matsukata-Ōkuma cabinet (September 1896 –January 1898). The rank and power of his targets seemed to have bothered him little. In 1904, he condemned the Katsura cabinet and criticized Inoue and Matsukata. For the latter transgression, the two sent him a letter "cutting off their relationship with him." It took the persuasive power of both Itō and Yamagata to patch up the breach.[64]

Miyoji not only sought to make money but was penurious as well. He was known as being "tight-fisted," "stingy," and "cold-blooded when it came to money." His niggardliness was basic in his decision not to enter the Seiyūkai in 1900. The cautious Miyoji was aware that it took money to maintain "an army."[65] When he first dealt with the Jiyūtō, the Tosa faction was in the commanding position. By 1900, however, the Kantō faction under Hoshi Tōru was dominant, and to build this dominance, Hoshi had spent an enormous amount of money.[66]

Hara, too, once smilingly told Kataoka Naoharu, an industrialist and politician (1859–1934), that men could not be

---

[63] *Hara nikki*, 7:94 (Dec. 27, 1916), 362 (March 30, 1918). See also Ishikawa, "Batsuzoku ni ōbantō," p. 48. Miyoji was given some kind of remuneration for his part in a real estate transaction involving the Honganji sometime in 1914; *ibid.*, 7:67 (June 20, 1914). This matter further contributed to his ill-repute. See *ibid.*, 7:201 (July 18, 1917).

[64] Ishikawa, "Batsuzoku no ōbantō," p. 48; *Suiusō nikki*, 2:447–448 (July 7, 1901); see also Uzaki, "Hyōmen ni noridashita," p. 43. *Hara nikki*, 2, sequel: 189–190, 192, 196 (Sept. 30, Oct. 11, Nov. 7, 1904). Hara seemed to enjoy writing about Miyoji's difficulties.

[65] *Asahi seiji keizai sōsho: sūmitsuin mondai*, quoted in Kurihara, *HIM*, 1:547; Uzaki, "Hyōmen ni noridashita," p. 44; Nakamura Kikuo, *Itō Hirobumi* (Tokyo, 1958), p. 157. In April 1898, Itō launched his third attempt to establish a party. He could not count on Jiyūtō support so he cried out, "I cannot depend on mercenary troops. I must have my own army." Hayashida Kametarō, *Nihon seitō shi* (Tokyo, 1927), 2:1–3.

[66] Masumi Junnosuke, *Nihon seitō shi ron* (Tokyo, 1966), 2:351–352; Toyabe Shuntei, *Zoku Meiji jimbutsu hyōron* (Tokyo, 1900), pp. 263–264.

moved without granting them official posts or money or, at the very least, "favors."[67] But it cannot be imagined that Miyoji ever would have placed himself in a position where he could be dunned for a political contribution of 20,000 yen.[68] In 1918, therefore, it was estimated that Miyoji was worth "several millions of yen," but he had no army of politicians.[69]

Miyoji, moreover, was not even willing to spend money to establish an "army" of bureaucrats. If he had been willing to do this, his power and influence doubtless would have been great. Yamagata, who had a large network of followers in the bureaucracy, was said to have "readily spent money" on others. Itō did not try to build a coterie of followers, so he did not have to spend money for this purpose. However, he did not overly concern himself with money.[70]

It was not only the attitude toward spending that set Miyoji apart from other Meiji leaders. There was a difference in style of spending. Hara dispensed money with grace. He would patiently listen to the petitioners' reasons for their need of funds so that they "would not lose face."[71]

There is one more important dimension to Miyoji's attitude toward money. He was so concerned about accumulating wealth that he tried to save money at public expense. He was willing enough to keep two or three concubines at a time. However, he

[67] Kataoka Naoharu, *Taishō Shōwa seijishi no ichi dammen: Zoku kaisōroku* (Tokyo, 1934), p. 210.

[68] Just prior to Katsura's death in October 1913, six or seven leaders of the Dōshikai met to discuss the future of the party. Katō and Gotō Shimpei were assessed 20,000 yen each to fill the party's empty treasury. Others contributed from 2,000 to 10,000 yen. Kataoka Naoharu, *Kaisōroku* (Kyoto, 1933), pp. 343–345.

[69] *Hara nikki*, 7:362 (March 30, 1918). This is evidence of Miyoji's sure money-making touch. Hara observed in 1904 that Miyoji had a fortune of 1 million yen; *ibid.*, 2, sequel: 190 (Sept. 30, 1904). Hoshi left only one house, which was sold for 70,000–80,000 yen. Maeda believes that if Hoshi had concentrated on his law practice, he could have left an estate of several millions of yen; Maeda, *Hoshi Tōru den* (Tokyo, 1948), p. 326. Cf. Nakamura Kikuo, "Hoshi Tōru to hambatsu seiji," *CK*, 80:393 (Jan. 1965). Hara, too, left very little: a house in Shiba Park, two country cottages, and "a few other things." See Masumi Junosuke, *Nihon seitō shi ron* (Tokyo, 1968), 4:258.

[70] Senryō Inshi (pseudo.), "Yamagata kō ron," *CK*, 25:93 (Oct. 1911); Miyake, *Yononaka*, p. 314. One critic wrote that if Miyoji had used his experience, intelligence, eloquence, and wealth, he easily could have become a party head. Itō Chiyū, quoted in Kurihara, *HIM*, 1:548.

[71] Uchida Nobunari, *Fūsetsu gojūnen* (Tokyo, 1951), pp. 60, 63.

sought to save money by housing them at the official residence. Significantly, he also enjoyed watching them fight for his attention. It is difficult to conceive of Yamagata keeping concubines in the prime minister's quarters. His long-time secretary, Irie Kan'ichi, recalled that Yamagata was scrupulous in drawing a line between public and private or personal matters. Yamagata had given Hoshi the large sum of money to manipulate party men. Hoshi never used any of it for personal use, justifying the high respect Yamagata had for him.[72]

PSYCHOLOGICAL FACTORS

The Japanese psychiatrist L. Takeo Doi has written widely on *amae*, a concept he considers a key to the understanding of Japanese personality structure. He holds that "all interpersonal relationships in Japan are tinged with the feeling of *amaeru* on the part of both partners either overtly or covertly." In other words, *amae* is "basic in the Japanese character structure," and there is a "social sanction . . . for expressing the wish to *amaeru*." He says that *amaeru* can be translated as "to depend and presume on another's love" or "to seek and bask in another's indulgence." This concept, he adds, describes "a child's attitude or behavior toward his parents, particularly his mother." However, it also pertains to the behavior of adults, such as the relationship between a master and a subordinate.[73]

---

[72] Uzaki, "Hyōmen ni noridashita," p. 44; Irie Kan'ichi, *Yamagata kō no omokage* (Tokyo, 1930), pp. 33–34, also p. 247 (supplement). Maeda gives conflicting accounts of the amount Hoshi received, but it was probably not more than 100,000 yen. Maeda, *Hoshi Tōru den*, p. 324, and *Hara Takashi den* I (Tokyo, 1943), p. 386. Cf. Hattori Shisō and Irimajiri Yoshinaga, *Kindai Nihon jimbutsu seiji shi* (Tokyo, 1955), 1:230. Hoshi wanted to create a united party with an absolute majority in the House of Representatives. To achieve this goal, Hoshi "bore the unbearable" (Maeda, *Hoshi Tōru den*, p. 323). In this sense, he was father of the conception that Hara later pushed to fulfillment. Cf. Najita, *Hara Kei*, pp. 12–13, 22–26.

[73] L. Takeo Doi, "Amae: A Key Concept for Understanding Personality Structure," in R. J. Smith and R. K. Beardsley, eds., *Japanese Culture: Its Development and Characteristics* (Chicago, 1962), pp. 132–139; "Giri-Ninjō: An Interpretation," in R. P. Dore, ed., *Aspects of Social Change in Modern Japan* (Princeton, N. J., 1967), pp. 327–334; "Psychoanalytic Therapy and 'Western Man': A Japanese View," *International Journal of Social Psychiatry, Congress Issue 1964*, pp. 13–18.

When a person feels that his desire to *amaeru* is not fulfilled, he is afflicted by *kodawari* or a sense that he is not accepted by others, and he becomes "inwardly disturbed over his personal relations." Closely related to this feeling is *suneru*, which describes a child or an adult pouting or sulking because "he is not allowed to *amaeru* as much as he wants to." This feeling in turn may cause a child or adult to *hinekureru* or to take "devious ways" to deny his wish to *amaeru*.[74]

Hiroshi Wagatsuma has taken this concept to analyze the novels of Ishiwara Shintarō. Wagatsuma sees the protagonists of these novels as "phallic characters" with an Oedipus complex who often are "incapable of mature heterosexual love [and] like small children . . . maintain a dependent attachment and need for love directed toward their mothers."[75]

According to analytic personality theories, emotional insecurity that leads to the inability to sustain meaningful relationships has its roots in early childhood. Unfortunately, documentation is lacking on the nature of Miyoji's early childhood, but Miyoji's behavior as an adult has led to the assumption that he was insecure. A further assumption is that his early environment, whatever the nature of it, greatly contributed to his insecurity. This must have been particularly true of his interaction with his parents, especially his mother. Miyoji, as we have seen, was very close to his mother. Whether this relationship was one in which he was overly attached to and dependent on his mother cannot be shown with certainty. Still, the patterns of his relationship with Itō suggest that Miyoji had a very strong need for *amae*. It is assumed that this strong need for *amae* was generated originally because of his relationship with his parents, especially with his mother.[76]

---

[74] Doi, "Amae," pp. 133–134.

[75] "A Psychoanalytic Study of Ishiwara Shintaro's Early Novels and Its Implications for the Understanding of Japanese Male Psychology," unpublished, p. 6.

[76] The childhoods of several Meiji leaders reveal interesting and consistent patterns. A number of them 'lost" their fathers when they were in their early teens or even younger. Their mothers are pictured as either having strong character or exerting great influence. The material suggests strong attachment to the mothers. This may indicate that Miyoji's experience in this respect is not unique.

The Other Itō: A Political Failure

It may be suggested that Itō served as Miyoji's parent figure in the political world for about thirty years (1877–1906). The descriptions of Miyoji's intimate relationship with Itō are sometimes couched in familial terms. "[Miyoji] was so favored by Itō that it was rumored that he was Itō's illegitimate son," wrote Maeda. "Miyoji was a *kobun* whom Itō raised from infancy," was Tokutomi's description.[77] The following comment concerning Miyoji was made by Hida Chiho, a mistress of Itō's, who was the proprietress of a Japanese-style restaurant:

> [Miyoji] was like a fashion-plate in his three-layered kimono of finely patterned silk crepe. . . . He always had light make-up on. What is more, he was [constantly] dabbing the tip of his nose with powdered paper. He derived pleasure from wearing undergarments matching those of his concubine Oume. . . . Because I was said to be "related" to Prince Itō, [Miyoji] would call out to me, "Mother dear, mother dear." This was too much even for a person like me.[78]

Miyoji's contemporaries not only described Itō's relationship with Miyoji in terms of parent-child but also discussed this relationship in terms of *amae*. For example, when Miyoji was chief cabinet secretary, Miyoji used to get his way with Itō by threatening to resign. He was also able to argue freely with Itō. Maeda insightfully noted that this was Miyoji's way of expressing *amae*. Baba in 1930 called Miyoji the greatest *sunemono* (warped man) of his age.[79] *Suneru*, as Doi points out, is the reaction associated with the frustration of the need for *amae*.

But let us return to Miyoji's reactions at the turn of the twentieth century, which led him to reject participation in party politics. Miyoji had cause to feel insecure about Itō's feelings toward him around 1900. In 1898, when Miyoji was no longer chief cabinet secretary, Itō had sided with Inoue Kaoru against him on the question of Itagaki's second tenure as home minister.

[77] Maeda, "Kempō no bannin," p. 191; Tokutomi, *Waga kōyū roku*, pp. 56–57.
[78] Hida Chiho, *Kusamomiji* (Tokyo, 1954), pp. 121–122. Hida may have been about twenty years Miyoji's junior. Masumi, *Nihon seitō shi ron*, 2:392.
[79] Maeda, *Seihen monogatari*, pp. 324–343, and "Kempō no bannin," p. 200; Baba, "Itō Miyoji ron," p. 203.

It has been said that Itō really did not heed Miyoji's advice and was listening to those Miyoji considered his enemies on the formation of the Seiyūkai in the summer of 1900.[80] Around this time, too, Miyoji became closer to Yamagata. This must have caused Itō some unhappiness because he brought this point up with Yamagata and this "caused an argument."[81] It is possible that Itō was expressing an *amae* type of emotional dependency with respect to Miyoji. Doi says that this type of relationship is uncommon and that the superior "guards against revealing it to himself and to others." It is also possible that there was a homosexual overtone in the relationship between the two, for, as Doi believes, "homosexual attachment is very similar to *amae*."[82] Wagatsuma also believes that the relationship between the mentor and his follower in Japan is often eroticized. He admits, however, that the problem is one of verification.[83] In any case, Miyoji had to admit to Itō that Yamagata never treated him as a *monkasei* (protégé) but only as a "visiting general." Finally, Itō, in his anger with Miyoji for not joining the Seiyūkai, had taken a bottle of *sake* to Miyoji to formalize a break in their relationship.[84]

The progressive coolness between Itō and Miyoji prevented Miyoji from manipulating Itō by *amae*.[85] Miyoji's attitudes and

---

[80] *Taiyō*, no. 13:27. (Nov. 1900). See also Uzaki, "Hyōmen ni noridashita," p. 43; Maeda, "Kempō no bannin," p. 200; Toshimitsu Tsurumatsu, *Toshimitsu Tsurumatsu ō shuki* (Tokyo, 1957), pp. 313–315, 426. Hara recorded that he took pains to discuss Seiyūkai organizational plans with Miyoji to avoid Miyoji's jealousy over their relationship with Itō. *Hara nikki*, 2:287 (July 30, 1900). See also *ibid.*, 2, sequel: 78 (May 21, 1903).

[81] *Suiusō nikki*, 2:460–461 (July 7, 1901).

[82] Doi, "Giri-Ninjō," p. 328. Conversation, Tokyo (Aug. 8, 1968). Doi also believes that a person may *amaeru* without being conscious of doing so.

[83] Personal correspondence, Feb. 9, 1969. Both Itō and Miyoji were aggressively heterosexual. Miyoji fathered his last child, a son, in 1907 when he was forty-nine. Kurihara, *HIM*, 2:223. In 1917, it was written of him that he had slowed down because of his age, but that he was still "quite active." Uzaki, "Hyōmen ni noridashita," p. 44. See also Ishikawa, "Batsuzoku no ōbantō," p. 48. On Itō, see Nakamura, *Itō Hirobumi*, p. 42.

[84] *Suiusō nikki*, 2:462 (July 7, 1901); Tokutomi, *Waga kōyū roku*, p. 144; Iwata Chūzō, "Itō kō to watakushi" (Tokyo, 1959), p. 14. Miyoji came back and was "forgiven."

[85] One source states that the relation between the two became strained in 1895 immediately after the Sino-Japanese war. Baba, "Itō Miyoji ron," 207. His

behavior at this time can be explained in terms of *kodawaru,* *suneru,* and *hinekureru*—the reactions of a person frustrated in his attempt to *amaeru.* His refusal to join the Seiyūkai and the fourth Itō cabinet are examples of *suneru.* His declarations of independence from Itō, especially when Itō suggested that he join the Privy Council and Katsura's first cabinet, are expressions of *hinekureru.*[86] Sometimes *hinekureru* preceded *kodawaru.* On one occasion, Itō telephoned Miyoji asking him to drop by. Miyoji wrote in his diary that he had a headache and did not wish to be disturbed by a "commonplace matter" (a cabinet-rank appointment), so he asked Itō to postpone the meeting to the next day. The following day, hidden among the dozens of lines of his diary entry was the plaintive remark, "There was no call from Itō."[87]

At times the emotions ran the gamut from *kodawaru* to *suneru* to *hinekureru.* Miyoji was concerned that Itō would "misinterpret" press accounts of his views and activities so he called on Itō to clarify matters. Later, he heard that Itō had scoffed at him for doing what he did. Miyoji angrily wrote in his diary, "Those who secretly disdain the scrupulousness of others will become also someday the object of great disdain. I record this now for the future to judge." In the same entry and within a few lines of the other, Miyoji consciously or unconsciously "demoted" Itō by talking down to him. Miyoji did this in one instance by using Itō's name without the courtesy of an honorific. He usually referred to Itō at this time as Marquis Itō (Itō kō). Here he merely stated, "I had directly advised Itō. . . ." In this way he denied his wish to *amaeru,* for as we have seen, *amae* is not usually expressed by a superior to a subordinate. In the second instance, he demeaned Itō by being overly courteous and referred to him as "honorable" Itō.[88]

---

biographers, speaking of a somewhat later period, admit to the "doubts" Itō entertained about Miyoji. Kurihara, *HIM,* 1:394–395.

[86] In both instances, he told his listeners that he would decide the matter on his own and he did not have to pay deference to Itō. Maeda, *Seihen monogatari,* pp. 471–473; *Suiusō nikki,* 1:218 (April 27, 1901).

[87] *Suiusō nikki,* 1:133–135 (April 10, 11, 1901).

[88] *Ibid.,* 1:202–203 (April 24, 1901). Ozaki Yukio recalled an incident in

Throughout this period, however, there is evidence that Miyoji never gave up his desire to *amae*, and he often expressed concern that Itō misunderstood him. Once when Itō was having problems with the House of Peers, a member of that body called on Miyoji. Miyoji was afraid that Itō would get a "false report" from "police spies," so he asked Okuda Gijin to inform Itō in the "greatest secrecy" of what "really happened."[89]

There is a fourfold significance in Miyoji's *amae* relationship with Itō. First, Miyoji's overwhelming need for *amae* and the frustration of this need by Itō made him react with sulking and with anger. In short, frustration of the need for *amae* triggered childish patterns of reaction. This in turn led to Miyoji's decision to eschew party politics and to remain a *kuromaku*. Miyoji believed that Itō desperately needed his help to make the Seiyūkai a success. By sulking and remaining aloof from the Seiyūkai, Miyoji was "hurting" Itō. Second, this decision, as we shall see, doomed him to be a political failure given the political trends of the times. Third, Miyoji's inability to rise above his childish reactions doubly assured his failure because these reactions made him unacceptable politically. Fourth, Miyoji was so habituated to taking a subordinate role that he could not be comfortable in any other. He was in an *amae* relationship with the three other men he called his *onjin* or benefactors. He probably came in contact with the first, Stout, when he was only twelve. It is easy to see why he could not break out of the mold. Miyake, describing Miyoji's dependency on Itō, remarked, "Habit is a frightening thing." Might it be possible also to suggest that Miyoji's masculine identity was so shaky that this factor reinforced his dependency on Itō? In any case, Toyabe's description of Miyoji as a "eunuchlike petty man" is intriguing.[90]

---

which Yamagata in a conversation with him ridiculed the deceased Itō by using highly honorific language toward him. *Minken tōsō shichijūnen* (Tokyo, 1952), p. 34. *Hinekure* was evident when Miyoji patronized Itō by saying that "Itō's bewilderment is truly pitiable," or "Itō's loss of popularity is truly regrettable," or, again, when he recorded that Itō was "indecisive" or "did not have the courage to carry out my suggestions." *Ibid.*, 1:41–43, 80, 166–167 (March 3, 13; April 20, 1901).

[89] *Ibid.*, 1:77 (March 13, 1901). See also *ibid.*, 1:184–187 (April 23, 1901).
[90] Miyake, *Yononaka*, p. 54. Toyabe, *Meiji jimbutsu hyōron*, p. 193.

The Other Itō: A Political Failure

The most influential years politically for Miyoji were between 1898 and 1912, according to Watanabe Ikujirō.[91] This statement is only partially valid. His connection with Itō and the Tosa faction of the Seiyūkai still made him useful. Katsura, one of the most promising nongenro politicians, respected him. But when he refused to enter the first Katsura cabinet, the two became estranged.[92] This break occurred sometime in May 1901. This marked the point when Miyoji was cut off from any possibility of ever holding public office. He still had a limited usefulness in serving as mediator between the Katsura government and the Seiyūkai.[93] However, within a few years, it became clear to Hara that Miyoji "recently has not been close to the government." By 1911, when Hara heard that Miyoji was "trying" to become a cabinet member, Hara dismissed that attempt as a "laughable matter."[94]

Hara, one of the most astute politicians of his day, was correct in judging Miyoji's trial balloon as "laughable." He saw that Miyoji was isolated politically. The roster of those whom Miyoji alienated reads like a who's who of modern politics in Japan.[95]

[91] "Itō Miyoji hakushaku ni tsuite," speech delivered Sept. 20, 1943, at the Peer's Club, Tokyo, p. 3.

[92] Tokutomi believed that Miyoji's refusal made Katsura feel that "people cannot be trusted," and that he never forgave Miyoji. Waga kōyū roku, pp. 145–146. See also Maeda, Seihen monogatari, pp. 543–545. Miyoji once complained in a letter to a friend that Katsura did not have the courtesy to pay his respects when Katsura came to Tokyo from his country home in Hayama. He also was peeved because Katsura did not accept his views. Undated, but probably sometime after March 10, 1902, quoted in Kurihara, HIM, 1:368–369. Hara also noted a coolness between the two. Hara nikki, 2, sequel: 11 (Oct. 21, 1902).

[93] Hara nikki, 2, sequel: 75–78 (May 15, 18, 19, 21, 1903). But Hara earlier said that the Seiyūkai was working through Count Inoue and was ignoring Miyoji. Ibid., 2:473 (Dec. 23, 1901).

[94] Ibid., 2, sequel: 191 (Oct. 9, 1904), 4:325 (Aug. 25, 1911). Saionji a bit earlier said that Miyoji had not done anything "worthy of notice," and yet strived to put himself up for promotion. Ibid., 4:231 (April 10, 1911).

[95] We have seen what Inoue, Matsukata, and Katsura thought of Miyoji. Yamagata became highly antipathetic toward Miyoji after their initial closeness around 1898–1900. He called Miyoji a "schemer who could not be trusted," and a "pettifogging lawyer." Hara nikki, 6:257 (May 18, 1915), 7:464 (July 31, 1918). See also ibid., 7:146, 201, 461 (April 4, July 18, 1917; July 27, 1918).

He was simply incapable of sustaining a meaningful relationship with his superiors, peers, and subordinates. He was supposed to be working closely with Hara on Seiyūkai affairs, but he spoke ill of Hara. He was contemptuous of Hayashi. Terauchi and Motono were dependent on him, but he could not refrain from criticizing them both. Katō became friendly with him, but Miyoji could not keep a civil tongue in his head.[96] Hara noted in March 1918 that Inukai and Miyoji were becoming friendly. A short time later Hara recorded a report that the relationship between Miyoji and Inukai "was not as of old" and that Inukai had recently "come to understand Miyoji's character."[97] Hara was correct when he sensed that Miyoji was able to draw close to a person quickly but could become estranged as quickly. He judged this to be a "peculiar kind of relationship."[98] Because of his attacks on others as well as his avariciousness, Miyoji was accused of lacking virtue and of being untrustworthy.[99]

Miyoji did have some supporters. Den Kenjirō, Okuda Gijin, and Gotō Shimpei were all said to have been Miyoji's *kobun.* But they drifted away, turned against him, or were shabbily treated.[100] Even when people were linked with Miyoji, observers

---

Even Itō felt that Miyoji was not "candid and open" in his relationship with him. *Suiusō nikki,* 2:384–385 (June 21, 1901). As his diary entries show, Hara really did not care for Miyoji. Terauchi felt that Miyoji had "betrayed" him. *Hara nikki,* 7:488, 493 (Sept. 4, 1918). Miyoji hated Ōkuma. Uzaki, "Hyōmen ni noridashita," p. 43. He clashed with Mutsu and Inoue Kowashi. Tokutomi, *Waga kōyū roku,* pp. 56–57, 251. Miyoji did not like Hoshi Tōru. Hirano Mineo, *Okazaki Kunisuke den* (Tokyo, 1938), p. 249. Suematsu Kenchō and all members of the Privy Council, with the exception of Kaneko Kentarō, did not "get along with him." *Hara nikki,* 7:461 (July 27, 1918).

[96] *Hara nikki,* 2:287, 323, (July 30, 1900, Feb. 22, 1901); *Suiusō nikki,* 1:167, 172–174, 197–198 (April 20, 21, 24, 1901); 7:372 (April 12, 1918); *ibid.,* 7:84 (Dec. 7, 1916).

[97] *Hara nikki,* 7:362, 373 (March 30; April 12, 1918). The two were drawn together in part by their common interests in calligraphy, swords, and paintings. Kurihara, *HIM,* 1:497–498.

[98] *Ibid.,* 7:362 (March 30, 1918). Much earlier, a puzzled Hara wrote, "It is difficult to understand [Miyoji's] motives." *Ibid.,* 2:323 (Feb. 22, 1901).

[99] Toyabe, *Meiji jimbutsu shokan,* pp. 175–176; Miyake, "Itō Miyoji ron," Ishikawa, "Batsuzoku no ōbantō," pp. 48, 50; Hara, 7:70 (Nov. 16, 1916) and 6:257 (May 18, 1915).

[100] Hara said that Miyoji always "spoke of" Den and Gotō as if they were his *kobun. Hara nikki,* 7:136 (March 2, 1917). See also *ibid.,* 2:422 (Sept. 14, 1901); Maeda, *Seihen monogatari,* pp. 490–491; Ishikawa, "Batsuzoku no ōban-

were prone to see the relationship as out of the ordinary. Hayashi Yūzō, for example, was said to be "mindlessly" supporting Miyoji.[101]

Miyoji was plainly an insecure man. We already have discussed one possible cause of his insecurity: a swift and abrupt drop in the standard of living of the Miyoji family in Nagasaki. Another cause may be related to his commoner background. His critics never let him forget his humble beginnings. One unkind journalist suggested that the Miyoji family was actually nationalized Chinese who served as interpreters and commercial agents in Nagasaki.[102] The critics also described the "rough," "unpolished," and "abrasive" aspect of his character; noted his unsystematic education and knowledge (while admitting his intelligence); and declared that he was not a true *bunjin* (man of letters). In a word, Miyoji was an uncouth bully boy.[103] The choice of the word *eunuch* to describe him was also not a capricious one.[104]

It was to live down this reputation that he dressed as a dandy and sought comfort in the refined hobbies of *bonsai* and the collecting of swords, paintings, and *objets d'art*. Still, his gnawing sense of insecurity constantly got the better of him and he struck out repeatedly. "In essence," wrote Hara, "when things do not

---

tō," p. 51; Kurihara, *HIM*, 2:165–166. In the period that Miyoji's biography describes the relationship between Miyoji and Gotō as being "friendly," Gotō tells Hara that Miyoji is not qualified to be prime minister. *Hara nikki*, 7:487 (Sept. 1, 1918). It was Hara who in the end secured the "cordial friendship if not the personal allegiance" of Den. Duus, *Party Rivalry*, p. 136. Motono Ichirō "worshipped" Miyoji and this seemed strange to Hara, for Miyoji was criticizing Motono. *Hara nikki*, 7:368, 372 (April 6, 12, 1918). Okuda Gijin was dismissed from a government post and Miyoji, who was supposed to be his *oyabun* (mentor), did not know about it. This too must have seemed unusual to Hara, for he made note of it. *Hara nikki*, 2, sequel: 11 (Oct. 21, 1902). Earlier, Miyoji expressed anger when Itō "stooped to working with a person [of the caliber] of Okuda. . . ." *Suiusō nikki*, 1:172 (April 21, 1901).

[101] *Taiyō*, 8, no. 4:34–35 (April 1902). Okazaki Kunisuke said that he enjoyed Miyoji's company, but he is talking about Miyoji in the context of his hobbies. "Itō shishaku no dōraku," p. 45.

[102] Uzaki, "Hyōmen ni noridashita," p. 41.

[103] Itō Chiyū, quoted in Kurihara, *HIM*, 1:548; Toyabe, *Meiji jimbutsu hyōron*, pp. 195–196, 203–204.

[104] See, for example, Toyabe Shuntei, "Itō Miyoji: Zokuri ka kangan ka," *Shuntei zenshū* (Tokyo, 1909), 1:352–355. Toyabe's father was a samurai.

go well for him, he criticizes others."[105] For Miyoji, things often did not go well.

The decision to avoid public office was made in 1898, and it was a considered, careful decision—whatever the unconscious motives may have been. Yet there are references to Miyoji's design for public office in the 1910's just as there were rumors in 1898 that he wanted to become president of the Jiyūtō. The very few instances in which Miyoji is directly connected with the references may be explained as trial balloons sent up by an incredibly insecure person trying to determine whether he was still politically acceptable. In most cases, however, his movements may be said to have been interpreted by his enemies as manifestations of Miyoji's ambitions. The immediate reaction then was to "head Miyoji off." This is the dimension of his political isolation and ineffectiveness.[106]

What Miyoji actually sought in this decade was status. He was still aspiring to play genrō. The Rinji Gaikō Chōsa Iinkai (Advisory Council on Foreign Relations) enabled him to satisfy this aspiration. The council was established on June 5, 1917. Its functions at that time were not spelled out. Hara wanted the council to be a "wholly informal" research and deliberative body which would lay down broad guidelines on matters relating to foreign affairs. An imperial ordinance would have sufficed to create an informal organ of this nature. Miyoji drafted the imperial rescript establishing the council.[107] In the rescript he

---

[105] *Hara nikki*, 7:368 (April 6, 1918).

[106] Ibid., 5:246 (June 6, 1913) and 7:201–202, 382, 458, 493, 496, (July 19, 1917; April 18, July 26, Sept. 4, 11, 1918); Miyake, "Itō Miyoji ron," p. 39; Uzaki, "Hyōmen ni noridashita," p. 41. An example of a completely isolated and therefore wholly ineffective person is Shimada Seijirō (1899–1930), author of the novel *Chijō*. He had a poverty-stricken childhood but was praised by all his associates as a child prodigy. He grew up to be a self-willed, egocentric adult who was hated even by his mother. He died in an asylum. Sugimori Hisahide's *Tensai to kyōjin no aida* (Tokyo, 1962) is a novel based on Shimada's life. It won the *Naoki* prize for 1962.

[107] For a discussion of its establishment and organization, see James W. Morley, *The Japanese Thrust into Siberia, 1918* (New York, 1957), pp. 23–27; also Kobayashi, *Suiusō nikki*, pp. 8–9, 206–252; *Hara nikki*, 7:187, 208 (June 16, July 23, 1917). An observer of the events noted that "students of the constitution had a hot controversy over the constitutionality of this Imperial Edict." Uichi Iwasaki, *The Working Forces in Japanese Politics* (New York, 1921), p. 34.

used the term *keiyoku* and proudly pointed out this fact to Yamagata, saying that this meant that the members of the council were therefore "on the same level as the genrō." Yamagata replied that such a use was "proper." Miyoji reacted with pleasure to this remark.[108]

Miyoji also had the members appointed as "ministers of state" and, on the day of their appointment, arranged to have the council dine with the emperor. Hara felt that the "ostentatiousness" of all this stemmed from Miyoji's "ambitions." Miyoji also sought to enlarge the council's functions to include deliberations on domestic affairs. He wanted the council to deal in details rather than in broad questions. He succeeded in changing the nature of its organization from that of an informal to a formal body.[109]

Immediately rumors spread that he desired to use membership in the council to become prime minister or ambassador plenipotentiary to the Paris peace talks.[110] Hara, however, perceptively noted that Miyoji's activities were indications of his ambitions to be promoted to count. An informal organ dealing in broad questions would not permit a member to achieve merit as would a formal body dealing in the details of all problems of the government, domestic and foreign. As Hara observed, "Miyoji is hastily seeking to achieve meritorious deeds."[111]

Miyoji's preference for status and security is also evident in his desire to be imperial household minister. Najita has noted correctly that the politicians of this decade believed that "a

[108] The term *keiyoku* comes from the *Shu ching*: "Open your mind and enrich my mind." James Legge, *The Chinese Classics* (Oxford, 1893–1895), 3:252; *Hara nikki*, 7:187 (June 16, 1917); Kobayashi, *Suiusō nikki*, p. 209. Yamagata, however, later "sneered" at the use of the word as a cheap way by which Miyoji sought to "better himself." *Hara nikki*, 7:200–201 (July 18, 1917).

[109] *Hara nikki*, 7:186–188, 207, 208, 232, 234, 376 (June 16, July 23, Sept. 11, 13, 1917; April 15, 1918).

[110] One critic wrote that from the fact that he is a member, "one can deduce that he has a scheme." Uzaki, "Hyōmen ni noridashita," pp. 44–45; Miyake, "Itō Miyoji ron," p. 39; *Hara nikki*, 7:201–202, 382 (July 19, 1917; April 18, 1918). Hara believed also that Miyoji wanted to use Inukai and him as a "stepping-stone to something." *Hara nikki*, 7:23 (Aug. 7, 1917).

[111] *Hara nikki*, 7:200–202, 205 (July 18, 1917); see also 7:187 (July 16, 1917). A decade earlier, Hara had recorded his disapproval of Miyoji's unseemly conduct in seeking a promotion in rank. *Ibid.*, 3:100 (Sept. 24, 1907).

clear separation existed between the spiritual realm of the Imperial Household and the mundane one of actual politics." It was a post which was "highly prized by aristocrats" and one to which Katsura was retired "under duress" in August 1912.[112]

Hara wrote in 1916 that Miyoji had wanted this position "for years."[113] When the Rinji Gaikō Chōsa Iinkai was most active, Hara told Yamagata that Miyoji had his eye on the post. Yamagata indicated that Miyoji would never get the job. This was also Yamagata's view in 1916. Miyoji never was appointed minister of the imperial household, but he became a count in September 1922, in "recognition of his services" on the council. He may even be said to have achieved a status "equal" to that of genro, for the council has been described as the "only political body in Japan which can effectively rival the genro in power."[114]

Miyoji, however, had been chasing a will-o'-the-wisp. The whole thrust of political development in Japan since the late Meiji had been toward the concentration of power in the parties.[115] Minobe Tatsukichi best summed up the reason for the

[112] Najita, *Hara Kei*, pp. 156–157, 93–94; also, p. 95.

[113] *Hara nikki*, 7:71 (Nov. 20, 1916). In 1913, he noted that Miyoji originally wanted to enter the cabinet but "it is now believed that he wants to become imperial household minister." *Hara nikki*, 5:246 (June 6, 1913).

[114] *Hara nikki*, 7:362 (March 30, 1918); see also 7:94 (Dec. 27, 1916); Kurihara, *HIM*, 1:455; Iwasaki, *The Working Forces*, p. 33. After Miyoji died, he was given the rank of *ju ichi i* (junior grade of the first court rank). All the genro received this rank. Ōkubo and Kido Takayoshi were promoted in May 1901, long after their deaths. Hara, Takahashi, Katō, Katō Tomosaburō, Tanaka Giichi, Hamaguchi Yūkō, Inukai, all of whom became prime minister, were given the lower rank, *shō ni i* (senior grade of the second court rank). Miyoji was eligible to be promoted. Promotions usually were made after death. Communication from the secretariat of the director of the Imperial Household Agency, January 31, 1969. So even as he lay dying on February 19, 1934, of bleeding ulcers, Miyoji must have had some satisfaction that in this one aspect he had equaled the genro.

[115] Najita, *Hara Kei*, pp. 185, 204; Duus, *Party Rivalry*, pp. 4, 235. Even the most pessimistic of the prewar interpreters, Bisson, believed that the "bureaucrats' decline . . . was an obvious fact by 1926. . . ." T. A. Bisson, "Democracy in Japan," Foreign Policy Association, *Information Service*, 6, no. 8:154, 155, 166 (June 25, 1930). Parties not only became more powerful relative to other organs in the government, but nonparliamentary elements grew progressively weaker in the Seiyūkai central party apparatus. Haruhiro Fukui, "The Japanese Liberal-Democratic Party and Policy Making," (Ph.D. dissertation, Australian National University, 1967), p. 27.

growing strength of the parties and the concomitant deterioration of the genro institution:

> The parliamentary system is a system of majority rule. Majority rule means that only numbers mean anything. Controlling numbers means that the power of an isolated individual . . . is extremely weak, and it is impossible for him to carry out his political views.[116]

The growing ineffectiveness of the genrō institution can be gauged by the increasing isolation, bewilderment, and cantankerousness of Yamagata. He saw his closest followers leave him one by one. Prime ministers no longer paid him the courtesy of consultation.[117] He was unaware of important political developments in Tokyo.[118]

In spite of this development, Miyoji, to satisfy status and security needs, continued to play the genrō. The vehicle through which he enacted this role was the Privy Council. To Watanabe, the twenty-three years from 1912 to 1934 were the years in which Miyoji exhibited the style "most peculiar to him." This he did by serving in the Privy Council as *kempō no bannin*, the watchdog of the constitution.[119] This role was essentially a negative one.

---

[116] Minobe Tatsukichi, *Gikai seiji no kentō* (Tokyo, 1934), p. 64.

[117] Katsura, Terauchi, Hirata Tōsuke, Kiyoura Keigo, "and others in the Yamagata faction" fell out with Yamagata. Katō, too, did not seek his advice. *Hara nikki*, 5:156, 159 (Dec. 13, 18, 1912); 6:106 (Aug. 14, 1914); 7:16, 35-42 (Sept. 29, Oct. 10, 11, 12, 1916). This is the mark of Hara's political sagacity. He keenly followed (and carefully and happily recorded) Yamagata's growing isolation and filled the vacuum by acting like a Yamagata follower. Yet he was able to retain his independence because he had never been a Yamagata *kobun* and Yamagata was a very lonely man.

[118] Yamagata did not know, for example, of the changes in the Rinji Gaikō Chōsa Iinkai engineered by Miyoji. *Hara nikki*, 7:376 (April 15, 1918). This does not mean that the genrō lost all influence. See Roger F. Hackett, "Political Modernization and the Meiji Genro," in Robert E. Ward, ed., *Political Development in Modern Japan* (Princeton, N. J., 1968), pp. 89-94. Cf. Bernard S. Silberman, who writes that bureaucratic development in Japan had by 1900 made it "no longer necessary to seek judgments by 'wise and knowing' men." "Bureaucratic Development and the Structure of Decision Making in the Meiji Period," *Journal of Asian Studies*, 27:93 (Nov. 1967).

[119] Watanabe, "Itō Miyoji hakushaku," p. 3. Miyoji was a member of the Privy Council for over thirty years (1899-1934). The deliberations were secret. The Tokyo newspapers, however, were able to report immediately and accurately

As Baba has pointed out, Miyoji's power was seen as a threat rather than as a "force for the orderly progress of the government."[120] Miyoji himself saw his role in negative terms. He likened himself to an old nail cast on the roadside. He told a listener that people should not hold him in disdain because of old age, for he could still inflict great damage and even "death" to anyone who stepped on him.[121] Typically, defiance could not prevent self-pity from bubbling over. Miyoji expressed "affection" for Prime Minister Tanaka Giichi (April 1927–July 1929), but at the same time was "sad" because Tanaka did not listen to his views on the China question (1927–1928).[122] Hardly anyone had been listening to him for thirty years.

CONCLUSIONS

The complex and unique factors that made Miyoji a political failure should give pause to anyone attempting to generalize about political motivations of whole groups. The perils are compounded when the historical dimension is added. A restatement into four general categories of the reasons for Miyoji's failure should serve to underscore the singularity of his case.

Miyoji was a commoner and he was not from Satsuma or Chōshū, although having a nonsamurai father and not coming from Satsuma or Chōshū were not serious handicaps in Meiji

on its proceedings. See Minobe, *Gikai seiji no kentō*, pp. 116–117; Harold S. Quigley, *Japanese Government and Politics: An Introductory Study* (New York, 1932), p. 93.

[120] Baba, "Itō Miyoji ron," p. 203. For a discussion of his roles on the question of the ratification of the Sino-Japanese postal exchange convention (February 1922) and the Taiwan Bank crisis (April 1927), see Kurihara, *HIM*, 1:515–532, 473, 476–478. See also Quigley, *Japanese Government and Politics*, pp. 112–113; Kenneth Colgrove, "The Japanese Privy Council," *American Political Science Review*, 25:883–888 (Nov. 1931); Minobe, *Gikai seiji no kentō*, pp. 227–229.

[121] Kurihara, *HIM*, 1:3 In 1927, Miyoji, age seventy, insulted Shidehara Kijūrō, age fifty-five, in an argument brought about by the Taiwan Bank crisis, although the argument itself had no connection with the crisis. Shidehara came close to physically attacking Miyoji. Shidehara Kijūrō, *Gaikō gojūnen* (Tokyo, 1951), p. 259.

[122] Kurihara, *HIM*, 1:479. More than a decade earlier, Miyoji was running to Matsukata, Yamagata, and Inoue, boosting Hara for the prime ministership. Hara's laconic comment was "I do not know how effective he is." *Hara nikki*, 6:65 (June 17, 1914).

Japan. Itō's father was a peasant. Miyoji himself became a privy councillor and a count. But one of the factors contributing to Miyoji's failure was that his behavior brought to the surface latent prejudices held against commoners by those of samurai background.[123] Miyoji's actions and attitude with respect to money; his inability to draw a line between what properly belonged to the public sector and what, if done in privacy, could be overlooked; his lack of self-discipline as manifested by his outbursts of temper—all doomed him to political isolation. After Itō's death in 1909, and perhaps even before, the weightiest single voice in Japanese government and politics was that of Yamagata, who prided himself on being a samurai's samurai. Miyoji greatly irritated Yamagata—a Yamagata who knew how to spend money "properly," who never committed the error of *kōshi kondō* (confusing private with public matters), and who exercised enormous self-discipline.[124] The fact that Miyoji never became minister of the imperial household is proof that Yamagata's reactions counted heavily while he lived. In essence, Miyoji was already a failure in the 1910's. He never achieved the primary goal he had set for himself: a position of high status coveted by aristocrats.

Another factor leading to Miyoji's political ineffectiveness was his unwillingness to accumulate what Eidheim has called "expertise" or political capital.[125] Political capital is accumulated by "spending," by dispensing the positions, money, and "favors" about which Hara talked. Miyoji was energetic enough behind the scenes but was incapable of the kind of spending necessary to be politically effective. To be sure, Miyoji was not unwilling to spend for other purposes. He once paid 300 yen to purchase

[123] Shibusawa Eiichi came from an affluent, educated, and cultured peasant family. Yet Shibusawa once was told by a samurai official that even educated peasants were "no better than vermin." William J. Chambliss, *Chiaraijima Village: Land Tenure, Taxation, and Local Trade, 1818–1884* (Tucson, Ariz., 1965), p. 116.

[124] Yamagata was known to have had a "terrible temper," but he "exercised extraordinary will-power and self-control to maintain his composure." Tokutomi Iichirō (Sohō), *Jimbutsu guroku* (Tokyo, 1928), p. 49.

[125] Harold Eidheim, "Entrepreneurship in Politics," in Frederik Barth, ed., *The Role of the Entrepreneur in Social Change in Northern Norway* (Bergen, 1963), pp. 80–81.

an ego-palliative letter sent by Yamagata to Inoue listing him as one of four possible candidates for the prime minister's post. Typically, Miyoji could not handle this kind of suggestion with finesse, for we see Yamagata angrily telling Hara that Miyoji had no talent but was showing the letter to others as if he were qualified to be prime minister.[126]

A third factor militated against Miyoji's success in politics. Miyoji was politically blind as well as a captive of political ideals a generation removed. Miyoji was always proud of his political acumen and his "insider's" knowledge of political developments. He liked to send long letters to Itō reporting political intelligence. He used to bore Hara with his long-winded political analyses.[127] Miyoji once showed Yamagata the contents of his diary and then recorded that Yamagata was "amazed" at the accuracy of his political insights.[128] However, Tokutomi says that he was shown in 1898 a report from Miyoji to Itō. He found that not only were Miyoji's interpretations wide of the mark but that he even had his facts wrong.[129] Hara also felt that Miyoji was unaware of what was "really" going on in the political world and that his views were "generally beneath notice."[130] He also hinted to Yamagata that Miyoji was out of touch with the times. Even before this conversation with Yamagata, he wrote that Miyoji was moved only by ideas in vogue twenty years before.[131]

[126] *Hara nikki*, 6:386 (March 6, 1916), 7:496 (Sept. 11, 1918). On another occasion, Miyoji meticulously recorded that he had spent 175.50 yen on his *bonsai* hobby. *Suiusō nikki*, 1:94 (March 21, 1901). At this time, it was estimated that 100 yen a month would enable a man to support a wife, two children, and three hired hands. Ishiguro Tadanori, in *Taiyō*, 7, no. 1:74–75 (1901).

[127] See, for example, letter dated October 28 in *Itō ke monjo*, (unpublished, National Diet Library), 26:166–170; *Hara nikki*, 7:459, 477 (July 27, Aug. 19, 1918).

[128] *Suiusō nikki*, 1:84 (March 14, 1901).

[129] The politician Noda Taikai was also present and he agreed. *Waga kōyū roku*, p. 11.

[130] *Hara nikki*, 7:460 (July 27, 1918), 132 (Feb. 23, 1917). Miyoji also seemed oblivious to the antipathy he aroused in others. *Ibid.*, 7:202, 246 (July 19, Oct. 3, 1917).

[131] *Ibid.*, 7:362 (March 30, 1918), 188 (June 16, 1917). Miyoji must have been delighted when he was described over a decade later as "a mysterious *kuromaku* (behind the black curtain) politician, a type *rare* nowadays." *Asahi seiji keizai sōsho: Sūmitsuin mondai*, quoted in Kurihara, *HIM*, 1:547 (italics, mine).

This was the time when Miyoji was deputy genrō as Itō's shadow. Little wonder, then, that Miyoji failed to see that the institution of genrō was not the viable one he had known, and he vainly sought this position for many years.

Moreover, he even failed to become a genrō in terms of style. If, as political scientists believe, followers and leaders "mentally identify with each other" to the point that followers "embody the values and ideal lifestyle" of the leaders, Miyoji and Itō must be excepted from this generalization.[132] In October 1909, before Itō left for Manchuria, where he met death at the hands of an assassin, he visited Miyoji at his home. There he picked up a brush and composed a poem for Miyoji. Freely rendered, it read,

> As I gaze upon the blue haze and the white dew,
> I sense a feeling of vastness.
> I have traveled a thousand miles,
> And everywhere the grass is alike fragrant.
> The whole world before me is fit to take my bones,
> For the hero, there is no native place.[133]

Surely, there was a world of difference between the Itō who composed the poem and a Miyoji who deliberately chose to stay within the safe and narrow confines of the Privy Council.

A fourth factor must be mentioned to explain Miyoji's political isolation. Katō Takaaki shared with Miyoji certain personal characteristics. Katō, like Miyoji, has been described as tenacious, blunt, precise, and supercilious.[134] Katō, however, became a party leader and prime minister. He achieved these positions because he made a deliberate choice to enter public office. Miyoji, even had he made a similar choice or had the scepter thrust into his hands, might not have succeeded. His personality flaws were greater, and these flaws were the more conspicuous and unforgivable because of his commoner background. Furthermore, in Miyoji's case, a feedback process was involved, a

---

[132] James C. Davies, "The Psychobiology of Political Behavior: Some Provocative Developments," Paper delivered at the Twenty-Third Annual Meeting of the Western Political Science Association (April 3–5, 1969), p. 4.

[133] Kurihara, *HIM*, 1:390–391.

[134] Duus, *Party Rivalry*, pp. 66–67.

process which explains in part Yamagata's relationship with him. Yamagata had recognized and used Miyoji's talents shortly before 1900. But when Miyoji's personality flaws made him ineffective politically, he became useless to Yamagata. This then sharpened the outlines of his defects, which further alienated Yamagata, rendering Miyoji even more ineffective.

Miyoji's failure to become minister of the imperial household must have embittered him. His actions in the Privy Council reflect, in part, this bitterness. But this failure is only one aspect of the kind of nearly total isolation he faced from around 1910 till his death in 1934. We see him striking out repeatedly against those he considered only too willing to "step on him." The imbalance of this man—in personality and behavior—was obvious to his contemporaries, so much so that in spite of his attempt to remain behind the "black curtain," one of them aptly characterized him as a "politician deformed like his *bonsai*."[135] In short, during what could have been years of retirement with honor, his sense of frustration and bitterness, his basic immaturity and narcissism, forced him into an unhappy and futile activism.

[135] Baba, "Itō Miyoji ron," p. 202.

372

KAYAHARA KAZAN AND
JAPANESE COSMOPOLITANISM

Akira Iriye

"We are Japanese; but we also must try to relate ourselves to the world. We must become cosmopolitan."[1] So wrote the journalist Kayahara Kazan (1870–1952) in 1911, at the midpoint in his life. "We Japanese," he said over three decades later, after the Pacific War, "must try to understand Japan. Besides Japan, we also must understand Asia. In addition, we must understand America and Europe."[2] All his life, he went on, he had been doing just that; he had been trying to know Japan better by learning more about the world. A man whose life spanned the years between the Meiji Restoration and the American occupation, Kayahara personified modern Japan's search for identity in a changing world, for a principle through which to relate one country to the whole of mankind, both geographically and historically. He tried to be both of Japan and of the world, and at the end of his life he at least had the satisfaction that his search had been sincere and meaningful, if not strikingly successful.

Kayahara was not an extraordinary man in terms of his intellect, experiences, or achievements. He had relatively few ideas, and he presented them more as preachments than as thoughtful analyses. But he was unusually self-conscious and articulate, and left voluminous records of his changing attitudes. He frequently traveled abroad and continued to ponder on the problem of Japan (and the Japanese) in the world. He asked many questions which modern Japanese intellectuals have never ceased to raise concerning the relationship between self, the

---

[1] Kayahara Kazan, *Kazan bunshō* (Tokyo, 1912), p. 180.
[2] Kayahara, *Nihon jinmin no tanjō* (Tokyo, 1946), p. 60.

small community, and the world. Most important, he was keenly interested in the behavior of Japanese abroad as he believed, rightly, that they became more self-conscious as they left their country and that without tracing the meaning of living abroad there could be no basis for comprehending the complexities of modern Japanese existence. For these reasons, Kayahara's life and thought lend themselves to a case study of cosmopolitanism, Japanese style, a central theme in modern Japanese history.

Kayahara Rentarō was born in Tokyo, son of a former lower samurai. His father died when he was young. As a child he stuttered, but overcame it, he says, through his own effort. In his teens he went to night school while studying English and Chinese classics on his own. During the day he worked as a clerk in the Dajōkan. Glimpses of the country's leaders discussing world affairs fascinated him, and he resolved one day to partake of world events. He loved to travel, and when he was about sixteen he traveled on foot along historical sites outside Tokyo and came on the area of Namamugi, where Englishmen had been murdered in 1862. This, he wrote later, made him long all the more for a trip abroad, but he had no money and had to bide his time. He sought to compensate for his lack of formal education by voluminous reading and for his inability to go abroad by turning to journalism.

During the 1890's, he was a young and earnest editor of Jiyūtō-connected newspapers in Yamagata and Akita, and his reformist and nationalistic writings, sprinkled with liberal references to Chinese classics and modern European writers, gained him increasing reputation. At the beginning of the new century, when he was editor of the *Jinmin shimbun* (*People's Daily*) in Nagano, he already was being compared to another renowned journalist, Tokutomi Sohō. Finally, in 1903, he was invited to join the editorial staff of the influential daily, *Yorozu chōhō*, and this gave him a long awaited opportunity to command a national audience. He wrote spirited articles during the Russo-Japanese War. It was very soon after the end of the war that he was sent by the paper to the United States and later to England. He was already in his mid-thirties, but he departed for America with all the youthful enthusiasm shared by his adventurous countrymen for whom the United States, as Katayama Sen exhorted them so often, was the place to go.[3]

"From the day I arrived in the United States till the day of my departure, I was simply overwhelmed by what I saw," Kayahara remarked of his life in America. "In every respect Japan and the United States were different."[4] He tried to understand these differences and relate them to a view of human civilization and history. Such attempts have been made by practically every Japanese visitor to a Western country. Kayahara did not have the literary gift of a Nagai Kafū or the scholarly discipline of an Asakawa Kan'ichi, his contemporaries who were at that time in the United States, and his observations did not benefit from the methods and concepts of modern sociology and psychology then being developed in the West. Rather, his chief mental equipment was a keen interest in different peoples, buttressed by massive but desultory reading among Western political writers and historical figures. But because he was an energetic reporter and left voluminous records of his observations both before and after his departure for America, his experiences and ideas provide the historian with fascinating raw material.

Before his departure for the United States in 1905, Kayahara had absorbed the clichés of the Meiji enlightenment and believed that "the new Japan is not so much an Asian as a Western nation." Asia represented reaction, conservatism, autocracy, and inequality, he wrote in 1895, whereas Europe stood for liberty, progress, individualism, and equality. Japan's task lay in using its left hand to receive the blessings of Western civilization and its right hand to distribute them among the Asian peoples suffering the oppression of their fossilized civilization. This simple image formed the basis of a book Kayahara wrote just before

---

[3] Kayahara's biographical details are gleaned from autobiographical passages in his books, particularly in their prefaces. See, in particular, *Tōhoku taisei-ron* (Yamagata, 1895); *Jinbutsu hyōron* (Shizuoka, 1901); *Dōchū seikan* (Tokyo, 1904). Some of the editorials Kayahara wrote for the *Yorozu chōhō* are included in his *Kōjō no ichiro* (Tokyo, 1904). Katayama Sen was a prolific writer best known for his articles and books describing how one could go to the United States. His *Tobei annai* (Tokyo, 1900) created a genre of "how to" pamphlets.

[4] Kayahara, *Kaigai bunshō* (Tokyo, 1912), preface.

leaving for his trip abroad. Traditionally, he said, civilization had moved eastward in Asia and westward in the West, in both instances culminating in the meeting place that was Japan. Before reaching Japan, Western civilization passed through America, and that was why they were the two most advanced countries in the world. "Japan and America are the most progressive countries in the world in the twentieth century," he wrote. The Japanese nation should keep its right hand extended across the Pacific in a firm grasp of friendship with America, while using its left to do for the rest of Asians what Perry had done for the Japanese.[5]

These were platitudes that Kayahara shared with most of his fellow journalists in Japan. There was another theme, however, which was at first barely audible but which he was to stress more and more loudly and persistently. This was the idea of peaceful economic expansion. It was by no means an original idea. The view that a nation's best interests were served in pursuit of economic goals through peaceful means, rather than in employing costly methods to satisfy irrational needs, derived spontaneously from the Japanese image of nineteenth-century Western progress. Meiji Japanese, in fact, were much less impressed with Western military power and colonialism than with the West's apparently absolute superiority in "peacetime warfare" and "peacetime competition." They were obsessed not so much by military confrontation as by commercial competition with the West. The only way to cope with the crisis, wrote numerous publicists whose voices Kayahara echoed, was for Japan to follow the West's example and try to expand economically. The world, he wrote in 1894, was "a battlefield for wars of intelligence and commerce." What the Japanese should do was to translate their expansive energy into action by going abroad and engaging in economic activities in the whole wide world. The twentieth century, he asserted ten years later, was "an age of national expansion and development." He exhorted his coun-

---

[5] Kayahara, *Tōhoku taisei-ron*, pp. 33, 35; Kayahara, *Sekai bunmei suii-shiron* (Tokyo, 1905), *passim;* Kayahara Rentarō and Fujiko, *Sayū shūchiku* (Tokyo, 1905), pp. 104, 131–132.

trymen, "Do not consider Japan your homeland. Take the entire world as your homeland." Where there was a will, there was an arena for energetic activity, and only by taking advantage of the opportunity would the Japanese people be able truly to measure up to the standards set by Westerners.[6]

This was the mental baggage with which he landed in Seattle in the fall of 1905. The rude shock of recognition was inevitable. Both his cultural monism, viewing his country as Westernized, and his peaceful expansionism, optimistically calling for his countrymen's emigration overseas, were brutally shaken during the first few weeks of his American sojourn. Not only was America as he actually saw it entirely different from what he had envisaged from books, but the facile idea of Japanese-American friendship and peaceful competition was mockingly laid bare by the anti-Japanese movement on the West Coast then reaching its climax. It is interesting to note that Nagai Kafū had just spent several months in the state of Washington and experienced a similar shock. "What a miserable life I led when I was on the West Coast of America," the novelist was to write. "All alone, I would just walk amid the pine trees that cover the new continent, feeling lonely and not knowing what else to do."[7]

The difference between Kafū and Kazan was that whereas the former sought solace in the fictitious world of nineteenth-century French literature in the search for a psychological point of contact between Japan and the West, the latter, without literary gift and imagination, resolved to reexamine his own intellectual past and trace the roots of the contrast between the West as he had been led to image it in Japan and as he actually encountered it. He persuaded himself that the views of the world that he had formed at home had been Western views accepted uncritically by the Japanese. No wonder the latter had fondly talked of the awakening and progress of Japan. No wonder that a Japanese

[6] Kayahara, "Kazanrō zatcho," appended to *Tōhoku taisei-ron*, pp. 32–33; Kayahara, *Dōchū seikan*, pp. 90–91. For a discussion of Meiji Japan's peaceful expansionism, see my "Heiwateki hattenshugi to Nihon," *Chūō kōron*, 84, no. 10:74–94 (Oct. 1969).

[7] Nagai Kafū, *Kafū zenshū*, Iwanami edition (Tokyo, 1964), 13:137–138.

visitor to the West should find himself bewildered. What was needed, Kayahara thought, was for the Japanese to make the study of the West their avocation and to do so through their own effort and observations, not through merely reading what Westerners had written about themselves. Only by doing so could they expect to have an understanding of the world. Only then would they be able to arrive at a balanced view of Japan, a view which was neither exclusively Western nor Japanese. Only thus would a true perspective emerge and would the Japanese be enabled to develop a cosmopolitan outlook and contribute to the understanding of world civilization.[8]

In trying to universalize the Japanese experience and overcome the parochialism of a Western-oriented outlook, Kazan was joining the scores of others who were at this time searching for a meaningful context of comparison between Japan and the West. The uniqueness of his views lay in his experiences among and observations of Japanese immigrants in the United States. Much of his thinking on East-West differences was derived from these observations. He was initially indignant over the failure of Americans to treat Japanese as their equals. Having believed these two peoples to be the most progressive in the world, it must have come as a rude shock to know that the Americans did not reciprocate the sentiment and that on the West Coast Japanese were living as outcasts. Why were the Americans, hitherto visualized as the epitome of civilization and progress, so imbued with prejudice? Should the Japanese submit to it, or should they resolutely resist it? Above all, how should one comprehend the historical significance of the anti-Japanese movement on the Pacific coast?

He developed some very explicit views on these questions and printed them on the pages of *Shinsekai* (*The New World*), a Japanese daily published in San Francisco (and Oakland, in the aftermath of the earthquake in 1906). Life on the West Coast for a time made him a racial determinist. Like so many Japanese visitors to the United States since then, he thought he found a clue to American history and society in its racial heterogeneity.

[8] Kayahara, *Kaigai bunshō*, preface.

The United States, he wrote in November 1906, had been founded by the Teutonic race for whom "one does not hesitate to accord a little respect" in view of its tradition of individual liberty, diligent work habits, and fair play. In fact, the Teutons and the Japanese were the only two great races in the world! But America had been peopled by latecomers such as Greeks, "who have long degenerated"; Slavs, who had just been beaten by the Japanese; Latins, "who are totally corrupt and impotent"; Spaniards, "who are superstitious and lazy"; Irish, "who cannot even build their own nation"; and Italians, "who always fight among themselves." West Coast agitators against Japanese were not Teutons, Kayahara said, but Irish and Italian Americans who were like asses in lion's skin.[9] With West Coast Americans thus disposed of as an inferior breed, it was easy for him to take the next step and say they should not have been there to begin with. "The sphere of activity of the European races should be limited to the Ural mountains in the East and the Rockies in the West," he declared. There was no reason why the whites should move farther westward, especially when the Japanese were expanding eastward and trying to engulf Hawaii and the Pacific slope with their influence. If, nevertheless, the Westerners should decide to dominate the Pacific coast and oppose Japanese settlement, a conflict between the white and yellow races was inevitable. "The Japanese on the Pacific coast and in San Francisco are the spearhead in the struggle between the two races. They are shouldering the historical responsibility for deciding whether the future world is to be a silver- [white] based world or a gold- [yellow] based world."[10]

Far from reiterating his faith in peaceful expansion, Kayahara now called for the use of force for, as he wrote in English, "Struggle is the law of life." He exhorted Japanese immigrants in California to "compete manfully" with Americans, remembering that "behind you stand the navy of 500,000 tons and the army of one million." The racial clash was a matter of life and death for the Japanese nation, and only through war could

[9] *Shinsekai*, Nov. 16, 1906.
[10] *Ibid.*, Nov. 28, 30, 1906 .

a young country such as Japan seek to have its rights protected and honor safeguarded. Should war come with the United States, it would serve to awaken the Americans from their sense of self-complacency and superiority, make them better understand Japan, and prove that Japan was the strongest and most civilized country in the world.[11]

Such extreme language never again was spoken by Kazan. It revealed the depth of his shock at discovering the racial diversity of mankind, but this kind of chauvinistic outburst was not typical of him. With the settlement of the San Francisco School Board Incident early in 1907, the Japanese community, including Kayahara, regained their calm, and in May he left for London. In a letter of farewell to the readers of the *Shinsekai* he said he would return if there were another immigration crisis, but he was never to do so.[12] By this time he had found a subject of more absorbing interest, and he was to spend the rest of his life thinking about it. This was the character of Japanese abroad, which was related to the over-all concern with the differences between Japan and the West.

The more he observed Americans and Japanese in the United States, the less he could help noticing fundamental differences between them. The racist rhetoric of his editorials perhaps concealed the genuine amazement at the discovery that the two peoples were entirely incompatible; they seemed to represent extreme poles of human experience. This amazement gradually gave rise to the pessimistic conclusion that the Japanese made very poor immigrants. They were poor linguists; Kayahara himself confessed that he hardly understood what Americans were saying. He noted, as had Nagai Kafū, that the Japanese in America communicated with each other in their native tongue, ate Japanese food, had little contact with Americans, and otherwise transplanted their old habits of life and thought to the new environment. They were homesick for Japan and never intended to settle in the United States permanently. Although his view of these immigrants was more charitable than that pictured in

[11] *Ibid.*, Nov. 11, 30, 1906.
[12] *Ibid.*, May 5, 1907.

Kafū's *Amerika monogatari* [*Stories of America*], in time he would come to believe that America's rejection of them was rooted in their rejection of America.[13] They did not seem interested in settling overseas and integrating themselves in the life of the host community. Instead, they apparently conceived of themselves as temporary sojourners, physically living in America but mentally conditioned by the values and habits of the home country. Under the circumstances there could be no substance to the vision of establishing little Japans overseas as Tokutomi Sohō had said in the 1890's, or of peaceful Japanese imperialism such as Kazan himself and others like Nitobe Inazō had been talking about.

Witnessing the difficulties of Japanese in America, Kayahara came to a conclusion about the differences between the two peoples. America had been founded by immigrants from Europe. The Japanese were poor immigrants. The contrast for him was fundamental. The Japanese were, in his words, sedentary, agricultural, immobile. The Americans, on the contrary, were migratory, commercial-industrial, mobile. These characteristics were historically determined. The West, the land of migrating peoples, was characterized by the struggle with nature and between races. Acquisitiveness, scientific and economic development, and individualism were the results. Asia lacked these things and was distinguishable by its harmony, collectivism, and traditionalism. No wonder the two were incompatible, and no wonder that Japan, the extreme Asian nation, and America, the extreme Western nation, were so different in every respect. At this time, however, Kayahara did not go on to conclude that because of such differences Japan was inferior to the West or that the gap was inseparable. He believed, as he wrote to an American friend, that Japan understood both Asia and the West and that this was its unique strength. For instance, the Japanese woman had the potentiality of becoming the most ideal woman in the world as a result of combining her traditional virtues, lacking in Western ladies, and the latter's good aspects. Westerners had individualism and the freedom of thought which, combined

[13] Kayahara, *Kokuminteki higeki no hassei* (Tokyo, 1918), p. 40.

with the strong tradition of familism in Japan, would produce an ideal social organization. Because the West and Asia were so different, it was imperative to add their merits and reject their shortcomings, and the Japanese were potentially capable of doing it.[14]

In order better to understand the West, Kayahara spent nearly three years (1907–1910) in Europe. Most of the views he already had formed in the United States were confirmed, although he noted differences among various countries of Europe. He was impressed with the pervading industrialism and commercialism of Europe, where people seemed to be permeated by the spirit of absolute equality, individual autonomy, and self-interest. The individualism and cosmopolitanism of Western materialism were in sharp contrast to Asia, which had neither individual autonomy nor a transnational community of interests but was distinguished by the presence of small groups such as classes and family units dictating a qualitative difference between men. Had Kazan read contemporary German sociology, he could have found more adequate concepts to describe what he was finding. At this time, at any rate, he was not sure that the two kinds of social organization could not be combined. Excesses of Western materialism and egalitarianism, for instance, could be remedied through the introduction of the spirit of harmony and mutual respect found in Asia. Japan, in particular, was in a position to develop its material life following the lead of the West while retaining the tradition of harmony between emperor and subject, rich and poor, parent and child, and young and old. Japan was thus historically at an important crossroad, where it could understand both the West and Asia and contribute to the creation of a civilization at a higher level than previously reached.[15]

Japanese abroad continued to attract Kayahara's attention. In Europe, as in America, they seemed to be at ease only among themselves. "Many of them come to the West merely to ex-

[14] *Shinsekai,* Mar. 24, 26, 1907; Kayahara, *Kaigai bunshō,* p. 131; Kayahara, *Chijinron* (Tokyo, 1913), *passim.*
[15] Kayahara, *Kaigai bunshō,* pp. 7, 53, 203–204.

change gossip with other Japanese," he remarked sarcastically. They were only superficially Westernized. Japanese in England, for instance, were "monsters wearing an Anglo-Japanese mask." Outwardly English gentlemen, inwardly they were still "barbarians from East Asia."[16] Students and professors from Japan absorbed book-learning in the West, without really comprehending the realities of European life. Nevertheless, the Japanese must resolutely try to remove obstacles in the way of their "peaceful expansion." Otherwise they would have no place to go in the world. Only by combating anti-Japanese tendencies could they hope to contribute to the making of a new world civilization.[17]

The polarity in Kazan's views of Japan and of Japanese abroad can readily be seen. Although he was proud of traditional values and institutions and confident that they had something to offer to the seemingly abysmal state of Western materialistic civilization, he was much less sanguine about the ability of the Japanese overseas to be the purveyors of the new dimension of human progress. How could he condemn Japanese in England as superficially Westernized barbarians and at the same time talk of Japan's ability to combine the virtues of the West and Asia? The two were never perceived as contradictory in his own mind because he was sure that *he* was not like other Japanese in Europe and truly understood the essences of Western and Japanese civilization. Pride in Japanese tradition but disdain for individual Japanese overseas has been a not uncommon reaction of Japanese intellectuals abroad, and Kayahara was psychologically at peace with such an internally contradictory image of the world.

Once back in Japan, however, he began watching his own country with the freshness of a visitor, and he came to take a much more critical view of Japanese society and develop a more consistent picture of the world. As he returned to the Tokyo office of the *Yorozu chōhō* and actively supported the developing movement against oligarchy and militarism, Kayahara

---

[16] *Ibid.*, pp. 19, 25.
[17] *Ibid.*, pp. 32, 233.

harped on the theme that the Japanese were too self-centered and parochial. This, to him, was essentially a perpetuation of the feudal ethos. The rapidity of national transformation after the Meiji Restoration had reinforced the warrior ethic of particularistic loyalties and blinded the leaders and people to the need to develop a more universalistic, cosmopolitan outlook. The Japanese were possessed with "a narrow, feudalistic nationalism" the like of which was not found in any other country. This left them ill-prepared for the struggle in a world dominated by the white peoples who were at once much more cosmopolitan and individualistic than the Japanese. Rather than acting as Japanese subjects and thinking only of themselves, they should learn to act as individuals in a wide world. Otherwise they would find themselves ostracized by all other countries.[18] Like Kafū, who returned to Japan after four years and was scandalized by the narcissism and parochialism of many Japanese, Kazan was critical of the "petty subjectivism" he found among his countrymen.

Fortunately for Kayahara, his writings commanded wide attention, as this was the time when the Japanese were showing a serious interest in the psychological and intellectual implications of overseas expansion. The years after the Russo-Japanese War saw the founding of such magazines as *Shin jidai* (*The New Epoch*, 1906), *Shokumin sekai* (*The World of Colonialism*, 1908), *Sekai no Nihon* (*Japan in the World*, 1911), and *Kaigai no Nihon* (*Japan Overseas*, 1911). Issue after issue of these publications pondered such questions as in what direction Japan should expand, how best the Japanese could be prepared for living abroad, and how they should behave among other peoples. Kayahara Kazan, as might have been expected, was the person ideally fitted to explicate these problems. He arrived on the scene at the right moment with the right kinds of experience. Apart from the ubiquitous Ōkuma Shigenobu, one probably encountered more writings by Kayahara on these subjects than by anyone else at this time. In 1911, for example, he wrote every lead article for *Sekai no Nihon*. His message in the articles, rang-

---

[18] Kayahara, *Kazan bunshō, passim.*

ing from "What is Meant by Japan in the World?" to "Youth and the World," was always the same: The Japanese must understand the world, not only by learning from its technology but also comprehending the psychology of Westerners. His observations of and conversations with Americans and Europeans gave him confidence and self-assurance. He was certain that he, at least, had looked into the Western mind from inside and understood how it viewed the world. That was why he was confident of his beliefs about Japan and the Japanese, for these were no longer parochial, ethnocentric views. He was still a convinced expansionist and reiterated time and again his call for peaceful economic expansion abroad. But he felt this must be buttressed by a new attitude toward the West and the world.

By 1913, Kayahara Kazan was boldly calling for national transformation along individualistic, democratic lines. What he termed "Kazanism" consisted of individualism, democracy (he used the word *demokurashii*), free trade, and imperialism "not as an instrument for exhibiting national glory but as an expression of national energy."[19] His overseas trip and reflection since returning home had made him a convinced Westernizer. The West he wanted his countrymen to emulate was the West of liberalism, capitalism, and internationalism. It was the world of bourgeois rationalism, commercial universalism, and tradition-free individualism—a world in which individuals and the nation were in a harmonious and complementary relationship and only economic forces defined the relationship among nations. This mixture of the English notion of the laissez-faire state and the German idea of Gesellschaft was presented as Kayahara's view of the West and as the opposite of what he saw in Japan. To him Japan still represented protectionism, war, and particularistic concerns. Unlike the governments in the West, he pictured the Japanese bureaucratic government as "pre-Renaissance," and its educational, financial, and continental policies as "anachronistic." "We must transform ourselves," he wrote. "The Japanese people must change their inner life, change their na-

---

[19] Kayahara, *Chijinron*, p. 4. See also Kayahara, "Kyokutō no keisei o ronjite kaigai hattensaku ni oyobu," *Kaigai no Nihon*, 1, no. 4: 139–143 (April 1911).

tional life, and change their outlook in international life." The expansion of Japan must be derived from the people's energy, not from the state's concern with national rights and prestige. The Japanese must learn to base their action on science, experimentation, and rational calculation of their interests.[20]

In thus calling for wholesale transformation of Japanese life, Kazan was parting company with those like Tokutomi Sohō who had begun talking of an inevitable racial war and asserting Japan's right to challenge the white-dominated definitions of what was good and plausible. Instead Kayahara's views reflected the realization, shared by some in the business world, that Japanese imperialism was becoming a burden and that political considerations underlying national policy had drained resources from the far more critical problem of raising the standard of living of the people at home. Continental policy, he said, had not helped to solve the problem; in order to save the people from exhaustion and revive their energy, the only source of national strength, Manchuria would probably have to be given up.[21] They were hardly breathing in a state which was archaic, and they needed to reorient their life toward more scientific and economic goals. The assumption here was that they could do so by getting rid of their inhibitions and resolving to compete with the Western nations on their own terms. "Peaceful, commercial, individualistic competition" among nations was the rule in the world, and whether they liked it or not the Japanese would have to rationalize their life unless they were willing to stagnate.[22] They had to see to it that in Japan the quietism of Asia would give way to the vitality of the West. This was truly "a

[20] Kayahara, *Chijinron*, pp. 219, 270. See also Kayahara, "Seinen to sekai," *Sekai no Nihon*, 2, no. 10: 1–3 (Oct. 1911).

[21] Kayahara, *Chijinron*, pp. 271–272. Kayahara's opposition to continentalism was rooted also in his conviction that Japan's future lay in the seas. He was a maritime expansionist and believed that continental commitments were diverting national energy from the far more rewarding pursuit of riches in the ocean. Such views followed from his "rational" expansionism, entailing a minimum of state intervention and carried out by individual Japanese. It cannot be denied, however, that sometimes his espousal of maritime destiny came close to sounding the refrain of naval thinkers like Satō Tetsutarō. See Kayahara, *Shin dōchū seikan* (Tokyo, 1913), p. 138.

[22] Kayahara, *Chijinron*, pp. 214–215.

fundamental transformation, a spiritual rebirth" of the nation.

The outbreak of war among the allegedly rational, peaceful nations of Europe did not shake Kazan's confidence in the rightness of his views. He had drawn an idealistic image of the West based largely on what he had seen of the United States, Britain, and Germany. Now the last two were fighting a brutal war, with the first maintaining a balance. True to his advocacy of "rational calculations of economic interests," Kayahara opposed Japan's siding with Britain. Should Germany lose, he thought, the world would fall under Anglo-Saxon domination, which would not serve Japan's interests at all as it would tend to relegate Japan to an isolated existence. A balance between the two giants of Europe, on the other hand, would be a good safeguard against such a possibility. In taking such a stand, he came into direct conflict with *Yorozu chōhō*'s editor in chief, Kuroiwa Ruikō, who insisted that Japan enter the war on the side of the allies. Kayahara resigned, and this proved to be the beginning of what he would call a life of hiding which lasted until his death.[23]

As is evident in this episode, Kayahara's attitude toward international events was devoid of moralistic concerns. Both Britain and Germany exemplified the best in the West as he saw it, and it was impossible if not senseless to argue which was better or had greater justice. In fact, he was not sure but that Germany came closer to being his ideal Western nation. He had admired Birmarckian social legislation and the political unity of Wilhelmian Germany, and the orderliness, scientific orientation, and work ethic of the German people. Because of his diagnosis of Japanese ills, which stressed the country's feudal and familial ethos and its artificial government forcing sacrifices on the people, it was natural that Germany should have presented the ideal opposite. There he saw an organic national community in which the leadership looked after the welfare of the people, and they in turn were imbued with the sense of belonging to a larger political entity. Segments of society were well integrated, benefits of civilization equitably distributed, and national life characterized by efficiency, orderliness, and organization. Given such a picture

[23] Kayahara, *Nihon kokumin ni yuigon su* (Tokyo, 1933), preface.

of Germany, Kazan could not accept the standard characterization of the war as between democracy and autocracy, peace and militarism, or freedom and oppression.[24]

Relieved of editorial duties, Kayahara decided to make another trip abroad. That he was beginning to have some doubts about the efficacy of democracy can be seen in his itinerary. This time he made the point of visiting Latin America in order, as he wrote, to see how republics functioned. As might be expected, he was disillusioned, and from this time on whenever he talked of democracy he evoked the memories of the sorry state of political institutions in these republics, where he found nothing but irresponsible political parties, revolutions not for ideals but for power and money, and despotic bureaucracies.[25] Nevertheless, he admitted that Chile, Argentina, and Brazil had more or less successful systems of self-government. Moreover, he felt that republican institutions, with all their shortcomings, were almost inevitable for young countries composed of immigrants and migrants. Latin Americans certainly seemed to be far better equipped to experiment with them than the Japanese. At any rate, the South American trip made him weary of extolling democracy for its own sake. His admiration for Germany's "minority-ruled democratic government," on the other hand, remained strong, even though this time he did not go to Europe. His renewed respect for social harmony, justice, and guaranteed livelihood which he visualized operating even in wartime Germany, makes one wonder if he had really subscribed to anything more than the rhetoric of freedom and liberty when he had earlier talked about them. He returned home more impressed with the need for "economic freedom" rather than "political freedom." This was not surprising, given his consistently economistic orientation, but the emphasis on livelihood and harmony was to crop

[24] Kayahara, *Kokuminteki higeki,* pp. 428–433. See also his *Shin eiyūshugi* (Tokyo, 1916). This book represents Kayahara's unabashed admiration for Germany. It also marks a sharp contrast to his economic expansionism, as it extols the virtue of particularistic nationalism and even advocates the use of force to solve the population crisis. This return to the theme Kayahara had expressed in 1906 lasted only briefly, and it can be taken as his temporary flirtation with the Germanic anti-Anglo-Saxonism. It left no trace in his writings till the 1930's.

[25] Kayahara, *Kokuminteki higeki,* p. 275 ff.

up from time to time whenever he felt the need to justify Japan's departure from the Anglo-Saxon norm of personal freedom.

The major reason for his wartime travel, however, was once again to observe conditions of Japanese living abroad. Here his views remained intact. When he revisited Japanese communities in the United States after a lapse of ten years, he found that the situation had not changed at all. "I discovered feudal Japan on the Pacific coast of the United States," he wrote. He never encountered a Japanese who knew what living among Westerners as an immigrant meant. There was no understanding of what constituted the American's drive toward acquisitiveness and self-autonomy. The Japanese in America stood outside America, their life was non-American, consequently they were in fact anti-American, and that was why they had provoked anti-Japanese sentiment. Their attitude had not changed; they were still living as though they were in Japan. If anything, their self-consciousness had increased. They were not living as immigrants in America, which should have been their attitude, for American civilization was built upon immigrants coming together for the creation of wealth. Japan's warrior ethic and Asia's "old and dead civilization" were not going to help in such a setting.[26] Whereas in 1906–1907 Kazan had urged Japanese immigrants to stand firm against American prejudice and talked of harmonizing Japanese and Western virtues, he now castigated them for lacking a philosophy of immigranthood. He lectured to them and harped on this theme so often that his talks were long remembered by Japanese in America.[27] They were perhaps too polite to point out that Kayahara's observations made some sense when referring to Japanese merchants and students in the United States, but that agricultural settlers had in fact been acquiring riches against the obstacles of restrictionist measures such as alien land acts.

In Latin America, Southeast Asia, and even Taiwan he noted the parochialism and lack of initiative on the part of Japanese. They were constantly homesick, longed for the day when they

[26] *Ibid.*, pp. 36, 39–40, 43, 47, 57.
[27] Ōtsuka Yoshi, *Ishokumin to kyōiku mondai* (Tokyo, 1933), p. 28.

would return to Japan, and never adapted themselves to the way of life of the host communities. They made poor business competitors against Westerners, they would not act unless supported by Japanese officials, and they had no philosophical comprehension of why they were abroad.[28] It is interesting to recall that Shimazaki Tōson was in Europe about this time. He was very proud to find Japanese doctors and nurses working among Westerners using medical implements they themselves had brought from Japan and impressing Europeans with their modern techniques.[29] Kayahara did not go to Europe, but to him such remarks would have sounded superficial. He knew that the Japanese were capable of imitating Westerners and learning the arts of Western civilization. But he felt that these facts did not alter the basic contention that the Japanese remained essentially unchanged. Psychologically they were still cut from the feudal cloth and their practice of modern medicine had not affected their inner motivation. Kayahara approvingly cited Carl Crow's observation that the Japanese were acutely sensitive to what foreigners thought of them and that the medical mission to Europe during the war was but one more example of the desire to be considered a civilized nation.[30] This was Westernization for the sake of reputation, not for the sake of fundamental, rational transformation of national life.

On his return to Japan he wrote two widely read articles for the magazine *Chūō kōron*. One was entitled "Sorrow on Returning Home: A Nation that Will Not Assimilate Itself to the World or Assimilate the World to Itself." He was very pessimistic about the Japanese, he wrote. They were petrified by rigid traditional values which found no point of contact with the rest of the world. They took old habits and attitudes with them whenever they went abroad, and even so they were always homesick. Their behavior was not sustained by "economic rationality" and thus their life overseas lacked permanence. "The Japanese people

[28] Kayahara, *Kokuminteki higeki*, pp. 25, 35 ff.

[29] Shimazaki Tōson, *Furansu dayori* (1915), in *Tōson zenshū*, Chikuma-shobō edition (Tokyo, 1967), 6:411.

[30] Kayahara, *Kokuminteki higeki*, p. 230; Carl Crow, *Japan and America* (New York, 1916), pp. 138–141.

must now seriously look at their inner life. It is not enough to talk of our merits and demerits. We must resolve to overcome ourselves, reveal our weaknesses mercilessly, and try to undertake a thorough, fundamental transformation of our lives."[31] The second article appeared a month later, in August 1918. Entitled "The Japanese People Fabricate Facts," it reiterated the argument that the Japanese had failed to become scientifically oriented, rationally profit-seeking merchants. "World life is commercial life. . . . The world is a means for creating wealth." The Japanese should have gone out to the world to seek wealth and then use it in order to realize the ideals of the nation. They had, in fact, no comprehension of what the nation stood for or of the economic orientation of the rest of the world. They had not become "world citizens."[32]

Thus Kayahara joined the chorus emanating from intellectual and journalistic circles calling for a new definition of national purpose and of Japan's relationship with the rest of the world. The chorus, all singing the coming of a new age, sang discordant tunes. Nitobe Inazō stressed the political aspect of the emerging internationalism as exemplified by the League of Nations, whereas Yoshino Sakuzō talked of mankind's new "moral consciousness" as the dominating factor in world affairs. Principles such as liberty, equality, fraternity, peace, and democracy, said Yoshino, were to be the "unmovable principles" governing the postwar world.[33] What proved to be the most persistent and influential theme in Japanese thinking after the war, however, was the notion of economism.[34]

[31] Kayahara, "Sokoku ni kaeru no hiai," *Chūō kōron*, 33, no. 7: 36–43 (July 1918). "Looking at one's inner life" became the theme on which Kayahara founded a new journal in 1919, called *Naikan*. Each month about 13,000 copies were printed and distributed. A typical issue contained several articles by Kayahara and very little else. They consistently promoted the notions of rationalism, economism, and cosmopolitanism.

[32] Kayahara, "Jijitsu o kazō suru Nihon kokumin," *Chūō kōron*, 33, no. 8: 60–72 (Aug. 1918).

[33] Yoshino Sakuzō, "Kokka seikatsu no isshin," *ibid.*, 35, no. 1: 117–156 (Jan. 1920). The best study of Nitobe's ideas is Kimitada Miwa, "Crossroads of Patriotism in Imperial Japan" (Ph.D. dissertation, Princeton University, 1967).

[34] Concerning postwar economic foreign policy, see my paper, "The Failure of Economic Expansionism, 1918–1931," presented at the Conference on Taishō Japan (Durham, N. C., 1969).

The idea that Japan's salvation lay in a fully integrated economic relationship with the rest of the world and in winning "peaceful warfare" was not new.[35] But the years after 1918 saw the growing conviction that economic competition was the only variable determining international affairs because of the passing of the "old diplomacy" and "the age of imperialism." With old-fashioned military conquests and predatory wars no longer thinkable, peoples of the world would turn their energy to more productive channels, curtail armament, and internationalize their economies. As Horie Kiichi wrote in 1922, nations now would have to coordinate their policies so as to march along the path of antimilitarism and anti-imperialism.[36] Another writer noted in the *Chūō kōron* that "nation-building through productive action" should be the goal for Japan. The Japanese should work with conscientiousness, intelligence, technology, and determination to maximize their productivity.[37]

It is evident that Kayahara's thought came very close to these views. He had long advocated similar opinions, and the postwar emphasis on economism in a sense brought to fruition his efforts of many years. His strength, as earlier, was that he was able to generalize about Japan and the world through his observation of Japanese overseas. It was with conviction gained through years of such observation that he could assert, as he did in 1918, "Our life must be made cosmopolitan. Our commerce, industry, and agriculture must have an international outlook." Above all, the Japanese must become world citizens. Only then would they be able to go anywhere in the world and compete confidently and successfully with other peoples. Only then could they truly be Japanese, truly be human. Parochial, particularistic, self-centered existence was no longer tenable. Instead of confining their consciousness to the narrow geographical limits and historical tradition of a nation, the Japanese must first of all try to view the whole world as their sphere of action, as their house,

[35] See Iriye, "Heiwateki hattanshugi"; Kuroda Ken'ichi, *Nihon shokumin shisō-shi* (Tokyo, 1942), p. 196 ff.
[36] Horie Kiichi, "Buryokuteki kyōsō kara kokusai keizaiteki kyōsō e," *Chūō kōron*, 37, no. 2: 20–30 (Feb. 1922).
[37] Sugimori Kōjirō, "Kokusai mugunbi to seisan rikkoku e," *ibid.*, pp. 85–88.

and then go back to Japan with a new perspective so as to find new meaning in national life and contribute to the progress of world civilization.[38] Such was Kayahara's message at the end of the war.

Although the generally economic orientation of Japanese foreign policy in the 1920's was sustained by the thought of men like Kayahara, he did not stop his relentless criticism of the Japanese mentality. He did not think the Japanese had taken his admonitions to heart; instead they still seemed to go the old unscientific, irrational way. It is doubtful whether it was the Japanese or Kazan himself who had not changed. He was in his fifties, and he had been repeating familiar messages for over ten years. Whatever he saw served to confirm his preconceptions. His writings for this period are nevertheless of some interest, as they show how a consistent critic of traditionalism dealt with specific issues of the 1920's. For instance, he was in China during the May 30, 1925, crisis. With refreshing insight he noted that the episode revealed Japanese lack and Chinese possession of economic rationalism. In his view, the Japanese were paying for their sentimentalism and emotionalism, and the anti-Japanese movement in China showed how the Chinese could utilize an economic weapon to respond to Japanese arrogance and racial prejudice. The Japanese were prone to appeal to political authority and military force to solve economic problems: "If they persist in settling all international disputes politically, they will always end up fighting wars." Because war would serve neither Japan's nor China's interests, one must view the Shanghai crisis with sympathy.[39]

The logical extension of such argument would have been to repudiate completely Japan's formal empire as an economic burden which irritated Chinese sensitivity. He stopped short of denouncing Japanese colonialism by name, but by the end of the decade he was willing to drop hints that he considered Japan's hold on Manchuria and even Korea to be an anachro-

---

[38] Kayahara, *Kokuminteki higeki*, pp. 58, 99, 425.
[39] Kayahara, *Tōkai igo Kayahara Kazan bunshū* (Tokyo, 1929), pp. 168–169, 172, 175–176, 382.

nism. He wrote, in January 1927, that the Taisho era had witnessed the transition from imperialism to pacifism and that the new era of Showa must be a period in which peace would become a reality through economic development and social progress. Unless the Japanese did away with imperialism and established the long-range goal of creating wealth through incessant effort, Japan would certainly become a third-rate nation. In 1928, Kayahara asserted that the Japanese in Manchuria really desired to leave, but that their homeland was not economically prepared to receive them back. If the Japanese should succeed in possessing "a psychological attitude like that of Westerners" and in becoming "businessmen," the colonies would have been liquidated and the Japanese enabled to "enjoy life rationally."[40] He did not state these ideas precisely in this way, but the scores of short essays he wrote in the second half of the decade leave no doubt what direction his thoughts were taking.

As with all those in and out of government who advocated economic foreign policy and peaceful expansion, Kayahara had the misfortune of witnessing the erosion of the postwar international system after 1929, as capitalist economies could no longer sustain a balance between international economic interdependence and their own domestic concerns. Economic life, far from producing peace and amity among nations, was becoming more and more particularistic and nationalistic. Peace came to be based not on commercial interdependence but on armament and collective security. Ironically, militarism and forceful expansionism brought about immediate economic benefits to the countries that resorted to them, as if to belie the fundamental assumptions of the preceding decade. But Kazan was undaunted. In a book written at the beginning of 1931, he reiterated the conviction that the Japanese still had not learned how to live rationally and humanly. That was why the national economy was bankrupt and Japan was fast becoming a have-not country. But

[40] *Ibid.*, pp. 391, 444–446, 448–449, 493. See also *Naikan*, 78: 26–27 (Sept. 1, 1926). Here he hinted that Japan's hold on Manchuria and Korea eventually would be shaken and that the Japanese people would have to undertake a different sort of expansion. In another issue of the journal he called for restoration of tariff and jurisdictional autonomy to China. *Ibid.*, 79: 2–3 (Oct. 1, 1926).

the remedy did not lie in resort to force but in rebuilding national life on the basis of "the will to live."[41]

Kayahara did make a few concessions to forceful expansionism and ultranationalism after the Manchurian incident. He wrote in 1933 that he had tried to be "a world citizen who was born in Japan," but that he had now become "a 100 percent Japanese." The nation "is the focus of a people's emotions," he said, and its maintenance and growth as a "cultural, spiritual, and moral entity" should be a cardinal objective of life. Moreover, an underdeveloped country like Japan could not hope to make progress without destroying the status quo. We must remember, he asserted, "that only through wars has the world's status quo been broken." So far one might see a classic case of apostasy. Similar ideas about the nation, war, and status quo were being repeated endlessly in post–1931 Japan. It was as if Kayahara had the dubious distinction of joining the exinternationalists who discovered all of a sudden that their internationalism had been derived from an image of the world which was nothing but a mirage. Beneath the surface declaration of his loyalty to the new order, however, Kazan managed to speak out for the same kinds of ideals that he had been urging on his countrymen for over two decades. "For the Japanese people, the Japanese nation is absolute," he wrote, "but this absoluteness is a subjective thing. If we objectively look at the world, we shall find that there are as many countries as there are stars." Japan was unique, and its distinguishing characteristic consisted of the people's martial spirit. They knew how to fight, but did not know how to live, work, and produce. Even the prized *yamato damashii* (Japanese spirit), according to Kayahara, had been an instrument for "rejecting and isolating the world." What was needed was not the revival of the policy of seclusion but a new nationalism, a new Japanese spirit which "embraced the world." The Japanese must become "international patriots, namely, patriots who do not forget the world." They must learn to base their total life on an economic foundation. All his life, he said, he had been

[41] Kayahara, *Ikin to hossuru Nihonjin ni uttau* (Tokyo, 1931), pp. 68, 109, 240.

trying to study Japan from a detached position; he had been "an international Lumpen proletariat, an international *rōnin*."[42] These remarks suggest that Kazan managed to maintain his integrity and autonomy with a minimum of rhetorical lip-service to the military.

Having led a life of self-imposed seclusion from public life for two decades, the transition to a life of almost total silence, which lasted till 1945, must not have been very painful. He had at any event fixed his ideas and repeated them so often that there was little use trying to adapt them to the new situation of war with China and the West. The Japanese defeat, however, seemed to Kayahara to be the final vindication of his argument that without more fundamental Westernization Japan would lose out in competition with the West. "Japan's unconditional surrender was Asia's last defeat by the West," he wrote shortly after the war. Further Westernization was the only way left for the salvation of Japan and Asia. This would entail social and psychological renovation, as the Japanese and Asians would have to learn from the Westerners' spirit of independence, individualism, egalitarianism, and struggle for life.[43]

It is easy to dismiss these ideas as trite, as sermonizing by an old man who was prone to see in everything a vindication of his ideas. Kayahara Kazen could be written off simply as a latter-day Fukuzawa Yukichi or Taguchi Ukichi without their

[42] Kayahara, *Nihon kokumin ni yuigon su,* pp. 7, 10, 27, 41, 87, 88, 121. In 1934, he published another book, entitled *Nihon no keizaiteki kokuze.* Here he called for a new totalitarianism which, however, was little different from the economic expansionism he had earlier advocated. Totalitarianism for him was simply the mobilization of national energy for economic development at home and cultural activities abroad. Despite his ability to retain long-felt convictions and adapt them to changing circumstances, it cannot be denied that Kayahara never openly challenged the new national and international order of the 1930's. It should be noted, however, that for him the decade seemed for a time to be a fulfillment of his dream: to make Japan an economically oriented nation. In *Nihon no keizaiteki kokuze* he asserted that the United States and Japan would never fight for they were economically complementary (p. 60).

[43] Kayahara, *Nihon jinmin no tanjō, passim.* Apart from the books mentioned in this study, Kayahara wrote several others, mostly recapitulating his familiar arguments. They include *Ningen seikatsu-shi* (1913), *Daisan teikoku-ron* (1914), *Nihon kokumin no seikatsu tetsugaku* (1921), and travelogues of the Inland Sea published in the late 1920's. Kayahara offers some explanation of these books in his *Ikin to hossuru Nihonjin ni uttau.*

scholarship and sophistication. But Kazan's ideas also serve to point up a theme around which modern Japanese history can be constructed. He was consistently interested in observing Japanese overseas. This was because, first, they exemplified the best and the worst in Japanese character and thus enabled the observer to draw conclusions about the nature of Japanese life. Second, Japan in modern times had inevitably to relate itself to the rest of the world, but the most direct relating was done by the Japanese who went to foreign countries. It was not simply "the coming of the barbarians" that "opened" Japan; it was also the going out of Japanese, which tested the ability of modern Japan to live in the world. Third, expansion whether by force or through peaceful methods, whether of Japanese goods, capital, or ideas, whether by colonization or emigration, was a perceived necessity which never left Japanese consciousness after the Meiji Restoration. The issue always was not whether to expand but how and where. The history of modern Japan in a sense was, then, a history of the expansion of Japan. The acuteness of Kayahara's observations lay in his ability to grasp this fact and his interest in determining to what extent Japan could be an expanding country by watching the men who did the expanding. He urged them to transcend their parochialism and develop a more universalistic outlook so as to communicate with other peoples. Despite his superficial and often contradictory image of the West, he was perfectly correct in his observation that modern Japan could truly belong to the world when overseas Japanese developed an ability to overcome their self-consciousness and regard all men as world citizens.

Kazan himself, however, never completely shed his provincialism. After all, he spent most of his years abroad living among and lecturing to his fellow countrymen. Most of the West was a closed book to him; he was a visitor who thought he understood America and Europe by watching but not working with Americans and Europeans. He visited a few families and read a few newspapers, but he never made an attempt to read current literature and scholarship in the West. His sole concern was with Japan in relationship to the rest of the world; he never pondered other nations' problems or international events without relating them to his central concern. He was interested in the expansion of Japan, but not in the expansion of the world. He was unique among his countrymen in his consistent advocacy of an internationalist outlook, but he was just as narrow as they in his preoccupation with the salvation of Japan. He was a parochial cosmopolitan, a particularistic universalist.

NAGAI RYŪTARŌ:
THE TACTICAL DILEMMAS OF REFORM

Peter Duus

In looking at the history of Japan between the two world wars, one is struck by the number of politicians who found it possible to participate in the politics of both the "liberal twenties" and the "fascist thirties." Many public men who got their start as moderate reformist politicians in the 1920's, whether as liberal democrats or as social democrats, not only gave vigorous support to the war effort but also joined in the formation of a "totalitarian" political structure in the late 1930's. As Tsurumi Shunsuke has pointed out, the overwhelming majority of the top leaders of the Imperial Rule Assistance Association were not "right-wing ultranationalists," but men drawn from the moderate middle ranges of the political spectrum—men like Ogata Taketora, Kiyose Ichirō, and Kawakami Jotarō, to name a few who survived into the postwar period as well.[1]

The spasm of remorse and recrimination following Japan's defeat has made it difficult to assess the role of these men dispassionately. On the whole it has been more tempting (and in some cases politically profitable) to condemn them for backsliding, opportunism, apostasy, and other moral weaknesses than to try to understand them. Even the efforts of Professor Tsurumi and his colleagues to explain the actions of these men through the concept of "ideological conversion" or "ideological defection"

NOTE: The author wishes to express his thanks to Professor Nagai Michio for his kind assistance in research for this essay. He lent the author many of his father's books, now very difficult to locate in libraries or bookstores, and also arranged interviews with several of his father's old political colleagues (Azuma Shun'ei, Matsumura Kenzō, and Miyake Shōichi.)

[1] Shisō no kagaku kenkyūkai, ed., *Tenkō* (Tokyo, 1962), 3:91.

(*tenkō*) have suggested obliquely either that they jettisoned their principles in the rush to join the war effort or that their original ideological commitments were "flawed."

All such assessments have an unreal quality about them for they portray politics as a stylized moral drama, in which choices are based solely on principle, and the paths toward good or evil are clearly distinguishable. Those who resist evil are to be praised, those who surrender to it are to be damned. But the actions of any man in political life—if he is neither completely a fanatic nor completely a scoundrel—are bound to be morally ambiguous, for he is constantly torn between doing what is right and staying in office. To think otherwise is to reduce political biography to caricature.

It would be useful, therefore, to abandon moral and ideological stereotypes in looking at the interwar years of Japanese politics, and try to discover instead what it was in the experience of the reformist politicians of the 1920's that may have attracted them in the late 1930's to the idea of a "new political order." This approach may not satisfy the "whiggish" propensities of many Japanese (and American) historians who ransack history to footnote the eternal struggle between the forces of democracy and the forces of authoritarianism, but it may lead to a more credible and certainly more human picture of the real choices these politicians faced.

An interesting case in point is that of Nagai Ryūtarō, one of the principal leaders of the Minseitō, who had risen to prominence in the 1920's as one of the chief Diet spokesmen of the "new liberalism." In 1940, he also became one of the most enthusiastic and least cynical supporters of the "new political order."[2] It is clear that he did not do so out of short-run expediency

[2] Nagai Ryūtarō (1881–1944) was the son of a former samurai family of Maeda han. His father was a school teacher with a fondness for *sake*, and until Nagai was fifteen his father lived apart from his family, which remained in Kanazawa City while he taught elsewhere. In 1897, Nagai entered Dōshisha Middle School but, owing to involvement in a student strike there, was forced to leave. He completed his secondary education at Kansei Gakuin, where he became a Christian. From 1901 to 1905, he attended Waseda University, graduating from the Faculty of Politics and Economics, where he studied under Abe Isoo, Ukita Kazutami, and others. From 1906 to 1909, he attended Manchester College,

or a desire to "hop on the bus" as many politicians did, for he
had been involved in discussions of how to pull such an organization together as early as 1936. Nor did he see himself as be-
traying his earlier role as a proponent of liberal reform. Rather,
his decision to help build a "new political structure" grew out of
an exasperation at the inability of the existing political system
to respond to the need for change. His participation in the IRAA
was not a denial or betrayal of his reformist outlook, but a re-
affirmation of it under new circumstances, and a last stab at
finding a modus vivendi for reform when other avenues of
political action had led to dead ends.

Like many others of his generation, Nagai entered politics
during the late 1910's in a state of high moral concern. He was
driven by the feeling that while the rest of the world was being
swept up in constant and often revolutionary change, Japan had
become tired, immobile, and stagnant. He laid much of the
blame for this on the older generation, who were immured in
the status quo. The majority of the country's leaders were "unable to change their views to keep pace with the constant and
steady progress of the world, or . . . unable to speak for fear of
public censure even if they [did] change their views." They
were merely content to "pass on ancestral customs, worship
ancestral religions, emphasize ancestral morality, and follow
ancestral customs, and . . . to regard it as virtuous to submit to

---

Oxford University, first receiving a scholarship on the recommendation of the
Japanese Unitarian group in Tokyo, and later as an exchange student from
Waseda. After his return to Japan, he received an appointment as instructor at
Waseda, and remained on the faculty there until he resigned for a career in
politics in 1917. While teaching social policy and colonial policy at Waseda, he
worked as editor of *Shin Nippon*, one of the leading liberal journals of the day
and also an organ for the views of Ōkuma Shigenobu, whose stern visage appeared on the magazine's cover every month. In 1917, Nagai tried unsuccessfully
to win a Diet seat from Kanazawa City as an independent candidate; in 1920,
he was successfully elected and remained a member of the Diet until his death
in 1944. He served as colonial minister under the Saitō cabinet, and as postal
minister and railroad minister under the first Konoe and Abe cabinets. The
standard biography of Nagai is Matsumura Kenzō, *Nagai Ryūtarō* (Tokyo, 1959).
The memoirs of his secretary of twenty years, Azuma Shun'ei, *Omitsusa* (Tokyo,
1968), also are full of useful biographical information.

all these even at the sacrifice of their own lives."[3] As a result politics were dull, complaisant, meaningless, or often sordid.

This feeling of malaise and disgust with politics had been with Nagai since his own youth, a period when the heated Diet struggles of the 1890's gave way to the "politics of compromise" during the early 1900's. For Nagai these years were not marked by the slow but steady progress of party power so much as a decline in the idealism which should leaven politics. He characterized the late Meiji as an era of "temporizing," best symbolized by Katsura Tarō, whom he regarded as a "man of no ideals who scurried hither and yon, pursuing makeshift solutions to problems as they arose." Nagai could not tolerate such muddling through, nor the apparent willingness of the political parties to accommodate themselves to it. He was almost obsessively concerned that the country move with the tides of progress and transform itself from a "passive" Japan to an "activist" Japan. He wanted no less than that Japan should develop "to the same level as the most advanced countries of the world," a level it clearly had not reached.[4] He was fond of likening his own times to the last days of the Bakufu, when the leaders of the country had failed to respond to "troubles at home and threats from abroad," and he called for a Taishō Restoration which would make possible a "national reconstruction" of Japan and the fulfillment of her "national mission" in the world.

By "national reconstruction" Nagai did not mean a violent overthrow of the existing order by force (as Kita Ikki did), but rather the establishment of a new set of priorities in government. Like other "new liberals" who turned their backs on the Meiji slogan of a "rich country and strong army," Nagai believed that the state should devote its energies not simply to the building of its own power but to the creation of a more just and egali-

---

[3] Nagai Ryūtarō, *kaizō no risō* (Tokyo, 1920), pp. 3–4; and *Nagai Ryūtarō-Shi daienzetsushū* (Tokyo, 1924), 1:102.

[4] Nagai Ryūtarō, *Zanpan* (Tokyo, 1914), pp. 197–199; Nagai Ryūtarō, "Taishō ishin no jitsu o ageyo," *Chūō kōron* (hereafter *CK*), 28, no. 3:24; Nagai Ryūtarō, "Reigo jukugo," *Shin Nippon* (hereafter *SN*), 3, no. 3:25–26; Nagai Ryūtarō, "Kaikyū seiji ka heimin seiji ka," *SN*, 5, no. 3: 73–74; Nagai Ryūtarō, *Enzetsushū*, 1:109.

tarian society as well.[5] This belief was nurtured, first of all, by Nagai's youthful conversion to Protestant Christianity, which instilled in him a sense of the equal moral worth of all men as "children of God." This moral egalitarianism dovetailed with, and was reinforced by, the idea of equality of opportunity which informed another important early influence on his life—late Meiji socialism. Under the convergence of these influences, he became committed to the doctrine that the state should intervene positively in social and economic life to promote the well-being of all members of society, especially "the poor, the oppressed, and the aggrieved," born without the advantages of status, wealth, or education.

Privately Nagai was fond of calling himself a supporter of "socialism," but it was clear that he meant the milder varieties of English and American socialism, which called for social melioration rather than class revolution. He was really an advocate of the general welfare state and its program—minimum wage laws, unemployment insurance, the recognition of trade unions, a more equitable distribution of the tax burden, old age pensions, accident insurance, and the like. Through the enactment of such measures, he hoped the state would guarantee the right of each of its members to exist securely and comfortably enough to "realize the true meaning of his existence" and to explore the full potentialities of his natural endowments.[6] Nagai's notion of "national reconstruction" was therefore not very different from the mixture of humanitarianism and state interventionism that has been prevalent among American and English social liberals since the turn of the century.

The demand for "national reconstruction" always was associated in Nagai's mind with the need for an expansion of the popular base of politics. Innocent of any managerial elitism, he worked from the assumption that because the people make up the nation they should have the responsibility and power to

[5] Cf. Matsumoto Sannosuke, *Kindai Nihon no seiji to ningen* (Tokyo, 1966), pp. 159–160.

[6] A fairly representative sample of Nagai's views on this matter may be found in Nagai, *Kaizō no risō*, pp. 3–20.

control its destiny.[7] It was obvious, however, that this was not
the case in Japan, where the Diet, ostensibly a mechanism for
popular control, represented not the people as a whole but a
special "privileged class." As he pointed out in 1914, there really
existed two public opinions within the country—one within the
Diet and the other outside it—and the former rarely reflected
the latter. "True popular opinion" was not heard in the Diet
because the political parties there represented only the "big
capitalists" and the "big landlords" who monopolized the right
to vote.[8] This subservience of the Diet and the parties to special
economic interests, both locally and nationally, made them in-
sensitive to the demands of the common people, particularly
the working classes, and left them merely spokesmen for the
well-to-do. The unfortunate result was that the people could
not "express their demands nor protest their hardships either to
the political parties or to the Diet in which those parties were
organized."[9] Nagai therefore became an ardent champion of an
expanded franchise, and ultimately of universal manhood suffrage, which he hoped would transform the "class politics" of
the day into truly "popular politics."

Like most of the other young Taishō liberals, Nagai's interest
in "national reconstruction" was not only humanitarian and
populistic, but also conservative. He wanted the country to
move in a new direction, but not so far that basic institutions
would be threatened. In part, he felt that "national reconstruction" was necessary for the preservation of the parliamentary
system, which he regarded as the best means for mediating the
clash of interests in society.[10] Unless the government were made
more responsive to popular aspirations and the political system
were altered to permit opportunities for greater popular participation, he feared a spreading indifference, if not hostility, toward parliamentary politics.

---

[7] Quoted in Matsumura, *Nagai*, p. 176.
[8] Nagai Ryūtarō, "Innai no gikai to ingai no gikai," *CK*, 29, no. 4:122–126.
[9] Nagai, *Kaizō no risō*, p. 106.
[10] Nagai, *Enzetsushū*, 1:117–118; Nagai Ryūtarō, "Gikai seiji no shimei no tame ni," *CK*, 35, no. 9: 53, 56–57.

Even more alarming was the possibility that failure to "popularize" both the political process and the content of government policy would make discontented elements among the populace prey to alien radicalism and "dangerous ideas." Even though "the awakening of the propertyless classes" and "class struggle" were still in their infancy in Japan, he wrote in 1921, "discontent and dissatisfaction" were "rife among the workers and the lower classes."[11] Social welfare policy and political democratization would "innoculate" the country against an epidemic of radicalism by satisfying the interests of the potentially discontent.

The other side of Nagai's drive to set new goals for Japanese politics was his desire that Japan should play a new and major role in world affairs. Whereas the older generation of politicians had thought in terms of "national survival," Nagai, like others who had seen Japan win her credentials as a great power in the Russo-Japanese War, spoke of Japan's "national mission" or "national destiny." He was attracted, however, neither by the notion that Japan should become the leader of a pan-Asian union to wrest control of the world from the West, nor by the idea that Japan's special vocation should be to achieve "harmony between Eastern and Western civilization." Emotionally committed to the destruction of "privilege" and the emancipation of the "oppressed" at home, he was drawn rather to the idea that Japan should help free the "colored peoples" of the world, particularly those of Asia, from the thrall of "Caucasian imperialism." Japan, being the "most intelligent" and "most powerful" of all the peoples threatened by the "white man's tyranny," was in the best position to encourage the efforts of colonial or exploited nationalities to establish their rights of self-determination.[12] Only

[11] Nagai Ryūtarō, "Shin gikaishugi o teishō su," *CK*, 36, no. 1: 108. For arguments in a similar vein, see *Kaizō no risō*, pp. 34–53; Nagai Ryūtarō, "Shakai seigishin no kakuritsu e," *Kensei kōron*, 3, no. 3: 46–54.

[12] A convenient summary of Nagai's position on this matter may be found in *Kaizō no risō*, pp. 181–196. See also, Nagai Ryūtarō, "Tai-Shi gaikō no konpon hōshin," *SN*, 4, no. 1: 10–14; Nagai Ryūtarō, "Sekai no futatsu taiseiryoku ni obiyakasaruru Nihon," *CK*, 34, no. 9: 40–46; Nagai Ryūtarō, *Sekai seisaku jukō* (Tokyo 1925), pp. 142–146.

she could smash the "delusion of white man's domination" and help to bring about independence and self-government for all the nationalities of the world.

Just what Nagai expected Japan to do in her role as champion of the oppressed peoples of Asia remained unclear. Despite the vehemence of his language, however, it is certain that at first he did not envisage it as a military role. By the end of the world war, with the growing demands of oppressed nationalities for independence, he felt Caucasian imperialism was in the process of natural disintegration and that the imperialist powers were spent and weakened by fighting among themselves. He looked forward to the emergence of a "true internationalism," in which every nationality would recognize the right of every other to exist and govern itself. In this situation, he had two prescriptions for Japanese foreign policy: First, it should avoid the "bureaucratic diplomacy" of the Kasumigaseki bureaucrats, who followed the lead of the imperialist powers and thus conveyed the impression that Japan was one of their number; second, it should be more sensitive to the nationalist aspirations of her Asian neighbors, particularly of China, where Japan's policy in the past had rested more on calculations of Japan's self-interest than on assessment of the feelings of the Chinese people.[13] Japan's special mission as "emancipator" of the oppressed peoples of Asia was therefore to be more facilitative than activist, and Nagai usually defined this mission in terms of whom Japan should protect Asia against rather than in terms of a positive and concrete method for doing so.

The question remains, how did Nagai expect his reform goals to be achieved? It is clear that he was proposing political action within the framework of "constitutional government," and was firmly committed to its procedures. Indeed, he constantly affirmed the superiority of parliamentary government as a means

[13] Nagai, *Enzetsushū*, 1: 79–100; Nagai Ryūtarō, "Shina taikan," *SN*, 6, no. 2: 22; Nagai Ryūtarō, "Chokugen," *SN*, 8, no. 2: 17; Nagai Ryūtarō, "Kokkashugi to kokusaishugi wa mujun sezu," *CK*, 36, no. 2: 59–64. See also Matsumura, *Nagai*, pp. 238–240, 260–271.

by which the conflicting interests of society could be reconciled. But within this framework there were alternative paths of political action. One was to take the "pragmatic" course of working within existing structures of political parties—the "established parties" which were on the verge of assuming the predominant role in constitutional politics. The other was to circumvent the "established parties" by politicizing the common people and bringing them to bear as a political force for reform. Nagai's disgust with the politicians of his day tempted him to try the latter route at first, but he was well connected enough to attempt the former as well. Throughout his career, he therefore found himself caught between the roles of loyal party regular and popular crusader for reform, and in both roles he encountered a growing sense of frustration.

The earlier, if not necessarily more authentic, side of Nagai's political personality was that of popular crusader. During most of his career he harbored the conviction, often publicly expressed, that the "rejuvenation" of Japanese politics would ultimately depend on the politicization of the masses. Convinced that the established parties were merely power brokers for special economic interests, he constantly was enticed by the vision of a political rebirth of Japan through the creation of a mass political movement dedicated to "national reconstruction" and the fulfillment of the "national mission."

Intellectually Nagai's interest in the development of a popular political movement rested on a faith that there was a latent political energy and power in the people, particularly in the lower classes, for it was they who ultimately were in the majority. In Europe, it was clear that the emergence of working-class parties had upset the classic liberal model of political competition between two parties, a conservative one supported by the old landed aristocracy and a liberal one supported by the new middle classes. It was not hard to surmise that eventually this pattern of "three-party politics" would give way to the triumph of the parties which took the side of the lower classes.[14]

[14] Nagai Ryūtarō, *Yasei* (Tokyo 1916), pp. 17–37; and *Kaizō no risō*, pp. 34–83.

Nagai very much felt that a similar political development should take place in Japan. In the early days of Taishō, he frequently called on the party politicians, especially the older liberals like Ozaki Yukio and Inukai Tsuyoshi, to abandon toothless slogans like "the destruction of *hanbatsu* government" and draw on the power of the masses by organizing political movements which would appeal to "those below the middle classes." "From the days of old," he wrote in an open letter to Inukai, "no one has ever lost by taking the side of the people. . . . They are in the great majority, and it is they who possess the ultimate power. Those who hold them will win, and those who do not will lose."[15] A mass-based political party would not only serve the cause of popular government; it was also politically expedient.

The attraction of the popular political movement as a political technique also grew out of Nagai's enormous talent as a political orator. In an era when the Diet debates were uninspiring and the mass media had not jaded popular appetites for theatricality in public figures, Nagai (like Ozaki Yukio, Shimada Saburō, and Nakano Seigō) belonged to that handful of politicians who bought fame by the mere "power of the tongue." Endowed with a dramatizing personality, he was able to make complex issues appear simple, to clothe ordinary ideas in florid raiment, and to convey to his listeners his own strong sense of conviction. His deep rich voice, his talent for pungent phrase making, his commanding public presence, and his unerring sense of timing electrified his audiences even during his student days at Waseda. He was no mere visceral spellbinder, however. He was a craftsman, who worked and reworked his speeches, polishing them until he achieved just the effect he wanted. Arima Yoriyasu was probably not far wrong when he commented that Nagai "lived for his speeches, so much so that I often had the illusion that even in normal conversations he was making an address. . . ."[16] But if Nagai may have struck Arima as slightly pompous, there

[15] Nagai Ryūtarō, "Kokumintō ni atau," *SN*, 2, no. 7: 18.

[16] Arima Yoriyasu, *Seikai dōchūki*, (Tokyo, 1952), p. 226. Some sense of Nagai's accomplishments as orator can be gleaned from reading Azuma, *Omitsusa*, pp. 124–140, and Matsumura Kenzō, *Sandai kaikōroku*, (Tokyo, 1964), pp. 322–327.

is no question of his popular appeal. His name drew overflowing crowds to political rallies in the provinces, and a collection of his speeches published in 1924 went through 142 printings in the next six years.

Given his power to attract and move audiences and his faith in the future of popular movements, it is not surprising that when Nagai first entered politics he attempted to build local support through a grass-roots reform movement, the Ishikawa-ken Rikken Seinentō (Ishikawa Prefecture Constitutional Youth Party). Originally begun as the Nagai Kōenkai (Association to Support Nagai Ryūtarō), which was formed by a number of local Waseda graduates to support his unsuccessful first attempt at a Diet seat in 1917, the organization expanded in the years that followed. Nagai's personal appeal and his promise as a "new man" with a political future provided its basic cohesion. But it was held together by other impulses as well. It attracted both those who admired Nagai's strong advocacy of political and social reform and those discontent with local politics, especially with the long domination of Kanazawa City by the Seiyūkai. During the early 1920's, it not only spearheaded attacks on local political corruption, but also became the center of the local popular movement for universal suffrage, organizing demonstrations in the prefecture and dispatching delegations to participate in the rallies at Tokyo. The organization, which experimented in cooperation with the local branch of the Yūaikai, also took a tolerant or sympathetic view of the budding tenancy and labor movements in Ishikawa Prefecture during the postwar recession years.[17]

Nagai was at first extremely optimistic about the future of political organizations like the Ishikawa Rikken Seinentō. He felt such a group might eventually become the nucleus of a "new party" which would fight for the cause of political reform. He reported in 1922 that he had found in his travels throughout the country a large number of "youth parties" aiming at building a

---

[17] Ishikawa-kenchō, ed., *Ishikawa-ken shi; gendai hen,* (Kanazawa City, 1962), 1: 97–100, 102–118. Some details on the organization also were provided in an interview with Azuma Shun'ei, 12/16/1968.

"central political force for national reconstruction" apart from and above the "established parties." With the passage of universal suffrage in the offing, he felt there was a possibility of welding these together in a "great reconstruction movement." If such a national "youth movement," rich in knowledge, vigor, spirit, and enthusiasm, were to attack the citadels of the privileged, determined to bring about a "Taishō Restoration," then the masses might rally around it.[18] In 1922, the Ishikawa Rikken Seinentō did indeed merge with similar groups in Toyama, Fukui, and Niigata, and in January 1925, a number of other groups joined this federation to form the Nihonkai Seinentō Remmei (Japan Sea Federation of Youth Parties) under Nagai's leadership. In his speech at the inauguration ceremonies of the new group, Nagai told its members that their "highest mission" was to act in concert with the other "new political forces" shortly to be enfranchised by universal suffrage in order to "bury the old Japan and to build the new."[19]

The vision of an alliance of reformist "youth" with the newly enfranchised masses was stimulated by the success of working-class parties in Europe during the early 1920's. Nagai was fond of encouraging his followers with the example of the Independent Labor Party in England, which had risen from humble beginnings under Keir Hardy to come to power under Ramsey MacDonald. But a more striking paradigm of success was the recent experience of the Italian Fascist Party, whose membership rose from 17,000 in 1919 to 4,500,000 three years later. Nagai clearly was fascinated with the achievements of Mussolini and his movement. In contrast to many left-wing and liberal commentators who denounced Mussolini as an "enemy of labor," Nagai regarded him as a political genius whose methods of political appeal showed the way working-class political movements would move in the future.

Nagai did not like everything about Mussolini, especially his

---

[18] Nagai Ryūtarō, "Minshū no yōkyū o taigen suru michi wa tada seinen minshūtō no sōzō aru nomi," *CK*, 37, no. 13: 65–74.
[19] Nagai Ryūtarō, *Nagai Ryūtarō-Shi daienzetsushū* (Tokyo, 1930), 2: 22–23, 44.

cavalier disregard for law and constitution, his high-handed treatment of the Italian parliament, and his overweening arrogance. Nor did he have any interest in the organizational panache of the Fascists. Unlike Nakano Seigō, another admirer of the European dictators, Nagai was far too committed to the parliamentary mechanism to propose building a black-shirt movement in Japan. Rather, he wanted to appropriate Mussolini's "spirit of leadership," his sensitivity to movements of mass opinion, and his political program to the reform of parliamentary politics in Japan. He felt that Mussolini had linked the two most important political impulses of the times to build popular support: the demand of the masses for equality of opportunity and economic stability, and the demand of the nation for a sense of its particular identity and purpose. By linking the cause of social democracy to a sense of "national mission" (as Nagai himself had), Mussolini appeared a far more accurate harbinger of the future than Wilson, the liberal hero, or Lenin, the hero of the radical left. Indeed, Nagai even went so far as to call Mussolini "the founder of a new stream of political thought."[20]

Perhaps inspired by the Italian example, from the late 1920's Nagai began to speak out for the need to organize a "nationalist mass party" which would build itself with the same kind of appeals as the Fascists. What he had in mind was a supraclass party able to attract genuine public support and public confidence by championing the causes of "national reconstruction" and the "national mission" rather than the interests of a special economic group.[21] Furthermore, he began to suggest that such "nationalistic mass parties" might emerge out of the matrix of conventional politics. Instead of building a movement from the grass-roots level, the "established parties" might be converted into a truly mass-based organization.

This shift in view, which indicated a cooling in his enthusiasm for the role of popular crusader, in part reflected the effects of

[20] Nagai Ryūtarō, *CK*, 37, no. 13:65–74; and *Nagai Ryūtarō-Shi kō-A yūben-shū*, (Tokyo, 1944), pp. 51–82.
[21] Matsumura, *Nagai*, pp. 302–307; Nagai Ryūtarō, *Watakushi no shinnen to taiken*, (Tokyo, 1938), pp. 281–290; Nagai Ryūtarō, "Minseitō wa kokkashugi taishūtō," *CK*, 43, no. 2: 75–77.

universal suffrage, or rather their absence. The extension of the franchise had failed to generate the alliance of "reformist" youth and the new voters he had anticipated, and the "proletarian parties" did not represent the common people so much as a left-wing minority. The masses had not risen to the occasion, and so one had to make do with the "established parties." But even more important, this shift in views was the result of Nagai's own growing involvement in the politics of the "established parties." In earlier days he had been a publicist on the fringes of politics, but as he gradually was absorbed into the political elite in the 1920's, he became more optimistic about changing it from within. Personal success bred a measure of tolerance for the conventional means of politics.[22]

Despite his early fulminations against the established parties, Nagai showed little hesitation to join one when the opportunity presented itself. After declining to run for a Diet seat in 1915, and after failing to win one in 1917, Nagai finally was successfully elected to the House of Representatives from his old home town, Kanazawa City, in 1920. Partly because of the reformist character of the Kenseikai (especially its advocacy of universal suffrage) and partly because of his long-standing association with Ōkuma and other Waseda men in the party, Nagai elected to enter the Kenseikai rather than the complaisant and powerful Seiyūkai which had just defeated the universal suffrage bill. Perhaps had he delayed his entry into politics for a decade or so, he might have found his way into the proletarian party movement, as many of the other "new liberals" did. (Indeed, he later commented—perhaps wistfully—that had Abe Isoo, one of his mentors at Waseda, gone into politics before him, he might have ended his career as a member of the Shakai Taishūtō.) But, as it was, he had little choice but to join an "established party," for it provided the only road to effective political action and political success in 1920.

Nagai's decision to enter the Kenseikai did not stifle his pungent and public criticism of the "established parties," nor his

[22] Nagai, *Watakushi no shinnen*, pp. 275–280; Matsumura, *Nagai*, p. 339 ff.

private contempt of many of his political bedfellows whom he regarded as mediocre, corrupt, and self-serving. Always a man of great moral earnestness, he remained a puritan in politics, and even a bit of a prig at heart. Although he did not hesitate to offer pork-barrel promises to local constituents, his political life was otherwise exceptionally fastidious. His personal popularity left him free of the need to build an electoral base by bribing voters or lavishly entertaining local "men of influence." With only modest campaign expenditures, he remained one of the top vote-getters in Ishikawa Prefecture until his death. Nor did he have to solicit what political funds he required, for enthusiastic supporters pressed money on him without being asked; even at the beginning of his career, he turned down a gratuitous offer of a villa for fear that strings might be attached. (Indeed, Nagai had such a strict notion of what was permissible for a man in public office that even when serving as cabinet minister he refused to let his son ride the train on his official ministerial railroad pass.) Furthermore, his personal puritanism—he rose every morning for a half-hour of Bible reading and private prayer—prevented him from getting involved in *machiai* politics or private scandal. Given these rigorous standards of personal behavior, it is not surprising that even when he had been in the political world for many years, he could not put off the feeling that it was like "a town where frauds and thieves and pickpockets gather."[23]

Nagai's refusal to succumb to private political vices and to accept the more unseemly folkways of his new profession did not impede his political career. The leaders of the Kenseikai and later the Minseitō—men like Katō Kōmei, Hamaguchi Yūkō, and Egi Yoku—were in many ways cut from the same mold. They also singled him out as a young man with promise from his first days in the Diet, when he won national fame for his ringing attack on Hara Kei as "the Lenin of the East." He was usually chosen to flay the government in interpellations or to

---

[23] Matsumura, *Nagai, passim.* Many details about Nagai's personality and private life were gotten from interviews with Nagai Michio, 12/14/1968, Azuma Shun'ei, 12/16/1968, and Matsumura Kenzō, 12/17/1968.

champion the party's position in Diet debates, and his popularity as a public speaker made him an asset in the campaigns of
party members less gifted than he in the art of public persuasion.
An open and genial man, who saved most of his passions and
pugnacity for his speeches, he also made few enemies within the
party.[24] Because he was uninterested in the competition for the
small rewards of party preference, he was able to stand above
the intraparty feuding that often cost ambitious young men
their careers. Consequently he was early tapped for positions
within the party, both when it was in power and when it was
out.

Nagai repaid this recognition of his talents with firm party
loyalty. Despite his continuing attacks on the political morality
of his fellows and his continuing interest in the "youth party"
movement in his own political bailiwick, he accepted the necessity of political action through the firm discipline of party
organization. He realized that, with the emergence of party
government and a two-party pattern in the Diet, working within
an "established party," no matter how lusterless many of its
members might be, was the best road to political success.
Throughout the 1920's, therefore, he stayed aloof from attempts
to form new reformist party groupings within the Diet, even if
they seemed to seek goals similar to his own. When a number of
the young "new liberals" in the Diet rallied around Inukai in
1923 to form the Kakushin Club, Nagai urged members of the
new party to disband and throw their votes to the Kenseikai instead. Working within an already established party, he felt, was
more likely to bring about "national reconstruction" through
universal suffrage and political democratization than organizing
new splinter groups. Similarily in 1927, when there were clan-
destine attempts to form a new party by certain young reformist
members of the Diet, Nagai abandoned it when it became clear
it would be only a minority faction.[25]

Party loyalty and political prudence paid off. By the early

[24] Baba Tsunego, *Seikai jimbutsu hyōron* (Tokyo, 1931), pp. 68–70.
[25] Nagai, *CK,* 37, no. 6: 115–126; Yamamura Kan'ichi, *Seijika yo doko e iku*
(Tokyo, 1929), pp. 402–412.

1930's, Nagai had risen to the top circle of the Minseitō leadership. Some even felt he might one day become its president. It was doubtless the feeling that his own personal future was linked closely with that of the party that led him to stick by the "established parties" in the face of "national emergency." When Adachi Kenzō and a number of Nagai's close political friends in the Minseitō bolted the party to form the Kokumin Dōmei (National People's League) in the wake of the Manchurian crisis and the October Incident in 1931, Nagai elected to stay on to work for political change within the party, a move he recommended to Adachi as well.

Nagai's own response to the growing national crisis was to preserve party control over the government through a coalition of the two major parties, which would leave political initiative in the hands of civilian politicians, yet create strong Diet support for a policy of domestic economic reform, national self-defense, and a strong foreign policy. He agreed to serve as colonial minister in Saitō Makoto's "national unity cabinet," which rested on a de facto coalition of the Seiyūkai and the Minseitō in the Diet. When moves were underway for a coalition of the parties in late 1933 and early 1934, Nagai again was active among those promoting the attempt.[26]

Rather interestingly, as evidence of his concern to reconcile his political tactics with a commitment to parliamentary institutions, he defended these actions by citing the experience of coalition cabinets in England during the First World War and later during the depression of 1929. There was no need to assume that "normal constitutional government" always required the alternation of political power between two parties, especially as majority party cabinets often were tempted to sacrifice the national interest to partisan concerns. The monopoly of power by one party encouraged it to perpetrate electoral abuses to preserve its Diet strength. Moreover, so long as there was an opposition party, no matter how small, a coalition government need not miss the healthy check of criticism in the Diet.[27]

[26] Matsumura, *Nagai*, pp. 293–300, 337–338.
[27] Nagai, *Watakushi no shinnen*, pp. 291–295.

At the same time, Nagai's confidence in the future of the established parties held firm through the crises of the 1930's when many were attracted to some form of antiparliamentarianism. Even as late as 1935, when the political parties were coming under attack from all directions, he wrote that the "existence of political parties" was "indispensable" to the "existence of the state." If there were no political parties, the government would attempt to win approval for its bills in the Diet through cajolery, bribery, or force, and political corruption would be far worse than it seemed to be at the time. Furthermore, it was only through political parties that the people were able to acquire an organized mode of debating and deciding national policy; without political parties, the people remained a formless throng unable to make their demands felt. The alternative to party politics was authoritarian rule, which eventually led either to violence against the rulers or complete stultification and subjection of the people.[28]

But by the late 1930's, especially after the dark year of 1936, there began to be a shift both in Nagai's mood and his political tactics. No longer did he speak so fervently of the need to defend party government or the conventional structure of party politics. To be sure, this reflected his growing sense of urgency about the fate of the nation, occasioned by the depression, Japan's deepening diplomatic isolation, and radical right-wing terrorism and violence. But these developments only served to catalyze the frustrations of a decade and a half in politics. For one, he no longer held out hope that the established parties could transform themselves into the kind of "nationalist mass party." They were too wedded to special interest groups, competing for the local economic advantage and struggling to control the local bureaucratic machinery in order to enhance their local power. He also began to see that the parties were not willing to bury the political ax in the interest of national unity. Whether because of policy differences or personal jealousy, the older party leaders were unwilling to make common cause to

[28] *Ibid.*, pp. 275–280; Nagai Ryūtarō, "Daisantō no muigi to yūigi," *CK*, 37, no. 6: 115.

preserve party control over the cabinet or to create unity on national policy. The tradition of party rivalry thwarted attempts at the kind of unionist or coalition politics Nagai had supported in the early 1930's. Although Nagai continued to remain a member of the Minseitō, occupying positions on its board of directors, he clearly felt that the declining effectiveness of the established parties to maintain a grip on political power or to deal with the pressing crises of the day called for a new type of political action.

Nagai therefore began to establish closer personal ties with extraparty political elements. His move in this direction was accelerated by the outbreak of the China War. Nagai welcomed the war as an opportunity for Japan to begin emancipating Asia from the grip of "Caucasian imperialism," but he knew that the outcome of the war would be decided not simply on the battlefield but on the home front as well. It would be necessary to rally the mass of the people behind the government, and at the same time to place the industrial resources of the economy under more rationalized control to avoid the wastefulness and inefficiency of free market competition.[29] This was a task for which the "established parties" were not equipped, and he began to throw his support to nonparty cabinets. Although he had decided not to join the Hayashi cabinet in 1936 on the grounds that it would mean "suicide" as a party politician, he readily agreed to hold the portfolios of postal minister and railroad minister under the first Konoe cabinet and then under the Abe cabinet. He used his position to help build the sinews of a "national defense" state, for example, by fighting through the passage of the Electrical Industries Control Bill, which placed more than six hundred private electrical companies under a system of unified national control.[30]

Nagai's participation in these nonparty cabinets not only reflected a weakening sense of party loyalty, but also eroded his relations with the Minseitō leadership, especially its president

[29] Nagai, *Watakushi no shinnen*, pp. 340–343; Nagai Ryūtarō, *Ajia saiken no gisen* (Tokyo, 1937), pp. 1–15.
[30] Matsumura, *Nagai*, pp. 357–424, 428–434.

Machida Chūji, who had hoped to become premier in 1937. But if Nagai found himself cut off more and more from the "established parties," he was by no means convinced that nonparty cabinets provided any great improvement in national leadership. Admittedly they were committed to "national interest" in a more obvious way, but resting as they did on alliances among civilian bureaucrats, the army, and the navy, they were plagued with the pull-and-haul of bureaucratic rather than economic "special interests." During the three years that followed the China incident, there had been five cabinets, all short-lived, weak, and rent by internal feuding. The uneasy compromise of non-party elites and the resulting lack of consistency in national policy indicated the continuing need for a "spirit of leadership" and a mode of political organization that would provide both popular support and national unity.[31]

For these reasons, coupled with his dwindling confidence in the "established parties," Nagai became active in the efforts to organize the "new political structure." In some ways, it marked a reversion to his old role as popular crusader. Indeed, the tone of his rhetoric in 1940 often recalled his earlier speeches to the Ishikawa Rikken Seinentō. Once again he was calling for a "second Restoration" to bring about the "reconstruction of Japan." But Nagai's years of working within the political establishment had not been without its effects, for it had muted and tempered the populist strain in him. The "national reconstruction movement" he was proposing in 1940 was not to be built from grassroots enthusiasm, but was to be a new national organization built from the top down. He was fully aware that access to power at the top of society was as important as participation at the bottom.

In its initial stages, the building of the "new political order" started as a project to organize a new political party around the leadership of Konoe Fumimaro. Nagai, who in earlier days had yearned for the appearance of a "politician who really governs with the people," perhaps thought he had finally found such a man in the "last of the Fujiwaras." Untainted by partisan en-

[31] Cf. Nagai's comments quoted in *ibid.*, p. 451.

tanglements, enjoying a reputation for "progressive views," and well connected with the *jūshin*, the military, and the parties, Konoe seemed in many ways the ideal man to stand above factional and party rivalry to lead the country through its time of crisis. Nagai had been one of his admirers since the mid–1920's, when his cooperation with the Katō government in 1925 helped to secure the passage of universal suffrage.

Nagai was involved in discussions of forming a Konoe-centered party in late 1936, but a concrete organizational effort did not get underway until the spring of 1940 on the initiative of Konoe's familiars, Arima Yoriyasu and Kazami Akira.[32] It had all the earmarks of the maneuverings which earlier had led to the formation of the "established parties." It was planned as a merger of disgruntled elements in the existing parties who sought to attach themselves to a powerful national political figure with access to the premiership. The new party was to be made up of the mainstream faction of the Seiyūkai, the Nagai and Sakurauchi factions of the Minseitō, and a number of small parliamentary splinter groups; the mainstream of the Minseitō and the Hatoyama faction of the Seiyūkai would be its opposition in the Diet. But when all the Diet parties voluntarily disbanded themselves in June and July of 1940, the plan to build a "new party" of the old style turned into a movement for an all-embracing political organization similar to a one-party state.

This alternative, however, was equally attractive to Nagai, who agreed with Konoe that the "new political structure" should be more than just a "clod of old political parties." It should provide organizational means to draw the masses into politics. In the long run he had in mind a national organization that would stretch down to every factory and hamlet, absorbing "leadership elements" and "progressive elements" from every strata of the people.

But first it was necessary to set up a "core body" around which this national organization could coalesce. Therefore the immedi-

---

[32] Details on these discussions may be found in Arima, *Seikai dōchūki*, pp. 117–118, 180–211; Kazami Akira, *Konoe naikaku*, (Tokyo, 1951), pp. 197–226; Kiya Ikusaburō, *Konoe-Kō hibun*, (Tokyo, 1950), pp. 39–60.

ate task was to bring together a "union of like-minded men" (*dōshiteki dantai*), comprised of progressive elements both within the Diet and without, which would act as a "propelling force" behind the eventual organization of the whole people. This core body, and the national organization which would emerge from it, was not to be an elitist group, nor simply an instrument for transmitting government orders to the people. Rather it was to serve as political broker between government and people—on the one hand, assuring that the "will of the people" was properly reflected in the formulation of national policy, and on the other hand, sharing with the government the "task of political leadership."[33] In short, Nagai was suggesting a political organization based on a kind of "democratic centralism."

In Nagai's view, this type of organization would have considerable advantages over the liberal model of "popular government." By eliminating political competion among partisan factions or parties, it would permit great national unity of purpose; by harmonizing the relationship between government and party, it would avoid the difficulties of chronic political instability which made long-range planning difficult; by being above class, it would eliminate the debilitating effects of internal political conflicts that arose when a political system encouraged particular social groups or classes to pursue separate interests. In short, Nagai felt that he had discovered a mechanism which would permit popular participation in politics and at the same time eliminate the divisive effects of party competition, factional struggle, or class conflict.

It is significant that Nagai believed that similar strong unified political systems had emerged not only in one-party states like Italy, Germany, and the Soviet Union, but also in the Western democracies where nearly dictatorial powers were exercised by the cabinet in England and the president in the United States. Unwilling to see the world locked in the struggle of "totalitarian-

---

[33] For Nagai's views on the character of the "new political structure," see Matsumura, *Nagai*, pp. 435–455. Nagai's comments in the discussions of the committee formed to organize the "new political structure" are to be found in Shimonaka Yasaburō, ed., *Yokusan kokumin undō shi*, (Tokyo, 1954), pp. 97–101, 110–111.

ism" against "democracy," Nagai instead saw it in the grip of a "world revolution" marked by the "liquidation of prewar liberal political systems" and "the establishment of new political systems which assume that the state and the people are bound in an inseparable relationship."[34]

Ironically, however, what finally emerged from the movement to establish a "new political order" was not a "core body" of the kind Nagai had envisaged, but rather the Imperial Rule Assistance Association. This was not a "union of like-minded men" but a catch-all political organization that drew into its ranks every shade of political opinion, from the veterans of the Shakai Taishutō to alumni of the Cherry Blossom Society. As a result, any effort at effective political action was stymied by its comprehensiveness, for beneath the holistic façade partisan conflict continued as usual. Nor was the new organization ever to have a chance to develop even a modicum of "democratic centralism," for from the beginning its functions were limited to assisting the government in policy research and in enforcement of government orders. It therefore was never able to act as a key element in the national decision-making process as Nagai had hoped it would. Whatever misgivings Nagai may have had about the final shape of the organization, he remained with it until his death from cancer as American fire-bomb raids were beginning at the end of 1944.

Was Nagai a political "convert" (*tenkōsha*)? It hardly seems useful to raise the question, for it implies that Nagai betrayed a clear-cut and deeply reasoned ideological commitment. Although this approach has much to commend it when applied to the Communists and other left radicals who made open recantations of their political faith in the early 1930's, it does not provide a satisfying framework of analysis in the case of men like Nagai, whose political experience was too enmeshed in practical affairs to admit of a precise assessment of the role ideology

---

[34] Nagai had pursued such arguments as early as 1933; for example, see Nagai Ryūtarō, "Kokka hijōji ni chokumen," *CK*, 48, no. 1: 44–47. See also Matsumura, *Nagai*, pp. 459–463; Nagai, *Kō-A yūbenshū*, pp. 301 ff.

played in their actions. Nagai's political attitudes were in any event too loose and ambiguous to be thought of as an "ism" which could be defected from. On the contrary, most of his fundamental political impulses were sufficiently vague to be compatible with a variety of policy positions. The cry for the "emancipation" of Asia, for example, was as easily squared with war against the Kuomintang government as it was with the policy of noninterference in China's domestic affairs during the 1920's—provided, of course, that like Nagai one regarded Chiang Kai-shek not as the heir of Sun Yat-sen but as a cat's paw of "Caucasian imperialism" and a traitor to the aspirations of the Chinese people. Needless to say, such a radical shift in policy had profound practical implications—and one can hardly deny the importance of these—but perhaps it is equally important to stress the emotional consistency that lay behind the logical contradictions.

Neither does it seem very useful to apply to Nagai's career the conventional vocabulary of Western political experience during the 1920's and 1930's—"democracy," "fascism," "totalitarianism," and the like—for this involves a misreading of Nagai's own perception of the issues facing Japan during this period. For him, the key problem was not the institutional question of "democracy" versus "fascism" or "totalitarianism" (though many liberal and left writers of the early 1930's phrased the problem this way), but the more fundamental political question of "change" versus "stagnation." The legitimacy of particular institutional forms, though not without importance, assumed a less critical concern in Nagai's mind than the need to find solutions to the pressing "dilemmas of growth" that Japan had been facing since the late Meiji period—the lack of a dynamic and decisive national leadership, the social tensions produced by a free market economy and a laissez-faire social policy, the mediocrity and corruption of Diet politics, and the absence of clear-cut national goals. Throughout his career this kind of problem ultimately engaged him more thoroughly than a commitment to the idealized models of the "classic" political liberalism many of the older generation of Japanese liberals adhered to.

Although he began his career believing that political democracy, social reform, and the national mission could be achieved within the conventional framework of Diet politics, he also was susceptible to experimentation within that framework. He never felt that it was possible to make a facile equation between "party rule" and "popular government" or even good government, nor was he convinced that the "established parties" constituted the only necessary vehicle for political action. On the contrary, he remained profoundly ambivalent toward the practice of party politics in Japan. Because he could see that there were alternative patterns to the "whig" model of popular government emerging in the West—whether in the form of the "three-party system," the mass movements of men like Mussolini (and later Hitler), the coalition politics of the British parties, or the expansion of presidential power in the United States—he was willing to attempt any political tactic he could justify to himself (and others) as in some sense achieving the goal of reform. If he could view men like Hitler and Mussolini as "true party politicians," it is unlikely that he saw any fundamental contradiction between his role in the movements of the 1920's and his role in organizing the "new political order" in 1940. Indeed, the later effort really flowed from the earlier one, albeit modified by his experience in the intervening years. In both cases, he was trying to overcome the contradiction between the myths which justified representative parliamentary institutions and the way they really worked.

It should be emphasized, however, that there was nothing inevitable about Nagai's progress from the politics of *minponshugi* to the politics of the *shintaisei*. After all, many whose political views were not very different from Nagai's in the 1910's and early 1920's followed quite different paths out of "Taishō democracy"—some like Ōyama Ikuo going into the proletarian party movement (and later exile), some like Yoshino Sakuzō shifting to an apolitical stance, and others like Nakano Seigō donning the black shirt. But even Nagai's original decision to cast his political fortunes with an "established party" did not automatically pave his way to the "new political order." It is conceivable that if the China incident had not occurred, or had it been settled quickly, he might have remained firmly committed to the "established parties," hoping to reform them from within during the late 1930's, as he had tried to earlier in the decade. But a growing feeling that Japan was facing a moment of national crisis and national opportunity unparalleled since the Meiji Restoration served to catalyze his accumulated political frustrations, and as the flow of events battered down the dikes of conventional politics, it is not surprising that Nagai tried to find some new vessel to ride the flood.

AKUTAGAWA RYŪNOSUKE
AND THE NEGATIVE IDEAL

Howard S. Hibbett

The death of Akutagawa Ryūnosuke (1892–1927) has remained such a vivid memory for the Japanese that over forty years later, in 1968, the happy event of the award of the Nobel Prize for Literature to Kawabata Yasunari was hailed as the biggest news from the *bundan* (the literary world) since Akutagawa's suicide. For Western readers, to whom he is best known as "the author of *Rashōmon*" (the macabre little story that was not quite the source of Kurosawa's celebrated motion picture of the same name), Akutagawa Ryūnosuke is merely the signature identifying a body of exotic, misanthropic work. Unfortunately, the ironist and superb stylist has thus far had an ironic fate abroad: He has been the most amply translated of modern Japanese writers, yet his work has been sadly diminished both by the hazards of translation and by the loss of a rich extraliterary context. But in Japan Akutagawa is still not only one of the most widely read authors of this century, but a man of legendary suffering whose personal life seems to have an inexhaustible if somewhat morbid fascination for his readers.

Moreover, Akutagawa's death has been interpreted as an event of broad historical significance. For example, the critic Nakamura Mitsuo declares, "His suicide was as significant as that of General Nogi, whom he disliked, for it too marked the end of an era."[1] Nakamura goes on to discuss Akutagawa's awareness of social change, of the "moral vacuum" of Taishō life, and of the feverish efforts of intellectuals to fill that void, chiefly by faith in salvation through Marxism. The failure of their "new

[1] *Nihon no kindai shōsetsu*, rev. ed. (Iwanami shoten, 1964), pp. 205–206.

morality" was to be one of the earlier lessons of the Shōwa era, and a sense of hopeless frustration soon became the prevailing mood among intellectuals. "Akutagawa, having perhaps a clearer premonition of what was to come than any of his contemporaries, said that he chose suicide because of a 'vague anxiety' over it" (10:343).[2]

This explanation for Akutagawa's suicide—and for his pervasive anxiety—continues to be stressed in critical and biographical writing about him. Even carefully qualified formulations tend to conclude with the symbolic role of Akutagawa as a martyr to his times. Thus Yamamoto Kenkichi, after acknowledging the difficulty of the problem, singles out a socially induced anxiety for explicit mention: "Why he committed suicide cannot be explained briefly because of the complexity of reasons. One may be permitted, however, to count as one of them his uneasiness as an intellectual who sensitively reacted to the tide of the days when social contradictions had become more and more conspicuous and the movements of the working classes gradually became intensified."[3] As the reiteration of such views suggests, Akutagawa's suicide has had a considerable influence on the self-image of the Japanese intellectual, the painfully conscious victim of post-Meiji history. To be sure, this kind of self-image had emerged even earlier, and may itself be counted as one of the reasons for Akutagawa's despair. A search for the real Akutagawa

[2] Parenthetical references throughout this paper are to *Akutagawa Ryūnosuke zenshū*, 11 vols. (Kadokawa shoten, 1967–1969), volume: page number only. This is the latest, though not in every respect the most complete, edition of the collected works. Two useful earlier editions of the same title are the more fully annotated and indexed one published by Chikuma shobō (8 vols., 1964–1965) and the latest of the Iwanami shoten editions (19 vols., 1954–1955). These collections should be supplemented by Kuzumaki Yoshitoshi, ed., *Akutagawa Ryūnosuke miteikōshū* (Iwanami shoten, 1968). For a convenient bibliographical guide to Akutagawa, see *Kindai bungaku kenkyū hikkei* (Gakutōsha, 1961), pp. 246–252. The most detailed biographical study is Morimoto Osamu, *Akutagawa Ryūnosuke denki ronkō* (Meiji shoin, 1964); but on Akutagawa's personality, see also Shiozaki Yoshio, *Sōseki, Ryūnosuke no seishin ijō* (Hakuyōsha, 1957) and two forthcoming studies: George DeVos and Hiroshi Wagatsuma, "Alienation and the Author," and Iwai Hiroshi, *Akutagawa Ryūnosuke* (*Patografi sōsho*, Kingō shuppan shinsha).

[3] "Characteristics of the Literature of the Shōwa Period," *Japan P.E.N. News*, 5:2 (1960).

—a desperately unhappy man but a man of impressive artistic accomplishments—will inevitably lead to the labyrinthine inter-relations among his actual life history, the legacy of his art, and a legend that seems as seductive as ever in present-day Japan.

For the younger generation in particular, Akutagawa epitomizes the attraction of the dazzling failure. Like Dazai Osamu, among others, he offers what might be called a negative ideal: that of the sensitive, brilliant young man who suffers from the oppressions of his family, his class, and his times, who struggles to create art, but whose despair finally leads to suicide. He represents a well-established, widely admired attitude, one reinforced by strong cultural traditions. His appeal for Japanese readers is enhanced by a cultural emphasis on identification with others, especially with the victims of heroic defeat; and there was already available to Akutagawa himself an abundance of striking models for negative choices, not least of suicide, many of which have remained attractive to succeeding generations.

But Akutagawa's life history also illustrates the concept of a socially unacceptable negative identity: "an identity perversely based on all those identifications and roles which, at critical stages of development, had been presented to the individual as most undesirable or dangerous, and yet also as most real."[4] For the understanding of his works as well as his life, it is necessary to take into account certain crucial psychological factors, usually either ignored or attributed wholly to hereditary or social influences. Akutagawa's enigmatic personality was expressed only obliquely in his writings, through an elaborately varied poetic vision of human frailty and suffering. It is difficult enough to grasp the reality of the man behind the literary masks or pictured in the famous photographs: the lean young aesthete with piercing eyes and a hint of a sardonic smile; the haggard, haunted figure of the later years; or, shortly before his suicide, the death's-head portrait clipped from a publicity film at the point where, pausing from agitated play with his children, he stares balefully into the camera, his anguished face shadowed

[4] Erik H. Erikson, "The Problem of Ego Identity," *Psychological Issues*, 1, no. 1: 131.

by a broad-brimmed sun hat, and puffs clouds of Mephisto-phelean smoke from his drooping cigarette. Again, there is the mystery of how Akutagawa's extraordinary strengths and weaknesses were fused in the service of artistic creativity. These problems hardly lend themselves to clear-cut solutions. But they lie behind any attempt to illuminate the relationship between the facts of his personal history and the wider implications of his life and work.

Akutagawa Ryūnosuke was born March 1, 1892, in the Tsukiji district of Tokyo, not far from the harbor. Tsukiji was still largely a foreign settlement—there were only two other Japanese households, according to his sister—though past its heyday as a center for the exotic crinoline and red-brick fashions of the Enlightenment. The name Akutagawa was that of his mother's family, who reared him; it became his legal surname only after his formal adoption by them some twelve years later. His father Niibara Toshizō had established a successful dairy business, an appropriate field for an enlightened Meiji entrepreneur, and gave his first son, after two daughters, the auspicious name of Ryūnosuke, signifying that he was born in the Year, Month, Day, and, if Akutagawa's own statement is not poetic license, even the Hour (around 8:00 A.M.) of the Dragon (10:351). As a further precaution, because both father and mother were at traditionally ill-omened ages, the baby was immediately protected by the old ritual of abandonment and recovery through a family friend —in this case, Matsumura Senjirō, the manager of one of the branch dairy shops.

Shortly after this formality, by which Ryūnosuke technically became a foundling, there occurred the most critical event of his early life, the source of one of the deepest fears that led eventually to his suicide. (One of his many aphorisms was to be "The first act of the human tragedy starts when an individual becomes the child of certain parents" [10:258]). On October 26, not quite eight months after she had given birth, his mother Fuku "suddenly went insane" (11:433). Thereafter, until her death ten years later, she apparently remained "a very quiet psychotic," as Akutagawa described her in his late essay "Tenki-bo" ("Necrology," 1926) (9:38). No doubt her overt madness began with a grave turn in a postpartum psychosis which earlier it had been possible to overlook. Among her more immediate reasons for being despondent was the death in 1891 of their first child, a six-year-old daughter, for which she felt guilty because the girl's illness had developed from a cold caught when they were on an outing together. Then there were the superstitious fears surrounding Ryūnosuke's birth, as well as the frustrations of a naturally timid and inarticulate woman whose enterprising husband was inclined, in the time-honored manner, to seek his pleasures elsewhere. Indeed, Toshizō is said to have had an illegitimate child by another woman in the same year that Ryū-nosuke was born. There is also a theory, based on some irregularities in the birth records, that Ryūnosuke himself was the illegitimate son of his mother's younger sister and Toshizō.

Akutagawa's reminiscences of his father mention the irascibility that was the only quality friends said they had in common. Niibara Toshizō's eventful career had begun when he left his provincial home—he came from a well-to-do family of farmers under the Mōri in Yamaguchi—and took part in the campaign to overthrow the Tokugawa regime. A few years after the Meiji Restoration he worked on a dairy farm south of Tokyo, and in 1883 opened his own establishment in Tsukiji. By the end of the next decade he had another dairy plant and grazing yard in the village of Shinjuku, on the northeastern outskirts of Tokyo, as well as a number of retail shops in other parts of the city. Though commoners, his ancestors belonged to a family which by hereditary right provided the village headman and which had included a scholar of Chinese in his grandfather's generation. Newly prosperous in the difficult years after the Restoration, the Niibara family, headed by Toshizō, was qualified for a link by marriage with the Akutagawa family, whose minor samurai status had been abolished along with their hereditary position as tea masters and cultural arbiters to the shogun. In an early photograph Toshizō is seen as a sturdy, determined-looking young man in formal kimono, his bowler hat on the table beside him. By contrast, a middle-aged picture of Akutagawa Michiaki, whose sister Toshizō married, shows a balding, plump, bespectacled gentleman in sober Victorian attire suitable to his station as a minor official in the Public Works Department of the Tokyo metropolitan government.

Michiaki was the head of the Akutagawa household, and therefore responsible for the marriage of his younger sister Fuku to Toshizō. After Fuku became insane, it was agreed that Ryūnosuke should be taken to live with Michiaki and his wife, whose only child had died, in their home beyond the Sumida River in the old Honjo district of the city. In fact, it was Michiaki's unmarried elder sister Fuki who had most to do with bringing Ryūnosuke up, and who was closest to him, if not always on the best of terms.

Growing up in the care of a spinster aunt old enough to be his grandmother, Akutagawa Ryūnosuke had the lonely privileges of the sole child in a small, middle-aged family of illustrious ancestry but declining fortunes. Some sixteen generations of forebears in service with the Tokugawa shoguns were claimed, ending with his grandfather who had remained a close attendant of the last shogun until the collapse of the Bakufu, and who is said to have been among those receiving the emperor's forces at the main gate when they entered Edo Castle. After that the Akutagawa family had subsided into genteel poverty, though Michiaki was able—at least until his business ventures after retirement—to maintain the dignity of a minor city official. But the strain of keeping up middle-class appearances helped to make Ryūnosuke acutely sensitive to his social status, his surroundings, and the polite deceit that he found in himself as well as in others.

Meanwhile, Fuyu, the youngest of the Akutagawa sisters (besides Fuki, Fuku, and Fuyu, there had been Fuji and Fumi, both now dead), had gone to Tsukiji to help in Toshizō's household. The ménage could not have been a comfortable one. Ryūnosuke's young aunt was to share the house with her mad sister, the quiet psychotic upstairs,for over a decade. In 1899, she had a child by Toshizō, and in the summer of 1904, a year and a half after her sister's death, legal matters were at last set in order by her marriage to Toshizō and Ryūnosuke's formal adoption into the Akutagawa family. This acknowledgment of the status quo probably made no great difference to him. At twelve, he had long since developed powerful feelings of shame and guilt, of self-doubt and doubt toward others. He had spent his childhood caught in a complicated double web of family relationships, each centered on a woman who had taken the place of his tragically blighted mother. Nothing could eradicate the distrust that was the deepest stratum of his personality.

Neither his younger half-brother Tokuji nor his three-year older sister Hisako seems to have been among Ryūnosuke's favorite playmates, nor were they ever mentioned affectionately in his writings. However, he continued visiting the Niibara household in the Shiba district, to which Toshizō had shifted his home and business in 1893. Apparently Toshizō regretted his decision to give up his son and, like Natsume Sōseki's foster father, tried repeatedly to ingratiate himself and cultivate a sound —and useful—filial relation. A model son, except for a certain "necessary" deviousness, Ryūnosuke was a brilliant student from the beginning of his school years, early demonstrating the promise of success that must have appealed to his success-minded father Toshizō. From about the time he entered elementary school at the age of six, he received private instruction in calligraphy, classical Chinese, and English. He was soon an obsessive reader, with a special taste for Edo and Meiji fiction.

Under the Westernized educational regime of the Third Middle School, of which he was to have prisonlike memories, Ryūnosuke began his voracious reading of European literature by way of English translation. Ibsen, Turgenev, Mérimée, and Anatole France were among his early favorites, helpful alike in illuminating the hidden emotions of people around him and in strengthening his lifelong defenses against vulgarians (such as his aggressive father) and against his own deep-seated feelings of physical and moral inferiority. Although he appears to have acquitted himself satisfactorily in the usual school sports and military exercises, even attaining the rank of captain in school drills, Ryūnosuke was a shy, thin boy who regarded himself as constitutionally inferior and had in fact been delayed a year in entering middle school because of a certain undefined ill health. But there is no doubt of his scorn for such traditional samurai arts as *kendō*, nor of his compensatory assertion of intellectual superiority. In later school years this unendearing trait became an essential element in his friendships, which, except for transient episodes of adolescent homosexual attachment, were fastidiously chosen on what he believed to be a purely intellectual basis. But his lofty arguments with schoolboy friends seemed to fulfill a need to dominate, or be dominated. The spirit of free intellectual antagonism was animated by strongly ambivalent emotions toward the narcissistic objects of his affection.

In 1910, at eighteen, Ryūnosuke was able to enter the First Higher School without examination, because of a new policy recognizing an excellent record at a middle school which was itself one of the best in Tokyo. That autumn the Akutagawa family gave up its house in Honjo and moved into a smaller one rented from Niibara Toshizō and standing in a corner of his Shinjuku dairy grounds. Ryūnosuke's three years at higher school seem to have been comparatively happy, although during the second year he lived in the school dormitory, which he disliked intensely. The marathon arguments of these years ("Whitman, free verse, creative evolution—the battlefields seemed limitless") were at once his chief pleasure, along with the reading that paralleled them, and an indispensable training for his hazy but proud intellectual ambitions (8:90–91). Although he had planned from the first to major in English literature, his interests at this time appear to have been more philosophical than literary, reflecting those of his friend Tsunetō Kyō—a classmate but four years his senior—and the current intellectual fashion of the "philosophical youth." Kant, Bergson, and Nishida Kitarō were favorite subjects of debate, though he also read Schopenhauer and Nietzsche, both very much to his taste, as well as the daring *fin de siècle* European poetry, drama, and fiction that was the rage in advanced literary circles. However, there is no indication that he shared his schoolmates' concern over the Kōtoku

Shūsui incident of 1910–1911, nor that he received the news of General Nogi's suicide with anything other than the cynicism later expressed in "Shōgun" ("The General," 1922). As for the Emperor Meiji, Ryūnosuke wrote to a friend that even he had been momentarily touched by his sister's tearful account of three little schoolchildren bowing for half an hour before the palace to pray for the emperor's recovery, and that, when he had picked up the black-bordered extra announcing the death, he felt a twinge of regret at having decided not to go down to the palace gate himself (1:269).

Shortly before his death Akutagawa Ryūnosuke composed an autobiographical mosaic of fifty-one linked sketches entitled *Aru ahō no isshō* (*A Fool's Life*, 1927): evocations of moods, impressions, or symbolic incidents, which reveal ominous memories of his past adult life—and the fragments he had shored against his ruins. Significantly, the first of these, "Jidai" ("The Age"), is a vision of himself at nineteen browsing through the European literary works ranged on the second-floor shelves of Maruzen bookstore. Thanks to the foreign ladder, he stands above the shabby throng of his countrymen and among the masters who had helped him to escape from the limitations of his own time and place. But in the second episode, "Haha" ("Mother"), a visit to a mental hospital reminds him of the menace of the past. Then he is seen in the stifling atmosphere of home and family, gasping for breath in his close love-hate relationship with his aunt Fuki. "Over and over he asked himself whether people who loved each other always made each other suffer" (10:164).

School friends played an increasingly important role in his life, although Tsunetō, his closest friend, chose to study law at the Imperial University in Kyoto, and Akutagawa followed the exemplary course by proceeding to the Tokyo Imperial University. In September 1913, he entered the English Department, where he maintained his reputation as a gifted student, partly by his continual absence from classes, and eventually completed a thesis on William Morris. He was graduated from the university on schedule in 1916, at the age of twenty-four, having meanwhile devoted most of his energies to literary activities, to the pleasures of gallery-and concert-going, and to other innocent forms of hedonism encouraged by the freedom of university life. In February 1914, with Kume Masao, Kikuchi Kan, and a few other coterie members, most of whom he had known since higher school days, he revived a student literary magazine called *Shinshichō* (*The New Tide*), which had already made history in its two earlier brief but noteworthy lives. Unlike Tanizaki Jun'ichirō, whose stories had appeared in the second series of *The New Tide* in 1910, Akutagawa did not attract public attention with these first works, nor did he leave the university to become a professional writer. But he discovered his vocation, and began the steady stream of writing that flowed beyond the third and fourth *New Tide* until his death thirteen years later.

Akutagawa's contribution to the first issue of the 1914 *New Tide* was a translation—from the English—of Anatole France's *Balthazar,* an ironically flavored tale of one of the Wise Men of the East. From this he turned to the similarly congenial *Celtic Twilight* of Yeats, of which he introduced several ghostly fragments. These translations were examples of what he found in Western writing to satisfy his taste for rich prose and for "mysterious stories" such as he had mentioned (with the adjective "MYSTERIOUS" in English) in letters to several friends the summer before, asking them to send him any they happened to run across (1:266, 270). Later in 1914, he translated bits of Gautier and Voltaire for *The New Tide.* He also began contributing to a poetry magazine: first a flowery essay on the Sumida River, full of romantic longings, literary associations, and images of death, and then a suite of twelve *tanka* called "Kyakuchū koi" ("Thoughts of Love while Traveling"). These poems seem to have been inspired by Akutagawa's "first love," Yoshida Yayoi, a niece of Matsumura Senjirō, his ceremonial foster father. Neither the girl nor his own family offered any encouragement, and one of Akutagawa's letters to Tsunetō comments wryly that his dreams of love are "entirely safe . . . for (1) girls are too vain, and (2) society is too fond of gossip"

(1:323). Youthful feelings of *Weltschmerz* are the subject of his first play, the one-act historical drama "Seinen to shi to" ("Youth and Death"), in the September *New Tide*. The barely recognizable plot was taken from the vast eleventh-century collection *Konjaku monogatari* (*Tales New and Old*), the literary merit of which Akutagawa was the earliest to recognize; but the manner was in the then fashionable vein of Maeterlinck. Meanwhile, the May issue had carried "Rōnen" ("Old Age"), an altogether polished and characteristic work, the first of his more than one hundred and fifty short stories.

The indignities of the aged proved to be a more sympathetic theme for Akutagawa than the suffering of the young. In his second story, "Hyottoko" ("The Comic Mask," 1915), a humiliating old age is cut off—as in "Rashōmon"—by sudden death. Mockery, ridicule, and distrust, not without an underlying pity, set the tone of all his early stories. From the first, the "author of *Rashōmon*" demonstrated not only stylistic finesse but a taste for scenes of degradation, and for bitter comedy at the expense of the grotesque and ugly.

In October 1914, Akutagawa and his family moved to a new, somewhat more spacious house in the quiet wooded suburb of Tabata, beyond the university. Except for a few years while he was teaching away from Tokyo, the Tabata house remained his home for the rest of his life. By October, the third *New Tide* also had expired, after eight issues, and Akutagawa and his friends had to find other outlets for their work until February 1916, when money from a joint translation of Rolland's *Vie de Tolstoi* enabled them to revive it once again. Thus the later famous "Rashōmon" appeared in the November 1915 issue of *Teikoku bungaku,* though it attracted hardly any critical attention. Of more immediate importance to his career was the fact that in the following month he was introduced by an old school friend to Sōseki's informal Thursday Club (Mokuyōkai) of friends and protégés who gathered once a week at his home.

That Akutagawa was impressed by Sōseki—not least by his outward assurance and sheer physical presence—was made very clear in his recollection of their meeting. "When I visited him

for the first time, I completely froze. Even now I have not altogether recovered from that mental sclerosis. And it was not just
ordinary embarrassment. . . . The fact is, I was confronted by
such a superior physique that a skinny fellow like me could not
help feeling oppressed, the way I feel at a medical examination"
(3:278). Later visits had their tense moments, too. Once Sōseki
told him to fetch a cigarette and, when the embarrassed Akutagawa was unable to find the box, gestured "fiercely" toward it
with his chin, as he went on talking to someone else (9:223).
Yet Sōseki's support, such as his letter praising "Hana" ("The
Nose," 1916) meant a great deal to him. (In addition to reas-
surance and cool praise, Sōseki gave him pointed criticism from
time to time—he once commented in English that a story was
"too laboured"—or simply advised him to continue working hard
[1:397].) Akutagawa became such a favorite that he was later
considered the logical candidate for marriage to Fudeko, the
eldest of the Natsume daughters. He was deeply moved by the
death of Sōseki in December 1916, and wrote in a letter, "I have
never known such sorrow. . . . I feel everything has become
desolate" (2:329).

By the end of 1916, Akutagawa had seen "The Nose" reprinted
in *Shinshōsetsu,* a major literary magazine, had fulfilled his first
request from an editor and received his first royalty payment,
and had published seventeen more stories, almost all of which
took their subjects from the past. But royalties were miniscule,
less than one yen a manuscript page, and Akutagawa's highly
wrought stories were seldom more than twenty or thirty pages
long. After his graduation from the university in July, he had
enrolled as a graduate student, though this status soon lapsed;
and on the first of December, commuting by train from lodgings
next to a washing-machine shop in Kamakura, he began teaching English (for sixty yen a month) at the naval engineering
academy at Yokosuka. Within the month Sōseki had died, and
talk of Akutagawa as the leading candidate for the hand of
Natsume Fudeko was ended by his formal engagement to Tsukamoto Fumiko, the sixteen-year-old daughter of a naval lieuten-

ant commander lost at sea when his ship was sunk by a mine off Port Arthur during the Russo-Japanese War.

As a recognized though ill-paid rising young author, Akutagawa followed Sōseki's advice to go on writing his elegant, mordant historical tales, advice all the more welcome since he had planned to do so in any case. But the variety of his subjects, sources, and methods is considerable, as if he felt obliged to try on one mask after another at the same time that he worked to enlarge his repertory of techniques. The most ambitious of his early stories was "Imogayu" ("Yam Gruel"), written on request for *Shinshōsetsu*. Again, a grotesquely exaggerated anecdote is worked out in deliberately revolting detail: The lowly samurai Goi ("fifth rank") is the butt of a series of jokes (including the sadistic trick of replacing his *sake* with urine), culminating in the effort of the cruel, physically and magically powerful warrior Toshihito to force on him an immense quantity of "a gruel made of sliced yams boiled in a broth of sweet arrowroot" (1.77). Goi had longed to gorge himself on the delicacy, but he loses his appetite from the fear and humiliation accompanying the promise of fulfillment of this humble ambition.

Akutagawa's mastery of this kind of story was by now apparent, even to his few unfriendly critics. (It was only later that "Yam Gruel" was interpreted as an anti-Marxist effort to persuade the poor to remain content with their lot.) But he also wrote some excellent stories with a contemporary Japanese setting, the finest of which was "Hankechi" ("Handkerchief," 1916), a character study casting an unflattering light on Nitobe Inazō, who had been principal of the First Higher School while he was a student there.

Akutagawa's first collection of short stories, entitled *Rashōmon*, was published in May of 1917, an event celebrated in late June by an elaborate dinner at a Nihombashi restaurant. A photograph shows some two dozen guests around a long table decorated with roses and sweetpeas; among those present is Tanizaki, in a natty double-breasted white suit, seated conspicuously in the place of honor across from Akutagawa. The book was so successful that a publisher produced a second volume of collected stories only half a year later. One of the more interesting of these was "Futatsu no tegami" ("Two Letters," 1917), a story about a psychologist who insists he is sane but keeps on meeting his *Doppelgänger*. It is Akutagawa's earliest account of a kind of madness that emerges as a major motif of his late works, and that he once said he himself had experienced.[5]

One of Akutagawa's most tranquil and productive periods was the year or so following his marriage to Tsukamoto Fumiko in February 1918. Fumiko was eight years younger, a pretty, round-faced girl of eighteen, still attending school. Akutagawa's many early letters to her are full of an affectionate tenderness suggesting his feelings toward his dead little sister rather than the dutiful politeness of a young man fulfilling his obligations to his family. But his more passionate concern seems to have been directed toward his writing, his reading, and his increasing circle of literary friends. Among the latter were several women whom he was later to describe, with characteristic egocentricity, as a source of intense pain in his life. And there was his aunt Fuki, who came to live with them and whose influence far outshadowed that of his young bride. Another shadow can be seen in Akutagawa's letters mentioning occasional worsening "neurasthenia" (*shinkei suijaku*). He had long suffered from depression and hypochondria; and in November, during an attack of influenza, he wrote a *haiku* ("A last look back—at the mountain village glowing with chrysanthemums in the fine autumn weather") as a "death verse" (3:358).

Akutagawa caught the flu again a few months later, during the spring epidemic in which his father Niibara Toshizō died. The account in "Necrology" is tinged with unexpected emotion, after the bitterness of his childhood memories. He seems to reveal a sense of guilt toward the father whose belated advances he had rejected, and whose authority and physical presence had helped to reinforce his awe of Sōseki. Also, like the narrator of

[5] *Akutagawa Ryūnosuke miteikōshū*, p. 431.

438

Kokoro, he must have felt guilty over his affinity to Sōseki as a moral and intellectual mentor, whose death he had profoundly mourned, in contrast to his feeling of distance from his actual father.

Akutagawa's first experience of the death of a close relative had come at ten, when his mother succumbed "probably more from emaciation than illness" (9:38). By the time he wrote "Necrology," he seems to have become aware of his own mixed feelings, always difficult for him to express, toward this ashen-faced, once beautiful woman who had haunted his childhood like a storybook ghost—and who indeed had the traditional justification for returning after death as the vengeful spirit of a jealous woman. Though divided from her by the gulf of madness, he felt a close identification with her, not least as sharing the same fatal weakness, and a corresponding difference from his vigorous father.

In April 1919, Akutagawa resigned his position at the naval engineering academy (and abandoned hope of a possible professorship at Keiō University) to become a full-fledged professional writer. He signed "a single piece of yellow paper"—a contract later bitterly regretted—to publish his newspaper work entirely in the *Osaka Mainichi* (10:169). His mock-patriotic statement that he had resigned as his contribution to strengthening the navy was prudently withheld by his new employer. However, he now had the freedom to devote all his time to literature, and returned with his wife and aunt to take up residence once again with his foster parents in Tabata. His second-floor study was called "Demon's Lair" ("Gakikutsu"), after his adopted *haiku* name of Gaki ("Hungry Demon" or "Devil of the Self"); there, on Sundays, after the fashion of Sōseki's Thursday Club, he held open house for the young writers and artists who were his friends.

By his late twenties Akutagawa had achieved fame, an impressive body of work, and the flattering conviction that he thoroughly understood himself. His assault on perfection seemed to be progressing satisfactorily, by his chosen means. Although he had tired of the shallow "rose-petal scented skepticism" of

Anatole France, he had only strengthened his defenses against his own emotions by cultivating a cold, rational, highly intellectual art (10:168). "All true artistic activity is conscious, for no matter what genius," he declared in an essay extolling the "complete" work of art, and the expressive means of accomplishing it. The artist must be fully aware of the effects which he produces, if not of why they are produced. "Art begins and ends in expression" (4:264–265).

Yet Akutagawa's rationalism was accompanied not only by the suppression of his feelings (fortunately his art was not so wholly conscious as he supposed), but also by a growing awareness of the shadows beneath its brilliant surface. More and more he turned away from his misanthropic historical pieces to portray an isolated modern man in realistic but poetic sketches. Some of them suggest that his lonely hero is driven by a hunger for intimacy, but even in these the popular romantic Japanese tale of parted lovers is attenuated to the point that the feeling of separation precedes, if not altogether precludes, any actual relationship.

Akutagawa's own several love affairs appear to have been marked by a sense of isolation rather than of amorous involvement. Apparently his strongest emotional tie, one of fear and hatred more than of love, was for the woman he called "a maniac's daughter," with whom he had only a brief affair.[6] This was Hide Shigeko, whom his friend Oana Ryūichi describes succinctly as "the daughter of a moneylender and a geisha, the wife of a stage-lighting technician, and an accomplished poetess."[7] She was one of several women at home in literary circles (another was Ishikawa Seiko, the flapperish younger sister of Tanizaki's first wife) in whom Akutagawa became interested after his return to Tokyo in 1919. Though Shigeko was no beauty, but a small trim lady who was at least a few years older than himself and who came to literary gatherings dressed in subdued kimono, she seems to have been on intimate terms with several of his friends as well, and soon appalled Akutagawa by her "animal

[6] Morimoto, *Akutagawa Ryūnosuke*, pp. 203–207.
[7] *Kujira no omairi* (Chūō kōronsha, 1940), pp. 91–92.

instincts." Later he congratulates himself on having escaped her, but in his imagination she remains his private Fury, the "goddess of revenge" whose tainted, death-laden image pursues him even in the last autobiographical writings before his suicide.

Meanwhile, Akutagawa's active literary career, though never so financially rewarding as to free him from worries over money, brought wider opportunities for travel and social life at the same time that it placed him under increasing pressure to lecture, grant interviews, and contribute to the swelling mass of Taishō literary journalism, in addition to meeting the deadlines of the various magazines in which he published his painstakingly written stories. In March 1920, his wife gave birth to the first of their three sons, named Hiroshi after Akutagawa's old school friend, the noted writer and literary entrepreneur Kikuchi Kan (or Hiroshi). Akutagawa's own reaction to this happy event, according to his later account, was a mixture of foreboding and guilt. The next March he was sent to China as a special correspondent for the *Osaka Mainichi,* a trip which began with three weeks in a Shanghai hospital suffering from pleurisy and which was followed, after his return in late July, by generally deteriorating health. An earlier visit to Nagasaki had already whetted his interest in the Chinoiserie of the Tokugawa period almost as much as in the vestiges of early Christian influence; and Akutagawa's assignment—simply to send back his impressions as a traveler—could not have been less demanding. No copy was sent, however, and the reports on the new and the old China by "the leading writer of the present literary world," so tantalizingly promised in the *Osaka Mainichi* in March, began to appear only in August, the month after his return.[8] The "new China," and Japan's active role on the Asian continent, were generally overlooked in favor of the old China, the intellectual and artistic circles to which he had access, and the pleasurable exotica that would appeal to any cultivated tourist.

Ever since his ill-fated trip to China, Akutagawa's mental and physical health declined more or less steadily. Life at home became even harder on his nerves after the birth in November

[8] Morimoto, *Akutagawa Ryūnosuke,* pp. 225, 242.

1922 of his second son Takashi; the next month he listed his complaints in a letter to a friend, with "neurasthenia" at the head, followed by "stomach spasms, intestinal catarrh, aspirin rash, and heart acceleration" (6:361). He also suffered intermittently from a severe case of piles, one of the more humiliating ailments, but his predominant symptom, in spite of heavy doses of sleeping medicines, seems to have been insomnia ("If I do not sleep for two nights, I am tired enough to be able to get some sleep the third night, but the night after that I am wide awake again" [9:313]).

The Akutagawa house in Tabata survived the earthquake of September 1923 without damage, and, unlike Kikuchi, Akutagawa was among those whose belief in the value of literature was not visibly disturbed by that catastrophe. Nevertheless, when he donned a sun helmet and went with Kawabata Yasunari and Kon Tōkō to view the corpses in the Yoshiwara pond, he was not only doing journalistic research but storing up impressions that reinforced his longstanding feelings of guilt and doom. Chance survival and massive exposure to death must have darkened his outlook, coloring his writings as well as strengthening the suicidal tendencies of his last critical years. Like other Taishō writers, he made no direct attempt, except in reporting, to deal with such a great and tragic event as the Kantō earthquake.

Still, in the post-earthquake years there was as dramatic a change in his writing as in Tanizaki's. After 1923, Akutagawa drew more and more directly on his own experience, without seeking to express his feelings through the world of history and fantasy for which he was famous. Except for a few stories published in the New Year issues of magazines, of which "Ikkai no tsuchi" ("A Clod of Earth") was most highly praised, all of his serious fiction in 1924 was closely autobiographical. "A Clod of Earth" is an accomplished portrait of the hard-working young widow of a farmer, drawn in a steel-gray realistic manner that was as foreign to Akutagawa as its proletarian subject. It did not prove to be the expected turning-point in his style and subject matter. A more significant development was the emergence of the tired but observant Yokosuka-bound narrator of "Mikan"

("Tangerines," 1919) as an alter ego with the plebeian name of Horikawa Yasukichi, an underpaid, overworked English teacher and part-time writer at the naval engineering academy in Yoko-suka, to which he endlessly commutes from Tokyo or Kamakura. Here, a twilight mood of romantic self-pity softens what might otherwise have been a satisfactorily dismal portrait of an op-pressed wage-slave.

In the summer of 1924, Akutagawa read extensively on social-ism (not only Marx and Lenin, but Kautsky and other lesser lights), a reflection of his sympathy with some of the principles, if not the literary tastes, of the growing number of writers of "proletarian literature," most of whom regarded him as hopeless-ly bourgeois. Akutagawa's left-wing sympathies were qualified by his sophisticated pessimism and by his distaste for the "tyran-ny of politics." Also, his socialist interests were inseparable from his engrossing and ever-worsening personal problems. He could no more fully accept the vision of a coming utopian society than he could give undivided loyalty to the old system by which he was still so strongly bound; nor could he view social evils and injustices without focusing on his own plight as a bedeviled writer. In any case, his Yasukichi pieces were coolly, if not cold-ly, received by critics of all persuasions, including those who were advocates of the I-novel. For them, Yasukichi was still too much his author's creation, all the more unnatural, in that he was obviously a self-portrait of the author, for his affected pose, his reticences, and his failure to confess any striking instances of sin or suffering.

Akutagawa had planned (and even begun) several more Yasu-kichi stories, but abandoned them in favor of a fairly straight-forward autobiographical attempt. Yet this too had a fictional element, however close to the actual facts of his experience and faithful to his current feelings toward them; and it offered an-other persona—a vain, sensitive, unhappy young man with the aristocratic name of Daidōji Shinsuke, fully aware of his petty bourgeois background and absorbed in recreating a singularly depressing childhood and youth. "Daidōji Shinsuke no hansei" ("The Early Life of Daidōji Shinsuke") appeared in January

1925, Akutagawa's only major work of that year, and in spite of a favorable critical reception was left unfinished. Though its six episodes form one of his longer narratives, taking Shinsuke from birth in Honjo to early college days, Akutagawa announced in a note at the end that he intended to continue the story to three or four times its present length. Incomplete as it is, and for all its exaggerations and chiaroscuro highlights and shadows, it remains his most substantial effort at autobiography. Not surprisingly, during a time of illness and growing despair, he felt unable to continue the account into his adult years, in which his private suffering contrasted poignantly with the achievements of his glittering career. Only as he came nearer death did he find the strength to sustain his tortured introspection, combining, in his posthumous works, a dramatic expression of self-loathing and graphic images of mental and physical torment.

Many of the troubles of the last few years of Akutagawa's life were especially painful to him because of his acute sense of responsibility. As head of the family, he was expected to solve the problems, including the financial ones, of all its members. Toward the end of 1924, for example, the death of an uncle was followed soon after by the lapse into critical tuberculosis of his wife's younger brother, who was supported by Akutagawa. Then there were more peripheral relationships, often almost as trying. In the spring of 1924, Akutagawa had served as matchmaker for the marriage between one of his friends and the sister of another; later the same year he found himself engaged in the melancholy task of presiding over their divorce. Also, in the summer of 1925, with the publication of a five-volume anthology of modern Japanese literature which he had edited to the highest standards, he was attacked by several authors for having neglected to obtain their permission or to distribute royalties. Apparently the royalties were too small to be worth distributing, possibly because the high literary standards resulted in low sales, but Akutagawa was distressed by the accusations and in the end sent each author a ten-yen gift certificate to the Mitsukoshi department store.

In July 1925, his wife bore a third son, to be named Yasushi.
Akutagawa spent the late summer in Karuizawa, more for con-
valescence than work, and most of the following January and
February at a hot-springs hotel in Yugawara, taking the waters.
Then in April, leaving his aunt and foster parents behind in
Tabata, he and his wife and youngest child went to live (first in
a hotel and later in a rented house) in her native village of
Kugenuma, where her brother was convalescing. Kugenuma was
on the ocean, not far south of Tokyo and almost too convenient
for visits from his literary friends. In a letter he complains of
having three times as many callers as at home (9:328). Besides
his usual physical ailments, he was suffering from various mental disturbances, including occasional hallucinations, and these
symptoms heightened his fear of inheriting his mother's madness. It seems that during the summer he decided to kill himself,
and that his wife, having been shown a suicide note entrusted
to his friend Oana, was aware of this decision.[9] Resignation to
death, along with the unaccustomed freedom of their new household, probably brought the sad renewal of intimacy that Akutagawa called their "second marriage" (10:176). Toward the end
of the year he seemed a good deal better, however, and began
writing more vigorously. On the second of January, 1927, they
went home to Tabata. This was already accounted the second
year of the new Shōwa era, the Taishō emperor having died, and
the reign name changed, only a week earlier—on Christmas Day,
1926.

By this time Akutagawa had fully recovered his creative vigor.
"Genkaku sambō" ("The Villa Genkaku"), in the January and
February *Chūō kōron,* is one of his finest stories. In March,
he published the bitter but hilarious novella *Kappa* as well as
"Shinkirō" ("Mirage"), one of the few works of which he seems
to have felt confident; in April, he began his most sustained
effort at literary criticism. The resulting series of essays make
up a small book under the self-deprecatory title *Bungeiteki na,
amari ni bungeiteki na* (*Literary, All Too Literary*), ironically
parodying Nietzsche's *Menschliches Allzumenschliches.* Each

[9] *Kujira no omairi,* pp. 100–101.

month also saw a number of shorter pieces, with some half dozen of them coming out in the July magazines, the last of his writings published during his lifetime. But several of his best works appeared only after his death, along with an unprecedented mass of eulogies and reminiscences.

It is no wonder that Akutagawa's 1927 works have a generally pathological tone, though they seem as varied and as firmly controlled as those of any year of his short career. "The Villa Genkaku" is at once the most complex and the most effectively macabre of his stories with a modern setting, and *Kappa* is his richest excursion into fantasy, a sardonic self-portrait against a background that satirizes all of contemporary Japan. "Mirage," on the other hand, is a slight, plotless account of two walks along the beach at Kugenuma, but in its dry, precise imagery and poetic sheen it reflects the influence of Shiga Naoya, whom he greatly admired and whose style of writing he advocated in a lengthy critical exchange with Tanizaki. But Akutagawa was depicting "an icy clear world of morbid nerves," as he described his mental state in one of his many suicide notes (10:346); and the everyday life he described in "Mirage" is pervaded by unease. "I sensed an eeriness in the very sunshine—something quite inexplicable" (9:79).

Tanizaki, nettled by Akutagawa's criticism of one of his intricately plotted tales, had asserted that architectonic strength, rather than the "purity" of having no "story," was exactly what modern Japanese fiction needed most. Akutagawa replied that what it really needed was more of the traditional poetic quality of Japanese fiction, a product of "the observant eye" and "the sensitive heart" (9:205). Tanizaki, however, was unkind enough to suggest that Akutagawa's own weakness was a deficiency of energy, and that the physical differences between them might have something to do with their differing views on art.

Still, as with Tanizaki's fiction, some of Akutagawa's strongest works were those in which his personal weaknesses found their most vivid expression. Among them were the prolific writings of his last, despairing months, ending with *A Fool's Life*, an artistic summation of his entire adult experience, and his aphoristic

Saihō no hito (*Man of the West*), on the figure he called "my Christ"—a poet and journalist of genius whose journalism "had reached the highest market price at the time he was crucified" (10:315). During the year before his death, Akutagawa had become more fascinated than ever by Christianity. This time Christianity meant something more personal to him than the Nagasaki exotica he had loved a decade ago "as a kind of art" or the martyrdom that had aroused in him "a morbid interest, like that aroused by the mentality of fanatics" (10:293). Yet he could never attain the religious faith for which he had a vague longing. For Akutagawa, "the Kingdom of Heaven of Christianity, filled with roses of soapy fragrance, had somehow vanished into thin air" (10:300). The Bible that lay by his death-bed, along with his manuscripts, was above all the last literary source for his own writings.

Another of these final manuscripts was "Haguruma" ("Cogwheels"), a lengthy poetic sketch in the manner he had come to regard as the "purest" form of prose fiction. This sketch is anything but trivial. It is a harrowing account of a nightmarish, hallucinatory period of torment, on the edge of death. But it is also a beautifully written work of art, at the opposite pole from the clinical document of schizophrenic suffering.

"Cogwheels" has the classic I-novel subject of a few days in the life of an author (in this case Mr. A, the author of *Hell Screen* and, more recently, of a rather gloomy autobiographical piece called "Necrology"), narrated by himself in a diarylike style as he spends most of his time at a hotel, trying to write. But it ends with a muffled *cri de coeur* that breaks off the scene of his "most frightening experience"—his wife runs upstairs to him thinking he has committed suicide—and conveys the intensity of the pressure of experience that lay behind the intricate, densely woven fabric of the story. For "Cogwheels" is an effective composition of fictionally heightened autobiographical incidents, although other writings confirm the existence of symptoms that, except for his sharp self-awareness, might well be considered textbook delusions of reference.

In Akutagawa's late works, his fears of madness and death

are as marked as his preoccupation with suicide. Suicide was, of course, a traditionally sanctioned solution to tragic dilemmas in Japanese society, and the literary world had been shaken only a few years earlier by one of the most dramatic of these: the double suicide of the novelist Arishima Takeo and his mistress, whose bodies had been found in his Karuizawa villa a month after their death. In one of his last letters, Akutagawa mentions that he too had originally felt the need for a woman as a "springboard" for the leap into death—and still envied the well-to-do who had a convenient villa (10:344–345).

Although he was neither wealthy nor afflicted with Arishima's peculiar blend of political and romantic despair, Akutagawa evidently found this suicide a tempting model for his own. It is impossible to say when he made, or decisively reaffirmed, his own choice of a way of death that had been carried out by such eminent literary predecessors as Kitamura Tōkoku and pictured in heroic terms in novels like Sōseki's *Kokoro*. But this fateful choice surely owes more to the strength and quality of his sense of vocation, together with his Strindbergian identity as a sick, mad artist, than to the frequently alleged fears of creative stagnation resulting from the pressures of political and social realities. Suicide itself was to be not only the denouement of his life, at a time personally, professionally, and socially ripe for it, but his ultimate work of art.

Akutagawa's preparations for suicide were characteristically meticulous. Some of his friends received unexpected gifts from him, personal belongings which he systematically distributed as mementos. To Tanizaki, at the height of their controversy over the pure novel, he sent several prized books from his own library, including a volume on Indian Buddhist sculpture that Tanizaki had particularly admired. But it was writing that sustained Akutagawa during these months and provided an extraordinary legacy in itself. In addition to completing several major works, he left a number of personal messages, among them the substantial "Aru kyūyū e okuru shuki" ("Note to an Old Friend") in which he elaborately analyzed his feelings about suicide ("My duty is to write everything honestly" [10:344]). The old friend

was Kume Masao, to whom he also entrusted the manuscript of
A Fool's Life, summing up the "poetry and truth" of his past
experience in a moving work of art. His purpose in committing
suicide is described in a letter to Oana as "settling the accounts
of a lifetime" (10:347).

In the "Note to an Old Friend," Akutagawa says that he wants
to write concretely—not like Mainländer, whose description is
skillful but abstract—of the process leading to death. But he
describes his motive as "simply a vague anxiety, an anxiety over
the future," and adds that he believes he already has analyzed
it fully (except for the "shadows of the feudalistic age" that
still hang over him) in *A Fool's Life*. He enumerates various
methods of suicide that he considered and then discarded, because they were painful, uncertain, unbecoming, or abhorrent
from an aesthetic standpoint; after fixing on drugs as the preferred method, he tried to learn all he could about toxicology.
Reluctantly he has decided to die alone, at home. "Finally, what
I planned was to prepare for suicide so adroitly that I would not
arouse the suspicions of my family. After several months I began
to feel fairly confident of this. . . . Coolly finishing these preparations, I am now merely playing with death" (10:343–346).

The last lines of the "Note to an Old Friend" are a searing expression of his feelings, of the suffering beneath his surface
calm: "I am now living in an icy clear world of morbid nerves
. . . . Still, nature is for me more beautiful than ever. No doubt
you will laugh at the contradiction of loving nature and yet
contemplating suicide. But nature is beautiful because it comes
to my eyes in their last extremity. I saw, loved, and also understood more than others. That gives me a certain satisfaction,
even in the midst of my incessant sufferings. Please do not publish this letter until some years after I die. It may be that my
suicide is not unlike a natural death" (10:346).

Shortly before dawn on July 24, 1927, as a light rain broke
several days of record heat, Akutagawa took a fatal dose of
barbiturates. He died in bed in the study-cottage which had
been built after the earthquake (his second-floor study having
begun to seem dangerous) but which had turned out to be un-

pleasantly damp and dark. By that evening all the newspapers carried several-column stories, with photographs and bold headlines ("AKUTAGAWA RYŪNOSUKE EULOGIZES DEATH AND COMMITS SUICIDE"); and Kume, after a little hesitation, held a press conference at which he read the "Note to an Old Friend." There was a good deal of quibbling over the punctuation, but the full text appeared in the next morning's papers. The legend of Akutagawa's death as the symbolic martyrdom of a Taishō intellectual already was afloat on the sea of journalism that had helped to sustain, at whatever peril, his own memorable career.

The apparent rationality of Akutagawa's decision to commit suicide was one of the reasons why the emotional shock-waves of this event radiated far beyond the narrow boundaries of the literary world. That such an eminent intellectual should have coldly and deliberately planned his own death seemed to imply a judgment against the wider world around him. Among the many epitaphs there are few that fail to interpret his death in broad social terms. In 1929, the young Miyamoto Kenji began his illustrious career as a left-wing political and literary activist by winning an essay contest, over the formidable competition of Kobayashi Hideo, with a subtle Marxist analysis of Akutagawa called "Haiboku no bungaku ("The Literature of Defeat"), echoing the title ("Defeat") of the last episode of *A Fool's Life*. Miyamoto interprets Akutagawa's work as the expression of his petty bourgeois class, barely mentioning the physiological factor emphasized by those skeptical of Marxist views, and sees his despair as the inevitable product of social disharmony.

Akutagawa's "last words" in literature expressed a feeling of despair toward man's happiness in social life. Like all pessimists, he had to find a conclusive comment on the eternal *Weltschmertz* with which man is burdened. This is not at all a new idea, or a new sentiment. It gives rise to the fatal logic of the petty bourgeoisie which views self-despair as the despair of society as a whole. Thus Akutagawa views the agony born

450

of and defined by his physiology and his social class as the eternal agony of humanity."[10]

Miyamoto's confident epitaph would no doubt have seemed persuasive to Akutagawa himself. Despite his proud but insecure claim to the privileges of genius, he was inclined to accept the deterministic physiological and social ideas of his day. Yet he was always dissatisfied with simple explanations, especially as propounded by those who seemed to him to have a naïve faith in human perfectability; his cloudy statements of suicide as "settling the accounts of a lifetime" or as the result of a "vague anxiety" allude to a richer and more meaningful interpretation of his life experience. Akutagawa's letters and memoirs suggest how he interpreted that experience, in a curious amalgam of self-loathing, self-pity, and excruciating self-awareness. The several "lives" of the alter egos in his autobiographical fiction, and fictionally enhanced memoirs, form a plausible composite portrait of the artist. But it is through his better known fiction, which is closer to fantasy, that Akutagawa's dark vision of himself and of the human condition has been universalized, influencing readers—and audiences—far from his own time and place, unacquainted with either the legend or the life.

For Japanese readers, life, legend, and legacy have combined to elevate his painfully formed negative identity to the status of a negative ideal. Akutagawa's death came as the consequence of a life marked by a precarious balance of health and sickness, of success and stagnation, of light and shadow; his final image as the doomed artist, alienated from and victimized by society, added another striking examplar to the stock of such images from the Japanese literary world. For a few later writers—Dazai Osamu is the best known—these images may have tipped the balance of their own lives toward self-destruction. The life and works of Akutagawa Ryūnosuke have enhanced the attraction of the dark forces that helped to shape them.

[10] Muramatsu Takeshi, Saeki Shōichi, Ōkubo Norio, eds., *Shōwa hihyō taikei,* 4 vols. (Banchō shobō, 1968), 1: 108.

INDEX

Index

Chile, 388

China: and the Ryukyus, 217, 229; Japan's war with, 10, 326, 328–29, 336n; Tientsin treaty with, 344; question of (1927–28), 368; and Kayahara Kazan, 393, 394n, 396; in the view of Nagai Ryūtarō, 406, 417, 422–23; Akutagawa sent to, 441

Chinese books: on sericulture, 143; cited by Miyazaki Antei, 148; cited by technologists, 150

Chinese calendar, 121

Chinese classics: studied by Tsunayoshi, 124; studied by Hashimoto Sanai, 236n; studied by Ōkubo, 274; studied by Mutsu, 314, 323; studied by Kazan, 374. See also individual works

Chinese historical "model," 171

Chinese language, used by Japanese, 31n, 88, 122n, 187, 211, 335–36, 342, 431

Chinese characters, used phonetically, 31n

Chinese influence, on the Japanese, 29, 31, 32n, 44, 48, 52, 87

Chinese literature, contrasted with Japanese, 30

Chinese thought, 46, 52, 107

Ch'ing dynasty, 167, 169, 178, 247

Chiryōchi (self-clarification), 162

Chisokuin, 105

Chōnin, 112

Chosa-gō, 224

Chōshū han, 8, 155, 260, 283–84; civil war of, 264; samurai of, 268; daimyo of, 269; and Kido Kōin, 272, 276–77, 298–99; troops of, in battle (1864), 273; cooperation of, with Satsuma, 302–03, 305; in the early Meiji period, 306; loyalists of, 313; and rōnin, 314; power struggles of, 316–17, 319–20

Chou dynasty, 288

"Christian" groups, 174

Christianity, 63, 68; and sin, 21–22; secret, in Osaka, 156; in the Ryukyus, 210–11, 213–14; proscribed, 216–17; tolerance of, urged, 240; of Nagai Ryūtarō, 400n, 403; and Akutagawa, 447

Chruchley, Frederic M., 340–41

Chrysanthemum and the Sword, The, 7, 266

Chu Hsi: school of, 158; ideas of, 160; commentaries on, 169; and Japanese education, 274. See also Shushigaku

Chūkō (humane imperial rule), 155

Chūkō-satsu ("Loyalty and Filial Piety Placard"), 118

Chūō kōron, 390, 392, 445

Chūsai, 157n. See also Ōshio Heihachirō

Civilization and Enlightenment movement, 10

Classes, of Tokugawa society, 2

Classic of Filial Piety, 67–68, 115, 118

Class, Status and Power, 208n

"Clod of Earth, A" ("Ikkai no tsuchi"), 442

Cogito ergo sum, 18

"Cogwheels" ("Haguruma"), 447

Coins. See Currency

Collected Works of Ōkubo, 270

Colonialism, Japanese, denounced, 393

Colonial minister, 401n, 415

"Colored peoples," and Japan's mission, 405

"Comic Mask, The" (Hyottoko), 435

Commissioner of construction (fushin-bugyō), 83–84

Commoners: urban, 9, 208n; in the Genroku period, 86, 126; in violent gangs, 112; ideas held by, 127; Itō Miyoji a, 363, 368

Company captains (ban-gashira), 74, 80–81, 83

Concubines, 97, 99–100, 354–55. See also Women

Confession, 53, 56

Conformity, 16

Confucian chroniclers, 106

Confucian classics, 87, 115, 117

Confucianism, 4–6, 162, 175–77, 197; taught by Ōshio Heihachirō, 25; and Ikeda Mitsumasa, 57, 82; of Kumazawa Banzan, 65; of Tsunayoshi, 85, 90, 97–98, 111, 114–16, 120, 124–25; Dazai Shundai a scholar of, 88; and the nō, 103; Hayashi Razan a scholar of, 114; of Ōkura Nagatsune, 129–30; and the technologists, 127, 140, 145–46, 150; Ōyōmei, of Ōshio Heihachirō, 155, 157, 167, 171; and late Ming loyalism, 169; in the Ryu-

Index

Electrical Industries Control Bill, 417
Emi Jimbei, 74
Emperor (Mikado), 40, 74, 87, 91,
104, 288, 290; palace of, burned,
109; Tsunayoshi's "loyalty" to, 119–
20; in the thought of Ōshio Heihachirō, 170, 172; injustice to, 176–77;
and the American treaty, 248–49,
254; court of, 251–52, 259; and the
succession crisis, 260; message of, to
Hotta, 256; personal rule by the
(goshinsei), 265; and Meiji states-
men, 294n, 306, 334; and Itō Miyoji,
365
"Emperor system," 259. See also Im-
perial family; Meiji emperor
"Engels-girls," 14
England, and Kayahara Kazan, 374;
385, 387; Japanese in, 383; Nagai's
view of, 403, 410, 415, 420
English language, 319, 339–40, 344,
374, 431, 436
Ennin, 6
Ennin's Travels in T'ang China, 6
Enryo ("not to push the self"), 20
Entrepreneurs, 25
Epidemic, 175
Erikson, Erik, 11–12, 285, 290, 336,
427n
Ethnocentrism, of the Japanese, 49
Etō Shimpei, 320
Europe: cultural change in, 10; need
of Japanese to understand, 373;
Kayahara's sojourn in, 382; Japanese
in, 390; Kayahara's failure to under-
stand, 397; working class parties of,
407, 410
Even Pass, 34, 38
Evil, 45–46, 48, 53, 55; in the thought
of Ōshio Heihachirō, 163–64, 170,
177, 179
"Evil religion" (jashūmon), 240n
Exclusion policy, 215. See also Seclu-
sion policy
Executive elder (shioki-karō). See Eld-
ers, executive
Exile, 92, 95–96, 99
Expansion, Japanese, 376, 384, 386n,
388n, 395, 396n, 397
Experts (kōsha), 137
Ezo. See Hokkaido (Ezo)

Face, 21

Falconry, 96, 125
Falcon's goose (taka no kari), 80
Family, 19; system, 43n
Famine, 3, 171–72
Fanaticism, 7. See also Sonnō jōi
Farmers: Ikeda Mitsumasa's policy
toward, 80–82; executed for break-
ing the "dog" laws, 95; as technolo-
gists, 127; Ōshio Heihachirō and,
156, 173–74, 177–78
Farm Family Profits (Nōka-eki), 130
Farming, commercial, 147–48
Father: role of, 279; as a daimyo figure,
285
"Father-mother": an official as, 285;
emperor as, 294n
Fertilizers, 132, 138–39
"Feudal conservatives," 295
Feudalism, 31, 158n, 261
Feudal lord. See Daimyo
Filial piety, 52, 117–19, 123, 279
Finance commissioner (kanjō bugyō),
110, 243–44
Finance Ministry, 320; office of the,
318
Fire: at Edo, 108; at Osaka and Kyoto,
109; set by Ōshio, 173–74
Fire God, 34
First Higher School, 432, 437
First minister (kampaku), 251
Fish, 95–96
Flood, 61, 69–70, 72, 109
Followers. See Kobun
Foochow, 213, 220
Fool's Life, A (Aru ahō no isshō), 433,
446, 449–50
Forcade, Théodore Augustin, 211–13
Foreign menace, 183, 190–91, 199n,
215–21, 223, 235, 240, 248, 252, 263
Foreign Ministry, 311, 352, 326–27
Foreign Office, 329
Foreign policy: Tokugawa Nariaki's
ideas on, 187; views of Abe Masa-
hiro on, 188n; and Shimazu Nari-
akira, 233; the pivotal issue in 1858,
234–35; and the Kyoto court, 247;
and Mutsu Munemitsu, 314, 318;
economic orientation of, 393
Former kampaku (taikō), 251, 255
Fortunetellers, 106
Four Books, 115, 121n
"Four Superior Lords," 3, 57

Index

472

Index

Index

Index

Sumida River, 434
Sumiyoshi Gukei, 121
"Summons" (*geki-bun*), 158n, 170, 173
Sumptuary laws, issued by Tsunayoshi, 118
Sumpu, 101
Sun Ch'in-feng, 168n
Sunemono (warped man), 357
Suneru, 356–57, 359
Sung, 169
Sun Goddess, 33–37, 39, 50–51, 53–55, 171; origin of, 42–43; younger brother of, 44
Sun Yat-sen, 422
Suō. *See* Itakura Shigemune
Supplement (*furoku*), 88
Suruga, 101, 119
Susanoo: stories about, 34–39; nature and personality of, 42–44, 46–47, 50, 55–56; behavior of, 53
Sū Tōkaku (Tsou Tung-kuo), 168n
Suzuki Chikara, 237, 240

Tabata suburb, 435, 439, 442, 445
Tabei, 84
Taboos, 41, 45
Tachi-sankon ceremony, 68
Tadasu (*kaku*), 164
Taguchi Ukichi, 396–97
Taikō, 251, 255
Taikyo (absolute spirit), 159–60
Taikyoku (ultimate source of ideal), 160
Taimen ("appearances"), 21
Taira no Masakado, 174
Tairō (great councillor), 65n, 84, 91, 94, 101, 119, 234, 256, 259–60, 262
Taishō era, 394, 423, 425
Taishō Restoration, called for, 402, 410
Taiwan Bank crisis, 368n
Taiwan: expedition (1874), 302–03; Japanese immigrants in, 389–90
Taiyō, 329
Tajima, 273
Takada han, 92
Takahashi Korekiyo, 348, 366n
Takahashi Taichirō, 196n, 199n
Taka loom, 151
Takamatsu, daimyo of, 185
Takarazuka all-girl revues, 14
Takasa Seifu, 304n
Takashima Shūhan, 188n
Takatsugi, 269

Takatsukasa Masamichi, 251–52, 253n, 255; forced to resign, 260
Takatsukasa Nobuko, 91, 101
Takatsukasa Norihira, 91
Tako tsubo bunka ("octopus-pot culture"), 16
Tales New and Old (*Konjaku monogatari*), 435
Tamarinoma (Antechamber), 242n
Tami hyakushō ("people and farmers"), 170
Tamura Takeaki, 103n
Tanaka Giichi, 366n, 368
"Tangerines" ("Mikan"), 443
Taniguchi Sumio, 57n, 61
Tanizaki Jun'ichirō, 14, 434, 437, 440, 446, 448
Tanka, 434
Tatebayashi castle, 90
Tanizaki, 446, 448
Taxes, in Okayama, 71–77, 79
Tax rate, standard (*mononari narashi*), 71
Technologists, 127, 137, 144, 149–53; literature of the, 128
Teikoku bungaku, 435
Temman district (Osaka), 156
Temmonkata (Bakufu astronomer), 121
Tempō no ran, 157
Tempō reforms, 215
Tendai: sect, 104; monks, 106n
Tenjō-no-ma, 68
Tenjuin, Lady, 76n
Tenkai (monk), 104, 114
"Tenkibo" ("Necrology"), 429
Tenkō ("ideological conversion"), 400
Tennōjiya, 173
Tenowokuwa, 131
Teppō-gashira (captain of the Musket Guard), 83
Terajima, 318
Terauchi Masatake, 336n, 362, 367n
Teruko. *See* Ikeda Teruko
Terumasa. *See* Ikeda Terumasa
Teutonic race, 379
Thursday Club (Mokuyōkai), 435, 439
"Three Dogs, the," 96
"Three houses." See *Sanke*
"Three-party system," 407, 423
"Three Wise Lords" (Sankenkō), 57n
Tientsin treaty, 344
Titsingh, Isaac, 101n
Toda family, 104n, 195, 204

477

Index